Peterson's
AP Chemistry

Peterson's
AP Chemistry

Brett Barker

THOMSON

PETERSON'S

Australia • Canada • Mexico • Singapore • Spain • United Kingdom • United States

About Thomson Peterson's

Thomson Peterson's (www.petersons.com) is a leading provider of education information and advice, with books and online resources focusing on education search, test preparation, and financial aid. Its Web site offers searchable databases and interactive tools for contacting educational institutions, online practice tests and instruction, and planning tools for securing financial aid. Peterson's serves 110 million education consumers annually.

For more information, contact Peterson's, 2000 Lenox Drive, Lawrenceville, NJ 08648; 800-338-3282; or find us on the World Wide Web at www.petersons.com/about.

Previously published as *ARCO Master the AP Chemistry Test.*

Editor: Wallie Walker Hammond; Production Editor: Alysha Bullock;
Composition Manager: Melissa Ignatowski; Manufacturing Manager: Judy Coleman.

ISBN: 0-7689-1828-6

Printed in the United States of America

10 9 8 7 6 5 4 3 2   07 06

First Edition

CONTENTS

Part I   Diagnosing Your Strengths and Weaknesses

Part II   AP Chemistry Strategies

Part III   AP Chemistry Review

Part IV   Practice Tests

Getting Started

There is no question that the AP Chemistry exam is one of the most rigorous tests offered by the College Board. Chances are, however, that if you are planning to take the AP Chemistry exam, you are the type of student who is ready to take on anything this test can dish out. You didn't take AP Chem by accident—you wanted to take it, and that's because you are the type of student who can handle challenges. So, although the test is difficult, don't be intimidated by it. You can beat this exam!

PREPARING FOR THE AP CHEMISTRY EXAM

Your first step is to understand that this test is not something to be taken lightly. Top athletes spend a great deal of time preparing their bodies for big competitions, and you, too, must prepare your mind for this exam. But most athletes don't train by themselves. They work out with an experienced coach who knows the keys to being successful. In preparation for the AP challenge, you will need a coach to help you learn the best strategies for the test. **Your teacher should be your first coach.** Due to the time constraints that teachers face and the extensive amount of material covered in this course, you will also need an assistant coach to help you prepare. This book can be that assistant coach, but it is not designed to replace your teacher. He or she knows the course, the material, and you, but unless your teacher can move in with you while you are preparing for the test, he or she can't provide you with all of the tools you will need to succeed. There aren't enough hours in the school day to teach you everything you need to know for the exam. This book can be your personal tutor. The material between its covers will help to familiarize you with all of the material covered on the exam, the structure of the exam, and strategies to prepare for and to take the exam and it can provide you with instant feedback about your performance. This book is also designed with the understanding that your time is valuable! You most likely have a very busy schedule before and after school, and the last thing you need is to add another time-consuming activity. Some of the information that you may have learned or that is in your textbook may go beyond the level of the AP exam. On other subjects, you may have learned less information than you need. This book attempts to get right to the point and to only review the material that you will need to know for the exam.

ROAD MAP

- *Preparing for the AP Chemistry Exam*
- *What the Exam Covers*
- *Getting to Know the Format of the Exam*
- *How the AP Chemistry Exam Is Scored*
- *Making a Study Plan*
- *10 Strategies for Acing the Exam*

WHAT THE EXAM COVERS

Each year, the College Board provides a content outline for the AP Chemistry course as well as a breakdown of the approximate percentage of the AP exam that will deal with certain topics. What follows is an outline of the content of the most recent exam.

Structure of Matter (20%)

- Atomic theory and atomic structure
  - Evidence for the atomic theory
  - Atomic masses; determination by chemical and physical means
  - Atomic number and mass number; isotopes
  - Electron energy levels: atomic spectra, quantum numbers, atomic orbitals
  - Periodic relationships, such as atomic radii, ionization energies, electron affinities, and oxidation states
- Chemical bonding
  - Binding forces
    - Types: ionic, covalent, metallic, hydrogen bonding, van der Waals theory (including London dispersion forces)
    - Relationships to states, structure, and properties of matter
    - Polarity of bonds, electronegativities
  - Molecular models
    - Lewis structures
    - Valence bond: hybridization of orbitals, resonance, and sigma and pi bonds
    - VSEPR
  - Geometry of molecules and ions, structural isomerism of simple organic molecules and coordination complexes; dipole moments of molecules; relation of properties to structure
- Nuclear chemistry: nuclear equations, half-lives, and radioactivity; chemical applications

States of Matter (20%)

- Gases
  - Laws of ideal gases
    - Equation of state for an ideal gas
    - Partial pressures
  - Kinetic-molecular theory
    - Interpretation of ideal gas laws on the basis of this theory
    - Avogadro's hypothesis and the mole concept
    - Dependence of kinetic energy of molecules on temperature
    - Deviations from ideal gas laws
- Liquids and solids
  - Liquids and solids from the kinetic-molecular viewpoint
  - Phase diagrams of one-component systems
  - Changes of state, including critical points and triple points
  - Structure of solids; lattice energies
- Solutions
  - Types of solutions and factors affecting solubility
  - Methods of expressing concentration (The use of normalities is not tested.)
  - Raoult's law and colligative properties (nonvolatile solutes); osmosis
  - Nonideal behavior (qualitative aspects)

Reactions (35-40%)

- Reaction types
  - Acid-base reactions; concepts of Arrhenius, Brønsted-Lowry, and Lewis; coordination complexes; amphoterism
  - Precipitation reactions
  - Oxidation-reduction reactions
    - Oxidation number
    - The role of the electron in oxidation-reduction
    - Electrochemistry: electrolytic and galvanic cells; Faraday's laws; standard half-cell potentials; Nernst equation; prediction of the direction of redox reactions
- Stoichiometry
  - Ionic and molecular species present in chemical systems: net ionic equations
  - Balancing of equations, including those for redox reactions
  - Mass and volume relations with emphasis on the mole concept, including empirical formulas and limiting reactants

- Equilibrium
  - Concept of dynamic equilibrium, physical and chemical; Le Chatelier's principle; equilibrium constants
  - Quantitative treatment
    - Equilibrium constants for gaseous reactions: *KP, K*
    - Equilibrium constants for reactions in solution
      - Constants for acids and bases: pK; pH
      - Solubility product constants and their application to precipitation and the dissolution of slightly soluble compounds
      - Common ion effect; buffers; hydrolysis
- Kinetics
  - Concept of rate of reaction
  - Use of experimental data and graphical analysis to determine reactant order, rate constants, and reaction rate laws
  - Effect of temperature change on rates
  - Energy of activation; the role of catalysts
  - The relationship between the rate-determining step and a mechanism
- Thermodynamics
  - State functions
  - First law: change in enthalpy; heat of formation; heat of reaction; Hess's law; heats of vaporization and fusion; calorimetry
  - Second law: entropy; free energy of formation; free energy of reaction; dependence of change in free energy on enthalpy and entropy changes
  - Relationship of change in free energy to equilibrium constants and electrode potentials

Descriptive Chemistry (10-15%)

- Chemical reactivity and products of chemical reactions
- Relationships in the periodic table: horizontal, vertical, and diagonal with examples from alkali metals, alkaline earth metals, halogens, and the first series of transition elements
- Introduction to organic chemistry: hydrocarbons and functional groups (structure, nomenclature, chemical properties). Physical and chemical properties of simple organic compounds should also be included as exemplary material for the study of other areas such as bonding, equilibria involving weak acids, kinetics, colligative properties, and stoichiometric determinations of empirical and molecular formulas.

Laboratory (5-10%)

These questions are based on common laboratory procedures that should have been learned as part of the course, such as:

- making observations of chemical reactions and substances
- recording data
- calculating and interpreting results based on the quantitative data obtained
- effectively communicating the results of experimental work

Students should be able to solve specific types of chemical calculations. The types of problems that might possibly be included on the exam include

- Percentage composition
- Empirical and molecular formulas from experimental data
- Molar masses from gas density, freezing-point, and boiling-point measurements
- Gas laws, including the ideal gas law, Dalton's law, and Graham's law
- Stoichiometric relations using the concept of the mole; titration calculations
- Mole fractions; molar and molal solutions
- Faraday's laws of electrolysis
- Equilibrium constants and their applications, including their use for simultaneous equilibria
- Standard electrode potentials and their use; Nernst equation
- Thermodynamic and thermochemical calculations
- Kinetics calculations

This may feel like too much information for you to ever master, and it is very rare that any teacher could make it through all of the recommended topics and activities within an academic year. In the next section, we will look at some details about how you'll be asked to apply your knowledge of the topics above, which should help to ease some of your fears.

GETTING TO KNOW THE FORMAT OF THE EXAM

The College Board reserves the right to make changes to the exam as it chooses; however, the structure of the exam has undergone only very slight changes in the years it's been offered. To keep abreast of the specific details about the AP Chemistry exam, refer to the College Board Web site at www.collegeboard.com/ap.

The exam is 180 minutes long and is divided into two sections. The first part, Section I, consists of 75 multiple-choice questions. There is a 90-minute time limit on Section I, and the results make up 45% of the total grade. The second part, Section II, is also 90 minutes long, makes up 55% of the total grade, and is broken into two sections. The first section is 40 minutes long; you may use calculators during this portion, but this is the only part of the exam on which you can use a calculator! It consists of two problems—in the first question, the problem is mandatory, but in the second question you get to choose between two different problems. These problems are calculation-based and are multipart problems. After 40 minutes, you will be instructed to put your calculator away and proceed to the second portion of Section II, Part B.

Part B is divided into three subsections. The first is a list of eight chemical equations, from which you will select five. In this subsection, you are provided with a written description of the reactants and conditions of a reaction, from which you must determine the product(s). You must also convert the entire equation into symbolic form (substituting symbols for written descriptions). The second subsection in Part B consists of two mandatory multipart questions. The content of these questions varies (later in this chapter you will see a list of previous topics). In the final subsection, you must select one of two questions. All of these parts of the AP exam are summarized in the table below:

Section I: Multiple Choice. 75 questions. 90 minutes. 45% of total grade
Section II: Free Response. 8 questions (you must answer 6). 90 minutes. 55% of grade.

Breakdown of the Free-Response Section

Part A			Part B		
40 minutes			50 minutes		
2 questions			4 questions		
40% of Section II; 22% of entire test			60% of Section II; 33 % of entire test		
Calculators (only calculators without alphabetic keyboards)			No calculators		
Question 1		Question 4	Question 5		Question 6
20% of Section II; 11% overall		15% of section 8.25 % overall	15% of section 8.25 % overall		15% of section 8.25 % overall
AND			AND		
Question 2	OR	Question 3	Question 7		Question 8
20% of Section II; 11% overall	OR	20% of Section II; 11% overall	15% of section 8.25 % overall	OR	15% of section 8.25 % overall

HOW THE AP CHEMISTRY EXAM IS SCORED
Multiple Choice

On the multiple-choice portion of the exam, there are 75 questions. Scores are determined according to the following formula:

Score = Correct Score – 0.25(Incorrect Score)

The reason for the strange equation is to prevent wild guessing. Take, for example, a student who bubbled in the same letter for every question. To be safe, she chooses "C" because it is in the middle of the five choices. On a test of 75 questions, with five possible responses (A–E) for each question, chances are that 15 of them will actually be C (15 will also be A, 15 will be B, etc.). That means that the student will have gotten 15 problems correct and 60 incorrect. Plugging these numbers into the equation will give you:

Score = Correct Score – 0.25(Incorrect Score) =
15 – 0.25(60) = 15 – 15 = 0

As you can see, this individual could have left all of the answers blank and still gotten the same score. There is no benefit to wild guessing. In Chapter 1, you will learn some techniques to take the "wild" out of guessing.

Free Response

The free-response questions are graded by a group of more than 100 AP Chemistry teachers and college chemistry professors who gather at the beginning of the summer to grade all of the exams. Scoring rubrics are carefully designed for each question, and the graders spend the week grading the tests in a very thorough, unbiased manner. The key to your success on the free response questions is your ability to write to these rubrics. While there is no way to predict in advance what topics will be covered in the free-response section (even though many people try), there are some strategies that will improve your chances. Hopefully, your teacher has had you practice writing AP-style essays, but even if he has not, you will still have an opportunity to try some in this book. You will also be able to evaluate your own performance using scoring rubrics that are similar to those used by the AP graders. This exercise will help you sharpen your writing skills and maximize your chances for a high score.

Your Composite Score

Once your multiple-choice and free-response scores have been calculated, each score will be used to calculate your composite score. This score ranges from 0 to 5, according to the scale shown below. Note the percentage of students receiving each score.

AP Grade	Qualification	Percent of students earning this score (from 1999 test)
5	Extremely well qualified	17.2
4	Well qualified	14.7
3	Qualified	25.3
2	Possibly qualified	22.0
1	No recommendation	20.8

One thing these numbers don't tell you is what it takes to get a 5 or a 4. The number of points to achieve these grades will differ slightly from year to year, but they remain relatively consistent over time. The Chemistry exam is intentionally made so that a score of 100% is extremely unlikely. In most administrations, scores of 50–60% usually receive scores of 5.

MAKING A STUDY PLAN

The fact that you bought this book is a step in the right direction for your success on the AP Chemistry exam. And there are some strategies that will help you get the most out of it. The following are two key questions you need to answer before you proceed:

1. How much time do I have before the AP exam?
2. How much time can I realistically devote to exam preparation?

Your answers to these questions will help you to set a pace for your review. If you have a long time before the test (two or three months), you can set a fairly relaxed pace. If you have a short time (one month or less), your pace will be more rigorous. Either way, the book is designed to be flexible and to accommodate a variety of situations. What follows is a brief description of the remainder of the book and how you can use it under different circumstances.

Overview of the Book
Part I
Diagnostic Test

Part II
Test-Taking Strategies and Essays through the Years

Part III
Review

Part IV
Full-Length Practice Tests

Read this section, and then go on to Chapter 1. These chapters contain vital information about the AP exam that will help you to develop sound test-taking strategies. Once finished, take the Diagnostic Test. Before you take it, however, you need to understand that the Diagnostic Test is **not** a practice AP exam! This book has two full-length practice AP Tests, but they do not appear until Part IV of the book. The Diagnostic Test is designed to resemble the approximate difficulty level of the AP exam and to reflect the content on the exam, but there are some significant differences in the structures of the two. The purpose of the test is to help you identify strengths and potential weaknesses, which you'll need to know to design your personal study plan. Once you finish the Diagnostic Exam, use these suggested guidelines to complete your test preparations.

The Complete Course

If you have plenty of time before the test (two or three months), it is recommended that you complete the entire course. There are twenty chapters, so if you divide these up over a two-month period, you would need to complete about two chapters a week. If you have a three-month period, this drops down to about one chapter every five or six days. You will receive the maximum benefit if you can complete the entire book. Even if you are planning to complete the entire book, it is recommended that you pick the most difficult areas first, especially those that you may not have covered much (or at all) in class. This way, if something happens and you don't have as much time as you thought, you've at least gone through the sections that will benefit you the most.

The Accelerated Course

If you are running out of time, you'll need to design an ambush approach to your studies. Don't attempt to complete the entire book. From the diagnostic test, select your weakest areas and plan to go through those first. Make a list of the topics you feel you can reasonably work through before the exam. Be very careful during this process. Do not skip sections you know very little about, figuring, "Oh, that probably won't be on the test." If it is on the content outline, it will be on the test! And, if you are especially unfortunate, the section you skip could end up as one of the mandatory essay questions. Even if you don't have time for all of the practice problems in a section, get through what you can. If you know certain topics very well, skip them. It's not ideal, but if you are reading this section (for the accelerated course) it is probably because you don't have time to do everything. Just remember, though, that every chapter you can work through is a bonus for you. Rather than be discouraged about not having enough time to finish everything, be encouraged about the sections you will finish. These are areas you wouldn't have known or would have done poorly on without your extra effort. Be positive!

10 STRATEGIES FOR ACING THE EXAM

Preparation for the Exam

1. Read the *AP Course Description for Chemistry* available from the College Board.

2. Take the Diagnostic Test.

3. Choose a place and time to study every day. Stick to your routine and plan.

4. Even though they are time-consuming, complete the *Practice Tests* in this book. They will give you just what they promise: **practice**—practice in reading and following directions, practice in pacing yourself, practice in understanding and answering multiple-choice questions, and practice in writing timed essays.

5. Complete all your assignments for your regular AP Chemistry class. Ask questions in class, talk about what you read and write, and enjoy what you are doing. The test is supposed to measure your development as an educated and analytical reader and writer.

The Night Before the Exam

6. Assemble what you will need for the test: your admission materials, four number 2 pencils, two pens, a watch (without an alarm), your approved calculator, and a healthy snack for the break. Put these items in a place where you will not forget them in the morning.

7. Don't cram. Relax. Go to a movie, visit a friend—but not one who is taking the test with you. Get a good night's sleep.

The Day of the Exam

8. Wear comfortable clothes. If you have a lucky color or a lucky piece of clothing or jewelry, wear it—as long as you won't distract anyone else. Take along a lucky charm if you have one.

9. If you do not usually eat a big breakfast, this is not the morning to change your routine, but it is probably a good idea to eat something nutritious if you can.

10. If you feel yourself getting anxious, concentrate on taking a couple of deep breaths. Remember, you don't have to answer all the questions, you can use EDUCATED GUESSES, and you don't have to get a perfect score on every part of the test.

Diagnosing Your Strengths and Weaknesses

PART
I

PREVIEW

Diagnostic Test

Diagnostic Test

The diagnostic test will help you identify your weak spots in the course. It is not designed to be a practice AP test. The questions may not resemble actual AP items. The purpose of the diagnostic test is to give you the opportunity to test your knowledge in a number of areas and, based on the results of this test, to plan your study time for the AP test accordingly.

The questions from each major topic area do not cover all of the subject areas in a chapter, so this test should in no way be viewed as a substitute for review. In addition, the answers on this test, unlike the other chapters, do not contain explanations. Each topic will be addressed and reviewed within specific, individual chapters. The answer key for the diagnostic test points out where in the chapter you can find the information. This should help you to identify weak points and customize your use of this book.

Good luck!

Diagnostic Test

Answer Sheet

If a section has fewer questions than answer ovals, leave the extra ovals blank.

1. Ⓐ Ⓑ Ⓒ Ⓓ Ⓔ	16. Ⓐ Ⓑ Ⓒ Ⓓ Ⓔ	31. Ⓐ Ⓑ Ⓒ Ⓓ Ⓔ	46. Ⓐ Ⓑ Ⓒ Ⓓ Ⓔ	61. Ⓐ Ⓑ Ⓒ Ⓓ Ⓔ
2. Ⓐ Ⓑ Ⓒ Ⓓ Ⓔ	17. Ⓐ Ⓑ Ⓒ Ⓓ Ⓔ	32. Ⓐ Ⓑ Ⓒ Ⓓ Ⓔ	47. Ⓐ Ⓑ Ⓒ Ⓓ Ⓔ	62. Ⓐ Ⓑ Ⓒ Ⓓ Ⓔ
3. Ⓐ Ⓑ Ⓒ Ⓓ Ⓔ	18. Ⓐ Ⓑ Ⓒ Ⓓ Ⓔ	33. Ⓐ Ⓑ Ⓒ Ⓓ Ⓔ	48. Ⓐ Ⓑ Ⓒ Ⓓ Ⓔ	63. Ⓐ Ⓑ Ⓒ Ⓓ Ⓔ
4. Ⓐ Ⓑ Ⓒ Ⓓ Ⓔ	19. Ⓐ Ⓑ Ⓒ Ⓓ Ⓔ	34. Ⓐ Ⓑ Ⓒ Ⓓ Ⓔ	49. Ⓐ Ⓑ Ⓒ Ⓓ Ⓔ	64. Ⓐ Ⓑ Ⓒ Ⓓ Ⓔ
5. Ⓐ Ⓑ Ⓒ Ⓓ Ⓔ	20. Ⓐ Ⓑ Ⓒ Ⓓ Ⓔ	35. Ⓐ Ⓑ Ⓒ Ⓓ Ⓔ	50. Ⓐ Ⓑ Ⓒ Ⓓ Ⓔ	65. Ⓐ Ⓑ Ⓒ Ⓓ Ⓔ
6. Ⓐ Ⓑ Ⓒ Ⓓ Ⓔ	21. Ⓐ Ⓑ Ⓒ Ⓓ Ⓔ	36. Ⓐ Ⓑ Ⓒ Ⓓ Ⓔ	51. Ⓐ Ⓑ Ⓒ Ⓓ Ⓔ	66. Ⓐ Ⓑ Ⓒ Ⓓ Ⓔ
7. Ⓐ Ⓑ Ⓒ Ⓓ Ⓔ	22. Ⓐ Ⓑ Ⓒ Ⓓ Ⓔ	37. Ⓐ Ⓑ Ⓒ Ⓓ Ⓔ	52. Ⓐ Ⓑ Ⓒ Ⓓ Ⓔ	67. Ⓐ Ⓑ Ⓒ Ⓓ Ⓔ
8. Ⓐ Ⓑ Ⓒ Ⓓ Ⓔ	23. Ⓐ Ⓑ Ⓒ Ⓓ Ⓔ	38. Ⓐ Ⓑ Ⓒ Ⓓ Ⓔ	53. Ⓐ Ⓑ Ⓒ Ⓓ Ⓔ	68. Ⓐ Ⓑ Ⓒ Ⓓ Ⓔ
9. Ⓐ Ⓑ Ⓒ Ⓓ Ⓔ	24. Ⓐ Ⓑ Ⓒ Ⓓ Ⓔ	39. Ⓐ Ⓑ Ⓒ Ⓓ Ⓔ	54. Ⓐ Ⓑ Ⓒ Ⓓ Ⓔ	69. Ⓐ Ⓑ Ⓒ Ⓓ Ⓔ
10. Ⓐ Ⓑ Ⓒ Ⓓ Ⓔ	25. Ⓐ Ⓑ Ⓒ Ⓓ Ⓔ	40. Ⓐ Ⓑ Ⓒ Ⓓ Ⓔ	55. Ⓐ Ⓑ Ⓒ Ⓓ Ⓔ	70. Ⓐ Ⓑ Ⓒ Ⓓ Ⓔ
11. Ⓐ Ⓑ Ⓒ Ⓓ Ⓔ	26. Ⓐ Ⓑ Ⓒ Ⓓ Ⓔ	41. Ⓐ Ⓑ Ⓒ Ⓓ Ⓔ	56. Ⓐ Ⓑ Ⓒ Ⓓ Ⓔ	71. Ⓐ Ⓑ Ⓒ Ⓓ Ⓔ
12. Ⓐ Ⓑ Ⓒ Ⓓ Ⓔ	27. Ⓐ Ⓑ Ⓒ Ⓓ Ⓔ	42. Ⓐ Ⓑ Ⓒ Ⓓ Ⓔ	57. Ⓐ Ⓑ Ⓒ Ⓓ Ⓔ	72. Ⓐ Ⓑ Ⓒ Ⓓ Ⓔ
13. Ⓐ Ⓑ Ⓒ Ⓓ Ⓔ	28. Ⓐ Ⓑ Ⓒ Ⓓ Ⓔ	43. Ⓐ Ⓑ Ⓒ Ⓓ Ⓔ	58. Ⓐ Ⓑ Ⓒ Ⓓ Ⓔ	73. Ⓐ Ⓑ Ⓒ Ⓓ Ⓔ
14. Ⓐ Ⓑ Ⓒ Ⓓ Ⓔ	29. Ⓐ Ⓑ Ⓒ Ⓓ Ⓔ	44. Ⓐ Ⓑ Ⓒ Ⓓ Ⓔ	59. Ⓐ Ⓑ Ⓒ Ⓓ Ⓔ	74. Ⓐ Ⓑ Ⓒ Ⓓ Ⓔ
15. Ⓐ Ⓑ Ⓒ Ⓓ Ⓔ	30. Ⓐ Ⓑ Ⓒ Ⓓ Ⓔ	45. Ⓐ Ⓑ Ⓒ Ⓓ Ⓔ	60. Ⓐ Ⓑ Ⓒ Ⓓ Ⓔ	75. Ⓐ Ⓑ Ⓒ Ⓓ Ⓔ

Diagnostic Test

Note: For all questions, assume that the temperature is 298 K, the pressure is 1.00 atmosphere, and solutions are aqueous unless otherwise specified.

Throughout the test, the following symbols have the definitions specified unless otherwise noted.

T = temperature	M = molar
P = pressure	m = molal
V = volume	L, mL = liter(s), milliliter(s)
S = entropy	g = gram(s)
H = enthalpy	nm = nanometer(s)
G = free energy	atm = atmosphere(s)
R = molar gas constant	J, kJ = joule(s), kilojoule(s)
n = number of moles	v = volt(s)
	mol = mole(s)

Directions: Each set of lettered choices below refers to the numbered statements immediately following it. Select the one lettered choice that best fits each.

1. A certain color of light has a wavelength of 550 nm. What is the energy possessed by a photon of such light?

   (A) 2.42×10^{-19}

   (B) 5.45×10^{14} J

   (C) 3.61×10^{-14} J

   (D) 3.61×10^{-19} J

   (E) 5.37×10^{-19} J

2. How will the time it takes to hard-boil an egg compare at higher altitudes?

   (A) It will take longer because of the lower boiling temperature of the water.

   (B) It will take longer because of the higher vapor pressure of the water.

   (C) It will take less time because of the higher boiling temperature of the water.

   (D) It will take less time because of the lower vapor pressure of the water.

   (E) It will take the same amount of time, regardless of the altitude.

3. Calculate the molar solubility of barium sulfate, $BaSO_4$, in 0.020 M sodium sulfate, K_2SO_4. K_{sp} for $BaSO_4$ is 1.08×10^{-10}.

   (A) 1.04×10^{-5}

   (B) 5.4×10^{-5}

   (C) 7.87×10^{-8}

   (D) 5.4×10^{-9}

   (E) 1.08×10^{-10}

4. $^{59}_{29}Cu \rightarrow {}^{0}_{+1}e +$ _____ If copper–29 undergoes a positron emission, what is the resulting product nuclide?

   (A) $^{59}_{29}Cu$

   (B) $^{58}_{28}Ni$

   (C) $^{58}_{30}Zn$

   (D) $^{57}_{29}Cu$

   (E) $^{60}_{29}Cu$

GO ON TO THE NEXT PAGE

5. Calculate the pH of a 0.10 M solution of HOCl, K_a = 3.5×10^{-8}.

   (A) 4.23

   (B) 8.46

   (C) 3.73

   (D) 1.00

   (E) 3.23

6. Determine the standard enthalpy of reaction for the combustion of hydrogen sulfide gas, which proceeds according to the reaction shown below:

   $2H_2S(g) + 3O_2(g) \rightarrow 2H_2O(l) + 2SO_2(g)$

   The standard enthalpies for the constituents are as follows:

Formula	$\Delta H°_f$ (kJ/mol)
$H_2S(g)$	−20
$H_2O(l)$	−285.8
$SO_2(g)$	−296.8

   (A) −575 kJ

   (B) −726 kJ

   (C) −963 kJ

   (D) −1125 kJ

   (E) −1320 kJ

7. Identify the type of organic compound shown:

   $$CH_3 \!-\!\!-\! C = O$$
   $$|$$
   $$CH_3$$

   (A) Aldehyde

   (B) Ester

   (C) Carbonyl

   (D) Ketone

   (E) Carboxylic acid

8. Which one of the following will not react?

   (A) $Ag + Au(NO_3)_3 \rightarrow$

   (B) $Cu + AgNO_3 \rightarrow$

   (C) $Pb + Cu(NO_3)_2 \rightarrow$

   (D) $Cd + Pb(NO_3)_2 \rightarrow$

   (E) $Ni + Cd(NO_3)_2 \rightarrow$

9. For the reaction $2A + B \rightarrow C$, experimental data was collected for three trials:

Experiment	[A] M	[B] M	Initial Rate M s^{-1}
1	0.40	0.20	5.5×10^{-3}
2	0.80	0.20	5.5×10^{-3}
3	0.40	0.40	2.2×10^{-2}

   What is the rate law of the reaction?

   (A) Rate = $k[A][B]$

   (B) Rate = $k[A]^0[B]^2$

   (C) Rate = $k[A]^2[B]^2$

   (D) Rate = $k[A]^2[B]^0$

   (E) Rate = $k[A][B]^2$

10. $4NH_3(g) + 5O_2(g) \rightarrow 4NO(g) + 6H_2O(g)$

    In the above reaction, 3.10 g of NH_3 reacts with 2.50 g of O_2. What is the theoretical yield of NO?

    (A) 1.88 g

    (B) 5.46 g

    (C) 8.20 g

    (D) 24.0 g

    (E) 120 g

11. $H_2O(g) + Cl_2O(g) \rightleftharpoons 2HOCl(g)$

    The reaction above is allowed to come to equilibrium at room temperature. At equilibrium, the partial pressure of H_2O is 296 mm Hg, Cl_2O is 15 mm Hg, and HOCl is 20 mm Hg. What is the value of K_p at this temperature?

    (A) 222

    (B) 11

    (C) 0.017

    (D) 0.090

    (E) 0.0045

12. A solution is made by dissolving 250.0 g of potassium chromate crystals (K_2CrO_4, molar mass 194.2 g) in 1.00 kg of water. What will the freezing point of the new solution be?

    Kf for water is 1.86 °C m^{-1}.

    (A) −8.87 °C

    (B) −7.18 °C

    (C) −5.73 °C

    (D) −3.2 °C

    (E) −1.86 °C

13. Copper is electroplated from $CuSO_4$ solution. A constant current of 2.00 amp is applied by an external power supply. How long will it take to deposit 1.00×10^2 g of Cu?

    (A) 21.1 hours

    (B) 10.0 min

    (C) 42.2 hours

    (D) 11.2 sec

    (E) 2.91 hours

14. Which molecule has a Lewis structure that does not obey the octet rule?

    (A) NO

    (B) CS_2

    (C) PF_3

    (D) HCN

    (E) CCl_4

15. Which of the following molecules has a trigonal pyramidal shape?

    (A) PCl_5

    (B) N_2O

    (C) NH_3

    (D) CCl_4

    (E) H_2O_2

16. Hydrogen gas, liberated from a reaction between hydrochloric acid and zinc, is bubbled through water and collected in an inverted graduated cylinder at 22°C. The pressure of the gas mixture is 765 mm Hg. The vapor pressure of water at 22°C is 20 mm Hg. What is the partial pressure of the hydrogen gas?

    (A) 22 mm Hg

    (B) 743 mm Hg

    (C) 745 mm Hg

    (D) 765 mm Hg

    (E) 785 mm Hg

17. Which set of quantum numbers (n, l, m_l, m_s) is NOT possible?

    (A) 1, 0, 0, ½

    (B) 1, 1, 0, ½

    (C) 1, 0, 0, −½

    (D) 2, 1, −1, ½

    (E) 3, 2, 1, ½

18. Which of the following explains why CH_3–O–CH_3 has a lower boiling temperature than CH_3CH_2OH?

    (A) Hydrogen bonding

    (B) Hybridization

    (C) Ionic bonding

    (D) Resonance

    (E) London dispersion forces

19. If 87.5% of a sample of pure ^{99}Rh decays in 48 days, what is the half-life of ^{99}Rh?

    (A) 6 days

    (B) 8 days

    (C) 12 days

    (D) 16 days

    (E) 24 days

GO ON TO THE NEXT PAGE

20. Which of the following explains why, at room temperature, I_2 is a solid, Br_2 is a liquid, and Cl_2 is a gas?

(A) Hydrogen bonding

(B) Hybridization

(C) Ionic bonding

(D) Resonance

(E) London dispersion forces

21. Which of the following reactions involves the largest increase in entropy?

(A) $AgNO_3(aq) + HCl(aq) \rightarrow AgCl(s) + HNO_3(aq)$

(B) $N_2(g) + O_2(g) \rightarrow 2NO(g)$

(C) $2NO(g) + O_2(g) \rightarrow 2NO_2(g)$

(D) $2KClO_3(s) \rightarrow 2KCl(s) + 3O_2(g)$

(E) $2SO_2(g) + O_2(g) \rightarrow 2SO_3(g)$

22. Determine the name of $[Cu(NH_3)_4]SO_4$.

(A) Tetraamminecuprate(II) sulfate

(B) Tetracupraammine (IV) sulfate

(C) Tetrasulfonoammine (IV) cuprate

(D) Amminecuprate (IV) sulfate

(E) Cupric ammonium sulfate

23. You are supposed to mix 250 ml of a 0.1 M solution of $Pb(NO_3)_2$ solution (molar mass = 331.2 g). You would need to mix _____ of $Pb(NO_3)_2$ with enough water to make 250 ml solution.

(A) 331.2 g

(B) 33.12 g

(C) 8.28 g

(D) 3.312 g

(E) 0.828 g

24. What is the hybridization around the central atom in the molecule $SiCl_4$?

(A) sp^3

(B) sp^2

(C) sp

(D) sp^3d

(E) sp^3d^2

Step 1)	$NO(g) + Cl_2(g) \rightleftharpoons NOCl_2(g)$	(fast equilibrium)
Step 2)	$NO(g) + NOCl_2(g) \rightarrow 2NOCl(g)$	(slow)

25. Which of the following rate laws is consistent with the reaction mechanism shown above?

(A) Rate = $k[NO][Cl_2]$

(B) Rate = $k[NO]_2$

(C) Rate = $k[NO][NOCl_2]$

(D) Rate = $k[NO]^2[Cl]$

(E) Rate = $k[NO]^2[Cl][NOCl_2]$

$$\ldots C_6H_5OH + \ldots O_2 \rightarrow \ldots CO_2 + \ldots H_2O$$

26. When the equation above is balanced, how many water molecules will be produced?

(A) 1

(B) 2

(C) 3

(D) 4

(E) 6

27. What type of emission is the isotope $^{14}_6C$ likely to undergo?

(A) Alpha decay

(B) Beta decay

(C) Positron emission

(D) Electron capture

(E) Nuclear fission

28. Which of the following is most likely to be a solid at room temperature?

(A) HF

(B) NH_3

(C) K_2S

(D) N_2

(E) H_2O

29. What is the percentage composition of Mg in the compound $Mg_3(PO_4)_2$?

(A) 21.92 %

(B) 23.57 %

(C) 27.74 %

(D) 32.32 %

(E) 48.70%

30. Five balloons are filled up with one mole each of hydrogen (H_2), helium (He_2), Nitrogen (N_2), Oxygen (O_2), and Argon (Ar) molecules. After some time has elapsed, which balloon will be the smallest?

(A) H_2

(B) He

(C) N_2

(D) O_2

(E) Ar

31. Which of these explains that the C—C bonds in benzene are all the same length?

(A) Hydrogen bonding

(B) Hybridization

(C) Ionic bonding

(D) Resonance

(E) London dispersion forces

32. What is the standard free energy change ($\Delta G°$) for the reaction shown below:

$$Fe^{3+}(aq) + Ag(s) \rightarrow Fe^{2+}(aq) + Ag^+(aq)$$

(A) –2.5 kJ

(B) 2.9 kJ

(C) 8.7 kJ

(D) 10.0 kJ

(E) 29 kJ

33. The vapor pressure of water at 50 °C is 92.5 mm Hg. If 400.0 g of sucrose ($C_{12}H_{22}O_{11}$ molar mass 342.3 g) is added to 900.0 g of H_2O at 50 °C, what will the vapor pressure of the solution be?

(A) 94.6 mm Hg

(B) 92.3 mm Hg

(C) 90.4 mm Hg

(D) 88.3 mm Hg

(E) 27.4 mm Hg

34. Which molecule listed below has two sigma (σ) and two pi (π) bonds?

(A) N_2

(B) C_2H_4

(C) N_2F_2

(D) HCN

(E) $C_2H_2Cl_2$

35. For the reaction $A + B \rightarrow C + D$, $\Delta H° = +40$ kJ and $\Delta S° = +50$ J/K. Therefore, the reaction under standard conditions is

(A) spontaneous at temperatures less than 10 K.

(B) spontaneous at temperatures greater than 800 K.

(C) spontaneous only at temperatures between 10 K and 800 K.

(D) spontaneous at all temperatures.

(E) nonspontaneous at all temperatures.

36. In which of the following systems would the number of moles of the substances present at equilibrium NOT be shifted by a change in the volume of the system at constant temperature?

(A) $SO_2(g) + O_2(g) \rightleftharpoons 2SO_3$

(B) $N_2(g) + 3\ H_2(g) \rightleftharpoons 2\ NH_3(g)$

(C) $NO_2(g) + SO_2(g) \rightleftharpoons SO_3(g) + NO(g)$

(D) $N_2O_4(g) \rightleftharpoons 2\ NO_2(g)$

(E) $CO(g) + 3H_2(g) \rightleftharpoons CH_4(g) + H_2O(g)$

37. Which one of the following electron configurations for the species in their ground state is NOT correct?

(A) Ca: $1s^2 2s^2 2p^6 3s^2 3p^6 4s^2$

(B) Bi: $[Xe]6s^2 4f^{14} 5d^{10} 6p^3$

(C) As: $[Ar]\ 4s^2 3d^{10} 4p^3$

(D) Br: $[Ar]\ 4s^2 3d^{10} 4p^5$

(E) P: $1s^2 2s^2 2p^6 3p^5$

GO ON TO THE NEXT PAGE

38. What is the oxidation state of Cr in the compound $K_2Cr_2O_7$?

    (A) +2

    (B) +3

    (C) +5

    (D) +6

    (E) +7

39. A 0.4647 g sample of a compound containing only carbon, hydrogen, and oxygen was burned in an excess of pure oxygen to yield 0.8635 g of CO_2 and 0.1767 g of H_2O. What is the empirical formula of the compound?

    (A) CHO

    (B) C_2H_2O

    (C) $C_3H_3O_2$

    (D) $C_6H_3O_2$

    (E) $C_3H_6O_2$

40. Which of the following is a conjugate acid/base pair?

    (A) HCl/OCl^-

    (B) H_2SO_4/SO_4^{2-}

    (C) NH_4^+/NH_3

    (D) H_3O^+/OH^-

    (E) H_3PO_4/PO_4^{3-}

Step 1)	$NO(g) + Cl_2(g) \rightleftharpoons NOCl_2(g)$	(fast equilibrium)
Step 2)	$NO(g) + NOCl_2(g) \rightarrow 2NOCl(g)$	(slow)

41. Which of the following rate laws is consistent with the reaction mechanism shown above?

    (A) Rate = $k[NO][Cl_2]$

    (B) Rate = $k[NO]_2$

    (C) Rate = $k[NO][NOCl_2]$

    (D) Rate = $k[NO]^2[Cl]$

    (E) Rate = $k[NO]^2[Cl][NOCl_2]$

42. When 0.200 L of 0.015 M $Pb(NO_3)_2$ is mixed with 0.300 L of 0.050 M KI, the value of Q will be _____ and the bright yellow precipitate, PbI_2, _____. (K_{sp} for PbI_2 is 9.8×10^{-9}).

    (A) less than K_{sp}; will form

    (B) greater than K_{sp}; will form

    (C) less than K_{sp}; will not form

    (D) greater than K_{sp}; will not form

    (E) equal to K_{sp}; will form

43. A crystal of NaCl is

    (A) soft, has a low melting temperature, and is a good electrical conductor.

    (B) hard, has a high melting temperature, and is a good electrical conductor.

    (C) soft, has a low melting temperature, and is a poor electrical conductor.

    (D) hard, has a high melting temperature, and is a poor electrical conductor.

    (E) soft, has a high melting temperature, and is a poor electrical conductor.

44. What effect will an increase in temperature have on the reaction below?

    $$2 SO_{3(g)} \rightleftharpoons 2 SO_{2(g)} + O_{2(g)}$$

    $$\Delta H° = +98.3 \text{ kJ per mole } SO_3$$

    (A) Shift the equilibrium to the right

    (B) Shift the equilibrium to the left

    (C) Will have no effect on the equilibrium

45. A 1.0–liter solution contains 0.25 M HF and 0.60 M NaF (K_a for HF is 7.2×10^{-4}) What is the pH of this solution?

    (A) 1.4

    (B) 3.5

    (C) 4.6

    (D) 2.8

    (E) 0.94

46. If a tree dies and the trunk remains undisturbed for 15,580 years, what percentage of original $^{14}_{6}C$ is still present? (half-life of $^{14}_{6}C$ = 5730 years)

(A) 5.20%

(B) 19.0%

(C) 2.20%

(D) 45.0%

(E) 15.2 %

47. What geometry does the molecule $SOCl_2$ exhibit?

(A) Pyramidal

(B) Trigonal bipyramidal

(C) Octahedral

(D) Trigonal planar

(E) Bent

48. In the rate law, Rate = $k[NO]^2[O_2]$, the reaction is _____ order for NO, _____ order for O_2, and _____ order overall.

(A) second; first; third

(B) second; zero; third

(C) first; second; third

(D) first; third; first

(E) third; third; third

49. A 6.00 L sample of an aqueous 0.108 M $MgCl_2$ solution at 30.0 °C will have an osmotic pressure of

(A) 8.05×10^2 mm Hg.

(B) 6.12×10^3 mm Hg.

(C) 2.04×10^3 mm Hg.

(D) 3.68×10^4 mm Hg.

(E) 1.02×10^3 mm Hg.

50. Which of the following is most likely to deviate from ideal gas behavior?

(A) Cl_2

(B) He

(C) Ar

(D) O_2

(E) CCl_2F_2

51. Which of the following shows the correct ranking of the highest to lowest first ionization energies for Na, P, Cl, K, Rb?

(A) Na > P > Cl > K > Rb

(B) Na > Cl > P > Rb > K

(C) Cl > P > Na > K > Rb

(D) Cl > P > Rb > K > Na

(E) Rb > K > Na > P > Cl

52. How many grams of silver nitrate ($AgNO_3$) are required to produced 44.0 g of aluminum nitrate ($Al(NO_3)_3$)?

$$6AgNO_3 + Al_2(SO_4)_3 \rightarrow 3Ag_2SO_4 + 2Al(NO_3)_3$$

(A) 105.3 g

(B) 132.0 g

(C) 169.9 g

(D) 213.0 g

(E) 264.0 g

53. A voltaic cell contains one half-cell with a zinc electrode in a $Zn^{2+}(aq)$ solution and a copper electrode in a $Cu^{2+}(aq)$ solution. At standard condition, $E° = 1.10$ V. Which condition below would cause the cell potential to be greater than 1.10 V?

(A) 1.0 M $Zn^{2+}(aq)$, 1.0 M $Cu^{2+}(aq)$

(B) 5.0 M $Zn^{2+}(aq)$, 5.0 M $Cu^{2+}(aq)$

(C) 5.0 M $Zn^{2+}(aq)$, 1.0 M $Cu^{2+}(aq)$

(D) 0.5 M $Zn^{2+}(aq)$, 0.5 M $Cu^{2+}(aq)$

(E) 0.1 M $Zn^{2+}(aq)$, 1.0 M $Cu^{2+}(aq)$

54. A 2.50 kg piece of copper metal is heated from 25°C to 225°C. How much heat, in kJ, is absorbed by the copper? The specific heat of copper is 0.384 J/g °C.

(A) 124 kJ

(B) 156 kJ

(C) 192 kJ

(D) 212 kJ

(E) 256 kJ

GO ON TO THE NEXT PAGE

55. If 25 mL of 0.75 M HCl are added to 100 mL of 0.25 NaOH, what is the final pH?

(A) 12.70

(B) 12.80

(C) 1.30

(D) 1.20

(E) 7.00

56. $2HF(g) \rightleftharpoons H_2(g) + F_2(g)$ $K_{eq} = 1.00 \times 10^{-2}$

1.00 mol HF, 0.500 mol H_2, and 0.750 mol F_2 are mixed in an evacuated 5.00 L flask. Which direction will the equilibrium shift to establish equilibrium?

(A) The equilibrium shifts to the right.

(B) The equilibrium shifts to the left.

(C) The system is at equilibrium.

57. Consider the following balanced equation:

$3 Ba(NO_3)_2 (aq) + Fe_2(SO_4)_3 (aq) \rightarrow 3 BaSO_4 (s) + 2 Fe(NO_3)_3 (aq)$

The net ionic equation to describe this balanced equation is

(A) $3Ba^{2+} (aq) + 3SO_4^{2-} (aq) \rightarrow 3BaSO_4 (s)$

(B) $6NO_3^{-} (aq) + 2Fe^{2+} (aq) \rightarrow 2Fe(NO_3)_3 (aq)$

(C) $3Ba^{2+} (aq) + 2NO_3^{-} (aq) + 2Fe^{3+} (aq) + 3SO_4^{2-} (aq) \rightarrow 3BaSO_4 (s) + 2Fe^{3+} (aq) + 6NO_3^{-} (aq)$

(D) $3Ba^{+} (aq) + SO_4^{3-} (aq) \rightarrow 3BaSO_4 (s)$

(E) $2Fe^{3+}(aq) + 3NO^{3-}(aq) \rightarrow 2Fe(NO_3)_3 (aq)$

58. Which of the following ionic compounds has the largest lattice energy, i.e., the lattice energy most favorable to a stable lattice?

(A) CsI

(B) LiI

(C) LiF

(D) CsF

(E) MgO

59. In a voltaic cell, a zinc electrode is placed in a solution that is 1.0 M for Zn^{2+}, while a copper electrode is placed in a 1.0 M Cu^{2+} solution. Calculate the cell potential for the voltaic cell. (Assume a salt bridge is in place.)

(A) 1.00 V

(B) 1.05 V

(C) 1.10 V

(D) 2.00 V

(E) 11.0 V

60. The K_{sp} of $PbSO_4$ (s) is 1.3×10^{-8}. Calculate the solubility (in mol/L) of $PbSO_4$ (s) in a 0.0010 M solution of Na_2SO_4.

(A) 1.3×10^{-10} M

(B) 4.5×10^{-6} M

(C) 1.3×10^{-5} M

(D) 1.3×10^{-7} M

(E) 1.3×10^{-3} M

61. A 6.50-L sample of carbon monoxide is collected at 55°C and 0.875 atm. What volume will the gas occupy at 1.10 atm and 20°C?

(A) 1.96 L

(B) 5.46 L

(C) 4.62 L

(D) 6.10 L

(E) 9.64 L

62. Name the following:

$$CH_3-CH_2-\underset{\underset{CH_2CH_3}{|}}{\overset{\overset{CH_3}{|}}{C}}-CH_3$$

(A) *n*-hexane

(B) 2-methyl-2-ethylbutane

(C) 3,3-dimethylpentane

(D) 2,2-diethylpropane

(E) 3-ethyl-3,3-dimethylpropane

63.

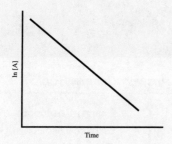

The graph shown is consistent with this type of reaction.

(A) Zero order

(B) First order

(C) Second order

(D) Third order

(E) Exothermic

64. When placed in a hot flame, copper nitrate crystals will turn

(A) yellow.

(B) violet.

(C) blue-green.

(D) orange.

(E) red.

Diagnostic Test

Answer Key

Number	Answer	Chapter/Topic	Number	Answer	Chapter/Topic
1.	D	Chapter 3 Atomic Structure	33.	C	Chapter 9 Solutions
2.	A	Chapter 8 States of Matter—Liquids and Solids	34.	D	Chapter 6 Molecular Geometry
			35.	B	Chapter 16 Thermodynamics
3.	D	Chapter 14 Additional Equilibrium Concepts	36.	C	Chapter 12 Equilibrium
			37.	E	Chapter 3 Atomic Structure
4.	B	Chapter 4 Nuclear Chemistry	38.	D	Chapter 10 Reaction Types
5.	A	Chapter 13 Acids and Bases	39.	C	Chapter 11 Stoichiometry
6.	D	Chapter 16 Thermodynamics	40.	C	Chapter 13 Acids and Bases
7.	D	Chapter 18 Organic Chemistry	41.	D	Chapter 15 Kinetics
8.	E	Chapter 10 Reaction Types	42.	B	Chapter 14 Additional Equilibrium Concepts
9.	B	Chapter 15 Kinetics			
10.	A	Chapter 11 Stoichiometry	43.	D	Chapter 8 States of Matter—Liquids and Solids
11.	D	Chapter 12 Equilibrium			
12.	B	Chapter 9 Solutions	44.	A	Chapter 12 Equilibrium
13.	C	Chapter 17 Electrochemistry	45.	B	Chapter 13 Acids and Bases
14.	A	Chapter 5 Chemical Bonding	46.	E	Chapter 4 Nuclear Chemistry
15.	C	Chapter 6 Molecular Geometry	47.	A	Chapter 6 Molecular Geometry
16.	C	Chapter 7 States of Matter—Gases	48.	A	Chapter 15 Kinetics
			49.	B	Chapter 9 Solutions
17.	B	Chapter 3 Atomic Structure	50.	E	Chapter 7 States of Matter—Gases
18.	A	Chapter 5 Chemical Bonding			
19.	D	Chapter 4 Nuclear Chemistry	51.	C	Chapter 3 Atomic Structure
20.	E	Chapter 8 States of Matter—Liquids and Solids	52.	A	Chapter 11 Stoichiometry
			53.	E	Chapter 17 Electrochemistry
21.	D	Chapter 16 Thermodynamics	54.	C	Chapter 16 Thermodynamics
22.	A	Chapter 14 Additional Equilibrium Concepts	55.	A	Chapter 13 Acids and Bases
			56.	B	Chapter 12 Equilibrium
23.	C	Chapter 9 Solutions	57.	A	Chapter 10 Reaction Types
24.	A	Chapter 6 Molecular Geometry	58.	E	Chapter 5 Chemical Bonding
25.	D	Chapter 15 Kinetics	59.	C	Chapter 17 Electrochemistry
26.	C	Chapter 10 Reaction Types	60.	C	Chapter 14 Additional Equilibrium Concepts
27.	B	Chapter 4 Nuclear Chemistry			
28.	C	Chapter 8 States of Matter—Liquids and Solids	61.	C	Chapter 7 States of Matter—Gases
29.	C	Chapter 11 Stoichiometry	62.	C	Chapter 18 Organic Chemistry
30.	A	Chapter 7 States of Matter—Gases	63.	B	Chapter 15 Kinetics
			64.	C	Chapter 14 Additional Equilibrium Concepts
31.	D	Chapter 5 Chemical Bonding			
32.	B	Chapter 17 Electrochemistry			

AP Chemistry Strategies

CHAPTER 1

The AP Test Structure

As part of your preparation for the AP Chemistry exam, you are taking a class. The purpose of the class is to teach you the content of the exam—the chemistry. While this is undoubtedly the most significant information to learn, there are some other things you can learn to prepare for the test. Remember, this is a one-shot deal—you only have one chance to prove what you have learned over the course of an entire year of school. Most of this book is devoted to review of the content of chemistry, but this chapter is designed to help you learn more about the actual AP test. You will learn about the question formats and the scoring process for the free-response questions. You will also learn some pacing, guessing, and test-taking strategies that can really boost your confidence—and your score!

REVIEW OF THE AP QUESTION TYPES

In the Introduction, we looked at the format of the exam—the two main portions of the test are multiple choice, worth 45 percent of the total grade, and free response, worth the remaining 55 percent. Now that you've had a chance to get a general feel for the test, let's begin to take a closer look at the test's design. There are certain types of questions that appear on the AP Chemistry exam. Becoming aware of these types of questions, as well as learning some strategies to answer them, can help you become more confident when you take the exam.

The main advantage of the multiple-choice section is that there are five answers to choose from, and the correct answer is always given to you! Properly written multiple-choice questions should not be easy to answer, however. Despite the fact that the correct answers are found somewhere in the five choices, the correct answer will be imbedded among what are known as distracters. Distracters are choices that are close to being correct but that are not the correct answer. The main difficulty comes from the amount of time you're given on this section. There are 75 questions to complete in 90 minutes. That's an average of 1 minute and 12 seconds per question—and without the benefit of a calculator! For those of you who spent long evenings working on problem sets that only had a handful of problems in them, this may have you concerned. Take heart, though, because there are some tricks you can learn to save you time, especially since you have the correct answers in front of you. So, one portion of this chapter is devoted to learning typical formats for multiple-choice questions on the chemistry exam and how best to approach each to save time and improve your performance.

The main difficulty of the free-response section is that the answers are not provided for you. You have the benefit of more time (and on part A, you can use a calculator), but you're on your own for coming up with a solution. For the free-response questions, it is important to become familiar with the scoring rubrics. Knowing how your answers will be graded can help you answer questions more efficiently and with a higher probability of earning points. Later in this chapter we will look at some strategies for writing effective free-response answers.

THE AP CHEMISTRY ANSWER SHEETS

For Section I of the test (the multiple-choice questions), you will be provided a test booklet and an answer sheet. The answer sheet is a bubble sheet, and the test booklet contains all of the multiple-choice questions. You are not allowed to use scratch paper on the test, and you will have to put your calculator away. Any extra writing you need to do (e.g., calculations) can be done in the margins of the test booklet—not on the answer sheet! As far as the bubble sheet goes, first make sure you're using a #2 pencil—that way, the marks you make will be dark enough for the scoring machine to read. In addition, you must make sure that your answers are neatly bubbled into the ovals.

For the free-response questions, you will be given a separate packet. The first part of the packet consists of your answer booklet. All answers are to be written here. You will also be given a green packet that contains the questions and a great deal of reference material—a periodic table, a table of standard reduction potentials, and several pages of formulas and constants (shown in tables 1.1 through 1.7).

SOME TEST-WISE STRATEGIES FOR AP SUCCESS

What makes some people better test-takers than others? The secret isn't just knowing the subject, it's knowing specific test-taking strategies that can add up to extra points. This means psyching out the test, knowing how the test-makers think and what they're looking for, and using this knowledge to your advantage. Smart test-takers know how to use pacing and guessing to add points to their score.

Pace Yourself

Remember, on the multiple-choice section you have about 1 minute and 12 seconds per question. But there will be some questions that won't take that long. Using less time on the easier questions will give you more time for the harder ones. Learning to pace yourself is extremely important. Here are some pacing guidelines you should remember:

Table 1.1   STANDARD REDUCTION POTENTIALS IN AQUEOUS SOLUTION AT 25°C

Half-reaction E((V)

$Li^+ + e^-$	$\rightarrow$	$Li(s)$	-3.05
$Cs^+ + e^-$	$\rightarrow$	$Cs(s)$	-2.92
$K^+ + e^-$	$\rightarrow$	$K(s)$	-2.92
$Rb^+ + e^-$	$\rightarrow$	$Rb(s)$	-2.92
$Ba^{2+} + 2e$	$\rightarrow$	$Ba(s)$	-2.90
$Sr^{2+} + 2e^-$	$\rightarrow$	$Sr(s)$	-2.89
$Ca^{2+} + 2e^-$	$\rightarrow$	$Ca(s)$	-2.87
$Na^+ + e^-$	$\rightarrow$	$Na(s)$	-2.71
$Mg^{2+}\ 2e^-$	$\rightarrow$	$Mg(s)$	-2.37
$Be^{2+} + 2e^-$	$\rightarrow$	$Be(s)$	-1.70
$Al^{3+} + 3e^-$	$\rightarrow$	$Al(s)$	-1.66
$Mn^{2+} + 2e^-$	$\rightarrow$	$Mn(s)$	-1.18
$Zn^{2+} + 2e^-$	$\rightarrow$	$Zn(s)$	-0.76
$Cr^{3+} + 3e^-$	$\rightarrow$	$Cr(s)$	-0.74
$Fe^{2+} + 2e^-$	$\rightarrow$	$Fe(s)$	-0.44
$Cr^{3+} + e^-$	$\rightarrow$	Cr^{2+}	-0.41
$Cd^{2+} + 2e^-$	$\rightarrow$	$Cd(s)$	-0.40
$Tl^+ + e^-$	$\rightarrow$	$Tl(s)$	-0.34
$Co^{2+} + 2e^-$	$\rightarrow$	$Co(s)$	-0.28
$Ni^{2+} + 2e^-$	$\rightarrow$	$Ni(s)$	-0.25
$Sn^{2+} + 2e^-$	$\rightarrow$	$Sn(s)$	-0.14
$Pb^{2+} + 2e^-$	$\rightarrow$	$Pb(s)$	-0.13
$2H^+ + 2e^-$	$\rightarrow$	$H_2(g)$	0.00
$S(^s) + 2H+ + 2e^-$	$\rightarrow$	$H_2S(g)$	0.14
$Sn^{4+} + 2e^-$	$\rightarrow$	Sn^{2+}	0.15
$Cu^{2+} + e^-$	$\rightarrow$	Cu^+	0.15
$Cu^{2+} + 2e^-$	$\rightarrow$	$Cu(s)$	0.34
$Cu^+ + e^-$	$\rightarrow$	$Cu(s)$	0.52
$I_2(s) + 2e^-$	$\rightarrow$	$2I^-$	0.53
$Fe^{3+} + e^-$	$\rightarrow$	Fe^{2+}	0.77
$Hg_2^{2+} + 2e^-$	$\rightarrow$	$2\ Hg(l)$	0.79
$Ag^+ + e^-$	$\rightarrow$	$Ag(s)$	0.80
$Hg^{2+} + 2e^-$	$\rightarrow$	$Hg(l)$	0.85
$2Hg^{2+} + 2e^-$	$\rightarrow$	Hg_2^{2+}	0.92
$Br_2(l) + 2e^-$	$\rightarrow$	$2Br^-$	1.07
$O_2(g) + 4H^+ + 4e^-$	$\rightarrow$	$2H_2O(l)$	1.23
$Cl_2(g) + 2e^-$	$\rightarrow$	$2Cl^-$	1.36
$Au^{3+} + 3e^-$	$\rightarrow$	$Au(s)$	1.50
$Co^{3+} + e^-$	$\rightarrow$	Co^{2+}	1.82
$F_2(g) + 2e^-$	$\rightarrow$	$2F^-$	2.87

Table 1.2 ATOMIC STRUCTURE

$\Delta E = h\nu$

$c = \lambda\nu$

$\lambda = \dfrac{h}{mv}$

$p = mv$

$En = \dfrac{-2.178 \times 10^{-18}}{n^2}$ joule

Table 1.3 EQUILIBRIUM

$K_a = \dfrac{\left[H^+\right]\left[A^-\right]}{[HA]}$

$K_b = \dfrac{\left[OH^-\right]\left[HB^+\right]}{[B]}$

$K_w = [OH^-][H^+] = 1.0 \times 10^{-14}$ at 25 °C

$\quad = K_a \times K_b$

$pH = -\log[H^+], \; pOH = -\log[OH^-]$

$14 = pH + pOH$

$pH = pK_a + \log\dfrac{[A-]}{[HA]}$

$pOH = pK_b + \log\dfrac{\left[HB^+\right]}{[B]}$

$pK_a = -\log K_a, \; pK_b = -\log K_b$

$K_p = K_c(RT)^{\Delta n}$

Where Δn = moles product gas − moles reactant gas

Questions Usually Go from Easiest to Most Difficult—You Should Too

While each successive problem may not be more difficult, you should keep in mind that the earlier problems tend to be the easiest. Work as quickly as you can through the beginning of the test. Don't get lulled into a false sense of security because you appear to be maintaining a good pace in the first part—it's going to get harder!

You Can Set Your Own Speed Limit

All right, how will you know what your speed limit is? Use the practice tests to check your timing and see how it affects your answers. If you've answered most of the questions within the time limit but also have a lot of incorrect answers, you'd better slow down. On the other hand, if you are very accurate in your answers but aren't answering every question in a section, you can probably pick up the pace a bit.

Table 1.4 THERMOCHEMISTRY

$\Delta S° = \sum S°$ products $- \sum S°$ reactants

$\Delta H° = \sum H°_f$ products $- \sum H°_f$ reactants

$\Delta G° = \sum \Delta G°_f$ products $- \sum G°_f$ reactants

$\Delta G° = \Delta H° - T\,\Delta S°$

$\qquad = -RT \ln K = -2.303\,RT \log K$

$\qquad = -n\,\mathcal{F}\,E°$

$\Delta G = \Delta G° + RT \ln Q = \Delta G° + 2.303 RT \log Q$

$q = mc\Delta T$

$C_p = \dfrac{\Delta H}{\Delta T}$

$\qquad E$ = energy

$\qquad \nu$ = frequency

$\qquad \lambda$ = wavelength

$\qquad p$ = momentum

$\qquad v$ = velocity

$\qquad n$ = principal quantum number

$\qquad m$ = mass

Speed of light, $c = 3.0 \times 10^8$ m s^{-1}

Planck's constant, $h = 6.63 \times 10^{-34}$ J s

Boltzmann's constant, $k = 1.38 \times 10^{-23}$ J K^{-1}

Avogadro's number $= 6.022 \times 10^{23}$ molecules mol^{-1}

Electron charge, $e = -1.602 \times 10^{-19}$ coulomb

1 electron volt per atom $= 96.5$ kJ mol^{-1}

It's Smart to Keep Moving

It's hard to let go, but sometimes you have to. Don't spend too much time on any one question before you've tried all the questions in a section. There may be questions later on in the test that you can answer easily, and you don't want to lose points just because you didn't get to them. Remember, all of the questions are worth the same amount of points—you won't get extra points for solving that really difficult problem. If you get stuck, it's better to bail and try for an easier question.

You're Going to Need a Watch

If you're going to pace yourself, you need to keep track of the time—and what if there is no clock in your room or if the only clock is out of your line of vision? It's a good idea to bring a simple, non-digital watch to the test. Don't use a watch alarm or else your watch will end up on the proctor's desk.

Table 1.5   EQUILIBRIUM CONSTANTS

K_a (weak acid)

K_b (weak base)

K_w (water)

K_p (gas pressure)

K_c (molar concentrations)

$S°$ = standard entropy

$H°$ = standard enthalpy

$G°$ = standard free energy

$E°$ = standard reduction potential

T = temperature

n = moles

m = mass

q = heat

c = specific heat capacity

C_p = molar heat capacity at constant pressure

1 faraday, $\mathcal{F}$ = 96,500 coulombs

P = pressure

V = volume

T = temperature

n = number of moles

D = density

m = mass

v = velocity

u_{rms} = root-mean-square speed

KE = kinetic energy

r = rate of effusion

M = molar mass

π = osmotic pressure

i = van't Hoff factor

K_f = molal freezing-point depression constant

K_b = molal boiling-point elevation constant

Q = reaction quotient

I = current amperes

q = charge (coulombs)

t = time (seconds)

$E°$= standard reduction potential

K = equilibrium constant

Gas constant, R = 8.31 J mol^{-1}K^{-1}

= 0.0821 L atm mol^{-1} K^{-1}

= 8.31 volt coulomb mol^{-1} K^{-1}

Boltzmann's constant, k = 1.38×10^{-23} J K^{-1}

K_f for H_2O = 1.86 K kg mol^{-1}

K_b for H_2O = 0.512 K kg mol^{-1}

STP = 0.000 °C and 1.000 atm

Faraday's constant, $\mathcal{F}$ = 96,500 coulombs per mole of electrons

Table 1.6   GASES, LIQUIDS, AND SOLUTIONS

$PV = nRT$

$$\left(P + \frac{n^2 a}{V^2}\right)(V - nb) = nRT$$

$PA = P_{total} \times XA$, where $XA = \dfrac{\text{moles A}}{\text{total moles}}$

$P_{total} = PA + PB + PC + \ldots$

$n = \dfrac{m}{M}$

$K = {}^\circ C + 273$

$\dfrac{P_1 V_1}{T_1} = \dfrac{P_2 V_2}{T_2}$

$D = \dfrac{m}{V}$

$u_{rms} = \sqrt{\dfrac{3kT}{m}} = \sqrt{\dfrac{3RT}{M}}$

KE per molecule $= \dfrac{1}{2} mv^2$

KE per mole $= \dfrac{3}{2} RTn$

$\dfrac{r_1}{r_2} = \sqrt{\dfrac{M_2}{M_1}}$

molarity, M = moles solute per liter solution

molality = moles solute per kilogram solvent

$\Delta T_f = iK_f \times \text{molality}$

$\Delta T_b = iK_b \times \text{molality}$

$\pi = \dfrac{nRT}{V} i$

Table 1.7   OXIDATION-REDUCTION; ELECTROCHEMISTRY

$Q = \dfrac{[C]^c [D]^d}{[A]^a [B]^b}$, where $aA + bB \rightarrow cC + dD$

$I = \dfrac{q}{t}$

$E_{cell} = E^\circ_{cell} - \dfrac{RT}{n\mathcal{F}} \ln Q$

$\qquad = E^\circ_{cell} - \dfrac{0.0592}{n} \log Q$ at 25°C

$\log K = \dfrac{nE^\circ}{0.0592}$

Learn to Be a Good listener

In Chapter 1, we told you that the fractional deduction for wrong answers makes random guessing a wash—statistically speaking, you're unlikely to change your score. This means that if you come to a question that you have absolutely no idea how to answer, you're probably better off skipping it and moving on rather than choosing an answer at random.

Educated Guessing Will Boost Your Score!

Although random guessing won't help you, anything better than random guessing will. On most questions, you should be able to guess better than randomly by using common sense and the process of elimination techniques that are developed throughout this book. Even if you aren't certain which answer is correct, you might be certain that one or more of the answer choices is definitely wrong. If you can eliminate one choice out of five, you have a 25 percent chance of guessing correctly. If you can knock out two choices, the odds go up to $33\frac{1}{3}$ percent. If you can knock off three, you have a 50/50 chance of guessing the right answer. With odds like these, it makes sense to guess.

The Easy Answer Isn't Always THE Best ANSWER

Make sure you read all of the choices before selecting your choice. Quite frequently, test-makers will put an attractive—but incorrect—answer as an (A) or (B) choice. Reading all of the choices decreases your chances of being misled, particularly in questions where no calculations are involved.

You Need to Work Quickly and Carefully

You're smart enough to know that with 90 minutes for 75 questions, you don't have time to dillydally. You also know that this is a high-stakes test. When you do a homework problem or even a problem on a chapter test in class, a careless error may not have devastating effects. However, too many careless mistakes on this test will lower your score in a hurry. Therefore, it's important to follow some simple guidelines as you prepare for the exam. These guidelines can help to minimize your careless errors and improve your rate for problem solving.

Know Your Stuff

While all of these strategies are helpful, there is no substitute for knowledge. If you don't know the material, your odds of getting correct answers are extremely limited. As we said in the last chapter, you may not know every bit of information on the exam, but it is important that you remember the information you have learned. The chapters in this book will help you to effectively and efficiently review that material.

Use Common Sense

It is always important to make sure your answers make sense. On multiple-choice questions, it might be readily apparent that you've made an error (e.g., none of the choices match your answer). However, on the free response, there is no immediate feedback about the accuracy of your answer. It is important to inspect your work to make sure it makes sense. For example, if you are solving an acid-base problem and your calculated pH is 15.3, you may want to look over your work! Before you solve a problem, think about what you would expect the answer to be prior to working it out. If there is a large discrepancy between your calculated answer and your prediction, you may have made an error.

Put down Your Calculator

You only get to use your calculator for one part of the test, so all calculations on the multiple-choice section must be done in your head or with pencil and paper. Couple this with the 1 or 2 minutes you'll have to answer each question and you can see how you might have difficulty crunching numbers by hand in such a short amount of time. One thing in your favor is that in 1996, when the College Board eliminated calculators from most of the test, the problems were rewritten so that the numbers were easier to work with. For example, in a stoichiometric conversion involving a compound like H_2SO_4, you might be given a mass of 100.1 g or 200.2 g to describe it. A quick determination of the molar mass of H_2SO_4 (98.1 g mol^{-1}) lets you see right away that you are dealing with a whole number of moles of sulfuric acid in the problem. On the portions of the exam where calculators are prohibited, you should expect to deal with numbers that are fairly easy to work with. However, you want to sharpen your skills for solving problems without a calculator. You don't want the AP exam to be your first time working without your calculator. Make sure that when you go through this book, *particularly the practice tests,* you do so without your calculator. Forcing yourself to work through the problems by hand will sharpen your skills and improve your speed.

Logarithms

There are several formulas that require the use of logarithms. Because logarithms are easy to work with on a calculator, you may never have learned much about what they actually are. Becoming familiar with a few properties of logarithms can help you work more quickly on some problems, especially pH problems. If you recall, the formula for the determination of pH is $pH = -\log[H^+]$. You usually are given some value for the concentration of hydrogen that is a small value like 1.0×10^{-3}. If you were to calculate an answer, you would find that $pH = -\log[1.0 \times 10^{-3}] = 3$. In other words, a pH of 3 is the same as 10^{-3}. Further investigation will show that a pH of 4 is equal to 10^{-4}. Care to make a prediction about the hydrogen ion concentration of a solution with a pH of 5? You got it—it's 10^{-5}. So, what if you have a $[H^+]$ of 2.4×10^{-4}? Well, you know that the value is greater than 1×10^{-4} and less than 1×10^{-3}. Therefore, the answer should be between pH = 3 and pH = 4. You can quickly rule out any choices that are not in this range.

MULTIPLE CHOICE
The Typical Multiple-Choice Question
The typical design of a question with five correct choices is to have one distracter that is very close to the correct answer, two that are still similar, and one that can usually be ruled out almost immediately. The structure of the distracters will vary according to the type of question that is being asked. For example, if a calculation is involved, the test-makers will often use various incorrect forms of the formulas to obtain the distracters. For example, take a problem that is a calculation using Charles's Law, which states that the ratio of volume to absolute temperature will remain constant for a gas at constant pressure:

What volume will an amount of nitrogen gas occupy at 77° if the gas occupies a volume of 400 ml at a temperature of 27°?

To solve this problem, you would first need to convert each temperature to kelvin. In doing so, you would have the following information:

$T_1 = 27° C = 300 K$

$T_2 = 77° C = 350 K$

$V_1 = 400$ ml

$V_2 = ?$

Since $\dfrac{V}{T} = k$ (constant), then $\dfrac{V_1}{T_1} = \dfrac{V_2}{T_2}$; rearranging the equation, we get $V_2 = \dfrac{V_1 T_2}{T_1}$.

At this point, let's look at the possible answers. The distracters are enclosed in parentheses.

(A) 1141 ml   (uses $\dfrac{(400)(77)}{27}$; note temperatures are in °C)

(B) 343 ml   (uses $\dfrac{(400)(300)}{350}$; note T is in kelvin but inverted)

(C) 140 ml   (uses $\dfrac{(400)(27)}{77}$; combination of choices A and B)

(D) 467 ml   (uses $\dfrac{(400)(350)}{300}$; correct answer)

(E) 1.33 ml   (uses $\dfrac{400}{300}$; missing T_2)

An important consideration: If you make any of the errors shown above, you will get one of the answers above, which can make you believe you have gotten the problem right! It's very important to know how you are going to proceed before you attempt to solve a problem.

The Use of Multiple Answers

Another version of multiple-choice questions that you will encounter on the exam is the use of multiple answers. This technique, used to various degrees in the chemistry exam, provides three different choices. The five possible answers involve different combinations of the three choices. Look at this sample question about periodicity:

As you move from left to right between elements 11 and 17,

  I. atomic radius decreases.

 II. ionization energy decreases.

III. electronegativity increases.

   (A) I only

   (B) II only

   (C) III only

   (D) I and III

   (E) I, II, and III

The problem with these questions is that if you are uncertain about one of the choices, they become increasingly more difficult to answer. For example, if you are not sure whether II is a correct answer, you may not know how to deal with choices (D) *and* (E). However, a second look might provide you with some clues about how to guess. For example, if you are only uncertain about number II but you are sure that I and III are correct, you can at least rule out (A), (B), and (C) as possible choices. This leaves you with a 50 percent chance of guessing correctly.

Reverse Multiple Choice

The AP exam usually starts out with yet a third type of question: something called a reverse multiple choice. That is, five choices are listed, and then several questions follow. You are supposed to answer each question with one of the choices from the list. For example, say you are given a problem about electron configurations. It might read something like this:

Questions 1–4

   (A) $1s^22s^22p^1$

   (B) $1s^22p^1$

   (C) $1s^22s^22p^63s^2$

   (D) $1s^22s^22p^73s^1$

   (E) $1s^22s^22p^6$

1. Corresponds to a noble gas
2. Represents an impossible configuration
3. Ground state configuration for Mg
4. Represents an atom in an excited state

In case you were trying to answer these, the answers are 1. (E), 2. (D), 3. (C), 4. (B).

A few things to remember about these problems: there are usually more choices than questions (that's to keep you from getting any right by process of elimination), and you may be able use answers more than once.

THE FREE-RESPONSE QUESTIONS

If you recall from the Introduction, the free-response portion of the test has two sections. In Section I, you are permitted to use a calculator, but in Section II, you are not. In Section I, there is one mandatory question and two additional problems from which you must choose one. Because you are allowed to use your calculator, anything goes. That is, the numbers won't be as convenient to work with as they are in the multiple choice. Also, because the correct answers are not somewhere in front of you, you will have to be much more alert about careless errors. In addition, you will need to attend to significant figures (see Chapter 2) when writing your answers. On Section II, you can count on one question giving you written descriptions of eight chemical reactions. You are provided with a description of the reactants and any special treatments (i.e., heating or electrolysis) and are asked to write out symbolic equations for five of them. On the remainder, you will be given two mandatory questions and two other questions, from which you will select one. These questions in Section II of the test are much more conceptual in nature and will resemble the format of the multiple-choice exam. Any questions requiring calculations will use numbers that are easy to work with. This is not to say that the questions are easy! They are very challenging. It just means that the calculations will not be the challenging part of the question.

Before we take a detailed look at free-response questions, you may be interested in knowing what topics appear most frequently in this section. In the table that follows, you will see the topics that have appeared in the Free Response portion of the AP Chemistry exam for the last three years. Following the table is a graphical summary of the table. *An important note:* Don't rely too heavily on this information. That is, don't skip your study of a section simply because it hasn't appeared very often. The questions are changed every year, and you never know when the College Board will decide to throw that one topic in there. However, you can use the information to help you create a personal study plan for the exam. You should see that some topics are almost always on the exam. If you're going to skip any sections or go lightly over them during your review, these would not be the best topics to skip. The other reason for giving you this information is to reduce anxiety. The more familiar you become with the exam, the less intimidated you will be by it. Minimizing your fear will help to maximize your confidence and, hopefully, your success!

Free-Response Topics Over the Years

In the table that follows, keep in mind that only the general topics are listed. There are some questions in the free-response questions that require you to integrate topic areas (e.g., free energy and equilibrium). In such instances, the primary topic of the question is listed. Also, there is no distinction of whether the question was a Section I (calculator) or a Section II (non-calculator) question. Finally, because the question with the eight reactions (from which you select five) appears every year, these have been omitted in the interest of space.

OVERVIEW OF THE FREE-RESPONSE PROBLEMS

Part A
Calculator Questions

Remember, in this section there are three questions, one required and two from which you select one. The first problem deals with some aspect of equilibrium and will consist of several parts, usually from five to seven. Each part is worth 1 or 2 points, for a total of 9 points. Average scores on this problem tend to be somewhere around 4. The two optional problems also contain multiple parts, with each worth 9 points. Scores on this question range from 4 to 5.

How to Improve Your Chances of Getting Points

There are some important factors to consider here. First, the graders are grading lots of papers—hundreds of them. Try putting yourself in their place. Picture yourself, after a long day of scoring chemistry papers, trying to grade a paper that is a mess, that is missing work, and that has some mistakes. Now picture yourself, after a long day of grading, scoring a paper that is neat and organized and that follows a logical progression. Can you picture it? Surely the second paper is likely to receive a warmer reception than the first. That's not to say that you can be completely incorrect and still get points for having attractive answers. However, there are opportunities for partial credit, that you want to take full advantage of. Graders don't take pleasure in deducting points from a paper, particularly when they think you might have known what you were doing.

 The second point to remember is that the grader does not know you. While this may be a rather obvious statement, there is a reason for mentioning it. Your teacher, despite his or her best attempts to be objective, may give you a little leeway on grading because he or she knows you and knows what you probably meant to say in your essays. The graders for the AP exam don't

	Main Topic	Details
1997	Acid-Base	*Ka*, *Kb*, concentration
	Electrochemistry	Half-reactions, cell potential
	Kinetics	Order, rate law, mechanism
	Bonding	Lewis structures, polarity
	Atomic theory/Bonding	Ionization energy, ionic radius
	Thermodynamics	ΔS, ΔG, *Kp*
	Nuclear	Decay, mass defect
	Laboratory procedures	Mass percent of an unknown soluble salt
1998	Equilibrium	*Ksp*
	Stoichiometry	Empirical formula, molar mass (freezing point depression), molar mass (vapor density)
	Thermodynamics	ΔH, ΔG
	Laboratory Procedures	Acid-Base titration
	Kinetics	Essays: graph interpretation (activation energy, rate, rate law)
	Equilibrium	Le Châtelier's
	Electrochemistry	Essays: electrochemical cell concepts
	Various topics	Essays: bonding, solubility, organic (isomers), oxidizing/reducing agents
	Equilibrium	*Ksp*
1999	Acid-Base	*K*, pH, *Kb*, titration
	Atomic structure	E, λ, ν, emission spectra
	Kinetics	Rate law, reaction mechanism
	Laboratory procedures	Determination of the molar mass by vapor density
	Thermodynamics	Essay: ΔH, ΔS, ΔG States of matter: solids, liquids
	Bonding	Lewis structures, bond lengths, molecular geometry
	Acid-Base	*K*, pH, *Kb*, titration
2000	Equilibrium	K_c, K_p, stoichiometry
	Electrochemistry	$E°$, ΔG, half-reactions, electrolytic cell
	Stoichiometry	Mass percent, water of hydration, redox titration
	Laboratory procedures	Molar mass determination by freezing point depression
	Thermodynamics	Hess's law, prediction of signs of entropy, free energy
	Kinetics	Rate law expression from data, reaction mechanism
	Atomic structure	Various questions about atomic structure
	Acid-Base	Various questions about strong acid/weak base titration

Occurence of Topics Since 1979

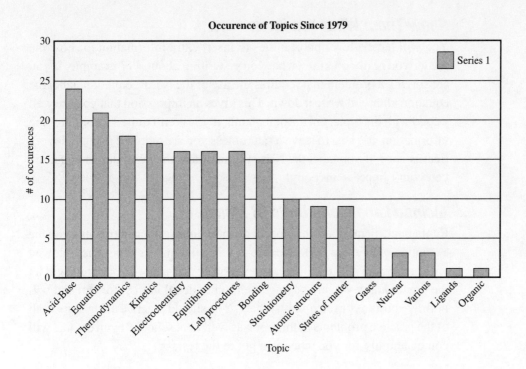

know you. They won't know what you probably meant—unless you write it down. You may know exactly how to answer every question, but if you don't write anything down, no one will ever know.

Be Neat

There's nothing more frustrating for a teacher or grader than trying to decipher chicken-scratch. You don't want the grader spending her time frustrated while trying to grade your work. Let her focus on the content rather than the form. The answers are not lengthy, so do your best to be neat and organized.

Show All of Your Work

One thing that many students resist is showing the steps in a calculation. They often figure that they have done the work on their calculator or in their heads so it isn't worth writing down. This test is not the time to be stubborn or to make a point. Write down all of your steps. There are times when the best of us make mistakes in a calculation. If you only show your answer, and it happens to be incorrect, the grader has no choice but to give you no credit for the entire question.

For some questions, your answer to one part will be used later in a different part. Let's say that you got the first part wrong but did the second part correctly. If you only show your answers, the incorrect answer from the first part will cause you to miss the second question as well. However, if you show all of the steps in the calculation, the grader can still award you full credit for the second part, even though the answer is incorrect. Writing down all of your steps makes sense.

Show Them What You Know

You will have a few opportunities to insert extra information to show the grader you really do know what you're writing about. For example, if you are solving a problem that requires the use of the Nernst equation, label the equation after you write it down. This gives an impression that you are well versed with the topic. On the other hand, if you aren't quite sure about some information, it's best to leave it out (unless you are required to put it down). For instance, if you label the Nernst Equation as the Schrödinger equation, you won't impress anybody!

Include Labels and Units Of Measure

Remember, all numbers that appear on the exam are measurements (with the exception of a few ratios). Because of this, all numbers should be followed with an appropriate unit of measure. Writing down all of your units will let the grader know you are paying attention to detail in the problem and will portray you as a conscientious student. You should practice using units in all of the practice problems in this book as well as at school. If you do, this will come naturally for you when you get to the test.

Significant Figures

The graders are allowed to take off one point per question for significant figures. This is a free point! It doesn't require you know anything about chemistry. The questions are hard enough without losing points for something like this. The graders are usually allowed to give you leeway of ±1 digit on your answers. If all else fails, keep in mind the number 3. Most textbooks and tests use three significant digits in their problems. More often than not, if you write your answers with three significant figures, you will be correct. In Chapter 2, we will review the rules for significant figures.

Choose Wisely

You don't get any more credit for selecting a more difficult question. This is also not an opportune time to challenge yourself. You have plenty of time to do that after you take the exam if you still feel compelled to do so. So, when given a choice between questions, read through each before deciding which one you will answer. Make sure you read all parts of all choices before making your decision. Some may start easy and then have a landmine (a really difficult part) buried toward the end. Others may start with a hard part and have easier parts at the end. You need to read all of the choices to make an informed decision.

Don't be tempted to answer both. You don't get any bonus points for answering extra questions on the test, nor should you waste time with such an attempt. You are far better off devoting your time to the required number of questions. If you begin to answer one question and change your mind, make sure you cross out or erase any portions that you may have started. This will prevent them from being accidentally graded.

Part B
Chemical Equations

In this section, you will begin with the reaction questions. Recall, you are given eight partial equations from which you are to select five. In each question, you are provided the reactants and any conditions of the reaction. You are then to write an equation for the reaction. The directions for this section tell you to assume that all solutions are aqueous unless otherwise indicated. You are also instructed to represent substances in solution as ions if the material is extensively ionized, and you should omit the formulas for any ions or molecules that are unchanged by the reaction (spectators, for instance). It is not necessary to balance the equations in this section. Don't waste the time doing that. Here is a sample problem that illustrates this portion of the test:

Sample: A sample of zinc powder is added to a solution of silver nitrate.
   Answer: $Zn + Ag^+ \rightarrow Zn^{2+} + Ag$

That is all that is necessary here. Note that, as directed, the equation is not balanced, the solution is assumed to be aqueous, the silver nitrate in solution is shown as ions, and the nitrate ion is omitted because it remains unchanged in the reaction. If you have time at the end of the test—but only if you have time—go back and add details to the equations, such as (aq), (g), or (l). These details are not required, but they help to establish you as a more knowledgeable and thorough student. Again, don't add anything you're not sure of. There are other factors to consider in this section, but these will be addressed in more detail in Chapter 10.

THE ESSAYS

These are not like the essays you write in English class. Most of the answers in this section are only a few sentences long. You don't get any extra points for writing long responses, so don't do it! Here are some other things to remember as you answer the essays.

Be Logical

Each question has several parts. Make sure you have read through each of these. In some questions, there is a logical progression from one question to the next. In your answers, be sure to reflect this overall structure. It helps the grader know that you are able to grasp the "big picture" in the problem. Before you attack the individual parts of the question, it helps to jot down an outline in your green packet (the one you aren't writing your answers on). This will help you to frame the question and develop a strategy to answer it.

Answer All Parts Separately

Do not write a giant paragraph that includes all of your answers. Address each subpart in a separate, lettered section.

Be Thorough

Don't assume that the grader knows anything (even though he probably knows everything about the topic). Making this type of assumption can cause you to omit important information from an answer. For example, if you were asked to identify the oxidizing agent for a reaction (for which an equation has been given), show the grader that you know what an oxidizing agent is. In your answer, you might write, "The oxidizing agent, or substance that causes another to lose electrons in a chemical reaction, is…" By writing your answer this way, you let the grader know that you understand the topic. There are times when partial credit can be awarded for correct descriptions of portions of the question. Don't lose these points just because you have assumed the grader already knows the information. *Of course he knows it.* You are trying to make sure he knows that *you* know it.

Don't Overdo It

Over the years, many students develop the "shotgun approach" to answering essay questions. A shotgun sprays a large amount of small lead shot around with the idea that some of it will hit the target. Likewise, these students will write down everything they know in hopes that some of it will answer the question. The AP graders are on to that game. It doesn't work. They do not want to wade through endless amounts of writing to try to find the pearls that are buried within. Be clear. Be concise. Say what you need to—and nothing else.

Summary: Know What You Are Up Against

- Familiarize yourself with the structure of the AP Chemistry exam. Knowing the test format will relieve test anxiety because you will know exactly what to expect on test day.

- Learn the given information. Your test booklet will provide you with important data and formulas. Don't waste time memorizing that information. Learn how to use it and know where you can find it during the test.

- Make sure you fill in the bubble sheet neatly. Otherwise, the scoring machine won't give you credit for your answers.

- Pace yourself. You must work quickly and carefully throughout the test. You can still get a very high score without answering all of the questions. Answer as many as you can as quickly as you can, and then go back and try to fill in the others.

- Remember that random guessing will have no effect on your score, but educated guessing will boost your score. So, if you've had time to read through a question and eliminate at least one choice, take a guess!

- In the free-response sections, be neat, thorough, and very clear. You do not want the graders having to guess what you wrote or what you meant.

- Remember—if you're working through this book, you're giving yourself the best preparation available for succeeding on the AP exam. Let your preparation give you the confidence you need to be calm and focused.

PART III

AP Chemistry Review

PREVIEW

Problem Solving and Measurement

A good portion of the AP Chemistry exam deals with calculations, either with or without the aid of a calculator. For all of these problems, there are two different components—the chemistry component and the math component. Most of this book is devoted to a review of the chemistry component of the problems, but this chapter is designed to review a few important mathematical skills that you will need to know as you work through the problems. Three skills that are critical to success on the AP Chemistry test use significant figures, scientific notation, and dimensional analysis.

In the second portion of this chapter, we will review laboratory equipment. In addition to an occasional question about laboratory procedure, the AP exam now contains an essay question that is entirely devoted to laboratory procedure. The College Board has a recommended series of labs, many of which you should have completed prior to taking the exam, and the exam will contain a description of one of these labs for you to analyze. In this book, you will find information about these labs in the chapters that correspond to their subject. The College Board also recommends that you should be familiar with a variety of laboratory equipment. So, in the last part of this chapter, you will find a list of the recommended labs as well as diagrams of the lab equipment. Make yourself familiar with the equipment by name and function.

DEFINING ACCURACY AND PRECISION

Students frequently have misconceptions about the definitions of accuracy and precision based on popular uses of the words. The term *accuracy* refers to how close a measured value is to the true value of a quantity. In other words, it describes how close you got. *Precision* describes how close your measurements are to each other, not how close they are to the actual value. That is, if your values are close together, they are considered precise, even if they are nowhere near the true value (accurate).

The distinction between accuracy and precision becomes extremely important when you consider real-world measurements. For example, if you try to measure the distance between two objects using a meter stick, the accuracy of your answer is limited. The smallest markings on the meter stick are millimeters. Therefore, you can definitely know the exact number of millimeters, and you can even estimate one more place after the decimal.

- *Defining Accuracy and Precision*
- *Using Significant Figures*
- *Reviewing Scientific Notation*
- *Using Dimensional Analysis to Organize Your Work*
- *Laboratory Component*

NOTE
The lab information presented in this book is certainly no substitute for the actual lab work, but it can serve to refresh your memory of those labs you have done and give you a basic idea of any labs you may not have had time to complete.

However, your value can be no more accurate than that as long as you are using a meter stick. It is possible that you may obtain a more sophisticated device, like a sonic range-finder, that can provide you with a more accurate measurement. The important thing to remember is that your data can be no more accurate than the device with which you are measuring. This concept is the foundation for the use of significant figures in calculations.

USING SIGNIFICANT FIGURES

In mathematics, most of the numbers you work with are pure numbers. They do not represent a real object or amount of any physical material. With numbers in chemistry, you are typically dealing with a quantity of something. Even when you obtain a ratio, the ratio is obtained from the division of two measurements. The point is that you are dealing with physical quantities. One of the dangers when solving a problem using real measurements is that you may come up with answers that suggest more accuracy than could possibly be obtained from the measuring devices used. However, there are some simple guidelines that will help you decide which digits are significant and which should be ignored.

Rules for Significant Figures:

1. All nonzero numbers are significant. (Example: 1, 2, 3, 4, 5… etc.)

2. Zeros between significant numbers are significant. (Example: 1002—Both zeros are significant.)

3. Zeros at the end *after* decimal are significant. (Example: 95.000—All zeros are significant. These represent measured amounts.)

4. Leading zeros (before significant numbers) are *not* significant (before or after the decimal). (Examples: 0.51 and 0.000007—None of these zeros are significant.)

5. Zeros at the end *before* the decimal are *not* significant. (Example: 1,875,000,000—None of these zeros are significant.)

For numbers that are written in scientific notation, only the root portion of the number is considered. (Example: 1.605×10^7 would have 4 significant digits.)

You Try It!

How many significant digits are present in each of the following?

_____1. 6.908 g _____2. 81801000 g _____3. 893.760 g

_____4. 56890 cm _____5. 8970000 cm _____6. 0.000136 cm

_____7. 345000 cm _____8. 0.008710 L _____9. 7890.0 L

Answers: 1. 4 (rule 2) **2.** 5 (rule 5—zeros at the end are place holders) **3.** 6 (rule 3) **4.** 4 (rule 5) **5.** 3 (rule 5) **6.** 3 (rule 4—zeros are place holders) **7.** 3 (rule 5) **8.** 4 (rule 4—first zeros are not significant; rule 3—last zero is significant) **9.** 5 (rule 3— last zero is significant; rule 2—middle zero is significant because it is between two significant numbers)

With a basic understanding of significant numbers, you can now understand how to determine significant numbers in calculations. Assume that you measure the density of an unknown substance. Remember the equation for density: $D = \frac{m}{v}$. The object had a mass of 25.35 g and a volume of 4.2 cm^3. Each of these measurements was taken by some measuring device and was measured as accurately as possible. If you substitute these numbers into the density equation, you get an answer of 6.03571429 g/cm^3. But just because the calculator gives all of those digits doesn't mean that your measurements are accurate. So, where do you draw the line in rounding those long numbers?

When measurements are used in calculations, it is important to keep track of the number of significant figures throughout the problem. This assures you that your answer will be no more accurate than the least accurate measurement. One important consideration for all problems is that the calculations should be completed before you round. Wait until you have an answer, and then round it to the proper place or number of significant figures.

Addition and Subtraction

The answer can only be as significant as the least accurate number (least place value).

Examples: 3.245 m + 3.98765 m + 5.98 m + 9 m = 22 m
6.234 g − 4.0 g = 2.2 g

You Try It!
1. 14.2 + 23.89 + 37.891   =
2. 345.178 − 4.58   =
3. 892.5 + 234 + 27.88   =
4. 94.234 − 2.7   =

Answers: **1**. 76.0; **2**. 340.60; **3**. 1154; **4**. 91.5

Multiplication and Division:

1. The answer can be only as significant as the least significant number involved (number of significant figures).

Samples: 78.35 m × 3400 m = 270 000 m^2 56.78 g ÷ 6.7 ml = 8.5 g/ml

2. Numbers that are written using scientific notation are treated the same way. The root portion of each number is what is counted.

Sample: 6.02×10^{23} atoms/mol × 1.4 mol = 8.4×10^{23} atoms

You Try It!
1. 3.08 J × 5.2 s   =
2. 0.075 kg ÷ 0.030 m   =
3. 4.50×10^{-7} m × 6.67×10^{14} s^{-1} =
4. 3.00×10^8 m s^{-1} ÷ 6.8×10^{-7} m   =

NOTE
The rules for significant figures are slightly different for addition, subtraction, multiplication, and division.

Answers: **1**. 16 J s **2**. 0.0023 kg m, or 2.3×10^{-3} kg m **3**. 3.00×10^8 ms^{-1} **4**. 4.4×10^{14} s^{-1}

REVIEWING SCIENTIFIC NOTATION

Many of the numbers you will deal with will either be very large (e.g., Avogadro's number — 6.02×10^{23}) or very small (e.g., Planck's constant — 6.63×10^{-34} J s). Rather than write these numbers with all of the zeros, it is much easier to use scientific (or exponential) notation

$$M \times 10^n$$

where M is a number equal to or greater than 1 and less than 10 M must have *one* significant digit to the left of the decimal point. n is any positive or negative integer.

To change a number into scientific notation:

1. Determine M by moving the decimal point so that you leave only one nonzero digit to the left of the decimal.

2. Determine n by counting the number of places that you moved the decimal point. If you move it to the left, the value of n is positive. If you move the decimal to the right, the value of n is negative.

Sample: Write the following numbers in scientific notation:
$105\ 000\ 000\ 000 = 1.05 \times 10^{11}$ $0.00000587 = 5.87 \times 10^{-6}$

You Try It!
Write the following numbers in scientific notation:

1. 400,780,000,000 =

2. 0.00052   =

Answers: 1. 4.0078×10^{11} 2. 5.2×10^{-4}

USING DIMENSIONAL ANALYSIS TO ORGANIZE YOUR WORK

There are a variety of problem-solving strategies that you will use as you prepare for and take the AP exam. Dimensional analysis, sometimes known as the factor label method, is one of the most important of the techniques for you to master.

Dimensional analysis is a problem-solving technique that relies on the use of conversion factors to change measurements from one unit to another. It is a very powerful technique but requires careful attention during setup. The conversion factors that are used are equalities between one unit and an equivalent amount of some other unit. In financial terms, we can say that 100 pennies is equal to 1 dollar. While the units of measure are different (pennies and dollars) and the numbers are different (100 and 1), each represents the same amount of money. Therefore, the two are equal. Let's use an example that is more aligned with science. We also know that 100 centimeters are equal to 1 meter. If we express this as an equation, we would write

$$100\ cm = 1\ m$$

TIP

You only need to worry about these on the free-response portion of the exam. On the multiple-choice portion, they do not try to trick you by having two answers that differ only by the number of significant digits.

Since these represent the same distance, the values can be thought of as equivalent. Therefore, we can say that

$$\frac{100 \text{ cm}}{1 \text{ m}} = 1$$

And, because each of these values is equal to the same thing, we can also say that

$$\frac{1 \text{ m}}{100 \text{ cm}} = 1$$

Since these two values are interchangeable, we now have a conversion factor that can be used to convert between meters and centimeters.

Sample: Convert 455 centimeters to meters.

Answer: First, set up the conversion factor to eliminate the centimeters unit and change it to meters. When you set up a problem like this, always begin by writing down your given (or starting) information. The next step is to set up the conversion factor so that the units in the denominator will cancel the units of the given. This can be accomplished by

$455 \text{ cm} \times \frac{1 \text{ m}}{100 \text{ cm}}$, which allows you to cancel units and solve the following problem:

$$455 \text{ cm} \times \frac{1 \text{ m}}{100 \text{ cm}} = \frac{455 \text{ m}}{100} = 4.55 \text{ m}$$

Sometimes, students prefer to use a slightly different setup, which can be especially helpful for longer stoichiometric conversions. Some call this technique the "egg carton" approach because the problem is set up in a grid that has slots to fill in quantities, much like the slots that hold eggs in an egg carton. The same problem above, written in the "egg carton" format, would look like this:

$$\frac{455 \text{ cm} \quad\quad 1 \text{ m}}{\hspace{3cm}} = 4.55 \text{ m}$$
$$100 \text{ cm}$$

Not all problems lend themselves to such a linear method, but you can still use the most important elements of this technique if you include units of measure with every quantity and carefully check to be sure that the units are canceling appropriately. To see a more complex example, let's look at a gas law problem.

CAUTION
While you are completing the calculation, check to make sure that all units are canceling. If they do not cancel, it is a warning that you have probably made an error in the setup or the solution of the problem.

Sample: What is the pressure of 2.0 moles of nitrogen gas (N_2) that occupies a volume of 1.5 L and is at 298 K?

Answer: Using the ideal gas equation, we know that $PV = nRT$. We also know that when we solve for P, our answer should come out to be in units of atmospheres (atm). When we set up and solve the problem, all units should cancel to give us atm.

$PV = nRT$, rearrange the equation to solve for P

$$P = \frac{nRT}{V} = \frac{(2.0 \text{ mol})\left(0.0821 \dfrac{\text{L atm}}{\text{mol K}}\right)(298 \text{ K})}{1.5 \text{ L}} \text{ ; canceling units, we see}$$

$$\frac{(2.0 \, \cancel{\text{mol}})\left(0.0821 \dfrac{\text{L atm}}{\cancel{\text{mol K}}}\right)(298 \, \cancel{\text{K}})}{1.5 \text{ L}} = \frac{48.9316 \, \cancel{\text{L}} \text{ atm}}{1.5 \, \cancel{\text{L}}} = 33 \text{ atm}$$

LABORATORY COMPONENT

The two sections that follow will provide you with a summary of the laboratory experiences and equipment the College Board recommends that you be familiar with. Further discussions of many of the labs will take place within the appropriate chapters. Emphasis will be placed on those labs that are most frequently referred to on the AP exam. Table 2.2 provides you with a list of the recommended equipment to help you remember the specific names for each piece. Words like "thingy" and "whatchamacallit" are not highly looked upon by the AP graders.

Table 2.1   Laboratory Exercises that are Recommended by the College Board

Lab	Equipment Used
Determination of the formula of a compound	crucible and cover, tongs, analytical balance, support stand, triangle crucible support, burner
Determination of the percentage of water in a hydrate	crucible and cover, tongs, test tube, analytical balance, support stand, triangle crucible support, wire gauze, burner
Determination of molar mass by vapor density	barometer, beaker, Erlenmeyer flask, graduated cylinder, clamp, analytical balance, support stand
Determination of molar mass by freezing-point depression	test tube, thermometer, pipet, beaker, stirrer, stopwatch, ice
Determination of the molar volume of a gas	barometer, beaker, Erlenmeyer flask, test tubes, graduated cylinder, clamp, analytical balance, thermometer, rubber tubing
Standardization of a solution using a primary standard	pipet, buret, Erlenmeyer flasks, volumetric flask, wash bottle, analytical balance, drying oven, desiccator, support stand, pH meter
Determination of concentration by acid-base titration, including a weak acid or weak base	pipet, buret, Erlenmeyer flasks, wash bottle, analytical balance, drying oven, desiccator, support stand and clamp, pH meter
Determination of concentration by oxidation-reduction titration	pipet, buret, Erlenmeyer flasks, wash bottle, analytical balance, drying oven, desiccator, support stand and clamp, pH meter as millivoltmeter
Determination of mass and mole relationship in a chemical reaction	beaker, Erlenmeyer flask, graduated cylinder, hot plate, desiccator, analytical balance
Determination of the equilibrium constant for a chemical reaction	pipet, test tubes and/or cuvettes, volumetric flask, analytical balance, spectrophotometer (Spec 20 or 21)
Determination of appropriate indicators for various acid-base titrations; pH determination	pipet, Erlenmeyer flasks, graduated cylinder, volumetric flask, analytical balance, pH meter
Determination of the rate of a reaction and its order	pipet, buret, Erlenmeyer flasks, graduated cylinder or gas measuring tubes, stopwatch, thermometer, analytical balance, support stand and clamp
Determination of enthalpy change associated with a reaction	calorimeter (can be polystyrene cup), graduated cylinder, thermometer, analytical balance
Separation and qualitative analysis of cations and anions	test tubes, beaker, evaporating dish, funnel, watch glass, mortar and pestle, centrifuge, Pt or Ni test wire
Synthesis of a coordination compound and its chemical analysis	beaker, Erlenmeyer flask, evaporating dish, volumetric flask, pipet, analytical balance, test tubes/cuvettes, spectrophotometer
Analytical gravimetric determination	beakers, crucible and cover, funnel, desiccator, drying oven, Meker burner, analytical balance, support stand and crucible support triangle
Colorimetric or spectrophotometric analysis	pipet, buret, test tubes and/or cuvettes, spectrophotometer, buret support stand
Separation by chromatography	test tubes, pipet, beaker, capillary tubes or open tubes or burets, ion exchange resin or silica gel (or filter paper strips, with heat lamp or blow dryer)
Preparation and properties of buffer solutions	pipet, beaker, volumetric flask, pH meter

Table 2.1 Continued	
Lab	**Equipment Used**
Determination of electrochemical series	test tubes and holder rack, beakers, graduated cylinder, forceps
Measurements using electrochemical cells and electroplating	test tubes, beaker, filter flasks, filter crucibles and adapters, electrodes, voltmeter, power supply (battery)
Synthesis, purification, and analysis of an organic compound	Erlenmeyer flask, water bath, thermometer, burner, filter flasks, evaporating dish (drying oven), analytical balance, burets, support stand, capillary tubes

Table 2.2   List of Equipment the College Board Recommends You Know

Analytical Balance	Desiccator	Graduated Cylinder	Test Tube
Barometer	Drying Oven	Hot Plate	Thermometer
Beaker	Electrodes	Ion Exchange Resin	Tongs
Buret	Erlenmeyer Flask	Meker Burner	Triangle Crucible Support
Burner	Evaporating Dish	Mortar and Pestle	
Calorimeter	Filter Crucibles and Adapters	pH Meter	Voltmeter
Capillary Tubes		Pipet	Volumetric Flask
Centrifuge	Filter Flask	Power Supply/Battery	Wash Bottle
Clamp	Forceps	Spectrophotometer	Watch Glass
Crucible	Funnel	Stirrer	Water Bath
Cuvettes	Gas Measuring Tubes	Support Stand	Wire Gauze
			Wire Loops

Summary: Tools for the Test

- *Accuracy* is about how close your measurements are to the actual, or true, value. *Precision* means that you are consistent in your measurements.

- There are five basic rules for determining whether or not digits are significant. These rules are important to know to earn all possible points during the free-response section of the test. Significant figures do not appear in the multiple-choice portion.

- Scientific notation provides a convenient way to write very large or very small numbers using powers of 10. You should be able to write, interpret, and perform calculations with numbers written using scientific notation.

- Dimensional analysis is a useful technique for organizing information in computations. By using this technique of canceling units and unit conversion, you can decrease your chances of making careless errors and can improve your score.

- Laboratory-based questions are becoming more common on the AP exam. You should review your old labs and look over the examples of the labs in this book. You should also know the names and uses for the equipment listed in this chapter.

While these are some of the tools you will need to continue with the book, they are by no means a comprehensive list. The more techniques you can learn and problem-solving strategies you can use, the more likely you are to experience success on the exam problems.

Atomic Structure

Just as the atom is the building block from which all materials are made, this chapter must be the building block upon which the rest of the book is made. The remaining chapters of this book are devoted to topics directly related to the behavior that can only be understood by first learning atomic structure. The information in this chapter will provide you with a solid foundation of knowledge upon which to build the remainder of your review. The AP exam has a few multiple-choice questions on the topics covered in this chapter and will periodically have one essay question as well. You will have a much easier time on the other sections of this book and the AP test if you can develop a firm understanding of atomic structure and its impact.

THE HISTORICAL DEVELOPMENT OF MODERN ATOMIC THEORY

The earliest known descriptions of atoms date back to between 460 and 370 B.C.E., when the Greek philosopher Democritus first proposed the idea that matter was composed of indivisible particles. He used the term *atomos* (indivisible) to describe these. Other philosophers, including Plato and Aristotle opposed Democritus's ideas, believing that matter was infinitely divisible—views that were widely held until the nineteenth century.

Dalton's Solid Sphere Model of the Atom

During the period between 1803 and 1807, John Dalton proposed a theory of the atomic nature of matter. Dalton's basic postulates stated that:

1. All matter is composed of extremely small particles called atoms.
2. Atoms of like elements are identical, while elements of different elements are different.
3. Atoms are neither created nor destroyed in chemical reactions, nor do they change forms.
4. Compounds are formed when atoms of different elements combine. Atoms will combine in certain fixed ratios with other atoms.

Thomson's Plum Pudding Model of Atomic Structure

These ideas remained relatively unchallenged until late in the nineteenth century when work with electricity uncovered additional aspects of atomic structure. The first discovery was that the atom, rather than being indivisible, actually consisted of small subatomic particles. The study of cathode rays uncovered the first subatomic particle, the negatively charged electron. While studying cathode rays, scientists also observed a second type of ray, the canal ray, which led to the discovery of a positively charged particle (later shown to be a proton). J.J. Thomson, a leading researcher in this area, proposed the second major model of atomic structure, the "plum pudding" model of the atom (named for a popular English dessert). The atom, he proposed, consisted of a positively charged, spherical mass (the pudding) with negatively charged electrons (raisins) scattered throughout.

Another of Thomson's significant contributions was the determination of the charge-to-mass ratio of the electron. This bit of evidence aided physicist Robert Millikan, in 1909, to determine the mass of the electron in his famous oil-drop experiment.

While Thomson and others were busy studying electrical phenomena, Henri Becquerel discovered a new phenomenon—radiation. (We will discuss radiation in more detail in Chapter 4.) The study of this new type of high-energy emission from materials was the principal focus of Ernest Rutherford. Rutherford's initial work discovered two new types of particles associated with the high-energy emissions, the alpha (α) particle and the beta (β). These are now known to be a helium nucleus and an electron, respectively (more on this in Chapter 4).

Rutherford's Discovery of the Nucleus

In 1910, Rutherford performed his famous gold-foil experiment, the results of which ended the brief reign of Thomson's plum-pudding model. In the experiment, he devised an ingenious apparatus to confirm current ideas about atomic structure. His design involved shooting a beam of alpha particles at a very thin sheet of gold foil. His hypothesis suggested that the distribution of charge and mass throughout a plum pudding atom should allow the positively charged alpha particle to blast right through the foil with little or no consequence. To his amazement, there were a significant number of particles that did not pass directly through the foil, but instead were deflected at various angles—some even straight backward! He ultimately concluded that the atoms in the foil must contain an extremely dense, positively charged core, sufficient to deflect the positively charged alpha particles. Rutherford's model, the third major atomic model, consisted of a dense positively charged nucleus, surrounded by tiny, negatively charged electrons in a large amount of empty space.

Apparatus for Rutherford's Gold-Foil Experiment

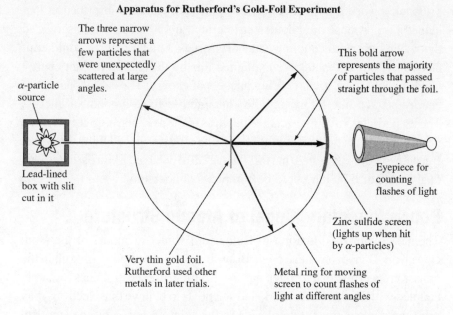

Figure 3.1—Schematic diagram of the setup in Rutherford's gold-foil experiment

Several years later, in 1919, Rutherford discovered the positively charged particle, the proton, that makes up the dense nucleus of an atom. It would be another thirteen years before James Chadwick discovered the neutrally charged neutron, the second component of the nucleus.

At this point, scientists knew of two fundamental components of atoms (and hence matter): the electron and the proton. They knew that protons were located in a dense region in the center of the atom and that that they were positively charged. They also knew that protons had a mass nearly 2000 times greater than that of an electron. In addition, they knew that the charge on an electron was equal in magnitude, but opposite in sign, to a proton (despite its much smaller size). The region outside the dense nucleus was mostly empty space; however, the electrons were believed to be scattered throughout the empty space. The exact positions and behavior of the electron were still uncertain.

MODERN ATOMIC THEORY
Planck's Quantized Energies and Einstein's Photoelectric Effect

In order to better understand how our existing model of the atom evolved, we must step back to about 1900, when physicist Max Planck discovered an unusual property of atoms. While studying the spectra emitted from glowing objects, Planck concluded that energy could be emitted or absorbed from atoms only in fixed amounts, or quanta. He proposed that this amount of energy (E) was directly proportional to the frequency (ν) of the electromagnetic wave. Mathematically, this is expressed in the formula

$E = h\nu$, where h, known as Planck's constant, is 6.63×10^{-24} J•s.

Planck's work provided Albert Einstein with valuable information that helped him propose the photoelectric effect in 1905. Einstein discovered that when light with certain frequencies struck a metal plate, it could emit electrons from the metal. He explained this by describing radiant energy (such as light) as a stream of tiny packets of energy. These tiny packets of energy behave like a tiny particle containing a fixed amount of energy. These "particles" of light became known as photons. This discovery created new problems for physicists whose existing models viewed light as a wave. Einstein's work suggested that this "wave" also behaved like a particle. This dual nature of light has yet to be completely understood.

Bohr's Planetary Model of Atomic Structure

The next major modification to Rutherford's nuclear model of the atom came from Danish physicist Niels Bohr. Bohr was attempting to explain the emission spectrum of hydrogen gas. At this time, the spectral lines research, coupled with Rutherford's work, led scientists to believe that electrons may orbit the nucleus much like planets in the solar system orbit the sun. But physicists could not explain how the electrons stayed in an orbit. Moving charged particles emit electromagnetic radiation that would result in an overall energy loss from the electron. Therefore, the electron should spiral into the nucleus of the atom. So Bohr suggested that there are distinct energy levels within an atom. Electrons will only be found in these allowed energy levels, and while in these regions they will not radiate. These levels correspond to specific distances from the nucleus. According to Bohr, electrons can jump to higher energy levels after absorbing specific amounts of energy. Likewise, electrons dropping from higher to lower energy levels will release certain amounts of energy in the form of photons. Electrons can only jump to an exact energy level (they may not stop "halfway" between). Additional data collected subsequent to Bohr's proposal did not support his model. Subsequently, much of the Bohr model has been discarded.

Shortly after Bohr's proposal, Louis de Broglie made an important proposal. He said that if waves have matter-like properties, then matter should have wavelike properties. It is not necessary for you to know the de Broglie equation, but you should understand that it predicted that matter of normal mass would create infinitesimally small waves. It is only matter with an extremely small mass, like an electron, and traveling at high speed that will emit appreciable wavelengths.

The Quantum Model of the Atom

The Heisenberg Uncertainty Principle

Using de Broglie's idea that matter has wave-like properties, Werner Heisenberg made an important proposal that bridged the gap between Bohr's model and the current quantum model. In Bohr's model, the electron was a particle in a fixed orbit around the nucleus. Heisenberg extended de Broglie's ideas to the electron, stating that only limited information about the electron's location and momentum could be gained. His assertion,

Table 3.1 Summary of the major contributors to the modern atomic theory

Name	Major Contribution(s)	Summary
John Dalton	Dalton's atomic theory	First quantitative evidence for discrete particles (atoms)
J. J. Thomson	Plum Pudding Model Charge-to-mass ratio of electron	Work with cathode rays discovered the positive and negative nature of the atom; also determined the charge-to-mass ratio for electrons
Max Planck	Quantized energy	Energy is released from atoms in discrete packets, or quanta.
Albert Einstein	Photoelectric effect	Duality of light; established relationships between energy and frequencies of light waves
Robert Millikan	Mass of an electron	His famous oil-drop experiment established the charge on an electron.
Ernest Rutherford	α, β, and γ emissions Gold Foil experiment Nuclear model of the atom	Determined the nature of radioactive particles. His gold-foil experiment established the presence of a positively charged nucleus and that the atom is mostly empty space.
Neils Bohr	Planetary model of electrons	Developed the idea of distinct energy levels where electrons could be found—similar to planets in the solar system
Werner Heisenberg	Heisenberg Uncertainty Principle	It is not possible to simultaneously know information about the location and momentum of an electron.
Erwin Schrödinger	Schrödinger equation	Established the field of wave mechanics that was the basis for the development of the quantum model of the atom

known as the Heisenberg uncertainty principle, states that it is not possible to know, simultaneously, information about the momentum and location of an electron. Therefore, it is impossible to conclude that electrons are found in well-defined circular orbits.

The Schrödinger Equation

At this point, the proposed model of atomic structure began to move in a different direction. Since it is not possible to pinpoint the exact location of an electron, the task turned to determining its probable location. In 1926, Erwin Schrödinger proposed an equation that now forms the basis for modern atomic theory. While the equation is too complex to study in detail, the suggestions made by it can be studied. The underlying premise is that we can use mathematical probability to determine the likelihood of finding electrons in a particular region. From this, we can begin to create a "map" of an atom based on these probabilities. This will be discussed in later in the chapter.

Since this time, a number of discoveries have been made regarding additional subatomic particles; however these are related to the domain of nuclear physics. The basic components of the atom that relate to its chemical behavior are the proton, neutron, and electron. It is to these that we now turn our attention.

THE PERIODIC TABLE OF THE ELEMENTS

In 1869, Dmitri Mendeleev was one of the first scientists to create a coherent arrangement of the elements. He did so by arranging elements in order of increasing atomic mass. He also created rows of elements that were arranged so that the vertical columns represented elements that shared similar characteristics. Much later, in 1913, Henry Mosely revised Mendeleev's chart so that elements were arranged by increasing atomic number rather than increasing atomic mass. This is the periodic table that you are familiar with today. Let's review the components and vocabulary associated with the modern Periodic Table of the Elements.

Subatomic Particles

While there are numerous subatomic particles, we will only look at those most relevant to chemistry: the proton, neutron, and electron.

Proton—a positively charged particle located in the atom's nucleus. The electrical charge has a magnitude of $+1.6 \times 10^{-19}$ coulombs (C); however, for simplicity, it is often referred to by its relative charge of $+1.0$ (charge relative to an electron). The mass of a proton is about 1.67×10^{-24} g. The gram is not a practical unit to describe the mass of subatomic particles, so instead we use the atomic mass unit, or *amu*. An amu is defined as 1/12 the mass of a carbon atom containing 6 protons and 6 neutrons. The mass of a proton is 1.0073 amu.

Neutron—a neutral particle located in the atom's nucleus. The mass of a neutron is 1.0087 amu, which is, for all practical purposes, the same as a proton.

Electron—a negatively charged particle* located outside of the atom's nucleus (we will look at this more closely later in this chapter). The electrical charge of an electron is -1.6×10^{-19} C, or a relative charge of -1.0 (charge relative to the proton). The mass of an electron is 5.486×10^{-4} amu, about 1836 times less than a proton.

*The electron is actually believed to have wave-like and particle-like properties, but, for convenience, we will refer to it as a particle.

Atomic Number is the term used to describe the number of protons in the nucleus of an atom. In a neutral atom, this will also describe the number of electrons.

Mass Number represents the total number of protons and neutrons in the atom.

Elements are described as atoms possessing the same number of protons. However, not all atoms of an element possess the same number of neutrons. These different varieties of an element that contain the same number of protons but different numbers of neutrons are known as *isotopes*. Isotopes will possess the same chemical properties, since they are determined by the number of electrons and protons, but they will have a different mass. In Chapter 4, we will look at how the number of neutrons affects the stability of the nucleus. All atoms of a specific isotope are known as *nuclides*. Isotopes are represented using a variety of symbols. Three of these are shown below:

Table 3.2

Style	Sample	Interpretation
Element name	Neon-20	Element name is followed by the mass number of the isotope
Element symbol	^{21}Ne	Element symbol with the mass number superscript and to the left.
Element symbol 2	$^{22}_{10}\text{Ne}$	Element symbol with the mass number superscript and to the left, and the atomic number subscript and to the left.

The atomic mass is a number that is used to describe the average mass of an element. It represents the weighted average of the mass of all isotopes of an element. Calculating the atomic mass requires knowledge of the mass numbers of each isotope for an element as well as each isotope's relative abundance. This latter quantity is determined experimentally with the help of a special piece of equipment known as a mass spectrometer. This is not a required calculation on the AP exam, but, for clarity, a sample calculation is shown below.

Sample: Neon has three isotopes, Neon-20, Neon-21, and Neon-22. The masses of each isotope and the relative abundances are shown in the table below:

Isotope	Mass (amu)	Relative abundance (%)
Neon-20	19.992	90.51
Neon-21	20.994	0.27
Neon-22	21.991	9.22

Answer: What this tells you is that if you scooped up a 100 g sample of Neon, 90.51 g of it would be Neon-20, 0.27 g would be Neon-21, and 9.22 g would be Neon-22.

Using a simple mean to calculate the atomic mass will not work since the isotopes are not present in equal amounts. Therefore, we must take into account the percentage of the total sample accounted for by each isotope. To complete the calculation, simply multiply the mass of the isotope by the relative abundance (expressed as a decimal) and add the total values:

Isotope	Calculation	Relative Mass (amu)
Neon-20	19.992×0.9051	18.0947592
Neon-21	20.994×0.0027	0.0566838
Neon-22	21.991×0.0922	2.0275702
Total		20.179

The modern periodic table of the elements can be written to display different amounts of information about the elements. The one you will be seeing in the book is designed to look like the one you will be able to use on the AP exam. This is the most basic periodic table, containing only the atomic number, the symbol, and the atomic weight of each element.

In each box of the periodic table, you will find the following information:

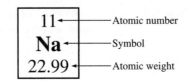

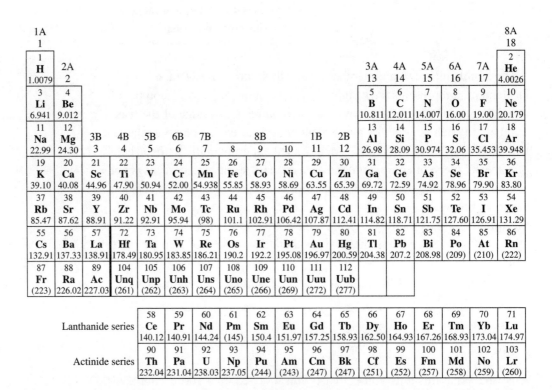

Figure 3.2—The Layout of the Periodic Table of the Elements

Different Sections of the Periodic Table

Now that you are familiar with the different parts of the table, let's begin looking at more specific information that can be gained by the table. A *Period* is defined as a horizontal row on the table. A *Group* or *Family* is defined as a vertical column on the table. Elements in the same group are chemically similar—that is, they behave the same in chemical reactions. In Figure 3.2, you will see some numbers written at the top of each column on the chart. The top set of numbers (with the A and B designations) is most commonly used in North America; however, the International Union of Pure and Applied Chemistry (IUPAC) developed a different numbering system using 1 through 18 (with bottom set of numbers). The elements in Groups 1A through 8A are known as the *representative elements*, while the elements in groups 1B through 8B represent the *transition elements*. Elements 1 through 92 are naturally occurring elements.

Most of the elements on the chart are metals. In Figure 3.3, all non-shaded elements are metals. The shaded elements are nonmetals. The elements that are on either side of the dark line separating the metals from the nonmetals have characteristics of both metals and nonmetals and are known as semimetals, or metalloids.

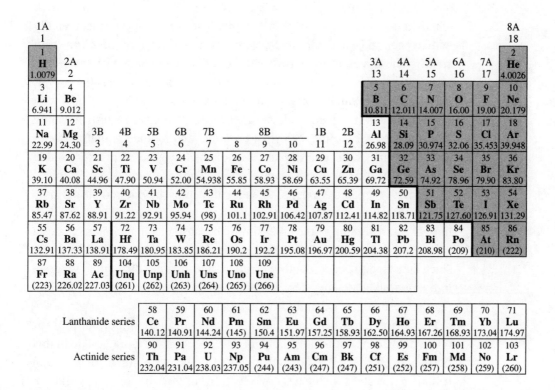

Figure 3.3—Classification of Materials on the Periodic Table

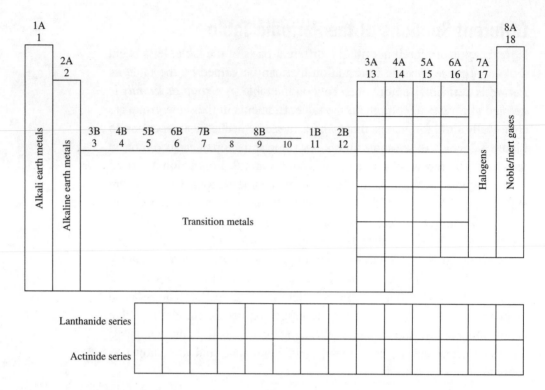

Figure 3.4—Special Groups of Elements on the Periodic Table

Looking at figure 3.4, you will note that some of the groups on the chart have specific names. Group IA elements are known as the ***alkali earth metals***. These materials are all soft, highly reactive metals that react readily with oxygen and water. Group 2A elements are known as the ***alkaline earth metals***. These metals are harder and more dense and have higher melting temperatures. They are also less reactive than the alkali metals. Group 7A, the ***halogens***, are highly reactive nonmetals. These tend to form salts with reactive metals (the name halogen is formed from Greek words meaning "salt formers"). Fluorine, chlorine, bromine, and iodine are diatomic elements. Group 8A, the ***noble gases***, are nonreactive gases with a very stable electron structure (more in the next section). The Lanthanides and Actinides are not really separate "groups" of elements at all. They fit into the periodic table at the place in the sixth and seventh period represented with the dark line. They are left out of the table simply because placing them in creates a very wide table. Most of the Lanthanides were not known until recently, since they tend to occur together in nature and are very difficult to separate into individual elements. The Actinides are quite radioactive, and for that reason most are not generally found in nature.

The periodic table of the elements is an extremely important tool for both chemists and students of chemistry. Much of the work you do in this book and on the AP exam will need to begin with some information found on this chart. In the next two sections of this chapter, you will look at how the electron structures of atoms can be determined indirectly from the periodic table.

THE QUANTUM MODEL OF THE ATOM

If you recall from the beginning of this chapter, some of the work that led to the development of the modern atomic theory was done by scientists Max Planck, Albert Einstein, Louis de Broglie, Werner Heisenberg, Niels Bohr, and Erwin Shrödinger. The first work centered around light (electromagnetic radiation), while the later work focused on the wavelike nature of matter. The AP exam does not probe too deeply into the theoretical considerations of any of these scientists, but some calculations have popped up on previous exams. Therefore, let's turn our attention to some of the equations associated with these scientists' work.

Relationships between Wavelength, Frequency, and Energy

Light is a form of electromagnetic radiation. Other forms of electromagnetic radiation include radio waves, microwaves, infrared rays, ultraviolet rays, X-rays, and gamma rays. All of these forms of radiation travel at the speed of light, but the individual properties of each type of radiation differ. Some of these properties are the wavelengths (λ), or distance between each wave; the frequency (ν), or the frequency of waves that pass by a certain point in a particular time interval; and energy (E).

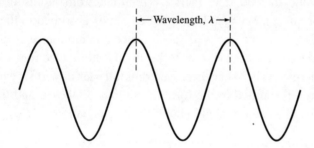

Figure 3.5—Depiction of a wavelength

The most basic calculation involving electromagnetic radiation describes the relationship between the frequency and wavelengths of each wave. All electromagnetic radiation travels at the speed of light (c), which is 3.00×10^8 m s^{-1}. If you think of frequency as the number of waves that pass by a point during any given time interval, you should be able to see that if the waves are farther apart (i.e., have a longer wavelength), fewer waves will pass by during that time interval. Conversely, if the waves are very close together (have a smaller wavelength), more waves will pass by a point in a given time interval. Therefore, frequency and wavelength are inversely related to one another. Mathematically speaking, this can be shown in the equation:

$$c = \lambda \nu$$

(Equation 3.1)

This is one of the equations you were provided with on the AP formula sheet. The units for c are m s^{-1}. Wavelengths are usually expressed in nanometers (nm) or angstroms (Å). The AP exam has used nanometers in the past. Frequencies are expressed in reciprocal seconds (s⁻¹). Problems typically provide one of the variables and ask for the other.

Sample: Calculate the frequency, in s⁻¹, of light with a wavelength of 540 nm.

Answer: First, the equation must be rearranged to solve for ν.

$$\nu = \frac{c}{\lambda}$$

You also need to remember that the distance units for c are in meters, whereas l is given in nm. Since those won't cancel directly, a conversion is necessary. Substituting into the equation, you get

$$\nu = \frac{3.00 \times 10^8 \, m^{s-1}}{540 \, nm \times \dfrac{10^{-9}}{1 nm} m} = 5.6 \times 10^{14} s^{-1}$$

You Try It!

What is the frequency, in s⁻¹, for light with a wavelength of 650 nm?

Answer: 4.6×10^{14}

Planck and the Quantum

Planck's work showed that energy is emitted from atoms in discrete amounts, or quanta. We also know that energy is absorbed in these same amounts. The difference between absorbance and emittance is that when energy is added to an atom (i.e., absorbed by the atom) electrons are forced to higher energy levels. When these electrons fall back down to lower energy levels, energy is emitted in the form of photons. Planck found that these energies could be summarized in the following equation:

(Equation 3.2)

$$E = h\nu$$

Where h is known as Planck's constant and has a value of 6.63×10^{-34} J s. This equation is also one of the equations provided on the AP exam. Energy is always emitted or absorbed in multiples of hn, which suggests that electrons move about between energy levels in an all-or-none fashion. That is, they either have enough energy to travel to a higher energy level or not. They do not travel halfway between intervals. This phenomenon is similar to the rungs on a ladder. You can only go up or down a ladder on the rungs. You cannot stop halfway between the rungs!

Sample: Calculate the amount of energy associated with a photon of light with a frequency of 6.23×10^{14} s⁻¹.

Answer: The equation is already set up to solve for E, so you just need to substitute the numbers. Planck's constant has a unit of J s, which will cancel the reciprocal seconds in the frequency, giving us units of Joules in our answer.

$$E = hn = (6.63 \times 10^{-34} \text{ J s})(6.23 \times 10^{14} \text{ s}^{-1}) = 4.13 \times 10^{-19} \text{ J}$$

You Try It! Calculate the amount of energy, in J, of a photon of light with a frequency of 4.6×10^{14} s^{-1}.

Answer: 3.0×10^{19} J

The Relationship between Energy and the Principal Quantum Number

Bohr was able to show that there is a clear relationship between the energy absorbed by (or released from) atoms. To do this he used the equation (provided for you on the AP exam)

$$En = -RH\left(\frac{1}{n^2}\right)$$

(Equation 3.3)

where R_H, known as the Rydberg constant, has a value of 2.18×10^{-18} J. The variable n represents the principal quantum number (discussed later in the chapter). If you look at this equation, you can see that as n approaches ∞, E approaches 0.

The Rydberg Equation

Because the amount of energy released (or absorbed) always is an interval of $h\nu$, it is possible to probe further into the energies emitted or absorbed by atoms as electrons move between different energy levels. The equation that allows us to determine this energy is known as the Rydberg equation, which can be written as

$$\Delta E = RH\left(\frac{1}{n_i^2} - \frac{1}{n_f^2}\right)$$

(Equation 3.4)

where R_H is the Rydberg Constant, 2.18×10^{-18} J, n represents the principal quantum number, and the subscripts i and f, represent the initial and final states. When the n_i is greater than n_f, that means that the electron is moving from a higher to a lower energy level and energy is being emitted. If you calculate ΔE under these conditions, you will see that the value you obtain is negative, which indicates energy is being lost. Conversely when $n_i < n_f$, the value of ΔE will be positive, indicating energy being absorbed. A very important note here: The Rydberg equation is not provided for you on the AP exam, but it is occasionally needed. On the 1999 exam, one of the free-response questions required the use of the equation. The Rydberg equation was derived from Bohr's equation, and it is possible to use Bohr's equation entirely. The way you do this, should you have to, is

$\Delta E = Ef - Ei$ (the change in energy from initial to final state)

If you know the energy levels that are associated with the initial and final states, you simply substitute for the E_f and E_i values:

$$Ef = -RH\left(\frac{1}{n_f^2}\right) \text{ and } Ei = -RH\left(\frac{1}{n_i^2}\right)$$

Each equation can be solved separately. So if you haven't memorized the Rydberg equation, you can always use this one.

Sample: How much energy is released from a hydrogen atom when an electron moves from $n_i = 4$ to $n_f = 2$?

Answer: Let's use the Rydberg equation first. We know the values of n_f and n_i, so we just need to plug and chug.

$$\Delta E = RH\left(\frac{1}{n_i^2} - \frac{1}{n_f^2}\right) = 2.18 \times 10^{-18} \text{ J} = \left(\frac{1}{4^2} - \frac{1}{2^2}\right) - \mathbf{4.10 \times 10\text{–}19 \text{ J}}$$

Because this equation is not given to you on the exam, let's take a look at the same problem using the equation that is provided.

$$\Delta E = E_f - E_i = E_2 - E_4$$

$$E_2 = -RH\left(\frac{1}{n_2^2}\right) = -2.18 \times 10^{-18} \text{ J}\left(\frac{1}{2^2}\right) = -5.45 \times 10^{-19} \text{ J}$$

$$E_4 = -RH\left(\frac{1}{n_4^2}\right) = -2.18 \times 10^{-18} \text{ J}\left(\frac{1}{4^2}\right) = -1.36 \times 10^{-19} \text{ J}$$

$$\Delta E = E_2 - E_4 = -5.45 \times 10^{-19} \text{ J} - (-1.36 \times 10^{-19} \text{ J}) = \mathbf{-4.09 \times 10\text{-}19 \text{ J}}$$

(Which, considering rounding, is the same as the previous answer.)

The final equation that we will consider is de Broglie's wave equation. This is the equation that describes the wavelike properties of matter. An extremely important consideration of this equation is that large moving objects produce wavelengths that are so small that they are negligible. However, small objects, like electrons, can produce significant wavelengths. The equation, which is given to you on the AP exam, is as follows:

(Equation 3.5)
$$\lambda = \frac{h}{mv}$$

where h is Planck's constant, m is the mass of the object, and v is the velocity (note this is a v written in italics, not the Greek symbol nu (ν) that is used to describe frequency). To illustrate the assertion about large and small objects, let's complete a sample problem that compares the wavelengths of each.

Sample: Compare the wavelengths between a 5 oz baseball (0.14 kg) moving at 100 miles per hour (about 45 m s^{-1}).

Answer: Using the de Broglie equation, we can substitute our given information to find the wavelength of the baseball:

$$\lambda = \frac{h}{mv} = \frac{6.63 \times 10^{-34}\,\text{Js}}{0.14\,\text{kg} \times 45\,\text{m s}^{-1}} = 1.1 \times 10^{-34}\,\text{m}$$

far too small be detected by anything!

(NOTE: Joule is a derived unit that originates from a Newton meter, which equals 1 kg m^2/s^2)

Now, compare that wavelength to an electron traveling at the same speed. The mass of an electron is about 9.11×10^{-31} kg.

$$\lambda = \frac{h}{mv} = \frac{6.63 \times 10^{\pm 34}\,\text{Js}}{9.11 \times 10^{\pm 31}\,\text{kg} \times 45\text{m s}^{\pm 1}} = 1.6 \times 10^{-5}\,\text{m,}$$

which is in the infrared region of the electromagnetic spectrum.

You Try It!

Calculate the wavelength of an electron (mass 9.11×10^{-31} kg) traveling at a speed of 3.65×10^6 m s^{-1}.

Answer: 1.99×10^{10} m = 1.99×10^{-1} nm

Although these calculations can be used to further investigate the work of Niels Bohr, these quantitative aspects of Bohr's work aren't tested on the AP exam. Therefore, let's skip ahead to the development of the quantum model of the atom, parts of which are tested on the exam.

QUANTUM NUMBERS

In order to begin to understand the behavior of atoms, we must first look at some of the details of the quantum mechanical model of the atom. Schrödinger's equation predicts the presence of certain regions in the atom where electrons are likely to be found. These regions, known as *orbitals*, are located at various distances from the nucleus, are oriented in certain directions, and have certain characteristic shapes. Let's look at some of the basic components of the atom as predicted by the equation, and at the same time we will review quantum numbers.

If you have four pieces of information about a house, you can find it just about anywhere in the United States. These four pieces are the Street Number, the Street Name, the City, and the State. So it is with atoms. There are four pieces of information from which you can identify a specific electron within any atom. These are known as quantum numbers, a list of which is shown below:

Principal quantum number (*n*)—This number describes the energy level in which the electron can be found. In our house analogy, this is equivalent to the State, which is the most general information about where the house is located. These correspond to regions that are found at specific distances from the nucleus of the atom. The principal quantum number, *n*, has a whole number, positive value, from 1 to 7 (*n* = 1, 2, 3…7). Lower values of *n* correspond to orbitals close to the nucleus and lower energy levels.

Azimuthal quantum number (*l*)—This number describes the shape of the orbital. The azimuthal quantum number can have values, from 0 to n-1, and these values correspond to certain orbital shapes. While the value can theoretically have a value as high as 6, we will see later that no values higher than 3 are found. The values that do exist, 0, 1, 2, and 3, correspond to particular shapes and are commonly designated as *s*, *p*, *d*, and *f* orbitals, respectively. In our house analogy, this quantum number would correspond roughly to the city. That is, it is a bit more specific than the State, but it still doesn't tell us exactly where the house is.

Magnetic quantum number (*m* or m_l)—This number describes the orientation of the orbital in space. The value of *m* is a range from –l to +l, including 0. In the house analogy, this quantum number is similar to the street name of the house. You can tell about where the house is from this information, but not exactly. In much the same way, you can determine which orbital an electron should be in from the magnetic quantum number, but you can't identify the specific electron.

Spin quantum number (*s*, or m_s)—This number describes the apparent spin of the electron. The term "apparent spin" is used since the atom behaves magnetically as though it were a spinning object, but the wavelike nature of the electron makes such spinning difficult to comprehend. Only two values for *s* are possible: $+\frac{1}{2}$ and $-\frac{1}{2}$ (corresponding to clockwise or counterclockwise spins). Finishing the house analogy, we can see that in an atom, no two electrons can have the same four quantum numbers. In much the same way, no two houses can occupy the exact same address at once.

The chart on the next page shows the possible quantum numbers for energy levels 1 through 4. We will use this as the basis for our consideration of other components of the model.

Before describing the patterns that occur in this arrangement, let's review a few terms.

Within an atom, electrons are arranged in specific regions of space based on the amount of energy they possess. These regions are known as *energy levels*, (or, in some places, *shells*). Each energy level is composed of one or more sublevel. A *sublevel*, (sometimes known as a *subshell*) is one or more orbitals of a particular shape. *Orbitals* are regions of space where there is approximately a 90 percent probability of locating an electron (based on the Schrödinger equation).

Table 3.3   Quantum states for the first four periods on the periodic table of the elements

n	l	m	S
1	0	0	$\pm\frac{1}{2}$
2	0	0	$\pm\frac{1}{2}$
	1	-1, 0, 1	$3\times\pm\frac{1}{2}$
3	0	0	$\pm\frac{1}{2}$
	1	-1, 0, 1	$3\times\pm\frac{1}{2}$
	2	-2, -1, 0, 1, 2	$5\times\pm\frac{1}{2}$
4	0	0	$\pm\frac{1}{2}$
	1	-1, 0, 1	$3\times\pm\frac{1}{2}$
	2	-2, -1, 0, 1, 2	$5\times\pm\frac{1}{2}$
	3	-3, -2, -1, 0, 1, 2, 3	$7\times\pm\frac{1}{2}$

We can see the relationship between these terms and quantum numbers by looking carefully at the table above. First, each unique value of n represents an ***energy level***. Each l value represents a specific ***sublevel*** within an energy level. Recall from the previous section that these sublevels are typically referred to using their common names $s, p, d,$ and f. Each unique combination of n and l values corresponds to a different sublevel. For example, for $n = 3$, and $l = 2$, this corresponds to the $3d$ sublevel of the atom. The m values tell us how many ***orbitals*** are found in a given sublevel. For instance, in the $3d$ sublevel there are 5 orbitals possible (for $3d$, $m = -2, -1, 0, 1, 2$). The spin quantum number tells us that there can be no more than 2 electrons in any orbital, which you will learn more about later in this chapter. Let's summarize what we know in a new chart.

Table 3.4   Quantum numbers and orbital configurations for the first 4 periods of the periodic table of the elements.

n	l	Sublevel	m	Number of orbitals	s	electrons in sublevel	electrons in energy level
1	0	$1s$	0	1	$\pm\frac{1}{2}$	2	2
2	0	$2s$	0	1	$\pm\frac{1}{2}$	2	8
	1	$2p$	−1, 0, 1	3	$3 \times \pm\frac{1}{2}$	6	
3	0	$3s$	0	1	$\pm\frac{1}{2}$	2	
	1	$3p$	−1, 0, 1	3	$3 \times \pm\frac{1}{2}$	6	18
	2	$3d$	−2, −1, 0, 1, 2	5	$5 \times \pm\frac{1}{2}$	10	
4	0	$4s$	0	1	$\pm\frac{1}{2}$	2	
	1	$4p$	−1, 0, 1	3	$3 \times \pm\frac{1}{2}$	6	
	2	$4d$	−2, −1, 0, 1, 2	5	$5 \times \pm\frac{1}{2}$	10	32
	3	$4f$	−3, −2, −1, 0, 1, 2, 3	7	$7 \times \pm\frac{1}{2}$	14	

In the table above, notice some patterns that are now apparent:

- The number of sublevels in the examples above is equal to the principal quantum number (this is only apparent for the first four energy levels).
- The number of orbitals in an energy level is equal to n^2.
- Since there are two electrons per orbital, the number of electrons possible in any energy level is $2n^2$.

Sample: Which element(s) has an outermost electron that could be described by the following quantum numbers $(3, 1, -1, +\frac{1}{2})$?

Answer: Begin with the 3. This represents the 3rd energy level, so the elements are surely in row 3. Now, look at the azimuthal quantum number, l, which is 1. This represents the 3p sublevel. So you know the electron is somewhere in the $3p$ sublevel. For our purposes, the other two numbers $(-1,$ and $+\frac{1}{2})$ don't tell us anything more. So the most we can say is that the element is somewhere between atomic numbers 13 and 18.

You Try It!
Which element(s) has an outermost electron that could be described by the following quantum numbers, $(4, 0, 0, +\frac{1}{2})$?

Answer: K or Ca

At this point we are ready to examine the shapes of the orbitals. Later you will learn more about the arrangement of electrons within atoms, but before you do that, let's look at the basic orbital configurations within an atom. The azimuthal quantum number determines the shape of the orbitals. Looking at

Table 3.3, you will note that the sublevels are labeled *s, p, d,* and *f.* While each of these sublevels can be found in more than one energy level, the basic shapes for each type are the same. In higher energy levels (higher *n* values), the shapes would just be larger. Figures 3.6–3.8 show the basic shapes for *s, p,* and *d* orbitals. Note that within a sublevel, what makes one orbital different from another is its orientation, determined by the magnetic quantum number (m_l)

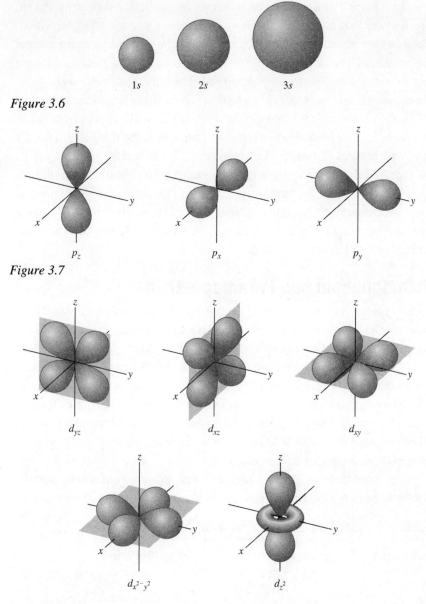

Figure 3.6

Figure 3.7

Figure 3.8

ELECTRON CONFIGURATIONS

At this point, you now have some background about the locations where electrons can be found in an atom, so let's move on to the task of describing the regions where they can be found in almost any atom. The specific arrangement of electrons within an atom is known as the electron configuration of an atom. There are three main rules that are used to guide the process of determining an atom's electron configuration.

First is the *Aufbau ("buildup") principle*, which states that electrons will fill orbitals of lowest energy first. Unfortunately, this order is not a linear sequence from 1 to 7. In our initial discussion of the Aufbau principle, we will look at a graphical representation of the energy levels within an atom. After that, we'll look at a simplified chart that is easy to remember.

Second is the *Pauli exclusion principle* (named after Wolfgang Pauli), which states that no more than two electrons can occupy a single orbital. Electrons are negatively charged particles. If you recall, like charges repel one another. The electron-electron repulsion becomes too great when more than two electrons occupy a single orbital. The only way that two electrons can overcome this electrostatic repulsion is by a slight magnetic attraction. This is the reason why electrons in the same orbital will have opposite spins.

Closely related to the Pauli exclusion principle is the third rule, *Hund's rule*, which states that when electrons occupy orbitals of equal energy (e.g., the five $3d$ orbitals), one electron enters each orbital until all the orbitals contain one electron. In this configuration, all electrons will have parallel spin (same direction). Second electrons then add to each orbital so that their spins are opposite to the first electrons in the orbital. Atoms with all outer orbitals half-filled are very stable.

Diamagnetism and Paramagnetism

Paramagnetism is a term used to describe an attraction to magnets. *Paramagnetic* elements are attracted to magnets. Diagmagnetism means repelled by magnets. *Diamagnetic* elements are weakly repelled by magnets. What distinguishes the two are the spins of the electrons in the orbitals. Paramagnetism occurs in elements with one or more unpaired electrons, which means that there is at least one orbital that contains a single electron. Most elements are paramagnetic. Diamagnetism occurs in elements where all electrons are paired. There are fewer atoms with this configuration (e.g., group IIA elements, or noble gases).

Using these three rules, let's look at a few examples of stable electron configurations for the first three periods of elements.

Table 3.5   Electron Configurations for Elements 1 to 20.

2nd Period	3rd Period	4th Period
Li = $1s^22s^1$	Na = $1s^22s^22p^63s^1$	K = $1s^22s^22p^63s^23p^64s^1$
Be = $1s^22s^2$	Mg = $1s^22s^22p^63s^2$	Ca = $1s^22s^22p^63s^23p^64s^2$
B = $1s^22s^22p^1$	Al = $1s^22s^22p^63s^23p^1$	Sc = $1s^22s^22p^63s^23p^64s^23d^1$
C = $1s^22s^22p^2$	Si = $1s^22s^22p^63s^23p^2$	Ti = $1s^22s^22p^63s^23p^64s^23d^2$
N = $1s^22s^22p^3$	P = $1s^22s^22p^63s^23p^3$	Etc.
O = $1s^22s^22p^4$	S = $1s^22s^22p^63s^23p^4$	
F = $1s^22s^22p^5$	Cl = $1s^22s^22p^63s^23p^5$	
Ne = $1s^22s^22p^6$	Ar = $1s^22s^22p^63s^23p^6$	

1st Period

H = $1s^1$ where the first 1 is equal to the energy level (or quantum number), the *s* is equal to the sublevel and the second 1 is equal to the number of electrons in the sublevel.

$$He = 1s^2$$

Orbital Diagrams

You may have noticed that in the section on quantum numbers, each sublevel (e.g., 2*p*) is composed of a certain number of orbitals. Orbitals can only hold up to two electrons, so the 2*p* sublevel is actually composed of 3 orbitals. However, if you look at the electron configurations of the 2*p*, for example, all of the 2*p* orbitals are summarized in one number—the total number of electrons in all 2*p* orbitals. Therefore, in nitrogen you have $2p^3$, but there is no description about where those electrons are within the 2*p* sublevel. Orbital diagrams provide us with a useful way to map the orbitals within individual orbitals. In these diagrams, boxes, or sometimes circles, are used to represent individual orbitals. Arrows are used to represent electrons, and the heads of the arrows indicate the spin. In Figure 3.9, note the orbital diagrams for the electrons in elements 1–10.

A shorthand notation is sometimes used to shorten the length of the configurations. In this notation, the symbol for the noble gas appears at the end of the period just before the element you are looking for, and then the remainder of the configuration will continue as above. For example, a shorter way to write the configuration for sulfur, element 16, would be: [Ne]$3s^23p^4$. Note—the noble gas is written in brackets.

Unusual Electron Configurations

There are a few electron configurations that don't follow the pattern listed above. These belong to some of the transition metals. For atoms with electrons

Figure 3.9

	1s	2s	2p			
Hydrogen	↑					
Helium	↑↓					
Lithium	↑↓	↑				*Note: According to the Pauli exclusion principle, the 3rd electron in lithium can't go in the 1s sublevel.*
Beryllium	↑↓	↑↓				
Boron	↑↓	↑↓	↑			*Note: Because of Hund's rule, the 5th electron must enter a separate orbital. Also note how spins are parallel.*
Carbon	↑↓	↑↓	↑	↑		
Nitrogen	↑↓	↑↓	↑	↑	↑	*Very stable: half-filled p orbitals*
Oxygen	↑↓	↑↓	↑↓	↑	↑	*The 8th electron is forced to pair up with another.*
Fluorine	↑↓	↑↓	↑↓	↑↓	↑	
Neon	↑↓	↑↓	↑↓	↑↓	↑↓	*Very stable: filled orbitals*

in the *d*-orbitals, there are two very stable configurations of electrons—when the *d*-orbitals are half-filled and when they are completely filled. This causes an unexpected configuration for some elements like chromium and copper. In the example below, notice the difference in electron configurations between element 23, vanadium, and element 24, chromium:

Vanadium: $[Ar]4s^23d^3$

You would expect that chromium would continue the pattern and have the configuration of $[Ar]4s^23d^4$. Instead, it is:

Chromium: $[Ar]4s^13d^5$

This is because in this configuration, the two sublevels, 4s and 3d, are half-filled—a very stable configuration. The same phenomenon is seen in copper:

Copper: $[Ar]4s^13d^{10}$

The completely filled *d* sublevel and half-filled 4s sublevel is a very stable configuration.

Electron Configurations and the Periodic Table

A careful inspection of the periodic table and Figure 3.10 will allow us to see some very clear relationships between the elements and their electron configurations. Note the configurations for H, Li, Na, and K (all group 1A elements). For each element, the last part of the electron configuration shows s^1, representing a single electron in the outer *s* orbital. The other groups of elements show similar patterns. The patterns help us to better understand certain properties of atoms that you will review in the next section. The periodic table is arranged according to the chart shown below:

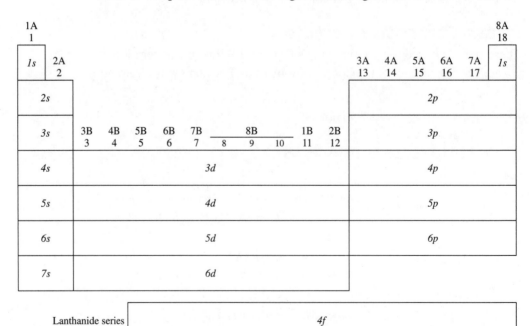

Figure 3.10–Patterns in outer shell electron configurations found in the periodic table of the elements.

When writing the electron configurations for an atom, there are a couple of shortcut techniques that can be used to help you remember the order in which the orbitals will fill up. The first is the chart in figure 3.10. If you were going to write the electron configuration for Selenium, Se, atomic number 34, you would first locate it on the periodic table. Second, you would begin going left to right across each period, filling in electrons as you go until you reach Se. Going across period one produces $1s^2$. Moving left to right across period 2 produces $2s^2$ and $2p^6$. Continuing on until you reach Se, you would end up with $1s^22s^22p^63s^23p^64s^23d^{10}4p^4$, or $[Ar]4s^23d^{10}4p^4$. At this point, you may be wondering if you should write the $3d$ orbitals before the $4s$ or after it. Writing it before is a way to show the configurations in order by energy level, whereas placing it after shows them in order of increasing energies. If you look at enough resources, you will find that it is done both ways, each source claiming that its is the correct way. In the past, the College Board has written them both ways, so be prepared for either. It is not incorrect to write them either way. What the questions on the AP exams of the past have been testing is whether you know the Aufbau principle, the Pauli exclusion principle, and Hund's rule.

1. You begin row 1 by writing $1s$.

   $1s$

2. In row 2, you are going to have two sublevels listed, $2s$ and $2p$.

   $1s$
   $2s$ $2p$

3. In row 3, you will have three sublevels, $3s$, $3p$, and $3d$.

   $1s$
   $2s$ $2p$
   $3s$ $3p$ $3d$

4. For the remaining rows, you are going to go up to f in energy levels 4 and 5, then begin going down. For example, in row 6, you only go to d, in row 7 only to p. There is no row 8.

5. To finish the chart, you will place arrows diagonally through the numbers so that the arrows begin on the right side of the chart and move diagonally to the left, dropping one level each column. When you follow the arrows to determine the order of filling, you begin at the top and move down to the left, and when you reach the end of the arrow, move back up to the arrow that is below the one you just finished. In other words, $1s$, then back to $2s$, then $2p$, $3s$, then $3d$, $4p$, $5s$, and so on.

$1s$
$2s$ $2p$
$3s$ $3p$ $3d$
$4s$ $4p$ $4d$ $4f$
$5s$ $5p$ $5d$ $5f$
$6s$ $6p$ $6d$
$7s$ $7p$

The second method uses what is often called the Aufbau chart. You can easily produce this from memory by constructing it as follows:

Sample: Write the electron configuration for Ba, atomic number 56.

Answer: $1s^2 2s^2 2p^6 3s^2 3p^6 4s^2 3d^{10} 4p^6 5s^2 4d^{10} 5p^6 6s^2$ or $[Xe]6s^2$

You Try It!
Write the electron configuration for Radon, Rn.

Answer: $1s^2 2s^2 2p^6 3s^2 3p^6 4s^2 3d^{10} 4p^6 5s^2 4d^{10} 5p^6 6s^2 4f^{14} 5d^{10} 6p^6$

PERIODIC TRENDS
Factors Affecting the Behavior and Structure of Atoms

There are two factors that are closely associated with the structure and behavior of atoms. The first of these is known as ***effective nuclear charge***. The nuclear charge is related to the number of charged particles (protons) in the nucleus. As the nuclear charge increases, there is an increase in the attractive force between the nucleus and the electrons. Nuclear charge increases from left to right across a period.

The second of these is known as ***nuclear shielding***. Nuclear shielding occurs when electrons in a lower energy level "shield" the electrons in a higher energy level from the effective charge of the nucleus. As a result, the attractive force felt by those outer electrons is less than it would be had those inner electrons not been present. As more energy levels fill, more shielding is seen between the nucleus and the outermost electrons in an atom. Therefore, nuclear shielding increases, going from top to bottom in a group. Increases in nuclear shielding are seen only after an energy level is filled and electrons begin to fill in a further energy level. Therefore, nuclear shielding does not change going from left to right across a period.

Variations in Atomic Radius

The atomic radius is the distance between the nucleus and the outermost electron. Atomic radii are measured in nanometers (10^{-9} meters). In some fields, atomic radii are measured in a unit known as an angstrom, Å (10^{-10} m, or $\frac{1}{10}$ of a nanometer). Hydrogen is the smallest atom, measuring only 0.037 nm, or 0.37 Å.

Trends in Atomic Radii

Periodic trends: Going from left to right across a period, atomic size tends to decrease. This occurs because of an increase in nuclear charge, which "pulls" the electrons in more tightly (thus making the atoms smaller). The noble gases are the smallest elements in each period.

   Group trends: Going from top to bottom in a group, atomic size increases. This is because electrons begin filling in energy levels that are farther from the nucleus (thus making the atoms bigger).

H							He
0.37							0.32
Li	**Be**	**B**	**C**	**N**	**O**	**F**	**Ne**
1.52	1.13	0.88	0.77	0.75	0.73	0.71	0.69
Na	**Mg**	**Al**	**Si**	**P**	**S**	**Cl**	**Ar**
1.86	1.60	1.43	1.17	1.10	1.04	0.99	0.97
K	**Ca**	**Ga**	**Ge**	**As**	**Se**	**Br**	**Kr**
2.27	1.97	1.22	1.22	1.21	1.17	1.14	1.10
Rb	**Sr**	**In**	**Sn**	**Sb**	**Te**	**I**	**Xe**
2.47	2.15	1.63	1.40	1.41	1.43	1.33	1.30

Figure 3.11—Atomic radii for the first five periods of the representative elements. All units are in Angstroms (Å)

Sample: Arrange the following atoms in order of increasing atomic radius: S, P, O

Answer: If you note the arrangement of these atoms, S and P are in the same period, while O and S are in the same group. Therefore, P is larger than S, and S is larger than O. Therefore O < S < P.

You Try It!
Arrange the following elements in order of decreasing radius: Si, Na, Mg.
Answer: Na > Mg > Si

Ionization Energy

Ionization energy is the amount of energy necessary to remove an electron from a gaseous atom. This quantity of energy will fluctuate in direct proportion to the amount of attraction between the nucleus and the electrons. When the force of attraction is strong, the ionization energy will be a larger number. When the force of attraction is weak, the ionization energy will be a small number.

Trends in Ionization Energies

Periodic trends—Ionization energies increase going from left to right across a period. This is because of the increase in nuclear charge. As the nuclear charge increases, the attraction between the electrons and the nucleus increases. This makes it more difficult to remove an electron from the atom.

Group trends—Ionization energies decrease going from top to bottom in a group. This is due to the increase in nuclear shielding. Within a group, as atomic number increases, the amount of shielding increases. This greater shielding causes a decrease in the amount of attraction between the nucleus and the electrons. As a result, it becomes easier to remove the outermost electrons of the atom.

H 1312							He 2372
Li 520	Be 899	B 801	C 1086	N 1402	O 1314	F 1681	Ne 2081
Na 496	Mg 738	Al 578	Si 786	P 1012	S 1000	Cl 1251	Ar 1521
K 2.27	Ca 1.97	Ga 579	Ge 762	As 947	Se 941	Br 1140	Kr 1351
Rb 376	Sr 503	In 558	Sn 709	Sb 834	Te 869	I 1008	Xe 1170

Figure 3.12—First ionization energies for the first five periods of representative elements. All units are in angstroms.

Multiple Ionization Energies

The energy required to remove one electron from the outermost energy level of an atom is known as the ***first ionization energy***. The energy required to remove the next electron (2nd electron) is known as the ***second ionization energy***. The energy required to remove the 3rd electron is the ***third ionization energy,*** and so on. By comparing multiple ionization energies of atoms, it is possible to determine the charge of an atom.

Elements in Group IA all have a single electron in their outermost energy levels. Due to the relatively small nuclear charge, it is fairly easy to remove this outer electron. However, once this electron is removed, the atoms all have electron configurations similar to a noble gas. Noble gases have some of the highest ionization energies. Therefore, a large amount of energy will be required to remove subsequent electrons. When these elements are involved in reactions, they will always lose one electron and no more (since additional electrons would be extremely difficult to remove).

Summary: Group IA elements have a small first ionization energy and a very large second ionization energy. They will lose one electron in a chemical reaction and have a 1^+ charge.

Elements in Group IIA all have two electrons in their outermost energy levels. Again, due to the relatively small effective nuclear charge, it is fairly easy to remove these outermost electrons. After removal of two electrons, however, these elements will have electron configurations like noble gases. Therefore, a large increase in ionization energies is seen between the second and third ionization energies. In reactions, these elements will lose two electrons.

Summary: Group IIA elements have relatively small first and second ionization energies and larger third ionization energies. They will lose two electrons in a chemical reaction and have a 2^+ charge.

In a similar fashion, elements in group IIIA will lose 3 electrons in a chemical reaction and acquire a 3^+ charge. Beyond Group III, however, the nuclear charge begins to be much greater, which makes removal of the outermost electrons quite difficult, especially for the elements with lower atomic numbers. As a result, these atoms will tend to resist giving up their outer electrons and instead tend to have a strong attraction for electrons of other atoms.

Sample: Which atom should have a smaller first ionization energy, oxygen or sulfur?

Answer: Since oxygen and sulfur are in the same group, you must recall the group trends. Since the outer electron in sulfur experiences more shielding, it will be easier to pull off. Therefore, S has the smaller first ionization energy

You Try It!

Which atom should have a larger first ionization energy: N or P?

Answer: N (less shielding)

Ionic Radius

Although there are patterns for the sizes of the ionic radii, these are not as easy to see as the patterns for other periodic trends. The patterns can really be divided into two main categories (other than periodic trends and group trends). These two categories are positively charged ions (cations), and negatively charged ions (anions). The main difference is that cations will lose electrons, leaving them with an increased effective nuclear charge per electron (more protons in the nucleus per electron). Anions will gain electrons, leaving them with a decreased effective nuclear charge. As a result, cations are *smaller* (more protons pulling fewer electrons) than their corresponding neutral atoms, and anions are *larger* (fewer protons pulling more electrons) than their corresponding neutral atoms. Therefore, in

Groups 1A through 3A, each ion is smaller than its corresponding neutral atom. All cations get smaller going across a period and larger going down a group. For groups 5A through 7A, the ions are larger than their corresponding atoms, however, they still get smaller going across the period and larger moving down a group.

Sample: Rank the following from smallest to largest: N^{3-}, Be^{2+}, O^{2-}

Answer: These elements are all in the same period. When beryllium loses two electrons, it will then lose them from the 2s orbital, leaving only 2 electrons in the 1s orbital. These will be acted on by 4 protons, however, making a very small ion. Oxygen and nitrogen will both be receiving electrons into 2p orbitals, however, oxygen has a larger effective nuclear charge. Therefore, the oxygen ion will be slightly smaller than the nitrogen ion. The answer, therefore, is: $Be^{2+} < O^{2-} < N^{3-}$

You Try It! Rank the following from smallest to largest: Mg^{2+}, Ca^{2+}, Al^{3+}

Answer: $Al^{3+} < Mg^{2+} < Ca^{2+}$

Electron Affinity

While ionization energy represents the amount of energy required to remove an electron from an atom, the *electron affinity* is the energy change that occurs when an electron is added to a gaseous atom. It is a measure of the amount of an atom's attraction for electrons. The values for an electron can be negative or positive. Negative values correspond to a release of energy, while positive values correspond to energy required to form an ion. For atoms that have a half-filled, or filled sublevel, or energy level, the addition of electrons is energetically unfavorable. Thus, the atoms with these configurations, groups 2A, 5A, and 8A, tend to have slightly negative or even positive electron affinity values. Atoms that are in the groups just to the left of these have much more negative electron affinities. This is because the addition of an electron will give these elements the stable half-filled, or filled sublevels.

H							He
−73							>0
Li	**Be**	**B**	**C**	**N**	**O**	**F**	**Ne**
−60	>0	−27	−122	>0	−141	−328	>0
Na	**Mg**	**Al**	**Si**	**P**	**S**	**Cl**	**Ar**
−53	>0	−43	−134	−72	−200	−349	>0
K	**Ca**	**Ga**	**Ge**	**As**	**Se**	**Br**	**Kr**
−48	−4	−30	−119	−78	−195	−325	>0
Rb	**Sr**	**In**	**Sn**	**Sb**	**Te**	**I**	**Xe**
−47	−11	−30	−107	−103	−190	−295	>0

Figure 3.13—Electron affinities of the first five periods of representative elements. All units are given in kJ/mol.

Sample: Why is it that sodium has a negative electron affinity while magnesium has a positive value?

Answer: Sodium only has a single electron in the 3s orbital. It can easily accommodate one more. Magnesium, on the other hand, has to add electrons to the 2p orbitals, which is not nearly as favorable.

You Try It!

Explain the difference in electron affinities between nitrogen and oxygen.

Answer: Nitrogen has a very stable $2p^3$ arrangement (one electron in each p orbital). Adding an electron means a loss in some of that stability.

Electronegativity

Electronegativity is a measure of the tendency of an element to attract additional electrons in a chemical reaction. Nonmetals (elements on the upper right portion of the periodic table) attract electrons more than metals because of their relatively higher nuclear charges and small shielding effects. The scale for measuring electronegativities goes from 0.7 to 4.0 (with 4.0 being the highest value). The element with the largest electronegativity is fluorine. This is because fluorine has the highest effective nuclear charge and the least amount of shielding. While the noble gases do have a higher nuclear charge, they are unable to react with other elements due to their electron configuration (this will be covered in Chapter 5). By definition, the attraction for other electrons has to be in a chemical reaction. The element with the smallest electronegativity is cesium. This is because its electrons are highly shielded and experience a small effective nuclear charge.

Trends in Electronegativities

H 2.1						
Li 1.0	Be 1.5	B 2.0	C 2.5	N 3.0	O 3.5	F 4.0
Na 0.9	Mg 1.2	Al 1.5	Si 1.8	P 2.1	S 2.5	Cl 3.0
K 0.8	Ca 1.0	Ga 1.6	Ge 1.8	As 2.0	Se 2.4	Br 2.8
Rb 0.8	Sr 1.0	In 1.7	Sn 1.8	Sb 1.9	Te 2.1	I 2.5
Cs 0.7	Ba 0.9	Tl 1.8	Pb 1.9	Bi 1.9	Po 2.0	At 2.2

Figure 3.14—Electronegativity values for the first six periods of representative elements.

Periodic trends—Electronegativities increase going from left to right across a period. This is due to the increasing nuclear charge, which causes a stronger attraction between the nucleus and electrons.

Group trends—Electronegativities decrease going from top to bottom in a period. This is due to the increased shielding, which weakens the attraction between the nucleus and the electrons.

Sample: Rank the following by increasing electronegativity: N, P, O

Answer: N and P represent group trends, while N and O represent periodic trends. N is more electronegative than P (less shielding), while O is more electronegative than N (greater effective nuclear charge). Therefore, $P < N < O$.

You Try It!
Explain why H has an electronegativity so much larger than Li.

Answer: H has only one electron. It has no shielding; therefore any electrons can be incorporated into the closest s orbital to the nucleus.

Summary of Periodic Trends

1. Going from left to right across a period, nuclear charge increases, while nuclear shielding is unaffected. As a result,

    a. atomic radius decreases.

    b. ionization energy increases.

    c. electronegativity increases.

2. Going from top to bottom down a group, nuclear charge is unaffected while nuclear shielding increases. As a result,

    a. atomic radius increases.

    b. ionization energy decreases.

    c. electronegativity decreases.

Atomic radius decreases
Ionization energy increases
Electronegativity increases

1A 1	2A 2	3B 3	4B 4	5B 5	6B 6	7B 7	8B 8	9	10	1B 11	2B 12	3A 13	4A 14	5A 15	6A 16	7A 17	8A 18
1 **H** 1.0079																	2 **He** 4.0026
3 **Li** 6.941	4 **Be** 9.012											5 **B** 10.811	6 **C** 12.011	7 **N** 14.007	8 **O** 16.00	9 **F** 19.00	10 **Ne** 20.179
11 **Na** 22.99	12 **Mg** 24.30											13 **Al** 26.98	14 **Si** 28.09	15 **P** 30.974	16 **S** 32.06	17 **Cl** 35.453	18 **Ar** 39.948
19 **K** 39.10	20 **Ca** 40.08	21 **Sc** 44.96	22 **Ti** 47.90	23 **V** 50.94	24 **Cr** 52.00	25 **Mn** 54.938	26 **Fe** 55.85	27 **Co** 58.93	28 **Ni** 58.69	29 **Cu** 63.55	30 **Zn** 65.39	31 **Ga** 69.72	32 **Ge** 72.59	33 **As** 74.92	34 **Se** 78.96	35 **Br** 79.90	36 **Kr** 83.80
37 **Rb** 85.47	38 **Sr** 87.62	39 **Y** 88.91	40 **Zr** 91.22	41 **Nb** 92.91	42 **Mo** 95.94	43 **Tc** (98)	44 **Ru** 101.1	45 **Rh** 102.91	46 **Pd** 106.42	47 **Ag** 107.87	48 **Cd** 112.41	49 **In** 114.82	50 **Sn** 118.71	51 **Sb** 121.75	52 **Te** 127.60	53 **I** 126.91	54 **Xe** 131.29
55 **Cs** 132.91	56 **Ba** 137.33	57 **La** 138.91	72 **Hf** 178.49	73 **Ta** 180.95	74 **W** 183.85	75 **Re** 186.21	76 **Os** 190.2	77 **Ir** 192.2	78 **Pt** 195.08	79 **Au** 196.97	80 **Hg** 200.59	81 **Tl** 204.38	82 **Pb** 207.2	83 **Bi** 208.98	84 **Po** (209)	85 **At** (210)	86 **Rn** (222)
87 **Fr** (223)	88 **Ra** 226.02	89 **Ac** 227.03	104 **Unq** (261)	105 **Unp** (262)	106 **Unh** (263)	107 **Uns** (262)	108 **Uno** (265)	109 **Une** (266)									

Atomic radius increases
Ionization energy decreases
Electronegativity decreases

Figure 3.15 Summary of periodic trends

Summary: Atomic Structure

- Our concept of an atom has changed quite a bit since Dalton first provided evidence for the existence of atoms. You should be familiar with the major contributions to the development of modern atomic theory. They do pop up on the test from time to time. Table 5.1 provides a good overview of these individuals and their contributions.

- The periodic table provides us with an excellent way to organize information about the elements. You should be familiar with the basic layout of the table as well as the names for specific groups of elements.

- The Quantum mechanical model of atomic structure is far too difficult to be explained in detail in an AP Chemistry course. However, some aspects of the theory are appropriate, and you should know them. These include the predicted number and shapes of orbitals in each energy level; the number of electrons found in each orbital, sublevel, and energy level; and the meaning of the four quantum numbers.

- Electron configurations provide us with a convenient way to map the positions of electrons. Most of the elements on the periodic table follow a very simple pattern in the buildup of electrons; however, there are a few exceptions, which you should try to memorize.

- Because of the arrangement of elements on the periodic table, there are several patterns that can be seen between the elements. These patterns, or periodic trends, can be observed for atomic radius, ionic radii, ionization energies, electron affinities, and electronegativities. You should be familiar with the periodic and group trends for each of these.

REVIEW QUESTIONS

Questions 1-4

    (A) F

    (B) O

    (C) Li

    (D) Na

    (E) K

1. Which element is the least electronegative?

2. Which element has the lowest ionization energy?

3. Which of the above has the smallest naturally occurring ion?

4. Which atom has the smallest atomic radius?

5. Which of the following pairs of atoms represents an isotope?

		Atomic number	Mass number
(A)	I.	8	18
	II.	9	18
(B)	I.	8	9
	II.	18	18
(C)	I.	8	18
	II.	18	36
(D)	I.	9	18
	II.	9	19
(E)	I.	6	12
	II.	12	18

In questions 6–8, refer to the electron configurations shown below.

    (A) $1s^22s^22p^63s^23p^4$

    (B) $1s^22s^22p^63s^23p^64s^13d^5$

    (C) $1s^22s^22p^83s^23p^6$

    (D) $1s^22s^22p^63s^23p^64s^23d^4$

    (E) $1s^22s^22p^63s^23p^6$

6. electron configuration of Cr

7. violates Pauli Exclusion Principle

8. noble gas configuration

In questions 9–11, select the scientists primarily responsible for the findings in each question.

   (A) Dalton

   (B) Einstein

   (C) Heisenberg

   (D) Thomson

   (E) Rutherford

9. Made important discoveries about the properties of cathode rays

10. Proposed the existence of a nucleus

11. Determined that it was impossible to know simultaneously information about the location and movement of electrons

12. Which set of quantum numbers (n, l, m_l, m_s) is not possible?

   (A) $1, 0, 0, \frac{1}{2}$

   (B) $1, 1, 0, \frac{1}{2}$

   (C) $1, 0, 0, -\frac{1}{2}$

   (D) $2, 1, -1, \frac{1}{2}$

   (E) $3, 2, 1, \frac{1}{2}$

Free Response

   (A) Chlorophyll a, a photosynthetic pigment found in plants, absorbs light with a wavelength of 660 nanometers.

   (i) Determine the frequency, in s^{-1}, of chlorophyll a.

   (ii) Calculate the energy of a photon of light with a wavelength of 660 nm.

   (B) In the Balmer series of hydrogen, one spectral line is associated with the transition of an electron from the fourth energy level ($n = 4$) to the second energy level ($n = 2$).

   (i) Indicate whether energy is absorbed or emitted as the electron moves from $n = 4$ to $n = 2$. Explain.

   (ii) Determine the wavelength of this spectral line.

   (iii) Indicate whether the wavelength calculated in (ii) is longer or shorter than the wavelength associated with an electron moving from $n = 5$ to $n = 2$. Explain.

ANSWERS

1. **The correct answer is (E).** Potassium will be the least electronegative element. The electronegativity value of an element is determined by the strength of attractions the atom has for other electrons in a chemical bond. Atoms with the highest electronegative values have a combination of a large effective nuclear charge and a small amount of shielding. In general, the elements at the upper right portions of the periodic table of the elements have the highest electronegativity values, while the elements in the lower left regions have the lowest values. Of the five choices, potassium has a combination of the smallest effective nuclear charge and the greatest amount of shielding.

2. **The correct answer is (E).** For the same reasons that it has the lowest electronegativity, potassium has the lowest ionization energy. The outermost electron has the most shielding between it and the nucleus with the smallest effective nuclear charge.

3. **The correct answer is (C).** Lithium has the smallest ion. When a lithium atom loses its outermost electron, it loses the entire second energy level. Its only remaining electrons are in the first energy level and have one more proton than helium with which to attract them.

4. **The correct answer is (A).** Fluorine has the smallest atomic radius. The fluorine atom has the highest effective nuclear charge of the elements in the list. Because there are no elements on the list with a greater effective nuclear charge or a smaller amount of shielding, fluorine will have the smallest atomic radius.

5. **The correct answer is (D).** Isotopes of an element have the same atomic number (numbers of protons), but different mass numbers (numbers of neutrons). The only choice that represents the same element is (D), where each isotope has 9 protons. One isotope has 9 neutrons, while the other has 10 neutrons.

6. **The correct answer is (B).** Although choices (B) and (D) each have 24 electrons, (B) is the better answer because of chromium's exceptional electron configuration. The chromium atom gains increased stability by promoting one of the 4s electrons to the vacant 3d orbital. This promotion creates half-filled orbitals, which increase stability.

7. **The correct answer is (C).** By placing 8 electrons in the 2p orbitals, (C) is in violation of the Pauli exclusion principle, which states that each orbital may only contain 2 electrons and that those must have opposite spins. Eight electrons exceed the maximum six.

8. **The correct answer is (E).** Choice (E) has the noble gas configuration (of Argon), which characteristically has filled s and p sublevels.

9. **The correct answer is (D).** Thomson's work with cathode ray's led to his eventual discovery of many important properties of the electron and his subsequent development of the "plum pudding" model of the atom.

10. **The correct answer is (E).** Rutherford, based on the results of his gold-foil experiment developed a model of the atom that included a positively charged dense core (the nucleus).

11. **The correct answer is (C).** The statement in 11 is the essence of the Heisenberg Uncertainty Principle.

12. **The correct answer is (B).** Choice (B) is an impossible configuration because of the value of the l quantum number. The value of l is only permitted to go from n-1 to 0. Therefore, l cannot have the same value as n.

Free Response

(A) Chlorophyll a, a photosynthetic pigment found in plants, absorbs light with a wavelength of 660 nanometers.

(i) Determine the frequency, in s^{-1}, of chlorophyll a.

The frequency can be determined using the equation below

$$\nu = \frac{c}{\lambda}$$

One important consideration is that the wavelengths and speed of light are expressed with different units of length. One of them will have to be converted before the frequency is calculated.

$$\nu = \frac{3.00 \times 10^{\pm 8}\,\text{m s}^{\pm 1}}{660\text{nm}\left(\dfrac{1\text{m}}{10^{9}\,\text{nm}}\right)} = 4.54 \times 10^{14}\,\text{s}^{\pm 1}$$

(ii) Calculate the energy of a photon of light with a wavelength of 660 nm.

To solve this one, you are going to multiply your answer from (i) by Planck's constant, h:

$E = h\nu = (6.626 \times 10^{-34}\,\text{J s})(\,4.54 \times 10^{14}\,\text{s}^{-1}) = 3.01 \times 10^{-19}\,\text{J}$

(B) In the Balmer series of hydrogen, one spectral line is associated with the transition of an electron from the fourth energy level (n=4) to the second energy level (n = 2).

(i) Indicate whether energy is absorbed or emitted as the electron moves from n=4 to n=2. Explain.

Energy is absorbed when an electron moves from a lower energy level to a higher energy level. When an electron moves from a higher energy to a lower energy level, the atom will release energy (in the form of a photon). That is what provides the driving force to move the electron. Since n = 4 corresponds to a higher energy level than n = 2, the atom will release energy in this transition.

(ii) Determine the wavelength of this spectral line.

The solution to this problem is a lengthy one. The energy level data will allow us to use the Rydberg equation, but this will only solve for E. In order to determine the wavelength, the energy (E) will be used to calculate the frequency, which can then be used to determine the wavelength.

The first step is to use the Rydberg equation to determine the energy emitted by the transition.

$$\Delta E = RH \left(\frac{1}{n_i^2} - \frac{1}{n_f^2} \right)$$

$$\Delta E = 2.18 \times 10^{-18} \left(\frac{1}{2^2} - \frac{1}{4^2} \right) = 4.01 \times 10^{-19} \text{ J}$$

The next step is to use the energy you just obtained to calculate the frequency.

$$v = \frac{E}{h} = \frac{4.01 \times 10^{-19} \text{ J}}{6.626 \times 10^{-34} \text{ Js}} = 6.05 \times 10^{14} \text{ s}^{-1}$$

Finally, you can use the frequency to determine the wavelength.

$$\lambda = \frac{c}{v} = \frac{3.0 \times 10^{8} \text{ ms}^{\pm 1}}{6.05 \times 10^{14} \text{ s}^{\pm 1}} = 4.96 \times 10^{\pm 7} \text{ m} = 496 \text{ nm}$$

(iii) Indicate whether the wavelength calculated in (ii) is longer or shorter than the wavelength associated with an electron moving from $n = 5$ to $n = 2$. Explain.

The transition from $n = 5$ to $n = 2$ is a larger transition than from $n = 4$ to $n = 2$, and, as a result, the photon will possess more energy. Because the photon has more energy, it will also have a higher frequency ($v = E/h$). This higher frequency corresponds to a shorter wavelength ($\lambda = c/v$).

4

Nuclear Chemistry

The AP exam requires you to know about nuclear equations, half-lives, radioactivity, and chemical applications of nuclear properties. This chapter begins with a brief review of the history of the nucleus and how we came to know about it and then moves into the required topics.

THE DISCOVERY OF RADIOACTIVITY

A simple, but working, definition of *radioactivity* is "the spontaneous decay of particles from the nucleus of an atom." Henri Becquerel first discovered radiation in 1896 while doing research on the fluorescence of different materials. One day, he set a sample of uranium ore in a drawer atop some unexposed photographic plates. Upon later developing the film, he discovered that the film had been exposed in the location where the ore had been sitting. He concluded that there must be some high-energy emissions emerging from the material. Becquerel did not wish to pursue this separate line of research, so he passed the work on to one of his graduate students, Marie Curie, and her husband, Pierre. The Curies painstakingly worked with large samples of the uranium ore to isolate the material responsible for the emissions (the material they isolated was radium).

RUTHERFORD DISCOVERS DIFFERENT TYPES OF RADIATION

The next major discoveries about radiation came from Ernest Rutherford. These experiments came before his famous "gold-foil" experiment. He discovered that an electrical field affected the emissions from radioactive material. By placing a sample of material near two charged plates (similar to the design of Thomson's cathode ray studies), he was able to observe the behavior of the radioactive emissions in an electric field. He accomplished this by firing a sample of radioactive material in a thin stream between two charged plates. He placed a photographic plate on the opposite side of the charged plates to observe the deflections of any particles.

From the deflections, he determined that some of the particles were positively charged, some were negatively charged, and some were not charged at all. He discovered that the positively charged particles were much more massive than the others, and when combined with electrons, they formed helium atoms. He called these particles **alpha particles** (α- particles), and

ROAD MAP

- *The Discovery of Radioactivity*
- *Rutherford Discovers Different Types of Radiation*
- *Different Types of Radioactive Emissions*
- *Radioactive Decay*
- *Half-Life*
- *Nuclear Reactions*

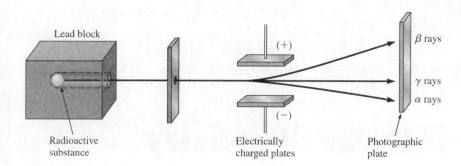

Figure 4.1

today we know them to be helium nuclei. The negatively charged particles were lighter and faster-moving than alpha particles and behaved like cathode rays. Rutherford called these **beta particles** (β-particles), and today we know them to be electrons. The third, neutral emission was determined to be extremely high-energy radiation, unaffected by an electrical field. These emissions became known as **gamma rays** (γ rays).

Alpha particles are relatively large and slow-moving and are easily stopped. Beta particles are much smaller, much faster, and about 100 times more penetrating than alpha particles. Gamma rays (often referred to as gamma photons) are massless and extremely fast and possess high energy. They are by far the most penetrating radiation—about 100 times greater than a beta particle, or 10,000 times more penetrating than an alpha particle.

The remainder of this chapter will be devoted to the process of radioactive decay.

DIFFERENT TYPES OF RADIOACTIVE EMISSIONS

There are five main types of emissions: alpha emission, beta emission, positron emission, electron capture, and gamma emission. Four of these produce changes in the elements undergoing decay, and the end result is a more stable atomic structure.

Alpha Emissions

These emissions result in the release of an alpha particle from the atom. Recall that an α-particle is a helium nucleus. The result in alpha decay is the atom's atomic number decreasing by two and the mass number decreasing by four. An example of an α-decay is

$$^{238}_{92}\text{U} \rightarrow {}^{4}_{2}\text{He} + {}^{234}_{90}\text{Th}$$

You Try It!
Fill in the missing isotope in the reaction that follows:

$$^{211}_{83}\text{Bi} \rightarrow {}^{4}_{2}\text{He} + \underline{\qquad}$$

Answer: $^{207}_{81}\text{Tl}$

Beta Emission

Although there are two types of β-particles (β+ and β-), the former is usually referred to as a **positron**, so we'll refer to only the β- particle as a beta particle. In a beta emission, a beta particle is ejected from the atom. A beta particle has all of the properties of an electron (virtually massless, negative charge), yet it is created by the conversion of a neutron in the nucleus to a proton and an electron (beta particle). The proton remains in the nucleus, and the beta particle is ejected from the nucleus. An example of a beta emission is

$$^{227}_{89}\text{Ac} \rightarrow ^{0}_{-1}\text{e} + ^{227}_{90}\text{Th}$$

Notice that since the number of nucleons in the atom does not change, the mass number remains unchanged. However, the gain of a proton increases the atomic number by one (and consequently changes the element).

You Try It!

Fill in the missing isotope in the reaction that follows:

$$^{209}_{82}\text{Pb} \rightarrow ^{0}_{-1}\text{e} + \underline{\hspace{1cm}}$$

Answer: $^{209}_{83}\text{Bi}$

Positron Emission

Positron emissions are also known as β+ emissions. The positron is known as an **antiparticle**. Antiparticles are the exact opposites of particles. The positron is the antiparticle to an electron and is represented by the symbol $^{0}_{+1}\text{e}$. The electron has virtually no mass and a charge of negative one (relative to a proton). A positron has virtually no mass and a charge of positive one. When an electron and its antiparticle, the positron, collide, they disintegrate and their matter is converted entirely into energy in the form of two gamma rays. In a positron emission, a proton in the nucleus is converted into a neutron and a positron. The neutron remains in the nucleus, and the positron is ejected. The life span of the positron is very brief since it will disintegrate upon collision with an electron. An example of a positron emission can be seen in the example showing the breakdown of carbon-11:

$$^{11}_{6}\text{C} \rightarrow ^{0}_{+1}\text{e} + ^{11}_{5}\text{B}$$

Notice that the number of nucleons doesn't change here, either. As a result, the mass number of the atom does not change. However, the conversion of a proton to a neutron decreases the atomic number by one (and changes the element).

You Try It!

Fill in the missing isotope in the reaction that follows:

$$^{58}_{29}\text{Cu} \rightarrow ^{0}_{+1}\text{e} + \underline{\hspace{1cm}}$$

Answer: $^{58}_{28}\text{Ni}$

Electron Capture

The fourth type of emission is called electron capture. In this process, an inner shell electron is pulled into the nucleus, and when this occurs, the electron combines with a proton to form a neutron. In electron capture reactions, the atomic number decreases by one, the mass number remains the same, and the element changes. One difference in this type of reaction is that the electron is written to the left of the arrow to show that it is consumed, rather than produced, in the process. An example of electron capture can be seen in the following reaction:

$$^{201}_{80}\text{Hg} + ^{0}_{-1}\text{e} \rightarrow ^{201}_{79}\text{Au}$$

You Try It!

Fill in the missing isotope in the reaction that follows:

$$^{68}_{32}\text{Ge} + ^{0}_{-1}\text{e} \rightarrow \underline{\hspace{2cm}}$$

Answer: $^{68}_{31}\text{Ga}$

Gamma Radiation

The fifth type of radioactive emission, gamma radiation, does not result in a change in the properties of the atoms. As a result, they are usually omitted from nuclear equations. Gamma emissions often accompany other alpha or beta reactions—any decay that has an excess of energy that is released. For example, when a positron collides with an electron, two gamma rays are emitted, a phenomenon usually referred to as **annihilation radiation.**

RADIOACTIVE DECAY

There are a variety of reasons why radioactive decay occurs, but the primary reason is increased nuclear stability. To briefly review, attractive forces must overcome electrostatic repulsions between the like-charged protons. These attractive forces are provided by gluons (but you needn't concern yourself with knowing about gluons). Neutrons seem to play a role in this attractive process as well, both by attracting neighboring nucleons (including protons) and by "diluting" the electrostatic repulsions between the protons, by spreading them out a bit. Small atoms tend to have stable structures with equal numbers of neutrons and protons. As atoms get larger, the number of neutrons exceeds the number of protons. There are also two other properties that seem to determine stability of atomic nuclei. These are based on a model of nuclear stability known as the shell model of the nucleus. Just as there are stable electron configurations, there seem to be stable configurations of nucleons. These two properties fall into two categories:

1. **Magic numbers—There are certain numbers of protons and neutrons that are found in the most stable nuclei.** These are known as the magic numbers for protons and neutrons. For protons, the numbers are 2, 8, 20, 28, 50, and 82. For neutrons, the numbers are 2, 8, 20, 28, 50, 82, and 126.

2. **Nuclei with even numbers of protons AND neutrons are more stable than atoms with odd numbers of neutrons.** It is believed that perhaps proton-

proton pairs and neutron-neutron pairs form stable relationships, much like electron-electron pairs in molecules. Above atomic number 83 (elements 84 and up), all elements are radioactive.

The Band of Stability

Figure 4.2 shows the pattern of stable nuclides of the elements. The shaded area of the graph indicates stable isotopes and is known as the belt (or band) of stability. Most radioactive isotopes are located outside this region. The figure may also help you to see that there are three main situations that determine the types of decay that elements are likely to undergo.

1. **Atoms whose nuclei are above the band of stability (high neutron-to-proton ratio) can lower their numbers of neutrons by undergoing beta emissions.** The typical pattern for these is that the mass number (number of neutrons + number of protons) is greater than the atomic weight. Remember that beta emissions convert neutrons into protons and beta particles.

2. **Atoms whose nuclei are below the band of stability (low neutron-to-proton ratio) can raise their numbers of neutrons by undergoing positron emissions, or electron capture.** The typical pattern here is that the mass number is less than the atomic weight. Remember that both processes involve the conversion of a proton into a neutron.

3. **Atoms with atomic numbers higher than 84 are too large to remain stable.** The easiest way to decrease size is to undergo alpha emission. Remember that alpha emissions eliminate two protons and two neutrons.

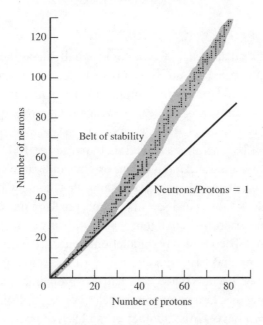

Figure 4.2

A large sample of radioactive material will spontaneously decay. Over time, the amount of the original sample will decrease and the amounts of products will increase. In the next section, you will look at the different ways this decay is described.

HALF-LIFE

A common way to describe the rate at which radioactive decay is occurring is a measurement known as the **half-life**. Half-life is defined as the time necessary for one half of a radioactive sample to undergo decay into new elements. Different isotopes have different decay rates. Some are as long or longer than 4.5 billion years (Uranium-238) to as short as 10 microseconds (astatine-215). It is not necessary to understand the factors that contribute to the length of the half-life, but you are expected to be able to perform various calculations involving half-life. There is also no way to really predict when an atom will undergo a single decay, but it is possible to observe large amounts of decay and come up with an average rate. If the amount of a radioactive substance is measured over time and the results are plotted, the resulting graph is known as a decay curve. Figure 4.3 shows the decay pattern more clearly.

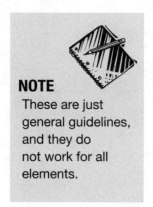

NOTE
These are just general guidelines, and they do not work for all elements.

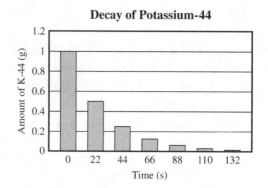

Figure 4.3

From a conceptual approach, we can look at half-life as the time it takes for $\frac{1}{2}$ of a sample to decay into some other substance. For instance, if we start out with 1.0 g of a radioactive sample, after one half-life has elapsed, we will be left with only 0.5 g of the original material. After two half-lives, we will have 0.25 g. After 3, 0.125 g. As you can see, this could go on for some time, but it is generally accepted that after about 10 half-lives have elapsed, there is a negligible amount of the original radioactive material left.

Most of the problems on past AP exams that contain half-lives are relatively simple to solve, using either conceptual or mathematical approaches. On the exam, you are not provided with any equations related to nuclear chemistry. Therefore, any calculations you will have to make should be fairly simplistic and easy to solve using a few simple rules. From a conceptual perspective, this that means half-life problems can be solved by repeatedly cutting the starting amount in half. For example, after one half-life, a sample will have $\frac{1}{2}$ the number of radioactive nuclei that it started with. After two half-lives, the sample will have $(\frac{1}{2})(\frac{1}{2})$, or $(\frac{1}{2})^2$, times the number of radioactive nuclei left. After three half-lives, the sample will have $(\frac{1}{2})(\frac{1}{2})(\frac{1}{2})$, or $(\frac{1}{2})^3$, times the number of radioactive nuclei left. If you haven't already spotted the pattern here, it is that the amount of sample left after time t will be

$$N_t = N_0(\tfrac{1}{2})^n \qquad \text{(Equation 4.1)}$$

where n = the number of half-lives that have elapsed during time interval t. This can also be rewritten as

$$\frac{N_t}{N_0} = (\tfrac{1}{2})^n \qquad \text{(Equation 4.2)}$$

which is the same thing as saying

$$\text{Fraction remaining} = (\tfrac{1}{2})^n \qquad \text{(Equation 4.3)}$$

Sample: If you start with 64 g of a material with a half-life of 10 years, how much will be left at the end of 40 years?

Answer: Conceptually, you can work through this step-by-step:

At end of	You will have left
10 years	32 g
20 years	16 g
30 years	8 g
40 years	4 g

Or you can use the formula

40 years = 4 half-lives, so
$$N_t = N_0(\tfrac{1}{2})^n = (64\text{ g})(\tfrac{1}{2})^4 = (64\text{ g})(1/16) = 4\text{ g}$$

The conceptual approach is particularly effective when solving problems that have half-lives that are whole number values. For more complex problems, we need to use some ideas borrowed from chemical kinetics. Radioactive decay can be described as a first order processes, which means it can be described with the following equation:

$$Rate = kNt \qquad \text{(Equation 4.4)}$$

where k is a constant, known as the decay constant, and N is the number of radioactive nuclei in the sample at time t. Note that the rate is proportional to the size of the sample.

By applying some basic calculus, we can integrate this equation into a new formula (it is not necessary for you to know how this was derived):

$$\ln\frac{N_t}{N_0} = -kt \quad \text{or} \quad \log\frac{N_t}{N_0} = \frac{-kt}{2.303} \qquad \text{(Equation 4.5, 4.6)}$$

where t is the time interval, k is the decay constant, N_0 is the initial number of nuclei, and Nt is the number of nuclei after time t. Mass values can be substituted for the N values since the mass will be proportional to the number of nuclei.

If you are going to be considering the half-life of a substance, then the quantities of nuclei will be related by the expression $Nt = \tfrac{1}{2} N_0$, or $2Nt = N_0$. Remember, after one half-life, the number of nuclei of a particular radioisotope will have decreased by half. This relationship will allow us to simplify the above expressions through substitution (again, it is not necessary for you to know the derivation) into the following expression:

(Equation 4.7)

$$k = \frac{0.693}{t^{\frac{1}{2}}} \text{ or } t_{1/2} = \frac{0.693}{k} \text{ (the number } 0.693 = \ln 2)$$

Sample: The half-life of Iodine-125 is 60 days. If the original sample had a mass of 50.0 grams, how much is left after 360 days?

Answer: If you compare the half-life to the time elapsed, you will see that the number of half-lives that elapse during the time interval is a whole number (60/360 = 6). The easiest way to approach this problem, then, is to use equation 4.1:

$$Nt = N0(1/2)^n$$

Given information
$N_0 = 50.0$ g
$n = 6$ half-lives   We can now substitute these values into
$Nt = ?$ the equation to solve for Nt
$Nt = 50.0 \text{ g}(1/2)^6 = 50.0 \text{ g } (1/64) = 0.781 \text{ g}$

You Try It!
Titanium-51 has a half-life of 6 minutes. If 98 g of the material are obtained, how many grams of the sample will remain after 1 hour?

Answer: 0.096 g

Sample: Iodine-131, a radioactive isotope of iodine, has a half-life of 8.07 days. A lab worker discovers that a sample of iodine-131 has been sitting on a shelf for 7 days. What fraction of the original nuclei is still present after 7 days?

Answer: To solve this problem, you will want to begin with the equation 4.6:

$$\log \frac{N_t}{N_0} = \frac{-kt}{2.303}$$

We will use this equation because we are concerned with the ratio of the initial to the final sample. We don't know k, so we can substitute the expression $k = \frac{0.693}{t^{\frac{1}{2}}}$ for k in the equation. Doing so will produce the new expression:

$$\log \frac{N_t}{N_0} = \frac{-0.693t}{2.303t^{\frac{1}{2}}} = \frac{-0.693 \, (7.0 \text{ days})}{2.303 \, (8.07 \text{ days})} = 0.2610$$

Therefore, we need to rearrange the equation so that

$$\frac{N_t}{N_0} = 10^{-0.2610} = 0.548; \; 0.548 \times 100\% = 55\%$$

We also could have used equation 4.5:

$$\ln \frac{N_t}{N_0} = -kt; \text{ substituting } k = \frac{0.693}{t^{\frac{1}{2}}} \text{ we obtain } \ln \frac{N_t}{N_0} = -\frac{0.693}{t^{\frac{1}{2}}}t$$

$$\ln \frac{N_t}{N_0} = \frac{0.693}{8.07 \text{ days}} (7 \text{ days}) = -0.601$$

$$\frac{N_t}{N_0} = e^{-.601} = 0.548 = 55\%$$

This is about what we predicted, so chances are we've done it correctly!

You Try It!
The half-life of phosphorus-30 is 2.5 min. What fraction of phosphous-30 nuclides would remain after 14 min?

Answer: 2.1%

Sample: If a 1.0×10^{-3} g sample of technetium-99 has a decay rate of 6.3×10^5 nuclei s^{-1}, what is its decay constant?

Answer: We want to use the formula: *Rate = kNt*

The first thing we will need to do is rearrange the equation to solve for *k*:

$$k = \frac{rate}{N_t}$$

We know the rate, but we still need to determine the number of nuclei present at time *t* (we only know the mass of the sample). To do this, we will need to determine how many technetium-99 atoms are present in 1.0×10^{-3} g of the substance). This is a mole-conversion problem (see Chapter 11).

$$1.0 \times 10^{-3} \text{ g } {}^{99}_{43}\text{Tc} \times \frac{1 \text{ mol } {}^{99}_{43}\text{Tc}}{99 \text{ g } {}^{99}_{43}\text{Tc}} \times \frac{6.02 \times 10^{23} \; {}^{99}_{43}\text{Tc nuclei}}{1 \text{ mol } {}^{99}_{43}\text{Tc}}$$

$$= 6.1 \times 10^{18} \; {}^{99}_{43}\text{Tc nuclei}$$

Now, we have all of the information we need to solve the problem:

$$k = \frac{rate}{N_t} = \frac{6.3 \times 10^5 \text{ nuclei / s}}{6.1 \times 10^{18} \text{ nuclei}} = 1.0 \times 10^{-13} \text{ s}^{-1}$$

You Try It!
A 2.8×10^{-6} g collection of plutonium-238 is decaying at a rate of 1.8×10^6 disintegrations per second. What is the decay constant (*k*) of plutonium-238 in s^{-1}?

Answer: 2.5×10^{-10} s^{-1}

TIP
Before beginning, it helps to consider what you are doing. If you know that the half-life is about 8 days and the sample is 7 days old, you know there should be just more than half of the sample present in the sample. When you finish your work, check to make sure your answer is close to your estimate.

Sample: What is the half-life of technetium-99?

Answer: We know from problem 3 that the decay constant of Tc-99 is 1.0×10^{-13} s^{-1}. We also know from equation 4.7 that

$$t_{1/2} = \frac{0.693}{k}$$

Therefore, by substitution, we will get

$$t_{1/2} = \frac{0.693}{k} = \frac{0.693}{1.0 \times 10^{-13} \text{s}^{-1}} = 6.9 \times 10^{12} \text{ s}$$

Depending on your needs, you might need to convert this into more suitable units. For instance,

$$6.9 \times 10^{12} \text{ s} \times \frac{1 \text{ min}}{60 \text{ s}} \times \frac{1 \text{ h}}{60 \text{ min}} \times \frac{1 \text{ day}}{24 \text{ h}} = 7.99 \times 10^7 \text{ days}$$

This still isn't a very useful amount since it is so large, so we can convert it further into years:

$$7.99 \times 10^7 \text{ days} \times \frac{1 \text{ yr}}{365.25 \text{ days}} = 2.2 \times 10^5 \text{ years}$$

You Try It!
A sample of curium-243 was produced for transport to a lab. When it was first produced, the activity of the sample was measured at 3012 dps (disintegrations per second). After 1.00 year, the lab needed to use the sample. The lead scientist measured the activity as 2921 dps. What is the half-life of curium-243?

Answer: 22.6 years

Radioactive Isotope Dating

Because radioactive isotopes seem to decay at very constant rates, they can be used as "clocks." One of the first radioactive dating techniques involved the use of the radioisotope carbon-14. Carbon-14 is produced in the upper atmosphere when neutrons (produced by cosmic rays from space) collide with nitrogen-14 molecules in the reaction shown below:

$$^{14}_{7}\text{N} + ^{1}_{0}\text{n} \rightarrow ^{14}_{6}\text{C} + ^{1}_{1}\text{H}$$

Carbon-14 incorporates into molecules just as Carbon-12 (ordinary carbon), including CO_2 gas. This carbon dioxide becomes incorporated into plants (and subsequently animals). It is assumed that the ratio of C-14 to C-12 within an organism is similar to the ratio in the atmosphere, about $1:10^{12}$ (it is believed to have been at this ratio for about 50,000 years). When a living organism dies, carbon no longer cycles into or out of it. Since Carbon-12 does not decay and Carbon-14 does, the change in ratio of C-12 to C-14 can be used to estimate the time of death of living organisms. There are other radioisotopes that are used for radioactive dating that include inorganic compounds in nonliving things, but the mechanisms for obtaining dates are similar. We will only examine C-14 dating.

The carbon-14 atom has a half-life of 5730 years and decays at a rate of 15.3 disintegrations per minute per gram of total carbon in living organisms. What this tells us is that if an organisms dies, the carbon-14 in it will decay at a rate of 15.3 disintegrations per minute per gram. As more carbon-14 decays, this rate will decrease. After one half-life has elapsed (5730 years), only half of the original C-14 will be left. This means that the total decay rate will be 7.65 disintegrations/minute/gram. After two half-lives, the disintegration will have dropped to 3.825, etc. Let's see how this information can be used to determine the date of an object.

Sample: How old is a piece of ancient wood that is giving off beta emissions from carbon-14 at the rate of 1.9 disintegrations/minute/gram?

Answer: We know that the rate of disintegrations is proportional to the number of nuclei. Therefore, we can substitute the activity for the N values in equation 4.6:

$$\ln \frac{N_t}{N_0} = -kt; \text{ substituting } k = \frac{0.693}{t^{\frac{1}{2}}} \text{ we obtain } \ln \frac{N_t}{N_0} = -\frac{0.693}{t^{\frac{1}{2}}}t$$

$$\ln \frac{1.9\text{dis}/\min/g}{15.3\text{dis}/\min/g} = -\frac{0.693}{t_{1/2}}t$$

$$-\frac{t_{1/2}}{0.693}\ln \frac{1.9\text{dis}/\min/g}{15.3\text{dis}/\min/g} = t = -\frac{5730\text{ y}}{0.693}\ln \frac{1.9\text{dis}/\min/g}{15.3\text{dis}/\min/g} = 1.7 \times 10^4 y$$

This object is about 17, 000 years old (rounded for significant digits).

You Try It!
A wooden artifact found in a mummy's tomb is found to have 9.4 disintegrations/min/g. How old is the artifact?

Answer: 4030 years old (rounded)

Transuranium Elements

In almost all of the previous examples, we have looked at nuclear reactions that occur by spontaneous decay. There are other types of nuclear reactions that can occur, known as **transmutation reactions**. These reactions can be induced by forcing a reaction between the nucleus of an element and nuclear particles (such as neutrons), or nuclei. Ernest Rutherford carried out the first transmutation by bombarding Nitrogen-14 nuclei with alpha particles. This resulted in the production of oxygen-17 and a proton, as shown below:

$$^{14}_{7}N + ^{4}_{2}He \rightarrow ^{17}_{8}O + ^{1}_{1}H$$

This process has been used to produce countless isotopes, including many radioactive isotopes. In addition, it has allowed scientists to produce elements with atomic numbers that are higher than that of the largest naturally occurring element, uranium. These elements are known as transuranium elements. In 1940, E. M. McMillan and P.H. Abelson of the University of California Berkeley produced the first transuranium element, neptunium (Np, Z=93), by bombarding uranium-238 with neutrons. The nuclei that captured the neutrons were converted to uranium-239, which decayed into neptunium-239 during a beta emission. The reaction is shown below:

Step 1: $^{238}_{92}U + ^{1}_{0}n \rightarrow ^{239}_{92}U$

Step 2: $^{239}_{92}U \rightarrow ^{239}_{93}Np + ^{0}_{-1}e$

NUCLEAR REACTIONS
Energy Relationships

Nuclear decay allows a nucleus to form products with lower energy. However, according to Albert Einstein's famous equation $E = mc^2$, any change in energy must be accompanied by a corresponding change in mass. In chemical reactions, this change in mass is negligible (though it does occur), but it is much more pronounced in nuclear reactions. If E changes by a certain amount, ΔE, then mass will have to change proportionally by an amount Δm (c being constant at all times). Thus,

(Equation 4.8)

$$\Delta E = (\Delta m)c^2$$

If we examine a specific reaction, we can see how this works. Take for instance,

$$^{238}_{92}U \rightarrow ^{234}_{90}Th + ^{4}_{2}He$$

The masses of each of the particles in the equation are

$$^{238}_{92}U = 238.0003 \text{ g mol}^{-1}, \quad ^{234}_{90}Th = 233.9942 \text{ g mol}^{-1},$$

$$\text{and } ^{4}_{2}He = 4.00150 \text{ g mol}^{-1}$$

The change in mass can be determined by subtracting the mass of the reactant (parent nuclei—in this case, uranium-238), from the combined masses of the products.

$$\Delta m = (233.9942 \text{ g} + 4.00150 \text{ g}) - 238.0003 \text{ g} = -0.0046 \text{ g}$$

To determine the energy change, we can now use Einstein's equation and solve for ΔE. Before we can do this, we must convert the mass to kilograms (because the energy unit of joules requires the mass in kilograms).

$$\Delta E = -4.6 \times 10^{-6} \text{ kg}(3.0 \times 10^8 \text{ m/s})^2 = -4.14 \times 10^{11} \text{ J}$$

This is an enormous amount of energy!

You will not be expected to perform these calculations on the AP exam, but you should appreciate from a conceptual level that there is an enormous amount of energy released during nuclear reactions. In addition, you should understand that the amount of energy released in nuclear reactions is much larger than that released in chemical reactions. The main reason is that during chemical reactions, the only energy released during a reaction will result from electrostatic forces between the protons and electrons in the atom. During nuclear reactions, the energy result is dependent on the energies associated with the strong nuclear force, which is many orders of magnitude larger than electrostatic forces. On the atomic level, we can see the effects of these strong nuclear forces when we look at the phenomena of binding energies and mass defect.

Binding Energy

It turns out that the mass of an individual atom is always less than the sum of its parts. That is, if you add up the masses of all the components of an atom, you will not get the total mass of the atom. As an example, let's look at oxygen-16.

Oxygen-16 contains 8 protons and 8 neutrons. Therefore, we would expect the mass to equal

mass of 8 protons +	mass of 8 neutrons =	total mass
8(1.0078252 amu) +	8(1.0086652 amu) =	16.1319232 amu
However, the actual mass of oxygen-16 is		15.9949150 amu

So, what happened to the 0.1370082 amu that should have been present? It turns out that when the neutrons and protons come together to form the nucleus, they form a more stable entity. This means that energy is released. When that energy is released, there must be a corresponding loss of mass. The more energy that is released, the more stable the nucleus is. In order to break apart a nucleus, you would have to add that much energy. The amount of energy you must add to break a nucleus into its constituent neutrons and protons is known as the **binding energy**. The difference in mass between the expected and actual masses is known as the **mass defect**.

It is not necessary to be able to perform these calculations for the AP exam. However, it is very important that you understand the underlying idea that large amounts of energy are released when atomic nuclei are broken apart. It is also important to understand that the difference in mass between the components of a nucleus and the actual mass of the nucleus can be accounted for by a change in the energy state of those components. The nature of that relationship is captured in Einstein's equation $E = mc^2$.

Nuclear Fission

We have seen so far that the process of heavy nuclei splitting apart (known as **fission**) is highly exothermic. In addition, the joining of lighter nuclei (known as **fusion**) is also a highly exothermic process. Fission is typically accomplished by bombarding heavy nuclei with slow-moving neutrons. Once the neutron is absorbed, the resulting unstable nucleus breaks into smaller nuclei. One of the most well known fissions involves the splitting of uranium-235, shown in the reaction below:

$$^{235}_{92}U + ^{1}_{0}n \rightarrow ^{139}_{56}Ba + ^{94}_{36}Kr + 3^{1}_{0}n$$

The neutrons produced by this fission reaction can potentially collide with other U-235 nuclei. The likelihood of the extra neutrons striking other nuclei increases as the mass of the sample increases. At a characteristic mass, the neutrons are assured to collide with U-235 nuclei, and as a result, a chain reaction begins. In this chain reaction, the neutrons from one fission will strike other nuclei and cause additional fission reactions. The mass at which a self-sustaining chain reaction will occur is known as the **critical mass**. Fission reactions are responsible for the production of nuclear power and for the design of nuclear weapons.

Nuclear Fusion

In a fusion reaction, light nuclei will combine to form heavier ones. While this process is quite commonplace on stars (including our sun), it is very difficult to accomplish in a laboratory setting. In order to fuse nuclei (such as hydrogen), extremely high temperatures are necessary (around 100 million degrees Celsius) to overcome the repulsive forces between nuclei. These temperatures are very difficult to achieve and to maintain long enough to achieve the reaction.

Summary:
Nuclear Chemistry

- Atomic nuclei are composed of neutrons and protons.

- For each nuclei, there are some isotopes that are more stable than others. The stability of each nucleus is determined by the ratio of neutrons to protons. The belt of stability can be used to estimate the stability of any given nucleus.

- To gain stability, neutrons undergo decay reactions: alpha emission, beta emission, positron emission, and electron capture are possible.

- Although it is not possible to predict when a single decay will occur, the overall rate of decay for any isotope is relatively consistent.

- The rate of decay can be used to determine the half-life of an isotope; that is the time during which one half of a radioactive sample is converted into a different material.

- The half-lives of certain materials, like carbon-14, can be used to determine the ages of artifacts.

- The sum of the masses of the individual components of an atom is greater than the actual mass of the atom. This is due to the mass that is converted into energy as the nucleons bind together.

- Nuclear fission is a process whereby unstable nuclei are bombarded by neutrons in order to split them into smaller nuclei.

- Nuclear fusion is a process where small nuclei are forced together with an extremely large amount of energy in an effort to join them into a larger nucleus.

REVIEW QUESTIONS

For questions 1–5, determine the missing information.

1. $^{230}_{90}\text{Th} \rightarrow ^{226}_{88}\text{Ra} +$ _____ The mechanism of this reaction is

   (A) alpha decay.

   (B) beta decay.

   (C) positron emission.

   (D) electron capture.

   (E) gamma photon emission.

2. $^{58}_{29}\text{Cu} \rightarrow ^{0}_{+1}\text{e} +$ _____ If copper-29 undergoes a positron emission, what is the resulting product nuclide?

   (A) $^{59}_{29}\text{Cu}$

   (B) $^{58}_{28}\text{Ni}$

   (C) $^{58}_{30}\text{Zn}$

   (D) $^{57}_{29}\text{Cu}$

   (E) $^{60}_{29}\text{Cu}$

3. $^{277}_{89}\text{Ac} \rightarrow ^{0}_{-1}\text{e} +$ _____ The missing product in the following equation is

   (A) $^{227}_{90}\text{Th}$

   (B) $^{227}_{89}\text{Ac}$

   (C) $^{227}_{88}\text{Ra}$

   (D) $^{223}_{87}\text{Fr}$

   (E) $^{228}_{89}\text{Ac}$

4. $^{68}_{32}\text{Ge} + ^{0}_{-1}\text{e} \rightarrow$ _____ What will the resulting product be when an electron is captured by a germanium-68 nucleus?

   (A) $^{68}_{33}\text{As}$

   (B) $^{69}_{32}\text{Ge}$

   (C) $^{68}_{32}\text{Ge}$

   (D) $^{68}_{31}\text{Ga}$

   (E) $^{72}_{34}\text{Se}$

5. $^{225}_{88}\text{Ra} \rightarrow ^{225}_{89}\text{Ac} +$ _____ What is the missing product in this reaction?

   (A) $^{0}_{+1}\text{e}$

   (B) $^{0}_{-1}\text{e}$

   (C) $^{4}_{2}\text{He}$

   (D) $^{0}_{0}\gamma$

   (E) $^{1}_{0}\text{n}$

6. If you begin with 300.0 g of a sample of a radioisotope and have 37.5 g remaining after a period of 90 minutes, what is the half-life of the radioisotope?

    (A) 90 minutes

    (B) 60 minutes

    (C) 30 minutes

    (D) 45 minutes

    (E) 3.4 minutes

7. Carbon-14 has a half-life of 5730 years. If you find a sample giving off 0.96 disintegrations/minute/gram, what is the age of the sample? (Originally the Carbon-14 gave off 15.3 disintegrations/minute/gram.)

    (A) 2.9×10^4 years

    (B) 2.3×10^4 years

    (C) 1.7×10^4 years

    (D) 9.9×10^3 years

    (E) 2.9×10^3 years

8. Strontium-90 is a radioactive isotope that was created by atomic weapons testing during World War II. The half-life of strontium 90 is 28.8 years. The first atomic weapons test took place in New Mexico on July 16, 1945. What fraction of the original strontium-90 remained in the desert on July 16, 2000?

    (A) 77 %

    (B) 50 %

    (C) 27%

    (D) 25%

    (E) 12.5%

9. For the types of radiation given, which of the following is the correct order of increasing penetrability?

    (A) Gamma rays < alpha particles < beta particles

    (B) Beta particles < alpha particles < gamma rays

    (C) Beta particles < gamma rays < alpha particles

    (D) Alpha particles < gamma rays < beta particles

    (E) Alpha particles < beta particles < gamma rays

10. If 87.5 percent of a sample of pure ^{99}Rh decays in 48 days, what is the half-life of ^{99}Rh?

    (A) 6 days

    (B) 8 days

    (C) 12 days

    (D) 16 days

    (E) 24 days

11. The radioactive decay of $^{19}_{8}O$ to $^{19}_{9}F$ occurs by the process of

    (A) beta particle emission.

    (B) alpha particle emission.

    (C) positron emission.

    (D) electron capture.

    (E) neutron capture.

12. The first part of the decay series of $^{240}_{94}Pu$ involves three alpha emissions followed by two beta emissions. What nuclide has been formed at this intermediate stage of the decay series?

    (A) $^{228}_{88}Ra$

    (B) $^{224}_{88}Ra$

    (C) $^{228}_{89}Ac$

    (D) $^{232}_{90}Th$

    (E) $^{228}_{90}Th$

Essay 1

The most common and stable form of oxygen is $^{16}_{8}O$, accounting for about 99.8% of all oxygen. Two of the many unstable isotopes of oxygen are $^{14}_{8}O$ and $^{21}_{8}O$. Each of these undergoes a radioactive decay, but the end products are different from each.

    (A) Identify the type of radioactive decay that oxygen-14 will undergo, and write a balanced nuclear equation for the process.

    (B) Identify the type of radioactive decay that oxygen-21 will undergo, and write a balanced nuclear equation for the process.

    (C) The decay of oxygen-21 is also accompanied by gamma ray emissions. Explain why it is not necessary to include this in the nuclear equation.

    (D) The most stable form of oxygen, $^{16}_{8}O$, has an atomic weight of $15.9\overline{9}$. However, adding the weights of its components (8 protons and 8 neutrons) gives a weight of 16.13. Account for this discrepancy between the predicted and actual weights.

Essay 2

    (A) Explain why beta particles are more potentially harmful to skin than alpha particles.

    (B) Explain why carbon dating is not a very useful technique for determining the age of objects that were never alive.

    (C) It has been proposed by some that transuranium elements, like Neptunium and Plutonium, were once present on earth in fairly significant quantities. Explain why they are not found today.

    (D) Fusion offers great promise as a clean, renewable energy source. However, for all of its promise, there are tremendous obstacles to be overcome before its use becomes possible. Explain why fusion is so much more difficult to accomplish than fission, a process already in widespread use for energy production.

ANSWERS

1. **The correct answer is (A).** You can tell that this is an alpha decay by the decrease of 4 in the mass number and 2 in the atomic number.

2. **The correct answer is (B).** Remember, positrons are formed from the conversion of a proton to a neutron and a positron. This will cause the atomic number to decrease by one but the mass number to remain unchanged.

3. **The correct answer is (A).** Beta emissions are the result of a neutron converting to a proton and an electron. The formation of the proton causes an increase in atomic number, but the mass number remains unchanged.

4. **The correct answer is (D).** The captured electron combines with a proton to form a neutron. This causes a decrease in the atomic number but no change in the mass number.

5. **The correct answer is (B).** Beta decay is the only decay that causes an increase in the atomic number.

6. **The correct answer is (C).** You can answer this conceptually or mathematically. Conceptually, try to determine if the number of half-lives is a whole number. Begin by successively dividing the sample in half. Half of 300 g is 150 g. Half of 150 g is 75 g. Half of 75 g is 37.5 g. Therefore, after 3 half-lives, the sample has decayed to its present amount. If 3 half-lives elapse in 90 minutes, each one must be 30 minutes. Mathematically, the problem is solved by using the equation $\ln \frac{N_t}{N_0} = -kt$; substituting $k = -\frac{0.693}{t_{1/2}}$, we obtain $\ln \frac{N_t}{N_0} = -\frac{0.693}{t_{1/2}} t$. Solving the equation for $t_{1/2}$ results in 30 minutes.

7. **The correct answer is (B).** You can solve the problem conceptually, beginning with a quick determination of the number of half-lives. Successive divisions of the disintegrations will determine the approximate number of half-lives: $15.3 \div 2 = 7.65 \div 2 = 3.825 \div 2 = 1.9125 \div 2 = 0.95625$. This is approximately 0.96, so about 4 half-lives have elapsed. Multiplying 5730 by 4 yields 22,920—which rounds to 2.3×10^4 years. The mathematical solution involves the equation $\ln \frac{N_t}{N_0} = -kt$; substituting $k = \frac{0.693}{t_{1/2}}$, we obtain $\ln \frac{N_t}{N_0} = -\frac{0.693}{t_{1/2}} t$. Substituting the data into the equation, we see that $\ln \frac{0.96 \text{ d/m/g}}{15.3 \text{ d/m/g}} \left(\frac{-5730}{0.693} \right) = 2.3 \times 10^4$ years.

8. **The correct answer is (C).** A quick inspection of the problem will tell you that the number of half-lives that have elapsed is not a whole number. Fifty-five years will have elapsed since July 16, 1945; however, two half-lives is equal to 57.6 years. Given the five choices, one answer is obviously correct, even without doing any calculations. If two half-lives had elapsed, the sample would be 25% of the original amount. Since the time elapsed is just shy of two half-lives, we would expect there to be slightly more than 25% of the original sample left. Therefore, 27% is the obvious answer. Mathematically, the problem can be solved using the following equation: Fraction remaining $= (1/2)n$. The value of n can be calculated by dividing the time elapsed by the half-life : 55 years $\div 28.8$ years $= 1.91$. This can be substituted for n, so that the fraction remaining $= (1/2)^{1.91} = 26.6$, which rounds to 27%.

9. **The correct answer is (E).** Alpha particles are the least penetrating particle because they have the greatest mass and the lowest velocity. Beta particles, being much smaller than alpha particles, travel much more quickly and meet less resistance due to their size, but they do encounter some resistance due to their charge. Gamma rays are the most penetrating since they have neither mass nor charge and travel at near light speed.

10. **The correct answer is (D).** Conceptually, you can see that 87.5 percent has decayed, which is the same as saying there is 12.5% remaining. You should recognize that 12.5% is one half of 25%, which is one half of 50%, which is one half of 100%. Thus, 3 half-lives have elapsed during the 48-day interval. Dividing the total time by the number of half-lives yields 16 days. Mathematically, use the equation $\ln \frac{N_t}{N_0} = -\frac{0.693}{t_{1/2}} t$. Substituting the given information, you get $\ln 0.125 = -\frac{(0.693)(48 \text{ days})}{\frac{1}{t^{\frac{1}{2}}}}$. Solving for $t_{1/2}$ yields 16 days.

11. **The correct answer is (A).** Beta decay is the only process that will increase the atomic number.

12. **The correct answer is (E).** The portion of the decay series described in the problem consists of the following reactions:

$$^{240}_{94}\text{Pu} \rightarrow {}^{4}_{2}\text{He} + {}^{236}_{92}\text{U} \qquad (\alpha\text{-decay})$$

$$^{236}_{92}\text{U} \rightarrow {}^{4}_{2}\text{He} + {}^{232}_{90}\text{Th} \qquad (\alpha\text{-decay})$$

$$^{232}_{90}\text{Th} \rightarrow {}^{4}_{2}\text{He} + {}^{228}_{88}\text{Ra} \qquad (\alpha\text{-decay})$$

$$^{228}_{88}\text{Ra} \rightarrow {}^{0}_{-1}\text{e} + {}^{228}_{89}\text{Ac} \qquad (\beta\text{-decay})$$

$$^{228}_{89}\text{Ac} \rightarrow {}^{0}_{-1}\text{e} + {}^{228}_{90}\text{Th} \qquad (\beta\text{-decay})$$

Essay 1

(A) Stable oxygen has an atomic weight of about 16 amu. Oxygen-14 has too few neutrons and so will need to increase the number of neutrons. This can occur by positron emission or electron capture. Positron emission is much more likely.

$$^{14}_{8}\text{O} \rightarrow {}^{0}_{+1}\text{e} + {}^{14}_{7}\text{N}$$

Alternative solution:

$$^{14}_{8}\text{O} + {}^{0}_{-1}\text{e} \rightarrow {}^{14}_{7}\text{N}$$

(B) Oxygen-21 has too many neutrons, so it will need to lose some. By undergoing beta emission, oxygen-21 can convert the neutrons to protons in the following reaction:

$$^{21}_{8}\text{O} \rightarrow {}^{0}_{-1}\text{e} + {}^{21}_{9}\text{F}$$

(C) Since gamma rays do not affect the chemical nature of the reactants or products, it is not necessary to include them.

(D) The difference in masses, known as the mass defect, is due to the conversion of mass that accompanies the formation of the nucleus. That is, the energy that is released as the more stable nucleus is formed by a conversion of mass according to the equation $\Delta E = c^2 \Delta m$.

Essay 2

(A) Beta particles are much smaller and travel much faster than alpha particles. They are about 100 times more penetrating than alpha particles and are more difficult to stop.

(B) Carbon dating relies on the ratio of carbon-14 to carbon-12 in organisms. Carbon-14, produced mostly in the atmosphere, is incorporated into living organisms through carbon dioxide formed from the radioactive isotope. When the organism dies, no more exchange of gases will take place, so at the time of death, the quantity of carbon-14 is fixed. If an organism was never a living organism, it is much less likely to (A) contain carbon, and (B) even if it does have carbon, it is much less likely to have incorporated the radioactive carbon dioxide.

(C) These elements are not present today because they have undergone decay into smaller elements. Over time, all larger radioactive elements will eventually decay into smaller, more stable elements.

(D) The very large repulsive force between nuclei must be overcome in order to allow fusion to occur. This requires enormous amounts of energy. Fission, on the other hand, requires much less energy because it is breaking apart already unstable nuclei.

Chemical Bonding

In this chapter, you will review the basic principles of chemical bonding. The underlying theme to remember as you go through this chapter is that chemical bonds form for a reason. Their formation is neither disorganized nor haphazard. Chemical bonds allow atoms to exist at lower energy states that are more stable. The main types of bonds fall into three categories: ionic, covalent, and metallic. Whether an atom will form ionic or covalent bonds depends on a variety of factors, the most important being its current electron configuration and the strength of the attractive force between the protons in the nucleus and the electrons. We will refer back to material from Chapter 3 (Atomic Structure) as we discuss these relationships. These same atomic properties will also determine more complex behavior, including the physical properties of ionic and covalent compounds, the shapes of the structures formed, and the attractive forces that will exist between the compounds. This chapter is going to focus on basic bonding principles and intermolecular forces (attractions or repulsions that occur between covalent or molecular compounds). Chapters 6, 7, and 8 will deal with the other topics.

The first thing we need to look at is the stability of the atom. Let's begin this by reviewing some details about electron configurations.

ROAD MAP

- *Lewis Symbols*
- *Octet Rule*
- *Ionic Bonds*
- *Covalent Bonds*
- *Using Lewis Structures to Determine Molecular Bonding*
- *Resonance Structures*
- *Intermolecular Forces*

LEWIS SYMBOLS

The electrons that are responsible for the formation of chemical bonds are the outermost electrons in an atom, also known as the valence electrons. During our present discussion, we are going to limit ourselves to the representative elements. Later in the chapter we will take on the much more challenging transition elements. For the representative elements, the outermost electrons are found in the s and p orbitals. G. N. Lewis devised a clever method for diagrammatically representing the valence electrons in an atom. His system uses the symbol of the element, around which dots are placed in symmetrical patterns. These dots can be used to better understand the transfer or sharing of electrons in bond formation. These structures, known as electron-dot structures, or Lewis-dot structures, are shown in Table 5.1. The table shows the dot structures for the eight groups, or families, of representative elements. All dot structures down a group in the periodic table are the same, with the exception of He, which only has two electrons. So although it is in group 8A, helium would have a dot structure identical to the group 2A elements.

Table 5.1   Details about the valence electrons for the Period 2 elements. The data in each column is applicable to all representative elements on the periodic table (except He, which will have the same information as group 2A elements).

Group number	Valence electrons	Outer shell electron configuration	Lewis Structure (Period 2) all periods are the same
1A	1	s^1	Li Li·
2A	2	s^2	Be Be
3A	3	s^2p^1	B ·B
4A	4	s^2p^2	C ·C·
5A	5	s^2p^3	N ·N·
6A	6	s^2p^4	O :O·
7A	7	s^2v^5	F :F:
8A	8	s^2p^6	Ne :Ne:

Although the dot structures are shown with a particular orientation and placement of dots, there is some flexibility to dot placement. The only rule that governs the placement of dots is that no more than 2 dots can be placed next to each other in a symbol (remember two electrons per orbital). There are some situations, for example, in which oxygen would be drawn with the symbol "·Ö·" or even "Ö:." The placement of dots will become more apparent when you begin making Lewis structures of molecules. Notice from the chart above that the number of dots (and therefore the number of electrons) is equal to the group number of the element. As we begin to discuss bonding, we will use dot structures to follow the movement of electrons.

OCTET RULE

The noble gases have a very stable structure. The reason for this, if you remember from Chapter 3, is that their full outer s and p orbitals provide the highest effective nuclear charge, which means a very tight hold on electrons. Ionization energies for the noble gases are the highest of any group. A closer look at groups 1A and 7A will also help to see the stability of the noble gases. Removal of an outer electron from a noble gas creates an element with an electron configuration of a group 7A element. The high electron affinities of the elements in these groups are evidence that these elements have a very great attraction for nearby electrons. A noble gas with the same electron configuration as a group 7A element would have an even greater attraction for electrons because of the extra proton in the nucleus. Because of this, any electron that is removed from a noble gas would be rapidly replaced from a surrounding atom.

Consider the opposite case, the addition of an electron. Adding an electron to a noble gas would mean adding an electron to a higher energy level (remember that *s* and *p* sublevels are filled in the noble gas configuration). This lone electron would have a similar configuration to a Group IA element; however, the atom would have a lower effective nuclear charge (because it will have one less proton than the corresponding Group 1A element). As a result, this outer electron would be very loosely bound to the atom and would be rapidly stripped away. Because the noble gas electron configuration is so stable, atoms tend to react in ways that will allow them to achieve this noble gas configuration. In order to achieve this number of electrons, atoms will gain, lose, or share electrons. And because noble gases have eight valence electrons, this pattern of reacting is called the *octet rule*.

Whether atoms gain, lose, or share electrons is determined by a number of factors, the main one being how tightly they hold on to their electrons. Think of it this way: the more tightly bound an electron is, the less likely it is to be taken away from an atom. Conversely, the less tightly bound an electron is, the more likely that electron is to be taken away. It is important to remember, however, that electrons don't just fall off or jump on to atoms in a vacuum—they have to come from somewhere and they must go somewhere. When we say that a sodium atom loses an electron, what must also be understood is that some other atom took that electron away from sodium. And, at an even deeper level, that other atom must have a pretty strong attraction for electrons (electron affinity or electronegativity) to be able to do that. Before we get into the more technical descriptions of ionic and covalent bonding, however, let's try to get a handle on the main ideas.

If one atom has a very weak attraction for its valence electron(s) (e.g., sodium, Na), and another atom has a very strong attraction for its valence electrons (e.g., fluorine, F), then the weakly held electron is likely to be stripped away from the first atom by the second atom (fluorine will strip sodium's valence electron). This will usually result in the formation of an ionic bond. If an atom with a weak attraction for its valence electron(s) (e.g., sodium, Na) is around another atom that also has a weak attraction on its valence electron(s) (e.g., Mg), then neither has enough attractive force to take the other's valence electron away. This means that under normal circumstances, these atoms won't react. But if both atoms have strong attractions for electrons, they will attract each other's electrons. The result of this type of atomic tug-of-war generally is that the two atoms will hold on to each other and share electrons. This type of interaction is the basis for a covalent (or molecular) bond.

IONIC BONDS

Ionic bonds are formed by electrostatic attractions between oppositely charged ions. These ions are formed when atoms of low ionization energy (weak attraction for valence electrons) lose one or more electrons to atoms with high electron affinity (strong attraction for electrons). At this point, we can use the octet rule to guide us through the process.

Let's begin with a very typical and simple example—the formation of sodium chloride (NaCl), ordinary table salt. Sodium is a group 1A element with one valence electron. The electron configuration of sodium is $1s^22s^22p^63s^1$. The outermost electron in the $3s$ orbital is weakly held. Chlorine, a group 7A element (halogen), has seven valence electrons. The electron configuration for chlorine is $1s^22s^22p^63s^33p^5$. The outermost electrons in the $3p$ orbitals are tightly held. Now, remember that the noble gas electron configuration, s^2p^6, is the most stable electron configuration. Careful examination of the electron configurations for sodium and chlorine will show that the loss of one electron by sodium will result in this configuration, and the gain of one electron by chlorine will also result in this configuration. Sodium will become isoelectronic (have the same electron configuration) to neon, while chlorine will become isoelectronic to argon.

Sodium: $1s^22s^22p^63s^1$ - electron $\rightarrow 1s^22s^22p^6$ = stable, octet

Chlorine: $1s^22s^22p^63s^33p^5$ + electron $\rightarrow 1s^22s^22p^63s^33p^6$ = stable, octet

Using dot structures to represent this equation, the reaction looks like this:

$$\text{Na} \,\,\overset{\frown}{+}\, \cdot\ddot{\text{C}}\text{l}: \longrightarrow \text{Na}^+ + \left[:\ddot{\text{C}}\text{l}:\right]^-$$

The simple transfer of an electron does not explain why the two atoms (now ions) bind together. To explain this, we need to look at the electrostatic interaction between the particles. Sodium, upon losing its electron, becomes a *cation*, or positively charged ion. Chlorine, upon gaining an electron, becomes an *anion*, or negatively charged ion. When the ions form, the result is that a negatively charged ion is next to a positively charged ion. These two oppositely charged particles will attract each other, providing the basis for the bond between the two ions. This example was convenient because sodium only needed to lose one electron to form an octet and chlorine only needed to gain one. This made for a perfect one-to-one transfer. However, a similar process can be used for other atoms that are less convenient. For example, take magnesium and chlorine. Magnesium, with a configuration [Ne]$3s^2$, must lose two electrons to become isoelectronic to neon. Chlorine, as you saw in the last example, only needs one electron. So, if magnesium is stripped of one electron by a chlorine atom, what becomes of its other electron? As we see in the example below, it can be stripped by another chlorine atom. This results in a compound composed of one magnesium ion and *two* chloride ions.

$$:\ddot{\text{C}}\text{l}\cdot \,\overset{\frown}{} \,\text{Mg} \,\overset{\frown}{} \,\cdot\ddot{\text{C}}\text{l}: \longrightarrow \left[:\ddot{\text{C}}\text{l}:^-\right]\left[\text{Mg}^{2+}\right]\left[:\ddot{\text{C}}\text{l}:^-\right]$$

The same pattern is followed when other combinations of ions produce larger compounds, like $AlCl_3$.

Properties of Ionic Compounds

We saw in the previous examples that the ions are held together by electrostatic attractions. What you have to remember is that positively charged particles attract any negatively charged particles—they are not specific. Likewise, negatively charged particles will attract any positively charged particles. As a result, when the sodium ion binds to the chloride ion, it will also bind to any other chloride ion in the vicinity. The chloride ions bind to the sodium ions in the vicinity. As a result, the ions begin sticking together in larger clusters, which we know as crystals. These crystals, composed of clusters of ions, are known as salts. In a salt, you won't find a single cation or anion, but rather large groupings of each. However, as you saw in the previous example of sodium chloride, the groupings of sodium and chlorine occur in one-to-one ratios (because of the octet rule). What this tells you in terms of crystalline structure is that while a sodium chloride crystal may contain vast numbers of sodium and chloride ions, they will be found in a 1:1 ratio. The resulting structures are known as a crystalline lattice:

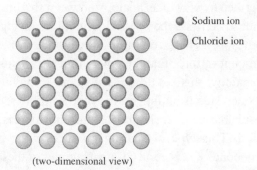

Sodium ion

Chloride ion

(two-dimensional view)

In the solid state, these substances are unable to conduct electricity (which requires a flow of electrons). This is only possible when these compounds are in the molten state or when they are dissolved in solution. The packing of the ions leads to crystalline structures. The relatively strong forces holding the ions together also give most of these structures high melting and boiling temperatures. The strength of the attractive force holding the ions together into the crystalline lattice is measured by the **lattice energy**, or the energy required to separate a mole of a solid ionic compound into its constituent gaseous ions. The larger the lattice energy, the stronger the attraction between the ions.

Transition Metals

Transition metals do not follow the octet rule simply because their outer electron structures involve both s and d orbitals. The transition metals form cations, so they are all losing electrons. The typical pattern for the loss of electrons in these elements is for the first electron(s) to come out of the s orbital and then for all remaining electrons to come out of the *d* orbitals. In addition, most of the transition metals can form more than one type of ion. An example would be copper, which can form ions of either 1^+ or 2^+ charge.

COVALENT BONDS

Remember, in ionic bonding, electrons from one atom are stripped away by electrons of another atom. This requires a large difference in the amount of attraction each atom has for its own electrons—one has to have a very strong attraction and the other a relatively weak attraction. Typically, ionic bonds form between metals and nonmetals. However, when both atoms have relatively strong attractions for electrons, neither atom can strip electrons away from the other. Instead, the electrons from one atom are attracted to the other and vice-versa. The orbitals of each atom will actually overlap, and the electrons will be "shared" between the atoms. This process will be described in much greater detail in Chapter 6.

There are two main ways that these electrons can be shared, and these will determine the characteristics of each molecule formed. Each of these two ways can be described by way of an analogy between sharing electrons and a tug-of-war game. The first type of sharing involves an equal sharing of electrons between atoms. That is, one atom attracts the other atom electrons with the same amount of force that the other atom attracts its electrons. In the tug-of-war analogy, this would be equivalent to having two evenly matched teams. Each side is pulling on the rope with the same amount of force, and as a result, the teams are bound together, but there is no movement in either direction. This type of sharing produces what are known as nonpolar covalent bonds. O_2, N_2, and Cl_2 are examples of these compounds.

The second type of sharing is where one team has a strength advantage over the other, and the rope begins moving toward that team. If the team has a *slight* advantage over the other, there will be a slight movement of the rope. If it has a *large* advantage, there will be a large movement of one team toward the other. In the case of covalent bonding, the factor that gives one team an advantage over the other is the electronegativities of each atom. Recall from Chapter 3 that electronegativity is the measure of the strength of the attraction an atom will have for the electrons of another atom during a chemical reaction. This means that compounds with high electronegativities will have strong attractions for electrons, and those with low electronegativities will have weak attractions.

If we look at our first example of the diatomic elements, O_2, N_2, and Cl_2, the electronegativities of each atom are the same (since they are the same element). We can look at methane gas, CH_4, to see an example of a weak attraction. The electronegativity for hydrogen is 2.1, and for carbon it is 2.5. The difference between carbon and hydrogen is relatively small; therefore the carbon atom will have only a slightly stronger attraction for hydrogen's electrons than hydrogen will have for carbon's. This uneven sharing of electrons is known as polarity. Hydrogen is slightly positive and carbon is slightly negative. If we look at the case of water, we see a much greater difference in electronegativities. Oxygen has an electronegativity of 3.5, which is much larger than hydrogen's 2.1. Consequently, water is a much more polar molecule than methane. So, polarity varies according to differences in electronegativities. On one end of the spectrum, there are nonpolar molecules with no difference in electronegativities between atoms. As the difference in electronegativities becomes greater, so does the polarity, the electrons are pulled more toward the atom with the higher electronegativity. Finally, if the difference in electronegativity between atoms becomes great enough, one atom simply removes the electron from the other, resulting in the formation of an ionic bond.

Polarity

In the last section, we learned how polar covalent bonds are formed. Let's look at an example and learn more of the consequences of forming these bonds. When two atoms share electrons unequally, they create what is called a **dipole**. A **dipole** is *a molecule that has a slightly positive end and a slightly negative end.* When two atoms form a polar covalent bond, the more electronegative element acquires a higher electron density. The less electronegative element acquires a lower electron density. This unequal distribution of the electrons causes one atom (the more highly electronegative) to acquire a partial negative charge while the other atom acquires a partial positive charge. It is not a full negative or positive charge because the electrons are not completely transferred from one atom to the other. A very common example of a polar covalent bond is seen in the water molecule. The highly electronegative oxygen atom attracts the hydrogen atom's electrons much more than the moderately electronegative hydrogen can attract oxygen's. As a result, we see a partial negative charge on the oxygen atom and a partial positive charge on the hydrogen atoms. Because of these polar bonds, the water molecule is said to be a polar molecule.

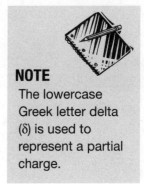

NOTE
The lowercase Greek letter delta (δ) is used to represent a partial charge.

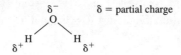

Metallic Bonds

In metals, the typical structure has numerous free-floating valence electrons that surround positively charged metal ions. Since the electrons are free to flow, metals are good conductors of electricity. The atoms in a metal are not tightly bound together (as they are in a salt). Instead they are free to move past one another, which gives metals the property of malleability (able to be shaped) and ductility (able to be drawn into thin wire). Ionic salts do not have these properties and will shatter if they are hammered or pulled.

USING LEWIS STRUCTURES TO DETERMINE MOLECULAR BONDING

In order to fully appreciate and understand molecular structure, you will need to be able to construct representations of various molecules. One of the easiest ways to do this is using Lewis structures. The procedure is a bit more complicated than for ionic compounds because of the increasing complexity of covalent compounds. The basic procedure for constructing Lewis diagrams of molecules consists of 4 steps:

1. Determine the total number of valence electrons for the entire molecule. For elements, use the group number from the periodic table. In the event that you have charged components (like polyatomic ions) in the molecule, add one electron for every negative charge on the ion (e.g., for SO_4^{2-}, add two electrons to the total because the ion has two more negative charges than a neutral species). For any positively charged components, subtract one electron from the total for each positive charge (e.g., for NH^+, subtract one electron from the total since it is going to be taking one away from the total). In this step, it doesn't matter where the electrons are coming from, just that you know the total.

2. Write a skeleton structure of the molecule. For this step, you will need to write the symbols for each atom in the molecule and connect each using a pair of dots or a dash. This is one of the more difficult steps since you are not told directly which atom is attached to which. In general, the chemical formula is written in the same order that the elements are connected in the molecule. When multiple atoms are connected to the same atom, the central atom is usually written first (e.g., in the CCl_4 molecule, the carbon is the central atom and the four chlorine atoms are bonded around it). Very often, the central atom is the least electronegative element.

3. Make octets around all surrounding atoms (not the central atom). Use the octet rule to fill in all 8 dots on all atoms surrounding the central atom (the one exception being hydrogen, which should only have two).

4. Put the rest of the electrons on the central atom. The remaining number of electrons is the total number (from step 1) minus the number you placed on the surrounding atoms in step 3. If you don't have enough electrons, you will need to determine if double or triple bonds are present. If you have too many electrons on the central atom, don't worry about it. You will see later in the chapter why this is possible.

Sample: Draw a Lewis structure for the molecule CF_4, carbon tetrafluoride.

1. Count the total valence electrons. Carbon has 4 and each fluorine has 7, for a total of $4 + (7 \times 4) = 32$

2. A skeleton structure will place the carbon as the central atom and with each fluorine atom around it. This formation is chosen because carbon appears first and is the least electronegative element.

$$\begin{array}{c} \text{F} \\ \text{F} : \ddot{\text{C}} : \text{F} \\ \text{F} \end{array}$$

3. Complete the octets around each fluorine atom.

$$\begin{array}{c} : \ddot{\text{F}} : \\ : \ddot{\text{F}} : \ddot{\text{C}} : \ddot{\text{F}} : \\ : \ddot{\text{F}} : \end{array}$$

4. After completing the octets for each fluorine atom, all 32 electrons have been used. Therefore, you're done.

You Try It!

Draw a Lewis structure for the molecule PCl_3.

Answer:
$$:\ddot{C}l:\ddot{P}:\ddot{C}l: \qquad :\ddot{C}l-\ddot{P}-\ddot{C}l:$$
$$\quad:\ddot{C}l: \qquad\qquad :\ddot{C}l:$$

Sample: Draw a Lewis structure for H_2CO.

1. The total number of valence electrons is 12. Each hydrogen has 1, the carbon has 4, and the oxygen has 6. $(2 \times 1) + 4 + 6 = 12$

2. This skeleton is a little more difficult, but you will discover that in carbon compounds, the carbon is usually the central element. Therefore, the skeleton diagram will look like:

$$\begin{array}{cc} H & H \\ H:\overset{\cdot}{C}:O & \text{or} \quad H-\overset{|}{C}-O \end{array}$$

3. Complete the valence shells (remember, only 2 electrons total for hydrogen, so it won't get any more).

$$\begin{array}{cc} H & H \\ H:\overset{\cdot\cdot}{C}:\overset{\cdot\cdot}{O}: & \text{or} \quad H-\overset{|}{C}-\overset{\cdot\cdot}{O}: \end{array}$$

4. Counting the electrons, we determine that with all 12 electrons used, there is an insufficient number for either carbon or oxygen. If oxygen receives an octet, then carbon is missing two electrons. Likewise, if you shifted the electrons so that carbon had an octet, oxygen would be missing two. The solution is to form a multiple bond. By creating a double bond between oxygen and carbon, all atoms have an octet.

$$\begin{array}{cc} H & H \\ H:\overset{\cdot\cdot}{C}::\overset{\cdot\cdot}{O} & \text{or} \quad H-\overset{|}{C}=\overset{\cdot\cdot}{O} \end{array}$$

You Try It!

Draw the Lewis structure for carbon dioxide, CO_2.

Answer: $\qquad \ddot{O}::C::\ddot{O} \quad$ or $\quad \ddot{O}=C=\ddot{O}$

RESONANCE STRUCTURES

There are some molecules for which satisfactory Lewis structures cannot be made. An example is sulfur trioxide, SO_3. Let's begin by making a Lewis structure of the compound:

1. Count the valence electrons. S = 6, O = 6, so $6 + (3 \times 6) = 24$

2. Draw the skeleton molecule.

3. Complete the octets.

4. After completing this portion, you may note that sulfur does not have an octet, which requires you to create multiple bonds. You may also notice that in creating the multiple bonds, there are actually three configurations that are equally possible.

So, which structure should be drawn? The answer is all three. Experimental evidence suggests that something different happens in molecules like SO_3—the measured bond lengths between each S and O are actually somewhere in between the length of a single and double bond. What is believed to happen in molecules such as this is a process known as delocalization, or resonance. The electrons shown in the double bond actually "spread out" so that they are equally shared among all constituents. This is the only explanation that seems to account for the intermediate bond lengths. When drawing resonance structures, it is appropriate to draw all possible Lewis structures. When looking at them, you should think of them as being superimposed on one another as opposed to being three distinct, isolated states.

Exceptions to the Octet Rule

Of course, now that you're getting the hang of it, you need to know about those ever-present exceptions to the rule. There are some cases in which the octet rule is not obeyed. You should be familiar with the examples, and there are some patterns you can learn to help you memorize this.

Odd Numbers of Electrons

Some molecules and ions have an odd number of electrons. That is, after all electrons are paired up as bonding pairs or lone pairs, there is an extra electron. The most common examples of these compounds contain nitrogen, such as NO and NO_2. In these cases, the extra electron should be placed into a multiple bond.

Molecules with Fewer Than Eight Valence Electrons

There are a few molecules in which an atom will have less than eight valence electrons. The most common examples of these contain H, Be, B, and Al. For example, boron trifluoride, BF_3, has a central boron atom surrounded by three fluorine atoms. After filling the octets around the fluorine atoms, there are two possible solutions. One is to leave boron with only six valence electrons, while the second is to draw resonance structures for the molecule. Experimental data suggests that the first solution is more correct because the bond lengths indicate single bonds.

Molecules with More Than Eight Valence Electrons

These are the most common exceptions to the octet rule. In these molecules, the atoms use empty d orbitals to hold more than eight valence electrons. These tend to form from large central atoms surrounded by small, highly electronegative elements (like F, Cl, and O). Some common examples are PF_5 and SF_6.

INTERMOLECULAR FORCES

The polarity of molecules like water has very significant effects on the behavior of these compounds. If you recall in ionic compounds, the oppositely charged ions attract each other and form large crystalline structures. A similar process occurs between polar molecules, but we describe these as intermolecular forces. There are three main intermolecular forces we need to examine. All three of these forces are known as van der Waals forces and are specifically called hydrogen-bonding forces, dipole-dipole interactions, and London dispersion forces.

Hydrogen Bonding

Hydrogen bonding will be seen in situations in which a hydrogen atom is bonded to a small, highly electronegative element with lone pair electrons. In hydrogen bonds, the hydrogen atom (with its partial positive charge), will be attracted to the lone pair electrons of the nearby partially negative atom. One of the more common and significant places where hydrogen bonding occurs is the water molecule. If two water molecules are near each other, the partially positive hydrogen atoms will be attracted to the lone-pair electrons of the nearby partially negative oxygen atoms. These electrostatic attractions will cause weak bonds to form between the water molecules. Hydrogen bonds, which are weak compared to covalent or ionic bonds, are the strongest of the intermolecular forces. They are responsible for a number of important chemical phenomena, some of which are listed in Table 5.2.

Table 5.2 Examples of the effects of hydrogen bonding.

Increased boiling temperatures	A perfect example is the difference between methane (CH_4), ammonia (NH_3), and water (H_2O). The dramatic difference in boiling temperatures of CH_4 (-162 °C), NH_3 (-33 °C), and H_2O (100 °C) is due to the greater hydrogen bonding between the more polar molecules.
Surface tension	Hydrogen bonding is not responsible for surface tension in all substances, but it is responsible for it in many substances. The tension found on the surface of liquids and the "rounding" of drops of liquids are due to an uneven amount of hydrogen bonding between the molecules on the surface with molecules beneath the surface and molecules in the air. This uneven attraction creates a net force that is inward.

Dipole-dipole Interactions

Dipole-dipole interaction is still caused by forces between polar molecules. However, this time the molecules are not limited to hydrogen-containing molecules. Any polar molecule can be attracted to any other polar molecule. Likewise, ions will also be attracted to polar molecules. The strength of these attractions will vary with the polarity of the molecules and will determine many physical properties similar to those listed in Table 5.2. In a dipole-dipole interaction, the atoms with partial positive charges are attracted to nearby atoms with partial negative charges (or lone-pair electrons).

London Dispersion Forces

London dispersion forces are the weakest of the intermolecular forces and occur between all molecules. These are the only types of intermolecular forces that are possible between nonpolar molecules and are caused by momentary dipoles. Experimental evidence suggests that electrons are not symmetrically distributed about the nucleus at all times. On average, the electrons may be spread out evenly around the nucleus, but there are brief instants when the electron density may be greater on one side of the atom than another. During these periods of time, the atoms develop a temporary or instantaneous polarity. The temporary polarity (which is the cause of the momentary dipole) allows for attraction between particles that are normally nonpolar. London dispersion forces tend to increase as the size and mass of the molecule increase.

Summary: Chemical Bonding

- Lewis symbols, or electron dot symbols, are useful ways to represent the valence electrons in many elements.

- Atoms form bonds that allow them to acquire a stable octet (or eight valence electrons).

- Ionic bonds, based on electrostatic attraction between oppositely charged particles, form when electrons are transferred from one atom to another.

- Ionic compounds are crystalline and tend to have high boiling points.

- Covalent bonds form between atoms with fairly similar electronegativities. Electrons are shared between atoms in covalent compounds. When the electrons are shared equally, the bond is nonpolar, and when they are shared unequally, the resulting bond is polar.

- Lewis structures can be used to draw the structures of covalent compounds. You should learn the rules for drawing these structures.

- Resonance structures exist for molecules in which electrons are delocalized.

- There are a few notable exceptions to the octet rule that you should be aware of: molecules with odd numbers of electrons, incomplete octets, and expanded octets.

- There are three main types of intermolecular forces you need to be aware of: hydrogen bonding, dipole-dipole interactions, and London dispersion forces. The first two only occur in polar molecules, whereas dispersion forces exist between all types of molecules.

- Intermolecular forces can be used to explain many physical properties of compounds.

REVIEW QUESTIONS

1. The energy required to remove an electron from a gaseous atom is known as

   (A) activation energy.

   (B) free energy.

   (C) ionization energy.

   (D) kinetic energy.

   (E) lattice energy.

2. The energy required to separate an ionic solid into gaseous ions is known as

   (A) activation energy.

   (B) free energy.

   (C) ionization energy.

   (D) kinetic energy.

   (E) lattice energy.

3. For which of the following molecules are resonance structures necessary to describe the bonding satisfactorily?

   (A) H_2O

   (B) SO_2

   (C) C_2H_6

   (D) HCN

   (E) PF_3

4. Which of the following has the most polar bond?

   (A) N_2

   (B) F_2

   (C) HF

   (D) HCl

   (E) PCl_3

5. Which of the following would most likely have the highest boiling point?

   (A) NH_3

   (B) CH_4

   (C) PCl_5

   (D) HF

   (E) LiCl

Use these answers for questions 6–8.

(A) Hydrogen bonding

(B) Hybridization

(C) Ionic bonding

(D) Resonance

(E) London dispersion forces

6. Is used to explain why bromine molecules are held together in the liquid state at room temperature.

7. Is used to explain why the boiling point of n–propanol, C_3H_7OH, is greater than the boiling point of propane, C_3H_8.

8. Is used to explain the fact that the S-O bonds in SO_3 are identical.

9. Which of the following elements, if placed as the central atom in a molecule, is capable of having more than 8 valence electrons?

(A) N

(B) F

(C) O

(D) Te

(E) H

10. Which molecule has a Lewis structure that does not obey the octet rule?

(A) NO

(B) CS_2

(C) PF_3

(D) HCN

(E) CCl_4

Free Response

Using the principles of chemical bonding and/or intermolecular forces, explain each of the following.

    (A) Neon has a boiling point of –246 °C, argon has a boiling point of –186 °C, and krypton has a boiling point of –153 °C.

    (B) In its metallic form, copper is used to make electrical wire because of its excellent conductivity, yet the compound copper II chloride, $CuCl_2$, does not conduct electricity.

    (C) H_2O has a boiling point of 100 °C, while the similar H_2S has a boiling point of –60 °C.

    (D) The melting point data in the Table below:

Melting point data for four lithium salts

Substance	Melting point (°C)
LiF	848
LiCl	610
LiBr	552
LiI	469

ANSWERS

1. **The correct answer is (C).**

2. **The correct answer is (E).**

3. **The correct answer is (B).** $\ddot{O}=\ddot{S}-\ddot{O}: \longleftrightarrow :\ddot{O}-\ddot{S}=\ddot{O}$

4. **The correct answer is (C).** H and F have the greatest difference in electronegativities.

5. **The correct answer is (E).** LiCl is an ionic solid. The others, all molecular compounds, will have lower boiling points.

6. **The correct answer is (E).** Bromine, Br_2, is a nonpolar molecule. The only intermolecular forces that are possible are London dispersion forces. The larger the molecule, the more interactions that are possible between atoms/molecules.

7. **The correct answer is (E).** The propane molecule is essentially nonpolar. The polar O-H bond in propanol allows for the formation of hydrogen bonds that will increase its boiling point.

8. **The correct answer is (D).** SO_3 has three resonance structures. The concept of resonance explains why all three of these bonds are identical as opposed to having one shorter S=O double bond and two longer S-O single bonds.

9. **The correct answer is (D).** Te is the only one with d orbitals capable of an expanded octet.

10. **The correct answer is (A).** NO has an odd number of electrons. It can't obey the octet rule. $\dot{N}=\ddot{O}$

Free Response

(A) Neon, argon, and krypton all are noble gases with increasing atomic number. London dispersion forces are responsible for the intermolecular forces that can cause attractions between the atoms. Dispersion forces increase as the size of an atom increases.

(B) The metallic bonds allow for free movement of valence electrons within elemental copper. This allows greater conductivity. Copper chloride, on the other hand, is an ionic solid, where the electrons are all held tightly within the crystalline structure of the compound. Tightly bound electrons can't support the flow of electric current.

(C) Although the molecules are structurally similar, the polarity of the bonds in each is dramatically different. Oxygen is a much more electronegative element than sulfur. Therefore, the polarity of each O-H bond is much higher than the polarity of the S-H bonds. This allows for a higher degree of hydrogen bonding between the water molecules and, hence, a higher boiling point.

(D) The trend in the table is that lithium is bonded to elements that become progressively larger. For ionic compounds, the strength of the bonds decreases as atomic size increases.

Chapter

Molecular Geometry

This chapter reviews molecular geometry and the two main theories of bonding. The model used to determine molecular geometry is the VSEPR (Valence Shell Electron Pair Repulsion) model. There are two theories of bonding: the valence bond theory, which is based on VSEPR theory, and molecular orbital theory. A much greater amount of the chapter is based on valence bond theory, which is based on VSEPR theory and uses hybridized orbitals, since this is the primary model addressed on the AP exam.

There are a few attributes of molecules that must be included in a discussion of molecular geometry. These include the three-dimensional arrangement of the atoms, the bond angles, the bond lengths, and the locations and effects of lone pairs of electrons. These issues are explained in the VSEPR model.

ROAD MAP

- *VSEPR Theory*
- *Molecular Geometry*
- *Dipole Moments*
- *Valence Bond Theory*
- *Sigma and Pi Bonds*
- *Molecular Orbital Theory*

VSEPR THEORY

As its name might suggest, VSEPR theory is based on the assumption that molecules will be constructed in ways that minimize electron pair repulsions. That is, pairs of electrons will repel each other to the farthest possible distance. With this understanding, there are some very clear patterns that emerge when looking at different types of molecular structures.

When constructing molecular models, it helps to review the Lewis structures for the molecule. If you recall from Chapter 5, Lewis structures display two types of electrons: bonding pairs (those shared between atoms) and nonbonding pairs (those that exist as lone pairs on an atom).

Electron-Pair Arrangements

Before looking at molecular geometry it is helpful to examine the way that VSEPR theory treats single atoms. According to the theory, the electrons are going to orient themselves as far away from one other as possible. In Table 6.1, you will notice the effect this has on different amounts of electron pairs.

The Relationship Between
Bond Angles and Nonbonding Electrons

The basic technique for predicting molecular geometries is to use one of the structures shown in Table 6.1 and insert atoms in the positions of some electron pairs while inserting lone pairs for the remainder. This will automatically reclassify some of the electron pairs as bonding pairs and

NOTE

Remember from Chapter 5, that there are some atoms that have more than an octet around them.

Table 6.1 Arrangements of Electrons Around Central Atoms

Electron Pairs	Electron-pair Arrangement	Geometry	Bond Angles
2	$180°$	Linear	$180°$
3	$120°$	Trigonal planar	$120°$
4	$109.5°$	tetrahedral	$109.5°$
5	$120°$ $90°$	Trigonal bipyramidal	$120°$ $90°$
6	$90°$ $90°$	Octahedral	$90°$ $180°$

others as nonbonding pairs. The bonding pairs determine the geometry of the molecule only, while the nonbonding pairs will contribute to the bond angles. Let's construct a model of a water molecule:

$$H - \ddot{O} - H$$

Figure 6.1

As you can see in the figure, there are two pairs of bonding electrons (one pair between each hydrogen and the central oxygen). There are also two pairs of nonbonding electrons. The electron pairs will orient themselves in a tetrahedral configuration. Since two of the pairs of electrons are going to be bonded to hydrogen atoms, the resulting molecule will be a shape known as "bent" (see table 6.2).

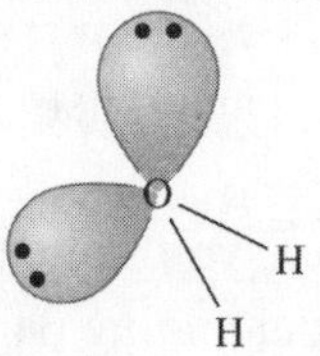

Figure 6.2

The water molecule helps to illustrate two important facets of VSEPR theory: that the molecular shape is not always going to be the same as the electron pair geometry and that the nonbonding pairs of electrons tend to have a larger effect on the overall molecule and are drawn larger as a result. This second point about the effect of the nonbonding pairs can be seen by comparing the bond angles of water, ammonia, and methane against the predicted bond angles of 109.5° (the predicted angle for a tetrahedral arrangement of electrons).

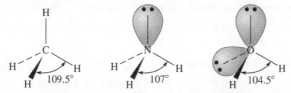

Figure 6.3

Each of these molecules has a tetrahedral arrangement of electrons. The difference between them is the number of nonbonding pairs in the molecule. As you have just seen, water has two nonbonding pairs of electrons and two bonding pairs. Ammonia (NH_3) has one nonbonding pair and three bonding pairs. Methane (CH_4) has no nonbonding pairs and four bonding pairs. As you can see in Figure 6.4, the bond angles between hydrogen atoms in methane are indeed 109.5°. However, ammonia is only 107 °, while water is 104.5°. The accepted explanation for this phenomenon is that the nonbonding electrons have a larger repulsive force than the bonding electrons. As a result, the bonding electrons between the hydrogen atoms and the central atoms are "squeezed" more tightly together. The more nonbonding pairs, the greater the decrease in bond angle. This same effect can be seen with multiple bonds. Multiple bonds also have the effect of compressing bond angles by exerting a greater repulsive force on neighboring electrons.

MOLECULAR GEOMETRY

The shapes of most molecules can be predicted using the six models for electron pair arrangements. What you need to do for each one is

1. Determine the number of electron pairs on the central atom—this determines the electron pair arrangements.

2. Determine the number of bonding pairs and nonbonding pairs. You should "ignore" the nonbonding pairs when determining the shape of the molecule (since they are not part of the molecule). The nonbonding pairs will only become significant if you need to determine information about bond angles.

Table 6.2, on the next three pages, lists representative structures and examples.

One thing to note that will save you some time memorizing information is that for molecules with no nonbonding pairs, the molecular geometry is identical to the electron pair geometry.

Samples: Determine the molecular geometries of the following molecules:
   a) CF_4 b) TeF_4 c) KrF_2

Answers:

a)   Drawing a Lewis structure lets you know quickly that there are four pairs of electrons surrounding the central atom and no nonbonding pairs. Therefore, the structure will be **tetrahedral.**

b)   Te has six valence electrons. The Lewis structure should indicate that four of these will be in bonding pairs with the fluorine atoms and the remaining two will exist as a nonbonding pair. Therefore, the structure shows 5 electron pairs, 1 of which is nonbonding, indicating a **seesaw** shape.

c)   Kr has eight valence electrons. The Lewis structure should indicate that two of these will be used in bonds with fluorine atoms, leaving six. These six will form three nonbonding pairs. Therefore, there are five electron pairs, two of which are bonding and three of which are nonbonding. The structure is **linear**.

You Try It!
Determine the molecular geometries of the following molecules:
   a) H_2Se b) BrF_3 c) SCl_4

Answers: a) bent   b) T-shaped   c) seesaw

Table 6.2

Electron Pairs	Electron pair arrangement	Bonding pairs	Nonbonding pair	Molecular geometry	Example
2	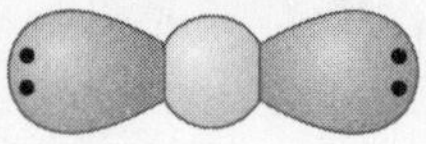 Linear	2	0	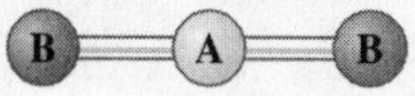 Linear	CO_2 BeH_2
3	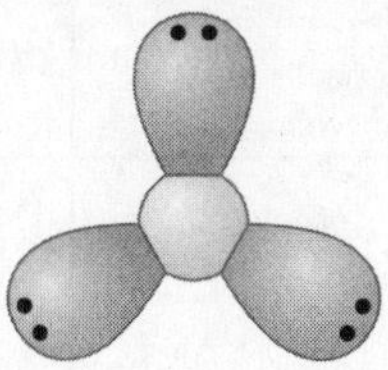 Trigonal planar	3	0	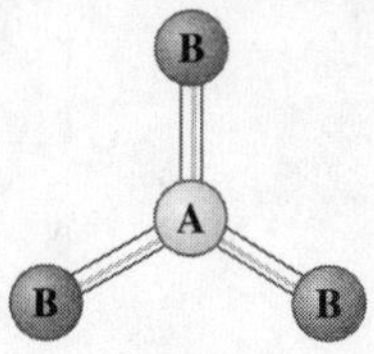 Trigonal planar	BCl_3 SO_3
		2	1	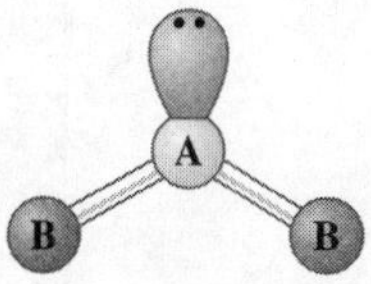 Bent	$SnCl_2$
4	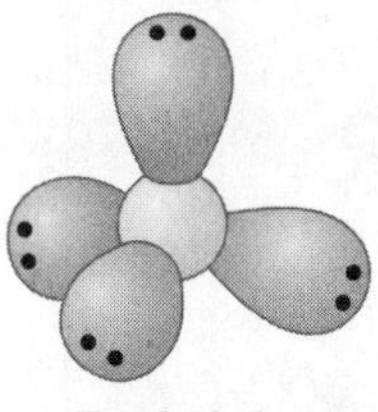 Tetrahedral	4	0	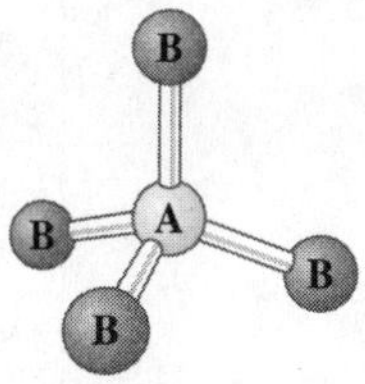 Tetrahedral	CH_4
		3	1	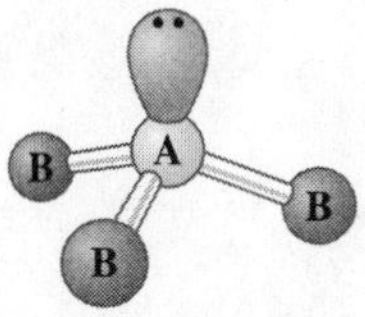 Trigonal pyramidal	NH_3
		2	2	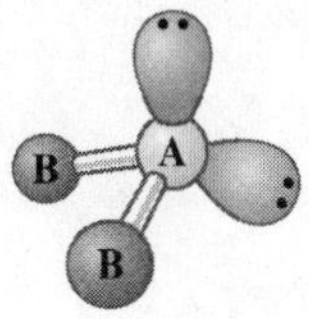 Bent	H_2O

Table 6.2 (Continued)

Electron Pairs	Electron pair arrangement	Bonding pairs	Nonbonding pair	Molecular geometry	Example
5	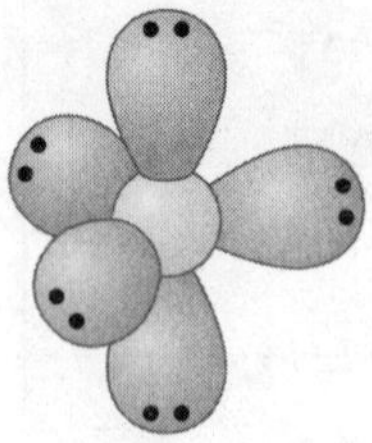 Trigonal bipyramidal	5	0	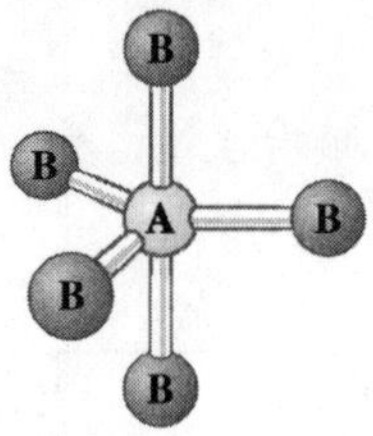 Trigonal bipyramidal	PCl_5
		4	1	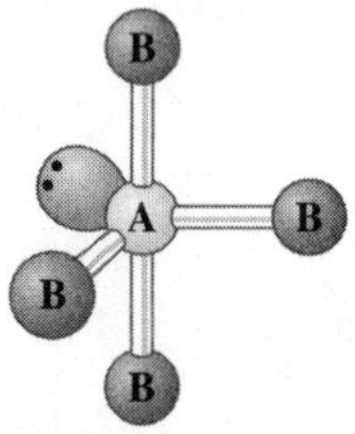 Seesaw	SF_4
		3	2	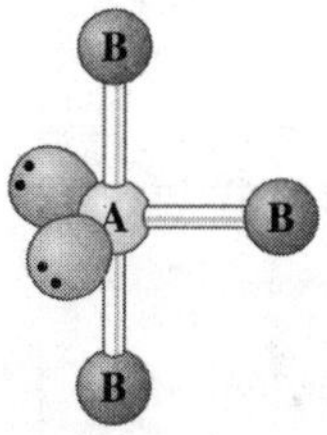 T-shaped	ClF_3
		2	3	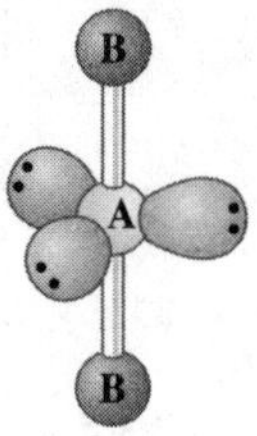 Linear	XeF_2

Table 6.2 (Continued)

Electron Pairs	Electron pair arrangement	Bonding pairs	Nonbonding pair	Molecular geometry	Example
	Octahedral	6	0	Octahedral	SF_6
6		5	1	Square pyramidal	BrF_5
		4	2	Square planar	XeF_4

DIPOLE MOMENTS

In Chapter 5, you learned about dipoles. A natural extension of that topic is a discussion of the dipole moment. If you recall, a dipole is created when there is an uneven distribution (or sharing) of electrons in a covalent bond between atoms of unequal electronegativities. The strength of a dipole depends partly on the degree of difference in electronegativities between the two atoms. That is, for two atoms whose differences in electronegativities are rather large, like H and F, the magnitude of the dipole will be larger than that of a bond between H and O (in which the electronegativity difference is not as large).

Dipoles, in addition to having a certain size, also exist in specific directions. For example, the dipole between H and F points toward F since F has a larger electronegativity and draws the electron density toward itself. So the dipole has both a size and a direction. Measurements that possess both a size and a direction are known as vectors. The magnitude of the dipole is usually expressed as the dipole moment. A dipole moment is defined as the product of the charge, Q, times the distance between the charges, r.

$$\text{Dipole moment} = Q \times r$$

The unit of measure for dipole moments is known as a debye (D).

You are not asked to calculate the dipole moment on the AP exam, but you do need to understand what it represents and how to work with it. What follows is a description of the types of information that usually appear on the AP exam for dipole moments.

Working with Vectors

If you are looking at the dipoles in a diatomic element, like O_2, you should quickly notice that there is no dipole moment. One oxygen atom pulls the other electrons toward it with a certain amount of force, but the other atom pulls back with an equal amount of force. Therefore, there is no net force between the two oxygen atoms—the forces cancel. For two different atoms, such as H and F, the electrons are definitely pulled more toward F than back toward H. As a result, there is a dipole moment toward the F:

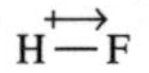

$$H \overset{\longleftrightarrow}{\rule{1cm}{0pt}} F$$

Figure 6.4

Any diatomic molecules containing two different elements will have dipole moments. More complex molecules have to be carefully considered before determining their dipole moments. For example, let's compare the molecules CO_2 and H_2O. Both contain three atoms, but the dipole moments are very different. As you just learned in the previous section, CO_2 has a linear molecular geometry. Since C and O have different electronegativity values, there will be a dipole between C and O. However, a closer look at the molecule, the dipoles, and the geometry reveal the nature of the dipole moment:

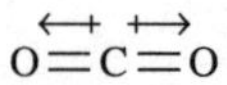

$$O \overset{\longleftrightarrow}{=} C \overset{\longleftrightarrow}{=} O$$

Figure 6.5

Because the magnitude of each dipole is equal and their directions are exactly opposed to one another, the two vectors cancel each other out. Therefore, the CO_2 molecule has no dipole moment. Now, consider the H_2O molecule. Since there is an electronegativity difference between H and O, there will be a dipole between each H and the oxygen atom. However, the molecular geometry of the water molecule is bent. This means that the vectors look like:

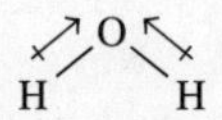

Figure 6.6

In this molecule, the vectors are not opposite each other and therefore do not cancel each other out. They will add together to produce a net dipole moment for the molecule:

Figure 6.7

A geometry that has angles in it does not necessarily mean the molecule has to have a dipole moment. Take, for instance, BF_3. The molecular geometry for this molecule is trigonal planar. There is a difference in electronegativities between boron and fluorine, so there will be dipoles between boron and fluorine. If you consider the molecular geometry, however, you will notice that the dipoles cancel each other out, giving the BF_3 molecule a dipole moment of zero:

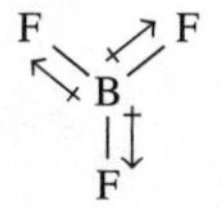

Figure 6.8

There are a few other items worth mentioning about dipole moments. In addition to the geometry of the molecule, you must consider the presence of nonbonding electrons. Nonbonding electrons also create a shift in electron density away from an atom and toward the nonbonding pair. These lone pairs will affect any molecules that contain nonbonding electrons. For example, if you look at the molecule NF_3, you might expect to see a rather large dipole moment. The shape of the molecule is trigonal pyramidal. Since there is a substantial electronegativity difference between N and F, the dipoles will be toward each fluorine atom. Therefore, there will be three dipoles moving downward, away from the nitrogen atom.

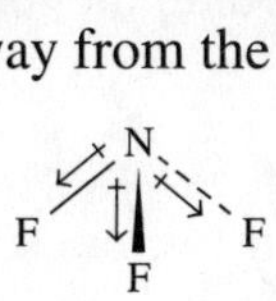

Figure 6.9

The dipole moment of the NF_3 molecule, however, is rather small, only about 0.2 D. The factor that reduces the effect of the fluorine atoms is the nonbonding pairs, which also create a force going upward (or opposite the net force of the fluorine atoms). This is nearly enough to cancel the force of the fluorine atoms:

Figure 6.10

Also, molecules are considered polar if they have a dipole moment and nonpolar if they have no dipole moment. Conversely, you could say that molecules that are polar have a dipole moment and molecules that are nonpolar do not have a dipole moment.

The AP exam does not ask you to calculate the dipole moments of any molecules. What it does ask—almost every year—are questions such as "Which of the following has the greatest dipole moment" or "Which of the following has no dipole moment." To answer those questions, you have to consider the geometry and the size of the attractions between the atoms.

Sample: Of the following molecules, which has the largest dipole moment?

    (A) CN^-

    (B) CO_2

    (C) N_2

    (D) HF

    (E) F_2

Answer: HF. N_2 and F_2 can be ruled out immediately since they are diatomic molecules and nonpolar. CO_2 is the only triatomic molecule here, but it is a linear molecule, and therefore it is nonpolar. Between CN^- and HF, the electronegativity differences between H and F are far greater than between C and N. Therefore, the dipole will be much larger between those two, creating a larger dipole moment.

You Try It!
Which of the following has a zero dipole moment?

    (A) HCN

    (B) H_2S

    (C) SO_2

    (D) NO

    (E) PF_5

Answer: PF_5

VALENCE BOND THEORY

The VSEPR model makes some assumptions. Primarily, it assumes that orbitals from neighboring atoms overlap and electrons are shared within the common region of space. Another assumption is that only unpaired electrons are involved in bonding. This latter assumption is where things get a bit sticky, so an alternative approach is needed. Take the fluorine atom, for instance, whose orbital diagram is shown below:

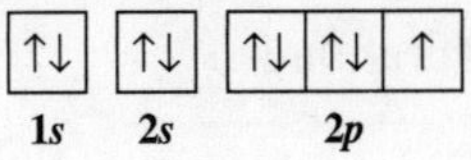

$$\boxed{\uparrow\downarrow}\ \boxed{\uparrow\downarrow}\ \boxed{\uparrow\downarrow\,|\,\uparrow\downarrow\,|\,\uparrow}$$
$$\text{1}s \qquad \text{2}s \qquad \text{2}p$$

Figure 6.11

Fluorine has one unpaired electron and, as you know, forms one bond. Similarly oxygen, whose orbital diagram is

$$\boxed{\uparrow\downarrow}\ \boxed{\uparrow\downarrow}\ \boxed{\uparrow\downarrow\,|\,\uparrow\,|\,\uparrow}$$
$$\text{1}s \qquad \text{2}s \qquad \text{2}p$$

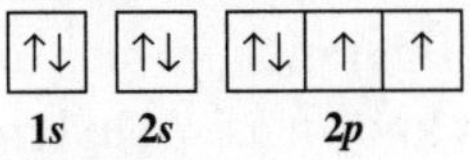

Figure 6.12

has two unpaired electrons and forms two bonds. Following this logic, you would expect that carbon, whose orbital diagram is

$$\boxed{\uparrow\downarrow}\ \boxed{\uparrow\downarrow}\ \boxed{\uparrow\,|\,\uparrow\,|\,}$$
$$\text{1}s \qquad \text{2}s \qquad \text{2}p$$

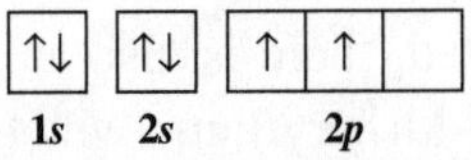

Figure 6.13

would only form two bonds. However, it is very rare that this occurs. Carbon most often forms four bonds. So, is the assumption about unpaired electrons incorrect, or is something else going on? It turns out that something else seems to be going on (though there is still a fair amount of argument about this). For your purposes on the AP exam, you can assume that what follows is an acceptable explanation.

The answer comes from a process known as hybridization of orbitals. The basic premise is that in order to gain the stability of additional covalent bonds, some electrons can be "promoted" to higher orbitals. While some energy is required to promote electrons to higher energy levels, the stability of the extra bonds compensates sufficiently to allow the process to occur. The four bonds of carbon can be explained by showing the promotion of an electron to a higher orbital, as seen in this new orbital diagram of carbon:

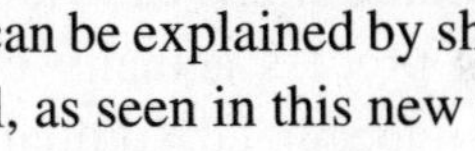

$$\boxed{\uparrow\downarrow}\ \boxed{\uparrow}\ \boxed{\uparrow\,|\,\uparrow\,|\,\uparrow}$$
$$\text{1}s \qquad \text{2}s \qquad \text{2}p$$

Figure 6.14

The diagram indicates that there are still separate *s* and *p* orbitals. Experimental evidence indicates that the bonds formed between carbon and other atoms (for example four hydrogen atoms) are all the same. That is, they all behave as though they are the same type of orbital. The accepted explanation for this is that the four orbitals form a new type of orbital known as a hybrid. In this case, because the new orbitals involve one *s* orbital and three *p* orbitals, the new orbitals are known as sp³ (pronounced "s-p-three"—don't mistake it for an exponent) hybridized orbitals, shown in the diagram below:

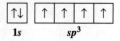

Figure 6.15

Other combinations of hybrid orbitals are possible. For example, boron, whose normal orbital configuration is

Figure 6.16

will promote a 2*s* electron to form hybrid orbitals, but there will still be an empty 2*p* orbital. This configuration, which involves combining one *s* orbital and two *p* orbitals, is known as *sp²* hybridization.

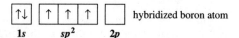

Figure 6.17

As you may have predicted, there is also an *sp* hybridized orbital. An example of this can be seen with beryllium (which can violate the octet rule). The normal beryllium orbital configuration is

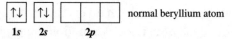

Figure 6.18

After promoting one of the *s* electrons to an unoccupied *p* orbital, the resulting orbitals become *sp* hybrids. This allows beryllium to form two bonds while leaving two unoccupied 2*p* orbitals.

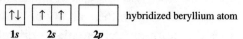

Figure 6.19

As you saw in Chapter 5, some atoms can violate the octet rule by using unoccupied *d* orbitals. This process actually occurs by hybridization—promoting electrons into the unoccupied *d* orbitals. For example, look at the hybridization of orbitals in the phosphorus atom as it is seen in PCl_5:

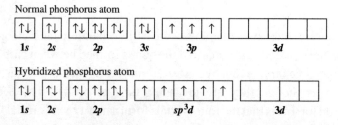

Figure 6.20

This type of hybridization is known as sp^3d (or dsp^3, depending on where you look). The remaining type of hybridization, known as sp^3d^2 (d^2sp^3), can be seen in the hybridization of sulfur in the compound sulfur hexafluoride, SF_6. In the diagram below, note how two electrons are promoted to the d orbitals:

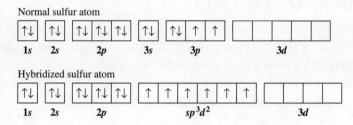

Figure 6.21

Conveniently, the shapes of the hybridized orbitals are identical to the shapes shown in Table 6.1. A quick summary is shown in Table 6.3:

Table 6.3

Hybridization	Number of hybridized orbitals	Geometry
sp	Two	Linear
sp^2	Three	Trigonal planar
sp^3	Four	Tetrahedral
sp^3d	Five	Trigonal bipyramidal
sp^3d^2	Six	Octahedral

Samples: Determine the hybridization of the central atom in the following molecules:

      a) CF_4 b) TeF_4 c) KrF_2

Answers:

a)   **$sp3$** The central carbon atom has two electrons in the $2s$ orbital and two unpaired electrons in the $2p$ orbitals. By promoting an electron from the s orbital to the unoccupied p orbital, carbon can form four sp^3 orbitals.

b)   **$sp3d$** The molecule requires four bonding pairs of electrons and one nonbonding pair. By promoting an electron to the d orbitals, Te will have five hybridized orbitals. In those sp^3d orbitals, one will contain a pair of electrons (the lone pair), while the other four will contain unpaired electrons (which will become bonding pairs with the fluorine atoms).

c)   **$sp3d$** By promoting one electron to a d orbital, krypton will have two unpaired electrons (that can bond to fluorine). The three remaining sp^3d orbitals will be filled by nonbonding pairs of electrons.

You Try It!

Determine the hybridization of the central atom in the following molecules:

a) AsF_5 b) BF_3 c) $SiCl_4$

Answers: a) sp^3d b) sp^2 c) sp^3

SIGMA AND PI BONDS

The bonds that you have seen so far are all known as sigma (σ) bonds. Sigma bonds are almost always single bonds that occur by orbitals that are directly overlapping along an axis. In the figure below, notice the four examples of σ bonds. Sigma bonds can form between neighboring orbitals, whether those are *s* orbitals, *p* orbitals, or hybrid orbitals.

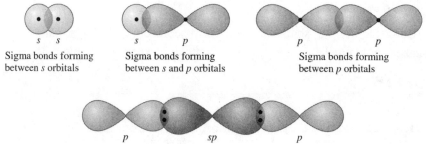

| Sigma bonds forming between *s* orbitals | Sigma bonds forming between *s* and *p* orbitals | Sigma bonds forming between *p* orbitals |

Sigma bonds between *p* orbitals and hybridized *sp* orbitals

Figure 6.22

The other type of bond that can form is a pi (π) bonds. Pi bonds are the type of bonds that make up multiple bonds and are formed when *p* orbitals on neighboring atoms align with one another in a parallel fashion. The electrons in the *p* orbitals distribute themselves above and below the axis (where the σ bond has occurred). Pi bonds are weaker than sigma bonds. Atoms that have only single available *p* orbitals can form a single π bond, where atoms with two available *p* orbitals can form two π bonds. The formation of pi bonds prevents molecules from rotating around the internuclear axis.

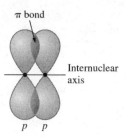

Figure 6.23

In summary, s bonds form single bonds and are much stronger than p bonds. Double bonds contain one σ bond and one π bond. Triple bonds are composed of one σ bond and two π bonds.

Sample: Ethylene gas, used in the ripening of fruits, has the formula CH_2CH_2. How many σ and π bonds are present in the molecule?

Answer: If you construct a Lewis diagram, you can see that the structure of the ethylene molecule contains single bonds between each carbon and two hydrogens and a double bond between the two carbon atoms. Therefore, between each carbon and hydrogen there is one σ bond, for a total of four. Between the carbon atoms, there is one σ bond and one π bond. In all, that makes *5 σ bonds and 1 π bond.*

You Try It!
List the number and types of bonds found in a molecule of hydrogen cyanide, HCN.

Answer: two σ bonds and two π bonds.

Bond Length, Bond Order, and Bond Dissociation Energy

Complete coverage of these topics would get a bit complicated at this point. The AP exam does not cover these at a very great depth, so you will only need a general idea of the topics to be successful. **Bond length** is the measured distance between the nuclei of the atoms involved in the bond. **Bond order** is the number of pairs of electrons in a bond. For example, in a H-H bond, the bond order is 1; in a O=O bond, the bond order is 2; and in a N$\equiv$N bond, the bond order is 3. **Bond dissociation energy** (also known as *bond enthalpy*) is the amount of energy necessary to break a chemical bond (energy is always required to break a chemical bond). The main idea is that the more tightly atoms are bound together, the shorter the bond becomes and the larger the bond dissociation energy becomes. As a general rule, this means that as the number of bonds between two atoms increases (that is, the bond order), the bond lengths get shorter and the bond energies greater.

MOLECULAR ORBITAL THEORY

If you are pressed for time, then skip this topic. It rarely appears on the AP exam, and it is rather complicated. However, because it has appeared on the test and it is mentioned in the required subject matter, it will be discussed in this book.

Molecular orbital theory is an alternative to valence bond theory that more adequately explains a few different phenomena. One of the inadequacies of the theory involves paramagnetic and diamagnetic properties of molecules. Recall from Chapter 3 that paramagnetism (attraction to a magnet) results from an odd number of electrons, while diamagnetism (non-attraction to a magnet) results from an even number of electrons. There are some cases where a few molecules with even numbers of electrons are very strongly attracted to magnets. Oxygen (O_2) is one of the better-known molecules to behave this way. Molecular orbital theory does a much better job explaining this than valence bond theory.

A **molecular orbital** is an allowed energy state where electrons can be found. Molecular orbitals form from overlapping atomic orbitals. When orbitals overlap, there are two possibilities for the region of space between the nuclei. The first is that the electron density is greater in that region than the rest of the orbital. When this condition occurs, the bond is quite stable, which provides a lower energy state than the individual orbitals possessed prior to overlapping. This is known as a **bonding orbital**. When orbitals exist along an axis between the two nuclei, they are known as σ **(sigma) bonding orbitals**. If the orbitals that were overlapping were 1s orbitals, they would be labeled σ_{1s} orbitals.

The second possibility is that the electron density in the overlapping regions between the nuclei is less than elsewhere. This region now has a higher energy than the overlapping orbitals and is known as an **antibonding orbital**. Similar to bonding orbitals, if an antibonding orbital exists on the internuclear axis, it is labeled as σ^{*}_{1s}. (Note: The * indicates antibonding.)

Orbital diagrams can be created for molecular orbitals much as they were created for atomic orbitals. Each molecular orbital possesses a certain amount of energy, and electrons are filled into these orbitals using the same rules as were used for atomic orbitals (aufbau principle, Pauli exclusion principle, and Hund's rule). You won't need to worry about anything past the second energy level, so you can look at a short list to determine the order of filling (from lowest to highest energies). The order of filling is

$$\sigma_{1}s \quad \sigma^{*}_{1}s \quad \sigma_{2}s \quad \quad \sigma^{*}_{2}s \quad \quad \pi_{2}p \quad \quad \sigma_{2}p \quad \quad \pi^{*}_{2}p \quad \quad \quad \sigma^{*}_{2}p$$

First, let's look at the simplest example, an H_2 molecule. In this molecule, two 1s orbitals will overlap. The electrons will fill in the σ1s orbital, as seen in the diagram below:

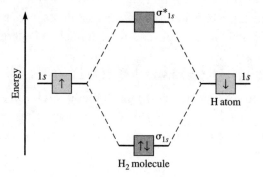

Figure 6.24

Another way to represent this is to use orbital diagrams that look like atomic orbital diagrams. The same H_2 molecule can be shown as follows:

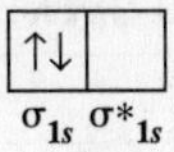

Figure 6.25

Bond Order

Earlier in this chapter, you learned the definition of bond order in the valence bond theory. In molecular orbital theory, the bond order is defined as one-half the difference between the number of electrons in bonding orbitals and the number of electrons in antibonding orbitals. Mathematically, this can be expressed as:

$$\text{bond order} = \tfrac{1}{2}(nb - na)$$

where nb is the number of electrons in bonding orbitals and na is the number of electrons in antibonding orbitals.

For hydrogen, the bond order is $\tfrac{1}{2}(2 - 0) = 1$. This is no different from what would be predicted in valence bond theory.

Electron Configurations for the Period Two Diatomic Molecules

To finish up this section on molecular orbital theory, let's look at the configurations for the elements from lithium to neon. These should provide you with sufficient examples to see the main principles behind molecular orbital theory.

Table 6.4. Molecular orbital configurations and other data about Period 2 elements. It is understood that each molecule has a complete s_{1s} and s^*_{1s} orbital. Note, that oxygen, fluorine, and neon have a slightly different order due to interactions between 2s and 2p orbitals.

Substance	Configuration	Bond order	Bond energy (kJ/mol)	Bond length (Å)	Magnetism
Li_2	σ_{2s} (↑↓), σ^*_{2s} ( ), π_{2p} ( )( ), σ_{2p} ( ), π^*_{2p} ( )( ), σ^*_{2p} ( )	1	110	2.67	Dia-
Be_2	σ_{2s} (↑↓), σ^*_{2s} (↑↓), π_{2p} ( )( ), σ_{2p} ( ), π^*_{2p} ( )( ), σ^*_{2p} ( )	0*	59	*	*
B_2	σ_{2s} (↑↓), σ^*_{2s} (↑↓), π_{2p} (↑)(↑), σ_{2p} ( ), π^*_{2p} ( )( ), σ^*_{2p} ( )	1	297	1.59	Para-
C_2	σ_{2s} (↑↓), σ^*_{2s} (↑↓), π_{2p} (↑↓)(↑↓), σ_{2p} ( ), π^*_{2p} ( )( ), σ^*_{2p} ( )	2	607	1.24	Dia-
N_2	σ_{2s} (↑↓), σ^*_{2s} (↑↓), π_{2p} (↑↓)(↑↓), σ_{2p} (↑↓), π^*_{2p} ( )( ), σ^*_{2p} ( )	3	945	1.10	Dia-
O_2	σ_{2s} (↑↓), σ^*_{2s} (↑↓), σ_{2p} (↑↓), π_{2p} (↑↓)(↑↓), π^*_{2p} (↑)(↑), σ^*_{2p} ( )	2	498	1.21	Para-
F_2	σ_{2s} (↑↓), σ^*_{2s} (↑↓), σ_{2p} (↑↓), π_{2p} (↑↓)(↑↓), π^*_{2p} (↑↓)(↑↓), σ^*_{2p} ( )	1	159	1.42	Dia-
Ne_2	σ_{2s} (↑↓), σ^*_{2s} (↑↓), σ_{2p} (↑↓), π_{2p} (↑↓)(↑↓), π^*_{2p} (↑↓)(↑↓), σ^*_{2p} (↑↓)	0*	4	*	*

*will not maintain diatomic structure

Summary:
Molecular Geometry

- VSEPR theory is the primary theory used to explain the structure of most molecules. The underlying assumption is that molecules form with geometries that try to minimize electron-electron repulsions.

- There are six main structures on which almost all molecules are based. These are the five geometries associated with electron pair arrangements, which are linear, trigonal planar, tetrahedral, trigonal bipyramidal, and octahedral.

- In molecules, both nonbonding pairs and double bonds compress bond angles.

- You should become familiar with the material in Table 6.2. During the test, you will need to be able to recognize the shapes of many molecules in a very short period of time.

- A dipole moment is a measure of the polarity of a molecule. Individual bond polarities are determined, and then the vectors are used to determine the net force.

- Valence bond theory predicts the hybridization or orbitals, which occurs when an atom promotes an electron from a lower to a higher energy level in order to form more bonding pairs. You should be familiar with the five types of hybridizations (sp, sp^2, sp^3, dsp^3, d^2sp^3).

- When orbitals overlap, bonds form. When the overlap is along the internuclear axis, this is known as a σ (sigma) bond. Sigma bonds can form between s, p, or hybridized orbitals. When the overlap is between parallel orbitals that lie perpendicular to the nuclear axis, this is known as a π (pi) bond.

- Sigma bonds are associated with single bonds, and pi bonds are associated with double and triple bonds.

- As the number of bonds between two atoms (bond order) increases, bond lengths get shorter and bond energies get greater.

- Molecular orbital theory is an alternative approach to bonding than valence bond theory. According to this theory, molecular orbitals form when orbitals overlap. This overlap gives rise to bonding orbitals and antibonding orbitals.

- Molecular orbitals fill in a prescribed sequence, although the sequence can vary based on the degree of interaction between s and p molecular orbitals (but you don't actually need to know any details about this).

REVIEW QUESTIONS

1. Types of hybridization exhibited by the C atoms in acetylene, C_2H_2, include which of the following?

   I. sp

   II. sp^2

   III. sp^3

   (A) I only

   (B) III only

   (C) I and II only

   (D) II and III only

   (E) I, II, and III

2. Which of the following diatomic molecules has the largest bond-dissociation energy?

   (A) Li_2

   (B) Be_2

   (C) B_2

   (D) N_2

   (E) O_2

3. Which of the follow diatomic molecules has the shortest bond length?

   (A) Li_2

   (B) Be_2

   (C) B_2

   (D) N_2

   (E) O_2

4. Which of the following diatomic elements contains only 1 sigma (σ) and 1 pi (π) bond?

   (A) Li_2

   (B) Be_2

   (C) B_2

   (D) N_2

   (E) O_2

5. In a molecule in which the central atom exhibits sp^3d hybrid orbitals, the electron pair arrangements form the shape of

   (A) a tetrahedron.

   (B) a square-based pyramid.

   (C) a trigonal bipyramid.

   (D) a square.

   (E) an octahedron.

6. Molecules that have planar configurations include which of the following?

    I. BF_3
    II. XeF_4
    III. NH_3

    (A) I only

    (B) III only

    (C) I and II only

    (D) II and III only

    (E) I, II, and III

7. The electron-dot structure (Lewis structure) for which of the following molecules would have one unshared pairs of electrons on the central atom?

    (A) H_2O

    (B) NH_3

    (C) CH_4

    (D) C_2H_2

    (E) CO_2

8. Which of the following molecules has a trigonal pyramidal shape?

    (A) PCl_5

    (B) N_2O

    (C) NH_3

    (D) CCl_4

    (E) H_2O_2

9. The AsF_5 molecule has a trigonal bipyramidal structure. Therefore, the hybridization of As orbitals should be

    (A) sp^2

    (B) sp^3

    (C) sp^2d

    (D) sp^3d

    (E) sp^3d^2

$$CCl_4, BeF_2, PCl_3, SbCl_5, XeF_4$$

10. Which of the following does not describe any of the molecules above?

    (A) Linear

    (B) Octahedral

    (C) Square planar

    (D) Tetrahedral

    (E) Trigonal pyramidal

11. The geometry of the H_2S molecule is best described as

    (A) trigonal planar.

    (B) trigonal pyramidal.

    (C) square pyramidal.

    (D) bent.

    (E) tetrahedral.

12. All of the molecules below display sp^3d hybridization EXCEPT

    (A) NF_3

    (B) PF_5

    (C) SF_4

    (D) BrF_3

    (E) $XeOF_2$

13. Pi bonding occurs in each of the following species EXCEPT

    (A) N_2F_2

    (B) C_2H_2

    (C) HCN

    (D) C_6H_6

    (E) CCl_4

14. Antibonding orbitals are found

    (A) between the nuclei of atoms.

    (B) surrounding the nuclei of atoms.

    (C) nowhere; they only exist theoretically.

    (D) on the outsides of atoms (the sides opposite the overlapping regions).

    (E) above the bonding orbitals.

15. Which of the following has a dipole moment of zero?

    (A) CCl_4

    (B) HCN

    (C) NO_2

    (D) NH_3

    (E) H_2O

Free Response

1. Use simple structure and bonding models to account for each of the following.

    (A) The bond length between the two carbon atoms is shorter in C_2H_2 than in C_2H_4.

    (B) The H-O-H bond angle is 104.5°, as opposed to the expected 109 °.

    (C) The bond lengths in the nitrate ion, NO_3^-, are all identical and shorter than a nitrogen-oxygen single bond.

    (D) The ethylene molecule, C_2H_4, does not rotate around the C-C axis.

2. Discuss briefly the relationship between the dipole moment of a molecule and the polar character of the bonds within it. With this as the basis, account for the difference between the dipole moments of CH_2Cl_2 and CCl_4

ANSWERS

1. **The correct answer is (A).** Only two hybridized orbitals are formed—one for the C-H bond and the other for the C-C bond. The remaining half-filled p orbitals are used to make the two π bonds, which complete the triple bond.

2. **The correct answer is (D).** Nitrogen has a triple bond and a bond order of 2. This makes it the strongest bond, requiring it to have the largest bond-dissociation energy.

3. **The correct answer is (D).** The triple bond in nitrogen is the strongest and will cause the nitrogen atoms to be the closest together.

4. **The correct answer is (E).** One σ bond and one π bond are characteristic of a double bond. The only double-bonded diatomic element listed as a choice is oxygen.

5. **The correct answer is (C).**

6. **The correct answer is (C).** BF_3 has a trigonal planar configuration, and XeF_4 has a square planar configuration. NH_3 has a trigonal pyramidal configuration.

7. **The correct answer is (B).** H_2O has two pairs, and all others have no unshared pairs.

8. **The correct answer is (C).**

9. **The correct answer is (D).** Make sure you read all choices carefully; choice (C) is a very close distracter, but it represents a nonexistent hybridization.

10. **The correct answer is (B).** Be careful on questions like this. $SbCl_5$ represents a trigonal bipyramidal structure, but this has been thrown in as a distracter. Of the five answer choices, four are represented, meaning the fifth choice, octahedral, must be the correct one.

11. **The correct answer is (D).** This is a characteristic structure for four electron pairs with two nonbonding pairs.

12. **The correct answer is (A).** Perhaps the biggest timesaving clue is that nitrogen is only a period 2 element. Since period 2 does not have d orbitals, it is not possible for nitrogen to promote an electron to a d orbital to form a bond. The long route to solving this problem would be to determine the hybridization of each separately.

13. **The correct answer is (E).** All the other choices have multiple bonds.

14. **The correct answer is (D).** Bonding orbitals exist in the overlapping region (where electron density is greatest). Antibonding orbitals exist opposite this region, or on the outsides of the atoms.

15. **The correct answer is (A).** All the other choices either contain bond angles that won't allow for cancellation of bond dipoles or different atoms (i.e., atoms with different electronegativities).

Free Response

1. (A) C_2H_2 has a triple bond between the two carbons, while C_2H_4 has double bonds. This allows for increased overlap and the formation of an additional pi bond. This has the effect of shortening the bond length.

    (B)   The two nonbonding pairs of electrons on the central oxygen atom exert a stronger repulsive force than the bonding pairs between oxygen and hydrogen. This has the effect of pushing the hydrogen atoms closer together, decreasing the H-O-H bond angle.

    (C)   A question that is worded this way should be a red flag that the test-makers may be asking about resonance structures, which, in fact, is happening here. There are three possible resonance structures. If the electron were localized to any one nitrogen and oxygen, the bond length of that bond would be shorter than the other two, and the other two would have bond lengths the same as a N-O single bond. Delocalization of the electron allows for the three resonance structures and also creates three equal bonds, each of which is less than a single bond but greater than a double bond.

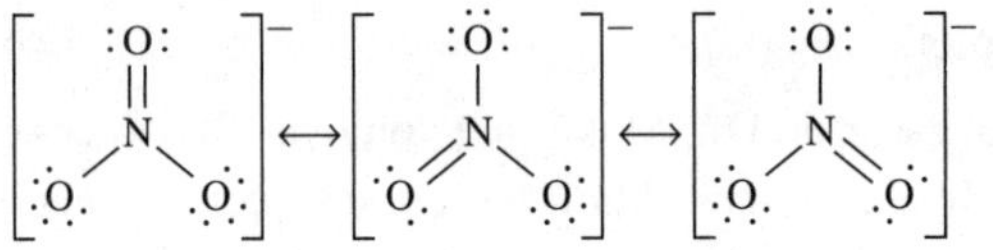

Figure 6.26

    (D)   The ethylene molecule, C_2H_4, is not able to rotate around the C-C axis because of the presence of the pi bond that forms from the overlap of the $2p$ orbitals of each carbon. The pi bonds prevent rotation and locks the molecule into its planar structure.

2. This question really has at least two distinct parts, the first about dipole moments, and the second to address the examples.

    The dipole moment of a molecule represents the combined effects of the individual vectors for each polar bond. A molecule can have very polar bonds, yet no dipole moment, if the configuration of the molecule is such that the vectors all cancel. It is the resultant of the individual vectors that determines the moment.

    In the CCl_4 molecule, the individual bond polarities are relatively large since there is a large difference in electronegativity between carbon and chlorine. However, the tetrahedral configuration of the molecule causes the individual polarities to cancel each other out. This is not the case in the CH_2Cl_2 molecule. This molecule also has a tetrahedral geometry, but the forces do not cancel out this molecule. The interactions between the carbon and hydrogen atoms are insufficient to cancel the dipoles between carbon and chlorine. As a result, there is a dipole moment for that molecule.

Chapter

States of Matters—Gases

This chapter is the first of two devoted to specific states of matter, and in it you will focus your attention on the gaseous state of matter. However, all of the states will be described within a larger framework that looks at the state of matter as a series of interrelated factors, including kinetic energy (or temperature), pressure, and intermolecular forces. Gases are usually described by a series of postulates known as kinetic molecular theory, which constitute the ideal gas law. To begin the chapter, you will look at a historical development of the ideal gas law, during which you will review some of the equations used to create the ideal gas law.

UNITS OF MEASURE

The three units described in the gas laws are temperature, volume, and pressure.

Temperature

Temperature is defined as the average kinetic energy of moving particles. In a hot object, the particles in the object are moving more (and hence possess more energy) than your hand. There will be a net flow of energy into your hand, and your hand will have the sensation of hotness. The opposite is true of cold objects. Energy flows from your hand into the object causing a cooling sensation in your hand.

In most instances, temperature is measured in the unit of °C (degrees Celsius), but for the description of any gas, it is imperative to use the Kelvin scale. The Kelvin temperature, also referred to as the absolute temperature, bears a direct relationship to kinetic energy. For example, 0 K (Note: It is not appropriate to use the ° symbol), known as **absolute zero,** represents zero kinetic energy. A doubling of Kelvin temperature represents a doubling of kinetic energy (e.g., 50 K to 100 K is twice the kinetic energy). This is not true for Celsius temperatures (50 °C to 100 °C is not a doubling of kinetic energy). Absolute zero, 0 K, is –273.15 °C, so the conversion from a Celsius temperature to a Kelvin temperature is:

(Equation 7.1)   Kelvin = Celsius + 273.15

(it is sufficient to use 273 in the problems you will have)

ROAD MAP

- *Units of Measure*
- *The Gas Laws*
- *The Ideal Gas Law*
- *Gas Density*
- *Dalton's Law of Partial Pressures*
- *Kinetic-Molecular Theory*
- *Graham's Law of Effusion*
- *Deviations from the Ideal Gas Laws*

Volume

Volume does not need such a lengthy discussion. The volume of a substance is simply the amount of space that it occupies. There are numerous units of measure that can describe volume, including cubic centimeters (cm^3), cubic meters (m^3), milliliters (mL), and liters (L). One cm^3 is equal to 1 mL. Ideal gas problems need to be solved in liters, since the ideal gas constant R uses liters as a unit (more on this later).

Pressure

Pressure is defined as the force per unit of area, that is

(Equation 7.2)

$$P = \frac{F}{A}$$

NOTE

This equation is provided for you in the AP formulas. Although the gas law questions on the AP exam usually provide the temperature in kelvins, you should be on the lookout for degrees Celsius.

For gases, this force can be a factor of their motion or their weight. Atmospheric pressure is caused by the weight of air particles that are attracted toward earth. Inside a sealed container, pressure is exerted by the collisions of particles on the sides of the container. By determining the force of those collisions on a given area, you can determine the pressure exerted by the particles. There are many units that describe pressure. The SI unit of pressure is the pascal, Pa. The kilopascal is a bit more practical as a unit, however, since a pascal is quite small. Other units of pressure include millimeters of Hg (mm Hg), torr, bar, and atmospheres. The relationship between the units is as follows:

1 atm = 760 mm Hg = 760 torr = 1.01 bar = 101.325 kPa

You might have noticed that torr and mm Hg have the same value. On the AP exam, units of pressure are usually atm in the ideal gas problems (R uses atm as the pressure unit) and mm Hg in partial pressure problems.

THE GAS LAWS

Many of the gas law problems on the AP exam are conceptual questions rather than calculations. Make sure you understand each of these topics at a conceptual level as well as at a mathematical level.

Boyle's Law

One of the earliest discoveries of the behavior of gases came from Robert Boyle in 1661. Boyle discovered that the volume of a gas is inversely proportional to the pressure placed on it. That is, in a system where volume is allowed to change, an increase in pressure will decrease the volume. Likewise, if you think of a closed system, such as a cylinder with a piston above it, pushing down on the piston (i.e., decreasing the volume) will have the effect of increasing the pressure. This relationship can be expressed mathematically as:

(Equation 7.3)

$$PV = \text{constant}$$

This condition, however, requires that temperature and the number of gas particles remain constant. A change in either of those will also change the pressure and volume. From a conceptual perspective, consider the piston as shown in Figure 7.1 again. If you think about a fixed number of particles inside the chamber, these particles are moving about, colliding with the sides of the container. As they do so, they exert a force. This force, as measured per unit of area that the particles are striking, represents the pressure exerted by the gas inside the piston. As the plunger is pushed down, note how the density of the particles increases. This means that the particles, still traveling the same speed, will not have to travel as far to collide with the sides of the container. As a result, the number of collisions they have will increase. This increase in collisions will cause an increase in pressure that is proportional to the change in volume.

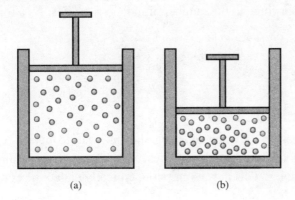

(a)   (b)

Figure 7.1

Charles's Law

The next discoveries about gases came from Jacques Charles, who in 1787 discovered what is today known as Charles's Law. This law states that for a fixed amount of gas at constant pressure, the relationship between volume and temperature is directly proportional. Written as a formula, Charles's law takes the form

$$\frac{V}{T} = \text{constant}$$

(Equation 7.4)

You probably have some familiarity with this law. Perhaps you have observed a balloon expanding on a hot day or a bag of microwave popcorn swelling as the contents begin to heat up.

Pressure and temperature relationships

You may have noticed that volume appears in both Boyle's and Charles's laws. If we make the assumption that pressure and volume are inversely related and volume and temperature are directly related, then we can say that pressure and temperature are inversely related, or

$$\frac{P}{T} = \text{constant}$$

(Equation 7.5)

TIP
Remember, Kelvin temperatures must be used for this to be accurate.

This relationship is frequently referred to as **Gay-Lussac's Law,** named after Joseph Louis Gay-Lussac, one of the early gas researchers. Gay-Lussac also performed some experiments that helped Amadeo Avogadro create what is now referred to as Avogadro's Law.

Avogadro's Law

In 1811, Avogadro formulated what is now known as **Avogadro's hypothesis,** which states that equal volumes of gases at the same temperature and pressure will contain equal numbers of molecules. It has been experimentally determined that 22.4 liters of any gas at 0 °C and 1 atm (standard temperature and pressure, STP) contain 1 mole of molecules (6.02×10^{23}). This hypothesis allows for the statement of **Avogadro's Law,** which says that the volume of a gas, kept at constant pressure and temperature, is directly proportional to the number of moles of the gas. As a formula, this reads

(Equation 7.6)
$$\frac{V}{n} = \text{constant}$$

Combined Gas Law

All four of these laws, when taken together, allow us to make a new formula that contains all four variables—pressure, volume, temperature, and the number of moles. This new expression, typically called the combined gas law, reads as follows:

(Equation 7.7)
$$\frac{PV}{nT} = \text{constant}$$

Since the outcome of the equation remains constant, you can use this equation to determine the behavior of a gas as conditions change (i.e., changing temperature, pressure, volume, or quantity of gas). To use the equation this way, it is helpful to rewrite it as

(Equation 7.8)
$$\frac{P_1 V_1}{n_1 T_1} = \frac{P_2 V_2}{n_2 T_2}$$

where the subscript 1 indicates the initial state of the gas and 2 represents the final state. This equation can be used to solve any problem where a change in conditions is indicated, regardless of how much information is given. For example, if only pressure and volume were given in the problem, the number of moles and temperature would simply be omitted. If only volume and temperature were given, then pressure and number of moles would be omitted. This equation (without the n) is provided in the AP formulas.

Sample: If 1.50 moles of a gas at 300 K and under a pressure of 1.5 atm occupy 0.5 liters, at what temperature will 3.00 moles of the same gas occupy 1.5 liters and exert a pressure of 3.0 atm?

Answer: To begin, you must set up the equation 9.8:

$$\frac{P_1 V_1}{n_1 T_1} = \frac{P_2 V_2}{n_2 T_2}$$

Problems like this have a lot of given information, and it is important you distinguish the initial conditions from the final conditions prior to substitution. While you're practicing, it is helpful to make a little chart or to write your given information in some organized fashion, but on the AP exam you usually won't have time to do this step on paper. Having practiced the technique should make you more careful about your work.

Given:

$P_1 =$	1.5 atm	$P_2 =$	3.0 atm
$V_1 =$	0.5 liters	$V_2 =$	1.5 liters
$n_1 =$	1.50 moles	$n_2 =$	3.00 moles
$T_1 =$	300 K	$T_2 =$	?

Rearranging the equation to solve for T_2, produces the expression:

$$T_2 = \frac{P_2 V_2 n_1 T_1}{n_2 P_1 V_1}$$

Substituting the given information into the equation produces

$$\frac{(3.0\ \text{atm})(1.5\ \text{liters})(1.50\ \text{mol})(300\ \text{K})}{(3.00\ \text{moles})(1.5\ \text{atm})(0.5\ \text{liters})} = 900\ \text{K}$$

If you have difficulty rearranging equations with this many variables, another technique is to substitute numbers directly in the equation and attempt to make the equation more manageable before rearranging. Solving the same equation, you can observe this technique:

$$\frac{P_1 V_1}{n_1 T_1} = \frac{P_2 V_2}{n_2 T_2}$$

$$\frac{(1.5\ \text{atm})(0.5\ \text{liters})}{(1.50\ \text{mol})(300\ \text{K})} = \frac{(3.0\ \text{atm})(1.5\ \text{liters})}{(3.00\ \text{moles})T_2}$$

This can be further simplified to

$$1.667 \times 10^{-3} = \frac{4.5}{(3.00)T_2}$$

The equation is much easier to rearrange now, giving

$$T_2 = \frac{4.5}{(3.00)(1.67 \times 10^{-3})} = 900 \text{ K}$$

You Try It!

$$3H_2 + N_2 \rightarrow 2NH_3$$

The Haber process is a method of producing ammonia from its elements hydrogen and nitrogen and takes place according to the reaction shown above. It is performed at high temperature and pressure. If 500 liters of ammonia are produced at 200 atmospheres and 800 K, what volume would the sample be at if the temperature was lowered to 300 K and the pressure decreased to 100 atm?

Answer: 375 liters

THE IDEAL GAS LAW

The ideal gas equation is not much of a stretch from what you have already seen with the combined gas law. If you recall, when the combined gas law was first presented, it was written in the form

$$\frac{PV}{nT} = \text{constant}$$

This constant can be replaced by a value, known as the ideal gas constant, R, to yield the equation

$$\frac{PV}{nT} = R$$

where the value of R is 0.0821 L-atm mol^{-1} K^{-1}. R can also have a value of 8.31 joules/mole Kelvin or 8.31 volt coulomb / mole K, but these latter forms of the gas equation are not used in solving gas law problems.

This equation can be rearranged to look more like the equation as you have learned it

(Equation 7.9)
$$PV = nRT$$

With this equation, it is possible to determine any property of a gas, if provided with the other three properties. An important thing to remember is the units of the ideal gas constant. Because R has units of L atm mol^{-1} K^{-1}, it is important that you have volumes in liters, pressure in atmospheres, and temperatures in kelvins. The problems generally are set up that way, but you should still be alert.

Sample: Determine the volume of 4.50 moles of an unknown gas that exerts 7.50 atm pressure at 350 K.

Answer: The given information is as follows:

$P = 7.50$ atm $T = 350$ K $n = 4.50$ mol $V = ?$

Rearrange the ideal gas equation to solve for V and substitute the given information:

$$V = \frac{nRT}{P} = \frac{(4.50 \text{ mol})(0.0821 \text{ L} \cdot \text{atm mol}^{-1} \cdot \text{K}^{-1})(350 \text{ K})}{7.50 \text{ atm}} = 17.2 \text{ L}$$

You Try It!

A gas is placed in a container at 5.00 atm and 300 K. If the volume of the container is 2.00 L, how many moles of gas must there be?

Answer: 0.406 mol

GAS DENSITY

The density of a gas can be measured in the same way as the density of a solid or liquid—by dividing its mass by its volume. Because the particles in a gas are very spread out, gas densities are very small numbers and are usually described in units of grams per liter as opposed to grams/mL or grams/cm^3 (as would be the case for solids or liquids). The AP exam occasionally has gas density questions on it, so you should be familiar with the method for solving them. The equation for calculating gas density can be derived from the ideal gas equation.

To begin, look at the ideal gas equation in its usual form

$$PV = nRT$$

By rearranging it, you will notice that the units on the left side of the equation now are moles per liter (which is getting close to grams per liter)

$$\frac{n}{V} = \frac{P}{RT}$$

You may also remember the expression below (if you don't, we'll review it in chapter 13)

$$n = \frac{m}{M} \quad \text{(this equation is provided for you on the AP exam)}$$

Substituting this value for n, you obtain

$$\frac{m}{VM} = \frac{P}{RT}$$

If you look carefully at this equation, you will note that the left side of the equation now contains mass divided by volume, which is equal to the density of a material. If we move the molar mass (M) to the right side of the equation, we get

$$\frac{m}{V} = \frac{PM}{RT}$$

Since $d = \frac{m}{V}$, we can substitute d into the equation, yielding

$$d = \frac{PM}{RT}$$

(Equation 7.10)

One of the laboratory procedures that you are expected to know involves the determination of molar mass from gas density. In the sample calculation that follows, you will solve for the density of a gas, but understand that a simple rearrangement of the equation allows you to solve for the molar mass.

Sample: A sample of oxygen gas, O_2, is in a container, inside which the pressure is 0.75 atm and the temperature is 323 K. Determine the density of this sample of O_2 in grams per liter.

Answer: The given information is listed as

$P = 0.75$ atm $T = 323$ K $M = 32.0$ g mol^{-1}

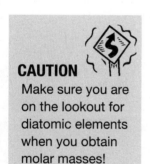

CAUTION
Make sure you are on the lookout for diatomic elements when you obtain molar masses!

Note that the molar mass was not given, but since it is needed, we can find it from the periodic table. If you have forgotten how to do this, see Chapter 13. Substituting our given information into the equation, we can solve for d:

$$d = \frac{PM}{RT} = \frac{(0.75 \text{ atm})(32 \text{ g mol}^{-1})}{(0.0821 \text{ L atm mol}^{-1} \text{ K}^{-1})(323 \text{ K})} = \mathbf{0.91 \text{ g L–1}}$$

You Try It!
A sample of butane gas, C_4H_{10}, was collected from a disposable lighter. What is the density of butane at 1.00 atm and 300 K?
Answer: 2.36 g L^{-1}

DALTON'S LAW OF PARTIAL PRESSURES

So far, we've limited our discussion to samples containing a single gas. Quite often, however, you are confronted with mixtures of gases (e.g., air). In 1801, John Dalton determined a relationship between gases in a mixture that is now referred to as Dalton's law of partial pressures. What he discovered is that the total pressure of a mixture of gases is equal to the sum of the pressures that each gas would exert if it were present alone. Expressed mathematically, this means that

(Equation 7.11) $P_t = P_A + P_B + P_C$ ... (This equation is given to you on the AP exam)

Where P_t is the total pressure, P_A is the pressure of gas A, and so on.

While it may be obvious to you, it is worth stating that the total number of moles of gas in the sample is also equal to the sum of the number of moles of each gas in the sample

$$n_t = n_A + n_B + n_C...$$

From this expression, it is possible to determine what percentage of a mixture is accounted for by a given substance. This is done by determining a quantity known as the mole fraction, which is defined as X_A (where A is a variable that represents a gas in the mixture):

$$X_A = \frac{n_A}{n_t}$$ (Equation 7.12)

This equation is useful because it allows us to determine the partial pressure of a gas if we know the total pressure and the amount present. The partial pressure of the gas will be proportional to the mole fraction of the gas in the mixture. This can be expressed as an equation

$P_A = P_t \cdot X_A$ (This equation is give to you on the AP exam) (Equation 7.13)

Finally, there is one more aspect of partial pressures that must be included. Most of the partial pressure problems that appear on the AP exam involve gases that have been collected over a liquid. (In other words, they have been collected by displacement of the liquid, usually water.) The significance of this is that in the container, along with the collected gas, is vapor from the liquid, so the pressure in the collection vessel is the sum of the pressure of the gas and the vapor. Since we know that the total pressure in the container is equal to the sums of the individual pressures, it is possible to determine the pressure of the gas using the expression

$$P_{gas} = P_t - P_{H_2O}$$ (Equation 7.14)

This equation can be used whether the gas is collected over water or some other liquid. If it is another liquid, substitute the vapor pressure of that liquid for the vapor pressure of water.

Sample: Oxygen gas is collected over water at 28 °C. The total pressure of the sample is 785 mm Hg. At 28 °C, the vapor pressure of water is 28 mm Hg. What pressure is the oxygen gas exerting?

Answer: Using equation 7.14, simply substitute the given values into the equation:

$$P_{gas} = P_t - P_{H_2O} = 785 \text{ mm Hg} - 28 \text{ mm Hg} = \textbf{757 mm Hg}$$

This problem is fairly representative of the partial pressure problems on the multiple-choice portion of the exam. On the free response, the questions are more complex.

You Try It!

Hydrogen gas, liberated from a reaction between hydrochloric acid and zinc, is bubbled through water and collected in an inverted graduated cylinder at 22 °C. The pressure of the gas mixture is 765 mm Hg. The vapor pressure of water at 22 °C is 20 mm Hg. What is the partial pressure of the hydrogen gas?

Answer: 743 mm Hg

Sample: A mixture of gases contains 1.5 moles of oxygen, 7.5 moles of nitrogen, and 0.5 moles of carbon dioxide. If the total pressure exerted by the mixture is 800 mm Hg, what are the partial pressures of each gas in the mixture?

Answer: To solve this problem, we need to use equations 9.12 and 9.13. The percentage of the total pressure exerted by each gas will be proportional to its percentage of the number of moles.

To begin, we can calculate the total number of moles (which is needed in equation 7.12). The total number is $= (1.5 \text{ mol } O_2) + (7.5 \text{ mol } N_2) + (0.5 \text{ mol } CO_2) = 9.5$ moles

This will be used to determine the mole fractions.

For oxygen, the calculation is completed by:

$$P_{O2} = P_t \bullet X_{O2} = 800 \text{ mm Hg} \left(\frac{1.5 \text{ mol}}{9.5 \text{ mol}} \right) = \textbf{126 mm Hg}$$

Repeating this process for nitrogen and carbon dioxide we find:

$$P_{N2} = P_t \bullet X_{N2} = 800 \text{ mm Hg} \left(\frac{7.5 \text{ mol}}{9.5 \text{ mol}} \right) = \textbf{632 mm Hg}$$

$$P_{CO2} = P_t \bullet X_{CO2} = 800 \text{ mm Hg} \left(\frac{0.5 \text{ mol}}{9.5 \text{ mol}} \right) = \textbf{42 mm Hg}$$

As a quick check, you can add the three partial pressures together—they should equal the total pressure:

126 mm Hg + 632 mm Hg + 42 mm Hg = 800 mm Hg.

You Try It!

A mixture of gases contains 1.00 moles H_2, 4.00 moles of O_2, and 1.50 moles N_2. If the total pressure of the mixture is 760 mm Hg, what is the partial pressure of the oxygen gas?

Answer: 468 mm Hg

KINETIC-MOLECULAR THEORY

The kinetic-molecular theory consists of five postulates about gases. These postulates are assumptions from which gas behavior is explained. Everything discussed so far in this chapter is consistent with kinetic-molecular theory. The five postulates of the theory are

1. The size of a gas molecule is negligible in comparison to the distance between gas molecules. That is, in a sample of a gas, most of the sample consists of empty space. Gas particles are very small and very far apart.

2. Gas molecules move randomly in straight-line paths in all directions and at different speeds. This means that in a sample of gas, there is an equal probability of finding gas particles with similar properties anywhere in the sample. You won't have a closed flask where all of the gas particles are on one side of the flask.

3. The attractive or repulsive forces between gas particles are considered very weak or negligible. This can be explained because the particles are moving quickly and are far apart.

4. When gas particles do collide, the collisions are elastic. An elastic collision is one in which the particles bounce off each other in such a way that the energy each particle leaves a collision with is exactly the same as the energy it had just before it collided. No kinetic energy is lost.

5. The average kinetic energy of a molecule is proportional to the absolute temperature.

In your AP Chemistry class you may have discussed the derivations for the equations that follow. The AP exam does not have any questions that require depth of understanding of the physics of particle movement. You are required to be familiar with and comfortable using a few equations, and we will discuss their use. Their origins are a combination of experimental data and some basic physics involving the properties of gas particles, such as force, velocity, and acceleration.

Kinetic Energy of a Gas Sample

Postulate 5 states that the average kinetic energy of a molecule is proportional to the absolute temperature. This also means that the kinetic energy of a sample of molecules will be proportional to the absolute temperature. The equation that describes this behavior is

$$KE_{avg} = \frac{3}{2}RT$$

(Equation 7.15)

This equation requires the use of one of the other values for R. Kinetic energy is measured in joules, so the expression on the right side of the equation must yield joules. The value of R, referred to as the molar gas constant in this expression, should be 8.31 J mol^{-1} K^{-1}. Thus, the expression will yield the joules per mole of a sample. If the average kinetic energy of an entire sample of gas is required, then the number of moles of gas must be entered into the equation. This equation, which is provided on the AP exam formula sheet, is

(Equation 7.16)
$$KE_{avg} = \frac{3}{2}nRT$$

Note how the units on the right will now equal joules. Also note how the average kinetic energy will be directly proportional to the absolute temperature.

Behavior of Single Molecules

Single gas molecules move randomly in straight-line paths. Each time they collide, either with another gas molecule or with the sides of a container, they will bounce off with no loss in kinetic energy (i.e., undergo an elastic collision). The kinetic energy of a particle can be determined using the following expression:

(Equation 7.17)
$$KE = \frac{1}{2}mv^2$$

where v is the velocity of the molecule. Velocity is a vector that represents distance traveled per time interval. The reason it is a vector is that the distance actually represents a change in the molecule's position through three-dimensional space, thereby giving it a distance and a direction. For your purposes, you needn't worry about this distinction. If you think of velocity as being equivalent to speed (speed is a scalar quantity—that is, it doesn't include the direction of motion), you'll be fine.

If you recall postulate 5 of the kinetic-molecular theory, the average kinetic energy of a molecule is proportional to the absolute temperature. Nothing is said about the mass or velocity, which are the terms in equation 7.17. What this means is that all gas particles present in a sample possess the same average kinetic energy, regardless of their size. This also means that in order for equation 7.17 to be valid, molecules of larger mass must be moving more slowly than small molecules.

Root Mean Square Velocity

An important consideration about energy and speed within a sample of a gas is that the particles within the sample do not all have the same energy or the same speeds. Instead, they possess a variety of speeds and energies. However, it has been observed that most of the particles in a sample tend to have speeds and energies near the average speeds and energies. There are increasingly fewer particles found farther away (either higher or lower) from the averages. The speed of an individual particle, possessing an average kinetic energy, is described as the root-mean-square (rms) molecular speed and can be described by the equation

(Equation 7.18)
$$u_{rms} = \sqrt{\frac{3RT}{M}}$$

Some important conceptual information you should know from this equation is that the speed of a molecule is directly related to the absolute temperature and inversely related to the molar mass. More massive particles are, on average, slower.

Sample: Calculate the rms speed of nitrogen gas (N_2) particles in a tank that has a temperature of 27 °C.

Answer: The first important thing to note is that the temperature is given in degrees Celsius and must be converted to Kelvin. The second important consideration is the units of the molar gas constant, R. The Joule is a unit of energy that represents a Newton meter (N-m) in physics. The Newton is a unit of force equivalent to the amount of force required to accelerate a 1 kg mass at 1 m/s^2. Why does this matter, you might ask? Because it means that a Joule can be described as a Newton meter, which is 1 kg m^2/s^2. Can you see the problem yet? The mass unit associated with Joules is the kilogram. Molar mass is usually expressed in grams/mole. To use the rms equation, you have to convert your mass units to kg.

Once you have converted the temperature to kelvins, you need only substitute the numbers into equation 9.18

$$u_{rms} = \sqrt{\frac{3RT}{M}} = \sqrt{\frac{3(8.31 \text{ J mol}^{-1} \text{ K}^{-1})(300 \text{ K})}{28.0 \times 10^{-3} \text{ kg mol}^{-1}}} = 517 \text{ m s}^{-1}$$

You Try It!
A sample of carbon dioxide was in a container, held at a constant 57 °C. What is the rms speed of the CO_2?

Answer: 432 m s^{-1}

GRAHAM'S LAW OF EFFUSION

It is important that you understand the difference between diffusion and effusion, although the terms are similar. Diffusion is the movement of particles from an area of high concentration (high partial pressure) to an area of low concentration (low partial pressure). A good example of diffusion would be when a student walks into a classroom wearing way too much fragrance—pretty soon, everyone becomes aware of it. The high concentration of particles on the person moves throughout the room to areas of lower concentration until the concentration becomes uniform (hopefully, by this time your nose will have become desensitized to the odor).

After reading the previous section, you may wonder why it takes so long for particles to spread around a room. After all, you just solved problems where speeds average around 400 to 500 meters per second. Molecules should be able to move across a room in a fraction of a second at that rate. They would—if there were no other molecules in the room. Because there are other particles, each molecule will encounter a number of collisions along the way. This continually changes the direction of molecules, which affects the time it takes for them to reach you.

CAUTION
While the AP exam tends to convert temperatures to kelvins for gas law problems, they will often leave them in Celsius, on kinetic-molecular theory questions. Be on the lookout for that. Any problems involving temperature of gases require absolute termperature, regardless of what you are given!

If a gas was placed in a container that had a tiny hole in it, and this container was placed into a second evacuated container, the gas would leak out of the hole and into the second container. This process, where a gas escapes through a tiny hole, is known as effusion. If you have ever woken up and been terribly disappointed by a helium balloon (the latex ones especially) lying on the floor instead of floating nicely as it had the day before, you have seen the results of effusion. The helium atoms effused through the tiny pores in the latex. Mylar balloons don't have as many pores, which slows the effusion. Graham's law of effusion states that when a gas, maintained at a constant temperature and pressure, leaks through a particular hole, the rate of effusion is inversely proportional to the square root of the molecular weight of the gas. The mathematical expression of Graham's law is derived from equation 7.18 and has the form

$$\text{Rate of effusion} \propto \frac{1}{\sqrt{M}}$$

This expression is rarely used in this form, but instead has been transformed into an expression that allows you to compare the rates of effusion of two gases. This equation, which is provided for you on the AP formula sheet, is

(Equation 7.19)

$$\frac{r_1}{r_2} = \sqrt{\frac{M_2}{M_1}}$$

From a conceptual standpoint, the equation tells you that larger molecules will effuse more slowly than smaller particles. Mathematically, the equation provides a number that tells you the ratio and the effusion rates of gases 1 and 2. If the ratio is greater than 1.00, gas 1 is effusing more quickly than gas 2. If the ratio is less than 1.00, gas 2 is effusing more quickly than gas 1.

Because both conceptual and numerical problems have appeared on the AP exam, let's do a sample problem of each type.

NOTE

Typically, the lighter gas is assigned as gas 1. This assures that your ratio will be greater than 1.00.

Sample: Equal numbers of moles of He(g), O_2(g), and CO_2(g) are placed in a glass vessel at room temperature. The vessel has a pinhole-sized leak, and the gases are allowed to effuse for a brief period of time. Rank order the gases remaining in the container, from the gas with the highest partial pressure to the gas with the lowest partial pressure.

Answer: Since you know that the rate of effusion is inversely related to the square root of the molar mass, you know that the larger the molar mass, the slower the rate of effusion. Therefore, the gas with the smallest molar mass will effuse at the greatest rate.

The trick in the question is that you are asked for the amounts that remain in the container. This means that the gas with the fastest rate of effusion will be the least plentiful gas in the container (more of it will have effused).

The molar masses of each gas are: He = 4 g mol^{-1}, O_2 = 32 g mol^{-1}, and CO_2 = 44 g mol^{-1}. Therefore, He will have the greatest rate of effusion, followed by oxygen, and finally CO_2. This means that helium will have the lowest partial pressure, followed by O_2, and finally CO_2, which will have the highest partial pressure.

You Try It!
A balloon is filled up with one mole of hydrogen (H_2) molecules. A second identical balloon is filled with one mole of He_2 molecules. After some time has elapsed, which balloon is smaller?

Answer: H_2, because the smaller molecules escape more quickly.

Sample: Two gases, SO_2 and NO_2, are placed in a container at a constant temperature and pressure. Calculate the ratio of effusion rates of the molecules.

Answer: The first thing to notice here is that the equation for calculating the ratio of effusion rates requires a distinction between gas 1 and gas 2. Since no such distinction is made in the problem, the decision about what to label each gas is arbitrary. However, because the lighter gas is typically labeled as gas 1, that's how we shall proceed.

You will use equation 7.19 to solve this:

$$\frac{r_1}{r_2} = \sqrt{\frac{M_2}{M_1}}$$

We will assign NO_2 as gas 1 and SO_2 as gas 2. Therefore,

$$\frac{\text{rate of effusion of } NO_2}{\text{rate of effusion of } SO_2} = \sqrt{\frac{M_{SO_2}}{M_{NO_2}}} = \sqrt{\frac{64.1 \text{ g mol}^{-1}}{46.0 \text{ g mol}^{-1}}} = 1.18$$

What this means is that NO_2 effuses at a rate 1.18 times greater than SO_2. This is because, on average, NO_2 particles move 1.18 times faster than SO_2 particles.

You Try It!
Calculate the ratio of effusion rates of helium (He) and neon (Ne) gases from the same container and at the same temperature and pressure.

Answer: 2.25

DEVIATIONS FROM THE IDEAL GAS LAWS

Most of the time, real gases approximate the ideal gas closely enough to use the ideal gas law equation. There are some circumstances, however, when the deviations between real and ideal gases become significant. The main sources for deviation arise from postulates 1 and 3. Postulate 1 asserts that the size of a gas molecule is negligible in comparison to the distance between gas molecules. Under most circumstances, this is true because the particles in a gas are very far apart. The distance between particles is also critical in postulate 3, which asserts that the attractive or repulsive forces between gas particles are negligible and also reasonable when the gas particles are very far apart. Problems start to occur, however, when the molecules get closer together. There are two situations when this will occur: high pressures and low temperatures.

When a gas is under high pressure, the distance between gas particles becomes much smaller, which allows for more opportunities for particles to interact. These interactions can be significant, especially when the gases are capable of intermolecular attractions. For example, a polar molecule, like SO_2 in the gaseous state, is capable of attracting other SO_2 molecules by dipole-dipole interactions if the particles get close enough together. High pressures force the molecules closer together and increase the likelihood of attractions, which decrease the ideal nature of a gas. (In the next chapter, you will examine in more depth the role of pressure on the state of a substance.)

Lowering the temperature also has an impact on the ideal nature of a gas. At low temperatures, the movement of gas particles begins to decrease. As the movement decreases, there are more opportunities for intermolecular attractions.

So, at high pressures or low temperatures, the behavior of gases will tend to deviate from ideal gas behavior. The amount of deviation also depends on the type of gas. Johannes van der Waals proposed an equation that was based on the ideal gas equation but that made corrections for the volume of a molecule (postulate 1) and the amount of molecular attraction (postulate 3). The van der Waals equation (which is provided for you on the AP exam) is

(Equation 7.20)

$$\left(P + \frac{n^2a}{V^2}\right)(v - nb) = nRT$$

where a and b are known as van der Waals constants and are different for each gas. The constant a is associated with the deviations due to molecular attractions, and constant b is associated with deviations due to molecular volumes. Values of a and b tend to increase as the mass and complexity of a gas increases. This should make sense since these conditions would be the most likely to affect postulates 1 and 3 of the kinetic-molecular theory.

Sample: The van der Waals constants for He and SO_2 are listed below.

Substance	a (L^2-atm mol^{-2})	b (L mol^{-1})
He	0.03412	0.02370
SO_2	6.714	0.05636

Assume that you have separate samples of 1.00 mole of the gas in a 22.4 L container at 273 K. If these gases were ideal gases, they would exert a pressure of 1.00 atm (per the equation $PV = nRT$). Using the van der Waals equation, calculate the pressures exerted by 1.00 moles of He and SO_2 in identical 22.4 L containers at 273 K.

Answer: This is a very long problem—and you won't be asked to solve a problem this complex on the AP exam. It can also show you the degree to which different gases deviate from ideal behavior.

Let's begin with He. The first thing you need to do is rearrange the equation to solve for P. This is easily done in two steps:

$$\left(P + \frac{n^2 a}{V^2}\right)(v - nb) = nRT\text{; divide each side by } (V - nb)$$

$$\left(P + \frac{n^2 a}{V^2}\right)(v - nb) = nRT\text{; next, isolate } P \text{ by subtracting } \frac{n^2 a}{V^2} \text{ from each side}$$

$$P = \frac{nRT}{(V - nb)} - \frac{n^2 a}{V^2}$$

Substitute the given information (Note: because of the units of a and b, it is necessary to use the ideal gas constant $R = 0.0821$ L-atm mol^{-1}K^{-1}):

$$P = \frac{(1.00 \text{ mol})(0.0821 \text{ L} - \text{atm mol}^{-1}\text{K}^{-1})(273 \text{ K})}{\left(22.4 \text{ L} - (1.00 \text{ mol})(0.02370 \text{ L mol}^{-1})\right)}$$

$$- \frac{(1.00 \text{ mol})^2(0.03412 \text{ L}^2 - \text{atm mol}^{-2})}{(22.4 \text{ L})^2}$$

$$P = 1.002 \text{ atm} - 6.80 \times 10^{-5} \text{ atm} = 1.002 \text{ atm}$$

In this case, the second value, 6.80×10^{-5} atm, is very small, which indicates that the main cause for the tiny deviation from ideal behavior is due to the volumes of the molecules rather than intermolecular attractions. This should make sense if you recall that a tiny atom, like He, is nearly incapable of creating any London dispersion forces.

Now for the second gas, SO_2. This is a much larger molecule, so we will predict some differences from He. Following the same procedure as you did for He, substitute the values for SO_2 into the final equation:

$$P = \frac{nRT}{(V - nb)} - \frac{n^2 a}{V^2}$$

$$P = \frac{(1.00 \text{ mol})(0.0821 \text{ L} - \text{atm mol}^{-1}\text{K}^{-1})(273 \text{ K})}{\left(22.4 \text{ L} - (1.00 \text{ mol})(0.05636 \text{ L mol}^{-1})\right)}$$

$$- \frac{(1.00 \text{ mol})^2(6.714 \text{ L}^2 - \text{atm mol}^{-2})}{(22.4 \text{ L})^2}$$

$$P = 1.003 \text{ atm} - 0.0134 \text{ atm} = 0.9896 \text{ atm}$$

The value of 1.003 atm is slightly larger than that of He, owing to the fact that the larger SO_2 molecules occupy more total space, which means they will experience more collisions with the container than He atoms. The much higher correction factor for molecular attractions (0.0134 atm) is higher than He because the much larger molecule is more capable of intermolecular interactions than He.

You Try It!

1.00 moles of nitrous oxide gas, N_2O, is introduced into a 22.4 L container at a temperature of 273 K. Determine the pressure using van der Waals equation. The van der Waals constants for N_2O are $a = 3.782$ L^2-atm mol^{-2}, and $b = 0.04415$ L mol^{-1}

Answer: 0.995 atm

Summary: States of Matter—Gases

1. The gas laws and the kinetic molecular theory describe gas temperatures using the Kelvin, or absolute, temperature scale. Gas volumes are usually described in liters, and gas pressures are described in terms of atmospheres, or mm Hg.

2. Boyle's law states that pressure and volume are inversely proportional at constant temperatures.

3. Charles's law states that volume and temperature are directly proportional at constant pressures.

4. Gay-Lussac's law states that pressure and temperature are directly proportional at constant volumes.

5. Avogadro's hypothesis states that equal volumes of gases at the same temperature and pressure will contain equal numbers of molecules. At STP, the volume of one mole of gas is approximately 22.4 liters.

6. Avogadro's law states that volume is directly proportional to the number of moles of a gas at constant temperature and pressure.

7. The ideal gas law, $PV = nRT$, describes the behavior of any ideal gas. The equation can be used to derive any of the other gas laws.

8. Dalton's law of partial pressures states that the total pressure in a mixture of gases is equal to the sum of the pressures that each individual gas exerts.

9. When gas samples are collected over a liquid, the total pressure exerted by the gas sample includes the vapor pressure of the liquid. In order to determine the pressure exerted by the gas alone, the partial pressure of the liquid must be subtracted.

10. The kinetic molecular theory consists of five postulates:
    - The size of a gas molecule is negligible in comparison to the distance between gas molecules.
    - Gas molecules move randomly in straight-line paths in all directions and at different speeds.
    - The attractive or repulsive forces between gas particles are considered very weak or negligible.
    - When gas particles do collide, the collisions are elastic.
    - The average kinetic energy of a molecule is proportional to the absolute temperature.

11. Graham's law of effusion states that the rate at which a gas effuses is inversely proportional to the molecular weight of the gas.

12. Under conditions of high pressure and low temperature, real gases begin to deviate from ideal gas behavior. The van der Waals equation can be used to determine the behavior of a real gas.

REVIEW QUESTIONS

1. A sample of helium gas is in a container at 30 °C. If the temperature is raised to 60 °C, the average kinetic energy of the atoms will change by a factor of

   (A) 1/2

   (B) $\sqrt{\dfrac{333}{303}}$

   (C) 333/303

   (D) 2

   (E) 4

2. Exactly 4.0 g of helium gas, He, is placed into a container at constant temperature and pressure. Next to the container of helium is a 28.0 g sample of nitrogen gas, N_2, placed in an identical container at the same temperature and pressure as the helium. From the list of statements below, select all that are TRUE:

   I. The number of atoms of He is identical to the number of molecules of N_2.

   II. The average kinetic energy of the He atoms is the same as the average kinetic energy of the nitrogen molecules.

   III. The average speed of the helium atoms is the same as the average speed of the nitrogen molecules.

   (A) I only

   (B) II only

   (C) III only

   (D) I and II only

   (E) I, II, and III

3. A sample of helium gas is collected in a container with a tiny hole in it. The helium gas (M = 4 grams) effuses at a rate of 0.2 moles per minute. If a sample of methane gas (M = 16 grams) is allowed to effuse under the same conditions, the rate of CH_4 effusion will be

   (A) 0.1 moles per minute.

   (B) 0.14 moles per minute.

   (C) 0.2 moles per minute.

   (D) 0.4 moles per minute.

   (E) 0.8 moles per minute.

4. A sample of 13.40 grams of a gas at 127.0 °C and 2.00 atmospheres pressure has a volume of 5.00 liters. What is the identity of the gas? Assume ideal behavior. The gas constant, R, is 0.0821 L atm mol^{-1} K^{-1}).

   (A) He (molar mass = 4.00 g)

   (B) N_2 (molar mass = 28.0 g)

   (C) O_2 (molar mass = 32.0 g)

   (D) Ne (molar mass = 20.2 g)

   (E) CO_2 (molar mass = 44.0 g)

5. If you collected a sample of 3.50 moles of hydrogen gas, H_2, and heated it in a 10.00 L container to a temperature of 300 K, how much pressure would the H_2 exert on the container?

   (A) 873 atm

   (B) 86.2 atm

   (C) 16.5 atm

   (D) 8.62 atm

   (E) 0.776 atm

6. 3.00 moles of nitrogen gas, N_2, and an unknown amount of hydrogen gas, H_2, are mixed together in a container. The total pressure in the container is 1000 mm Hg. If the partial pressure of nitrogen in the container is 750 mm Hg, how many moles of hydrogen gas must be present?

   (A) 0.5 moles

   (B) 1.0 moles

   (C) 1.5 moles

   (D) 2.0 moles

   (E) not enough information

7. A chunk of calcium carbide is placed into a container of water, and the acetylene gas that is formed is bubbled through water into an inverted graduated cylinder. The pressure inside the graduated cylinder is 800 mm Hg, and the temperature is 27 °C. What is the partial pressure exerted by the acetylene gas? (The vapor pressure of water at 27 °C is 27 mm Hg.)

   (A) 800 mm Hg

   (B) 827 mm Hg

   (C) 27 mm Hg

   (D) 773 mm Hg

   (E) 54 mm Hg

8. A sample of carbon dioxide gas, CO_2, is in a container, inside which the pressure is 1.25 atm and the temperature is 300 K. What is the density of this sample of CO_2 in grams per liter?

   (A) 0.022 g L^{-1}

   (B) 1.42 g L^{-1}

   (C) 2.23 g L^{-1}

   (D) 5.00 g L^{-1}

   (E) 24.8 g L^{-1}

9. An unknown quantity of methane gas, CH_4, is held in a 2.00-liter container at 77 °C. The pressure inside the container is 3.00 atm. How many moles of methane must be in the container?

   (A) 0.21 moles

   (B) 0.95 moles

   (C) 1.05 moles

   (D) 4.8 moles

   (E) 0.5 moles

10. Which of the following is most likely to deviate from ideal gas behavior?

    (A) H_2

    (B) He

    (C) Ne

    (D) N_2

    (E) CCl_4

Free Response

1. Three large, identical balloons are filled with 22.4 L of gas at STP. The three gases are helium (He), hydrogen (H_2), and sulfur hexafluoride (SF_6). What follows is a list of statements about those three balloons. Comment on the accuracy of the statements, using specific details to support your argument/comments.

   (A) Because hydrogen is the smallest particle, the balloon with hydrogen will contain the largest number of moles of gas.

   (B) The kinetic energies of the molecules compare as follows:
       $SF_6 < He < H_2$

   (C) SF6 will deviate the most from ideal gas behavior.

   (D) One day after filling the balloons, all three will have decreased in size by the same amount.

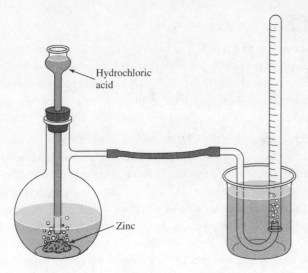

Figure 7.2

2. A small sample of mossy zinc was placed into a reaction vessel, as shown in Figure 7.2. Hydrochloric acid was added, and the hydrogen gas that was generated was bubbled through water into a gas collection tube filled with water. When the reaction reached completion, the gas collection tube was nearly full. The gas was allowed to sit for several minutes. The collection tube was then adjusted so that the level of water in the tube was equal to the level of the water outside the tube. The volume of gas was determined to be 47 mL, and the temperature of the water was 22 °C. The barometric pressure in the laboratory was 745 mm Hg. The vapor pressure of water at 22 °C is 19.4 mm Hg.

(A) Calculate the number of moles of hydrogen gas produced.

(B) Explain why it was necessary to allow the gas to sit in the tube for several minutes before determining its volume.

(C) Explain why it was necessary to adjust the level of the tube so that water levels inside and outside of it were the same.

(D) Explain why the vapor pressure of water is given.

ANSWERS

1. **The correct answer is (C).** The big trap here is the degrees Celsius. The fact that the second temperature is exactly two times greater than the first temperature makes it very attractive to think that the kinetic energy will double. Wrong! The kinetic energy is proportional to the absolute temperature scale. On this scale, the ratio of 60/30 becomes (60 + 273)/(30 + 273) or 333/303.

2. **The correct answer is (D).** There are two ways that you can gain support for I. First, the mass of each sample represents one mole of the gas. Knowing that there is one mole in each container allows you to say that the number of particles in each container is the same. However, a second way to get the same answer is Avogadro's hypothesis, which states that equal volumes of gases at the same temperature and pressure will contain equal numbers of molecules. Because the containers are the same size (volume) and at the same temperature and pressure, you can assume they have equal numbers of particles. Support for II comes from the kinetic-molecular theory, which states that the average kinetic energy of gas particles is proportional to the absolute temperature. Because the containers are at the same temperature, it can be said the gases have the same average kinetic energies. There is no support for III, however. Kinetic energy is measured using the formula $\frac{1}{2}mv^2$, where v represents the speed of the particles. Kinetic molecular theory tells us that the product of these numbers will be the same for both gases, but because the masses of each gas are different, it is impossible for them to have the same speeds. Nitrogen, the heavier gas, will, on average, travel much slower than helium.

3. **The correct answer is (A).** There is a quick way to solve this and also a long way. The quick way is to remember that Graham's law states that the rate of effusion is inversely proportional to the square root of the molar mass. You can see pretty quickly that the molar mass of methane is 4 times that of helium. The square root of 4 is 2, meaning that helium will diffuse two times faster than methane. The longer way is to actually set up the equation $r^1/r^2 = \sqrt{M_2 / M_1}$ and solve for r^2.

4. **The correct answer is (E).** Using the ideal gas equation $PV = nRT$, and solving for n, you get 0.3045 moles. Dividing the mass of the sample by the molar mass yields 44.0 g, which is the molar mass of CO_2.

5. **The correct answer is (D).** Another ideal gas equation. This time, all values are in the appropriate units, so you just need to plug and chug.

6. **The correct answer is (B).** You know that $P_A = P_t x_A$. If you try setting this up for the hydrogen, it gets a little more complicated. Always remember what you are given in a problem. You know how many moles of nitrogen gas you have. You also know the total pressure and the partial pressure of nitrogen. Therefore, you can use the given information to figure out the total number of moles in the mixture. Once you know this, you can quickly determine the amount of hydrogen. 750 mm Hg = 1000 mm Hg (3/x). Solving for x, you find it to be 4. That means there are four moles in the mixture. Three of these are nitrogen, so the other one must be hydrogen. Note: There are other ways to solve this problem—this one is relatively straightforward and easy to solve, so it was selected.

7. **The correct answer is (D).** Remember, whenever you collect a gas sample over water (or another liquid), the total pressure reflects the pressure of the gas sample AND the vapor pressure of the water. To determine the pressure of the gas, you must subtract the vapor pressure of the water from the total pressure. $P_{gas} = P_t - P_{water} = 800$ mm Hg $- 27$ mm Hg $= 773$ mm Hg

8. **The correct answer is (C).** Density can be calculated using the equation $d = PM/RT$. All values are already in the units of R, so plug and chug. (1.25 atm)(44.0 g/mol)/(0.0821 L atm/mol K)(300 K) = 2.23 g/L

9. **The correct answer is (A).** Ideal gas equation. Temperature is in Celsius, so it will need to be converted to Kelvin. $n = PV/RT = (3.00$ atm)(2.00 L)/(0.0821 L atm/mol K)(350 K) = 0.21 moles

10. **The correct answer is (E).** When considering particles, remember that larger or more complex molecules will most likely deviate from ideal gas behavior. This is due both to their increased volume and to their increased likelihood of molecular attraction.

Free Response 1

(A) Wrong! Avogadro's hypothesis tells us that equal volumes of gases at constant temperature and pressure will contain equal numbers of moles of the gases. These balloons all have equal volumes, and each is at the same temperature and pressure. Therefore, size has nothing to do with this.

(B) Wrong again! One of the postulates of kinetic-molecular theory is that the average kinetic energy of a gas is directly related to the absolute temperature of the gas. Mass and volume have nothing to do with it. The gases are all at the same absolute temperature; therefore, they will all have the same average kinetic energies.

(C) This statement is correct. The sulfur hexafluoride molecule has a much larger volume than the other molecules and is much more likely to experience molecular attractions than the other two molecules. These two factors will make this molecule most likely to deviate from the key postulates in the kinetic-molecular theory (that size of the molecule is negligible and that molecular attractions are negligible).

(D) Wrong! Graham's law of effusion states that the rates of effusion are inversely related to the square root of the molar mass. This means that smaller particles will effuse more quickly than larger particles. All three balloons will get smaller at different rates, which means they will be different sizes on the next day (hydrogen will be smallest, followed by helium, and then sulfur hexafluoride).

Free Response 2

(A) This is a laboratory procedure that you are expected to have per-formed and know for the AP exam. While setting up this calculation, we will actually be answering some of the following questions. You will use the ideal gas equation to solve the problem. Therefore, you will need to know the pressure, volume, and temperature of the gas. The pressure of the gas will equal the total pressure of the mixture minus the vapor pressure of water (which is present in the gas collection tube, along with the hydrogen). The total pressure of the gas is equal to the atmospheric pressure in the room. Therefore, the pressure of the hydrogen gas is equal to 745 mm Hg – 19.4 mm Hg = 725.6 mm Hg (726 mm Hg). Remember, the ideal gas equation requires atmospheres, so this will need to be converted to atmo-spheres. 726 mm Hg $\times$ 1 atm/760 mm Hg = 0.955 atm. The volume of the mixture is 47 mL, but the ideal gas equation requires liters, so this will need to be converted to liters. 47 mL = 4.7×10^{-2} L. The tempera-ture of the gas is assumed to be the temperature of the water, which is 22 °C. This will need to be converted to K. 22 °C = 295 K. Now you are ready to substitute your data into the equation: $PV = nRT$; $n = PV/RT = $ (0.955 atm)(4.7×10^{-2} L)/(0.0821 L atm/mol K)(295 K) **= $1.85 \times 10{-3}$ mol H2**

(B) The gas must sit in the tube so that the temperature of the gas will equilibrate with the temperature of the water. This is necessary because the temperature of the water is the only known temperature and therefore is the temperature used in the gas equation.

(C) When the water level inside the tube is the same as the water level outside the tube, this is an indicator that the gas pressure inside the tube is equal to the air pressure outside the tube. Because in your lab there is no way to directly measure the gas pressure inside the tube, this allows you to determine the pressure by direct comparison to atmospheric pressure. Atmospheric pressure can therefore be substi-tuted into the gas equation.

(D) The vapor pressure of water must be given because the gas in the collection tube is actually a mixture of hydrogen gas and water vapor. By subtracting the vapor pressure of water, you can determine the partial pressure of the hydrogen gas in the mixture.

Chapter

8

States of Matter—Liquids and Solids

In the previous two chapters, you looked at the basic composition of matter and the characteristics of the gaseous state of matter. One common theme in each of those chapters was the presence of intermolecular forces that occur between particles. In Chapter 5, you were introduced to the three main types of these forces: hydrogen bonding, dipole-dipole interactions, and London dispersion forces. In Chapter 7, you saw how real gases don't behave quite like ideal gases. That is, real particles do have mass and volume and exert attractions on other particles. This accounts for deviations between real behavior and ideal behavior. It also explains why gases under different combinations of pressure and temperature can be liquefied. In this chapter, we will revisit intermolecular forces and discuss their roles in the liquid and solid states. In addition, we will look at the effects of chemical bonding on the behavior of solids. We will also look at different diagrams that are useful when studying the different states of matter.

GENERAL CHARACTERISTICS OF GASES, LIQUIDS, AND SOLIDS

Before you continue, you should have a good feel for the differences between the three main states of matter at the particle level. Figure 8.1 provides a graphic representation of what is described in the next three paragraphs.

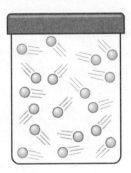 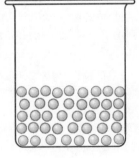 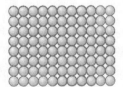

Figure 8.1

ROAD MAP

- *General Characteristics of Gases, Liquids, and Solids*
- *Energy and Phase Changes*
- *Heating Curves*
- *Vapor Pressure*
- *Phase Diagrams*
- *The Solid State*

NOTE

Occasionally, *plasma*, the gaseous mixture of ions and electrons that exists at extremely high temperatures, is classified as a fourth state of matter. Because it is irrelevant to our discussion, we are limiting the topic to the three clearly recognized states.

Gases, you will recall from Chapter 7, are characterized by particles that are free to move about in constant, random, straight-line motion. Under normal atmospheric conditions, the particles are very spread out. Gases can be thought of as being fluid, not in the sense that they are liquids, but that they can flow. They can flow freely because the particles can move past one another with ease. Because there is a large amount of empty space between the particles, gases are highly compressible. Gases essentially fill any container they are placed into.

In liquids, the particles are much closer together. Liquids still share some of the same characteristics as gases. Although the particles are much closer together than they are in the gaseous state, they are generally free to slide past one another. Remember, the forces holding the particles together in the liquid state are not chemical bonds but intermolecular forces. They can keep the particles together, but not tightly enough to prevent them from moving. Because the particles can slide past one another, liquids can flow. This will allow them to take the shape of any container that they are placed into, but unlike gases, they are not able to change their volume to fill the container. Particles of a liquid are much closer together than a gas. As a result, liquids are almost completely incompressible.

Solids are neither fluid nor compressible. The particles in a solid, which might be atoms, molecules, or ions, depending on the material, are tightly packed together into a rigid structure. The movements in a solid are limited to oscillations, or vibrations. Solids will maintain their shape without a container.

In the previous chapter, you looked at the van der Waals equation as a way of taking into account the sizes of particles as well as molecular attractions. In this chapter, these properties become even more important in the consideration of liquids and solids.

ENERGY AND PHASE CHANGES

So far, we have talked about the three different phases of matter, but in a disconnected way, as though the three states have nothing to do with one another. As you will see, however, the three states are very much connected to one another. Energy is the thread that binds them all together and separates them. There are some terms associated with the transitions from one state of matter to another that you should be familiar with.

Melting, also known as fusion, is the term used to describe a change from the solid state to the liquid state. A certain amount of energy is necessary to break the particles from the rigid solid state into this fluid state. If you take an ice cube from the freezer and set it on the counter, you will witness melting as the cube changes from the solid state to the liquid state. The higher kinetic energy of the particles on the counter and in the air will continue to transfer energy to the ice cube, causing it to melt.

If the little puddle of water is put into a small container and placed back into the freezer, the water, now at a higher kinetic energy than the air in the freezer, will lose energy to the air particles in the freezer. When the particles have lost sufficient energy, they will no longer be able to overcome the attractive forces that will cause them to change back into a rigid solid structure once again. This process of moving from the liquid state to the solid state is known as *freezing*. One thing you have to be careful of is associating the word freezing with cold. Many things you are familiar with, like ice cubes, don't freeze until they become cold. This is not true for all substances, however. Picture molten lava running down the sides of a volcano. As it cools, it is freezing, but you would hardly consider it to be cold! You will also learn later in this chapter that terms like "boiling" and "freezing" are related to pressure as well as to temperature.

If you have ever seen dry ice "melt," you may have noticed that there is no puddle left behind. The word "melts" is in quotes because the process that dry ice undergoes is not known as melting. Dry ice, or solid carbon dioxide, at normal atmospheric pressure passes directly from the solid state to the gaseous state, without passing through the liquid state. This process is known as *sublimation*. The reverse process is possible as well. The conversion of a gas into a solid is known as *deposition*.

When a liquid changes to a gas, the process is known as *vaporization* (remember the term vapor is used to describe a gas that is normally a solid or liquid at room temperature). Had our melted ice cube sat on the counter for an extended amount of time, the water would have eventually vaporized into water vapor. (We frequently call this evaporation.) When the reverse process occurs, that is, when a gas converts into a liquid, the process is known as *condensation*. A few types of condensation that you are probably quite familiar with would be the formation of liquid on the outside of cold drink glasses and dew forming on grass or plants.

HEATING CURVES

A heating curve provides you with a nice summary of the previous information while also presenting you with some new information. Heating curves are obtained from the gradual heating of a substance from the solid state to the gas state at a constant atmospheric pressure. As you'll see in a later section, changes in pressure have an impact on changes of state. For now, we will limit ourselves to atmospheric pressure.

You may have done a lab at one point where you made a heating curve for water or a similar substance. The way you would do this would be to obtain a sample of ice at a temperature below zero and begin to slowly heat it while closely monitoring the temperature. Heating curves are sometimes plotted with temperature over time. The diagram we are referring to has temperature plotted against energy. If you follow Figure 8.2, you will see that initially, the added heat is used to change the temperature of the ice, but, at this point, no melting takes place. Once the temperature of the ice reaches 0 °C, it will begin to melt. There is a period of time, however, when the ice is melting and heat is continually added, but the temperature does not increase. This is seen as the first plateau on the graph. What is happening during this plateau, and why doesn't the temperature change? The temperature remains constant because all of the energy that is being added to the system is being used to break the strong attractive forces that lock the particles in the rigid solid state. The amount of energy that is required to completely convert the solid to the liquid is known as the ***heat of fusion***.

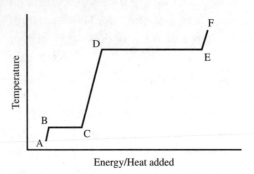

Figure 8.2

Once all the particles have broken free from this solid state (i.e., the solid has melted), then the added heat causes an increase in the motion of the particles and a subsequent increase in temperature. This temperature increase will continue at a fixed rate (determined by the type of substance). While the substance is getting hotter, a small number of particles are evaporating, but the bulk of the material remains in the liquid state. Once the water or other material reaches its boiling temperature (at atmospheric pressure), vaporization will take place. Once again, however, the heating curve experiences a plateau. As long as there is liquid present, the temperature of the liquid/vapor mixture remains at the boiling temperature (for water, 100 °C at 1.00 atm pressure). The heat that is being added is used to break apart the intermolecular attractions holding the particles together in the liquid state. The quantity of heat required to completely convert the liquid to a gas is known as the ***heat of vaporization***. The greater the intermolecular attractions between particles in the liquid state, the greater the heat of vaporization will be. Because of the large amount of hydrogen bonding between water molecules, the heat of vaporization for water is very large. If you've ever been burned by steam, you know it is extremely painful. That's because as the water vapor hits you and condenses, all of the heat that was absorbed in the vaporization process is released during condensation.

There is a similar type of plot known as a ***cooling curve***. This provides the same data, except it involves heat being removed, or lost from the system, rather than heat being added. It is essentially a mirror image of the heating curve—all parts are exactly the same and represent the same processes, only in reverse. These types of graphs occasionally appear on the AP exam. You should know how to read and identify all of the parts on them.

Sample:

The questions that follow are based on Figure 8.3.

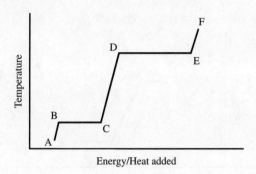

Figure 8.3

Identify the locations on the heating curve of the following processes or quantities:

    A. Melting

    B. Vaporization

    C. A mixture of solid and liquid exists

    D. The substance just begins to boil

    E. The heat of vaporization

    F. Condensation

    G. The substance is totally in the liquid state

Answers:

    A. Line BC. Melting begins at point B and continues until point C is reached.

    B. Line DE. During vaporization there is no temperature change. The process of vaporization begins to occur right at point D.

    C. Line BC. Melting begins at point B, when the substance begins to convert to liquid. It does not become completely liquid until point C.

    D. Point D.

    E. Line DE. The heat of vaporization is the amount of energy added between points D and E that represents all energy used to overcome all intermolecular forces holding the substance in the liquid state.

    F. Line ED. Although condensation can occur at temperatures below the boiling temperature, a heating curve is not designed to show changes. Those are more apparent in a phase diagram (discussed later in the chapter). Condensation begins at point E, where energy is released as particles begin to rejoin into the liquid state.

    G. Line CD. During this period, all added energy increases the temperature of the liquid.

You Try It!

Examine the cooling curve in Figure 8.4, and answer the questions that follow.

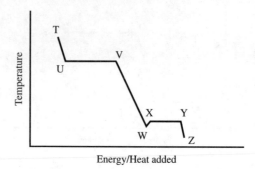

Figure 8.4

Identify the locations on the heating curve of the following processes, or quantities:

    A. Freezing

    B. Condensation

    C. A mixture of solid and liquid exists

    D. The heat of vaporization

    E. The substance is totally in the liquid state

Answers:

A. Freezing: W to Y

B. Condensation: U to V

C. A mixture of solid and liquid exists: W to Y

D. The heat of vaporization: U to V

E. The substance is totally in the liquid state: V to W

VAPOR PRESSURE

In the previous chapter, you learned that in a sample of a gas, the individual gas particles had various amounts of kinetic energy. Some had more than average, some had less. The same is true for any collection of particles, even liquids and solids. If you consider a container of water, this means that some of the water molecules have more kinetic energy than others. Since the particles are constantly in motion, they collide with one another, transferring some kinetic energy as they do (these collisions are not elastic). Occasionally, at the surface of the water, a particle gains enough kinetic energy to overcome the attractive forces exerted on it by neighboring water molecules. When it does, it escapes from the water into the air, becoming a gaseous molecule. The amount of energy required to break free from the water is known as *escape energy*. This process can occur at any temperature, however, one thing that should be remembered is that at higher temperatures, a larger percent of molecules in the liquid will be able to attain the escape energy (they're already closer to it in a hotter liquid). Another thing that should be remembered is that when a molecule possessing a higher kinetic energy leaves, the total kinetic energy of the water decreases. This is why evaporation is considered a cooling process. If you have ever felt a breeze blow by when you are wet, either with sweat or with water, you know that you get cooler. In dry climates, like the desert Southwest, many homes use evaporative coolers. These cooling systems use a large fan and special pads that are housed in a unit atop the house that are constantly soaked with water. Hot air from the outside, with the help of the large fan, is cooled through evaporation as it passes through the web pads. The cooled air is then blown into the house.

Now consider a container of water that is sealed, like a tightly sealed jar that is half-filled with water. If you leave the jar on a shelf for an extended period of time, the level of water should remain constant (assuming there is a good seal on the jar). Does this mean that evaporation is not taking place in the jar? Certainly not! Here's how it works: Particles on the surface still leave the liquid and begin to enter the gas (air) above the liquid. However, in the sealed jar they have nowhere to escape to, so they will continually bounce around up in the top of the jar. Some may bounce off of the lid; others may bounce off the glass, while some will collide with other molecules of gas in the air space. And then there are those that will collide with the water surface. Some of the water molecules that strike the surface, especially those that have lost some kinetic energy due to collisions, will not have sufficient energy to leave again. That is, they will reenter the liquid state. For a period of time after the jar is sealed, the number of particles moving from the liquid to gas state will exceed the number of particles returning from the gas state to the liquid state. However, as the number of particles entering the gas state increases, so will the number of gas particles entering the liquid state. This will happen until the particles in the jar reach a certain point, known as *dynamic equilibrium*, where the rates at which particles are leaving and reentering the liquid will be equal. Many people share the misconception that everything stops at this point. Nonsense! It only looks that way because the rate at which evaporation and condensation occur are equal, but both processes are still occurring. If you're not convinced, poke a hole in the bottom of a Styrofoam cup. Then try filling it with water. If you fill it faster than it can drain, it will fill up. If you fill it up slower than it can drain, it will stay empty. But if you fill it up at the exact same rate as it is draining, the water level will stay the same, even though it is filling and draining at the same time.

The particles that have entered the gas state are now bouncing around in the top part of the jar. As they do so, they are colliding with everything around them. This creates *vapor pressure,* which is the pressure exerted by the vapor when the liquid and gas states are in dynamic equilibrium.

Factors Affecting Vapor Pressure

If you think about it a bit, the factors that affect vapor pressure should not come as any surprise. The first one is temperature. As temperature increases, so does the average kinetic energy of the particles in the liquid (and the gas above it). As a result, more particles can reach escape energies and those that have escaped can exert more force (due to their increased energy) on their surroundings. If you recall from the chapter on gases, for any problem where a gas was collected over a liquid (like water), you had to take into account the vapor pressure of water. That's because you had a closed container over the water catching the gas. While it was catching the gas, it was also catching the water vapor that had escaped from the liquid. You also may have noticed that the amount of water vapor was listed for given temperatures. That was because the vapor pressure of water (or any liquid) is affected by temperature.

Another thing that affects vapor pressure is *volatility*. A volatile liquid is defined as a liquid that attains relatively high vapor pressures at normal temperatures. An easy way to think of it is that liquids evaporate quickly at room temperature. If you've ever seen a gasoline spill on the ground on a hot day, you may have noticed that it dries up quickly. Gasoline is a volatile liquid and evaporates quickly. In a closed container, it acquires a high vapor pressure. Things that don't evaporate quickly, like cooking oil, have a very low volatility. There are some solids that are considered volatile, such as solid room deodorizers and mothballs (which contain naphthalene or para-dichlorobenezene). These materials sublime; therefore, they can be considered to have a vapor pressure at standard temperatures and pressures.

Relationship between Boiling Point and Vapor Pressure

You may have been a little confused by the sudden switch from cooling curves to vapor pressure, but here is where the two topics come together. When does a liquid boil? If you are thinking of your experience with water, you may answer, "When it gets hot enough" or "When it reaches the boiling temperature." However, neither of these is really correct. A liquid boils when the vapor pressure of the liquid equals the external pressure. If you're talking about an open container, like a pot on a stove, external pressure means atmospheric pressure. When the two pressures are equal, that's when you see the bubbles start to form in the boiling liquid. Now, if the atmospheric pressure happens to be 1.00 atmospheres and the water is pure, then water will boil at 100 °C. However, water can be made to boil at room temperature if you drop the pressure low enough (like in a bell jar over a vacuum pump). By affecting the boiling temperature, vapor pressure affects the way food is cooked (no, this isn't trivia time—this has actually been on previous AP exams!). At high elevations, there is less atmospheric pressure. That means that the vapor pressure of the water does not have to be as high for boiling to occur. If you recall from the heating curve, once the water starts to boil, it won't get any hotter. That means at higher altitudes, water boils at a lower temperature than at lower altitudes. It takes longer to cook foods at high altitudes. There is also a cooking device known as a pressure cooker. These are pots that seal up tightly so that the pressure above the liquid can build up higher than atmospheric pressure (there are valves that prevent them from exploding). Because the external pressure is higher, the liquid in the pot can heat above the normal boiling temperature and cook more quickly.

Pressure does not have nearly the same affect on the melting/freezing point of a liquid as it does on the boiling point.

Sample: If you lived on top of a very high mountain and you made a cup of hot coffee using water boiled in an open pot on the stove, how would it's temperature compare to a cup of coffee made at sea level?

Answer: It would be lower. At high altitudes, the vapor pressure reaches equilibrium with the atmospheric pressure and lower temperatures (because of the decreased atmospheric pressure at high altitudes). At sea level, water boils at a higher temperature.

You Try It!
How will the time it takes to hard-boil an egg compare at higher altitudes?

Answer: It will take longer because of the lower boiling temperature of the water.

Other Properties of Liquids

We've looked at the vapor pressure of liquids, but we haven't really discussed in detail the factors that contribute to the vapor pressures or volatilities that are characteristics of liquids. The factors are all based on the intermolecular forces from Chapter 5. Perhaps a few things will start to fall into place for you. In the last section, we were looking at the molecular processes that occur during evaporation. If you recall, a particle had to possess enough energy to escape from the liquid state to enter the gas state. But what keeps it from leaving? In other words, what is keeping it in the liquid state? Most of this can be answered with the key words *intermolecular attractions*. The stronger the attractive forces are that hold particles together, the more force will need to be exerted to pull them apart. Looking back at some of the questions in Chapter 5 about boiling points, this might make more sense to you now. Consider the examples of methane, ammonia, and water. Water is the only liquid at room temperature. (Don't confuse ammonia with ammonium hydroxide, the solution we called "household ammonia.") Why? Because it is a very polar molecule, it is capable of forming strong hydrogen bonds between neighboring molecules. It takes a lot more energy to get the particles apart. That's why it remains in the liquid state at higher temperatures than the others. Ammonia is capable of some hydrogen bonding, but not at the same degree as water. Its boiling temperature is between water and methane. Methane has the lowest boiling point because it is a nonpolar molecule, bound only by dispersion forces.

Viscosity

Intermolecular attractions are the primary cause of this phenomenon, *viscosity*, or the thickness of a liquid. In general, liquids containing larger molecules or liquids with greater intermolecular forces between molecules are thicker liquids. Motor oil and corn syrup are fairly viscous liquids. Increasing the temperature of a liquid generally decreases its viscosity.

Surface Tension

Cohesive forces between particles in a liquid cause the phenomenon known as *surface tension*. The term "cohesive" refers to the forces between particles of a substance. It's what we've been calling intermolecular attractions. Surface tension occurs because there is an uneven attraction between particles on the surface of a liquid.

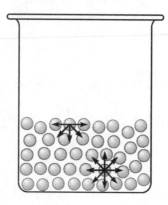

Figure 8.5

These uneven forces on the surface cause the molecules to pack more tightly together and create a more rigid surface.

Another type of force that can occur is known as *adhesion*, or adhesive force. These are the forces that bind different substances together. An example of adhesive forces (other than adhesive tape!) is the way that water adheres to different materials. When you first learned how to read a graduated cylinder, you had to learn to compensate for the *meniscus*, or the curved part on the surface of the liquid. The meniscus forms when you put water into a graduated cylinder because the adhesive force between the water molecules and the glass is stronger than the cohesive forces holding the water molecules together.

PHASE DIAGRAMS

For the most part, our discussion about states of matter and phase changes has been limited to temperature effects. The heating and cooling curves are illustrations of temperature effects on state. In the section on vapor pressure, you were introduced to the idea that variations in pressure can also cause changes in state. When water boils at low temperatures, it clearly illustrates that there are really two external factors involved in changes of the state of water: temperature and pressure. In this section, you will begin to review the effects of pressure on state. This will be done with the help of phase diagrams, which are diagrams that provide a graphical representation of the states of matter for a substance under all variations of temperature and pressure.

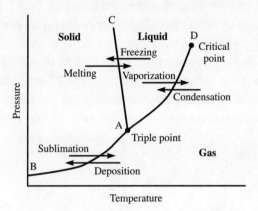

Figure 8.6

Phase diagrams contain a variety of information at various levels of complexity. The broadest distinctions are the three large areas that are contained on the graph. Referring to Figure 8.6, most of the left side of the chart (those portions above and to the left of the lines connecting points B-A-C) represents those temperatures and pressures at which the substance being shown exists as a solid. On the right, below the lines connecting B-A-D, are the temperatures and pressures at which the substance exists as a gas. The V-shaped region between the lines connecting C-A-D represents the liquid state. The lines themselves represent the temperatures and pressures at which the states on either side are in equilibrium. For example, the line B-A represents the temperatures and pressures where the gas state and the solid state are in equilibrium. Line A-C represents the temperatures and pressures at which the solid and liquid states are at equilibrium, and the curve A-D represents the equilibrium states between liquid and gas.

Two other special features on the diagram are designated by black dots. The dot at point D, known as the ***critical point***, represents the ***critical temperature*** and the ***critical pressure*** (the point at which the liquid state no longer exists, regardless of the amount of pressure). The other dot represents the intersection of the three lines, known as the ***triple point***. The triple point represents the temperature and pressure at which all three phases coexist simultaneously.

Although they aren't labeled, all of the phase changes listed earlier in the chapter are also detectable on the phase diagrams. The equilibrium lines, mentioned earlier in this section, represent those places where phase changes occur. For example, at any of the locations along line A-C, a transition from left to right represents melting.

The phase diagram in Figure 8.6 is the diagram for water, which is not representative of most substances. The main difference is the transition from solid to liquid, line A-C. For most substances, this will have a slightly positive slope. You will note that in the diagram for water, the slope is negative. The positive slope for most substances means that as pressure increases, so does the melting temperature. This should make sense on an intuitive level. Increasing pressure will squeeze the particles closer together, meaning it will take more energy to break them apart. Water, however, is one of the few substances whose liquid state is more compact than the solid state. In the solid state, water is less dense than it is in the liquid state, which is why ice floats on top of water. The reason that ice expands is because the crystals in solid H_2O arrange themselves in an organized hexagonal structure that takes up more space than the less organized, but more compact, arrangement of the liquid water molecules.

Sample: Use Figure 8.7 to answer the following question.

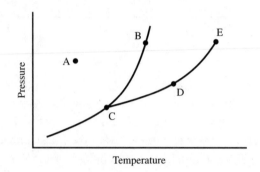

Figure 8.7

Which point represents the equilibrium between the liquid and gas phases during vaporization?

Answer: The correct answer is D. The entire line from C to the critical point E represents equilibrium between the liquid and gas phases.

You Try It!
Referring to Figure 8.7, indicate the point on the graph that represents a pure solid below its melting point.

Answer: The correct answer is A.

THE SOLID STATE

The particles in a solid are held together with sufficient force to maintain a rigid structure. In some cases, these forces consist of intermolecular forces, while in others, chemical bonds. Solids are typically classified according to the types of forces that hold the particles together. When classified this way, the four types of solid are molecular, ionic, covalent network, and metallic.

Molecular Solids

Just like the name suggests, these solids are composed of molecules that are held together by intermolecular forces of attraction. Ice would be a perfect example. Relative to the other solids, these tend to have much lower melting temperatures. This is easy to remember because they are not held together with chemical bonds, whereas the others are.

Ionic Solids

Ionic solids are actually crystalline salts composed of oppositely charged ions that are held together by electrostatic attraction (ionic bonds). If you recall from Chapter 5, the charged particles indiscriminately bond to other oppositely charged particles, forming large groupings of charged particles. The arrangements tend to be highly regular, a result of the similar attractions and repulsions that each specific ion has in the crystal. A *crystal lattice* is composed of a number of identical subunits, known as *unit cells*, that stack like building blocks around and about each other in a highly ordered fashion. The ionic bonds are very strong bonds, and, as a result, ionic solids have high melting points. As you read in Chapter 5, the strength of the bonds is usually measured in terms of the lattice energy, or energy required to separate a mole of a solid ionic compound to a mole of gaseous ions. The stronger the attraction is between the ions in a crystalline solid, the larger the lattice energy. Another characteristic of salts is that they are fairly easy to shatter. The reason for this is that the unit cells are arranged along planes, and when the crystal is hit, these planes will slide past one another slightly, causing electrostatic repulsions between neighboring ions. These repulsions, which occur when ions that were aligned with oppositely charge ions prior to being hit, move slightly so that they are briefly realigned with like-charged ions.

Covalent Network Solids

These solids are formed from atoms that are bonded covalently into large structures. These are some of the strongest solids due to their very stable covalent bonds. Some of the most common examples are graphite (carbon atoms), diamond (carbon atoms), and quartz (silicon dioxide). These mostly have high melting temperatures. Many of these structures, like diamond, are extremely hard and resist shattering. The atoms in the solid do not necessarily determine the properties of the solid. For example, graphite and diamond are both composed of carbon atoms, yet their properties are entirely different. This is due to the arrangement of the carbon atoms in the solid. In diamond, the carbon atoms arrange themselves in rigid three-dimensional structures, whereas in graphite, the carbon atoms arrange themselves in long flat sheets.

Metallic Solids

Metallic solids have a very wide variety of properties. Their structures tend to be highly ordered; the metal atoms arranging themselves into regularly packed structures, with the loosely held valence electrons delocalized about the nuclei. While melting points vary a tremendous amount (melting temperatures range from below room temperature to above 3500 °C), there are some characteristics that are shared. Most metals are good conductors of electricity due to the loosely held valence electrons. In addition, metals are malleable (they can be hammered/molded into different shapes) and ductile (they can be drawn into wires). This is because the atoms are free to slide past each other and are not restricted by rigid ionic or covalent bonds.

Sample: In which of the following processes are covalent bonds broken?

   (A) $Br_2(l) \rightarrow Br_2(g)$

   (B) $H_2O(s) \rightarrow H_2O(g)$

   (C) $KCl(s) \rightarrow KCl(l)$

   (D) $SiO_2(quartz) \rightarrow SiO_2\ gas(g)$

   (E) $Cu(s) \rightarrow Cu(l)$

Answer: The correct answer is (D). SiO_2 (quartz) is a covalent network solid. Therefore, in its crystalline form, the rigid solid structure is maintained by covalent bonds. The other examples only involve the breaking of various intermolecular forces.

You Try It!

Select the process that would require the most energy:

   (A) $Au(s) \rightarrow Au(l)$

   (B) $CH_3OH(l) \rightarrow CH_3OH(g)$

   (C) $SrCl_2(s) \rightarrow SrCl_2(l)$

Answer: The correct answer is (C). Melting a stable ionic compound will require much more energy than breaking most intermolecular forces, especially the vaporization of an alcohol, choice (B), and the melting of a soft metal like gold.

Summary: States of Matter— Liquids and Solids

- Gases are characterized by their low density, high compressibility, and fluidity.

- Liquids are virtually incompressible and fluid and maintain a constant volume.

- Solids are incompressible and maintain a constant volume.

- Melting and freezing are terms to describe the conversions between the solid and liquid states. The amount of energy that is absorbed or released in this process is known as the heat of fusion.

- Vaporization and condensation are terms used to describe the conversions between the liquid and gaseous states. The amount of energy absorbed or released in this process is known as the heat of vaporization.

- When matter converts directly from the solid to the gaseous state it is known as sublimation. The reverse is called deposition.

- Heating curves are graphical representations of the temperature changes of a substance as it changes state from solid to gas, plotted as a function of energy absorbed (or time). Cooling curves show the reverse of this process.

- The vapor pressure of a substance in a closed system is the pressure exerted by a vapor that is in dynamic equilibrium with the liquid state. Intermolecular forces are the main factors that determine vapor pressure.

- The boiling point of a liquid is the point at which the vapor pressure of the liquid is equal to the external pressure. As a result, the boiling temperature is affected by pressure, including pressure changes due to altitude.

- Phase diagrams are graphical representations of the relationships between pressure, temperature, and the state of a substance. You should be able to read and interpret phase diagrams for the AP exam.

- Solids are usually described according to the forces that hold the particles together. The four types of solids are molecular solids, ionic solids, covalent network solids, and metallic solids.

REVIEW QUESTIONS

1. 1-propanol, $CH_3CH_2CH_2OH$, boils at 97 °C and ethyl methyl ether, $CH_3CH_2OCH_3$, boils at 7 °C, although each compound has an identical chemical composition. The difference that is responsible for the higher boiling temperature is

   (A) molar mass.

   (B) hydrogen bonding.

   (C) density.

   (D) specific heat.

   (E) enthalpy.

2. Which of the following is true at the triple point of a pure substance?

   (A) The temperature is equal to the normal melting point.

   (B) All three states have identical densities.

   (C) The solid-liquid equilibrium will always have a positive slope moving upward from the triple point.

   (D) The vapor pressure of the solid phase always equals the vapor pressure of the liquid phase.

   (E) The pressure is exactly one-half the critical pressure.

For questions 3–5, use the key below. Select the description that best describes the substance.

   (A) A network solid with covalent bonding

   (B) A molecular solid

   (C) An ionic solid

   (D) A metallic solid

3. Dry ice, solid carbon dioxide, CO_2

4. Diamond, solid C

5. Brass, a mixture of copper and zinc

6. The critical temperature of a substance is the

   (A) temperature at which the vapor pressure of the liquid equals normal atmospheric pressure.

   (B) highest temperature at which a substance can exist in the liquid state, regardless of pressure.

   (C) temperature at which boiling occurs at 1.0 atmosphere of pressure.

   (D) temperature and pressure where solid, liquid, and vapor phases are all in equilibrium.

   (E) Point at which pressure and temperature are less than 0.

7. When the liquid metal mercury, Hg, is placed in a small tube, the meniscus actually curves upward, just the opposite of water. The reason for this is that

(A) the cohesive force is greater than the adhesive force.

(B) the adhesive force is greater than the cohesive force.

(C) the density of mercury is much larger than water.

(D) the density of mercury is much greater where it is in contact with the glass.

(E) mercury is less volatile than water.

Questions 8–11 refer to the phase diagram shown below:

Figure 8.8

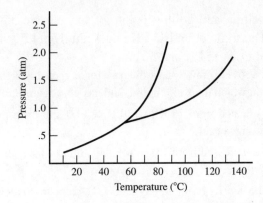

Figure 8.9

Use the key to answer questions 8–10

(A) Sublimation

(B) Condensation

(C) Solvation

(D) Fusion

(E) Freezing

8. If the temperature increases from 10 °C to 60 °C at a constant pressure of 0.5 atm, which process occurs?

9. If the temperature decreases from 100 °C to 60 °C at a constant pressure of 1.5 atm, which process occurs?

10. If the pressure increases from 0.5 atm to 1.5 atm at a constant temperature of 100 °C, which process occurs?

11. The normal boiling point of the substance is approximately

(A) 55 °C

(B) 65 °C

(C) 75 °C

(D) 85 °C

(E) 95 °C

12. Which of the following explains why, at room temperature, I_2 is a solid, Br_2 is a liquid, and Cl_2 is a gas?

    (A) Hydrogen bonding

    (B) Hybridization

    (C) Ionic bonding

    (D) Resonance

    (E) London dispersion forces

Free Response

Question 1

The normal melting and boiling points of oxygen are 55 K and 90 K, respectively. The triple point is 54 K and 1 mm Hg (1.5×10^{-3} atm). The critical point of O_2 is 154 K and 50 atm.

(A) Use the data above to draw a phase diagram for oxygen. Label the axes and label the regions in which the solid, liquid, and gas phases are stable.

(B) If oxygen is heated from 75 K to 130 K at 1.00 atm pressure, describe any changes that may occur.

(C) If pressure is increased from 1.00 atm to 40 atm at a constant temperature of 110 K, describe any changes that may occur.

(D) How does the density of liquid oxygen, $O_2(l)$, compare to the density of solid oxygen, $O_2(s)$? Explain your answer using both the data and your phase diagram.

Question 2

Give scientific explanations for each of the following items:

(A) Students working in a lab in a mountainous region of Nevada measure the boiling temperature of water as 93 °C, while students in San Diego, California, measure the boiling temperature of water as 100 °C. Both groups have accurate thermometers.

(B) Pioneers in the hot, dry, desert Southwest used to dampen their bed sheets at night to keep cooler while they slept.

(C) Graphite, C(s), is a very soft material used as a dry lubricant and in the production of pencil "leads." Diamond, also C(s), is an extremely hard material, often used in the production of industrial drill bits and saws.

ANSWERS

1. **The correct answer is (B).** In 1-propanol, the oxygen is bonded to a carbon and a hydrogen, whereas in ethyl methyl ether, the oxygen is bonded to two carbons. The more polar O-H bond allows for greater hydrogen bonding than the C-H bonds alone.

2. **The correct answer is (D).** Because the triple point represents the temperature and pressure at which solid, liquid, and gas all coexist, the vapor pressures will be identical at this point.

3. **The correct answer is (B).**

4. **The correct answer is (A).**

5. **The correct answer is (D).** Brass, being an alloy, is simply a mixture of the two metals. Because it is a mixture, the metals still retain their properties as metals.

6. **The correct answer is (B).**

7. **The correct answer is (A).** The cohesive forces between mercury atoms are much stronger than the adhesive forces of mercury and glass. This creates a strong surface tension in mercury as well as the upward bulge in the test tube. In water, the adhesive forces are greater, which causes the molecules on the edge of the test tube to cling to the glass while the rest hang down from the sides. This is why water curves in the opposite direction.

8. **The correct answer is (A).** Refer to line 8 in the diagram.

9. **The correct answer is (E).** Refer to line 9 in the diagram.

10. **The correct answer is (B).** Refer to line 10.

11. **The correct answer is (D).** Refer to dotted line 11. Note that this is the temperature at which liquid and vapor states are in equilibrium at 1 atm pressure.

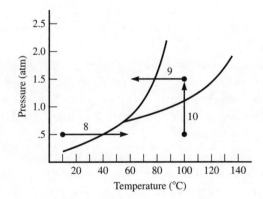

Figure 8.10

12. **The correct answer is (E).** These are nonpolar diatomic molecules. The only intermolecular force between them is London dispersion force. The largest molecule, I_2, will have the greatest forces, followed by Br_2 and I_2.

Free Response

Question 1

(A) See Figure 8.11.

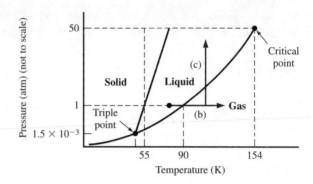

Figure 8.11

(B) Note line (b) in Figure 8.11. The liquid oxygen will vaporize to oxygen gas under these conditions.

(C) Note line (c) in Figure 8.11. The oxygen gas will condense to liquid oxygen.

(D) The density of liquid oxygen is lower than solid oxygen. You can tell this by the positive slope of the equilibrium line separating the solid and liquid states. Increasing pressure along this line leads to an increase in the melting temperature, indicating a more dense state with additional intermolecular attractions.

Question 2

(A) At higher elevations, atmospheric pressure is lower. As a result, the boiling point (which is the point at which the vapor pressure is at equilibrium with the atmospheric pressure) will also be lower. In San Diego, the city is essentially at sea level, where you would expect to find atmospheric pressures very close to 1.0 atmosphere.

(B) This process takes advantage of the cooling effects of evaporation. As the water evaporates from the sheet (which it is guaranteed to do, given the hot, dry climate), the average kinetic energy of the water molecules still in the sheet will decrease. This decrease in average kinetic energies is felt as a decrease in temperature, or a cooling.

(C) While both forms of carbon are network solids, the structure of graphite is large sheets of molecules that easily slide past one another. In diamonds, however, the carbon atoms bond both vertically and horizontally, allowing for much more rigid three-dimensional structures, some of the hardest known.

Solutions

In the last two chapters, you reviewed properties of solids, liquids, and gases. In this chapter, you will review the processes that occur when two different substances mix together to form a homogeneous mixture. Remember from your general chemistry class: homogeneous mixtures are uniform throughout, while heterogeneous mixtures have separate parts (or phases). An example of a homogeneous mixture is salt water. The salt and water are mixed together, but you can't distinguish the salt from the water. Homogeneous mixtures are also called solutions. An important characteristic of a solution (homogeneous mixture) is that you can separate it using ordinary means. The salt can be separated from the water by evaporating the water away. Heterogeneous mixtures have distinct parts, like a handful of iron filings mixed in with a handful of sugar. Like homogeneous mixtures, the materials have not reacted chemically—they just happen to be in the same place at the same time. The sugar and iron can easily be separated either with a magnet (attract the iron) or by throwing the mixture in water (dissolves the sugar).

There are two major divisions in a discussion of solutions: solution formation and solubility equilibria. The first topic deals with the mechanisms by which solutions form—different ways to describe solutions, factors that affect solution formation, and some of the physical properties of solutions. Those are the domain of this chapter. Solubility equilibria are discussed in Chapter 14, after you've had a chance to review the concept of equilibrium.

MEASURING CONCENTRATION

A solution is a mixture of two or more things that blend together in a uniform way. When this occurs, one material dissolves in the other. The material that is dissolving is known as the *solute*. The substance that it is dissolving in is called the *solvent*. There are a variety of ways to describe the amount of solute that is found in the solvent.

Popular Terminology

You may see concentration described in common terms out in the real world. For example, you might see a bottle of vinegar that says 5% on it. That means that out of 100% of the solution, 5% is actually vinegar (acetic acid). Other percentages are given by mass. The concentrated hydrochloric acid that you use in the lab is purchased in bottles that are 37% HCl. That means that for

ROAD MAP

- *Measuring Concentration*
- *Solvation*
- *Colligative Properties*

every 100 g of solution, 37 g are actually HCl. Still another popular description of solutions is parts per million (ppm). This is used to describe very dilute solutions, for example, the amount of available chloride ion found in a swimming pool of water. On the AP exam, you are unlikely to encounter these terms, but they help to give you a broader understanding of units of concentration.

Chemistry Terminology

The three typical ways to describe solutions in chemistry are the mole fraction, molarity, and molality. The term normality is occasionally used, but the College Board specifically states that it is not on the test, so we'll skip it. The **mole fraction** is the same mole fraction we discussed in chapter 9. The mole fraction of substance A is expressed as:

(Equation 9.1)

$$X_A = \frac{\text{moles A}}{\text{total moles}}$$

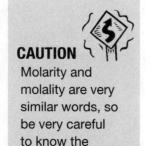

CAUTION

Molarity and molality are very similar words, so be very careful to know the difference.

Molarity describes the number of moles of solute per liter of solution. Many students get this last part mixed up. They think it means per liter of solvent. No! To clarify, we can consider an example of making a solution. If you wanted to make a 2.0 *M* solution of sodium hydroxide (NaOH), you would weigh out 2.0 moles (80.0 g) of solid sodium hydroxide and transfer it to a 1.00 liter volumetric flask. You would then add water until you had exactly 1.00 liters of solution. You don't add 1.00 liters of water! To calculate molarity, you simply divide the moles of solute by the liters of solution. For substance A, the molarity would be

(Equation 9.2)

$$M_A = \frac{\text{moles A}}{\text{liters of solution}}$$

Sample: Your lab partner has just made a solution for you to use in a lab but says she forgot the molarity. She remembers that she weighed out 83.0 g of KI and added enough distilled water to equal 500 ml of solution. What is the molarity of the KI?

Answer: First, remember that molarity is expressed in moles of solute per liter. You know that the mass is expressed in a gram value, so the first thing to do is convert that to moles. Once you've done that, you will be able to determine the molarity.

$$83.0 \text{ g KI} \times \frac{1 \text{ mol}}{166 \text{ g KI}} = 0.5 \text{ mol}$$

At this point, you are ready to substitute your information into the molarity equation:

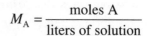

$$M_A = \frac{\text{moles A}}{\text{liters of solution}} = \frac{0.5 \text{ mol KI}}{0.5 \text{ liters of solution}} = 1.0 \, M \text{ KI}$$

Your lab partner has mixed a 1.0 *M* solution of KI.

You Try It!
You are supposed to mix 250 ml of a 0.1 M solution of $Pb(NO_3)_2$ solution (molar mass = 331.2 g). You would need to mix _____ g of $Pb(NO_3)_2$ with enough water to make 250 ml solution.

Answer: 8.28 g

Molality is a bit different. It is calculated as the moles of solute per kilogram of solvent. Two main differences here: first, you are measuring units of mass instead of units of volume, and second, you are using only the amount of solvent in the denominator. That's where the confusion usually comes from with molarity. With molarity, you are dividing the moles by the amount of *solution*, whereas in molality, you are dividing the moles by the amount of *solvent*. To calculate the molality of a solution where substance A is dissolved in some solvent, you would use the equation

$$m_A = \frac{\text{moles A}}{\text{kilograms of solvent}}$$

(Equation 9.3)

The AP formula sheet does not use the variable for molality because it would be the same as mass. Instead, the sheet writes the word "molality" in the equation.

For dilute aqueous solutions (solutions where water is the solvent), the molarity and molality are very similar. This is because 1.00 L of water has a mass of 1.00 kilogram (at 4 °C, anyway).

Because molality is only based on mass values, it does not vary with the temperature of the solution. Molarity, on the other hand, does vary slightly due to changes in the volume of a solution at different temperatures.

Sample: What is the molality of a solution that has 27.0 g of potassium chromate (K_2CrO_4, molar mass 194.2) dissolved in 110.0 g of water?

Answer: There is more than one way to solve this problem. There are certain steps in common with all of them, however. The first step we'll perform is to determine the number of moles in 27.0 g of K_2CrO_4:

$$27.0 \text{ g } K_2CrO_4 \times \frac{1 \text{ mol}}{194.2 \text{ g } K_2CrO_4} = 0.139 \text{ mol } K_2CrO_4$$

The molality requires us to know the moles of solute per kilogram of solvent. We will convert our information into moles per g of solvent, and then into kilograms.

$$\frac{0.139 \text{ mol } K_2CrO_4}{110 \text{ g } H_2O} \frac{1000 \text{ g}}{1 \text{ kilogram}} = 1.26 \text{ } m$$

Note: This final step could also have been calculated without the conversion factor by expressing the mass of water in kilograms:

$$\frac{0.139 \text{ mol } K_2CrO_4}{0.110 \text{ kg } H_2O} = 1.26 \text{ } m$$

NOTE
One important note about the AP exam formula sheet: on the formula sheet, the symbols for molar mass and molarity are nearly identical. The only difference is that the molar mass is a bold italic ***M***, while the molarity is just an italic *M*. Make sure you know your formulas well enough that you don't confuse the two.

You Try It!

A solution is prepared by dissolving 25.0 g of methanol (CH_3OH, molar mass 32.0 g) with 80 g of ethanol (C_2H_5OH, molar mass 46.1 g). What is the molality of the solution?

Answer: 9.77 m

SOLVATION

Solvation is the name of the process where a solute is dissolved by a solvent. An easy example to start with is the dissolving of a polar solute, like NaCl, in a polar solvent, H_2O. When the sodium chloride crystals are added to water, the polar water molecules are immediately attracted to the crystals. At the same time, the particles in the crystal are also attracted to the water, but the water molecules are free to move about while the sodium and chloride ions are bound to the rest of the crystal. The water molecules are attracted to the ions on the surfaces of the crystal. The oxygen atom in the water molecule, with its partial negative charge, is attracted to the positively charged sodium ions, while the hydrogen atoms, with their partial positive charges, are attracted to the negative chloride ions. If the attractions between water and the ions in the crystal are sufficient, the ions will be removed from the crystalline lattice and will move out into the liquid (i.e., be "dissolved").

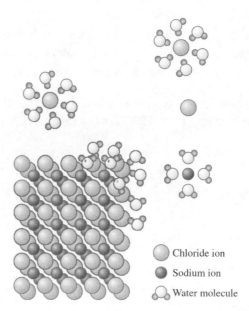

○ Chloride ion

● Sodium ion

◯ Water molecule

Figure 9.1

What happens next is very similar to the equilibrium you read about in the last chapter between the liquid and vapor in a closed container. When the salt is added to the water, the water has no salt dissolved in it. Within a short time, the water is filled with a number of sodium and chloride ions. To really understand what happens next, think of the following example: Picture yourself throwing a handful of salt into a small container of water. You can probably imagine that no matter what you do to the water, there will be a pile of salt in the bottom of the container. Not all of it will dissolve. (This is a lot like what happens when you try to make chocolate milk with too much chocolate and not enough milk. No matter what you do, there is always that big glob of chocolate on the bottom!) The large quantity of salt begins to dissolve into the water. However, as the sodium and chloride ions, surrounded by water molecules, move about in the solution, occasionally they will collide with the salt crystals. Sometimes they will bounce off, while other times they will get stuck to the crystal again. The greater number of sodium and chloride ions that are dissolved in the water, the greater the probability that some will collide with the salt crystal. So while the crystal is dissolving in the water, it is simultaneously being reformed.

The reason for using the example of the big pile of salt in the water is to make you aware of the equilibrium that occurs. You may be tempted to think that once the salt stops dissolving (i.e., when it just sits in the bottom of the container) all activity has stopped in the container. Don't think it! Remember the equilibrium system between water and water vapor? Remember that when that system looked like it was not doing anything, it was really in dynamic equilibrium? Remember that the vapor was forming at the same rate as the liquid? Well, the same thing is occurring here. The crystals are being dismantled at the same rate that they are being reconstructed. As a result, you don't see any changes taking place.

A solution that is in this state, where it has dissolved as much solute as it possibly can at a given temperature, is called a *saturated solution*. What if you only put a small pinch of salt into a large container of water? Do you think it would all dissolve? If you said yes, you're right. Do you think you could get a little more salt to dissolve in the large container of water? If you said yes, you'd be right again. Solutions that are not yet saturated, that is, solutions that can dissolve more solute, are known as *unsaturated solutions*. There is a third type of solution, known as a *supersaturated solution*. These solutions actually have more dissolved in them than they can hold at a given temperature. The way these solutions are typically made is to heat the solvent (which will allow you to dissolve more solute), saturate the solution, and then very carefully cool the solution. Most supersaturated solutions are very unstable. By dropping in a small seed crystal or by scratching the glass inside the container (which creates vibrations in the solution and tiny pieces of glass), you can usually get the solute to rapidly precipitate out of the solution.

You may have mixed some solutions before where, upon adding the solvent to the solute, the temperature began to increase. Sodium hydroxide releases a great deal of heat when dissolving. So do Epsom salts (magnesium sulfate). There are even some substances, such as ammonium nitrate, that get cold when dissolving. Where does this heat come from? It is known as the *heat of solution*, and there are three separate processes that determine how much heat will be generated and also whether the process will be exothermic or endothermic. At this point in the review, we have not yet discussed enthalpy, H. A more detailed description will occur in chapter 16. For our purposes in this chapter, you really only need to remember two things. First, enthalpy represents the heat associated with a process. (Later we will talk about the heats associated with chemical reactions, but at this point we're limiting the focus to heats of solution, $H_{solution}$, also abbreviated H_{soln}.) The second thing you need to remember is that an ***exothermic*** process, one that releases heat, has a negative enthalpy ($\Delta H_{soln} < 0$). An ***endothermic*** process is one that requires heat or takes it from the environment ($\Delta H_{soln} > 0$). The dissolving of sodium hydroxide is exothermic and ammonium nitrate is endothermic.

The heat of solution is determined by three separate enthalpies associated with solvation. The first is the energy associated with pulling the solute apart. The second is associated with pulling the solvent apart, so that it can accommodate the solute. The third is the heat associated with solute and solvent interactions. If these interactions are very favorable, then dissolving is likely to occur. If they are not, dissolving is not likely to occur. Returning to our salt water example, this process is likely to occur because there is such a strong attraction between the polar water molecules and the sodium and chloride ions. However, if you throw a handful of salt into a cup of cooking oil, very little is likely to happen. That's because the attraction between the solute and solvent is so much less than the attractions between the molecules in the oil and the sodium and chloride ions for each other. As a result, salt, a polar substance, won't dissolve in a nonpolar solvent.

Like Dissolves Like

Though there are some exceptions, in most cases the rule "like dissolves like" applies. That is, polar solvents (like water) can dissolve polar solutes (like salts), and nonpolar solvents (like gasoline) can dissolve nonpolar solutes (like grease). These solvent-solute interactions have other effects on the properties of solutions that are the topic of the upcoming section on colligative properties.

The Effects of Temperature and Pressure on Solubility

In the previous section, you read about saturated, unsaturated, and super-saturated solutions. These terms are all related to the amount of solute that is dissolved into a solvent. However, you probably also know that the temperature of a solvent affects the amount of solute that can dissolve in it. The degree to which the temperature affects dissolving is something specific to each substance, but for most solid solutes, an increase in temperature will lead to an increase in solubility. There are some substances that actually decrease in solubility with increased temperature, but these are the exception rather than the rule.

The effect of temperature is opposite for gases dissolved in water. Gases become less soluble at higher temperatures. One of the main reasons that carbonated soft drinks are usually served with ice (even when they are already cold), is to keep them cold longer. This not only makes for a more refreshing drink, it maintains higher levels of dissolved CO_2 in the beverage.

Many people who try to get more drink for their money by ordering a soft drink without ice often find out that they have a warm, flat, syrupy mess by the time they get near the bottom of the cup.

Pressure only affects solutions of gases dissolved in liquid solvents. If you have ever watched a glass of soda, you probably saw the bubbles floating to the top of the liquid. These were bubbles of dissolved carbon dioxide coming out of the solution. Because the glass is open, the carbon dioxide that bubbles out of the liquid will move into the surrounding air. Over time, nearly all of the CO_2 will be gone. However, you know that a can of soda can sit on the shelf for a very long time and still remain carbonated. The reason is the container is closed. While that's probably obvious to you, what is going on inside the can may not be.

The process inside a sealed container of a liquid-gas solution is very similar to the process of equilibrium between the liquid and vapor states that we discussed in Chapter 8. The gas that is dissolved in the liquid begins to come out of solution and enter the air space above the liquid. Over time, more and more particles begin to enter this space. However, as time progresses, gas molecules will reenter the solution. The system will come to equilibrium, at which point the rate at which gas particles are leaving solution will be the same as the rate at which particles are returning to solution. If the pressure above the liquid was suddenly increased, the molecules above the surface would exert more force and therefore return to solution more quickly. The rate of dissolving would increase while the rate of gas formation would decrease until a new equilibrium was reached. Usually, carbonated beverages are bottled at slightly higher pressures than standard atmospheric pressure. The hiss you hear when you open the bottle or can is the high pressure air rushing out of the container, coming to equilibrium with the atmospheric pressure.

COLLIGATIVE PROPERTIES

In Chapter 8, you reviewed heating and cooling curves in addition to phase diagrams. You also looked at factors that affect the boiling temperatures of different substances. Those substances in Chapter 8 were all pure substances. In this section, we'll look at how the behaviors of solutions differ from those of a single substance. These properties that are affected by the presence (and amount) of a solute are known as colligative properties. The five colligative properties are vapor-pressure reduction, boiling point elevation, freezing-point depression, vapor-pressure reduction, and osmotic pressure.

Vapor-Pressure Reduction

When a nonvolatile solute is added to a solvent, the vapor pressure of the resulting solution will be lower than the vapor pressure of the pure solvent. Why does this occur? To answer this, you have to remember back to our discussion of the equilibrium between vapor and liquid in a closed system. If you recall, equilibrium is reached when the rate that particles are escaping the liquid is equal to the rate that the particles are returning to the liquid. Also recall that these transitions take place on the surface of the liquid. Now, suppose you add a nonvolatile solute to the solvent. (The AP curriculum specifies that only the effects of nonvolatile solutes are required.) Because the solute is nonvolatile, it will not enter the gaseous phase above the liquid. What this means is that at the surface of the liquid, where particles of the solvent can escape, there are now some particles of the solute mixed in with the solvent. As a result, the number of solvent molecules that are able to escape will be less than the number that could have escaped in the pure solvent (they are blocked by the solute particles). The addition of a nonvolatile solute decreases the ability of solvent molecules to form vapors. This means that not as much vapor can form, which also means that there will be fewer gaseous molecules returning to the liquid state. Thus, the vapor pressure is reduced.

One of the first to investigate the mathematical relationship between the vapor pressure reduction and the amount of solute was François Raoult. The mathematical relationship he determined is known as ***Raoult's law***. What the law states is that the partial pressure of the solvent over a solution equals the vapor pressure of the pure solvent times the mole fraction of solvent in the solution. As an equation, this becomes

(Equation 9.4)

$$P_A = P°_A X_A$$

where $P°_A$ is the vapor pressure of pure solvent and X_A the mole fraction of the solvent. Put very simply, if the mole fraction is equivalent to 99% of the pure solvent concentration, the new vapor pressure will be 99% what it was before the solute was added. Note, the decrease of 1% would also equal the mole fraction of the solute. Thus, the decrease in vapor pressure would be 1%.

Sample: A solution of sugar water is made by dissolving 200.0 g of sucrose, $C_{12}H_{22}O_{11}$ (molar mass 342.3 g), in 710.0 g of pure water at 25 °C. The vapor pressure of water at 25 °C is 23.76 mm Hg. Calculate the vapor pressure of the sugar water, assuming all of the sucrose dissolves in the water.

Answer: We're going to use Raoult's law to solve the problem, but we need to determine the mole fraction of water first. Therefore, we need to determine the number of moles of sucrose present in the solution, and then the number of moles of water present.

For the number of moles of sucrose

$$\text{Moles sucrose} = 200.0 \text{ g sucrose} \times \frac{1 \text{ mol sucrose}}{342.3 \text{ g sucrose}} = 0.5843 \text{ mol sucrose}$$

$$\text{Moles water} = 710.0 \text{ g water} \times \frac{1 \text{ mol water}}{18.01 \text{ g water}} = 39.42 \text{ mol water}$$

The mole fraction of water

$$X_{H_2O} = \frac{mol\ H_2O}{mol\ H_2O\ +\ mol\ sucrose}$$

$$= \frac{39.42\ mol\ H_2O}{39.42\ mol\ H_2O\ +\ 0.5843\ mol\ sucrose} = 0.9854$$

Now that we have this number, we can use the Raoult's law:

$$P_{H_2O} = P°_{H_2O}X_{H_2O} = (23.76\ mm\ Hg)(0.9854) = 23.41\ mm\ Hg$$

The vapor pressure has been lowered 0.35 mm Hg by the addition of sucrose.

You Try It!
Glucose, $C_6H_{12}O_6$, is commonly mixed with water to make intravenous feeding solutions. What would be the vapor pressure of a solution where 60.0 g of glucose (molar mass 180.16 g) is dissolved in 700.0 g H_2O at 22°C? The vapor pressure of pure water at 22°C is 19.83 mm Hg.

Answer: 19.66 mm Hg

Ideal Solutions

Like gases, solutions can also be thought of as ideal. Raoult's law only works for ideal solutions. Ideal solutions are described as those solutions that follow Raoult's law. Solutions that deviate from Raoult's law are nonideal. What makes a solution deviate from ideal behavior? The main reason is intermolecular attractions between solute and solvent. When the attraction between solute and solvent is very strong, the particles attract each other a great deal. This makes it more difficult for solute particles to enter the vapor phase. As a result, fewer particles will enter that state and the vapor pressure will be lower than expected. Remember, Raoult's law operates on the assumption that the reason for a decrease in the number of particles leaving the solution is that fewer can be on the surface in order to leave. If, in addition to this, the solute particles are also holding more tightly to the solvent particles, then fewer will leave the surface than expected. The most ideal solutions are those where the solvent and solute are chemically similar.

If the attraction between the solute and solvent is less than the attraction between solvent particles or between solute particles, then more particles will be able to leave the liquid and the vapor pressure will be higher than predicted. You should definitely keep these two conditions in mind as we go into the next section.

Boiling Point Elevation

If you remember, the boiling point for a substance is the point where the vapor pressure of the liquid equals the external pressure above the liquid. Changing the external pressure changes the boiling temperature, as we saw in examples of different boiling temperatures at different altitudes. Now you have just learned that adding a nonvolatile solute to a solvent decreases the vapor pressure of the solution. That means that if you are going to try to boil a *solution*, you will have to heat it to a greater temperature than you would a pure solvent. To increase the amount of particles leaving the solution to a level equal to that of the pure solvent, you have to add more heat to the solution. In other words, the liquid won't boil until you've added that extra heat (i.e., raised its temperature).

From the conceptual level, that's why the boiling temperature increases when you add a solute to a solvent. That's why you pour antifreeze into a car radiator (it allows the temperatures of the water to increase past the normal boiling temperature). From a mathematical level, however, there is another consideration you must make. When you are solving problems about boiling point elevation, you need to know how much the temperature is going to increase and what it is going to be after a certain amount or type of solute is added. For this, it is important to consider the nature of the solute.

Electrolytic Solutes

If you throw a scoop of table sugar into water and heat it, will it have the same effect as a scoop of table salt? Not quite. The reason is that when sugar is dissolved, the crystals break apart into individual sucrose molecules. When salt dissolves, because it is an ionic solute (also known as an ***electrolyte***), it does something a little different. It breaks into two types of particles, sodium ions and chloride ions, which means that there will be twice as many particles released into the solution as with sugar. A salt like magnesium chloride, $MgCl_2$, will release three particles, one magnesium ion and two chloride ions. When you calculate the boiling point elevation, you must take the nature of the solute into account. The way you do this is with the ***van't Hoff factor*** (i). For your purposes you can assume that the van't Hoff factor is equal to the number of ions that are produced from each unit of solute dissolved. For sucrose, i is 1; for sodium chloride, i is 2; and for magnesium chloride, i is 3. This is an oversimplification of the van't Hoff factor, but this explanation is more than sufficient for the AP exam. The equation for calculating the boiling point elevation, ΔT_b, for a solution, which is given to you on the AP exam, is

(Equation 9.5)
$$\Delta T_b = iK_b m$$

where i is the van't Hoff factor, K_b is the boiling point elevation constant, and m is the molality (*not* the mass; on the AP exam, the equation is written with the word *molality*, instead of m). K_b is specific to the solvent and is expressed in various units. The problems in this book and others use °C m^{-1} as units for K_b. The AP formula sheet uses K kg mol^{-1}. However, because a change of 1 degree Celsius is identical to a change of 1 kelvin and the units for molality are mol kg^{-1}, you should see that the units are really identical to one another. This applies to K_f, the freezing-point depression constant, as well.

Sample: A cook adds 50.0 g of salt (NaCl, molar mass 58.4 g) into a pot containing 1.00 kg of water. She then brings it to a boil. What will be the temperature of the boiling salted water (assuming that pure water boils at 100°)? K_b for water is 0.512 °C m^{-1}.

Answer: You will use the boiling-point elevation formula to solve this. Because sodium chloride is an electrolyte, it will be necessary to use the van't Hoff factor in this problem. Each NaCl dissociates into one Na^+ ion and one Cl^- ion. Therefore the van't Hoff factor will be 2.

Before we can substitute the data into the equation, we also need to know the molality of the solution. To calculate the molality, we need to determine the number of moles of salt per kilogram of water. The first step will be to calculate the number of moles of salt.

$$\text{Moles NaCl} = 50.0 \text{ g NaCl} \times \frac{1 \text{ mol NaCl}}{58.4 \text{ g NaCl}} = 0.856 \text{ mol NaCl}$$

Now, you're ready to determine the molality

$$\text{Molality} = \frac{\text{moles NaCl}}{\text{kg H}_2\text{O}} = \frac{0.856 \text{ mol NaCl}}{1.000 \text{ kg H}_2\text{O}} = 0.856 \, m$$

Now that the molality is known, you can determine the boiling point elevation

$$\Delta T_b = iK_b m = (2)(0.512 \text{ °C } m^{-1})(0.856 \, m) = 0.877 \text{ °C}$$

Therefore, the new boiling point will be 100 °C + 0.877 °C = 100.877, or 100.9 °C.

You Try It!

A solution is made by mixing 255 g of strontium nitrate ($Sr(NO_3)_2$, molar mass 211.6 g) in 1.00 kg of water. If the boiling point of pure water is assumed to be 100.0 °C, calculate the predicted boiling point of the strontium nitrate solution. K_b for water is 0.512 °C m^{-1}.

Answer: 101.9 °C (Remember, the van't Hoff factor will be 3.)

Freezing-Point Depression

In addition to raising the boiling temperature of a solution, the presence of a solute will cause a decrease in the freezing temperature of a solution. The decrease in freezing temperature, known as the freezing-point depression, ΔT_f, is best explained using a phase diagram, like those you reviewed in lesson 10. If you refer to Figure 9.2, note how the addition of a nonvolatile solute shifts the position of the curve separating the liquid and gas states.

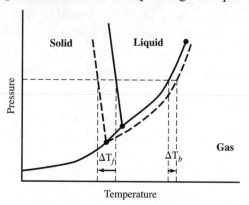

Figure 9.2

This represents the vapor-pressure reduction that you already read about. If you trace it down to lower temperatures, however, you will notice that it now meets the line separating the solid and gas states at a lower position. Keep in mind that above the line (represented by the dotted line in the figure), this still represents the equilibrium between gas and liquid. Note that the triple point has also changed. The new freezing/melting point for the substance must shift to the left and begin at the point where the new dotted vapor pressure line crosses. As a result, the freezing temperatures for the substance change. Just as the presence of dissolved solute particles disrupted the vaporization process, they also disrupt the freezing process. The added particles inhibit the solvent's ability to crystallize and therefore shift the freezing temperature. Like the boiling-point elevation, freezing-point depression is also affected by the number of solute particles released during solvation. As a result, the formula for the freezing-point depression will also have to include the van't Hoff factor. The equation is written as

(Equation 9.6) $$\Delta T_f = iK_f m$$

where i is the van't Hoff factor, K_f is the freezing-point depression constant, and m is the molality. K_f varies with the solvent.

Sample: A "cool dip" (cold pool that is next to a hot tub) can be made by dissolving large amounts of salt in water and then chilling it. The resulting solution can be cooled below 0 °C, the normal freezing temperature of water. If a salt water solution was made with 300 g of salt (NaCl, molar mass 58.4 g) dissolved in 1.00 kg of water, how cold could the salt water get before freezing? K_f for water is 1.86 °C m^{-1}.

Answer: Once again, the solute is an electrolyte, so the van't Hoff factor must be used. Since NaCl will dissociate into one Na^+ and one Cl^- ion, the value of i is 2.

The next step is to determine the molality of the solution. To do this, we need to divide the moles of NaCl by the kilograms of solvent. First, however, we must know the number of moles of NaCl. This can be calculated by

$$\text{Moles NaCl} = 300 \text{ g NaCl} \times \frac{1 \text{ mol NaCl}}{58.4 \text{ g NaCl}} = 5.14 \text{ mol NaCl}$$

The molality, therefore, will be

$$\text{molality NaCl} = \frac{5.14 \text{ mol NaCl}}{1.00 \text{ kg H}_2\text{O}} = 5.14 \, m$$

The last step is to calculate the freezing point depression,

$$\Delta T_f = iK_f m = (2)(1.86 \text{ °C } m^{-1})(5.14) = 19.1 \text{ °C}$$

The lowest the temperature can get, therefore, is $0 \text{ °C} - 19.1 \text{ °C} = -19.1 \text{ °C}$

You Try It!

A solution is made by dissolving 250.0 g of potassium chromate crystals (K_2CrO_4 molar mass 194.2 g) in 1.00 kg of water. What will the freezing point of the new solution be? K_f for water is 1.86 °C m^{-1}.

Answer: −7.18 °C

Osmotic Pressure

You may remember learning about osmosis in a biology class. The term describes the movement of water across semi-permeable membranes. Semi-permeable membranes allow certain sizes, or types, of particles to pass through, but not others. In chemistry, the term can refer to any solvent; however, most applications of the concept that are relevant to you involve water. The movement of water across the membrane helps to restore equilibrium to the system. In a system where two concentrations of a solution are separated by a semi-permeable membrane, water can flow back and forth through the membrane. Water, on the side of the membrane with the lower solute concentration, passes through the membrane to the side with the higher solute concentration. Likewise, water can pass from the side with higher solute concentration to the side with lower solute concentration. However, the presence of additional solute particles on the side with higher concentration reduces the amount of solute particles that are able to pass through the membrane to the side with lower concentration (much like the solute particles preventing the escape of solvent from the liquid to vapor phase). This creates a net flow of solvent into the area of highest solute concentration. However, the net flow of water also creates an increase in pressure on the side of the membrane with higher concentration of solute.

The cause of this increase in pressure can vary depending on the system. If the system is an open container with a membrane separating the sides, the flow of water to one side will increase the volume on that side. That will cause the water to rise to a higher level. The mass of solution pushing down (due to gravity) provides the pressure in this case. If the system consists of the solutions on the inside and outside of a living cell, the membrane of the swelling cell will exert a pressure. The origin of the pressure makes no difference to us. The important thing is that the increased pressure increases the flow of water back into the area of lower concentration. Thus, the pressure will continue to increase until equilibrium is established. The amount of pressure that is required to just establish equilibrium, or to stop the net flow of water, is known as ***osmotic pressure***, π. Osmotic pressure can be calculated using an equation that is very similar to the ideal gas law equation. The equation, also provided for you on the AP exam, is

(Equation 9.7)

$$\pi = \frac{nRT}{V} i$$

where R is the ideal gas constant and T is the absolute temperature. The equation is often simplified so that the n/V is converted to the molarity, M. Rewritten, it appears as

(Equation 9.8)

$$\pi = MRTi$$

Sample: A solution is made by placing 220.0 g of glucose ($C_6H_{12}O_6$, molar mass = 180.16 g) in a volumetric flask and adding distilled water to equal 1.00 L of solution. Calculate the osmotic pressure at 25 °C. Glucose is a nonelectrolyte.

Answer: Because you are given a mass of glucose and a volume of solution, you can determine the molarity of the solution, which allows us to use Equation 11.8. In order to determine the molarity of the solution, you will need to determine the number of moles of glucose in the solution.

$$220.0 \text{ g glucose} \times \frac{1 \text{ mol glucose}}{180.16 \text{ g glucose}} = 1.221 \text{ mol glucose}$$

From this, you can determine the molarity of the solution

$$\text{Molarity} = \frac{\text{moles solute}}{\text{liters of solution}} = \frac{1.221 \text{ mol glucose}}{1.00 \text{ L solution}} = 1.221 \text{ mol L}^{-1}$$

$$\pi = MRTi = (1.221 \text{ mol L}^{-1})(0.0821 \text{ L atm mol}^{-1} \text{ K}^{-1})(298 \text{ K})(1) = 29.9 \text{ atm}$$

You Try It!
If you were to add 50.0 g of sodium chloride, an electrolyte (NaCl, molar mass 58.44 g), to enough water to make 1.00 L of solution, what would be the osmotic pressure of the solution at 22 °C?

Answer: 41.4 atm

NOTE
The units for molarity have been left as mol L^{-1} so you can see how the units of R, the ideal gas constant, will cancel them.

Because glucose is a non-electrolyte, the van't Hoff factor is 1.

Applications of Colligative Properties

One of the laboratory requirements for the course, and also the topic of former test questions, is the determination of the molar mass of a substance from the freezing-point depression. Actually, any of the colligative properties can be used to determine the molar mass, but the only one that you are required to know is the freezing-point depression method. It is easier to illustrate the technique within the framework of a problem, so the discussion of this process will be done within a sample problem.

Sample: 100 grams of an unknown substance was dissolved in 900 g of water. The freezing temperature of the solution was determined to be $-3.76\ °C$. What is the molar mass of the unknown substance? Assume that $K_f = 1.86\ °C\ kg\ mol^{-1}$.

Answer: First of all, the value of K_f (or K_b for that matter) will be given to you. The values for water are included on the AP equation sheet. Second, you need to set up your equation.

Beginning with the formula for calculating the freezing point depression

$$\Delta T_f = iK_f m$$

you must determine what you have been given and what you need to use to solve the problem. Because a formula is not present, nor is the van't Hoff factor, you have to assume that it is not needed. Because of this, you will drop it from the equation. The equation now becomes

$$\Delta T_f = K_f m$$

We have been given K_f and ΔT_f. If you substitute the given information right now, you will know the molality of the solution. You'll be halfway there at that point.

$$\frac{\Delta T_f}{K_f} = m = \frac{3.76\ °C}{1.86\ °C\ kg\ mol^{-1}} = 2.02\ mol\ kg^{-1}$$

This tells us that there are 2.02 moles of the unknown substance dissolved in each kg of water. The problem is that the substance isn't dissolved in 1 kg of water. It's dissolved in 900 g. In the next step, you need to figure out how many moles are dissolved in the 900 g of water. This is accomplished by simply multiplying the values together (using common units, however).

$$2.02\ mol\ kg^{-1} \times 0.900\ kg = 1.82\ mol$$

At this point, you now know that 100 g of the substance is equal to 1.82 mol, so you can easily calculate the molar mass of the solute as follows:

$$n = \frac{m}{M}; M = \frac{m}{n} = \frac{100\ g}{1.82\ mol} = 54.9\ g\ mol^{-1}$$

You Try It!

1.00 g of a nonelectrolyte is dissolved in 100.0 g of pure water. What is the molar mass of the solute if the freezing point of the solution is $-0.103\ °C$? K_f for H_2O is $1.86\ °C\ m-1$.

Answer: 181 g

Summary: Solutions

- Solutions are homogeneous mixtures.

- Solutions are usually measured in different concentration units. The two most common are molarity, moles of solute per liter of solution, and molality, moles of solute per kilogram of solvent.

- The process of dissolving, solvation, occurs when the attractive forces between solvent and solute exceed the attractive forces between solvent and solvent or solute and solute.

- In the process of dissolving, there is a maximum amount of solute that can be dissolved in a solvent at any given temperature. When this maximum is reached, the rate of dissolving is at equilibrium with the rate of crystallization. At this point, the solution is saturated. No additional solute will dissolve (actually dissolving still occurs, but since it is in equilibrium with crystallization, there is no net change in the amount of solute).

- A solution that has less than the amount of solute required to reach equilibrium is unsaturated, and a solution with excess solute is supersaturated. Neither of these conditions is at equilibrium.

- Many times, the dissolving process generates heat, which is to say it is exothermic. Occasionally solution formation is endothermic.

- Increases in temperature are usually associated with increased solubility of solid solutes and decreased solubility of gaseous solutes. Decreases in temperature are associated with decreased solubility of solid solutes and increased solubility of gaseous solutes.

- Increases in pressure increase the solubility of gaseous solutes, but have little effect on solid solutes. Similarly, decreases in pressure decrease the solubility of gases in liquids and have little effect on solid solutes.

- There are four main colligative properties, or properties of a solvent that are affected by the presence of a solute: vapor-pressure reduction, boiling-point elevation, freezing-point depression, and osmotic pressure.

- In general, the addition of solute to a solvent decreases the vapor pressure, increases the boiling point, decreases the freezing point, and increases the osmotic pressure of the solvent.

- In Raoult's law, solutions are believed to be ideal. That is, the vapor pressure of a solvent is directly proportional to the mole fraction of solute.

- In solutions where the solute-solute interactions, or solvent-solvent interactions, affect the vapor pressure, Raoult's law is not observed and the solutions cannot be classified as ideal.

- Solutions where the solvent and solute are chemically similar are the most ideal solutions.

REVIEW QUESTIONS

1. An aqueous solution of potassium iodide, KI, is heated from 25 °C to 85 °C. During the time period while the solution is being heated, which of the following is true?

   (A) The mole fraction of solute decreases.

   (B) The mole fraction of solvent increases.

   (C) The density of the solution is constant.

   (D) The molarity of the solution is constant.

   (E) The molality of the solution is constant.

2. If you were trying to increase the amount of dissolved carbon dioxide gas, $CO_2(g)$, in water, which set of conditions would allow you the highest levels of dissolved CO_2?

	Pressure of $CO_2(g)$ above $H_2O(l)$ (atm)	Temperature of $H_2O(l)$(°C)
(A)	10.0	90
(B)	10.0	10
(C)	5.0	90
(D)	5.0	10
(E)	1.0	10

3. Which of the following pairs of liquids forms the most ideal solution (the solution that most closely follows Raoult's law)?

   (A) $C_6H_{14}(l)$ and $H_2O(l)$

   (B) $CH_3CH_2CH_2OH(l)$ and $H_2O(l)$

   (C) $CH_3CH_2OH(l)$ and $C_6H_{14}(l)$

   (D) $C_6H_6(l)$ and $C_6H_5CH_3(l)$

   (E) $H_3PO_4(l)$ and $H_2O(l)$

4. Which of the following solutions has the lowest freezing point?

   (A) 0.50 m $C_{12}H_{22}O_{11}$

   (B) 0.50 m KNO_3

   (C) 0.50 m $MgSO_4$

   (D) 0.50 m Na_3PO_4

   (E) 0.50 m K_2CrO_4

5. 100.0 milliliters of a 4.00 molar solution of KBr (molar mass 119.0 g) would contain _____ of KBr.

   (A) 2.98 g

   (B) 4.76 g

   (C) 47.6 g

   (D) 476 g

   (E) 500 g

6. An aqueous solution of silver nitrate ($AgNO_3$, molar mass 169.9 g) is prepared by adding 200.0 g $AgNO_3$ to 1,000 g H_2O. If K_f for H_2O is 1.86 °C m^{-1}, the freezing point of the solution should be

   (A) 0.00 °C

   (B) – 0.219 °C

   (C) – 0.438 °C

   (D) – 2.19 °C

   (E) – 4.38 °C

7. A solution of glucose (molecular weight 180.16) in water (molecular weight 18.01) is prepared. The mole fraction of glucose in the solution is 0.100. What is the molality of the solution?

   (A) 0.100 m

   (B) 0.162 m

   (C) 3.09 m

   (D) 6.17 m

   (E) 10.0 m

8. Your teacher has asked you to prepare 1.00 liter of a 0.100-molar aqueous solution of sodium hydroxide (molar mass 40.0 g). You should weigh out

   (A) 4.00 g NaOH and add 1.00 liter of distilled H_2O.

   (B) 2.50 g NaOH and add 1.00 liter of distilled H_2O.

   (C) 4.00 g NaOH and add 1.00 kilogram of distilled H_2O.

   (D) 4.00 g NaOH and add distilled H_2O until the solution has a volume of 1.00 liters.

   (E) 2.50 g NaOH and add distilled H_2O until the solution has a volume of 1.00 liters.

9. Which of the following aqueous solutions has the highest boiling point?

   (A) 0.10 M sodium fluoride, NaF

   (B) 0.10 M nitric acid, HNO_3

   (C) 0.10 M ammonium hydroxide, NH_4OH

   (D) 0.10 M magnesium chloride, $MgCl_2$

   (E) 0.20 M glucose, $C_6H_{12}O_6$

10. The vapor pressure of water at 50 °C is 92.5 mm Hg. If 400.0 g of sucrose ($C_{12}H_{22}O_{11}$ molar mass 342.3 g) is added to 900.0 g of H_2O at 50 °C, what will the vapor pressure of the solution be?

    (A) 94.6 mm Hg

    (B) 92.3 mm Hg

    (C) 90.4 mm Hg

    (D) 88.3 mm Hg

    (E) 27.4 mm Hg

11. How much pure water (H_2O molar mass 18.01 g) would 81.1 g of iron (III) chloride ($FeCl_3$, molar mass 162.2) be dissolved in to make a solution with a molality of 1.5 *m*?

    (A) 333 kg

    (B) 333 g

    (C) 3.33 kg

    (D) 666 g

    (E) 500 ml

12. What is the osmotic pressure of a 0.100 molar saline solution (NaCl dissolved in H_2O) at 27 °C?

    (A) 0.22 atm

    (B) 0.44 atm

    (C) 2.5 atm

    (D) 4.9 atm

    (E) 9.8 atm

Free Response

Question 1

A 0.562 g sample of an unknown substance was dissolved in 17.4 g benzene. The freezing point of the solution was 4.075 °C. The freezing point of pure benzene is 5.455 °C. For benzene, $K_f = 5.065$ °C m^{-1}, and $K_b = 2.61$°C m^{-1}. Assume that the solute is a nonelectrolyte.

    (A) What is the molality of the solution?

    (B) What is the molar mass of the unknown?

    (C) If the boiling temperature of pure benzene is 80.2 °C, what is the boiling temperature of the solution?

    (D) What is the van't Hoff factor? Explain whether the use of one was necessary in these calculations.

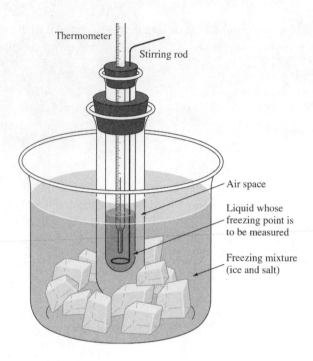

Thermometer

Stirring rod

Air space

Liquid whose freezing point is to be measured

Freezing mixture (ice and salt)

Question 2

A high school student was going to determine the molar mass of an unknown compound using the freezing-point depression technique. A sample of solvent was first chilled to its freezing temperature in a small test tube that was placed within a second test tube as shown in the diagram. Following the initial trial, a carefully measured amount of water was added to the test tube and the tube and its contents weighed. A small amount of solute was weighed and added to the test tube containing the water. The freezing temperature was measured again in the same way as the initial trial with the pure water. Assume that:

- the solute was a nonelectrolyte.
- the temperature of the liquid in the small test tube was uniform throughout.
- a graduated cylinder and an analytical balance are available.

(A) Write the equation(s) needed to calculate the molar mass of the solute.

(B) List the measurements that must be made in order to calculate the molar mass of the solute.

(C) Explain the purpose of placing the test tube containing the liquids inside the larger test tube.

(D) The student determines the molar mass of the solute to be 170 g mol^{-1}. Show the set-up you would use to calculate the percent error for the experiment if the mass of the unknown was actually 180 g mol^{-1} (it is not necessary for you to perform the calculation).

(E) If the student had used the molarity rather than the molality in the determination of the molar mass, how would this have affected his results.

ANSWERS

1. **The correct answer is (E).** The molality, because it is only dependent on the mass of the solute and solvent, does not change as temperature changes. Volume does vary with temperature, which is why choices (C) and (D) are not appropriate. Mole fractions are unaffected by volume changes, but they do remain constant during heating (unless vaporization accompanies the heating).

2. **The correct answer is (B).** Gases are most soluble in liquids at lower temperatures and when higher partial pressures of the gas are present above the liquid. Choice (B) represents the conditions of highest pressure and lowest temperature.

3. **The correct answer is (D).** The two liquids shown in D represent the most chemically similar elements listed. The others in the list will experience more intermolecular forces.

4. **The correct answer is (D).** While at first glance all of the solutions may look similar, on closer inspection there are important differences. With the exception of sucrose, the other solutes are electrolytes. This means they will separate into ions when they dissolve. The van't Hoff factor must be considered when determining freezing points. Sodium phosphate, Na_3PO_4 will separate into 4 ions, $3\,Na^+$ and $1\,PO_4^{-3}$. That will create more solute particles in the solution than any of the others, which will lower the freezing point.

5. **The correct answer is (C).** A 4.00 molar solution of KBr would contain 4 moles of KBr per liter. This is the equivalent of $4\text{ mol} \times 119\text{ g/mol} = 476$ g of KBr. Because we are only going to obtain 100.0 milliliters of the solution (1/10 of a liter), the amount of KBr will be 1/10 the amount. Hence, $0.10\text{ L} \times 476\text{ g/L} = 47.6$ g.

6. **The correct answer is (E).** 200 g $AgNO_3$/169.9 g/mol = 1.177 mol $AgNO_3$; 1.177 mol $AgNO_3$/1.00 kg H_2O = 1.1777 m; $\Delta T_f = iK_f m = (2)(1.86\text{ °C }m^{-1})$ $(1.177\ m) = -4.38$ °C. The van't Hoff factor of 2 was needed because of the dissociation of $AgNO_3$ into one Ag^+ ion and one NO_3^- ion.

7. **The correct answer is (D).** If the mole fraction of glucose is 0.100, that means that the mole fraction of water must be $1.00 - 0.100 = 0.900$. Knowing this, you can determine the mass of the solvent, and from that the molality. 0.900 mol $H_2O \times 18.01$ g mol^{-1} = 16.209 g H_2O. molality = mol glucose / kg H_2O = 0.100 mol / 0.016209 kg H_2O = 6.17 m.

8. **The correct answer is (D).** It's very important that you remember the definition of molarity: molarity is the number of moles of solute per liter of solution. That means that the contents of the solute and solvent must equal 1.00 liter. In this problem, the solution is to be 0.100–molar, which means that there are 0.100 moles of solute per 1.00 liter. $0.100\text{ mol} \times 40.0$ g mol^{-1} = 4.00 g.

9. **The correct answer is (D).** The solute that produces the most particles in solution will produce the solution with the highest boiling point. (E) is a tempting choice because the concentration is twice that of any other. Glucose, however, is not an electrolyte. (A), (B), and (C) will all have van't Hoff factors of 2, while $MgCl_2$ has a van't Hoff factor of 3, which will produce the greatest boiling point elevation.

10. **The correct answer is (C).** This is a vapor-pressure reduction problem. The first step is to determine the mole fraction of water in the solution. This will then be used to determine the vapor pressure of the solution. 400 g sucrose × 1 mol/342.3 g = 1.169 mol sucrose; 900 g H_2O × 1 mol/18.01 g = 49.972 mol H_2O; mole fraction = mol H_2O / mol sucrose + mol H_2O = 49.972 mol/(1.169 mol + 49.972 mol) = 0.9771; $P_A = P_{H_2O}X_A$ = (92.5 mm Hg)(0.9771) = 90.4 mm Hg.

11. **The correct answer is (B).** Molality is moles of solute per kilogram of solvent. Therefore, you first need to calculate the number of moles of $FeCl_3$ that are in 81.1 g. After a quick eyeballing you might notice that 81.1 is half of 162.2, which means that you have 0.5 moles of $FeCl_3$. With this information, you can use the molality equation to calculate the answer: molality = moles $FeCl_3$/kg H_2O; 1.5 m = 0.5 mol $FeCl_3$/X kg H_2O; × kg H_2O = 0.5 mol $FeCl_3$/1.5 m; X = 0.333 kg H_2O, or 333 g.

12. **The correct answer is (D).** You need to use the van't Hoff factor in this because NaCl is an electrolyte. Therefore, you will use $\pi = MRTi$ = (0.100 mol L^{-1})(0.0821 L atm mol^{-1} K^{-1})(300 K)(2) = 4.9 atm.

Free Response

Question 1

(A) 0.272 m. The molality is calculated as the number of moles of unknown per kilogram of benzene. Because the number of moles of the unknown substance is not known, the molality will be calculated from the freezing-point depression of the solution. This is done using the equation $\Delta T_f = K_f m$. Because the solution is a nonelectrolyte, the van't Hoff factor is unnecessary. This expression can be rearranged to yield $\Delta T_f = K_f = m$. Molality is determined to be (5.455 °C – 4.075°C) / 5.065 °C m^{-1} = 0.272 m.

(B) 119 g mol–1. The molar mass of the unknown is calculated from the molality of the solution. According to the given information, 0.562 g is dissolved in the benzene. In part A, it was determined that the molality of the solution is 0.272 m. This tells you that there are 0.272 moles of unknown per kilogram of benzene. We know that we have 0.562 g unknown per 17.4 g of benzene. These two pieces of information will allow us to calculate the molar mass of the unknown. The molality=moles unknown/kg benzene; this can be rewritten as molality = (grams solute)(molar mass) / kg benzene. This can be rearranged to yield the final equation: molar mass = grams solute / (molality)(kg benzene). Substituting in the data, we get molar mass = 0.562 g / (0.272 m)(0.0174 kg benzene) = 119 g mol–1.

(C) 80.9 °C. The boiling temperature of the solution is calculated using the boiling point elevation equation: $\Delta T_b = K_b m$. The van't Hoff factor is not needed since the solute is a nonelectrolyte. From part (A) we know the molality, so the data can be substituted directly into the equation: ΔT_b = (2.61 °C m^{-1})(0.272 m) = 0.710 °C. The elevated boiling temperature will be 80.2 °C + 0.710 °C = 80.9 °C.

(D) The van't Hoff factor is in the calculations for colligative properties of solutions. Because the number of solute particles in solution affects these factors, an adjustment must be made for electrolytic solutes. This is due to the fact that electrolytes, when dissolved, yield as many particles as the number of ions in the solute. For example, the electrolyte sodium chloride, NaCl, will dissolve to yield one sodium ion, Na^+, and one chloride ion, Cl^-, per sodium chloride. Because the problem declared that the unknown solute was a nonelectrolyte, no van't Hoff factor was needed.

Question 2

(A) Molar mass can be calculated in two steps. First the molality is determined from the freezing point depression, using the expression $\Delta T_f = K_f = m$. Once the molality is known the equation to determine the molar mass will be derived from the molality equation. Since molality = moles solute/kg solvent, and moles solute = grams solute / molar mass solute, we can substitute (grams solute/molar mass solute) for moles solute in the molality equation. This produces the equation molality = (grams solute/molar mass solute) / kg solvent. Rearranging this equation, we obtain molar mass solute = grams solute / (molality)(kg solvent).

(B) In order for this to work, you need several measurements. To calculate the molality, two temperature readings are required. The first is for the pure solvent, and the second for the solution. Subtracting these values will produce ΔT_f. The value of K_f is also needed, but it is obtained from a reference book, not the experiment. In order to complete the calculations, two other pieces of data are required. The first is the mass of the solute. The second is the mass of the solvent. By using these two values, along with the molality (just calculated), we will be able to calculate the molar mass of the unknown.

(C) The purpose of the outer test tube is to slow down the rate of temperature decrease to allow for more uniform cooling and also greater accuracy of the temperature at the freezing point. Submerged directly in the water, the test tube with the solution will cool too rapidly.

(D) The percent error is determined by using the equation: |measured result – theoretical result|/theoretical result × 100%. The absolute value is used because we are not concerned if the error was above or below the theoretical value—only about how much it is above or below the theoretical value. If the numbers were substituted into this equation, it would read |170 g mol^{-1} – 180 g mol^{-1}|/180 g mol^{-1}× 100%.

(E) Molarity and molality are different measures, although there are some conditions where they are very similar. Molality depends on the mass of the solvent and molarity depends on the volume of the solvent. Since volume is affected by temperature, there may be some fluctuations in the volume of a solution as it heats or cools. Mass, and therefore molality, is unaffected by temperature changes. Another area where problems can possibly arise is the definitions. For molarity, the solute is added and the volume of the solute + solvent shall equal 1.00 L (or some other amount). For molal concentrations, the solute is added to 1.00 kg of water. There are a couple of conditions where the difference between molality and molarity is very small. The main one worth noting is when the amount of solute is small, relative to the amount of water. Water has the unique property that, by definition, 1.00 L of water is equal to 1.00 kg of water (only at 4 °C, but the numbers are still very close at other temperatures). Therefore, if a tiny amount of solute is placed in a container and water is filled until 1.00 liter of solution is produced, the amount of water will be very close to 1.00 liter, and therefore 1.00 kg. Therefore, in the special case where a solution is very dilute and the solvent is water, molality and molarity are nearly the same. This is a fairly dilute solution, so the error would have been very small if molarity was used.

Reaction Types

This chapter is divided into two major sections. The first, nomenclature, is a review of material you should have learned in your first-year chemistry course but that you will be expected to know for the AP exam. In the second section, you will review the major types of chemical reactions.

NOMENCLATURE

Nomenclature, or the naming system, is fairly uniform. The body that is most widely recognized for developing and maintaining the rules for naming compounds is the International Union of Pure and Applied Chemistry (IUPAC). The rules that you will need to be familiar with were developed by IUPAC. In this chapter, you will only be reviewing the procedures for naming inorganic compounds. Organic compounds, whose naming system is quite a bit different, will be addressed in Chapter 18. There are different procedures for naming ionic and covalent compounds. We'll begin with ionic compounds.

Ionic Compounds

Ionic compounds are composed of two or more atoms that have lost or gained electrons to become charged particles. The oppositely charged particles are held together by electrostatic attractions. In general, ionic compounds consist of a metallic cation (positively charged ion), bonded to a nonmetallic anion (negatively charged ion) or a negatively charged polyatomic ion. Polyatomic ions are stable arrangements of atoms that are covalently bonded together but that maintain a net charge. Most of the polyatomic ions are negatively charged. The ammonium ion, NH_4^+, is one of the only positively charged polyatomic ions. Table 10.1 shows a list of some of the more common polyatomic ions.

As you saw in Chapter 5, the ratio of ions in an ionic compound is determined by the charges on the ions. In a salt, the ions will combine to form compounds with a net charge of zero. Before listing the specific rules for naming compounds, let's review a few things about ions and electrical charges.

- Metals in groups 1A and 2A on the periodic table form cations with the same positive charge as their group numbers (1A = 1+, and 2A = 2+).

Table 10.1 Common Polyatomic ions

Charge	Formula	Name
1+	NH_4^+	ammonium
2+	Hg_2^{2+}	mercury (I)
1-	BrO_3^-	bromate
	$C_2H_3O_2^-$	acetate
	ClO^-	hypochlorite
	ClO_2^-	chlorite
	ClO_3^-	chlorate
	ClO_4^-	perchlorate
	CN^-	cyanide
	HCO_3^-	hydrogen carbonate, (common name is bicarbonate)
	HSO_4^-	hydrogen sulfate, (common name is bisulfate)
	$H_2PO_4^-$	dihydrogen phosphate
	MnO_4^-	permanganate
	NO_2^-	nitrite
	NO_3^-	nitrate
	OH^-	hydroxide
	SCN^-	thiocyanate
2-	CO_3^{2-}	carbonate
	$C_2O_4^{2-}$	oxalate
	CrO_4^{2-}	chromate
	$Cr_2O_7^{2-}$	dichromate
	HPO_4^{2-}	hydrogen phosphate
	SO_3^{2-}	sulfite
	SO_4^{2-}	sulfate
3-	AsO_4^{3-}	arsenate
	PO_4^{3-}	phosphate
	PO_3^{3-}	phosphite

- Most transition metals, as well as the metals in groups 3A–6A, have multiple charges possible, however, there are four very commonly used elements that have only one charge and should be memorized: Ag^+, Zn^{2+}, Cd^{2+}, and Al^{3+}. If you locate these on the periodic table, you will find that they are very close to one another.

- For the representative metallic elements in groups 3A–6A, most have two positive charges that follow a pattern. The two charges consist of a charge equal to the group number and a second charge equal to the group number minus two. For example, the element tin, Sn in group 4A, can have two charges, 4^+ (its group number) and 2^+ (its group number minus two).

Binary Ionic Compounds

Binary ionic compounds are compounds composed of two monatomic ions. These usually are a metallic cation and a nonmetallic anion. When naming these compounds, there are a few rules that need to be followed:

- Cations that only have one possible charge bear the same name as their neutral atoms. For example, a lithium atom, a group 1A element, can only have a 1^+ charge. A lithium ion is referred to as simply a "lithium" ion.

- Cations that can have more than one charge are named by placing a Roman numeral equal to the positive charge after the name of the element. For instance, the element copper can have two possible charges, 1^+ and 2^+. A Cu^{2+} ion is called a copper (II) ion. The Roman numeral is placed in parentheses.

- Monatomic anions are named after the element, but the ending has been modified and an "–ide" ending added as a replacement. For example, the S^{2-} ion becomes a "sulfide ion." There are no clear rules that can be followed about which part of the root to remove before adding the "–ide" ending, so it is easiest to memorize these anions. There aren't very many, so it is not that large a task. The charges on the monatomic anion are usually equal to the negative result of 8 minus the group number. For example, oxygen, a group 6A element, has a charge of $-(8-6)$, or -2. The reason for this is that it is how many negatively charged electrons are acquired in the formation of a stable octet (8 valence electrons).

- Binary acids, acids that are formed from a hydrogen ion bonding to a monatomic anion, are named by placing the term "hydro-" in front of the root of the anion ending in "-ic." For instance, HCl is called hydrochloric acid.

These are the main rules that are used to name binary ionic compounds. In most cases, the procedure is quite simple. For example, LiCl is named lithium chloride. Lithium is a group 1A element, so its name doesn't change, and the chloride comes from adding an "–ide" ending to a monatomic, nonmetallic anion. There are some cases, however, where the procedure is not as readily apparent. These are the compounds formed from the metals with more than one possible charge. For example, the compound $FeCl_3$ has an iron ion in it. Iron has more than one possible ionic charge, so its name requires the use of a Roman numeral. This is a fairly easy one to figure out because you know that a chloride ion has a 1^- charge. You also know that the net charge in an ionic compound is zero. Therefore, if it takes three chloride ions (with a total charge of 3^-) to neutralize one iron ion, the iron ion must have a charge of 3^+. Therefore, the name would be written as iron (III) chloride. In the next section, we'll look more closely at this process of determining the Roman numerals to assign cations with more than one possible charge.

NOTE
The subscript 2 tells you how many chloride ions are present. One (1) is not written as a subscript.

Writing Formulas for Binary Ionic Compounds

The formula for an ionic compound actually represents the simplest ratio of ions within a crystal. It is important to remember that the formulas you write for the exam must represent the simplest ratio of ions. There are two main ways to write the formulas for ionic compounds. The first method uses conservation of charge, while the second is a shortcut method often called the crisscross method.

In the conservation of charge method, you come up with the simplest ratio of ions to have a net charge of zero. This is basically a trial and error method, but, if you do it enough, you will discover patterns that make the process very efficient. It will be easier to review this with a few different examples.

Sample: Determine the formula for lithium chloride.

Answer: To begin, you need to determine the charges on each ion. Lithium, a group 1A element, has a charge of 1^+, and the chloride ion has a charge of 1^-. So, we begin by looking at the two ions, Li^+ and Cl^-. You should quickly notice that a charge of 1^+ will exactly balance a charge of 1^-. Therefore, for every one Li^+, there will be one Cl^-. As a result the formula will read $LiCl$.

Sample: Determine the formula for magnesium chloride.

Answer: Magnesium, a group 2A element, has a charge of 2^+. Chloride has a charge of 1^-. This time we have Mg^{2+} and Cl^-. If one chloride ion combines with a magnesium ion, there will still be a net charge of 1^+. Therefore, in order to balance the 2 positive charges of magnesium, you will need to have two chloride ions, each with a 1^- charge. The formula for magnesium chloride will be $MgCl_2$.

Sample: Determine the formula for magnesium oxide.

Answer: Magnesium is Mg^{2+}. Oxide represents the oxygen ion with a charge of 2^-, or O^{2-}. If you look at this example, only one magnesium ion is needed to balance the charge of one oxide ion. Therefore, the formula is MgO.

Sample: Determine the formula for aluminum oxide.

Answer: Aluminum has a charge of 3^+ and oxygen has a charge of 2^-. In the previous examples, you could manipulate the quantities of one of the ions to make the charges balance. Clearly, that won't work here. In this example, you need to balance the charges by changing the quantities of both ions. If you double the quantity of aluminum, the two aluminum ions will have a total charge of $2(3^+)$—or 6^+. If you look at the negative charge of 2^-, you might quickly see that 2 goes into 6 three times. If you triple the quantity of oxygen, you will have a charge of $3(2^-)$ or 6^-. Now the positive and negative charges are balanced. The final formula must have two aluminum ions for every three oxide ions, or Al_2O_3.

The Crisscross Method

The crisscross method of formula writing makes writing formulas for compounds like aluminum oxide an easier process. In this method, the first step is to write the ionic symbols next to each other. Once this is done, the number of the charge on the cation is written as a subscript for the anion and the number of the charge on the anion is written as a subscript for the cation.

Sample: We'll use aluminum oxide again:

$$Al^{3+} \diagdown O^{2-} \longrightarrow Al_2O_3$$

Answer: Notice how the arrows crisscross as they move toward the subscript position. That is where the name comes from. The method makes formula writing for ionic compounds quick and easy. There is one thing you need to pay attention to as you use this method, as the next example will demonstrate.

Sample: Write the formula for tin (II) oxide.

Using the crisscross method, we see that

$$Sn^{2+} \diagdown O^{2-} \longrightarrow Sn_2O_2$$

The first thing to point out is the charge on tin. While tin has more than one possible charge, you know it has to be two in this case because of the Roman numeral (II) that appears in the name. The formula Sn_2O_2 does not represent the smallest ratio of ions. You should notice that if each one of these subscripts is reduced by $\frac{1}{2}$, the new formula will be SnO. You can only reduce these subscripts if all subscripts in a formula can be reduced by the same amount (this will be more critical with ternary ionic compounds).

Going back to the previous section, where you were looking at how to determine the Roman numerals written after some elements, you may see how this can be done using the crisscross method. To determine the Roman numeral, you use a reverse crisscross technique to determine the charge on the cation. This charge then becomes the value of the Roman numeral. While you can probably eyeball a solution to these, we'll list a set of rules that will work for all examples:

a. Determine the total (–) charge by multiplying the charge on each anion by the total number of anions present.

b. The total (–) must equal the total (+).

c. Determine the (+) charge on each cation by dividing the total (+) charge by the number of cations present in the compound (subscript).

d. This answer is the charge that should be written as a Roman numeral in the name.

Sample: Write the name of PbO_2.

Answer: Following the four rules:

a. Determine the total (–) charge by multiplying the charge on each anion by total number of anions present (**2 × 2– = 4–**).

b. The total (–) must equal the total (+) (**4– = 4+**).

c. Determine the (+) charge on each cation by dividing the total (+) charge by number of cations present in compound (subscript) (**4+ ÷ 1 = 4**).

d. This answer is the charge that should be written as a Roman numeral in the name (**lead (IV) oxide**).

You Try It!

Write the formulas for the following compounds:

1. Calcium oxide	7. Nickel (II) oxide
2. Magnesium iodide	8. Hydrobromic acid
3. Chromium (III) oxide	9. Calcium sulfide
4. Sodium bromide	10. Silver chloride
5. Tin (IV) oxide	11. Lead (II) fluoride
6. Zinc iodide	12. Cadmium bromide

Answers:

1. CaO	4. NaBr	7. NiO	10. AgCl
2. MgI_2	5. SnO_2	8. HBr	11. PbF_2
3. Cr_2O_3	6. ZnI_2	9. CaS	12 $CdBr_2$

Write the names represented by the following formulas:

1. Na_2S	7. Hg_3N
2. AlN	8. MnO
3. $MgBr_2$	9. FeO
4. Co_2S_3	10. Ba_3N_2
5. CuI_2	11. H_2S
6. SrI_2	12. BeI_2

Answers:

1. sodium sulfide	7. mercury (I) nitride
2. aluminum nitride	8. manganese (II) oxide
3. magnesium bromide	9. iron (II) oxide
4. cobalt (III) sulfide	10. barium nitride
5. copper (II) iodide	11. hydrosulfuric acid
6. strontium iodide	12. beryllium iodide

Ternary Ionic Compounds

Ternary ionic compounds are ionic compounds containing one or more polyatomic ions. The possible combinations are a monatomic cation bonded to a polyatomic anion, a polyatomic cation bonded to a monatomic anion, or a polyatomic cation bonded to a polyatomic anion. There are additional rules that must be added to the rules in the previous section:

- Since polyatomic ions already have specific names, these names are not changed when the ion becomes part of a compound. For example, if the sulfate ion, SO_4^{2-}, combines with a calcium ion, Ca^{2+}, the resulting compound, $CaSO_4$, is called calcium sulfate.

- Because the atoms in a polyatomic ion are a stable unit, if more than one ion is needed to balance the charge of the oppositely charge ion, parentheses are placed around the polyatomic ion to indicate that the subscript placed outside the parentheses refers to the entire polyatomic ion. For example, if the hydroxide ion, OH^-, combines with a lithium ion, Li+, the resulting formula is LiOH. However, if the hydroxide ion combines with a magnesium ion, Mg^{2+}, the resulting formula will be $Mg(OH)_2$. The parentheses indicate that there are two hydroxide ions required to balance the 2^+ charge of the magnesium ion. Leaving out the parentheses would create the formula $MgOH_2$, which only indicates the presence of an extra hydrogen atom.

- For ternary acids, the prefix "hydro-" is dropped. The acid is named according to the polyatomic ion. If the polyatomic ion ends in "-ate," the acid is named using the root of the polyatomic ion ending in "-ic," followed by the word "acid." For example, when H+ combines with the nitrate ion, NO_3^-, the resulting acid is called nitric acid. If the polyatomic ion ends in "-ite" the acid is named using the root of the polyatomic ion ending in "-ous," followed by the word "acid." For example, when H+ combines with the nitrite ion, NO_2^-, the resulting acid is called nitrous acid.

The crisscross or conservation of charge methods are used in the same way to determine the ratio of ions in the compound.

You Try It!

Write the formulas for the following compounds:

1. potassium acetate	7. perchloric acid
2. calcium hydrogen sulfate	8. lithium phosphate
3. strontium nitrite	9. ammonium oxide
4. nickel (II) sulfate	10. sodium hydrogen phosphate
5. manganese (III) cyanide	11. zinc oxalate
6. zinc hydroxide	12. ammonium carbonate

Answers:

1. $KC_2H_3O_2$ 2. $Ca(HSO_4)_2$ 3. $Sr(NO_2)_2$ 4. $NiSO_4$

5. $Mn(CN)_3$ 6. $Zn(OH)_2$ 7. $HClO_4$ 8. Li_3PO_4

9. $(NH_4)_2O$ 10. Na_2HPO_4 11. ZnC_2O_4 12. $(NH_4)_2CO_3$

Write the names for the compounds represented by the following equations:

1. $Pb(OH)_2$

2. $Al_2(SO_4)_3$

3. $NaHCO_3$

4. $Co(NO_3)_2$

5. $CrCO_3$

6. H_2SO_3

7. $Sn_3(PO_4)_4$

8. $Mg(OH)_2$

9. $Fe(C_2H_3O_2)_3$

10. NH_4NO_2

11. $Mn_3(PO_3)_2$

12. $NaHSO_4$

Answers:

1. lead (II) hydroxide

2. aluminum sulfate

3. sodium hydrogen carbonate

4. cobalt (II) nitrite

5. chromium (II) carbonate

6. sulfurous acid

7. tin (IV) phosphate

8. magnesium hydroxide

9. iron (III) acetate

10. ammonium nitrite

11. manganese (II) phosphite

12. sodium hydrogen sulfate

MOLECULAR COMPOUNDS

The nomenclature for molecular compounds is much less complicated than for ionic compounds. Molecular compounds are formed from covalently bonded nonmetallic elements. The formula for a molecule represents a stable unit of atoms, unlike a formula for an ionic compound, which only represents the simplest whole number ratio of ions. As a result, molecular formulas cannot be simplified like formulas for ionic compounds. An example would be hydrogen peroxide, H_2O_2. Although the formula could be reduced to HO, this would be inappropriate because H_2O_2 is a molecule. Changing the structure to HO would change the chemical composition.

Another source of difficulty is that the atoms in molecules do not form ions. Therefore, the use of Roman numerals is not possible. And because nonmetals have multiple oxidation states possible (nitrogen has 8), it is too difficult to determine the possible combinations of atoms in a molecule. All of this is meant to illustrate why a different naming system is required for molecular compounds.

The rules for naming molecules are very simple:

- The second atom in the molecule is always written with an "-ide" ending.
- The first atom in the molecule is given the name of the element.
- Prefixes are used to indicate the number of atoms of each type are in a compound. These prefixes, listed in Table 10.2, should be committed to memory.
- Prefixes are written before the names of all atoms with one exception: if there is only one of the first atom in the molecule.
- When determining the name of a molecular compound from the formula, the subscript determines the prefix you will use in the name.

Table 10.2

Number	Prefix
1	mono-
2	di-
3	tri-
4	tetra-
5	penta-
6	hexa-
7	hepta-
8	octa-
9	nona-
10	deca-

Sample: Write the formula for the compound dinitrogen pentoxide.

Answer: Since "di-" = 2, there will two nitrogen atoms in the molecule. "Penta" is 5, so there will be 5 oxygen atoms. The resulting formula will be **N2O5**

Sample: Write the name of the compound SO_3.

Answer: There is only one sulfur atom. Because it is the first atom in the formula, no prefix will be used. There are three oxygen atoms, so the prefix "tri-" will be used. The resulting name will be sulfur trioxide.

You Try It!
Write formulas for the following compounds:

1. nitrogen dioxide
2. carbon monoxide
3. dinitrogen monoxide
4. silicon dioxide
5. sulfur hexafluoride
6. phosphorous pentachloride
7. silicon monocarbide
8. carbon disulfide
9. dinitrogen trioxide
10. tetrasulfur dinitride
11. dihydrogen mononitride
12. tetraboron monocarbide

Answers:

1. NO_2 2. CO   3. N_2O 4. SO_2 5. SF_6 6. PCl_5
7. SiC   8. CS_2 9. N_2O_3 10. S_4N_2 11. H_2N 12. B_4C

Write the names of the following compounds:

1. NF_3
2. S_2Cl_2
3. CF_4
4. BCl_3
5. P_4H_{10}
6. O_2F_2
7. SF_4
8. B_2O_3
9. Si_3N_4
10. B_2O_3
11. ClO_7
12. SiF_4

Answers:

1. nitrogen trifluoride
2. disulfur dichloride
3. carbon tetrafluoride
4. boron trichloride
5. tetraphosphorous decahydride
6. dioxygen difluoride
7. sulfur tetrafluoride
8. diboron trioxide
9. trisilicon tetranitride
10. diboron trioxide
11. chlorine heptoxide
12. silicon tetrafluoride

CHEMICAL EQUATIONS

A chemical equation is a way to represent, in symbols, a chemical reaction. By using combinations of symbols to represent chemicals and processes, you can express in a universal language the events in a chemical reaction. Before reviewing the different types of reactions, it will be helpful to review some of symbols that are used in chemical equations.

A basic chemical equation consists of a few components. In every reaction, there is at least one reactant and one product. In order to better illustrate the features of a chemical equation, we will use an example of a chemical reaction that has two reactants and two products. In the equation, the formulas of each reactant and product will represent the chemicals. The reactants are placed on the left side of the equation and the products on the right side of the equation. An arrow ($\rightarrow$) placed in the center, between the reactants and products, indicates a reaction is taking place. A plus (+) sign on the left side of the equation, placed between the reactants (if there are more than one), is used to signify that the reactants are added together. A plus (+) sign on the right, or products side, of the equation signifies that the products are separate entities. An example of a chemical reaction is the addition of sodium metal to water to form sodium hydroxide and hydrogen gas. When written as a chemical equation, this word equation is translated to

$$Na + H_2O \rightarrow NaOH + H_2$$

This type of equation is often called a *skeleton equation*. It indicates which reactants were involved and what products were formed, but little else. The addition of a few more symbols can provide much more information. What's missing in the chemical equation that was present in the word equation is the states of the chemicals. The word equation specified sodium metal and hydrogen gas, yet the chemical equation does not indicate this. By rewriting the equation, we can convey this information:

$$Na(s) + H_2O(l) \rightarrow NaOH(aq) + H_2(g)$$

These symbols are frequently added to chemical equations to provide the states of the reactants and products. Solids are represented by (s), liquids by (l), aqueous solutions (solutions where water is the solvent) by (aq), and gases by (g).

Another issue with the skeleton equation above is that the reaction, as written, violates the law of conservation of matter. According to the equation, one sodium atom reacts with one oxygen atom and two hydrogen atoms to produce one sodium atom, one oxygen atom, and three hydrogen atoms. A hydrogen atom has been created, in direct violation of the law of conservation of matter. In reality, this is not how the chemicals react. The reaction really takes place like this:

$$2Na(s) + 2H_2O(l) \rightarrow 2NaOH(aq) + H_2(g)$$

If you count up the atoms of each element on either side of the arrow, you see that there are now 2 sodium atoms, 4 hydrogen atoms, and 2 oxygen atoms on the left side of the arrow and 2 sodium atoms, 4 hydrogen atoms, and 2 oxygen atoms on the right side of the arrow. Matter has been conserved! In case you have forgotten, the coefficients in front of a component in an equation tell you how many of the atoms or molecules are present. 2Na means two sodium atoms, and $2H_2O$ represents two water molecules. Subscripts, like the 2 after the H in $2H_2O$, indicate the number of atoms of the element that are in the molecule (in water, the 2 means there are two hydrogen atoms). This type of equation, where matter is conserved, is known as a **balanced equation**. In the next section we will review the procedures for balancing equations.

The other symbols that can add information to an equation are shown in Table 10.3:

Table 10.3

Symbol	Meaning
$\xrightarrow{\Delta}$ or $\xrightarrow{heat}$	Reactants are heated
$\xrightarrow{50\ atm}$	Reaction is carried out at a certain pressure
$\xrightarrow{100\ °C}$	Reaction is carried out at a specific temperature
$\xrightarrow{MnO_2}$	A catalyst is used in the reaction
$\downarrow$	Product is a solid precipitate
$\uparrow$	Product is a gas
$\rightleftharpoons$	Reaction can proceed in both directions, neither direction ending in completion.

Balancing Equations

In the upcoming chapters, the chemical equations you will be working with will be balanced equations. That is because the topics covered in these chapters are all concerned with quantitative aspects of chemical reactions. In this chapter, you are looking at different reaction types and learning how to predict the outcomes of various reactions. As you just read, chemical reactions must be balanced in order to follow the law of conservation of matter. The process is, in principle, just an elementary form of record keeping to assure that there are equal numbers of atoms of each element going into and coming out of a chemical reaction. In practice, balancing equations is not always as easy. Many reactions are quite simple and require very little to balance them, but some are quite complex. There are a few procedures that you should follow while balancing equations as well as a few strategies that will allow you to balance equations more quickly.

Rules for Balancing Equations

The bottom line is that you must adjust the equation so that the number of atoms of each element is the same on each side of the equation. There are some rules that must be followed while balancing equations:

- You can only change the coefficients that appear before an element or compound.
- You are never allowed to change any subscripts in a formula. Changing subscripts changes the chemical nature of the substance, whereas changing a coefficient simply changes the amount of a substance.
- Coefficients should be written as the lowest numerical ratios.

Sample: $Zn + HCl \rightarrow ZnCl_2 + H_2$

Answer: If you look at this equation, there is one zinc atom on the left side and one on the right side. At the moment, all zinc atoms are accounted for. While looking at the zinc chloride on the right side, you may have noticed the subscript 2 by the chlorine. There are two chlorine atoms in zinc chloride, but only one on the reactant side of the equation. You can begin by placing a coefficient of 2 in front of HCl:

$$Zn + 2HCl \rightarrow ZnCl_2 + H_2$$

This gives you the two chlorine atoms that you need, but it has now also given you two hydrogen atoms on the reactants side. A visual inspection of the products indicates that you need two hydrogen atoms to balance the equation, so hydrogen is now balanced.

A quick tally of the atoms indicates that all are balanced. Mentally, you should go through a process similar to the chart below:

Table 10.4

Reactants	Products
Zn = 2 atoms	Zn = 2 atoms
H = 2 atoms	H = 2 atoms
Cl = 2 atoms	Cl = 2 atoms

The basic process of balancing equations is, by nature, a trial and error affair, but you can streamline the process by using a few different strategies.

The most important approach is to begin by balancing substances that only appear once on each side of the equation. Elements that appear more than once are more difficult. Quite often, you may find that by balancing the easiest elements first, the others will balance themselves. One element that often appears in more than one compound in an equation is oxygen. It is a good idea to wait on the oxygen atoms until the end.

A second strategy is to look for any polyatomic ions. If a polyatomic ion appears on each side of the equation, you can treat it like an individual element while balancing the equation.

Sample:

$$NaHCO_3 + H_2SO_4 \rightarrow Na_2SO_4 + H_2O + CO_2$$

Answer: In this equation, you should notice two things. First, oxygen appears in several places in the equation. Second, the sulfate ion is present on each side of the equation. Our first step is to look for an element that appears only once. Sodium is a good starting point. You will very often find that metal cations are the best place to start. We begin by placing a 2 in front of the sodium atom on the reactants side of the equation:

$$2NaHCO_3 + H_2SO_4 \rightarrow Na_2SO_4 + H_2O + CO_2$$

Placing this 2 in front of sodium balances the sodium atoms, but it also adds two additional hydrogen atoms, two carbon atoms, and six oxygen atoms (all from the bicarbonate ion). Carbon is another atom that appears only once on each side. There are now two carbon atoms on the reactants side and only one on the products side. We can continue by placing a 2 in front of the carbon dioxide molecule, CO_2, on the products side.

$$2NaHCO_3 + H_2SO_4 \rightarrow Na_2SO_4 + H_2O + 2CO_2$$

The carbon atoms and the sodium atoms are now balanced. Time to pick another element. Our choices are hydrogen, oxygen, and sulfur. Since sulfur is tied up in a sulfate ion, we will leave that one alone for now. Hydrogen is the next easiest element. On the reactant side of the equation, there are a total of 4 hydrogen atoms (2 in sodium bicarbonate and 2 in sulfuric acid). On the

TIP

This mental checklist helps you keep track of the atoms you are trying to balance. As reactions become more complex, it may help you to write this list down on paper.

products side, there are only 2. We can balance the hydrogen by placing a coefficient of 2 in front of the water molecule on the products side:

$$2NaHCO_3 + H_2SO_4 \rightarrow Na_2SO_4 + 2H_2O + 2CO_2$$

At this point, we have balanced everything except sulfur and oxygen. Here is where we can take advantage of the sulfate ion. Because sulfate appears on each side of the equation, you can treat it as a single element. There is one on the reactant side and one on the product side, so it's balanced. When we check the oxygen atoms, we can ignore the oxygen atoms in the sulfate ions for now. On the reactant side, we have 6 oxygen atoms. On the products side, we have 2 in the water molecule, and 4 in the carbon dioxide molecules, for a total of 6. Doing some quick mental checking, we see that all of the atoms in the equation are now balanced. By waiting to balancing the oxygen atoms, they balanced themselves!

Another helpful strategy is to look for odd numbers of atoms on one side of the equation. If there is an odd number of atoms on one side of the equation but an even number on the other, there is no way to balance the equation by adding coefficients in front of the even-numbered element. An even number multiplied by any number will always be even. In these equations, you need to work on the odd side. When you multiply an odd number by an even, the product is always even. An example of this sort is shown below:

$$Cl_2 + AlI_3 \rightarrow AlCl_3 + I_2$$

For both chlorine and iodine, each has an odd number of atoms on one side of the equation and an even number on the opposite. If we look at chlorine, Cl_2, on the reactants side, there is no coefficient you can put in front of it to make it an odd number. So our efforts are best spent on the other side of the equation. Because balanced equations must show the lowest whole number ratio of reactants and products, you should always start with the smallest coefficient possible. If we put a coefficient of 2 in front of the $AlCl_3$, it will give us an even number of chlorine atoms. It also gives us 2 aluminum atoms, making aluminum out of balance.

$$Cl_2 + AlI_3 \rightarrow 2AlCl_3 + I_2$$

The next step will be to balance chlorine and aluminum. To get 6 chlorine atoms on the reactants side, we must put a coefficient of 3 in front of the Cl_2. You will find that this is a fairly common pattern in balancing (finding the least common multiple). Next, we need to put a 2 in front of the AlI_3 to balance the aluminum.

$$3Cl_2 + 2AlI_3 \rightarrow 2AlCl_3 + I_2$$

Everything is balanced now, except for iodine. There are 6 on the left and only 2 on the right. This is easily remedied by placing a coefficient of 3 in front of I_2:

$$3Cl_2 + 2AlI_3 \rightarrow 2AlCl_3 + 3I_2$$

Doing a quick check, all atoms are now balanced and the coefficients are in the simplest whole number ratio.

The last strategy for balancing equations is used for balancing combustion reactions. Later in the chapter, we will discuss combustion reactions, but for now, assume that a hydrocarbon is reacting with oxygen to form carbon dioxide and water vapor. These are particularly nasty reactions to balance as the coefficients can get quite large. There is a shortcut that makes the process very simple if the fuel contains only carbon and hydrogen. The steps to balancing this type of combustion reaction are shown in the example below of the combustion of benzene, C_6H_6:

$$C_6H_6 + O_2 \rightarrow CO_2 + H_2O$$

Step 1: Balance the carbon and hydrogen atoms. To do this, you will need to place a coefficient of 6 in front of the CO_2 and a coefficient of 3 in front of the water.

$$C_6H_6 + O_2 \rightarrow 6CO_2 + 3H_2O$$

Step 2: Count the number of atoms on the right side of the equation. (You are going to have to cheat a little bit here to make this work out). In this equation, there are a total of 15 oxygen atoms on the right side of the equation (12 in CO_2 and 3 in H_2O).

Step 3: Take the number of oxygen atoms from the right side of the equation and place a coefficient in front of the O_2 on the left side that is that number over 2. For this, you will make a coefficient of 15/2 (don't worry—you're not going to leave it like that):

$$C_6H_6 + \frac{15}{2} O_2 \rightarrow 6CO_2 + 3H_2O$$

Step 4: Change the 15/2 coefficient to a whole number, multiplying it by 2. When you do that, however, you have to multiply everything by 2 as well. When finished, you should have something like this:

$$2C_6H_6 + 15O_2 \rightarrow 12CO_2 + 6H_2O$$

This shortcut will save you a lot of trial and error!

You Try It!
Balance the following equations.
1. $Au_2O_3 \rightarrow Au + O_2$
2. $Na_3PO_4 + ZnSO_4 \rightarrow Na_2SO_4 + Zn_3(PO_4)_2$
3. $MnO_2 + HCl \rightarrow MnCl_4 + H_2O$
4. $CaO + P_4O_{10} \rightarrow Ca_3(PO_4)_2$
5. $C_6H_5OH + O_2 \rightarrow CO_2 + H_2O$
6. $(NH_4)_2S + Co(NO_3)_2 \rightarrow CoS + NH_4NO_3$
7. $Al + O_2 \rightarrow Al_2O_3$
8. $C_2H_6 + O_2 \rightarrow CO_2 + H_2O$

Answers:

1. $2Au_2O_3 \rightarrow 4Au + 3O_2$
2. $2Na_3PO_4 + 3ZnSO_4 \rightarrow 3Na_2SO_4 + Zn_3(PO_4)_2$
3. $MnO_2 + 4HCl \rightarrow MnCl_4 + 2H_2O$
4. $6CaO + P_4O_{10} \rightarrow 2Ca_3(PO_4)_2$
5. $C_6H_5OH + 7O_2 \rightarrow 6CO_2 + 3H_2O$
6. $(NH_4)_2S + Co(NO_3)_2 \rightarrow CoS + 2NH_4NO_3$
7. $4Al + 3O_2 \rightarrow 2Al_2O_3$
8. $2C_2H_6 + 7O_2 \rightarrow 4CO_2 + 6H_2O$

MAJOR REACTION TYPES

There are a few different ways to classify chemical reactions. We will look at the most traditional method of classifying reactions, which divides reactions into five categories, based on the behavior of the chemicals during the reactions:

1. *Combination (synthesis) reactions*—two or more substances reacting to form a single compound

2. *Decomposition Reactions*—reactions in which a single compound is broken down into two or more simpler products

3. *Combustion reactions*—reactions where oxygen reacts with another substance, often producing energy in the form of heat and light

4. *Displacement reactions (Single replacement reactions)*—chemical reactions in which atoms of one element replace the atoms of a second element in a compound

5. *Metathesis reactions (Double-replacement reactions)*—chemical change that involves an exchange of positive ions between two compounds

Combination or Synthesis Reactions

These are reactions in which two or more substances combine to form a single product. A general equation for a combination reaction is:

$$A + B \rightarrow AB$$

Example: $N_2(g) + 3H_2(g) \rightarrow 2NH_3(g)$

NOTE: The characteristic feature of these reactions is that only one product is formed. No other type of reaction has this outcome.

Decomposition Reactions

These are reactions in which a single compound is broken down into two or more simpler products. The products of a decomposition reaction can be any combination of elements and compounds. It is usually difficult to predict the products of decomposition reactions, but if a simple binary compound breaks down, the products will usually be the constituent elements. (Constituent elements are those elements that make up a compound.) Most decomposition reactions require energy to occur. A general equation for a decomposition reaction is

$$AB \rightarrow A + B$$

Example: $2\,HgO(s) \xrightarrow{\Delta} 2\,Hg(l) + O_2(g)$

NOTE: The distinguishing feature of these reactions is that there is a single reactant. No other reaction has a single reactant.

Combustion Reactions

These are reactions where oxygen reacts with another substance, often producing energy in the form of heat and light. These reactions typically involve hydrocarbons, which are compounds of hydrogen and carbon. When hydrocarbons react with oxygen, they generate water vapor and either carbon dioxide or carbon monoxide as products. For the combustion of hydrocarbons, there are two types: complete and incomplete.

Complete combustion occurs when there is ample oxygen and the reaction generates carbon dioxide and water as products. A general equation for the complete combustion of a hydrocarbon is

$$C_xH_y + O_2 \rightarrow CO_2 + H_2O$$

Example: $2\,C_6H_6 + 15\,O_2 \rightarrow 12\,CO_2 + 6\,H_2O$

Incomplete combustion occurs when there is insufficient oxygen. Carbon monoxide and water are generated as products. A general equation for the incomplete combustion of a hydrocarbon is

$$C_xH_y + O_2 \rightarrow CO + H_2O$$

Example: $C_2H_4 + 2O_2 \rightarrow 2CO + 2\,H_2O$

Metathesis Reactions

The term metathesis literally means "to transpose." The term "double replacement" is often used to describe these reactions because the cations switch places with each other. These are chemical reactions that involve an exchange of positive ions between two compounds and that generally take place between two ionic compounds in an aqueous solution. The driving force that causes these reactions to occur is a decrease in the number of ions from the reactants to products. This will occur when a stable product forms from the ionic reactants. The three types of stable products that can form are a precipitate (or an insoluble solid), a gas (gaseous materials will bubble out of the solutions and leave the reaction mixture), or a stable molecule (a weak electrolyte, or nonelectrolyte, such as water). A general equation for a double-replacement reaction is

$$AB + CD \rightarrow AD + CB$$

Example: $BaCl_2\,(aq) + K_2CO_3\,(aq) \rightarrow BaCO_3\,(s) + 2\,KCl\,(aq)$

Note how the barium and potassium ions have simply been exchanged between the two negative ions. Also note that on both sides of the equation there are two ionic compounds. This is a good indicator that an equation represents a double-replacement reaction.

Precipitation Reactions

One of the three types of metathesis reactions is driven by the production of an insoluble solid. While we are going to go much more in depth about solubility in Chapter 14, there are some basic rules you can learn now that will provide you with more than enough information to predict the products of chemical reactions. These basic rules, usually referred to as solubility rules, are listed in Table 10.5. When reading the chart, keep in mind that all the solutions listed are aqueous solutions (water is the solvent). The term "insoluble" is not exactly correct. All materials are soluble to a certain degree, though, for some materials, the degree of solubility is so small it is negligible. In these cases, we refer to the material as insoluble. You will learn more about this in Chapter 14.

Table 10.5 Solubilities of common ions

Soluble compounds	Exceptions
All compounds of the alkali metals (Group IA) are soluble.	
All salts containing NH_4^+, NO_3^-, ClO_4^-, and $C_2H_3O_2^-$ are soluble.	
All chlorides, bromides, and iodides (salts containing Cl^-, Br^-, or I^-) are soluble	Halides where Ag^+, Pb^{2+}, and Hg_2^{2+} are the cations are insoluble
All sulfates (salts containing SO_4^{2-}) are soluble	Sulfates with the cations Hg^{2+}, Pb^{2+}, Ca^{2+}, Sr^{2+}, and Ba^{2+}.

Insoluble compounds	Exceptions
All hydroxides (OH^- compounds) and all metal oxides (O^{2-} compounds) are insoluble.	Hydroxides and metal oxides combined with Group IA elements and Ca^{2+}, Sr^{2+} and Ba^{2+}.
NOTE: When metal oxides do dissolve, they react with water to form hydroxides.	Group IA and NH_4^+ compounds are are soluble
For example:	
$Na_2O(s) + H_2O(l) \rightarrow 2NaOH(aq)$	
All compounds that contain PO_4^{3-}, CO_3^{2-}, SO_3^{2-}, and S^{2-} are insoluble	

When you attempt to determine products of a precipitation reaction, you need to think back to what the solutions look like. For example, suppose you have two beakers, one containing an aqueous solution of lead (II) nitrate, $Pb(NO_3)_2$, and the other containing an aqueous solution of potassium iodide, KI. Prior to mixing, the contents of the containers look something like the diagram in Figure 10.1:

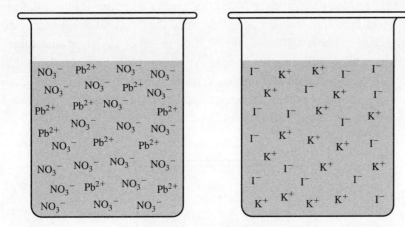

Figure 10.1

Each beaker contains a soluble salt, which means that each ionic salt will dissolve in the water. Crystalline $Pb(NO_3)_2$, when added to water, dissolved. The same happened to KI. In each beaker, since the salts are soluble, the ions are dissolved in water and floating about. In the first beaker, if a lead ion encounters a nitrate ion, it may stick together briefly, but because the salt is soluble, it will quickly dissolve into solution again. The same is true for the KI beaker. If you dump some of each beaker into a third beaker, you are going to mix all four of the ions together like in Figure 10.2:

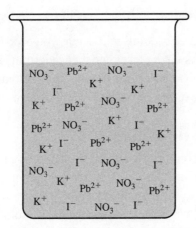

Figure 10.2

At this point, all four ions are free to interact, so there will be two interactions that were not possible before. The first is K^+ and NO_3^- ions, and the second Pb^{2+} and I^- ions. To determine what will happen next, you need to refer to table 10.5, the solubility rules. If you look up the first possible pairing of ions, K^+ and NO_3^-, you can determine if potassium nitrate is an insoluble product. For two reasons, it is not: all salts made from group 1A elements are soluble, and all nitrates are soluble. The next possible product then is lead (II) iodide. For this compound, the table says that all iodides are soluble except those formed with Ag^+, Pb^{2+}, and Hg^{2+}. Therefore, lead (II) iodide is an insoluble product. What that means, in terms of our beaker, is that when lead ions encounter iodide ions, they will stick together (see Figure 10.3). They will continue to stick together in larger and larger numbers until visible crystals appear. You have probably seen the bright yellow precipitate, lead (II) iodide. What will be left in the beaker is an aqueous solution of potassium nitrate and any leftover lead or iodide ions (this will be discussed in Chapter 11).

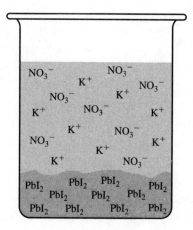

Figure 10.3

The reaction that we have just described can be written as:

$$Pb(NO_3)_2(aq) + 2KI(aq) \rightarrow PbI_2(s) + 2KNO_3(aq)$$

To determine if these reactions will occur, you need to write the equation as though the cations switch places and then determine if either of the newly formed products is insoluble. If it is not, then the reaction will not occur (unless one of the next two products—water or a gas—is formed).

Neutralization Reactions

These reactions will only be discussed briefly at this point, since they will be discussed in detail in Chapter 13. In neutralization reactions, an acid and a base are combined to form a salt and water. These reactions apply to acids that dissociate to form free hydrogen ions in solution and bases that dissociate to form free hydroxide ions. For example, when hydrochloric acid, HCl, is combined with sodium hydroxide, NaOH, the reaction proceeds as follows:

$$HCl(aq) + NaOH(aq) \rightarrow H_2O(l) + NaCl(aq)$$

Some other neutralization reactions can occur that are not as obvious as this one, but these will be addressed in Chapter 13.

Gas-forming Reactions

These reactions are also acid-base interactions. One of these that may immediately come to mind in this category is a reaction that you more than likely did as a child—mixing vinegar and baking soda. Now that you are an AP chemistry student, you know that you were really mixing acetic acid, $HC_2H_3O_2$, and sodium bicarbonate, $NaHCO_3$. When these two substances are mixed, the reactions proceeds as follows:

$$HC_2H_3O_2(aq) + NaHCO_3(aq) \rightarrow NaC_2H_3O_2(aq) + H_2CO_3(aq)$$

Although the sodium bicarbonate is a solid when it is added to the acetic acid, it must dissolve in the aqueous solution before the reaction can occur. That is why it is shown as (aq) in the reaction. Now that you have written this out, you may be trying to figure out where the gas is. The gas is produced when the unstable product, carbonic acid, decomposes to form water and carbon dioxide gas:

$$H_2CO_3(aq) \rightarrow H_2O(l) + CO_2(g)$$

If you combine the two equations, you can see that the reaction is a neutralization reaction and produces a gas:

$$HC_2H_3O_2(aq) + NaHCO_3(aq) \rightarrow NaC_2H_3O_2(aq) + H_2O(l) + CO_2(g)$$

IONIC EQUATIONS

The equations you have been looking at up to this point have been known as ***molecular equations***. They are called this because all of the substances are written as though they are molecules, even when they may not presently be in that state. For example, in the previous section, two substances we were discussing were lead (II) nitrate and potassium iodide. In the example that used the two substances, both were in an aqueous solution. When the two solutions were mixed, the reaction occurred and crystalline lead (II) iodide was formed. However, if you had taken the crystalline forms of each reactant, $Pb(NO_3)_2$ and KI, and thrown them together, they would have sat there for an indefinite amount of time with little or no reaction occurring. The two materials need to be dissolved (or in a molten state) for the reaction to occur. In the equation for the reaction, though, the materials are written as though they were molecules:

$$Pb(NO_3)_2(aq) + 2KI(aq) \rightarrow PbI_2(s) + 2KNO_3(aq)$$

Potassium nitrate, KNO_3, is written as a molecule, even though that material can't form in water. For this reason, there is another type of equation that is often used to describe reactions that involve ions. It is known as an ***ionic equation***. Instead of writing the formulas for the substances as molecules (or salts), we will write the formulas for the ions that would be present in aqueous solution. If the previous equation is rewritten as an ionic equation, it will become

$$Pb^{2+}(aq) + 2NO_3^-(aq) + 2K^+(aq) + 2I^-(aq) \rightarrow PbI_2(s) + 2K^+(aq) + 2NO_3^-(aq)$$

Note that in the ionic equation, nitrate ions on the reactant side of the equation acquired a coefficient of 2. This is because when $Pb(NO_3)_2$ dissociates, it forms one Pb^{2+} ion and two NO_3^- ions. Also notice that the lead iodide, PbI_2, is written as a solid on the products side of the equation. All precipitates will be written this way. Although this doesn't appear in the previous example, when nonelectrolytes or weak electrolytes like water appear in an ionic equation, they are written in their appropriate state, such as $H_2O(l)$.

Net Ionic Equations

If you look at the equation in the previous example, there are a few ions that haven't done anything. Let's look at the equation again, with these highlighted so you can see that they do nothing:

$$Pb^{2+}(aq) + \boxed{2NO_3^-(aq)} + \boxed{2K^+(aq)} + 2I^-(aq) \rightarrow PbI_2(s) + \boxed{2K^+(aq)} + \boxed{2NO_3^-(aq)}$$

Ions that haven't done anything are known as **spectator ions**. Just like spectators watch a football game without taking part in it, these spectator ions "watch" the reaction without taking part in it. The equation can be rewritten without the spectator ions. When it is written this way, it is known as a net ionic equation. The previous equation, written as a net ionic equation, is

$$Pb^{2+}(aq) + 2I^-(aq) \rightarrow PbI_2(s)$$

This equation only shows the ions that are actually involved in the reaction. It also helps to point out other reactions that are possible. For example, any soluble lead salt, when combined with any soluble iodide salt, will produce the insoluble lead (II) iodide.

You Try It!

Write net ionic equations from the following pairs of reactants. Use the solubility to determine the products when necessary. All pairs will react to form products.

1. $H_2SO_4(aq) + BaCl_2(aq)$
2. $Pb(NO_3)_2(aq) + MgSO_4(aq)$
3. $NaOH(aq) + HNO_3(aq)$
4. $Sr(C_2H_3O_2)_2(aq) + NiSO_4(aq)$
5. $Fe(OH)_3(s) + HClO_4(aq)$

Answers:

1. $Ba^{2+}(aq) + HSO_4^-(aq) \rightarrow BaSO_4(s) + H^+(aq)$
2. $Pb^{2+}(aq) + SO_4^{2-}(aq) \rightarrow PbSO_4(s)$
3. $H^+(aq) + OH^-(aq) \rightarrow H_2O(l)$
4. $Sr^{2+}(aq) + SO_4^{2-}(aq) \rightarrow SrSO_4(s)$
5. $Fe(OH)_3(s) + 3H^+(aq) \rightarrow Fe^{3+}(aq) + 3H_2O(l)$

Single Replacement Reactions

These reactions are part of a larger category of reactions known as **redox reactions** (redox is short for oxidation–reduction). Sometimes these are called displacement reactions. These are chemical reactions in which atoms of one element replace the atoms of a second element in a compound. A general equation for a single–replacement reaction involving a metal (A), replacing a metallic cation in solution (B) is:

$$A + BC \rightarrow AC + B$$

Example: $Zn(s) + 2AgNO_3(aq) \rightarrow Zn(NO_3)_2(aq) + 2Ag(s)$

Whether one metal will replace another metal from a compound is determined by the reduction potential of the metal, found on a table of standard reduction potentials (like the one available to you on the AP exam). If the metallic element is higher on the chart than the cation, it will replace it. If it is not higher on the chart, no reaction will occur.

For a nonmetal (D), replacing a nonmetallic anion, the general form of the reaction is

$$D + BC \rightarrow BD + C$$

Example: $Cl_2 + 2NaBr \rightarrow 2NaCl + Br_2$

These reactions are typically limited to the halogens. The procedure for predicting the outcome of these reactions is the same as for the metals. The halogens also appear on the table of standard reduction potentials, but for reasons we will discuss in Chapter 17, the halogens get more reactive as you go up the table of reduction potentials. An easy way to remember the reactivities of the halogens is they are less reactive going down the group (as atomic number increases).

You Try It!

Predict the outcome of the following reactions. Not all substances may react. When a reaction does occur, write the complete and balanced equation, followed by the net ionic equation.

1. $Fe + NaCl(aq) \rightarrow$
2. $F_2 + AlCl_3(aq) \rightarrow$
3. $K + CuSO_4(aq) \rightarrow$
4. $Pb + KCl(aq) \rightarrow$
5. $Mg + HCl(aq) \rightarrow$

Answers:

1. No reaction
2. $3F_2 + 2AlCl_3(aq) \rightarrow 2AlF_3(aq) + 3Cl_2$; $3F_2 + 6Cl^- \rightarrow 6F^- + 3Cl_2$
3. $2K + CuSO_4(aq) \rightarrow K_2SO_4(aq) + Cu$; $2K + Cu^{2+} \rightarrow 2K^+ + Cu$
4. No reaction
5. $Mg(s) + 2HCl(aq) \rightarrow MgCl_2(aq) + H_2(g)$; $Mg + 2H^+ \rightarrow Mg^{2+} + H_2$

OXIDATION-REDUCTION REACTIONS

Redox reactions are not limited to single replacement reactions. They really describe a wide variety of reactions, but each shares the common theme of involving an *oxidation* and a *reduction*. An oxidation occurs when a substance loses electrons and becomes more positively charged. Earlier in the book we discussed a similar phenomenon in the formation of ionic compounds. Substances don't just lose electrons for no reason. They lose electrons because another substance takes them. When a substance acquires additional electrons and becomes more negatively charged, it is called a *reduction*. An oxidation cannot take place without a reduction, so these processes must occur simultaneously. These reactions describe the simultaneous oxidation and reduction of materials, which has earned them the name oxidation-reduction reactions.

Two terms you should be familiar with are *oxidizing agent* and *reducing agent*. An oxidizing agent is a substance that oxidizes another substance. This means it is causing the other substance to lose electrons. The only way to do this is for the oxidizing agent to gain the electrons or become reduced. Therefore, oxidizing agents oxidize other materials while they are being reduced. Similarly, a reducing agent is a substance that reduces other materials by becoming oxidized. In other words, reducing agents are giving away electrons. We are going to look at this more closely in Chapter 17, but there is one important application for this chapter. The table of standard reduction potentials that you are given on the AP exam is a helpful way to predict the outcome of redox reactions. The way it is set up, the strongest reducing agents are at the top of the chart (have the most negative values), and the strongest oxidizing agents are located at the bottom of the chart (have the most positive values).

Oxidation Numbers

An oxidation-reduction reaction has to be accompanied by a change in the oxidation state of the reactants. Sometimes, these changes aren't that obvious. It helps if you learn how to follow the oxidation states of an element during a chemical reaction. In ionic compounds, it is very obvious where the electrons have been transferred. However, in molecular compounds, electrons are being shared. Oxidation numbers are really fictitious creations that help us better understand atomic behavior. If you remember back to Chapter 5 when we discussed covalent bonds, you may recall that electrons are being shared between atoms in a covalent bond. In many cases, one atom is more electronegative than the other, resulting in a polar bond. When you determine the oxidation number of an atom, you pretend that the more electronegative element actually got the entire charge of the electron and the less electronegative element lost it. Therefore, in a water molecule, the more electronegative oxygen would be assigned both of the electrons from the hydrogen atoms, giving it an oxidation number of –2. Hydrogen would have an oxidation number of +1. Oxidation numbers are usually written with the sign of the charge written before the number

TIP

If you have trouble remembering the definitions of the terms oxidation and reduction, just remember the little mnemonic device: "LEO says GER" which stands for Losing Electrons is Oxidation, and Gaining Electrons is Reduction

instead of after it. This is so you don't confuse them with real charges found on ions. There are some rules that are followed to simplify the process of assigning oxidation numbers:

1. The oxidation number of an element in its normal state is zero. A piece of copper, Cu, would have an oxidation number of 0. Chlorine gas, Cl_2, will also have an oxidation number of zero. Even though some elements are diatomic, remember that the electrons in those bonds are shared evenly, so no number is assigned.

2. Oxidation numbers for monatomic ions are the same as their charges. K^+ has an oxidation number of +1, and O^{2-} has an oxidation number of –2.

3. In a binary compound, the more electronegative element is assigned a negative oxidation number equal to the charge it would have in simple ionic compounds. For example, in CCl_4, the chlorine atoms are assigned oxidation numbers of –1 because in ionic compounds, chloride ions have a 1^- charge.

4. For any electrically neutral compound, the sum of the oxidation numbers will always equal zero. For any ionic species (like polyatomic ions), the sums of the oxidation states of the elements will equal the charge of the ion. In CCl_4, if each chlorine is assigned a –1 oxidation number, then carbon must be assigned a +4 so the net charge will be zero. In a polyatomic ion, like nitrate, NO_3^-, oxygen is the more electronegative element, so it will be assigned a –2 oxidation number. Because there are three oxygen atoms in a nitrate ion, the total oxidation state for oxygen is –6. Since the sum of the oxidation states must equal the charge of the ion, nitrogen must have an oxidation number of +5 so that the sum will be -1: $-6 + 5 = -1$

Sample:

Assign oxidation numbers to all atoms in the following:

A. SF_6

B. $Cr_2O_7^{2-}$

C. P_2O_5

Answers:

A. Fluorine is always going to have to have an oxidation number of –1. It is the most electronegative element, so nothing will ever have a higher electronegativity. Therefore, the 6 fluorine atoms will give a total of $6(-1) = -6$. Because this is a neutral molecule, the sum of sulfur's oxidation number and the six fluorines must be zero. That means sulfur must be +6.

B. Oxygen is more electronegative, so it will have the negative oxidation number. It will have the charge it has in ionic compounds, which is 2–. Oxygen will always have a –2 oxidation number, except when it appears as a peroxide ion (O_2^{2-}), where it will have a –1. Since there are 7 of them, the total will be $7(-2) = -14$. The sum of the two chromium atoms and oxygen must equal the charge of the ion (2–). Therefore, each chromium must have a +6 oxidation number. $2(+6) + 7(-2) = -2$.

C. P_2O_5 is a neutral molecule in which oxygen is the more electronegative element. With 5 oxygen atoms, the total negative oxidation number is $5(-2) = -10$. Since there are two phosphorous atoms, each will have an oxidation state of +5.

You Try It!
Assign oxidation numbers to the atoms in the following:

A. PbS

B. MnO_4^{2-}

C. N_2O_5

Answers
A. Pb = +2, S = –2   B. Mn = +6, O = –2   C. N = +5, O = –2

One of the main purposes for using oxidation numbers is to follow the movement of electrons during an oxidation-reduction reaction. Doing so helps to predict the products and determine the outcomes of such reactions. There are a few different ways to analyze redox reactions, but we will focus on only one: the *ion-electron method* (also called the *half-reaction method*). The procedure requires that you know the reactants and products of the reaction, but, by going through the process, you will gain a better understanding of the mechanisms by which these reactions proceed.

Understanding the Oxidation-Reduction Process

These reactions all proceed by the transfer of electrons from one substance to another. Part of understanding the process is recognizing when these transfers are taking place. For example, if you look at the equation for the reaction that takes place between magnesium metal and hydrochloric acid, you may not notice the transfers unless you learn to look for them. The equation is written as:

$$Mg(s) + 2HCl(aq) \rightarrow MgCl_2(aq) + H_2(g)$$

You've probably seen this reaction, and you may have even performed it. There are no charged particles visible. However, let's begin by looking at the oxidation states of each substance in the reaction. Rewriting the equation with the oxidation states written above each element, we can see that there are a few changes:

$$\overset{0}{Mg(s)} + \overset{+1}{2HCl(aq)} \rightarrow \overset{+2}{MgCl_2(aq)} + \overset{0}{H_2(g)}$$

You can see that magnesium has lost two electrons and hydrogen has picked up one electron. Another way to see the process is to write an ionic equation, like you learned in the last section:

$$Mg(s) + 2H^+(aq) + 2Cl^-(aq) \rightarrow Mg^{2+}(aq) + 2Cl^-(aq) + H_2(g)$$

Looking at the ionic equation, you can see that electrons are actually being transferred. If we write the net ionic equation, you will see that the only atoms participating in the reaction are those whose oxidation numbers have changed.

$$Mg(s) + 2H^+(aq) \rightarrow Mg^{2+}(aq) + H_2(g)$$

In this reaction, you may be able to see the movement of electrons just by looking at the equation. Some other equations are more difficult and will require you to follow a series of procedures to complete them. We will begin to look at those rules using this relatively easy example.

The first step in balancing the equation is to write an unbalanced net ionic equation for the reaction. We'll dispense with the states for now.

$$Mg + H^+ \rightarrow Mg^{2+} + H_2$$

The second step requires you to separate the equation into two separate half-reactions. A half-reaction only shows what is going on in half of the reaction. The first half-reaction shows the oxidation and the second half-reaction the reduction.

Oxidation: $Mg \rightarrow Mg^{2+}$
Reduction: $H^+ \rightarrow H_2$

In the third step, you need to make sure you have the same number of each atom on each half of the equation.

Oxidation: $Mg \rightarrow Mg^{2+}$ (this one doesn't change)
Reduction: $2H^+ \rightarrow H_2$

In the fourth step, you need to add electrons to the equation to balance the charges. Write them in the equation as though they are elements with the symbol e^-.

Oxidation: $Mg \rightarrow Mg^{2+} + 2e^-$
Reduction: $2H^+ + 2e^- \rightarrow H_2$

You may be able to look at these two equations and think, "Hey, magnesium lost two electrons, and the hydrogen atoms gained two electrons." Coincidence? Nope. That's why this method is helpful. It explains where the electrons go, and how this dictates the outcome of the reaction. In this simple reaction, we left out a few steps because they weren't required. We'll finish this section by tackling two more challenging examples that will require you to use all of the rules.

Reactions in Acidic Solutions

In this first reaction, an acidified solution of potassium dichromate, $K_2Cr_2O_7$, reacts with a solution of potassium chloride, KCl. This type of problem periodically appears on the AP exam. The skeleton equation for this reaction is

$$Cr_2O_7^{2-} + Cl^- \rightarrow Cl_2 + Cr^{3+}$$

Step 1: Just like the last example, we need to begin by writing the unbalanced skeleton equation in ionic form:

$$Cr_2O_7^{2-} + Cl^- \rightarrow Cl_2 + Cr^{3+}$$

Step 2: Same as last time—convert the reaction into half-reactions.

Oxidation: $Cl^- \rightarrow Cl_2$
Reduction: $Cr_2O_7^{2-} \rightarrow Cr^{3+}$

(If you don't recognize it, the oxidation state of chromium has changed from +6 to +3)

Step 3: At this point, things get a little different. Balance the atoms other than O in each half-reaction.

$$Oxidation: 2Cl^- \rightarrow Cl_2$$
$$Reduction: Cr_2O_7^{2-} \rightarrow 2Cr^{3+}$$

Step 4: This step was not in the previous example. For reactions in an acidic medium, add H_2O to balance the oxygen atoms. In doing this, you will create some hydrogen atoms. You will need to balance those next, by adding H+ ions to the other side of the equation. All of these species are present in acidic solutions.

$$Cr_2O_7^{2-} \rightarrow 2Cr^{3+} + 7H_2O$$

You have to balance the hydrogen atoms now, so add H^+ to the other side

$$14H^+ + Cr_2O_7^{2-} \rightarrow 2Cr^{3+} + 7H_2O$$

Step 5: Add electrons to the half-reactions to balance the charges

$$Oxidation: 2Cl^- \rightarrow Cl_2 + 2e^-$$

(The total number of negative charges on the left side is 2 and on the right is 0. We need to add $2e^-$ to the right to balance the charges.)

$$Reduction: 14H^+ + Cr_2O_7^{2-} + 6e^- \rightarrow 2Cr^{3+} + 7H_2O$$

The total charge on the left is 12^+, obtained from 14^+ on hydrogen plus 2^- on the dichromate ion. The total charge on the right is 6^+, from the two chromium (III) ions. To balance the charges on the right and left, we must add $6e^-$ to the left, making the total charge 6^+, the same as the right side.

Step 6: At this point, you need to remember what we said about oxidation and reduction. One substance is oxidized and the other reduced. As the equations exist right now, the chloride ions have lost 2 electrons, but the chromium atoms have gained 6 electrons. That's impossible! The 6 electrons had to come from the chloride ions. In step 6, therefore, we need to equalize the number of electrons in each half-reaction. We need to increase the total number of electrons lost by the chloride ions to 6. To do this, we have to multiply the entire half-reaction by 3.

$$Oxidation: 6Cl^- \rightarrow 3Cl_2 + 6e^-$$
$$Reduction: 14H^+ + Cr_2O_7^{2-} + 6e^- \rightarrow 2Cr^{3+} + 7H_2O$$

Step 7: In the final step, you're going to combine the two half–reactions. After you have done this, you want to double check to make sure that all charges are balanced and that the number of atoms is balanced. Once you have done that, remove the electrons, and you're left with the balanced net ionic equation.

$$14H^+ + Cr_2O_7^{2-} + 6Cl^- + 6e^- \rightarrow 2Cr^{3+} + 3Cl_2 + 7H_2O + 6e^-$$
$$net\ ionic\ equation: 14H^+ + Cr_2O_7^{2-} + 6Cl^- \rightarrow 2Cr^{3+} + 3Cl_2 + 7H_2O$$

Reactions in Basic Solutions

Occasionally, you will have problems where the reaction takes place in a basic medium. In these problems, when you reach step 4, you add the water molecules to balance the oxygen atoms, and then add the hydrogen atoms to balance the hydrogen atoms in water (that's the same as what you normally do in step 4 for an acidic solution). After that, however, you add hydroxide (OH^-) ions on both sides of the equation to balance out the hydrogen atoms. After you do this, there will be H^+ ions and OH^- ions on the same side of the equation. You combine them together to form water molecules (as many as you can form) and cancel the number of water molecules that appear on both sides of the equation. In this example, we will look at a reaction that takes place in basic solution. If you're pressed for time, you can probably skip this—these rarely appear on the exam.

The skeleton equation: $MnO_4^- + I^- \rightarrow MnO_2 + IO_3^-$

Step 1: Write the unbalanced ionic equation.

$$MnO_4^- + I^- \rightarrow MnO_2 + IO_3^-$$

Step 2: Convert the reaction into half–reactions.

$$\text{Oxidation: } I^- \rightarrow IO_3^-$$

(Iodide has changed oxidation states from –1 to +5.)

$$\text{Reduction: } MnO_4^- \rightarrow MnO_2$$

(The oxidation state of manganese has changed from +7 to +4.)

Step 3: Balance the atoms other than oxygen.

Both atoms are already balanced

Step 4: Balance the oxygen atoms with water.

$$\text{Oxidation: } 3H_2O + I^- \rightarrow IO_3^-$$
$$\text{Reduction: } MnO_4^- \rightarrow MnO_2 + 2H_2O$$

Next, balance the hydrogen atoms with H^+.

$$\text{Oxidation: } 3H_2O + I^- \rightarrow IO_3^- + 6H^+$$
$$\text{Reduction: } MnO_4^- + 4H^+ \rightarrow MnO_2 + 2H_2O$$

This next part is what's different for a basic solution, adding OH^- ions to both sides of the equation for every H^+.

$$\text{Oxidation: } 3H_2O + I^- + 6OH^- \rightarrow IO_3^- + 6H^+ + 6OH^-$$
$$\text{Reduction: } MnO_4^- + 4H^+ + 4OH^- \rightarrow MnO_2 + 2H_2O + 4OH^-$$

Now, you form water molecules where you can add $H+$ and $OH-$ together.

$$\text{Oxidation: } 3H_2O + I^- + 6OH^- \rightarrow IO_3^- + 6H_2O$$
$$\text{Reduction: } MnO_4^- + 4H_2O \rightarrow MnO_2 + 2H_2O + 4OH^-$$

Finally, we will cancel the extra water molecules and proceed to step 5.

$$\text{Oxidation: } I^- + 6OH^- \rightarrow IO_3^- + 3H_2O$$
$$\text{Reduction: } MnO_4^- + 2H_2O \rightarrow MnO_2 + 4OH^-$$

Step 5: Add electrons to each half–reaction to balance the charges.

$$\text{Oxidation: } I^- + 6OH^- \rightarrow IO_3^- + 6e^- + 3H_2O$$
$$\text{Reduction: } MnO_4^- + 3e^- + 2H_2O \rightarrow MnO_2 + 4OH^-$$

Step 6: Modify the half–reactions, so the total electrons are the same.

$$\text{Oxidation: } I^- + 6OH^- \rightarrow IO_3^- + 6e^- + 3H_2O$$
$$\text{Reduction: } 2MnO_4^- + 6e^- + 4H_2O \rightarrow 2MnO_2 + 8OH^-$$

Step 7: Combine the half reactions and balance all electrons and atoms. We'll remove any excess water molecules or hydroxide ions in this step.

$$2MnO_4^- + 6e^- + 4H_2O + I^- + 6OH^- \rightarrow 2MnO_2 + 8OH^- + IO_3^- + 6e^- + 3H_2O$$

$$\text{net ionic equation: } 2MnO_4^- + H_2O + I^- \rightarrow 2MnO_2 + 2OH^- + IO_3^-$$

You Try It

Balance the following redox reactions, using the half-reaction method. Write your answers as net ionic equations.

A. $Mn(s) + H_2SO_4(aq) \rightarrow MnSO_4(aq) + H_2(g)$

B. $Pb(s) + AgNO_3(aq) \rightarrow Pb(NO_3)_2(aq) + Ag(s)$

C. $MnO_4^-(aq) + Cl^-(aq) \rightarrow Mn_2^+(aq) + Cl_2(aq)$ in acidic solution

Answers:

A. $Mn(s) + 2H^+(aq) \rightarrow Mn^{2+}(aq) + H_2(g)$

B. $Pb(s) + 2Ag^+(aq) \rightarrow Pb2^+(aq) + 2Ag(s)$

C. $2MnO_4^-(aq) + 10Cl^-(aq) + 16H^+(aq) \rightarrow 2Mn^{2+}(aq) + 5Cl_2(g) + 8H_2O$

What You Are Going to Be Accountable for on the AP Exam

This topic rarely appears in the multiple-choice portion of the AP exam. It is always found in the Free Response section of the test, where you are presented with 8 reactions, from which you must select 5. You are given the reactants and conditions for eight different possible reactions. The reactants are written as words, and you are to translate them into symbols. Each of the five reactions that you write is worth 3 points. Over the years, averages on this section are usually between 6 and 7 out of 15. What that means to you is if you get two of these correct, you are doing about as well as someone who has a cumulative score of 3 on the AP exam. Many of the reactions may seem very strange, but you shouldn't panic when you get to this part. There are some strategies you can use to help you improve your chances on this section.

1. The instructions say that you are to assume that solutions are aqueous unless otherwise indicated. This means it is not necessary to write (*aq*) next to each reactant and product in solution. The same is true for the phases of the substances. You do not need to write (*s*), (*l*), or (*g*).

2. The instructions also say to represent substances in solution as ions if the substances are extensively ionized. That means that if the substance dissolves, you should use an ionic equation to describe the constituent ions.

3. The instructions also say to omit formulas for any ions or molecules that are unchanged by the reaction. This is the equivalent of using a net ionic equation.

4. Finally, the instructions say that you need not balance the equation. Don't interpret this as saying "…but we'll be really impressed with you if you do!" It does not. There are a few places on the exam where you can show off your equation-balancing prowess, but this is not one of them.

5. Of the 3 points for each question, one of the points is for correctly writing the reactants. The other two points are for correctly writing the products. There are some things you should know about how these points are awarded. First, if you include any spectator ions on the reactant side, you will lose the reactant point for that question. If a reaction is written as a molecular equation instead of an ionic equation, you will only earn one point, even if the products are correct. When you write the charges for ions, they must be correct or you won't earn any points.

Now that you have some awareness of what will be expected of you on the AP exam, let's review the material in the chapter. There are far too many chemical reactions to worry about memorizing individual reactions. Instead, you should focus your attention on learning the identifying characteristics of the different types of reactions so that you can more effectively predict the possible products. In addition, you should learn the basic mechanisms for each type of equation to help you with your response.

SUMMARY OF THE FIVE MAIN REACTION TYPES

Table 10.6 summarizes the distinguishing characteristics of the different reaction types.

Table 10.6

Reaction Type	General Equation	Distinguishing Characteristics
Combination	$A + B \rightarrow AB$	On the exam, these will usually have two elements as reactants.
Decomposition	$AB \rightarrow A + B$	You're only given a single reactant. You'll most likely be given a set of conditions as well (i.e., heating, etc.)
Single Replacement	$A + BC \rightarrow AC + B$ Or $D + BC \rightarrow BD + C$	A neutral element combined with an ionic compound (usually in solution).
Metathesis (double replacement)	$AB + CD \rightarrow AD + CB$	These will have different combinations we will look at in more detail. A key feature though is the presence of two binary reactants (usually both ionic, but not always).
Combustion	$CxHy + O_2 \rightarrow CO(2) + H_2O$	The two in CO_2 is written in parentheses because sometimes CO is a product. Not all combustion reactions involve hydrocarbons. These questions usually use the word "burn" in the conditions of the reaction

TIP

An easy mnemonic device to remember the diatomic elements is Dr. Brinclhof. If you spell the last name this way, BrINClHOF, you should quickly recognize the seven diatomic elements: Br(omine), I(odine), N(itrogen), Cl(chlorine), H(ydrogen), O(xygen), and F(luorine)

Combination

In combination reactions, the reactants combine to form a single product. Because a combination of an element and a compound or two compounds would be difficult to classify as a combination reaction, the reactions on the AP exam that are combination reactions tend to use two elements. So, if you encounter two elements on the exam, they will undergo a combination reaction.

Sample: Magnesium metal is heated strongly in the presence of nitrogen gas.

Answer: When you read this, you have to know that nitrogen gas is a diatomic element. You also have to assume that strong heat means the reactants probably wouldn't react otherwise. When you write the reactants and products, you do not need to write the states of conditions of the reaction.

$$Mg + N_2 \rightarrow Mg_3N_2$$

The formula Mg_3N_2 was obtained by using the crisscross method. You can use the periodic table on this part of the exam, so you should really make an effort to memorize the common charges of ions, or oxidation states, by an elements position on the chart.

Decomposition

These are probably the easiest to detect, even if they aren't the easiest to determine the products for. The reason they are easiest to detect is there will only be a single reactant. You will usually be told something is being done to it, like heating, but no other reactant is mentioned. There may be a catalyst mentioned, but it will be labeled as a catalyst.

Sample: Potassium chlorate crystals are heated strongly in the presence of the catalyst manganese dioxide.

Answer: There's only one reactant, so this must be a decomposition reaction. The main problem is to try to determine the correct products. Usually, decomposition reactions are going to produce gases and salts. If nothing else, you are guaranteed one point if you can correctly write the formula of the reactant!

$$KClO_3 \rightarrow KCl + O_2$$

Combustion Reactions

The key term to look for in these questions is the word "burn." Combustion reactions can occur with different types of materials, but the most common and the most widely used on the AP exam is combustion of hydrocarbons. While the products are easily predictable, you have to have an understanding of organic chemistry nomenclature (we will discuss that in chapter 20) to be able to write the formulas of the reactants.

In all of these combustion reactions, the hydrocarbon reacts with oxygen. If sufficient oxygen is available for the hydrocarbon to react completely with the oxygen, a complete combustion occurs, where the products are CO_2 and H_2O. If insufficient oxygen is present, carbon monoxide, CO, will form instead. Occasionally, the AP questions will specify an "excess of oxygen gas" to let you know that a complete combustion is expected.

Sample: Butane gas is burned in air.

Answer: Past AP exams have used the word "air" in combustion questions. Assume that the word air represents oxygen when you answer the question. The only other difficult part on a question like this will be remembering the structure of butane. The reaction proceeds as

$$C_4H_{10} + O_2 \rightarrow CO_2 + H_2O$$

Occasionally, other compounds will be burned besides hydrocarbons. If the compound contains carbon, assume that one of the products is likely to be carbon dioxide (or carbon monoxide).

Sample: Carbon disulfide vapor is burned in oxygen.

Answer: $CS_2 + O_2 \rightarrow CO_2 + SO_2$

Double Replacement Reactions

These will take a variety of forms. The one thing they will all have in common is that two compounds will be reacting. What those compounds are will give you clues about how the reaction will proceed.

Precipitation Reactions

In these reactions, you will see two salt solutions added together. You need to use the solubility rules to determine the insoluble solid. Remember that in these reactions there are spectator ions, so make sure you leave them out of your equation.

Sample: A test tube containing a solution of silver nitrate is added to a beaker containing a solution of sodium chromate.

Answer: First thing to do is look at the possible products here: sodium nitrate and silver chromate. If you remember your solubility rules, you will know that silver chromate is the solid here. Therefore, the reaction will look like

$$Ag^+ + CrO_4^{2-} \rightarrow Ag_2CrO_4$$

Remember, silver is one of the four metals that only have one charge. If you forget the charge, it does appear on the reduction potentials chart. Also note that the spectator ions are omitted.

Neutralization Reactions

In a neutralization reaction, an acid or a base will combine to form neutral products. There are several variations here, but we have not yet gone over the specifics of acid-base chemistry. At this point, we will only look at a simple neutralization between a strong acid and a strong base. In chapter 15 we will take a deeper look at acid-base chemistry.

Strong Acid and Strong Base

These are like the examples we looked at earlier in the chapter. An acid and a base react to yield water and a salt.

Sample: A solution of hydrochloric acid is added to an equimolar solution of sodium hydroxide.

$$H^+ + OH^- \rightarrow H_2O$$

Gas-forming Reactions

In these reactions, a gas is formed as a product, which drives the reaction. A very common example is used in the identification of limestone.

Sample: A piece of solid calcium carbonate is added to a solution of dilute hydrochloric acid.

$$CO_3^{2-} + H^+ \rightarrow H_2O + CO_2$$

While HCO_3^- is an acceptable answer for a product, it is very unstable and rapidly decomposes to form water and carbon dioxide.

Displacement Reactions

These reactions will take a few different forms, but there are some things in common. The main thing is the presence of an element and a compound. Usually, the element will be a metal, but sometimes it will be a halogen. The compound will either be a dissolved salt or water. You will be able to use the chart of standard reduction potentials on this section, so you should be able to determine the activity of the elements. You should make a point of memorizing the cutoff points for the replacement of hydrogen. In general, the materials above hydrogen on the chart will replace H in acids, but only those from sodium through the top will replace H in liquid water.

One type that is a bit more complex but that shows up a fair amount is the addition of a metal to a strong oxoacid solution (usually nitric or sulfuric). The reason these are selected as often as they are is that they violate the typical rules for the replacement of hydrogen in solution. This is because the acids act as strong oxidizing agents that will ionize the metal. Copper or silver typically appear on the exam because they won't react with other acids but they will with the oxoacids. Both metals are oxidized by these acids.

Sample: A piece of calcium metal is dropped into a container of pure water.

Answer: Notice how one of the reactants is a single element. This is your clue that this may be a replacement. Next, you need to decide if calcium is capable of replacing the hydrogen in water. Looking at the list of reduction potentials, you notice that calcium is above sodium on that list, so it will replace the hydrogen. The reaction, therefore, is

$$Ca + H_2O \rightarrow Ca^{2+} + OH^- + H_2$$

First, notice that the equation is not balanced. It does not need to be. Second, notice how the calcium hydroxide is written in ionic form instead of molecular. This is a requirement for the AP exam. Hydrogen gas is a molecular compound and should be written as such.

Sample: A strip of magnesium ribbon is lowered into a test tube of silver nitrate solution.

Answer: Again, notice the single element as a reactant and a solution of an ionic compound as the other reactant. These are clues for a replacement. You should check to make sure that magnesium is capable of replacing silver in solution. A quick glance at the reduction potentials indicates that it will easily replace silver, so the reaction should be completed.

$$Mg + Ag^+ \rightarrow Mg^{2+} + Ag$$

Notice, the nitrate ion is not written, as it is only a spectator ion. Also notice that the charges are not balanced. That's okay; you don't have to balance the equation. It's very important that you know the charges of the elements. For some of the elements, the table of reduction potentials shows the charges, but this won't help you as much with the transition metals.

Sample: Chlorine gas is bubbled through a solution of sodium iodide.

Answer: A careful look here will show you an element and a dissolved salt for reactants. Another careful look will help you recognize that the element is a halogen, which means it is going to replace the anion from solution, in this case iodide. Sodium is a spectator in this reaction and will be omitted.

$$Cl_2 + I^- \rightarrow Cl^- + I_2$$

Sample: A small piece of copper metal is dropped into a beaker containing concentrated nitric acid.

Answer: You have probably seen this reaction, either as a live demonstration or in a video. It is a very dramatic reaction. When the metal is placed in the acid, it begins to get very hot, it fizzes, the nitric acid turns green, and a very poisonous brown gas is formed. Chemically, the reaction is written as

$$Cu + H^+ + NO_3^- \rightarrow Cu^{2+} + NO_2 + H_2O$$

Had the reaction occurred in dilute nitric acid, the product nitrogen dioxide, NO_2, would be replaced with nitrogen monoxide, NO. Notice that this is not a typical replacement, where hydrogen gas is released. These gases are characteristic of the reaction. If sulfuric acid was used instead of nitric acid, the gas would be SO_2.

Flowchart to Determine a Compound Formula When Given a Name

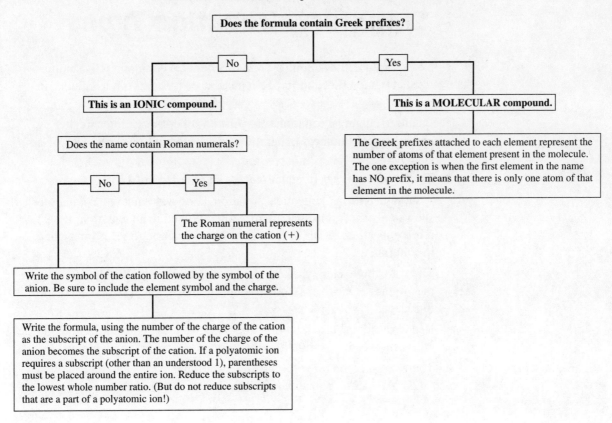

Figure 10.4

Flowchart to Determine a Compound Name When Given a Formula

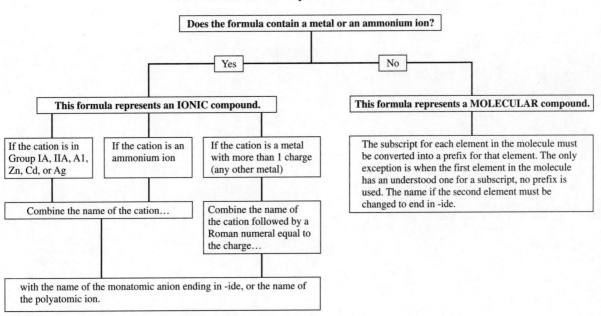

Figure 10.5

Summary: Reaction Types

- Nomenclature, the naming system for chemical compounds, is summarized in figures 10.4 and 10.5. Nomenclature for acids is not included in the chart.

- Balanced chemical equations obey the law of conservation of matter by placing equal numbers of atoms of each element on both sides of a chemical equation.

- The five main types of equations are summarized in Table 10.6.

- A shortened form of chemical equation, known as a net ionic equation, shows only the atoms that are directly involved in an equation. It also represents all materials as they exist in the reaction (e.g., as ions when in solution, etc.).

- There are three main types of metathesis reactions, all distinguished by the products. One forms a precipitate, another a nonelectrolyte, and the third a gas.

- Redox reactions, also known as oxidation-reduction reactions, include all reactions where oxidations and reductions occur simultaneously.

- There are specific rules for writing equations that need to be followed on the AP exam. You should be familiar with these rules.

REVIEW QUESTIONS

Because this topic only appears as Free Response questions, no multiple-choice questions are included in this chapter. As you work through these, don't try to memorize them. The reactions change every year, and they are very diverse. Make sure you are learning how to write your answers and also the major principles that guide all reactions. Learning these will help you better predict the products of any reaction.

Give the formulas to show the reactants and the products for the following chemical reactions. Each occurs in aqueous solution unless otherwise indicated. Represent substances in solution as ions if the substance is extensively ionized. Omit formulas for any ions or molecules that are unchanged by the reaction. In all cases a reaction occurs. You need not balance the equations.

1. A clean piece of magnesium ribbon is burned in nitrogen gas.

2. A beaker of ammonium sulfate solution is added to a saturated solution of barium hydroxide.

3. A sample of solid calcium fluoride is mixed with dilute sulfuric acid.

4. A crucible containing solid ammonium carbonate is heated.

5. A pea-sized chunk of sodium metal is dropped into a beaker of water.

6. Ammonia gas is added to a container of boron trifluoride gas.

7. A beaker containing dilute hydrochloric acid is poured into a beaker containing a solution of potassium sulfite.

8. Solid sodium oxide is sprinkled into a container of pure water.

9. A clean iron rod is submerged in a solution of iron(III) sulfate.

10. Silver turnings are dropped into a container of dilute nitric acid (6M) solution.

11. Ethanol is burned completely in air.

12. A solution of potassium iodide is added to an acidified solution of potassium dichromate.

13. A solution of potassium carbonate is added to a container of dilute hydrochloric acid.

14. A sample of potassium sulfite solution is mixed with an excess of dilute hydrochloric acid.

15. Tin(II) chloride solution is slowly poured into an acidified solution of potassium permanganate.

16. A solution of ammonia is added to a solution of ferric chloride.

17. A test tube of hydrogen peroxide solution is gently heated.

18. Crystals of dinitrogen pentoxide are stirred into water.

19. Copper (II) sulfide crystals are strongly heated in oxygen gas.

20. A concentrated solution of ammonia is added to a solution of zinc iodide.

21. Solid lithium hydride is added to water.

22. A solution of tetraaminecopper (II) sulfate is combined with an excess of nitric acid solution.

23. An excess amount of chlorine gas is slowly passed over hot iron filings.

24. Methanol is burned in oxygen.

25. Hydrogen sulfide gas is bubbled through a solution of mercury (II) chloride.

ANSWERS

1. $Mg + N_2 \rightarrow Mg_3N_2$ Two elements—suggests a combination reaction.

2. $NH_4^+ + SO_4^{2-} + Ba^{2+} + OH^- \rightarrow BaSO_4 + NH_3 + H_2O$ (or $NH_4^+ + OH^-$) The AP exam frequently includes questions with an ammonia solution (what you're dealing with as products in this reaction). Ammonia and water are actually in equilibrium with the ammonium and hydroxide ions.

3. $H^+ + SO_4^{2-} + CaF \rightarrow HF + CaSO_4$

4. $(NH_4)_2CO_3 \rightarrow H_2O + CO_2 + NH_3$ You know it has to be a decomposition, so the challenge is to figure out what products will form. They have to be gases/vapors, so you start with ammonia gas. Any time you have a carbonate in a decomposition, figure it will probably decompose to carbon dioxide gas. After those are gone, that leaves you with enough materials to produce water vapor.

5. $Na + H_2O \rightarrow Na^+ + OH^- + H_2$ You've probably seen this reaction at some point. The reactants should tip you off that it has to be a replacement reaction. The displaced hydrogen ions will combine to form hydrogen gas.

6. $BF_3 + NH_3 \rightarrow BF_3NH_3$ In the ammonia molecule there is a nonbonding pair of electrons that can react in a variety of ways. Later in the book, you will learn about complexes that can form with ammonia. In this reaction, boron trifluoride is a molecule that is usually represented with only 6 electrons around the central boron, making it a perfect mate for the ammonia molecule. As tempted as you might be to try to apply a double replacement strategy here, remember that they are both molecular substances. This suggests another approach: a combination reaction.

7. $H^+ + SO_3^{2-} \rightarrow HSO_3^-$ A double replacement reaction (KCl is soluble)

8. $Na_2O + H_2O \rightarrow Na^+ + OH^-$ A very characteristic reaction for metal oxides. Soluble metal oxides (like this one) are known as basic anhydrides because they dissolve in water to form basic solutions. You can also treat it like a double replacement reaction.

9. $Fe^{3+} + Fe \rightarrow Fe^{2+}$ The reactants should tip you off that this has to be a single replacement reaction. This is a redox reaction, where iron is reduced. These are the only two possible oxidation states for iron.

10. $Ag + H^+ + NO_3^- \rightarrow Ag^+ + NO$ (or NO_2) $+ H_2O$ Remember, nitric acid is a strong oxoacid, making it a strong oxidizing agent. Even though silver won't react with most acids, it will react with nitric acid. In these reactions, look for the metal to be oxidized. Most likely, NO will be the product because of the dilute solution of nitric acid, but it is also possible that some NO_2 will form. In cases like this, the graders usually won't mark you down for listing both (or either one separately).

11. $C_2H_5OH + O_2 \rightarrow CO_2 + H_2O$ Classic complete combustion reaction.

12. $H^+ + I^- + Cr_2O_7^{2-} \rightarrow I_2 + Cr^{3+} H_2O$ Questions pop up periodically that contain an acidified solution of potassium dichromate (or potassium permanganate) or either of those two added to an acidified solution of some other compound. This is a redox reaction similar to the examples in the chapter. The H^+ and H_2O come from the acidic solution.

13. $H^+ + CO_3^{2-} \rightarrow CO_2 + H_2O$ Double replacement reaction. Remember, carbonates tend to form CO_2.

14. $H^+ + SO_3^{2-} \rightarrow H_2O + SO_2$ Another double replacement. A different gas is formed, but note the similarity to number 13.

15. $Sn^{2+} + H^+ + MnO_4^- \rightarrow Sn^{4+} + Mn^{2+} + H_2O$ Another redox reaction in acidified solution. Look back to the redox section, if you have trouble here.

16. $Fe^{3+} + NH_3 + H_2O \rightarrow Fe(OH)_3 + NH_4^+$ The ammonium ion is in solution.

17. $H_2O_2 \rightarrow H_2O + O_2$ Decomposition of hydrogen peroxide. This is a very common reaction and is the reason why hydrogen peroxide has a very poor shelf life.

18. $N_2O_5 + H_2O \rightarrow H^+ + NO_3^-$ Nonmetallic oxides are often called acid anhydrides. Most, particularly those where the nonmetal has a higher oxidation state, produce acids when dissolved in water.

19. $CuS + O_2 \rightarrow CuO + SO_2$ You could also have Cu as a product, or Cu_2O. Sulfur dioxide must be present as the other product.

20. $Zn^{2+} + NH_3 \rightarrow Zn(NH_3)_4^{2+}$ OR $Zn^{2+} + NH_3 + H_2O \rightarrow Zn(OH)_2 + NH_4^+$
There are two possible outcomes here. One is the formation of a complex ion and the other is the formation of insoluble zinc hydroxide. Either would be given credit. On this problem, remember the ammonia and water solution is in equilibrium and can be written as $NH_3 + H_2O$, or $NH_4^+ + OH^-$. Either is considered correct. The implications on the reaction are when the ammonia is in the NH_3 state, the formation of the complex is favored. The other, NH_4^+ state, frees the hydroxide ions to form the insoluble solid.

21. $LiH + H_2O \rightarrow Li^+ + OH^- + H_2$ Just like pure metals in water, metal hydrides will also produce basic solutions. This one behaves like a double replacement reaction.

22. $H^+ + Cu(NH_3)_4^{2+} \rightarrow Cu^{2+} + NH_4^+$ If the name of the compound confused you, we'll be going over complex ions later. This is a redox reaction.

23. $Fe + Cl_2 \rightarrow FeCl_3$ Remember, two elements are reactants. There's not much to do except combine them.

24. $CH_3OH + O_2 \rightarrow CO_2 + H_2O$ (CO also acceptable)   Combustion reaction.

25. $H_2S + Hg^{2+} \rightarrow HgS + H^+$ Formation of a precipitate.

Chapter

11

Stoichiometry

This chapter should be thought of as more of a starting point than a self-contained unit. Stoichiometry is just a strange word that refers to record keeping during chemical reactions. It is the calculations that illustrate the relationships between reactants and products in chemical reactions. The ideas from this chapter will be used in the next several chapters.

THE MOLE

Fundamental to any discussion of the amount of reactants and products must be the mole. The mole (abbreviated as mol) is a term used to describe an amount of particles, typically atoms, molecules, or formula units. The English language includes many terms that describe specific numbers. For example, a dozen doughnuts means 12 doughnuts. One gross of something is 144. The mole is just a much bigger number. A mole represents 6.02×10^{23} particles, also known as Avogadro's number of particles. If you remember from earlier in the book, the atomic mass unit was based on 1/12 the mass of a carbon-12 atom. Well, Avogadro's number is based on the number of atoms in a 12 g sample of carbon-12 atoms. This also relates to the second way to describe moles. One mole of a substance will weigh, in grams, the same amount as the weight expressed in atomic mass units. The mass of a water molecule is 18.01 amu, so the molar mass (the mass of one mole of water molecules) is 18.01 g. As covered in Chapter 7, one mole of any gas at STP will have a volume of 22.4. So, moles help demonstrate the relationship of the number of particles, mass, and volume of different substances.

ROAD MAP

- *The Mole*
- *Determining Chemical Formulas*
- *Calculations in Chemical Reactions*
- *Limiting Reactants*

Calculating the Molar Mass of a Substance

To calculate a molar mass, add the total weights of all atom(s) in an element or compound. These weights are obtained from the Periodic Table of the Elements.

Sample: Calculate the gram formula mass of $K_2Cr_2O_7$.

Answer:

$$
\begin{array}{l}
K - 2 \times 39.10 = 78.20 \\
Cr - 2 \times 52.00 = 104.00 \\
\underline{O - 7 \times 16.00 = 112.00} \\
294.20 \text{ g } K_2Cr_2O_7
\end{array}
$$

You Try It!

1. Calculate the gram formula mass of Na_2CrO_4.
2. Calculate the gram formula mass of C_9H_{18}.
3. Calculate the gram formula mass of $Ba_3(PO_4)_2$.

Answers:
1. 162.00 g   2. 126.27 g   3. 601.93 g

Mole Calculations

The most basic mole calculation is the mole-to-mass (or mass-to-mole) conversion. It is simply a matter of using dimensional analysis and the molar mass of the substance to make the conversion.

Converting Moles to Grams

To convert a mole value to a mass value you will need to multiply by the molar mass.

$$\text{Moles of given substance} \times \frac{\text{molar mass of given}}{1 \text{ mol given}} = \text{mass of given}$$

Sample: How many grams are in 7.20 mol of dinitrogen trioxide?

Answer: First calculate the molar mass of dinitrogen trioxide

N: 2×14.01 g N = 28.02 g N

O: 3×16.00 g O = 48.00 g O

$28.02 + 48.00 = 76.02$ g N_2O_3

Next insert the molar mass into the equation:

$$7.20 \text{ mol } N_2O_3 \times \frac{76.02 \text{ g } N_2O_3}{1 \text{ mol } N_2O_3} = 547.34 \text{ g } N_2O_3$$

You Try It!

1. Find the mass in grams of 3.32 mol K.
2. Find the mass in grams of 5.08 mol $Ca(NO_3)_2$.
3. Find the mass in grams of 4.52×10^{-3} mol $C_{20}H_{42}$.

Answers:
1. 129.81 g   2. 833.6 g   3. 1.28 g

Converting Grams to Moles

This procedure is very similar to the mole to gram conversion, except in this one you divide by the molar mass.

$$\text{Mass of given substance} \times \frac{1 \text{ mol given}}{\text{molar mass of given}} = \text{moles of given}$$

Sample: Calculate the number of moles in 922 g of iron (III) oxide, Fe_2O_3.

Answer: First, calculate the molar mass of Fe_2O_3:

Fe: 2×55.85 g Fe = 111.7 g Fe

O: 3×16.00 g = 48.00 g O

111.7 g Fe + 48.00 g O = 159.7 g Fe_2O_3

Next, convert 922 grams into moles:

$$922 \text{ g } Fe_2O_3 \times \frac{1 \text{ mol } Fe_2O_3}{159.7 \text{ g } Fe_2O_3} = 5.77 \text{ mol } Fe_2O_3$$

You Try It!

1. Calculate the number of moles 187 g Al.
2. Calculate the number of moles in 333 g SnF_2.
3. Calculate the number of moles in 847 g $(NH_4)_2CO_3$.

Answers:

1. 6.93 moles   2. 2.12 moles   3. 8.81 moles

Other Mole Calculations

The calculations shown in the previous two sections as well as the calculations in this next section are summarized in a convenient chart, Figure 11.1. In this figure, the mole is inside a star in the center of the diagram. In the calculations above, when converting from moles to grams, you simply follow the arrow from the star to either one of the left corners (upper left if the substance is an element, lower left if it is a compound). For example, to convert from moles of an element to grams of that element, follow the arrow from the star to the upper left corner. Notice that above the arrow it says "× atomic mass" if you read it in the direction you are moving. That means you take the number of moles × the atomic mass to obtain the mass of the element. If you are converting in the other direction, from grams of the element to moles, you follow the arrow back to the middle, which says "/ atomic mass." This means to take the mass you are given and divide it by the atomic mass of that element to determine the number of moles. Sometimes, you will need to do other calculations using the mole. These are based on the other two equalities for moles, which are that 1 mole is equal to 6.02×10^{23} particles and 1 mole of a gas at STP occupies a volume of 22.4 liters. These two relationships are also found in Figure 11.1 and are read the same way as the mass to mole examples. The following is a brief look at these problems.

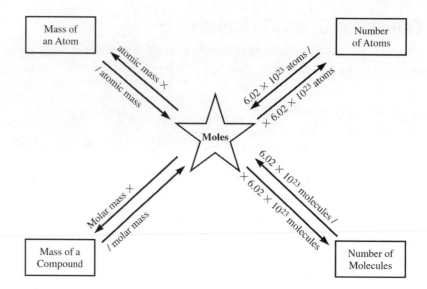

Figure 11.1

Moles to Particles

Sample: How many atoms of magnesium are in a sample of magnesium containing 2.75 moles of magnesium atom?

Answer: To make this conversion, using the chart in Figure 11.1, simply multiply the moles of magnesium by Avogadro's number (6.02×10^{23} particles).

$$2.75 \text{ moles Mg} \times 6.02 \times 10^{23} \text{ atoms Mg} = 1.66 \times 10^{24} \text{ atoms}$$

Particles to Moles

To go in the other direction, you just divide by Avogadro's number.

Sample: If you have 4.86×10^{22} molecules of water, how many moles of water do you have?

Answer:
4.86×10^{22} molecules H_2O / 6.02×10^{23} molecules
If you used dimensional analysis, this same procedure would be done with the calculation

$$4.86 \times 10^{22} \text{ mc } H_2O \times \frac{1 \text{ mol } H_2O}{6.02 \times 10^{23} \text{ mc } H_2O} = 0.0801 \text{ mol } H_2O$$

Moles to Volume

In these calculations, you will convert from the number of moles of a gaseous substance to the number of liters of that substance. Again, you can use Figure 11.1 to assist you with your calculation.

Sample: What is the volume of 0.372 moles of oxygen gas?

Answer: You would use the chart to move from moles to liters, which means you will need to multiply by 22.4 liters.

$$0.372 \text{ moles} \times \frac{22.4 \text{ liters}}{1 \text{ mol}} = 8.33 \text{ liters}$$

NOTE: This same result can be obtained using the ideal gas law $PV = nRT$

Volume to Moles

This is simply the converse—determining the number of moles of gas present in a certain volume. The procedure requires dividing by 22.4 liters instead of multiplying.

Sample: How many moles of helium gas, He, are contained in a balloon that has a volume of 15.8 liters?

Answer:

$$15.8 \text{ liters} \times \frac{1 \text{ mol}}{22.4 \text{ liters}} = 0.703 \text{ moles}$$

Additional Calculations

The chart can also be used to make more complex calculations. If, for example, you were trying to determine the volume, in liters, of hydrogen gas in a sample of 2.23 g H_2, you would begin on the upper left corner of the chart, convert grams to moles, and then move from the moles to the volume. It involves two separate calculations rather than the single calculations in the examples. To solve the problem just mentioned, you could combine the two steps into a single equation or solve it in two steps. Here is an example of it solved in a single equation using dimensional analysis.

$$2.23 \text{ g } H_2 \times \frac{1 \text{ mol}}{1.01 \text{ g}} \times \frac{22.4 \text{ liters}}{1 \text{ mol}} = 49.5 \text{ liters}$$

DETERMINING CHEMICAL FORMULAS
Percent Composition

This next type of problem occurs quite frequently on the AP exam. This calculation is the stepping-stone toward determining the empirical or molecular formula for a compound. The procedure allows you to determine the percentage by mass that a given substance exists in a compound or what percentage of a compound is composed of a particular substance. In the procedure, you need to determine the mass percentage of each element that is in the compound. You do so with the following calculation:

$$\text{Mass \% of substance} = \frac{\text{mass of substance in compound}}{\text{molar mass of compound}} \times 100\%$$

Sample: Determine the percentage composition for each element in the compound iron (II) carbonate ($FeCO_3$).

Answer: This requires you to determine the mass percentage of each component in the compound. The first step is to calculate the molar mass of the substance.

Fe: 1×55.85 $= 55.85$ g

C: 1×12.01 $= 12.01$ g

O: 3×16.00 $= 48.00$ g

Molar mass $FeCO_3 = 115.86$

Next, you will divide the molar mass of each substance by the molar mass of the compound.

$$\text{Mass \% Fe} = \frac{55.85 \text{ g Fe}}{115.86 \text{ g FeCO}_3} \times 100\% = 48.20\%$$

$$\text{Mass \% C} = \frac{12.01 \text{ g Fe}}{115.86 \text{ g FeCO}_3} \times 100\% = 10.37\%$$

$$\text{Mass \% O} = \frac{48.00 \text{ g Fe}}{115.86 \text{ g FeCO}_3} \times 100\% = 41.43\%$$

You Try It!

Calculate the percent composition of $Mg_3(PO_4)_2$.

Answer: Mg = 27.74%   P = 23.57%   O = 48.70%

Empirical Formulas

An empirical formula shows the simplest ratio of atoms in a molecule (or an ionic compound). For a molecular substance, the empirical formula only tells you the ratio of atoms, so it may not be very helpful at identifying the nature of a substance. For example, take any of the group of hydrocarbons known as the alkenes. All of the different compounds have a 1-to-2 ratio of carbon to hydrogen. Ethene is C_2H_4, propene is C_3H_6, and butene is C_4H_8. If you reduce all of the subscripts, they each come out to CH_2. Knowing the empirical formula helps to tell you that this substance is an alkene, but it doesn't tell you which one. How can you determine what a compound is from the empirical formula? The molecular weight will solve your problem. If you know the empirical formula and the molecular weight, you can determine the molecular formula for a compound. The first type of calculation we will look at is the determination of the empirical formula. The second type is the determination of a molecular formula.

Determining an Empirical Formula

Analysis of a compound containing potassium, chromium, and oxygen determines that in a 3.34 g sample, 0.89 g is potassium, 1.18 g is chromium, and 1.27 g is oxygen, what is the empirical formula of the compound?

Our first step will be to calculate the number of moles of each compound.

$$K: 0.89 \text{ g K} \times \frac{1 \text{ mol K}}{39.10 \text{ g K}} = 0.0228 \text{ mol K}$$

$$Cr: 1.18 \text{ g Cr} \times \frac{1 \text{ mol Cr}}{52.00 \text{ g Cr}} = 0.0227 \text{ mol Cr}$$

$$O: 1.27 \text{ g O} \times \frac{1 \text{ mol O}}{16.00 \text{ g O}} = 0.0794 \text{ mol O}$$

The next step is to divide all of the numbers of moles by the smallest one.

$$K: \frac{0.0228 \text{ mol}}{0.0227 \text{ mol}} = 1.00$$

$$Cr: \frac{0.0227 \text{ mol}}{0.0227 \text{ mol}} = 1.00$$

$$O: \frac{0.0794 \text{ mol}}{0.0227 \text{ mol}} = 3.50$$

At this point, you need to make a decision. If the outcome of your calculation produces all integers within a small degree of experimental error, you are ready to use these numbers as the subscripts in the empirical formula. If they are not, then you need to determine what you can multiply all of the numbers by to produce all integers. In most cases, it is fairly obvious. For instance, in our example, you can see that by doubling 3.50, it becomes 7.00—an integer. Therefore, to complete the empirical formula, you need to multiply all of the numbers by 2. This produces the empirical formula $K_2Cr_2O_7$.

Since this is an ionic compound, the empirical formula is the only formula that is possible. However, for a molecular compound, it is possible to have an empirical formula that does not represent the molecular formula. Here is a look at such an example. In the first problem, we will also show the procedure for beginning with a percentage composition, which is quite typical for these problems.

Sample: The percentage composition of citric acid found in lemons and other fruits is 37.5% C, 58.3 % O, and 4.20% H by mass. What is the molecular formula of citric acid if the molecular mass is 192.14 g?

Answer: The first step is to calculate the empirical formula. To begin, we need to determine the number of moles of each element. However, the percentage composition does not tell us a mass. To get around this, the commonly used technique is to assume that you have a 100.0-gram sample of the substance. Because 100.0 grams is equal to 100%, you can simply take the percentages and say that the masses are equal to that same amount in grams. From there, the problem proceeds just like the previous example.

$$\text{C: } 37.5 \text{ g} \times \frac{1 \text{ mol C}}{12.01 \text{ g C}} = 3.122 \text{ mol C}$$

$$\text{H: } 4.20 \text{ g} \times \frac{1 \text{ mol H}}{1.01 \text{ g H}} = 4.158 \text{ mol H}$$

$$\text{O: } 58.3 \text{ g} \times \frac{1 \text{ mol O}}{16.00 \text{ g C}} = 3.644 \text{ mol O}$$

The next step is to divide all numbers by the smallest number:

$$\text{C: } \frac{3.122 \text{ mol}}{3.122 \text{ mol}} = 1.000$$

$$\text{H: } \frac{4.158 \text{ mol}}{3.122 \text{ mol}} = 1.332$$

$$\text{O: } \frac{3.644 \text{ mol}}{3.122 \text{ mol}} = 1.167$$

This is a good example of one that does not jump off the page at you. The numbers are definitely not integers; neither can they be explained by experimental error. A closer look displays a pattern, however. If you look at the H, .332 is extremely close to the decimal equivalent of the fraction 1/3. The 0.167 ending in oxygen is extremely close to the decimal equivalent of the fraction 1/6. Because 6 is a multiple of 3, the solution appears to require all values to be multiplied by 6. Therefore, the empirical formula for citric acid is

$$(C_{1.000}H_{1.332}O_{1.167})6 = C_6H_8O_7$$

The next step is to compare the weight of the compound in the empirical formula to the molecular weight. The molecular weight of $C_6H_8O_7$ is

C: 6×12.01 g   = 72.06

H: 8×1.01 g   = 8.08

O: 7×16.00 g   = 112

72.06 + 8.08 + 112 = 192.14 g

For this formula, the empirical formula has the same mass as the molecular formula, so they must be the same. The molecular formula of citric acid is $C_6H_8O_7$. So that you can see what happens when the two aren't the same, we'll do one more example. In this one, however, we will skip the first steps and go right to the final step.

Sample: The empirical formula of a compound is CH_2O. The molar mass of the compound is 180.18 g. Find the molecular formula for this compound.

Answer: First, we need to calculate the molar mass of CH_2O:

C: 1×12.01 = 12.01 g
H: 2×1.01 = 2.02 g
O: 1×16.00 = 16.00 g

$12.01 + 2.02 + 16.00 = 30.03$ g

You can probably eyeball this one and know the molecular formula, but we'll solve it formally so you can see the procedure. In order to determine how many times you will have to multiply each subscript, you need to determine the ratio of the empirical formula and the molecular formula. Dividing the molecular formula by the empirical formula does this:

$$\frac{\text{molecular formula mass}}{\text{empirical formula mass}} = \frac{180.18 \text{ g}}{30.03 \text{ g}} = 6$$

Therefore, you need to multiply each subscript in the empirical formula by 6.

$$(CH_2O)6 = C_6H_{12}O_6$$

The molecular formula of the compound is $C_6H_{12}O_6$.

CALCULATIONS IN CHEMICAL REACTIONS

This section begins to look at chemical reactions rather than single substances. Using the techniques in this section, you will be able to convert from a given amount of one substance to an amount of any other substance in a reaction. By having this ability, you will be able to better predict the outcome of many different chemical reactions. We'll begin with the most basic procedure of converting from moles of one substance to moles of another and work our way toward converting quantities of one substance to quantities of another.

Mole-to-Mole Conversions

The most important step to all of these calculations is the use of a value known as the *mole ratio*. The mole ratio is the ratio of moles of one substance to moles of second substance. It is determined by the ratios of the coefficients from the balanced chemical equation. The mole ratio is used in all conversions since it allows you to switch from values that describe the given substances to values that describe the unknown substance. To facilitate this process, there is another chart, figure 11.2, that provides guidelines for solving most problems. In this first type of calculation, we will use the mole ratio to convert from units of moles of the given substance to moles of the unknown substance. We're going to omit the states of the reactants and products so that you can focus your attention on the coefficients.

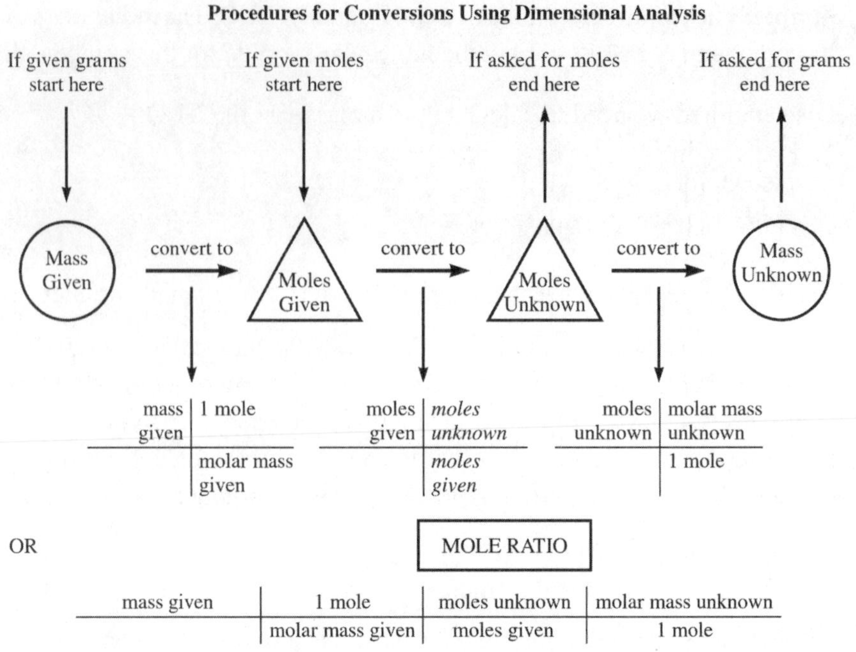

Procedures for Conversions Using Dimensional Analysis

If given grams start here   If given moles start here   If asked for moles end here   If asked for grams end here

Mass Given   convert to   Moles Given   convert to   Moles Unknown   convert to   Mass Unknown

$$\frac{\text{mass given} \mid 1 \text{ mole}}{\text{molar mass given}} \qquad \frac{\text{moles given} \mid moles\ unknown}{moles\ given} \qquad \frac{\text{moles unknown} \mid \text{molar mass unknown}}{1 \text{ mole}}$$

OR   MOLE RATIO

$$\frac{\text{mass given}}{} \Bigg| \frac{1 \text{ mole}}{\text{molar mass given}} \Bigg| \frac{\text{moles unknown}}{\text{moles given}} \Bigg| \frac{\text{molar mass unknown}}{1 \text{ mole}}$$

Figure 11.2

Sample:

$$2C_2H_6 + 7O_2 \rightarrow 4CO_2 + 6H_2O$$

In the equation above, determine the number of moles of carbon dioxide produced if 3.5 moles of ethane, C_2H_6, react with an excess of oxygen.

Answer: In the problem, first note the use of the term excess. Whenever you see this, the reason you are being told about an excess of a reactant is so you know that the other reactant can react completely to yield the maximum amount of product. In some later examples in this chapter, you will see what happens when there is a limited amount of a reactant.

The next thing to determine are the given and unknown substances. In this problem, ethane is the given substance and carbon dioxide is the unknown. Our task will be to convert from moles of ethane to moles of carbon dioxide. We will do this using the mole ratio, which is based on the equality of 2 moles C_2H_6 = 4 moles CO_2. In simple terms, the ratio tells you that you will always produce twice as many moles of CO_2 as the number of moles of ethane. To solve the problem, we will use the mole ratio as the conversion factor to change units from ethane to carbon dioxide.

$$3.50 \text{ moles } C_2H_6 \times \frac{4 \text{ moles } CO_2}{2 \text{ moles } C_2H_6} = 7.00 \text{ moles } CO_2$$

Mole-to-Mass or Mass-to-Mole Calculations

In these calculations, you will be converting either from moles of the given substance to grams of the unknown or from grams of the given substance to moles of the unknown. Either way, you will need to use the mole ratio as the mechanism for crossing over from one substance to the next. Other than the step with the mole ratio, these calculations are the same as the calculations from earlier in the chapter that converted mass to moles or moles to mass for a single substance. We'll use the same equation from the sample problem to continue with this example.

Sample: Moles to Mass

$$2C_2H_6 + 7O_2 \rightarrow 4CO_2 + 6H_2O$$

In the reaction shown above, how many grams of oxygen gas are required to completely react with 3 moles of ethane, C_2H_6?

Answer: Before you can determine the number of grams of oxygen, you need to know the number of moles of oxygen that will be required. You know that for every 2 moles of C_2H_6, you need 7 moles of O_2. Therefore we can begin with the mole ratio

$$3 \text{ mol } C_2H_6 \times \frac{7 \text{ moles } CO_2}{2 \text{ moles } C_2H_6} = 10.5 \text{ mol } O_2$$

Now that you know you will need 10.5 mol O_2, you can calculate the mass of the O_2.

$$10.5 \text{ mol } O_2 \times \frac{16.00 \text{ g } O_2}{1 \text{ mol } O_2} = 168.0 \text{ g } O_2$$

Sample: Mass to Moles

$$2C_2H_6 + 7O_2 \rightarrow 4CO_2 + 6H_2O$$

In the equation above, how many moles of water vapor can be produced from the combustion of 147.0 g of ethane, C_2H_6?

Answer: First, you need to know how many moles of ethane are being burned. Once you know this, you can use the mole ratio to determine the moles of water vapor.

$$147.0 \text{ g } C_2H_6 \times \frac{1 \text{ mol } C_2H_6}{30.08 \text{ g } C_2H_6} = 4.89 \text{ mol } C_2H_6$$

Now that you know the moles of C_2H_6, you can convert to moles of H_2O.

$$4.89 \text{ mol } C_2H_6 \times \frac{6 \text{ mol } H_2O}{2 \text{ mol } C_2H_6} = 14.67 \text{ mol } H_2O \text{ will be produced}$$

Mass-to-Mass Conversions

These are by far the most common conversions that you will be required to know. In these problems, you are given the mass of one substance and asked for the mass of another substance. The procedure is really just the two previous procedures blended together. The sample problem will demonstrate the procedures for solving these problems.

Sample:

$$4Al + 3O_2 \rightarrow 2Al_2O_3$$

In the reaction shown above, how many grams of aluminum are required to produce 192.0 grams of Al_2O_3? Assume there is adequate oxygen for a complete conversion of aluminum.

Answer: The three steps you are going to follow are:

1. Convert grams of Al_2O_3 to moles of Al_2O_3.

$$192.0 \text{ g } Al_2O_3 \times \frac{1 \text{ mol}}{101.96 \text{ g}} = 1.883 \text{ mol } Al_2O_3$$

2. Convert moles of Al_2O_3 to moles of Al (mole ratio step)

$$1.883 \text{ mol } Al_2O_3 \times \frac{4 \text{ mol Al}}{2 \text{ mol } Al_2O_3} = 3.766 \text{ mol Al}$$

3. Convert moles of Al to grams of Al

$$3.766 \text{ mol Al} \times \frac{26.98 \text{ g}}{1 \text{ mol}} = 101.6 \text{ g Al are required}$$

This procedure can also be set up as a one-step dimensional analysis problem as follows:

$$\frac{192.0 \text{ g } Al_2O_3}{} \left| \frac{1 \text{ mol } Al_2O_3}{101.96 \text{ g } Al_2O_3} \right| \frac{4 \text{ mol Al}}{2 \text{ mol } Al_2O_3} \left| \frac{26.98 \text{ g Al}}{1 \text{ mol Al}} \right. = 101.6 \text{ g Al}$$

Note how all units except g Al cross cancel.

Other Conversions

Once you know this basic procedure, you can also convert from any quantity of one substance to any quantity of another. The secret is to combine the two charts to one larger chart. Because the mole ratio is the place that must be included in all calculations of this type, you must know the number of moles of the given substance to be able to convert to the unknown substance. It doesn't matter what starting unit you have (i.e., liters, atoms, g), you will use the procedures in Figure 11.1 to convert to moles. Once you know the moles, you use the mole ratio to change from one substance to the other. At that point, you use Figure 11.1 again to convert to whatever ending unit you desire. If you are converting from grams of the given to grams of unknown, or any intermediate step, you can use Figure 11.2 to do so.

LIMITING REACTANTS

In this section, we will further investigate relationships between substances in chemical reactions. Up to this point, we have been assuming that there is a sufficient amount of each chemical to complete the reaction. However, much of the time the amounts of chemicals don't work out so nicely. There may be a deficiency of one substance that limits the amount of product that can be formed. An analogy, one that has perplexed consumers for years, is the hot dog and bun dilemma. Many packages of popular hot dogs come with 10 hot dogs. Most packages of buns come with 8 buns. Although you probably know what's coming, let's go through it anyway. You can't make 10 complete hot dogs here. Even though you have 10 hot dogs, you only have enough buns for 8, so the most hot dogs you can make is 8. You will have 2 bun-less hot dogs left over. The bun is what we would call a ***limiting reactant*** in this reaction. The yield, or number of complete hot dogs, is limited because of the number of buns that we have. This very same principle applies to chemical reactions as well. The yield is limited by the amount of each reactant. Once a reactant is used up, the reaction will stop, and any amount of the other reactant(s) left over will remain in the reaction vessel. In the first sample problem, we will determine the limiting reactant in a chemical reaction.

In the last chapter, we looked at the reaction between lead (II) nitrate and potassium iodide, where the yellow precipitate lead (II) iodide was formed. We will use this reaction to look at limiting reactants. To refresh your memory, the reaction proceeds as follows:

$$Pb(NO_3)_2(aq) + 2KI(aq) \rightarrow PbI_2(s) + 2KNO_3(aq)$$

From the balanced equation, you can see that it is necessary to have twice as many moles of potassium iodide as lead nitrate for the reaction to complete. What if you only had 1.5 moles of KI, and 1 mole of $Pb(NO_3)_2$? Since the ratio of KI to $Pb(NO_3)_2$ is 2-to-1, if you only have 1.5 moles of KI, you could only combine with 0.75 moles of $Pb(NO_3)_2$. Therefore, you would have 0.25 moles of unreacted $Pb(NO_3)_2$ left in the reaction vessel after all KI had reacted. In this example, KI was the limiting reactant.

It's fairly easy to conceptualize the idea of limiting reactants when you are given moles of the reactants. When you are given grams, it is not always so easy to see. When you have to solve limiting reactant problems, it is always necessary to determine the number of moles of each substance and compare that to the required ratios from the balanced chemical equation. Let's use the same reaction, but use masses instead of moles.

Sample: A solution of lead (II) nitrate containing 286.4 g of $Pb(NO_3)_2$ is added to a solution of potassium iodide containing 138.9 g of KI.

    (A) How many grams of solid PbI_2 will be formed during the reaction?

    (B) What is the limiting reactant?

    (C) How many grams of the excess reactant will be remaining?

Answers:

(A) A typical way to solve this problem is to calculate the number of moles of product that can be produced from each quantity of reactant. The answer that is the smallest will indicate the limiting reactant.

$$286.4 \text{ g Pb(NO}_3)_2 \times \frac{1 \text{ mol}}{331.22 \text{ g}} \times \frac{1 \text{ mol PbI}_2}{1 \text{ mol Pb(NO}_3)_2} = 0.865 \text{ mol PbI}_2$$

$$138.9 \text{ g KI} \times \frac{1 \text{ mol}}{166.01 \text{ g}} \times \frac{1 \text{ mol PbI}_2}{2 \text{ mol KI}} = 0.418 \text{ mol PbI}_2$$

Because KI is only capable of producing 0.418 mol of PbI_2, it is the limiting reactant. The amount of PbI_2 that will be formed in this reaction is

$$0.418 \text{ mol PbI}_2 \times \frac{461.02 \text{ g}}{1 \text{ mol}} = 192.71 \text{ g PbI}_2$$

(B) KI is the limiting reactant.

(C) To determine the amount of excess reactant, we need to determine how much $Pb(NO_3)_2$ was actually used during the reaction and subtract this from the starting amount.

$$0.418 \text{ mol PbI}_2 \times \frac{1 \text{ mol Pb(NO}_3)_2}{1 \text{ mol PbI}_2} \times \frac{331.22 \text{ g Pb(NO}_3)_2}{1 \text{ mol Pb(NO}_3)_2} = 138.4 \text{ g}$$
$$Pb(NO_3)_2$$

This answer tells us that 138.4 grams of $Pb(NO_3)_2$ will actually react with KI and that the remainder, $(286.4 \text{ g} - 138.4 \text{ g}) = 148 \text{ g}$ will remain in solution. If more KI were added to the reaction vessel, more precipitate would form.

The amount of PbI_2 calculated in part (A), 192.71 g, is known as the **_theoretical yield_** of the substance. That is the maximum amount that can form based on the stoichiometric relationships between reactants and products. The actual reaction will more than likely produce less than this, for a variety of reasons (which are unimportant to us).

You Try It!

Solid aluminum reacts vigorously with aqueous copper (II) chloride. Use the reaction below to answer questions (A), (B), and (C).

$$2Al(s) + 3CuCl_2(aq) \rightarrow 2AlCl_3(aq) + 3Cu(s)$$

43.17 g of solid aluminum are added to an aqueous copper (II) chloride solution containing 302.51 g of $CuCl_2$.

    (A) Which is the limiting reactant?

    (B) What is the theoretical yield of Cu?

    (C) How many grams of excess reactant are left in the reaction vessel?

Answers:

(A) $CuCl_2$ (B) 2.25 mol = 143.0 g Cu   (C) 2.7 g Al

Summary: Stoichiometry

- A mole is equal to 6.02×10^{23} particles. The mass of one mole of particles is known as the molar mass of a substance, and the volume of one mole of gas particles at STP is equal to 22.4 liters.

- The molar mass of a substance is calculated by adding the weights of the atoms of each element multiplied by the number of atoms of that element in the compound.

- The molar mass of a substance is used to convert from moles to grams of a single substance or grams to moles of a single substance.

- Avogadro's number, 6.02×10^{23} is used to convert from moles to particles or particles to moles for a single substance.

- Molar volumes can be determined by using the equality 22.4 liters = 1 mol, provided the gas is at STP.

- The percentage composition of a compound tells you, by percentage, the mass of each element in a compound. It also allows you to determine empirical and molecular formulas.

- The empirical formula is the simplest whole number ratio of elements in a compound. The molecular formula tells you the actual numbers of each atom in a compound.

- The same basic formulas for mole conversion with one substance are used to compare two substances in a chemical reaction. The only difference is that one substance must be converted to another using the *mole ratio* before the calculation can be completed.

- A limiting reactant is a reactant that is completely used up in a chemical reaction and that prevents the remainder of the other reactant(s) from forming products.

- The *theoretical yield* of a reaction is the amount of product that is predicted using the stoichiometric ratios of moles from the balanced chemical reaction.

REVIEW QUESTIONS

1. In which of the following compounds is the mass ratio of nitrogen to oxygen closest to 0.58 to 1.00?

   (A) N_2O

   (B) NO

   (C) NO_2

   (D) N_2O_3

   (E) N_2O_5

2. How many grams of strontium nitrate, $Sr(NO_3)_2$, contain 40 grams of oxygen atoms?

   (A) 212 grams

   (B) 96 grams

   (C) 62 grams

   (D) 24 grams

   (E) 88 grams

3. 1.00 mole of four different compounds containing element X were analyzed and found to contain 36.0 grams, 54.0 grams, 72.0 grams, and 108 grams, respectively. A possible atomic weight of X is

   (A) 13.5

   (B) 18.0

   (C) 25.0

   (D) 72.0

   (E) 108.0

4. The simplest formula for an oxide of chromium that is 61.9% chromium by weight is

   (A) CrO_3

   (B) CrO_2

   (C) CrO

   (D) Cr_2O

   (E) Cr_2O_3

5. A hydrocarbon gas with an empirical formula CH_2 has a density of 2.51 grams per liter at STP. A possible formula for the hydrocarbon is

   (A) CH_2

   (B) C_2H_4

   (C) C_3H_6

   (D) C_4H_8

   (E) C_5H_{10}

6. When magnesium metal is heated in air, one product of the reaction is found to contain 72.2% Mg by mass and 27.8% N by mass. What is the empirical formula for this compound?

   (A) MgN

   (B) Mg_2N

   (C) MgN_2

   (D) Mg_2N_3

   (E) Mg_3N_2

7. A piece of solid sodium metal with a mass of 7.67 grams is added to an excess of hydrochloric acid. What volume of hydrogen gas is produced from this reaction if it takes place at STP?

   (A) 22.4 liters

   (B) 11.2 liters

   (C) 7.46 liters

   (D) 5.60 liters

   (E) 3.74 liters

8. ___$Al(s)$ + ___$HCl(g) \rightarrow$ ___$AlCl_3(s)$ + ___$H_2(g)$

   If 2 moles of aluminum metal shavings react with hydrogen chloride gas, how many moles of H_2 can be formed?

   (A) 2

   (B) 3

   (C) 4

   (D) 5

   (E) 6

9. $3Cu(s) + 8HNO_3(aq) \rightarrow 3Cu(NO_3)_2(aq) + 2NO(g) + 4H_2O$

   Copper reacts with dilute nitric acid according to the balanced equation above. If 2 moles of copper metal are allowed to react with an excess of nitric acid, how many grams of NO gas can be formed?

   (A) 90.0 g

   (B) 80.0 g

   (C) 40.0 g

   (D) 20.0 g

   (E) 1.5 g

10. __ $C_6H_{12}(l) +$ __ $O_2(g) \rightarrow$ __ $CO_2(g) +$ __ $H_2O(l)$

   According to the reaction represented above, how many moles of O_2 are required to produce 2 moles of H_2O?

   (A) 2 moles

   (B) 5/2 moles

   (C) 3 moles

   (D) 7/2 moles

   (E) 4 moles

11. In a very violent reaction known as the thermite reaction, powdered aluminum metal reacts with iron (III) oxide to form molten iron and aluminum oxide. How many moles of aluminum metal are required to produce 13.96 g of molten iron?

   (A) 0.0500 mole

   (B) 0.0625 mole

   (C) 0.125 mole

   (D) 0.250 mole

   (E) 0.500 mole

12. $4NH_3(g) + 5O_2(g) \rightarrow 4NO(g) + 6H_2O(g)$

   In the reaction above, 3.10 g of NH_3 reacts with 2.50 g of O_2. What is the theoretical yield of NO?

   (A) 1.88 g

   (B) 5.46 g

   (C) 8.20 g

   (D) 24.0 g

   (E) 120 g

Free-Response
Question 1

You are given three unknown hydrocarbon compounds (unknowns A, B, and C), each containing only carbon and hydrogen. Using the data below, answer the questions that will eventually allow you to determine the identities of the unknowns.

   (A) Complete combustion of 1.00 g of unknown A resulted in the formation of 1.39 liters of CO_2 (at STP) and 2.23 g of H_2O. What is the most probable molecular formula of unknown A?

   (B) Determine the molecular weight of unknown B if the vapor density of B at STP is 3.13 grams per liter.

   (C) The empirical formula for unknown B is CH_2. Determine the molecular formula.

   (D) 1.00 g of unknown C contains 0.817 g carbon. The complete combustion of 1.00 mole of unknown C requires 5 moles of O_2. What is the most likely molecular formula of unknown C?

Question 2

The following questions refer to a laboratory activity designed to determine concentration of lead ions in a solution of lead (II) nitrate using gravimetric analysis. In the experiment, a 50.0 mL sample of the $Pb(NO_3)_2$, solution was added to an excess of potassium iodide solution. The resulting precipitate, PbI_2, was collected by vacuum filtration, dried in a drying oven, and weighed. Assume that

- both solutions were pure.
- no decomposition took place in the drying oven.
- the filter did not allow any PbI_2 to pass through..
- all lead is lead (II).
- an analytical balance was used to weigh the product.

   (A) If 2.310 g of PbI_2 were collected, how many grams of lead (II) nitrate must have been in the 50.0 mL sample?

   (B) What was the molarity of the lead (II) nitrate solution?

   (C) How many grams of lead (II) ions were in the lead (II) nitrate solution?

   (D) What is the minimum number of moles of potassium iodide that must be present in solution to assure a complete precipitation of all lead from solution?

   (E) If the solid PbI_2 on the filter paper was not thoroughly rinsed with distilled water prior to drying, what implications would that have on your answer in question (a)? Defend your response.

ANSWERS

1. **The correct answer is (D).** On a problem like this, you need to work quickly. You know that the ratio of nitrogen to oxygen is supposed to be 0.58 to 1.00. Begin by writing the atomic masses of nitrogen and oxygen, and then multiply them by ratios in the formulas. If you round 0.58 to 0.6, this will save time during the initial problem solving. That gives you a ratio of 3 to 5 to work with. You will quickly rule out most choices. When you get to the last one, you can double check. N_2O_3 yields the approximate ratio of 28/48, which equals 0.58 to 1.

2. **The correct answer is (E).** If you use the periodic table, you can determine the molar mass of $Sr(NO_3)_2$ at 211.64. During the AP exam, you can save time by rounding the masses. A quick glance at the answers shows that none of them are that close together. Therefore, when determining the molar mass or strontium nitrate, you can round Sr to 88 and N to 14; O is already 16. The round of mass of 212 is going to be close enough to get the correct answer. From this, you can determine the mass percentage of oxygen by dividing 96 by 211.64 (212). The mass percentage is 45.4 % (dividing by 212 yields 45.3%). If you known that oxygen is 45.4% by mass of the compound, then you just need to figure out what 40 grams is 45.4% of. Dividing 40 grams by .454 yields 88 grams.

3. **The correct answer is (B).** In this one, you are just looking for multiples of an answer. Notice that all of these numbers are multiples of 18.

4. **The correct answer is (B).** This is similar to question 2. The quickest way to figure it out is to write 52 (the mass of Cr) over 16 (the mass of O). You know that the mass of chromium in the compound divided by the mass of the compound must equal 0.619, so you can eyeball different combinations to see which one would be close. When you think you have one, you can do the math to confirm it. For example, if you look at CrO_3, you can fairly quickly determine the molar mass: $52 + (3 \times 16 = 48) = 100$. $\frac{52}{100}$ is clearly not the ratio you are looking for. So try another. CrO_2 yields $\frac{52}{84} = .619$.

5. **The correct answer is (D).** Remember, all gases at STP have a volume of 22.4 liters per mole. Therefore if the density is 2.51 grams per liter, all you need to do is determine the mass in 22.4 liters. You can do this with a proportion:

$$\frac{2.51 \text{ g}}{1 \text{ L}} = \frac{x \text{ g}}{22.4 \text{ L}}; x = 56.2 \text{ g, the mass of } C_4H_8.$$

6. **The correct answer is (E).** There are two ways to work a problem like this. One is the correct way, and the other is a quick eyeballing (if you're short on time). In the eyeballing, you would write the rounded mass of Mg (24 amu) over the rounded mass of N (14 amu). Then look quickly at the multiples in the problem to see which ones produce mass percents around 75%, and 25% (this will get you very close). The correct way to solve the problem, which can also be done very quickly if you've been practicing, is as follows:

$$72.2 \text{ g} \times \frac{1 \text{ mol}}{24.3 \text{ g}} = 2.97; \quad \frac{2.97}{1.99} = 1.5 \times 2 = 3$$

$$27.8 \text{ g} \times \frac{1 \text{ mol}}{14.0 \text{ g}} = 1.99; \quad \frac{1.99}{1.99} = 1.0 \times 2 = 2$$

7. **The correct answer is (E).** Some problems on the AP exam are going to be like this. You need to determine the balanced equation for a reaction even on the multiple-choice section of the test.

 This reaction is $2Na + 2HCl \rightarrow 2NaCl + H_2$

 The mole ratio of Na to H_2 is 2:1.

 The calculation is going to be $7.67 \text{ g} \times \dfrac{1 \text{ mol}}{23 \text{ g}} \times \dfrac{1 \text{ mol H}_2}{2 \text{ mol Na}} = 0.167 \text{ mol H}_2$.

 If one mole occupies 22.4 L, then 0.167 mole = 3.74 L.

8. **The correct answer is (B).** First you have to balance the equation: $2Al + 6HCl \rightarrow 2AlCl_3 + 3H_2$. Now this becomes a very simple mole-to-mole

 conversion: $2 \text{ mol Al} \times \dfrac{3 \text{ mol H}_2}{2 \text{ mol Al}} = 3 \text{ mol H}_2$

9. **The correct answer is (C).** $2 \text{ mol Cu} \times \dfrac{2 \text{ mol NO}}{3 \text{ mol Cu}} \times \dfrac{30 \text{ g NO}}{1 \text{ mol Cu}} = 40 \text{ g}$

10. **The correct answer is (C).** The balanced equation is $C_6H_{12}(l) + 9O_2(g) \rightarrow 6CO_2(g) + 6H_2O(l)$. Therefore, the calculation is $2 \text{ mol H}_2O \times \dfrac{9 \text{ mol O}_2}{6 \text{ mol H}_2O} = 3 \text{ mol O}_2$

11. **The correct answer is (D).** The equation for the reaction is $Fe_2O_3 + 2Al \rightarrow Al_2O_3 + 2Fe$. The calculation, therefore, is $13.96 \text{ g Fe} \times \dfrac{1 \text{ mol Fe}}{55.85 \text{ g Fe}} \times \dfrac{2 \text{ mol Al}}{2 \text{ mol Fe}} = 0.250 \text{ mol}$

12. **The correct answer is (A).** If you encounter a problem in which two masses are given, suspect a limiting reactant problem. In this problem, the limiting reactant is O_2. You can determine this with the calculation shown below or eyeball it. The molar mass of NH_3 is about 17 g. The molar mass of O_2 is 32 g. If you look at the balanced equation, you will see that you need more moles of oxygen than ammonia. You can also look at the masses you have and know that you have less moles of oxygen than ammonia. That tells you that oxygen is the limiting reactant. The formal calculation is

 $3.10 \text{ g NH}_3 \times \dfrac{1 \text{ mol NH}_3}{17 \text{ g NH}_3} \times \dfrac{4 \text{ mol NO}}{4 \text{ mol NH}_3} = 0.182 \text{ mol NO}$

 $2.50 \text{ g O}_2 \times \dfrac{1 \text{ mol O}_2}{32 \text{ g O}_2} \times \dfrac{4 \text{ mol NO}}{5 \text{ mol O}_2} = 0.0625 \text{ mol NO}$

 Knowing that O_2 is the limiting reactant, you can just complete the calculation

 using the value from O_2: $0.0625 \text{ mol NO} \times \dfrac{30 \text{ g}}{1 \text{ mol NO}} = 1.88 \text{ g NO}$

Free Response
Question 1

(A) In this problem, you know a few things. The most important is that each compound contains only hydrogen and carbon. What's important about that is it means that all of the carbon in carbon dioxide comes from the hydrocarbon and all of the hydrogen in water comes from the hydrocarbon. Therefore, we can work backwards to get our answer. The first thing to do is to pick either carbon dioxide or water to analyze, since we know something about both. Arbitrarily, we'll pick carbon dioxide. You have a volume at STP, which means you'll have to use the 1 mol = 22.4 liters of gas relationships. We have 1.39 liters of gas, which means we have 1.39 liters $\times \frac{1 \text{ mol}}{22.4 \text{ liters}} = 0.0621$ mol CO_2. This means we have 0.0621 mol C.

For water, we have 2.23 g $\times \frac{1 \text{ mol}}{18.02 \text{ g}} = 0.124$ mol H_2O. This means we have twice as many moles of hydrogen atoms, or 0.248 mol H. Now we can see that we have 0.0621 mol C and 0.248 mol H. We have 4 times as many moles of hydrogen, so the empirical formula for the compound is CH_4. Because we know the amount of unknown that was analyzed, we can use that information to determine the molecular formula of the unknown. We could set up an equation and solve for an unknown, but instead we'll just try to confirm that CH_4 is also the molecular formula. In doing so we use the calculation below to see if we obtain the correct amount of CO_2 or H_2O:

$$1.00 \text{ g } CH_4 \times \frac{1 \text{ mol } CH_4}{16.1 \text{ g } CH_4} \times \frac{1 \text{ mol } CO_2}{1 \text{ mol } CH_4} = 0.0621 \text{ mol}$$

Since this matches our value from before, this must be the molecular formula of the compound.

(B) Because this one is at STP, it makes it a bit easier. You can also solve for vapor densities that are not at STP by using the ideal gas equation and solving for density (if you do not remember how to do this, review chapter 9). However, because this one is at STP, we know that one mole of the gas will occupy 22.4 liters. Using this information and the density of the vapor, we can determine the molar mass of B using the equation

$$\frac{3.13 \text{ g B}}{1 \text{ L B}} \times \frac{22.4 \text{ L}}{1 \text{ mol B}} = 70.1 \text{ g mol}^{-1}$$

(C) The mass of $CH_2 = 14.0$ g mol^{-1}; $\frac{70.1 \text{ g mol}^{-1}}{14.0 \text{ g mol}^{-1}} = 5$. Therefore we need to multiply everything in the empirical formula by 5. The molecular formula for B is C_5H_{10}.

(D) If 1.00 g of the unknown contains 0.817 g carbon, the mass percent of carbon is 81.7%, leaving the remaining 18.3% as hydrogen. Therefore, we need to use the procedures for determining an empirical formula from a percentage composition. The problem will progress as follows (remember with percents, assume a 100 g sample):

$$81.7 \text{ g C} \times \frac{1 \text{ mol}}{12.01 \text{ g C}} = 6.80 \text{ mol}; \quad \frac{6.80}{6.80} = 1$$

$$18.3 \text{ g H} \times \frac{1 \text{ mol}}{1.01 \text{ g H}} = 18.12 \text{ mol}; \quad \frac{18.12}{6.80} = 2.66$$

At this point, you need to determine integers that are multiples of 1 and 2.66. Some quick calculations determine that $3 \times 2.66 = 7.98$, which is well within experimental error of 8. Therefore, the empirical formula must be C_3H_8. To determine the molecular formula, we can use the information in the problem. 1 mole of the combustion of unknown C requires 5 moles of O_2. The balanced equation for the complete combustion of C_3H_8 requires 5 moles of O_2. The next possible formula, C_6H_{16}, requires 10 moles. The number of moles of oxygen will continue to increase, so the molecular formula must be C_3H_8.

Question 2

(A) 1.656 g $Pb(NO_3)_2$ This is a mass-to-mass conversion. You must begin by writing the complete, balanced equation for the reaction:

$$Pb(NO_3)_2 \text{ (aq)} + 2KI(aq) \rightarrow PbI_2(s) + 2KNO_3(aq)$$

Proceed with the conversion:

$$2.310 \text{ g PbI}_2 \times \frac{1 \text{ mol PbI}_2}{461.0 \text{ g PbI}_2} \times \frac{1 \text{ mol Pb}(NO_3)_2}{1 \text{ mol PbI}_2} \times$$

$$\frac{331.2 \text{ g Pb}(NO_3)_2}{1 \text{ mol Pb}(NO_3)_2} = 1.660 \text{ g Pb}(NO_3)_2$$

(B) 0.100 M. This is a molarity calculation, which, if you recall, requires you to divide the moles of solute by the liters of solution. We already know that we have 50 mL of solution (or 0.050 L solution), so we just need the number of moles of $Pb(NO_3)_2$ represented by 1.660 g.

$$1.660 \text{ g Pb}(NO_3)_2 \times \frac{1 \text{ mol}}{331.2 \text{ g}} = 5.01 \times 10^{-3} \text{ mol}$$

The molarity is $M = \dfrac{5.01 \times 10^{-3} \text{ mol}}{0.05 \text{ L}} = 0.100 \text{ M}$

(C) The grams of lead can be determined from the grams of lead (II) nitrate from the answer to part (a) and the mass percentage of lead in that compound.

$$\text{Mass \% Pb} = \frac{207.2 \text{ g}}{331.2 \text{ g}} = 0.6256 \text{ (62.56\%)}$$

You can use this figure to determine the amount of lead in solution:

$$1.660 \text{ g Pb}(NO_3)_2 \times 0.6256 = 1.038 \text{ g Pb}$$

(D) $1.660 \text{ g Pb(NO}_3)_2 \times \dfrac{1 \text{ mol Pb}(NO_3)_2}{331.2 \text{ g Pb}(NO_3)_2} \times \dfrac{2 \text{ mol K}}{1 \text{ mol Pb}(NO_3)_2} = 1.00 \times$

10^{-2} mol KI

(E) Failure to adequately rinse the lead (II) iodide thoroughly will increase the likelihood that the solid will be contaminated with some of the solvent (KI(aq) or KNO_3(aq)). Upon drying, this will increase the mass of the solid (which will be a mixture of solid $Pb(NO_3)_2$, solid KI, and solid KNO_3). The increased mass will lead to an overestimation of the amount of lead (II) iodide formed, which will cause an overestimation of the amount of starting material in the lead (II) nitrate solution.

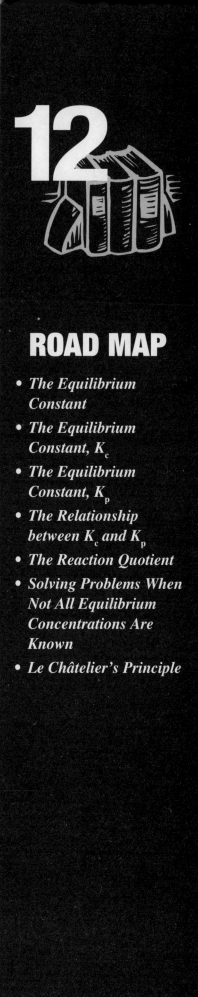
Equilibrium

Up to this point, we have been looking at chemical reactions that have a start and a finish. That is, the reactants are combined, and a certain amount of product is formed. After that, the reaction is finished—no more products will be formed. In addition, these reactions tend to be irreversible. If a piece of sodium is placed into a container of chlorine gas, a very violent reaction ensues, from which a white powder (salt) is formed. This white powder is not readily converted back to sodium and chlorine. It can be done, but it is not an easy transformation.

Many reactions, however, do not run to completion. They will reach a point where they stop, but in this chapter you will learn that when they are in this state they are not really stopped at all. These reactions, where the products can readily reform the reactants, are known as reversible reactions. The way these reactions proceed is analogous to the systems in equilibrium that were discussed in Chapters 7 and 9 (vapor equilibrium and solutions). In the next three chapters, you will study the equilibrium of chemical reactions and learn more about the factors associated with it. The focus of this chapter is to introduce the equilibrium constant, which provides data about the relationships between reactants and products in a system at equilibrium, and Le Châtelier's principle, which allows you to predict the effects of different stressors on reaction equilibria.

THE EQUILIBRIUM CONSTANT

Chemical Equilibrium is the situation where the concentration of reactants and products remains constant. This occurs when opposing reactions happen at the same rate. That is, the conversion of reactants to products is proceeding at the same rate as products are converted to reactants. A system must be closed (not allow for the escape of reactants or products) to achieve equilibrium. This is very similar to our discussion of the liquid-vapor equilibrium in Chapter 7.

Example: A reversible reaction takes the form:

$$X \rightleftharpoons Y$$

At equilibrium, X forms Y at the same rate as Y forms X. Therefore, the concentration of $[X]$, will remain constant. Likewise, $[Y]$ will also remain constant.

ROAD MAP

- *The Equilibrium Constant*
- *The Equilibrium Constant, K_c*
- *The Equilibrium Constant, K_p*
- *The Relationship between K_c and K_p*
- *The Reaction Quotient*
- *Solving Problems When Not All Equilibrium Concentrations Are Known*
- *Le Châtelier's Principle*

NOTE
The concentration of a substance is shown by placing brackets, [ ], around it.

CAUTION
The constant ratio does NOT mean the reaction has stopped.

Once a reaction has reached equilibrium, the rates of the forward and reverse reactions will remain constant (providing that environmental conditions remain constant). This can be expressed mathematically as:

$$\frac{[Y]}{[X]} = \text{constant}$$

THE EQUILIBRIUM CONSTANT, K_c

There are two main ways to describe the equilibrium of a reaction. The first is in terms of the concentrations of reactions and products. The expression that describes the equilibrium of a reaction where the concentrations of the materials are known is K_c. When the reactants and products are in the gaseous state, we can also use the equilibrium constant expression, K_p, where partial pressures are used instead of concentration units. Solids and pure liquids (like water) are omitted from equilibrium expressions because their concentrations do not change during chemical reactions.

Let's begin by looking at how the equilibrium constant, K_c, is derived from a balanced chemical equation. Let's use a reaction written in the form

$$aA + bB \rightleftharpoons cC + dD$$

The equilibrium constant can be calculated using the general expression:

(Equation 12.1)

$$K_c = \frac{[C]^c[D]^d}{[A]^a[B]^b}$$

In this reaction, the coefficients from the balanced equation become the exponents in the equilibrium constant expression. The concentrations of the products go in the numerator, and the concentrations of the reactants go in the denominator.

Sample 1: Write the equilibrium constant expression, K_c, for the following reaction:

$$2CO_2(g) \rightleftharpoons 2CO(g) + O_2(g)$$

Answer: Using equation 12.1, we determine K_c to be

$$K_c = \frac{[CO]^2[O_2]}{[CO_2]^2}$$

Sample 2: Write the equilibrium constant expression, K_c, for the following reaction:

$$Ni(s) + 4CO(g) \rightleftharpoons Ni(CO)_4(g)$$

Answer: Because Ni is a solid, it will not be entered into the equation.

$$K_c = \frac{[Ni(CO)_4]}{[CO]^4}$$

NOTE
The standard convention places the product in the numerator.

NOTE
The subscript c represents concentration.

You Try It!

Write the equilibrium constant expression, K_c, for the following reactions:

(a) $H_2(g) + I_2(g) \rightleftharpoons 2HI(g)$

(b) $2NH_3(g) + 3CuO(s) \rightleftharpoons 3H_2O(g) + N_2(g) + 3Cu(s)$

(c) $NH_4Cl(s) \rightleftharpoons NH_3(g) + HCl(g)$

Answers: (a) $K_c = \dfrac{[HI]^2}{[H_2][I_2]}$ (b) $K_c = \dfrac{[H_2O]^3[N_2]}{[NH_3]^2}$ (c) $K_c = [NH_3][HCl]$

THE EQUILIBRIUM CONSTANT, K_p

The equilibrium constant, K_c, is used to describe the concentrations of reactants and products at equilibrium. When the reactants and products are gases, it is often useful to use the expression K_p instead, where the subscript p represents pressure. In this expression, the equilibrium is described in terms of the partial pressures of the reactants and products. The equilibrium constant expression, K_p, for the reaction

$$aA + bB \rightleftharpoons cC + dD$$

would be written

$$K_p = \frac{(P_C)^c (P_D)^d}{(P_A)^a (P_B)^b}$$

(Equation 12.2)

where P represents the partial pressure of each substance.

Sample: Write the equilibrium constant, K_p, for the following mixture of gases at equilibrium:

$$2CO_2(g) \rightleftharpoons 2CO(g) + O_2(g)$$

Answer: Using equation 12.2, we determine K_p to be

$$K_p = \frac{(P_{CO})^2 (P_{O_2})}{(P_{CO_2})^2}$$

You Try It!

Write the equilibrium constant, K_p, for the following mixture of gases at equilibrium:

$$2\,NO_{(g)} + O_{2(g)} \rightleftharpoons 2NO_{2(g)}$$

Answer: $K_p = \dfrac{(P_{NO_2})^2}{(P_{NO})^2 (P_{O_2})}$

THE RELATIONSHIP BETWEEN K_c AND K_p

The ideal gas law can be used to convert between concentration (K_c) and pressures (K_p). If you recall from Chapter 7, the ideal gas law is $PV = nRT$. You do not need to know the derivations of these equations, but you should know how to use both equations 12.3 and 12.4.

(Equations 12.3 and 12.4)
$$K_p = K_c(RT)^{\Delta n} \qquad K_c = K_p\left(\frac{1}{RT}\right)^{\Delta n}$$

Where Δn = (total moles of gaseous products) – (total moles of gaseous reactants),

R = ideal gas constant (0.0821 L atm mol^{-1} K^{-1}), and T is temperature in Kelvin.

Sample: A 3:1 starting mixture of hydrogen, H_2, and nitrogen, N_2, comes to equilibrium at 500°C. The mixture at equilibrium is 35.06% NH_3, 96.143% N_2, and 0.3506% H_2 by volume. The total pressure in the reaction vessel was 50.0 atm. What is the value of K_p and K_c for this reaction?

$$N_{2(g)} + 3H_{2(g)} \rightleftharpoons 2NH_{3(g)}$$

Answer:

1. Note that the 3:1 information is irrelevant in this problem—remember that we are only concerned with the equilibrium conditions in this problem. It doesn't matter what the starting conditions were. Once equilibrium is established, the quantities of the constituents are determined by K.

2. Use Dalton's law of partial pressures to determine the partial pressure of each gas at equilibrium (% of mixture multiplied by the total pressure). Remember, the law states that the total pressure exerted by a mixture of gases is equal to the sums of the individual pressures that each gas exerts. The pressures exerted by the gases in this mixture will equal their percentage of the total pressure. To determine the partial pressures, we will multiply each percentage of gas by the total pressure:

P_{NH_3} = 0.03506 × 50.0 atm = 1.75 atm
P_{N_2} = 0.96143 × 50.0 atm = 48.1 atm
P_{H_2} = 0.003506 × 50.0 atm = 0.175 atm

3. Use the partial pressures to calculate K_p

$$K_p = \frac{\left(P_{NH_3}\right)^2}{\left(P_{N_2}\right)\left(P_{H_2}\right)^3} = \frac{(1.75)^2}{(48.1)(0.175)^3} = \mathbf{11.9}$$

4. Once you have calculated K_p, you can use the value in equation 12.4 to determine the value of K_c.

$$K_c = K_p\left(\frac{1}{RT}\right)^{\Delta n} = 11.9\left(\frac{1}{0.0821 \times 773}\right)^{-2} = \mathbf{4.79 \times 10^4}$$

Note: Δn has a negative value because the moles product – moles reactant = 2 – (1+3) = -2

You Try It!

$$2NO(g) + Cl_2(g) \rightleftharpoons 2NOCl(g)$$

In the above reaction, the total pressure of the mixture of gases at equilibrium is 1.55 atm. The percentages of each gas in the mixture are as follows: NOCl = 77.4%, NO=3.20 %, and Cl_2 = 19.4%. Calculate K_p and K_c for the reaction.

Answer: $K_p = 1.9 \times 10^3$; $K_c = 4.65 \times 10^4$

Calculating the Equilibrium Constant for Equilibrium Reactions Involving Concentration Changes

The equilibrium constant for a reaction works just as it is advertised—it is always constant. It doesn't matter how much of the reactants or products are present at the beginning of the reaction; when equilibrium is reached, if the equilibrium constant is calculated, it will always be the same. In these next calculations, we will be calculating K_c from the concentrations of the reactants and products at equilibrium. When concentrations (or pressures) are known, use equations 12.1 and 12.2 to determine K.

Sample:

At high pressure (1000 atm) and temperature (450°C), nitrogen and hydrogen gases come to equilibrium according to the reaction shown below:

$$N_2(g) + 3H_2(g) \rightleftharpoons 2NH_3(g)$$

If, at equilibrium, the concentration of nitrogen (N_2) is 2.95 M, the concentration of hydrogen (H_2) is 7.68 M, and the concentration of ammonia (NH_3) is 5.78 M, what is the K_c?

Answer:

$$K_c = \frac{[NH_3]^2}{[N_2][H_2]^3} = \frac{(5.78)^2}{(2.95)(7.68)^3} = \textbf{2.50} \times \textbf{10}^{-2}$$

You Try It!

At 425 °C, gaseous hydrogen iodide (HI) partially decomposes into hydrogen (H_2) and iodine (I_2) gases. What is the value of K_c at 425 °C if the concentrations of the constituents are [HI] = 7.06×10^{-3} M, [H_2] = 9.58×10^{-4} M, and [I_2] = 9.58×10^{-4} M?

Answer: $K_c = 1.84 \times 10^{-2}$

Conceptual Interpretation of the Equilibrium Constant

When you are solving mathematical chemistry problems, such as equilibrium problems, it is easy to lose the meaning of the problems. It is important to develop a conceptual understanding of the material that can guide you as you work through the math problems. Let's take a moment to review some basic ideas about equilibrium constants before we move on to more difficult problems.

Since the expression for K is in the general form:

$$K = \frac{\text{Products}}{\text{Reactants}}$$

we can make some assumptions about the reaction by examining the value of K.

For reactions where K is very large ($K>1$), we can conclude that the amount of product is much larger than the amount of reactants. Therefore, the reaction to the right is favored (equilibrium is favored to the right). Conversely, if K is quite small, ($K<1$) it tells us that the amount of reactants is much greater than the amount of products. Therefore, equilibrium is favored to the left. Keep these ideas in mind when you see values for K.

THE REACTION QUOTIENT

Earlier in the chapter, you read that regardless of the initial concentrations of reactants in an equilibrium reaction, the value for the equilibrium constant will always be the same. The equilibrium constant is determined at equilibrium when the rates of the forward reaction and reverse reaction are the same. If the two reactants are put in a reaction vessel and there is initially no product(s), the reactants will react for a period of time. After a while, the amount of product will begin to build up, but while this is happening the product(s) will begin forming the reactants. This process will continue until the rates are the same. Using the same logic, if only the products of the previous reaction were placed in the reaction vessel, the reverse reaction would proceed until the time when the reactants had accumulated in sufficient quantity to begin forming products at the same rate as the reverse reaction. The concentrations of reactants and products will change until equilibrium is reached.

There are times when you will be given information about the reactants and products when they have not reached equilibrium. Under these conditions, a value known as the reaction quotient can be calculated. The value of the reaction quotient, Q, when compared to the equilibrium constant, will indicate the direction the reaction is proceeding. The reaction quotient is calculated using the same expression as K, but the concentrations of the reactants and products are not equilibrium values. For the reaction

$$aA + bB \rightleftharpoons cC + dD$$

the reaction quotient, Q, is calculated with the expression:

(Equation 12.5)
$$Q = \frac{[C]^c [D]^d}{[A]^a [B]^b}$$

The value of Q can be helpful in determining the direction of a reaction in a nonequilibrium state. For instance, if the value of Q is greater than K, it means that the equation is top-heavy or that there are too many products (or not enough reactants). In this case, the reaction will have to proceed to the left to lower Q toward the value of K. If Q is smaller than K, there are too many reactants and not enough products, which means the reaction will need to shift to the right to reach equilibrium. If Q and K are equal to one another, the reaction is at equilibrium.

Sample:

$$N_2(g) + 3H_2(g) \rightleftharpoons 2NH_3(g)$$

In the reaction shown above, the value of K_c at 500 °C is 6.0×10^{-2}. At some point during the reaction, the concentrations of each material were measured. At this point, the concentrations of each substance were $[N_2] = 1.0 \times 10^{-5}$ M, $[H_2] = 1.5 \times 10^{-3}$ M, and $[NH_3] = 1.5 \times 10^{-3}$ M. Calculate the value of Q, and determine the direction that the reaction was most likely to proceed when the measurements were taken.

Answer: To solve this problem, you need to begin by determining the value of Q using equation 12.5:

$$Q = \frac{[C]^c [D]^d}{[A]^a [B]^b} = \frac{[NH_3]^2}{[N_2][H_2]^3} = \frac{\left(1.5 \times 10^{-3}\right)^2}{\left(1.0 \times 10^{-5}\right)\left(1.5 \times 10^{-3}\right)^3} = 6.67 \times 10^7$$

The value of Q is nearly 9 orders of magnitude larger than K. Therefore, the only way that equilibrium will be reached is if the reaction proceeds toward the left. That will decrease the numerator, increase the denominator, and decrease the value of Q.

SOLVING PROBLEMS WHEN NOT ALL EQUILIBRIUM CONCENTRATIONS ARE KNOWN

Occasionally, not all equilibrium concentrations are known. When this occurs you must use equilibrium concepts and stoichiometry concepts to determine K. What you are trying to do in these problems is determine the amounts of materials at equilibrium. In Chapter 11, you learned that the balanced chemical equation shows you the relative amounts of reactants and products during the chemical reaction. For a reaction at equilibrium, the logic is the same. The mole ratios still apply. There is one major difference, however, between the stoichiometry of reversible and irreversible reactions. For reversible reactions, the reactants will not be completely converted to product(s), which is the case in irreversible reactions (keeping in mind limiting reactants, of course). So, in the stoichiometry of equilibrium, the mole ratios are still used to determine the relative amounts of each substance. However, because the reactants are not completely converted to products (and vice versa), the ratio will only help us to determine the difference between the starting and ending amounts of a substance. This process will be illustrated in the next sample problem. Using a table and following some basic steps can simplify solving these problems:

Step 1. Write a balanced equation for the reaction.

Step 2. Create a table with three rows and as many columns as there are constituents (reactants and products). The three rows should be labeled "Start" (for initial concentration or pressure), "Δ" (change in concentration or pressure), and "Finish" (equilibrium concentration or pressure).

Step 3. Fill in all known parts of the table.

Step 4. For any substances where the initial and equilibrium concentrations are known, determine the change in concentration (Δ).

Step 5. Use the stoichiometric relationships (mole ratios) in the reaction to fill in the remaining blanks (review Chapter 11 if you have forgotten this).

Step 6. Once the table is completed, use the values to determine the equilibrium constant.

Sample 1:

The equilibrium reaction referred to is

$$H_2(g) + I_2(g) \rightleftharpoons 2HI(g)$$

When 2.00 mole each of hydrogen (H_2) and iodine (I_2) are mixed in an evacuated 1.00 L vessel, 3.50 mole of HI are produced. What is the value of the equilibrium constant, K_c?

Step 1. The equation is already balanced.

Steps 2 and 3. Create a table; fill it in with the known values:

	H_2	I_2	2HI
Start	2.0 M	2.0 M	0
Δ			
Finish			3.50

Note: *The volume of the vessel is used to calculate the concentrations.*

Don't forget, you can put a "0" in the start for HI since there is none initially present. You always need to carefully examine your given information. Quite often there is material that is given that is not explicitly stated. In this problem, you are not told that there is no HI to start with, but you are told that H_2 and I_2 are combined in an evacuated vessel. That means nothing else is in there. In other words, the starting concentration of HI is zero.

Step 4. The only substance you can calculate the change (Δ) for is HI, so fill in the table for it.

	H_2	I_2	2HI
Start	2.0 M	2.0 M	0
Δ			+3.50
Finish			3.50

Step 5. Use the mole ratios from the balanced equation to fill in the remaining blanks. You can use the ratios because you know, from the balanced equation, that if 3.50 moles of HI are produced, one-half that amount of each reactant must have been used up (mass still has to be conserved).

$$3.50 \text{ mol HI} \times \frac{1 \text{ mol H}_2}{2 \text{ mol HI}} = 1.75 \text{ mol H}_2$$

$$3.50 \text{ mol HI} \times \frac{1 \text{ mol I}_2}{2 \text{ mol HI}} = 1.75 \text{ mol I}_2$$

Because H_2 is being converted into HI, this number should be a negative number to indicate the decrease in quantity. The same goes for I_2. You can see here that because the reaction is at equilibrium, not all of the starting materials are converted into the product HI. However, because of the law of conservation of mass, you know that whatever amount of product was gained must correspond to an equivalent loss of reactants.

	H_2 (mol)	I_2 (mol)	2HI (mol)
Start	2.0	2.0	0
Δ	−1.75	−1.75	+3.50
Finish	0.25	0.25	3.50

Step 6. The quantities from the "Finish" row are used to calculate K_c.

$$K_c = \frac{[HI]^2}{[H_2][I_2]} = \frac{(3.50)^2}{(0.25)(0.25)} = 196$$

You Try It!

Nitric oxide gas, NO, and oxygen gas, O_2, react to form the poisonous gas nitrogen dioxide, NO_2, in the reaction shown below:

$$2NO(g) + O_2(g) \rightleftharpoons 2NO_2(g)$$

10.0 moles of NO and 6.00 moles of O_2 are placed into an evacuated 1.00 L vessel, where they begin to react. At equilibrium, there are 8.80 moles of NO_2 present. Calculate the value of K_c, assuming that the temperature remains constant throughout the reaction.

Answer: 33.6

Determining Equilibrium Concentrations When Only Initial Concentrations Are Known

In this next section, we will look at a situation in which you have information about the starting materials, but no information about the quantities at equilibrium. If you are thinking ahead, you may see that in the charts you have just been reviewing, if you don't know the quantities at equilibrium, each substance will be represented by a variable. There are two main ways to handle these problems. The first we will look at is to set up an equation and solve for x. This is by far the easier of the two. In the next sample we will look at how to solve such a problem.

Sample 2:

$$H_2(g) + I_2 \rightleftharpoons 2HI$$

0.500 mol of H_2 and 0.500 mole of I_2 are added to a 1.00-liter reaction vessel. The mixture is heated to 498 °C and allowed to reach equilibrium according to the reaction shown above. At this temperature, $K_c = 49.7$. What is the composition of the reaction mixture at equilibrium in this system?

Answer: To begin, you will need to make a chart with all of the information. This chart will be slightly different however, because no ending amounts are known.

$H_2(g) + I_2 \rightleftharpoons 2HI$			
	H_2	I_2	2HI
Start	0.50	0.50	0
Δ	-x	-x	+ 2 x
Finish	0.50 −x	0.50 − x	2x

Before continuing, you should take note of a few things. First, because the reaction vessel is 1.00 liter, we can substitute the number of moles for the molarity. Second, because we don't know the equilibrium concentrations of the two known substances (H_2 and I_2), we must represent the decrease in each substance with the variable x. Finally, the ration 2/1 written in the Δ row for HI represents the mole ratio of HI to the other reactants.

At this point, we're ready to substitute the values into the equilibrium expression for K_c.

$$K_c = \frac{[HI]^2}{[H_2][I_2]} \qquad 49.7 = \frac{(2x)^2}{(0.50 - x)^2}$$

At this point, you need to think before proceeding. Don't jump right in and start multiplying numbers and variables. If you look carefully, you will notice that the values on the right are both squared. This means that you can take the square root of both sides and get rid of those squares. The result of this is

$$\sqrt{49.7} = \sqrt{\frac{(2x)^2}{(0.50 - x)^2}}$$

which is rewritten as $\pm 7.05 = \frac{(2x)}{(0.50 - x)}$.

Both + and − 7.05 values must be considered since they are both mathematical possibilities.

$\pm 7.05(0.50 - x) = 2x$, which we then can solve as two equations:

$+3.525 - 7.05x = 2x$ $\qquad$ and $\qquad$ $-3.525 + 7.05 = 2x$

Solving for x, we find that the two equations produce the following solutions:

$$3.525 = 9.05x \qquad -3.525 = -5.05x$$
$$\text{and}$$
$$0.39 = x \qquad 0.70 = x$$

The second answer can't be correct because a value of x that large will produce negative concentrations of H_2 and I_2 at equilibrium. Therefore, the answer, 0.39, is accepted as the answer for x. At this point, the value must be substituted back into the table to obtain the equilibrium concentrations.

Solving for x, we get 0.11 mol H_2, 0.11 mol I_2, and 0.78 mol HI

You Try It!
0.500 moles of NO gas are placed into a 1.00-liter reaction vessel. The gas is heated to an extremely high temperature, where it decomposes according to the reaction shown below:

$$2NO(g) \rightleftharpoons N_2(g) + O_2(g)$$

At equilibrium, $K_c = 2.4 \times 10^3$. Determine the equilibrium composition of the mixture at equilibrium.

Answer: 5.1×10^{-3} mol NO, 0.25 mol N_2, 0.25 mol O_2

In the last sample problem and the **You Try It!** problem, the problems were designed so that the values of x could be obtained by finding the square roots of each side of the equation. There are some problems where this is not the case and you must calculate x using the quadratic equation. While you may have worked with these kinds of problems in your course, they will not be included in this book because they don't appear on the AP exam.

LE CHÂTELIER'S PRINCIPLE

Le Châtelier's Principle states that if a system at equilibrium is disturbed, it will react in such a way as to minimize the disturbance. What causes these disturbances? Changes in pressure, concentration, and temperature can affect the constituents in a reaction, each of which is discussed in detail below.

Refer to the general reaction shown below in the discussion that follows:

$$aA + bB \rightleftharpoons cC + dD$$

Effects of Changing Concentration

Adding A or B to the mixture will create an increased concentration of A or B. The reaction will respond by trying to "use up" the excess; in other words, the rate of the forward reaction will increase until equilibrium is reestablished. Likewise, adding C or D will cause the reverse reaction to speed up.

Sample: Which direction will the reaction shift if substance A is added to the reaction vessel?

Answer: Adding A or B will cause a shift in equilibrium to the right. This will use up the extra A until equilibrium is reestablished.

Effects of Changing Pressure

If the pressure of a system containing gaseous molecules is increased, then the number of molecules must be reduced to relieve the stress. The reaction will shift to the side with the smallest number of moles of gaseous molecules. If the number of moles is the same in the forward and reverse reaction, then no change will occur. In order for pressure changes to affect the direction of the reaction, the pressure must be increased by either decreasing the volume of the container or by changing the partial pressures of the individual gases in the mixture. For example, adding an inert gas to the reaction vessel will not affect the reaction. It will increase the total pressure of the system, but it will not affect the partial pressures of the gases involved in the reaction.

Sample: In the reaction

$$2Cl_2(g) + 2H_2O(g) \rightleftharpoons 4Cl(g) + O_2(g)$$

in which direction will the reaction shift if the pressure increases?

Answer: If you count the number of moles of gas on each side of the equation, you will note that the left side of the reaction contains 4 moles of gas, while the right side has 5 moles. An increase in pressure will favor the side with the fewest number of moles, so the reaction will shift to the left (the reverse reaction is favored).

Effects of Changing Temperature

The effect a change in temperature will have on a system depends on the enthalpy of reaction. Enthalpy is a concept that will be discussed in detail in Chapter 16, but you will be able to understand this concept with just a small amount of information. There are two main types of reactions: endothermic and exothermic. Endothermic reactions require heat in order to occur, while exothermic reactions release heat. Enthalpy is a measure of the amount of heat liberated or absorbed in a chemical reaction that occurs at constant pressure. It can be measured, and it is described by the symbol H (ΔH for a reaction which involves a change in enthalpy). A negative value for ΔH means the reaction is exothermic, while a positive value for ΔH represents an endothermic reaction. The important thing to remember is that a change in temperature of a reaction at equilibrium will cause the reaction to shift in the direction that will undo the change of temperature. An important note about temperature changes is that because the shifts are based on the energetics (enthalpies) of the reactions, the shifts will cause changes in rates that will affect K. Changes in temperature will change the value of K.

Let's refer to the previous equation to illustrate:

$$aA + bB \rightleftharpoons cC + dD$$

If you write the equation with the word "heat" in it, you can then treat the equilibrium the same as you do for a change in concentration. If the forward reaction is endothermic, ($\Delta H > 0$), write "heat" as a reactant. If the reaction is exothermic, ($\Delta H < 0$), write "heat" as a product.

Sample 1: What effect will an increase in temperature have on the reaction below?

$$2\,SO_3(g) \rightleftharpoons 2\,SO_2(g) + O_2(g) \qquad \Delta H° = +196.6 \text{ kJ per 2 moles } SO_3$$

First, note that the reaction is endothermic ($\Delta H > 0$). It can be rewritten as

$$\text{Heat} + 2SO_3(g) \rightleftharpoons 2SO_2(g) + O_2(g)$$

The addition of heat will cause the reaction to proceed in a direction that will use up heat. In this reaction, the highly endothermic forward reaction will use up the heat and will hence be favored. The reaction will shift to the right, and K will increase at the higher temperature.

Sample 2: What effect will an increase in temperature have on the reaction below?

$$2NO(g) + O_2(g) \rightleftharpoons 2NO_2(g) \qquad \Delta H° = -113 \text{ kJ}$$

Answer: Note that the reaction is exothermic ($\Delta H < 0$). It can be rewritten as

$$2NO(g) + O_2(g) \rightleftharpoons 2NO_2(g) + \text{Heat}$$

Since the reaction will shift to use up the heat, you can see that the reverse reaction will be favored. The reaction will shift to the left. For exothermic reactions, K is smaller at higher temperatures.

Catalysis

Catalysts do not affect equilibrium concentrations. The addition of a catalyst speeds up the rate of both the forward and reverse reactions. At equilibrium, these reaction rates are equal. The effect of the catalyst is to make these equal rates faster.

You Try It!

Combining carbon monoxide gas, CO, and hydrogen gas, H_2, in the reaction shown below, produces methanol, CH_3OH:

$$CO(g) + 2H_2(g) \rightleftharpoons CH_3OH(g) \qquad \Delta H° = -21.7 \text{ kcal}$$

Which direction will the reaction proceed after the following disruptions to the equilibrium?

  (a) Some of the methanol vapor is condensed and removed from the reaction vessel.

  (b) The pressure is increased by decreasing the volume of the reaction vessel.

  (c) The temperature is increased.

Answers: (a) shift right   (b) shift right   (c) shift left

Summary: Equilibrium

- Chemical equilibrium occurs in reversible reactions when the rate of the forward reaction is equal to the rate of the reverse reaction.

- The equilibrium constant, K, describes the relationship between the reactants and products of a reversible reaction at equilibrium.

- K_c describes equilibrium in terms of the concentrations of reactants and products.

- K_p describes equilibrium in terms of the partial pressures of the reactants and products.

- The reaction quotient, Q, is used to describe the relationships between the reactants and products in a system that is not necessarily in equilibrium.

- When the value of $Q < K$, the reaction proceeds to the right; when the value of $Q > K$, the reaction proceeds to the left; and when $Q = K$, the reaction is at equilibrium.

- Le Châtelier's Principle states that when a system at equilibrium is disturbed, it will react in a way that minimizes the disturbance.

- A change in the concentration of reactants or products will cause the reaction to shift in the direction that compensates for the addition or loss of material. For example, if the concentration of a reactant is increased, the reaction will proceed to the right, toward the formation of more product. This will use up the excess reactant and restore equilibrium.

- A change in pressure of a gaseous mixture will shift equilibrium to the direction that compensates for the pressure change. Increases in pressure will shift the reaction to the side of the reaction that has fewer moles of gas, while decreases in pressure favor the side of the reaction with more moles of gas.

- The effects of temperature changes are related to the enthalpy of the reaction. In response to a temperature increase, an endothermic reaction ($\Delta H > 0$) will shift to produce more products, which will use up the excess heat. An exothermic reaction ($\Delta H < 0$) will shift to product more reactants, which uses up the heat in the reverse reaction (or by slowing down the forward reaction, slows down the production of additional heat).

REVIEW QUESTIONS

1. $2\,CO_2\,(g) \rightleftharpoons 2\,CO\,(g) + O_2\,(g)$

   After the equilibrium represented above is established, some pure $O_2\,(g)$ is injected into the reaction vessel at constant temperature. After equilibrium is reestablished, which of the following has a lower value compared to its value at the original equilibrium?

   (A) K_{eq} for the reaction
   (B) The total pressure in the reaction vessel
   (C) The amount of $CO_2\,(g)$ in the reaction vessel
   (D) The amount of $O_2\,(g)$ in the reaction vessel
   (E) The amount of $CO\,(g)$ in the reaction vessel

2. $2SO_2(g) + O_2(g) \rightleftharpoons 2SO_3(g)$ $\qquad \Delta H° = -197\ kJ$

   Which of the following changes alone would cause a decrease in the value of K_{eq} for the reaction represented above?

   (A) Decreasing the temperature
   (B) Increasing the temperature
   (C) Decreasing the volume of the reaction vessel
   (D) Increasing the volume of the reaction vessel
   (E) Adding a catalyst

3. $N_2(g) + 3H_2(g) \rightleftharpoons 2NH_3(g) + energy$

   Some N_2 and H_2 are mixed in a container at 200 °C, and the system reaches equilibrium according to the equation above. Which of the following causes an increase in the number of moles of NH_3 present at equilibrium?

   I. Decreasing the volume of the container
   II. Raising the temperature
   III. Adding a mole of Ar gas at constant volume

   (A) I only
   (B) II only
   (C) I and III only
   (D) II and III only
   (E) I, II, and III

4. $I_2(g) + Br_2(g) \rightleftharpoons 2IBr(g)$

   In the reaction shown above, 0.50 moles of Br_2 and 0.50 moles of I_2 are placed in an evacuated 1.00 liter vessel and allowed to reach equilibrium. What is the value of K_c if the vessel contains 0.84 moles of IBr at equilibrium?

   (A) 2.0
   (B) 8.8
   (C) 11.0
   (D) 110
   (E) 131

5. $4CuO(s) + CH_4(g) \rightleftharpoons CO_2(g) + 4Cu(s) + 2H_2O(g)$

   Which is the correct set up to determine K_c for the reaction above?

   (A) $\dfrac{[CO_2][Cu]^4[H_2O]^2}{[CuO]^4[CH_4]}$

   (B) $\dfrac{[CuO]^4[CH_4]}{[CO_2][Cu]^4[H_2O]^2}$

   (C) $\dfrac{[CO_2][H_2O]^2}{[CH_4]}$

   (D) $\dfrac{[CO_2][H_2O]^2}{[CuO]^4[CH_4]}$

   (E) $\dfrac{[CO]^2[Cu]^4[H_2O]^2}{[CuO]^4[CH_4]}$

6. In which of the following systems would the number of moles of the substances present at equilibrium NOT be shifted by a change in the volume of the system at constant temperature?

   (A) $SO_2(g) + O_2(g) \rightleftharpoons 2SO_3$

   (B) $N_2(g) + 3 H_2(g) \rightleftharpoons 2 NH_3(g)$

   (C) $NO_2(g) + SO_2(g) \rightleftharpoons SO_3(g) + NO(g)$

   (D) $N_2O_4(g) \rightleftharpoons 2 NO_2(g)$

   (E) $CO(g) + 3H_2(g) \rightleftharpoons CH_4(g) + H_2O(g)$

7. $Cu_2S(l) + O_2(g) \rightleftharpoons 2Cu(l) + SO_2(g); \Delta H = -250$ kilojoules

   The reaction above is used in the mining industry to extract copper from copper ore. Once the mixture is allowed to establish equilibrium at temperature T and pressure P, the equilibrium can be shifted to favor the products by

   (A) increasing the pressure by decreasing the volume of the reaction vessel at constant T.

   (B) increasing the pressure by adding an inert gas such as helium.

   (C) decreasing the temperature.

   (D) allowing some gases to escape at constant T and P.

   (E) adding a catalyst.

8. An evacuated 1.00-liter vessel is injected with 0.777 moles of sulfur trioxide gas, SO_3. The vessel is then heated to a high temperature where the SO_3 partially decomposes to form the products SO_2 and O_2 in the reaction shown below:

$$2SO_3(g) \rightleftharpoons 2SO_2(g) + O_2(g)$$

The temperature is kept constant, and the amount of SO_3 in the vessel at equilibrium is 0.520 mol. What is the value of K_c at this temperature?

(A) 0.031

(B) 0.062

(C) 0.125

(D) 0.257

(E) 31.9

9. A 3.00-liter reaction vessel is filled with carbon monoxide gas, CO, and chlorine gas, Cl_2. The mixture is heated to 670 K and allowed to reach equilibrium according to the balanced equation shown below:

$$CO(g) + Cl_2(g) \rightleftharpoons COCl_2(g)$$

At equilibrium, the mixture contains 0.036 moles CO, 0.075 moles Cl_2, and 1.11 moles $COCl_2$. What is K_c at this temperature?

(A) 8.11×10^{-4}

(B) 2.43×10^{-3}

(C) 12.0

(D) 411

(E) 1.23×10^3

10. $H_2O(g) + Cl_2O(g) \rightleftharpoons 2HOCl(g)$

The reaction above is allowed to come to equilibrium at room temperature. At equilibrium, the partial pressure of H_2O is 296 mm Hg, Cl_2O is 15 mm Hg, and HOCl is 20 mm Hg. What is the value of K_p at this temperature?

(A) 222

(B) 11

(C) 0.017

(D) 0.090

(E) 0.0045

11. For the reaction shown below, $K_p = 2.8 \times 10^{-2}$ at 400 K.

$$2NH_3(g) \rightleftharpoons N_2(g) + 3H_2(g)$$

What is the value of K_c at this temperature?

(A) 1.3×10^{-5}

(B) 2.6×10^{-5}

(C) 8.5×10^{-4}

(D) 1.3×10^{-2}

(E) 30

12. At 373 K, the reaction shown below has an equilibrium constant, $K_c = 2.19 \times 10^{-10}$.

$$COCl_2(g) \rightleftharpoons CO(g) + Cl_2(g)$$

After placing a mixture of gases in the reaction vessel, the concentrations were measured to be $[COCl_2] = 3.50 \times 10^{-3}$ M, $[CO] = 1.11 \times 10^{-5}$ M, and $[Cl_2] = 3.25 \times 10^{-6}$ M. Which statement below accurately describes the reaction?

(A) The reaction is at equilibrium.

(B) The reaction is not at equilibrium, and it is proceeding to the left.

(C) The reaction is not at equilibrium, and it is proceeding to the right.

(D) The reaction quotient is equal to K_c.

(E) The reaction quotient is less than K_c.

Free-Response

Question 1

Sulfur trioxide gas, one of the causes of acid rain, is produced in the upper atmosphere when oxygen reacts with sulfur dioxide gas in the reaction shown below:

$$2SO_2(g) + O_2(g) \rightleftharpoons 2SO_3(g) \qquad \Delta H° = -197 \text{ kJ}$$

The gases are placed in a reaction vessel and allowed to come to equilibrium at temperature T, pressure P, and volume V. Predict and explain the effects that each of the following will have on the equilibrium composition of the reaction:

(A) The partial pressure of $SO_3(g)$ is increased by the addition of $SO_3(g)$.

(B) The pressure in the vessel is increased by the addition of He.

(C) The total pressure in the vessel is increased by decreasing the volume of the vessel.

(D) The temperature of the system is decreased.

(E) The partial pressure of $O_2(g)$ is decreased.

Question 2

A 1.00 liter evacuated reaction vessel was filled with 0.034 mol each of H_2 and I_2 gases. The reaction proceeded to equilibrium according to the equation shown below. The equilibrium constant, K_c, at temperature T, was 45.0.

$$H_2(g) + I_2(g) \rightleftharpoons 2HI(g)$$

(A) What is the equilibrium composition of the mixture?

(B) Determine K_p for the reaction mixture described in part (A), if the temperature T is 500 °C.

(C) After equilibrium had been established, 0.008 mol of HI was injected into the reaction vessel, and the system was allowed to reestablish equilibrium. Determine the new composition of the equilibrium mixture after the new equilibrium is established.

ANSWERS

1. **The correct answer is (E).** A large percentage of the multiple-choice equilibrium questions are based on Le Châtelier's principle, like this one. If pure oxygen is injected into the reaction vessel, the concentration of one of the products increases, which will drive the reaction to the left. You need to look for answers that are consistent with that shift. The amount of carbon monoxide will have to decrease because it is required to react with the excess oxygen to restore equilibrium.

2. **The correct answer is (B).** This is another Le Châtelier problem. Because it is an exothermic reaction ($\Delta H° < 0$), you can think of the reaction as having heat as another product. An increase in temperature will drive the reaction to the left. This will cause an increase in the concentration of reactants (and a subsequent decrease in products), which will decrease the value of K_{eq}.

3. **The correct answer is (A).** A decrease in pressure, caused by a decreased volume, will cause the reaction to shift in the direction that has fewer particles, which is to the right. This is the only choice that is true. Raising the temperature of an exothermic reaction will drive the reaction to the left, which will decrease the number of moles of NH_3; adding an inert gas like argon will have no effect on the reaction because it won't affect the partial pressures of any of the reaction components.

4. **The correct answer is (D).** This requires the use of a chart, which is shown below:

$I_2(g) + Br_2(g) \rightleftharpoons 2IBr(g)$		
	I_2	Br_2	$2IBr$
Start	0.50 mol	0.50 mol	0 mol
Δ	$-\frac{1}{2}(0.84)$	$-\frac{1}{2}(0.84)$	+0.84 mol
Finish	0.08 mol	0.08 mol	0.84 mol

Because the volume of the vessel is 1.0 liter, the number of moles is the same as the concentration (molarity). Therefore, we're ready to substitute the numbers into the equilibrium constant expression:

$$K_{eq} = \frac{[IBr]^2}{[I_2][Br_2]} = \frac{(0.84)^2}{(0.08)(0.08)} = 110$$

5. **The correct answer is (C).** The solids CuO and Cu must be omitted from the equation.

6. **The correct answer is (C).** The equation in choice (C) is the only one in which the number of moles of products is the same as the number of moles of reactants. As a result, it won't shift in response to pressure changes due to changes in volume.

7. **The correct answer is (D).** There are two things that you should note about this equation. First, it is exothermic; second, it involves a heterogeneous equilibrium (it has two solids and two gases). Therefore, the equilibrium expression is $\frac{[SO_2]}{[O_2]}$. A decrease in the temperature will cause a shift toward the products. One of the bigger tricks in this question is the use of solids. If you are looking at the number of moles of each substance, and not paying attention to the states, you will be mislead into thinking that a pressure change will have an affect on this. It won't, because there are equal numbers of moles of the only gaseous components.

8. **The correct answer is (A).** This is another chart problem. Set it up as follows:

$2SO_3(g) \rightleftharpoons 2SO_2(g) + O_2(g)$			
	$2SO_3$	$2SO_2$	O_2
Start	0.777 mol	0	0
Δ	-0.257	$+\frac{2}{2}(0.257)$	$+\frac{1}{2}(0.257)$
Finish	0.520 mol	0.257	0.1285

Now the substitution: $K_c = \dfrac{[SO]^2[O_2]}{[SO_3]} = \dfrac{(0.257)^2(0.1285)}{(0.520)^2} = 0.031$

9. **The correct answer is (E).** Be careful, there was huge trap in this problem—one that the AP exam occasionally throws in. In this problem, the volume of the reaction vessel is not 1.0 liter. Therefore, to get the concentrations of the reactants and products, you must use the number of moles divided by the volume (n/3 liters). Look out for this on the AP exam. The rest of the problem is as follows:

$$K_c = \frac{[COCl_2]}{[CO][Cl_2]} = \frac{\left(\dfrac{1.11}{3}\right)}{\left(\dfrac{0.036}{3}\right)\left(\dfrac{0.075}{3}\right)} = 1.23 \times 10^3$$

10. **The correct answer is (D).** This is a straightforward K_p problem.

$$K_p = \frac{\left(P_{HOCl}\right)^2}{\left(P_{H_2O}\right)\left(P_{Cl_2O}\right)} = \frac{(20)^2}{(296)(15)} = 0.090$$

11. **The correct answer is (B).** Conversion of K_p to K_c: $K_c = K_p\left(\frac{1}{RT}\right)^{\Delta n}$ where Δn = (number of moles products – number of moles reactants) = ((1+3) – 2) = 2. The equation then becomes

$$K_c = 2.8 \times 10^{-2}\left(\frac{1}{(0.0821)(400)}\right)^2 = 2.6 \times 10^{-5}$$

12. **The correct answer is (B).** This is a reaction quotient, Q, problem. You need to calculate Q and then compare it to the equilibrium constant, K. The calculation is as follows:

$$Q = \frac{[CO][Cl_2]}{[COCl_2]} = \frac{(1.1 \times 10^{-5})(3.25 \times 10^{-6})}{(3.50 \times 10^{-3})} \quad 1.0 \times 10^{-8}.$$

This is considerably larger than K. Therefore, the reaction is not at equilibrium, and it must be moving toward the left (which will increase the reactants, decrease the products, and decrease Q until it equals K).

Free Response

Question 1

(A) The addition of SO_3 to the reaction vessel will increase the concentration of SO_3 and drive the reaction to the left, causing the production of more SO_2 and O_2, increasing their partial pressures and concentrations.

(B) The addition of an inert gas will not affect the equilibrium partial pressures and, as a result, will not cause a shift in the equilibrium.

(C) Increasing the pressure by changing the volume will cause the reaction to shift to the right. This will allow the number of particles to decrease, which will reduce the pressure.

(D) This is an exothermic reaction ($\Delta H < 0$). A decrease in temperature will drive the reaction to the right in an attempt to generate more heat. Thus, the amount of SO_3 will increase.

(E) Decreasing the partial pressure of O_2 will cause the equilibrium to shift to the left in order to restore equilibrium. This will cause an increase in SO_2 and a decrease in SO_3.

Question 2

(A) You need to set up a table for this one.

$H_2(g) + I_2(g) \rightleftharpoons 2HI(g)$			
	H_2	I_2	$2HI$
Start	0.034	0.034	0
Δ	-x	-x	+2/1x
Finish	$0.034 - x$	$0.034 - x$	$2x$

The next step is to set up the equilibrium expression:

$$K_c = \frac{[HI]^2}{[H_2][I_2]}; \qquad 45 = \frac{(2x)^2}{(0.034 - x)^2}$$

You can take the square root of both sides to determine the value of x:

$$\sqrt{45} = \sqrt{\frac{(2x)^2}{(0.034 - x)^2}}; \qquad \pm 6.71 = \frac{(2x)}{(0.034 - x)}$$

Solving for + and – 6.71, we find x to be

$$0.228 - 6.71x = 2x \qquad -0.228 + 6.71 = 2x$$
$$0.228 = 8.71x \qquad -0.228 = -4.71x$$
$$0.026 = x \qquad 0.049 = x$$

0.049 must be rejected because it would cause H_2 and I_2 to have negative concentrations. Therefore, $x = 0.026$. Substituting this back into the values in the table provides:

0.008 mol H_2, 0.008 mol I_2, and 0.052 mol HI

(B) $K_p = K_c(RT)^{\Delta n}$; $\qquad K_p = 45[(0.0821)(773\ K)]^0$; $\qquad K_p = 45$

K_p is the same as K_c. There is no difference in the number of moles of reactants and products. Therefore, the partial pressures will be proportional to the concentrations.

(C) You need to make another table. One thing to be careful of is that in this problem, you don't have any starting materials equal to zero.

$H_2(g) + I_2(g) \rightleftharpoons 2HI(g)$			
	H_2	I_2	$2HI$
Start	0.008	0.008	0.060
Δ	+ 0.5x	+ 0.5x	–x
Finish	0.008 + 0.5x	0.008 + 0.5x	0.060 –x

Because you are starting with some hydrogen and iodine, you have to add the new amount to the original amount. In the calculation that follows, K_c remains the same since we are at the same temperature.

$$K_c = \frac{[HI]^2}{[H_2][I_2]}; \qquad 45 = \frac{(0.060 - x)^2}{(0.008 + 0.5x)^2}$$

Taking the square root of each side:

$$\sqrt{45} = \sqrt{\frac{(0.060 - x)^2}{(0.008 + 0.5x)^2}}; \qquad \pm 6.71 = \frac{(0.060 - x)}{(0.008 + 0.5x)}$$

Finish solving for x (–6.71 is excluded because it yields a negative value for x):

$$+6.71(0.008 + 0.5x) = 0.06 - x$$
$$4.355x = 6.2 \times 10^{-3}$$
$$x = 1.45 \times 10^{-3}$$

Substituting for the values in the table:

$8.7 \times 10^{-3} = H_2,\ I_2;\ HI = 0.059$

13

Acids and Bases

DEFINITIONS OF ACIDS AND BASES

There are three definitions for acids and bases that you must be familiar with: Arrhenius, Brønsted-Lowry, and Lewis. In the following section, you will review the meaning and application of these different definitions.

Arrhenius

Arrhenius definitions are the earliest and the most simplistic of acid base definitions. Of the three definitions, arrhenius definitions are the least inclusive, but the most commonly known acids and bases can be defined by Arrhenius.

An **Arrhenius acid** is a substance that, when dissolved in water, increases the concentration of H^+ ions in the solution.

$$\textbf{Example: } HCl(g) \xrightarrow{H_2O} H^+(aq) + Cl^-(aq)$$

An **Arrhenius base** is a substance that, when dissolved in water, increases the concentration of OH^- ions in the solution.

$$\textbf{Example: } NaOH(s) \xrightarrow{H_2O} Na^+(aq) + OH^-(aq)$$

In the Arrhenius definitions for acids and bases, the strength of the acid or base is determined by the degree of ionization. For example, HCl is considered a strong acid because when it is placed in water it completely ionizes to H^+ and Cl^-. The strongest acids and bases are all Arrhenius acids and bases.

Brønsted-Lowry

While the Arrhenius definitions focus on the H^+ and OH^- ions, the Brønsted-Lowry definitions focus on the behavior of protons—that is, the transfer of a proton from one substance to another.

A **Brønsted-Lowry** acid is a substance that transfers a proton to another substance. Since a hydrogen ion is a proton, all Arrhenius acids are Brønsted-Lowry acids. However, the slight difference in definitions allows us to consider additional substances as acids. We can also consider reactions that do not occur in aqueous solutions.

$$\textbf{Example: } NH_3(g) + HCl(g) \rightarrow NH_4Cl(s)$$

Notice how HCl still acts as an acid, but in this reaction it is doing so without being dissolved in water.

A **Brønsted-Lowry** base is substance that accepts a proton from another substance. This is a significant change from the Arrhenius definition. Arrhenius bases possess an OH^-, whereas Brønsted-Lowry bases need not. In the example below, notice how ammonia increases the concentration of hydroxide ion in the resulting solution without donating a OH^- ion. It does so by accepting a proton from water.

$$NH_3(aq) + H_2O(l) \rightleftharpoons NH_4^+(aq) + OH^-(aq)$$

Another significant difference between definitions is that Brønsted-Lowry acids and bases need not be molecular substances. There are a variety of reactions in which ions donate or accept protons. In the sample below, note how the cyanide ion (CN^-) acts as a base by accepting a proton and the bicarbonate ion (HCO_3^-) acts as an acid by donating a proton.

$$CN^-(aq) + HCO_3^-(aq) \rightleftharpoons HCN(aq) + CO_3^{2-}(aq)$$

Amphoterism

An **amphoteric substance** is a substance that acts as an acid in some reactions and a base in others. In the two reactions below, note how water donates a proton (making it an acid) in the first reaction, while in the second reaction it receives a proton (making it a base).

$$NH_3(aq) + H_2O(l) \rightleftharpoons NH_4^+(aq) + OH^-(aq)$$

$$HCl(g) + H_2O(l) \rightarrow H_3O^+(aq) + Cl^-(aq)$$

Conjugate Acid-Base Pairs

One very important thing to remember is that an acid and base are always present in these reactions. In order for a molecule or ion to donate a proton, there has to be another ion or molecule to receive it. In addition, in reversible acid-base reactions, the roles of the substances as proton donor or acceptor will switch in the reverse reaction. In the example below, note how water (a Brønsted-Lowry base in this reaction) accepts a proton to form a hydronium ion in the forward reaction. In the reverse reaction, the hydronium ion (Brønsted-Lowry acid) donates a proton and, after losing the proton, becomes the water molecule once again.

$$H_2CO_3(aq) + H_2O(l) \rightleftharpoons H_3O^+(aq) + HCO_3^-(aq)$$

Also note how H_2CO_3 donates a proton in the forward reaction to form a bicarbonate ion, which then will accept a proton in the reverse reaction.

These pairs of substances—H_2O/H_3O^+ and H_2CO_3/HCO_3^-—differ only by the presence (or absence) of a proton, which classifies them as **conjugate acid-base pairs**. A **conjugate acid** is formed when a proton is added to a Brønsted-Lowry base. Therefore, in the previous example the conjugate acid is the hydronium ion, since it was formed by the addition of a proton to the water molecule (the Brønsted-Lowry base in the forward reaction). Removing a proton from a Brønsted-Lowry acid forms a **conjugate base**. In the previous example, HCO_3^- is the conjugate base of H_2CO_3.

Sample: In the chemical reaction shown below, identify the Brønsted-Lowry acid, Brønsted-Lowry base, conjugate acid, and conjugate base.

$$H_3PO_4(aq) + NO_2^-(aq) \rightleftharpoons HNO_2(aq) + H_2PO_4^-(aq)$$

Answer:
Brønsted-Lowry acid: H_3PO_4—donates a proton
Brønsted-Lowry base: NO_2^-—accepts a proton
Conjugate acid: HNO_2—formed by the addition of a proton to NO_2^-; will donate a proton in the reverse reaction
Conjugate base: $H_2PO_4^-$—formed by the removal of a proton from H_3PO_4; will accept a proton in the reverse reaction
NOTE: Removing a proton from an acid produces a conjugate base, and adding a proton to a base produces a conjugate acid.

You Try It!
In the chemical reaction shown below, identify the Brønsted-Lowry acid, the Brønsted-Lowry base, the conjugate acid, and the conjugate base.

$$NH_3(aq) + H_2O(l) \rightleftharpoons NH_4^+(aq) + OH^-(aq)$$

Answer:
Brønsted-Lowry Acid: H_2O—donates a proton
Brønsted-Lowry Base: NH_3—accepts a proton
Conjugate acid: NH_4^+—formed by adding a proton to a base
Conjugate base: OH^-—formed by removing a proton from an acid

Strengths of Acids and Bases

Before continuing on to the last definition of acids and bases, it will be helpful to consider the definitions for strong and weak acids within the context of the Brønsted-Lowry model of acids and bases. The definitions are really an extension of the Arrhenius ideas. In the Arrhenius definitions, strong acids and bases were those that ionize completely. Most Brønsted-Lowry acids and bases do not completely ionize in solution, so the strengths are determined based on the degree of ionization in solution. For example, acetic acid, found in vinegar, is a weak acid that is only about 1% ionized in solution. That means that when acetic acid, $HC_2H_3O_2$, is placed in water, the reaction looks like

$$HC_2H_3O_2(aq) + H_2O(l) \rightleftharpoons C_2H_3O_2^-(aq) + H_3O^+(aq)$$

This equation can actually provide you with a wealth of information if you know how to interpret it. Because the acetic acid is only about 1% ionized, it means that the reaction to the left is much more favored than the reaction to the right. In the reaction going to the right, $HC_2H_3O_2$ is the acid and H_2O is the base. In the reaction going to the left, H_3O^+ is the acid and $C_2H_3O_2^-$ is the base. Because the reaction going to the left is favored, it means that H_3O^+

is a stronger acid than $HC_2H_3O_2$. It also means that $C_2H_3O_2^-$ is a stronger base than H_2O. In acid-base equilibrium reactions, the dominant direction of the reaction is from the stronger acid and base to the weaker acid and base.

To summarize, strong acids yield weak conjugate bases while weak acids yield relatively strong conjugate bases.

How Strength Relates to the Molecular Structure

There are a few trends about acid strengths that you should be familiar with. If you consider the acid HA, the bond between H and A will have to be broken in order for the hydrogen ion to be donated. The easier it is to break this bond, the more acidic the substance HA. For binary acids (those containing only hydrogen and a nonmetallic element), there are two main factors that determine the ease of this process: the polarity of the bond between H and A and the size of A. The factors can be summarized as follows:

- The larger molecule A is, the stronger the acid will be.
- The more polar the bond between H and A is, the stronger the acid will be.

For acids containing oxygen, known as oxoacids, the rules are similar but have a slight difference. In the oxoacids, the hydrogen atom is bonded to an oxygen atom, which is, in turn, bonded to something else. Quite often, the general symbol to describe them is HOX, where X is some element. For example, the structure of perchloric acid, seen in figure 13.1, shows the positioning of the acidic hydrogen atom (the one that will come off). Note how the oxygen atom it is bonded to is also bonded to a chlorine atom. For the oxoacids, the basic rules for determining the strengths of the acids are as follows:

- The more electronegative element X is, the stronger acid HOX will be.
- When comparing acids where X is bonded to additional oxygen molecules (for instance, comparing perchloric acid, $HClO_4$, to chloric acid, $HClO_3$), the more additional oxygen atoms that are bonded to X, the stronger the acid will be ($HClO_4$ is stronger than $HClO_3$).

For polyprotic acids (acids where more than one proton can be removed), each successive proton becomes more difficult to remove. In H_2SO_4, the first proton readily dissociates, forming the HSO_4^- ion. The additional electron density on the ion has a stronger hold on the additional hydrogen ion, so it is held much more tightly. Therefore, for polyprotic acids, the anions formed by the dissociation of the acidic hydrogen are always less acidic than their parent molecule.

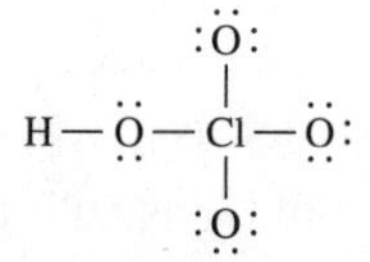

$$\text{H}-\overset{..}{\underset{..}{\text{O}}}-\overset{\overset{\displaystyle :\overset{..}{\text{O}}:}{|}}{\underset{\underset{\displaystyle :\overset{..}{\text{O}}:}{|}}{\text{Cl}}}-\overset{..}{\underset{..}{\text{O}}}:$$

Figure 13.1

Lewis Acids and Bases

The Lewis concept of the acid is included in the AP curriculum but is not emphasized as much as the other two descriptions. As a result, we will just look at the main ideas.

The Lewis concept deals with the behavior of electron pairs in chemical reactions. The same electron pairs we looked at when we discussed molecular geometry (see Chapter 6) can be involved in many reactions. Substances that can form a covalent bond by accepting an electron pair from another substance are known as **Lewis acids**. Substances that can form a covalent bond by donating an electron pair to another substance are known as **Lewis bases**. Be careful that you don't mix these up with the Brønsted-Lowry acids and bases. It is easy to do since the words "donate" and "accept" are used, except they are associated with the opposite species (Brønsted-Lowry acids *donate* protons, while Lewis acids *accept* electron pairs).

When you are working on problems with Lewis acids and bases, it is often useful to use Lewis diagrams (or at least modified Lewis diagrams) to determine the behavior and location of the electron pairs. In the reaction shown in Figure 13.2, note how the electron pair from nitrogen (in ammonia) is donated to boron (in BF_3). This transfer of the electron pair allows for the formation of a covalent bond.

Figure 13.2

In the previous example, note that the success of the reaction depended upon the acid (BF_3) having an incomplete octet. Many substances, including metal ions that have incomplete octets, can act as Lewis acids in the presence of Lewis bases.

Sample: Identify the Lewis acid and base in the reaction shown below.

$$CN^-(aq) + H_2O(l) \rightleftharpoons HCN(aq) + OH^-(aq)$$

Answer:
Acid: H_2O (gained a pair of electrons in the reaction)
Base: CN^- (donated a pair of electrons)

You Try It!
In the following reaction, identify the Lewis acid and the Lewis base.

$$B(OH)_3(aq) + H_2O(l) \rightleftharpoons B(OH)_4(aq) + H^+(aq)$$

Answer:
Acid: $B(OH)_3$
Base: H_2O

NOTE
The hydrogen ion (H^+) is often written in acid-base examples and problems because it is simplistic. In actuality, a positively charged hydrogen ion will bind to a polar water molecule to form a hydronium ion (H_3O^+). The expressions (H^+) and (H_3O^+) can be used interchangeably.

THE pH CONCEPT
Self-Ionization of Water

A sample of pure water will contain a small quantity of ions (H^+ and OH^-) produced from the self-ionization of water. These ions exist only for a brief time period before rejoining to form water molecules. At any given moment, only a very small proportion of the sample of water exists as ions (only about one of every billion particles). The following equation describes this process:

$$H_2O(l) \rightleftharpoons H^+(aq) + OH^-(aq)$$

Using the equilibrium expression that you reviewed in Chapter 12, the equilibrium constant for the self-ionization of water can be expressed as

$$K = \frac{\left[H^+\right]\left[OH^-\right]}{\left[H_2O\right]}$$

However, since the concentration of liquid water is constant and so large relative to the concentration of ions, it can be omitted from the equilibrium expression. At 25 °C, the equilibrium expression can be rewritten as

(Equation 13.1)
$$K_w = [H^+][OH^-] = [H^3O^+][OH^-] = 1.0 \times 10^{-14}$$

where the subscript "w" in the equilibrium constant expression stands for "water." Because the amounts of hydrogen and hydroxide ions are equal in water (and any neutral solution)

$$[H^+] = [OH^-] = 1.0 \times 10^{-7}M$$

Since the equilibrium constant expression (K_w) remains constant, an increase in one ion will only occur at the expense of a decrease in the other. An increase in [H^+] must be accompanied by a corresponding decrease in [OH^-], such that the product of the two will equal 1.0×10^{-14}. The reverse will occur as well—a decrease in [H^+] will be accompanied by an increase in [OH^-]. Use the table below to help you remember the relationships between these two ions.

Solution			
Neutral	[H^+]	=	[OH^-]
Acidic	[H^+]	>	[OH^-]
Basic	[H^+]	<	[OH^-]

The pH Scale

pH stands for the *power* of *Hydrogen* ion concentration in a solution. The numerical values for pH range from 0 to 14 and can be calculated using the equation below:

$$pH = -\log[H^+]$$

(Equation 13.2)

We can use the $[H^+]$ for a neutral solution to show how the pH equation works (recall that in a neutral solution $[H^+] = 1.0 \times 10^{-7}$):

$$pH = -\log[H^+] = -\log(1.0 \times 10^{-7}) = 7$$

A pH of 7 is representative of neutral solutions. In acidic solutions, where the $[H^+] > 1.0 \times 10^{-7}$, pH values less than 7 are obtained. Likewise, in basic solutions, pH values greater than 7 are obtained.

Sample: An unknown solution has a hydrogen ion concentration of 5.40×10^{-6} *M*. Calculate the pH and determine if the solution is acidic or basic.

Answer: $pH = -\log[H^+] = -\log(5.40 \times 10^{-6}) = 5.27$

The pH is less than 7, so the solution is acidic. You can determine whether a solution is acidic or basic by "eyeballing" the $[H^+]$. Any exponents less than −7 will yield an acidic pH, while exponents greater than −7 will yield a basic pH.

You Try It!

An unknown solution has a hydrogen ion concentration $[H^+]$ of 7.64×10^{-11} *M*. Calculate the pH and determine if the solution is acidic, basic, or neutral.

Answer: $pH = -\log[H^+] = -\log(7.64 \times 10^{-11}) = 10.1$, so the solution is basic.

Calculating the Hydrogen Ion Concentration

There are a few variations on pH problems that you might encounter. The simplest variation is a reversal of the pH equation to solve for the hydrogen ion concentration. To solve these problems, rearrange the pH equation to solve for $[H^+]$.

$$[H^+] = 10^{-pH}$$

(Equation 13.3)

Sample: What is the hydrogen ion concentration of a solution with a pH of 2.4?

Answer: $[H^+] = 10^{-pH} = 10^{-2.4} = 4.0 \times 10^{-3}$ *M*

You Try It!

An unknown base has a pH of 10.6. Determine the $[H^+]$ of the solution.

Answer: $[H^+] = 10^{-pH} = 10^{-10.6} = 2.5 \times 10^{-11}$ *M*

Relationship between pH and [OH⁻]

The second variation is to determine either the pH or the hydrogen ion concentration of a solution when given the hydroxide ion concentration, [OH⁻], for the solution. To solve these problems you need to utilize the equilibrium constant expression for the self-ionization of water (K_w). This expression will allow you to convert from the hydroxide ion concentration, [OH⁻], to the hydrogen ion concentration [H⁺]. The [H⁺] can then be used to calculate pH if necessary. One of the free response questions on the 1999 exam required this calculation.

Sample: Orange juice has a hydroxide ion concentration of 6.3×10^{-12} M. Determine the pH of orange juice.

Answer: This will require two steps:

First, the hydroxide ion concentration will be used to calculate the hydrogen ion concentration. Next, the obtained value will be used to determine pH.

$$K_w = [H^+][OH^-] = 1.0 \times 10^{-14}$$

Solve for [H⁺]:

$$[H^+] = \left[H^+\right] = \frac{1.0 \times 10^{-14}}{6.3 \times 10^{-12}} = 1.6 \times 10^{-3} \ M$$

Use this value to calculate the pH:

$$pH = -\log[H^+] = -\log(1.6 \times 10^{-3}) = \mathbf{2.8}$$

You Try It!

Household ammonia has a hydroxide ion concentration of 7.9×10^{-3} M. Calculate the pH of household ammonia.

Answer: [H⁺]=1.3×10^{-12} M; pH = 11.9

Calculation of pOH

In addition to the pH value, a solution can also be described according to its pOH (power of hydroxide ion concentration). Because of the relationship between hydrogen ions and hydroxide ions, there are many similarities between pOH and pH. First, note the similarity between the calculation of pH and pOH in the equation below:

(Equation 13.4)
$$pOH = -\log[OH^-]$$

Similarly, the [OH⁻] can be calculated by rearranging the pOH equation:

(Equation 13.5)
$$[OH-] = 10^{-pOH}$$

Finally, there is a relationship that allows easy conversion between pH and pOH:

(Equation 13.6)
$$pH + pOH = 14$$

Sample: A solution of potassium hydroxide has a hydroxide ion concentration of 2.5×10^{-5} M. What are the pH, [H$^+$], and pOH of the solution?

Answer: There is more than one way to solve this problem. One possible solution would use the given [OH$^-$] to calculate the [H$^+$], use the calculated [H$^+$] to determine the pH, and then use the pH to determine the pOH. Another would be to use the [OH$^-$] to determine the pOH, then use the pOH to determine the pH, and finally use the pH to determine the [H$^+$]. While there are still other variations possible, we will select the second one and solve the problem.

$$pOH = -\log[OH^-] = -\log(2.5 \times 10^{-5}) = 4.6$$
$$pH = 14 - pOH = 14 - 4.6 = 9.4$$
$$[H^+] = 10^{-pH} = 10^{-9.4} = 4.0 \times 10^{-10} \text{ M}$$

You Try It!
Drain cleaner, a strong base, has a pH of 13.0. Calculate the pOH, [OH$^-$], and [H$^+$].

Answers:
pOH = 1.0;   [OH-] = 1.0×10^{-1} M;   [H+] = 1.0×10^{-13} M

WEAK ACIDS AND BASES

When a strong acid or base undergoes a complete ionization in solution, the concentrations of the newly formed ions can be understood using basic stoichiometry principles. This is because essentially all of the acid is converted to ions. With weaker acids and bases, equilibrium is established between the ions, much like the equilibria studied in the last chapter. The concentrations of the ions must be determined by using an equilibrium constant, K. The equilibrium constants used to describes acid-base equilibria are in the same form as K_c from the last chapter. We'll use the dissociation of acetic acid to begin our description of the new equilibrium constant.

The equation that describes the ionization of acetic acid in water takes the form

$$HC_2H_3O_2(aq) + H_2O(l) \rightleftharpoons H_3O^+(aq) + C_2H_3O_2^-(aq)$$

If you were going to determine the equilibrium constant, K_c, for this reaction, you would set it up as follows:

$$K_c = \frac{\left[H_3O^+\right]\left[C_2H_3O_2^-\right]}{\left[HC_2H_3O_2\right]}$$

Water is omitted from the expression because its concentration is not likely to be affected by this equilibrium. When the equilibrium constant, K_c, is written for an acid-base equilibrium, it is known as the acid-dissociation constant, K_a. The generic equation for the acid-dissociation constant is written with the symbol HA to represent the acid. Thus for the reaction

$$HA(aq) + H_2O(l) \rightleftharpoons H_3O^+(aq) + A^-(aq)$$

The acid dissociation constant, K_a is expressed

(Equation 13.7) $\qquad K_a = \dfrac{\left[H_3O^+\right]\left[A^-\right]}{\left[HA\right]}$, which is generally shortened to $K_a = \dfrac{\left[H^+\right]\left[A^-\right]}{\left[HA\right]}$

Calculating the pH of Weak Acid Solutions

You've already seen how to calculate the pH of a solution containing a strong acid. This was relatively easy because the acid completely dissociated. That meant for every mole of acid, you generated a mole of hydrogen ions (for monoprotic acids). With weak acids, the process is not as simple, but you will notice that it is very similar to the calculations you did in the last chapter for K_c. We'll review the procedure using the equilibrium of acetic acid in water, shown below:

$$HC_2H_3O_2(aq) \rightleftharpoons H^+(aq) + C_2H_3O_2{}^-(aq)$$

In a 0.10 M solution of acetic acid, $HC_2H_3O_2$, what are the concentrations of hydrogen ion, H^+, and acetate ion, $C_2H_3O_2{}^-$? What is the pH of the solution if $K_a = 1.7 \times 10^{-5}$?

As you approach the problem, you need to think about what it is you are calculating. The solution is 0.10 M acetic acid solution. That means that 0.10 mol acetic acid was dissolved in enough water to make 1.00 liter of solution. Some of that 0.10 mol has dissociated, however. Because we don't know how much, we have to determine the amount using the expression for K_a. This will allow us to determine the concentrations, and eventually the pH. We will begin by setting up a chart like the ones you used in the last chapter.

$HC_2H_3O_2(aq) \rightleftharpoons H^+(aq) + C_2H_3O_2{}^-(aq)$			
	$HC_2H_3O_2$	H^+	$C_2H_3O_2{}^-$
Start	0.10	0	0
Δ	$-x$	$+x$	$+x$
Finish	$0.10 - x$	x	x

In the calculations, we have omitted the self-ionization of water. Since the equilibrium concentration of hydrogen ion $[H^+]$ is so small (1.0×10^{-7}), it is negligible compared to the molarity of the acetic acid.

The next step is to substitute the values into the equation for K_a.

$$K_a = \frac{\left[H^+\right]\left[C_2H_3O_2{}^-\right]}{\left[HC_2H_3O_2\right]} \qquad 1.7 \times 10^{-5} = \frac{(x)^2}{0.10 - x}$$

At this point, we need to consider a very important idea. As the equation stands, we need to use the quadratic equation to solve it. You're not going to want to spend your precious time on the AP exam (or even now) cranking out quadratic equations, so we're going to make an estimate. The only catch is that we always have to check to make sure that we can get away with the shortcut. The shortcut is to assume that the value for x is going to be so small that subtracting it from 0.10 won't make a dent in it. For example, pretend that x is 0.00001. Subtract that from 0.10. You get 0.09999, which is essentially 0.1. So, we're going to forget about the x in the denominator of the fraction. When we have solved for x, we'll go back and see if we can get away with it. Our new equation is

$$1.7 \times 10^{-5} = \frac{(x)^2}{0.10}$$

We can rearrange this so that

$$x^2 = 1.7 \times 10^{-6}$$

and then solve for x by taking the square root of both sides

$$x = 1.3 \times 10^{-3}$$

If we check back to our assumption, we see that $0.10 - x = 0.10 - 0.0013 \approx 0.10$; good enough! Now to finish the problem:

$$x = [H^+] = [C_2H_3O_2^-] = 1.3 \times 10^{-3}\ M$$

Solving for pH, we use the pH equation:

$$pH = -\log[H^+] = -\log(1.3 \times 10^{-3}) = 2.9$$

You Try It!

Propionic acid, $HC_3H_5O_2$ has a K_a of 1.3×10^{-5}. If you started with a 0.25 M solution, of propionic acid, what would be the concentrations of hydrogen ions, H^+, and propionate ions, $C_3H_5O_2^-$. What would be the pH of the solution?

Answer:

$[H+] = [C_3H_5O_2^-] = 1.8 \times 10^{-3}$
pH = 2.7

Polyprotic Acids

For polyprotic acids, the K_a for the initial hydrogen ion is usually much higher than the K_a for the second, or third hydrogen ions. For example, in phosphoric acid, H_3PO_4, the value of K_a for the first hydrogen ion is 6.9×10^{-3}. For the second ionization, the hydrogen will come off the $H_2PO_4^-$ ion, and the K_a for this is 6.2×10^{-8}. The third ionization, which converts HPO_4^{2-} to H^+ and PO_4^{3-}, has a K_a of 4.8×10^{-13}. Just because there are three hydrogen atoms on phosphoric acid does not mean that all three will come off easily or that they will contribute to the acidic character of the substance. This example is fairly typical, and from it we will make a helpful generalization about polyprotic acids: when you want to determine the hydrogen ion concentration of one of these, use the K_a from the first ionization (sometimes referred to as K_a1). The other values are so much smaller that they are negligible.

Base Equilibria

So far, we've been looking at the equilibria of weak acids, from which we developed the acid-dissociation constant, K_a. There is a similar process for weak bases. Let's use the weak base, ammonia. In solution, ammonia establishes the equilibrium shown below:

$$NH_3(aq) + H_2O(l) \rightleftharpoons NH_4^+(aq) + OH^-(aq)$$

Following the same process we used to look at the equilibrium of the acid, let's set up the equilibrium constant expression for this reaction:

$$K_c = \frac{\left[NH_4^+\right]\left[OH^-\right]}{\left[NH_3\right]}$$

Again, because the concentration of water is constant, we can say that $K_c = K_b$ for this reaction. If written in a generic format, where B is to represent the base, the equilibrium takes on the following form:

$$B(aq) + H_2O(l) \rightleftharpoons HB^+(aq) + OH^-(aq)$$

The base-dissociation constant, K_b, is written as

(Equation 13.8)
$$K_b = \frac{\left[HB^+\right]\left[OH^-\right]}{[B]}$$

The base-dissociation constant expression can be used to calculate the concentrations of ions just like the acid-dissociation expression. The problem-solving strategy is identical.

SALT SOLUTIONS

If you remember from Chapter 10, we said that if an acid and base are mixed together, a neutralization reaction occurs that produces water and a salt. In this section, we are going to look a bit more closely at the salts that form in neutralization reactions (and salts in general). If you remember, a neutralization reaction takes the form:

$$HA(aq) + BOH(aq) \rightarrow H_2O(l) + BA(aq)$$

From this you can see that the cation from the salt comes from the base and the anion comes from the acid. Salts can act as Brønsted-Lowry acids or bases to produce solutions that are acidic or basic. The salts react with water in a reaction known as hydrolysis to yield either a conjugate acid and a hydroxide ion or a conjugate base and a hydrogen (hydronium) ion. If you know the origins of the components of a salt, you can make some predictions about the pH of the solution formed from a hydrolysis of a salt ion.

Salts from Strong Acids and Bases

To understand a little bit about how this works, look at the dissociation of hydrochloric acid, a strong acid.

$$HCl(aq) + H_2O(l) \rightarrow H_3O^+(aq) + Cl^-(aq)$$

The reaction only goes in the forward direction (if any movement occurs in the reverse direction, the amount is so slight that it is negligible). This means that chloride ions are very weak bases, so weak that they can be thought of as having no basic character. In a similar reaction, look at the dissociation of sodium hydroxide, a strong base,

$$NaOH(aq) + H_2O(l) \rightarrow Na^+(aq) + OH^-(aq)$$

This reaction only goes in the forward direction. As a conjugate acid, sodium is completely ineffective. Now, put the two substances, HCl and NaOH together,

$$HCl(aq) + NaOH(aq) \rightarrow H_2O(l) + NaCl(aq)$$

The salt formed, NaCl, is quite soluble in water, but we have just seen that neither of the ions is capable of behaving as an acid or a base. As a result, a solution of salt water (made by dissolving sodium chloride in water) has a neutral pH.

Salts created from the conjugates of strong acids and bases will produce neutral solutions.

Salts from Strong Acids and Weak Bases

You already know that the conjugate base of a strong acid is extremely weak. The conjugate acid of a weak base, however, is relatively strong. Therefore, the conjugate ion from the weak base will hydrolyze to produce an acidic solution. The weaker the base, the stronger the conjugate acid will be. An example would be NH_4Cl. The NH_4^+ ion, the cation from a base, hydrolyzes water as shown below:

$$NH_4^+(aq) + H_2O(l) \rightleftharpoons NH_3(aq) + H_3O^+(aq)$$

Salts from Weak Acids and Strong Bases

From the first example, we know that the conjugate acids of strong bases are weak. The conjugate bases of weak acids, however, are relatively strong. Therefore, the anions from the weak acids will hydrolyze water to form basic solutions. An example would be $NaC_2H_3O_2$. The acetate ion, the anion from the weak acid, hydrolyzes water as shown below:

$$C_2H_3O_2^-(aq) + H_2O(l) \rightleftharpoons HC_2H_3O_2(aq) + OH^-(aq)$$

Salts from Weak Acids and Weak Bases

This one is not as clear-cut as the others. Both species will hydrolyze water. The question here is which one will do it more? The only way to really predict the nature of the solution is to look at the K_a of the cation and the K_b of the anion. If K_a is bigger, the solution will be acidic, but if K_b is bigger then the solution will be basic.

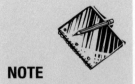

THE RELATIONSHIP BETWEEN K_a AND K_b

NOTE
The weaker the acid, the stronger the conjugate base.

In the previous section, you saw further evidence of the relationships between acids, bases, and their conjugates. The relationship between acids and their conjugate bases and bases and their conjugate acids will allow us to better see another relationship between K_a and K_b. If you consider the acetic acid equilibrium again,

$$HC_2H_3O_2(aq) \rightleftharpoons H^+(aq) + C_2H_3O_2(aq) \qquad K_a = 1.7 \times 10^{-5}$$

Next, consider the hydrolysis of water by acetic acid's conjugate, the acetate ion,

$$C_2H_3O_2(aq) + H_2O(l) \rightleftharpoons HC_2H_3O_2(aq) + OH^-(aq)$$

What if you wanted to calculate the *Kb* for this equilibrium? As it turns out, you don't have to. There is a relationship between these two expressions that may not have been obvious when you looked at them in this way. If we place them on top of one another, you might see something different:

$$HC_2H_3O_2(aq) \rightleftharpoons H^+(aq) + C_2H_3O_2\,(aq)$$

$$C_2H_3O_2^-(aq) + H_2O(l) \rightleftharpoons HC_2H_3O_2(aq) + OH^-(aq)$$

If you add the two equations together, you will find that the net equation is

$$H_2O(l) \rightleftharpoons H^+(aq) + OH^-(aq)$$

Perhaps you recognize this equation from the beginning of the chapter. If you don't, it is the equation for the self-ionization of water, from which K_w was derived. What you've now seen are three equations. The first is an equation that would be used to calculate the K_a of acetic acid. The second is the equation used to calculate K_b for the conjugate base. The third, which is derived from these two, is the formula for calculating K_w. There is a very clear relationship between K_a, K_b, and K_w. The three constants are all related in equation 13.9, shown below:

(Equation 13.9) $$K_w = K_a K_b$$

If you wanted to determine K_b for the acetate ion, you could use the K_a of its conjugate acid, acetic acid. The K_a of acetic acid is 1.7×10^{-5}.

$$K_b = \frac{K_w}{K_a} = \frac{1.0 \times 10^{-14}}{1.7 \times 10^{-5}} = 5.9 \times 10^{-10}$$ which makes acetate a pretty weak base.

You Try It!
HF is a fairly weak acid with a K_a of 6.8×10^{-4}. What is the K_b for the F^- ion?

Answer: 1.5×10^{-11}

THE COMMON-ION EFFECT

You will see this topic appear twice, once in this chapter and once the next chapter. For now, you will see how this phenomenon affects acid-base equilibria. In the next chapter, you will see its effects on solubility equilibria. The common-ion effect is not too different from what its name suggests. If you have an equilibrium system and add a solute to it that contains one of the ions in the equilibrium, it will cause the equilibrium to shift. That is the common-ion effect (common because the solute has an ion in common with the equilibrium system). From a conceptual standpoint, this can be addressed using Le Châtelier's principle. For example, consider our favorite equilibrium system below:

$$HC_2H_3O_2(aq) \rightleftharpoons H^+(aq) + C_2H_3O_2^-(aq)$$

We can add a couple of different things to the mixture that will affect it and demonstrate the common-ion effect. One of them would be sodium acetate, $NaC_2H_3O_2$. Another would be hydrochloric acid. Think about this for a moment, keeping in mind Le Châtelier's principle. If sodium acetate is added to the mixture, it will dissociate into sodium ions and acetate ions. The increase in concentration of the acetate ions will drive the reaction to the left, which will further inhibit the dissociation of acetic acid. Adding hydrochloric acid will have the same effect because it will increase the concentration of protons, which will also drive the reaction to the left. Sodium acetate and hydrochloric acid have two features that allow them both to cause the common-ion effect to occur. First, they are both strong electrolytes, and second they each have an ion in common with the acetic acid equilibrium. These are the key ingredients that cause the common-ion effect.

Quantitative Treatment of the Common-Ion Effect

Having a conceptual understanding of the effect is a good starting point, but we still need to be able to understand the quantitative relationships between the different components in the equilibrium mixture. In this section, we will see how to deal with the common-ion effect in acid-base equilibrium problems. You will find that these problems are very similar to the weak acid problems earlier in the chapter.

In this sample, we will see what happens when we make a solution that contains both acetic acid and sodium acetate (which was used in our previous example). Suppose you make a solution that contains 0.30 mol $HC_2H_3O_2$ and 0.30 mol $NaC_2H_3O_2$ dissolved in 1.00 liter of solution. Let's compare the pH of this sample to the pH of a solution that only has 0.30 mol $HC_2H_3O_2$. If the conceptual explanation in the last section is valid, we should predict that the pH of the solution with the sodium acetate will be higher (less acidic) than the acetic acid-only solution. To begin, let's set up the equation for the equilibrium reaction:

$$HC_2H_3O_2(aq) + H_2O(l) \rightleftharpoons H_3O^+(aq) + C_2H_3O_2^-(aq)$$

There are a few things that you need to pay attention to as you set this problem up. First, the sodium need not be written in the equation because it doesn't do anything (it's a spectator). Second, unlike the previous weak acid problems, these problems aren't starting out with no products. The common ion in this reaction is the acetate ion, which is a product of the acetic acid dissociation. When you set up your chart, you need to include all amounts of all substances present at the start of the reaction. We're going to omit water in our chart because it is not part of the equilibrium expression.

Let's make the chart.

	$HC_2H_3O_2(aq) + \rightleftharpoons H_3O^+(aq) + C_2H_3O_2^-(aq)$		
	$HC_2H_3O_2$	H_3O^+	$C_2H_3O_2^-$
Start	0.30	0	0.30
Δ	-x	+x	+x
Finish	0.30 − x	x	0.30 + x

At this point, you are ready to plug these values into the K_a expression. We saw earlier in the chapter that the K_a for acetic acid was 1.7×10^{-5}.

$$K_a = \frac{[H_3O^+][C_2H_3O_2^-]}{[HC_2H_3O_2]}; \qquad 1.7 \times 10^{-5} = \frac{x(0.30 + x)}{0.30 - x}$$

Like the previous problems, we are going to assume that x is small enough that adding or subtracting it from or to 0.30 will make an insignificant difference. That will allow us to solve for x.

$$1.7 \times 10^{-5} = \frac{0.30 + x}{0.30}$$

$$1.7 \times 10^{-5} = x$$

If we check our earlier approximation, we see that $0.30 - 1.7 \times 10^{-5} = 0.30$ so we can go with that.

Substituting our x back into the equation for the $[H_3O^+]$ (which we have to do to get the pH), we get $[H_3O^+] = 1.7 \times 10^{-5}$.

If we use this hydronium ion concentration, we can determine the pH:

$$pH = -\log[H_3O^+] = -\log(1.7 \times 10^{-5}) = 4.77$$

Now, let's compare that to the pH of a 0.30 M solution of acetic acid. Because you have already done this type of calculation, we'll just show the set-up and solution with no further explanation.

	$HC_2H_3O_2(aq) \rightleftharpoons H^+(aq) + C_2H_3O_2^-(aq)$		
	$HC_2H_3O_2$	H^+	$C_2H_3O_2^-$
Start	0.30	0	0
Δ	−x	+x	+x
Finish	0.30 − x	X	x

$$K_a = \frac{\left[H_3O^+\right]\left[C_2H_3O_2^-\right]}{\left[HC_2H_3O_2\right]} \qquad 1.7 \times 10^{-5} = \frac{(x)^2}{0.30 - x}$$

$$1.7 \times 10^{-5} = \frac{(x)^2}{0.30}$$

$$x = \sqrt{\left(1.7 \times 10^{-5}\right)(0.30)}$$

$$x = [H_3O^+] = 2.26 \times 10^{-3}$$

$$pH = -\log[H_3O^+] = -\log(2.26 \times 10^{-3}) = 2.65$$

So, by adding sodium acetate to the solution, the pH of the acetic acid solution changed from 2.65 to 4.77. This was caused by the addition of a common ion from a strong electrolyte and behaved according to Le Châtelier's principle.

This same process can be seen in bases. Consider the equilibrium of a weak base ionization, as shown below

$$NH_3(aq) + H_2O(l) \rightleftharpoons NH_4^+(aq) + OH^-(aq)$$

The addition of a strong electrolyte containing either an ammonium ion (NH_4^+) or a strong base (containing OH^-) will shift the equilibrium to the left. It will also shift pH in the other direction, which will make the basic pH less basic.

BUFFERS

The term "buffer" is usually used to describe a buffered solution, which is a solution that resists changes to pH when acids or bases are added to it. You know enough chemistry right now to know that there are limits to the amount of acid or base that a solution can buffer. You can probably imagine that a 100 ml beaker of buffered solution won't be much good if you mix it with a liter of concentrated hydrochloric acid! The amount of acid of base that a buffered solution can "handle" before appreciably changing pH is known as the **buffer capacity**. The purpose of this section is to review the nature of buffers and how this relates to the buffer capacity.

What you saw in the last section was an example of how the presence of certain ions in solution can regulate the pH of a system. In the acetic acid/sodium acetate example, we started with a weak acid and then added a salt containing the conjugate base of the weak acid to the solution. This pairing of the weak acid and the conjugate base modified the pH of the solution. This is the principle behind buffered solutions. If an acid was added to the solution containing the acetic acid/acetate conjugates, the hydronium ions from the acid would combine with the acetate ions to form more acetic acid. So, what should have amounted to an increase in hydronium ions in the solution was foiled by the acetate ions.

The ability to drive the reaction to the left, and thereby remove the hydronium ions from solution, hinges on two factors. First, there has to be enough of the conjugate base to combine with the acid. Second, the K_a of the acid has to be small enough that the reaction doesn't move quickly to the right. In other words, when the protons combine with the conjugate base, they will remain that way (the acid is weak enough that it does not readily ionize).

In a basic solution, the principle is similar. The conjugate acid of the weak base combines with excess hydroxide ion to drive the reaction toward the weak base. The same factors govern the process: the amount of the conjugate acid and the K_b of the base.

Buffers can be made that will resist changes to pH by acids and bases. To illustrate this, let's look at an example of a buffer that is composed of HX, a weak acid, and X$^-$, the conjugate base of the weak acid. Normally, the solution would exist in equilibrium as shown below (water has been omitted to make the relationships more obvious):

$$HX(aq) \rightleftharpoons H^+(aq) + X^-(aq)$$

When you look at this equilibrium, though, you have to remember that the acid has been spiked with a salt that will increase the concentration of X$^-$ to much higher levels than would normally be found (from the dissociation of the acid). That means that the concentration of H$^+$ ions is relatively much smaller than the concentration of X$^-$. If an acid is added to the mixture, the equilibrium will be shifted to the left as excess hydrogen (hydronium) ions combine with the conjugate base:

$$HX(aq) \rightleftharpoons H^+(aq) + X^-(aq)$$

The disproportionate arrow sizes indicate that the reaction is moving much more to the left after an acid is added. If a strong base is added instead of an acid, the hydroxide ion in the base will react with the acid in a neutralization, as shown below:

$$OH^-(aq) + HX(aq) \rightleftharpoons H_2O(l) + A^-(aq)$$

The amount of acid or base that a buffer is able to neutralize before changing pH, the buffering capacity, is related to the amount of weak acid/ conjugate base or weak base/conjugate acid present in the buffer solution. The greater the concentration of the conjugate pairs, the more resistant to a change in pH the buffer will be. In the next section, we'll look at some quantitative aspects of buffer solutions.

Quantitative Aspects of Buffers

On the AP exam, acid-base questions appear on a regular basis, and buffer calculations are among the most common of those questions to pop up. One of the things you are expected to be able to do is calculate the pH of a buffer solution, and though you may not realize it yet, you have already done this calculation. In the previous example of the common ion effect, when you calculated the pH of the solution made with the 0.30 *M* acetic acid and the 0.30 *M* sodium acetate, that was a buffer solution. That is the first type of buffer calculation you are expected to know. The second type of calculation is to determine the effect of adding a strong acid or base to a buffer, and the third type is to determine how to prepare a specific buffer. Let's take the second type of problem now, where you will see how to calculate the effect of adding a strong acid or base to a buffer solution.

As long as we already have mixed up a batch of the acetic acid/sodium acetate buffer, we might as well use it. We'll set up two different reaction vessels. To the first one, we will add 0.01 mol of gaseous HCl, and to the second we'll add 0.01 mol of solid NaOH.

Vessel 1: Addition of a strong acid, HCl, to a buffer solution

Two things are going to occur in the vessel, and solving the problem requires you to look at both. First, the acid will immediately dissociate into H^+ ions and Cl^- ions. Second, we will assume that the H^+ from the HCl will react completely with the acetate ion. This has an important implication for our starting conditions. If we make these two assumptions, then the starting concentration of acetate, $C_2H_3O_2^-$, will be $(0.30 - 0.01) = 0.29\ M$ because it reacts with the H^+ from hydrochloric acid. This reaction forms acetic acid, so the amount of acetic acid in the solution will increase after the addition of hydrochloric acid to $(0.30 + 0.01) = 0.31\ M$. In the next part of the problem, we need to look at the effect of the ionization of acetic acid, which requires the use of an equilibrium calculation.

$HC_2H_3O_2(aq) \rightleftharpoons H^+(aq) + C_2H_3O_2^-(aq)$			
	$HC_2H_3O_2$	H^+	$C_2H_3O_2^-$
Start	0.31	0	0.29
Δ	$-x$	$+x$	$+x$
Finish	$0.31 - x$	x	$0.29 + x$

$$K_a = \frac{\left[H_3O^+\right]\left[C_2H_3O_2^-\right]}{\left[HC_2H_3O_2\right]}; \qquad 1.7 \times 10^{-5} = \frac{x(0.29 + x)}{0.31 - x}$$

Assuming x is much smaller than 0.31 or 0.29,

$$1.7 \times 10^{-5} = \frac{0.29x}{0.31}$$

$$x = \frac{\left(1.7 \times 10^{-5}\right)0.31}{0.29} = 1.8 \times 10^{-5}$$

Substituting this for x, we see that $H^+ = 1.8 \times 10^{-5}$.

Therefore, we can use this value to calculate the pH of the solution,

$$pH = -\log[H^+] = -\log(1.8 \times 10^{-5}) = 4.74$$

If you recall from the earlier problem, the pH of the solution prior to the addition of the HCl was 4.77.

If you had added 0.01 mol HCl to pure water, the pH would have been

$$pH = -\log[H^+] = -\log(0.01) = 2.0$$

Quite a bit different!

Vessel 2: Addition of a strong base, NaOH to a buffer solution

In this example, we're adding 0.01 mol NaOH to the buffer solution. Before we begin with the math, let's consider what is going to happen in the vessel. Right after the sodium hydroxide is added, it will dissociate completely into sodium and hydroxide ions because it is such a strong electrolyte and a strong base. We are also going to assume that the hydroxide ions react completely with the acetic acid to yield water and acetate ions. This will cause an increase in the concentration of acetate ions at the expense of a decrease in the concentration of acetic acid. The setup will be the opposite of the addition of acid. Let's begin the calculation with an equilibrium calculation:

	\multicolumn{3}{c}{$HC_2H_3O_2(aq) \rightleftharpoons H^+(aq) + C_2H_3O_2^-(aq)$}	
	$HC_2H_3O_2$	H^+	$C_2H_3O_2^-$
Start	0.29	0	0.31
Δ	$-x$	$+x$	$+x$
Finish	$0.29 - x$	x	$0.31 + x$

Make sure you aren't getting mixed up about the changing concentrations of the buffer constituents and the signs in the Δ column. The change in concentration that occurs because of the addition of strong acid or base takes place in a separate reaction to the one in the equilibrium calculation table. The effects of these changes are reflected in the different amounts in the "start" row of the table. The other events shown in the table only describe the equilibrium of the acetic acid solution, which will always increase the concentration of acetate ion.

With that out of the way, let's finish the calculation. Set up the expression of K_a to solve for x.

$$K_a = \frac{[H_3O^+][C_2H_3O_2^-]}{[HC_2H_3O_2]}; \qquad 1.7 \times 10^{-5} = \frac{x(0.31 + x)}{0.29 - x}$$

Assuming x is much smaller than 0.31 or 0.29,

$$1.7 \times 10^{-5} = \frac{0.31x}{0.29}$$

$$x = \frac{(1.7 \times 10^{-5})0.29}{0.31} = 1.60 \times 10^{-5}$$

Substituting this for H^+, we find that the pH of the solution is

$$pH = -\log[H^+] = -\log(1.60 \times 10^{-5}) = 4.80$$

As you can see, the buffer solution maintained the pH within a relatively small range. The buffer solution only has a pH of 4.77, the buffer with HCl was 4.74, and the buffer with NaOH was 4.80. All of these were only slight changes in the pH.

Henderson-Hasselbalch Equation

This equation is used to directly calculate the pH of a buffer without using an equilibrium calculation. It is important that you know how to do equilibrium calculations before you use this equation. The equation makes the calculation much faster, but there are frequently conceptual questions about acid-base equilibria that require a solid understanding of the topic. Therefore, make sure you truly understand what you are doing before using this calculation. The problems that use the Henderson-Hasselbalch equation can be solved using equilibrium calculation tables as well.

So what is this equation? Let's take a moment to show the derivation, so it will make more sense to you. We'll begin with the formula for K_a that we've been using:

$$K_a = \frac{[H^+][A^-]}{[HA]}$$

If we rearrange this equation, we can solve for [H$^+$]. This will allow us to later use it to calculate pH.

$$[H^+] = K_a \frac{[HA]}{[A^-]}$$

Before going on to the next step, we need to look at a new variable. So far, you've learned about pH and pOH. Remember, these were obtained by taking the –log of the [H$^+$] and [OH$^-$], respectively. Here, we're going to introduce two new terms: pK_a, and pK_b. These terms are used to describe the K_a and K_b in small, positive numbers, rather than very small exponents (much like the pH values of 0-14 represent the small [H$^+$] ion amounts of $1 - 1 \times 10^{-14}$). pK_a is calculated as the $-\log K_a$, and pK_b is the $-\log K_b$. You will need these terms to understand the rest of the derivation, which we'll continue now:

We can take the negative log of both sides of the equation to reveal a familiar relationship

$$-\log[H^+] = -\log K_a \frac{[HA]}{[A^-]}$$

If we substitute pH for –log[H$^+$], and factor the right side, we end up with:

$$pH = -\log K_a - \log \frac{[HA]}{[A^-]}$$

A careful look at this expression should reveal the value for pK_a that we mentioned earlier when we showed that $pK_a = -\log K_a$. If we substitute that and add the log, we get

$$pH = pK_a + \log \frac{[A^-]}{[HA]}$$

(Equation 13.10)

This equation is known as the Henderson-Hasselbalch equation and is provided for you on the AP formula sheet. You can use it to calculate the pH of a buffer. There is a similar form of the equation that is rewritten to address the hydroxide ion concentration:

$$\text{pOH} = \text{p}K_b + \log\frac{\left[\text{HB}^+\right]}{[\text{B}]}$$

where B is the base and HB^+ is the protonated base.

To show how the equation is used, let's use the previous calculation to show how the equation could have been used instead of the equilibrium calculation method.

If you recall, we were using a buffer that was composed from 0.30 mol $\text{HC}_2\text{H}_3\text{O}_2$ and 0.30 mol $\text{NaC}_2\text{H}_3\text{O}_2$ dissolved in 1.0 liter of solution. The K_a of acetic acid is 1.7×10^{-5}. Using the Henderson-Hasselbalch equation to determine the pH, we get

$$\text{pH} = \text{p}K_a + \log\frac{\left[\text{A}^-\right]}{[\text{HA}]} = -\log(1.7 \times 10^{-5}) + \log\left(\frac{0.30}{0.30}\right) = 4.77$$

The equation to determine the pH after addition of the acid would become

$$\text{pH} = \text{p}K_a + \log\frac{\left[\text{A}^-\right]}{[\text{HA}]} = -\log(1.7 \times 10^{-5}) + \log\left(\frac{0.29}{0.31}\right) = 4.74$$

The equation to determine the pH after addition of the base would become:

$$\text{pH} = \text{p}K_a + \log\frac{\left[\text{A}^-\right]}{[\text{HA}]} = -\log(1.7 \times 10^{-5}) + \log\left(\frac{0.31}{0.29}\right) = 4.80$$

All three produced identical answers to the equilibrium calculation tables that we used.

ACID-BASE TITRATIONS

An acid-base titration is a procedure that is used where a base of known concentration is added to an acid of unknown concentration (or vice-versa) in order to determine the concentration of the unknown. In addition, it is possible to determine the K_a of the acid being titrated (or K_b of the base) as well as an appropriate indicator. Acid-base titrations are often the topic of AP exam questions and are frequently used in the laboratory questions. You should know about titrations from a conceptual level, be able to perform calculations for titrations, and know how to properly perform one in the laboratory. We'll begin with the conceptual explanation of titrations.

There are a few main types of titrations: 1) a strong acid titrated with a strong base (or a strong base titrated with a strong acid); 2) a weak acid titrated with a strong base; 3) a weak base titrated with a strong acid; and 4) a polyprotic acid titrated with a strong base. Each one of these produces characteristic results and will need to be discussed separately. For the solutions of weak acids and bases, the process is complicated by the common-ion effect.

Strong Acid with a Strong Base

One of the most common titrations of this type is the titration of hydrochloric acid, HCl, with sodium hydroxide, NaOH. If you remember from Chapter 10, this is a neutralization reaction. However, you should also remember from Chapter 11 that in order for a complete neutralization to occur, the reaction must use appropriate stoichiometric ratios. When we first look at the process, we will do so with two solutions of known concentration, but you will see that this process can be used to determine the concentration of one of the solutions.

The way that this procedure is typically done is to obtain a sample of strong base that has been standardized (the exact concentration determined) and place it into a buret. Frequently, questions appear on the test that deal with the procedures for titrations. One procedural question that has come up more than once involves the cleaning of the buret prior to the titration. After thorough cleaning with water and distilled water, the buret should be rinsed with the solution that is going in it. This is done by running several small amounts of the solution through the tip prior to the titration. This assures that the concentration of every drop in the buret is constant. The base is slowly added to the acid and the pH is recorded after the additions. In most modern high school labs, the pH is constantly being recorded with a digital pH meter or a computer probe.

The purpose of determining the pH is to create a **titration** curve for the reaction. A titration curve is a graph of the pH plotted against the amount of titrant (what's in the buret). Figure 13.5 shows the titration curve for a strong acid titrated with a strong base. With digital pH meters, this plotting must be done by hand, but with computer probes, the computer usually plots the curve while you are performing the titration.

Hopefully you have had the opportunity to do titrations in your laboratory, but if you haven't (or if you were lost while you were trying to do them!), here's a little refresher. During the initial stages of the titration, there is very little change in pH. You add relatively large amounts of base to the flask or beaker containing the acid, and the pH increases only slightly. However, almost all at once, the pH sharply rises from a low, acidic pH to a high, basic pH. The graph goes straight up at this point and the stoichiometric amounts of acid and base are equal. This point is known as the equivalence point of the titration. In this titration, at the equivalence point, the pH of the solution is 7.0. Remember HCl and NaOH react to form water and NaCl. Since neither Na^+ nor Cl^- can hydrolyze water, the pH is completely neutral, or 7. The typical procedure is to use an indicator solution that will change colors during this time of the titration. Once the equivalence point is passed, the solution quickly becomes basic because all of the excess H^+ ions from the HCl have combined with OH^-. Subsequent additions of sodium hydroxide will create an excess of OH^-.

The titration curve for a strong acid with a strong base look like the one in Figure 13.5, and you should be familiar with the shape. If you plotted the curve for a strong base being titrated with a strong acid, the curve would be a mirror image of Figure 13.5—the curve would start with a high pH and gradually slope downward until at the equivalence point, it would drop sharply to an acidic pH and then continue its gradual descent.

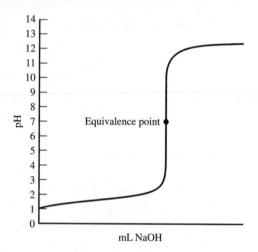

Figure 13.5

Weak Acids with Strong Base

For weak acids being titrated with a strong base, there are three main differences in the titration. The first is that the pH at the beginning of the titration is higher simply because the acid is not as strong as a strong acid. As with strong acids, the pH rises slowly at first and then begins to rise quickly near the equivalence point. However, near the equivalence point, when the change becomes most rapid (vertical on the titration curve), the range of pH values is much smaller than the range for a strong acid/strong base pairing. For the third main difference, the pH at the equivalence point is not 7.

The main reason for the unusual behavior is the composition of the weak acid. The conjugate base of the weak acid creates a buffering effect. As the hydroxide ions from the base react with the acid, the concentration of the conjugate base increases. When the base has reacted with all of the hydrogen ions from the acid, the solution contains an excess of the conjugate (salt). If you recall from the previous section, the conjugate base of a weak acid will hydrolyze water to create a basic solution. So, instead of being neutral at the equivalence point, the pH will be basic. Adding additional base will only enhance this effect.

For the titration of a weak base with a strong acid, the effect is fairly similar. The main difference is that the pH will be lower than 7 at the equivalence point. As the hydrogen ions in the acid neutralize the hydroxide from the base, the concentration of the conjugate acid from the base will increase. If you recall, the conjugate acids of weak bases will hydrolyze water to create acidic solutions. This will cause the pH at the equivalence point to be acidic. Addition of further acid to the mixture will enhance this effect.

Of considerable difference with the titrations of weak acids and weak bases are the buffering effects of the conjugate salts. The titration curves all contain a buffering region near the equivalence point where most of the solution consists of the conjugate base (for a weak acid titration; a conjugate acid for a weak base titration):

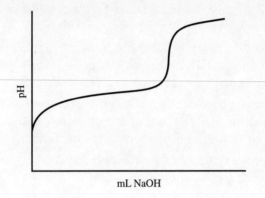

Figure 13.6

Summary: Acids and Bases

- Arrhenius acids increase the concentration of H^+ ions in solution, while Arrhenius bases increase the concentration of OH^- in solution. The strongest acids and bases are Arrhenius acids and bases.

- Brønsted-Lowry acids donate protons in solution. Brønsted-Lowry bases accept protons in solution. The definitions for Brønsted-Lowry acids and bases are more broad and allow for the consideration of many more substances than either of the other two definitions.

- When a Brønsted-Lowry acid donates a proton, the remaining anion is known as a conjugate base. When a Brønsted-Lowry base accepts a proton, the protonated base is known as a conjugate acid.

- Strong acids and bases ionize completely in solution, while weak acids and bases partially ionize. The partial ionization of weak acids and bases creates solutions in which an equilibrium is established.

- Lewis acids are substances that form a covalent bond by accepting an electron pair from another substance.

- Lewis bases are substances that form a covalent bond by donating an electron pair to another substance.

- The pH scale consists of a range of values from 0–14 that describe the concentration of hydrogen ions in a solution. The equation used to calculate pH is $pH = -\log[H^+]$.

- The neutral pH of 7 is based on the fact that water self-ionizes to form hydronium (hydrogen) ions and hydroxide ions in equal amounts. The concentration of these ions is equal to 1.0×10^{-7}, which corresponds to a pH of 7.

- The concentration of hydroxide ions can be expressed using pOH values.

- The hydrogen ion concentration of weak acids must be determined by considering the equilibrium concentrations of all ions in the equilibrium mixture.

- K_a is the term used as the equilibrium constant for weak acid equilibria.

- K_b is the term used as the equilibrium constant for weak base equilibria.

- The salts of strong acids and strong bases produce neutral solutions. Salts from strong acids and weak bases yield acidic solutions, while salts from weak acids and strong bases yield basic solutions.

- The common-ion effect is observed when an equilibrium system is disrupted by the addition of a salt containing one of the ions in the equilibrium mixture. The effect of this addition, as predicted by Le Châtelier's principle, is to shift the equilibrium away from the common ions.

- Buffer solutions are created by pairing a weak acid with a salt of its conjugate base or a base with a salt of its conjugate acid. Buffer solutions maintain a relatively stable pH when small amounts of acids or bases are added.

- An acid base titration is a procedure that is typically used to determine the concentration of an unknown acid or base solution. In a titration, a strong or base or known concentration is added to a base or acid of unknown concentration. An indicator solution is typically utilized to mark the equivalence point, or the point at which the stoichiometric amounts of acid and base are equivalent.

REVIEW QUESTIONS

Multiple Choice

1. A molecule or an ion is classified as a Lewis base if it

   (A) donates a proton to water.

   (B) forms a bond by accepting a pair of electrons.

   (C) forms a bond by donating a pair of electrons.

   (D) accepts a proton from water.

   (E) has resonance Lewis structures.

2. What is the $H^+(aq)$ concentration in 0.05 M HClO (aq) ? (The K_a for HClO is 3.0×10^{-8})

   (A) 1.5×10^{-9}

   (B) 2.5×10^{-10}

   (C) 3.9×10^{-9}

   (D) 3.9×10^{-5}

   (E) 3.9×10^{-3}

3. A 50.0 mL sample of 0.15 M NaOH is added to 50.0 mL of 0.10 M $Ba(OH)_2$. What is the molar concentration of $OH^-(aq)$ in the resulting solution? (Assume that the volumes are additive.)

   (A) 0.10 M

   (B) 0.13 M

   (C) 0.18 M

   (D) 0.36 M

   (E) 0.55 M

4. A bottle of distilled vinegar purchased at a supermarket was titrated with a 0.50 M NaOH solution to determine the content of acetic acid, $HC_2H_3O_2$. For 20.0 milliliters of the vinegar, 24.0 milliliters of 0.50-molar NaOH solution was required. What was the concentration of acetic acid in the vinegar if no other acid was present?

   (A) 1.60 M

   (B) 0.800 M

   (C) 0.600 M

   (D) 0.400 M

   (E) 0.250 M

5. $HCN(aq) + H_2O(l) \rightleftharpoons H_3O^+(aq) + CN^-(aq)$

   In the equilibrium represented above, the species that act as bases include which of the following?

   I.   CN

   II. H_2O

   III. HCN^-

   (A) II only

   (B) III only

   (C) I and II

   (D) I and III

   (E) II and III

6. What volume of 0.150-molar HCl is required to neutralize 25.0 milliliters of 0.120-molar $Ba(OH)_2$?

   (A) 20.0 mL

   (B) 30 0 mL

   (C) 40.0 mL

   (D) 60.0 mL

   (E) 80.0 mL

7. For oxoacids that vary only by the number of oxygens (i.e., HAO, HAO_2, HAO_3), which of the following occurs as the number of oxygen atoms increases?

   (A) It is impossible to predict the acid strength.

   (B) The strength of the acid increases.

   (C) The strength of the acid decreases only if A is a nonmetal.

   (D) The strength of the acid decreases only if A is a metal.

   (E) The strength of the acid decreases whether A is a nonmetal or a metal.

Questions 8–10 refer to the following diagrams:

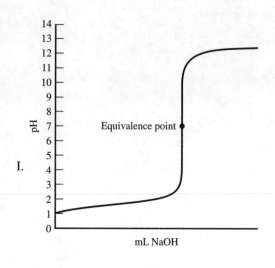

I.

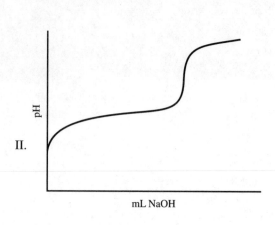

II.

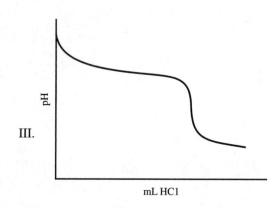

III.

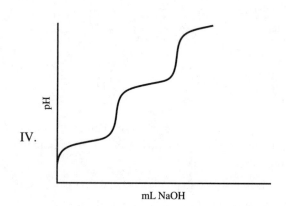

IV.

8. Could represent the titration curve of $HC_2H_3O_2$

   (A) I

   (B) II

   (C) III

   (D) IV

   (E) None of the graphs are an accurate representation.

9. Could represent the titration of a polyprotic acid

   (A) I

   (B) II

   (C) III

   (D) IV

   (E) None of the graphs are an accurate representation.

10. Could represent the titration of NH_3

    (A) I

    (B) II

    (C) III

    (D) IV

    (E) None of the graphs are an accurate representation.

Questions 11 and 12 refer to aqueous solutions containing 1:1 mole ratios of the following pairs of substances. Assume all concentrations are 1 M.

    (A) NH_3 and NH_4Cl

    (B) $HC_2H_3O_2$ and $NaC_2H_3O_2$

    (C) HCl and KCl

    (D) KOH and NH_3

    (E) NH_3 and HCl

11. Represents an acidic solution that is not a buffer

12. Represents a buffer at pH < 7

Free Response

Question 1

    (A) 4.60 g of formic acid, $HCHO_2$, is mixed with enough pure water to create 1.00 liters of solution. K_a for formic acid is 1.7×10^{-4}. Calculate the pH of the solution.

    (B) 100 mL of 0.1 M HCl solution is mixed with 100 mL of the formic acid solution described in part (A). Calculate the $[H_3O^+]$ of the resulting solution.

    (C) A new solution was mixed with 0.10 mol of formic acid, $HCHO_2$, and 0.15 mol of sodium formate, $NaCHO_2$, dissolved in enough water to make 1.00 liter of solution. What is the pH of the resulting solution?

    (D) If 0.005 mol HCl is bubbled through 1.00 liter of the solution described in part (C), what is the pH of the resulting solution?

Question 2

A 50.00 mL sample of 0.25 M benzoic acid, $HC_7H_5O_2$, is titrated with 0.199 M NaOH solution. The K_a of benzoic acid is 6.3×10^{-5}.

(A) What is the pH, pOH, and $[H_3O^+]$ of the benzoic acid solution prior to the titration?

(B) How many milliliters of NaOH are required to reach the equivalence point?

(C) What is the pH of the solution at the equivalence point?

(D) Which of the following would be the best indicator to use for this titration?

Methyl red	$K_a = 1 \times 10^{-5}$
Cresol red	$K_a = 1 \times 10^{-8}$
Alizarin yellow	$K_a = 1 \times 10^{-11}$

Justify your response.

ANSWERS

Multiple Choice

1. **The correct answer is (D).** By definition, Lewis acids donate protons to form chemical bonds, and Lewis bases accept protons to form chemical bonds.

2. **The correct answer is (D).** The following equilibrium calculation table can be constructed:

$HClO(aq) \rightleftharpoons H^+(aq) + ClO^-(aq)$			
	HClO	H^+	ClO^-
Start	0.05	X	x
Δ	$-x$	$+x$	$+x$
Finish	$0.05 - x$	$+x$	$+x$

$$K_a = \frac{\left[H^+\right]\left[ClO^-\right]}{[HClO]}; \; 3.0 \times 10^{-8} = \frac{(x)(x)}{(0.05 - x)} = \frac{x^2}{(0.05 - x)}$$

$$x = \sqrt{0.05\left(3.0 \times 10^{-8}\right)} = 3.9 \times 10^{-5}.$$

Double-checking the shortcut, $0.05 - 3.9 \times 10^{-5} = 0.050$; we were justified with the assumption that x could be disregarded.

3. **The correct answer is (C).** The total $[OH^-]$ of the solution will equal the hydroxide ion concentration of NaOH, added to that of $Ba(OH)_2$. The biggest misleading factor here is that the barium hydroxide will donate two hydroxide ions to solution. That means the problem will be solved as:

(0.050 L NaOH)(0.15 mol NaOH/1.00 L) +

(2 mol OH-/mol $Ba(OH)_2$)(0.050 L $Ba(OH)_2$)(0.10 mol $Ba(OH)_2$/L) = 0.0175 moles OH-

Don't forget the last step: You only have 100 mL so (0.0175 mol OH)/0.10 L solution = 0.18 M

4. **The correct answer is (C).** At the equivalence point, the amount of hydroxide from the base is balanced with the H^+ of the acid. This can be determined using the equation below:

(0.50 M NaOH)(0.024 mL) = 0.012 mol NaOH

0.012 mol NaOH = (0.020 mL)[H^+]

[H^+] = 0.60 M

5. **The correct answer is (C).** Bases in this reaction would be considered the substances that are accepting protons (Brønsted-Lowry definition). In the forward reaction, H_2O receives a hydrogen to become a hydronium ion. In the reverse reaction, CN^- receives a proton to become HCN. HCN donates a proton, which makes it an acid.

6. **The correct answer is (C).** Neutralization will occur when the number of moles of hydrogen ions added to the base equals the number of moles of hydroxide ions present in the base. The trick in this question is that barium hydroxide dissociates to form two moles of hydroxide ion per mole of $Ba(OH)_2$. The calculation would look as follows:

   $(0.150 \text{ mol/L HCl})(X \text{ L}) =$
   $(0.120 \text{ mol/L } Ba(OH)_2)(2 \text{ mol } OH^-/\text{mol } Ba(OH)_2)(0.025 \text{ L } Ba(OH)_2)$
   $x = 0.040 \text{ L} = 40.0 \text{ mL}$

7. **The correct answer is (B).** For oxoacids, as the number of oxygen atoms attached to atom A in the molecule increases, it becomes easier to remove the proton. This will increase the acidity of the oxoacid.

8. **The correct answer is (B).** The curve shown as choice II is the most like a weak acid. The characteristics that differentiate it from a strong acid are the slight initial increase in pH at the initial addition of base and the elongated region prior to and after the equivalence point. This is where the conjugate base exhibits a buffering effect.

9. **The correct answer is (D).** Polyprotic acids display more than one equivalence point. The diagram in IV is a typical example of a polyprotic acid.

10. **The correct answer is (C).** Choice III is the only possible base among four choices, making it the only possible answer. It is also representative of a weak base because of the initial drop in pH and the elongated regions around the equivalence point.

11. **The correct answer is (C).** HCl is a very strong acid, which means that the chloride ion is a very weak conjugate base. This means the solution is not a buffer solution. The potassium chloride is really a distracter in this question. Although Cl^- is present in each salt, the common-ion effect is only seen in equilibrium systems. The reverse reaction for the dissociation of either of these two would be so slight it would be negligible. However, because KCl does nothing to neutralize the acid, the solution would be both acidic and not a buffer.

12. **The correct answer is (B).** In this answer, the common-ion effect is seen with the addition of sodium acetate. The $HC_2H_3O_2/C_2H_3O_2^-$ equilibrium creates a buffer, which is also acidic.

Free Response

Question 1

(A) **pH = 2.4** In order to calculate pH, you must know the $[H^+]$ concentration. The K_a expression will allow you to determine the $[H^+]$ if you know the concentration of $HCHO_2$. In order to solve this problem, you need to determine the molarity of the formic acid and then use this value to calculate the $[H^+]$ and, ultimately, the pH. The calculation proceeds as follows:

$$4.60 \text{ g HCHO}_2 \times \frac{1 \text{ mol HCHO}_2}{46.0 \text{ g HCHO}_2} =$$

0.10 mol $HCHO_2$ in 1.00 liters solution = 0.10 M.

	$HCHO_2(aq) \rightleftharpoons H^+(aq) + CHO_2^-(aq)$		
	$HCHO_2$	H^+	CHO_2
Start	0.10 mol	0	0
Δ	-x	+x	+x
Finish	$0.10 - x$	+x	+x

$$K_a = \frac{[H^+][CHO_2^-]}{[HCHO_2]}; \qquad = 1.7 \times 10^4 = \frac{(0.10)(x)}{(0.10-x)} = \frac{0.10x}{0.10}$$

$$x = [H^+] = \sqrt{1.7 \times 10^{-5}} = 4.1 \times 10^{-3}$$

$$pH = -\log[H^+] = -\log(4.1 \times 10^{-3}) = 2.4$$

(B) $[H_3O^+] = 1.7 \times 10^{-4}$

$$HCHO_2 \rightleftharpoons H^+ + CHO_2^-$$

In this problem, you are going to be dealing with the common-ion effect. Assume that all of the H^+ from the HCl is going to push the equilibrium to the left.

	$HCHO_2(aq) \rightleftharpoons H^+(aq) + CHO_2^-(aq)$		
	$HCHO_2$	H^+	CHO_2^-
Start	0.10 mol	0.10	0
Δ	−x	+x	+x
Finish	$0.10 - x$	$0.10 + x$	+x

$$K_a = \frac{[H^+][CHO_2^-]}{[HCHO_2]}; \qquad = 1.7 \times 10^4 = \frac{(0.10)(x)}{(0.10-x)} = \frac{0.10x}{0.10}$$

$$x = [H^+] = [H_3O^+] = 1.7 \times 10^{-4}$$

(C) **pH = 4.0** This is a buffer solution containing a weak acid and its conjugate base. In this problem, you set up the equilibrium calculation table with amounts for $HCHO_2$ and CHO_2^- in the start column.

$HCHO_2(aq) \rightleftharpoons H^+(aq) + CHO_2^-(aq)$			
	$HCHO_2$	H^+	CHO_2^-
Start	0.10 mol	0	0.15
Δ	$-x$	$+x$	$+x$
Finish	$0.10 - x$	x	$0.15 + x$

$$K_a = \frac{[H^+][CHO_2^-]}{[HCHO_2]}; \qquad = 1.7 \times 10^4 = \frac{(x)(0.15 = x)}{(0.10 - x)} = \frac{0.15x}{0.10}$$

$$x = [H^+] = 1.1 \times 10^{-4}$$

$$pH = -\log[H^+] = -\log(1.1 \times 10^{-4}) = 4.0$$

(D) **pH = 3.9** In this problem, you have to assume that the acid will ionize and the H^+ ions will react completely with any formate ions in solution. Therefore, the starting concentration of formate ion should be decreased and the starting concentration of formic acid increased.

Initial $[HCHO_2] = 0.10$ mol $+ 0.005 = 0.105$

Initial $[CHO_2] = 0.15$ mol $- 0.005 = 0.145$

$HCHO_2(aq) \rightleftharpoons H^+(aq) + CHO_2^-(aq)$			
	$HCHO_2$	H^+	CHO_2
Start	0.105 mol	0	0.145
Δ	$-x$	$+x$	$+x$
Finish	$0.105 - x$	x	$0.145 + x$

$$K_a = \frac{[H^+][CHO_2^-]}{[HCHO_2]}; \qquad = 1.7 \times 10^4 = \frac{(x)(0.145 + x)}{(0.105 - x)} = \frac{0.145x}{0.105}$$

$$x = [H^+] = 1.2 \times 10^{-4}$$

$$pH = -\log[H^+] = -\log(1.2 \times 10^{-4}) = 3.9$$

The Henderson-Hasselbalch equation also produces

$$pH = pK_a + \log\frac{[A^-]}{[HA]}$$

$$pH = -\log(1.7 \times 10^{-4}) + \log\left(\frac{0.145}{0.105}\right) = 3.9$$

Question 2

(A) **[H+] = 8.9 × 10-4; pH = 3.1; pOH = 10.9**. Prior to the titration, the pH of the benzoic acid solution must be determined using an equilibrium calculation table.

Initial concentration of benzoic acid: 0.05000 L 0.25 M = 0.0125 mol $HC_7H_5O_2$

$HC_7H_5O_2(aq) \rightleftharpoons H^+(aq) + C_7H_5O_2^-(aq)$			
	$HC_7H_5O_2$	H^+	$C_7H_5O_2^-$
Start	0.0125	0	0
Δ	$-x$	$+x$	$+x$
Finish	$0.0125 - x$	x	x

$$K_a = \frac{\left[H^+\right]\left[CHO_2^-\right]}{\left[HCHO_2\right]}; \qquad 6.3 \times 10^{-5} = \frac{(x)(x)}{(0.0125 - x)} = \frac{x^2}{0.0125}$$

$$x = \sqrt{(0.0125)(6.3 \times 10^{-5})} = 8.9 \times 10^{-4}$$

[H+] = 8.9×10^{-4}

pH = $-\log(8.9 \times 10^{-4}) = 3.1$

pOH can be calculated from the equation pH + pOH = 14

pOH = 14 – pH = 10.9

(B) **NaOH = 62.8 milliliters**. In the titration, the equation for the neutralization is

$$HC_7H_5O_2(aq) + OH^-(aq) \rightarrow H2O(l) + C_7H_5O_2^-(aq)$$

The equivalence point will be reached when the number of moles of NaOH equals the number of moles of $HC_7H_5O_2$. This is calculated as follows:

Amount of benzoic acid to be neutralized:

0.0500 L $HC_7H_5O_2$ 0.25 M $HC_7H_5O_2$ = 0.0125 mol $HC_7H_5O_2$

Therefore, 0.0125 mol of NaOH are required to reach the equivalence point.

$$0.0125 \text{ mol NaOH} \times \frac{1 \text{ L soln}}{0.199 \text{ mol NaOH}} = 0.0628 \text{ L or 62.8 milliliters.}$$

(C) **pH = 8.20**. At the equivalence point, the equation has essentially reversed itself. Prior to titration, the equilibrium was as follows:

$$HC_7H_5O_2(aq) \rightleftharpoons H^+(aq) + C_7H_5O_2^-(aq)$$

Upon addition of the NaOH, the OH- ions react completely with the benzoic acid in a reaction that can be considered irreversible:

$$HC_7H_5O_2(aq) + OH^-(aq) \rightarrow H_2O(l) + C_7H_5O_2^-(aq)$$

The reaction uses up all OH- and converts all $HC_7H_5O_2$ to $C_7H_5O_2^-$. The benzoate ions then will establish an equilibrium system as follows:

$$C_7H_5O_2^-(aq) + H_2O(l) \rightleftharpoons HC_7H_5O_2(aq) + OH^-(aq)$$

The next step is critical. When you determine the starting concentration of benzoate ion, you must do so by dividing the number of moles of benzoate by the volume of the new solution, which will consist of the 50.00 mL of the original solution + 62.8 mL of added solution. The neutralization created 0.0125 mol $C_7H_5O_2^-$, so the molarity is

$$\frac{0.0125 \text{ mol } C_7H_5O_2}{(0.050 \text{ L} + 0.0628 \text{ L})} = 0.111 \text{ M } C_7H_5O_2^-$$

Now, an equilibrium table can be constructed as follows:

$C_7H_5O_2^-(aq) \rightleftharpoons HC_7H_5O_2(aq) + OH^-(aq)$			
	$C_7H_5O_2^-$	$HC_7H_5O_2$	OH^-
Start	0.111	0	0
Δ	-x	+x	+x
Finish	0.111 − x	x	x

At this point, the calculation becomes a little different. Because the benzoate ion is a base, the equilibrium constant expression must be the base ionization constant, K_b. You haven't been given the value of K_b, however, so you will have to generate it using equation 13.8:

$$K_w = K_aK_b; \qquad K_b = \frac{K_w}{K_a} \qquad K_b = \frac{1.0 \times 10^{-14}}{6.3 \times 10^{-5}} = 1.6 \ 10^{-10}$$

Now, the equilibrium expression can be set up:

$$K_b = \frac{[HC_7H_5O_2][OH^-]}{[C_7H_5O_2]} \qquad 1.6 \times 10^{-10} = \frac{(x)(x)}{(0.0167 - x)}$$

Making the assumption that x will be quite small, we can then solve for x:

$$x = \sqrt{(1.6 \times 10^{-10})(0.0167)} = 1.6 \times 10^{-6}$$

At this point, you know that the $[OH^-] = 1.6 \times 10^{-6}$. There is more than one way to proceed from here. Two of the more obvious ways are to use the hydroxide concentration to calculate the pOH, and then convert that to a pH value. The other way is to convert the hydroxide ion concentration to the hydrogen ion concentration and calculate the pH directly. We will use the latter to calculate the pH.

$[OH^-] = 1.6 \times 10^{-6}$

$[OH^-][H^+] = 1.0 \times 10^{-14}$

$[H^+] = \dfrac{1.0 \times 10^{-14}}{1.6 \times 10^{-16}} = 6.25 \times 10^{-9}$

$pH = -\log[H^+] = -\log(6.25 \times 10^{-9}) = 8.20$

(D) Because the pH at the equivalence point is 8.20, the best indicator to use (of the three listed) is cresol red. With a K_a of 1×10^{-8}, the pK_a would be 8. This suggests that it will be effective in the pH ranges near 8. Because this is a titration of a weak acid, the equivalence point will be found in a more narrow range of pH values than for a strong acid. The other two indicators are effective at pH values that may be too low (methyl red) or too high (alizarin yellow) to detect the equivalence point.

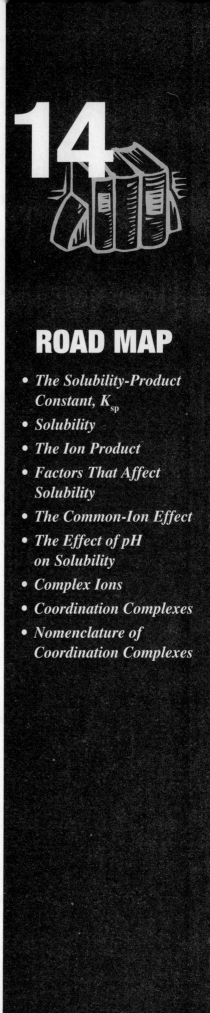

14

Additional Equilibrium Concepts

In this chapter, we will extend the concepts of equilibrium that have been discussed in previous chapters. In Chapter 9 we discussed the concept of equilibrium in relation to saturated solutions in which an equilibrium was established between solvated ions and undissolved solute. In Chapter 10 we discussed the solubility of different salts when we looked at the formation of precipitates. In this chapter you will see the connection between these two ideas with the introduction of the solubility product constant, K_{sp}, which is a quantitative means of describing solubility equilibria. This measure helps to predict and explain the precipitation of different salts from solution. You will also see how the common-ion effect, temperature, and pH affect solubility.

THE SOLUBILITY-PRODUCT CONSTANT, K_{sp}

So far, you have learned about a number of different equilibrium constants, including K_p, K_c, K_a, K_b, and K_w. In this section, you will learn about another equilibrium constant, K_{sp}. If you recall from Chapter 9, when a soluble solute is placed into a solvent it will dissolve until the solution becomes saturated. At the point of saturation, an amount of solid solute exists in equilibrium with the surrounding solution. One thing you will learn in this chapter is that even when a substance is considered insoluble, a small amount of the substance will still dissolve. One of the insoluble substances you learned about in Chapter 9 was the bright yellow precipitate lead (II) iodide, PbI_2. If we assume for a moment that it is soluble in very small amounts (which it is), we can consider the equilibrium shown below:

$$PbI_2(s) \rightleftharpoons Pb^{2+}(aq) + 2I^-(aq)$$

This equilibrium is known as a **heterogeneous equilibrium**, which is to say that it consists of substances that are in different states (phases). If you recall from Chapter 12, the equilibrium constant expressions for such equilibria do not contain the concentrations of liquids or solids. The equilibrium expression for this reaction will describe the degree to which the solid dissolves in solution, which is another way to say the degree to which it is soluble. And since the solid is not shown in the equilibrium expression, the equilibrium constant will express the product of the concentrations of the dissolved solute ions. For this reason, the equilibrium constant is referred to

ROAD MAP

- *The Solubility-Product Constant, K_{sp}*
- *Solubility*
- *The Ion Product*
- *Factors That Affect Solubility*
- *The Common-Ion Effect*
- *The Effect of pH on Solubility*
- *Complex Ions*
- *Coordination Complexes*
- *Nomenclature of Coordination Complexes*

as the solubility-product constant. For this equilibrium, the solubility-product constant, K_{sp} is

$$K_{sp} = [Pb^{2+}][I^-]^2$$

One important consideration is the absence of the solid from the expression. Even though the solid (PbI_2) is not shown in the equilibrium expression, it must be present in the solution in order for the system to be at equilibrium. In problems involving K_{sp}, you will usually encounter the information that some undissolved solid remains, which is your cue to know that it is okay to use the K_{sp} expression.

The value of K_{sp} for PbI_2 at 25 °C is 9.8×10^{-9}. Small numbers like this are a good indicator that the material is not very soluble.

SOLUBILITY

It is important to make the distinction between solubility and the solubility product constant. **Solubility** refers to the amount of a substance that can dissolve to form a saturated solution. The solubility of a substance is usually expressed in grams solute per liter of solution (g/L). Sometimes, however, it is described in moles solute per liter of solution, in which case it is referred to as the **molar solubility** of the substance. At any given temperature, the solubility-product constant, K_{sp}, for a solute remains constant. The solubility of a solute is not necessarily constant because it is affected by the concentrations of other dissolved substances. In the next section we will look at some factors that affect the solubility of a solute.

One type of calculation that you may be asked to perform is the determination of the concentration of an ion in solution when given the K_{sp}, or you may be asked to calculate the K_{sp} when given the concentration of an ion in solution. The two sample problems that follow will demonstrate these techniques.

Sample 1: Solid calcium phosphate, $Ca_3(PO_4)_2$, is added to a sample of pure water at 25 °C and stirred for an extended period of time until it is certain that equilibrium has been established. After several days, a small amount of solid calcium phosphate is still present on the bottom of the reaction vessel. An analysis of the solution shows that the concentration of calcium ion is 3.42×10^{-7} M. Calculate K_{sp} for $Ca_3(PO_4)_2$.

Answer: The first thing you need to do is write the balanced equation for the equilibrium:

$$Ca_3(PO_4)_2(aq) \rightleftharpoons 3Ca^{2+}(aq) + 2PO_4^{3-}(aq)$$

From the balanced equation, the equilibrium expression can be written as:

$$K_{sp} = [Ca^{2+}]^3[PO_4^{3-}]^2$$

We know the concentration of Ca^{2+}, but we will have to use stoichiometric relationships to determine the concentration of PO_4^{3-}:

$$[PO_4^{3-}] = \left(\frac{3.42 \times 10^{-7} \text{ mol } Ca^{2+}}{L} \right) \left(\frac{2 \text{ mol } PO_4^{2-}}{3 \text{ mol } Ca^{2+}} \right) = 2.28 \times 10^{-7} \text{ M}$$

With this value, you can now calculate K_{sp}:

$$K_{sp} = [Ca^{2+}]^3[PO_4^{3-}]^2 = (3.42 \times 10^{-7})^3(2.28 \times 10^{-7})^2 = \mathbf{2.07 \times 10{-}33}$$

Calcium phosphate is not a very soluble compound.

Sample 2: The K_{sp} for silver chromate, Ag_2CrO_4, is 1.12×10^{-12}. What is the molar solubility of Ag_2CrO_4?

Answer: You still must start out by writing the solubility equilibrium and solubility product expression:

$$Ag_2CrO_4(s) \rightleftharpoons 2Ag^+(aq) + CrO_4^{2-}(aq) \qquad\qquad K_{sp} = [Ag^+]^2[CrO_4^{2-}]$$

Next, you will set up an equilibrium calculation table:

$Ag_2CrO_4(s) \rightleftharpoons 2Ag^+(aq) + CrO_4^{2-}(aq)$			
	Ag_2CrO_4	$2Ag^+$	CrO_4^{2-}
Start		0	0
Δ		$+2x$	$+x$
Finish		$2x$	x

Substituting the values into the K_{sp} expression:

$$K_{sp} = [Ag^+]^2[CrO_4^{2-}]$$

$$1.12 \times 10^{-12} = [2x]^2[x] = 4x^3$$

Solving for x, we find that x is

$$x = \sqrt[3]{\frac{1.12 \times 10^{-12}}{4}} = 6.5 \times 10^{-5}$$

Since x is the stoichiometric equivalent of Ag_2CrO_4, the molar solubility will be **$6.5 \times 10{-}5$ M.**

THE ION PRODUCT

Before we begin considering shifts in an equilibrium system, we need a quantitative way to describe the state of the system at any time, whether it has established equilibrium or not. In Chapter 12, you learned about the reaction quotient, Q, which was used to describe equilibrium systems. In solubility equilibria, we're not really dealing with a quotient—just a product. Because the expression is the product of the concentrations of two different ions, the equilibrium expression that describes solubility equilibria is known as the **ion product**. Q is calculated in the same way as K_{sp}, except it does not necessarily describe a system at equilibrium. Referring to our initial example, for the equilibrium shown below:

$$PbI_2(s) \rightleftharpoons Pb^{2+}(aq) + 2I^-(aq)$$

the ion product is

$$Q = [Pb^{2+}][I^-]^2$$

The value of Q can be interpreted according to three possible relationships between Q and K_{sp}:

$Q > K_{sp}$	This condition means that the concentration of ions is higher than it is at equilibrium. The way to get rid of the excess ions is for them to form additional solid (precipitate). This process will occur until $Q = K_{sp}$
$Q < K_{sp}$	This means that the concentration of ions is smaller than it should be. The way to increase the concentration of ions is for more of the solid to dissolve until $Q = K_{sp}$
$Q = K_{sp}$	The solution is at equilibrium. That means the solution is saturated and there is some solid present.

These relationships can be used for more than just describing the status of a solid and its constituent ions. Another useful application is to determine if a precipitate will form from two different solutions. For instance, silver nitrate is soluble in water. Potassium chromate is also soluble (as are all potassium salts). If these two solutions are mixed together, two possible products can form: potassium nitrate and silver chromate. Potassium nitrate is soluble, but silver chromate is not. But what if very dilute solutions of each were added together? Is there a point at which the solutions would be so dilute that no precipitate would form? The ion product tells us that the answer is a definite, "Yes." In order for a precipitate to form, the value of Q must exceed Ksp. If it does not, no precipitate will form. Let's take a look at a problem that shows this.

Sample: Will a precipitate form when 0.10 L of 1.0×10^{-4} M $AgNO_3$ is mixed with 0.10 L of 2.5×10^{-4} M K_2CrO_4?

Ksp for $Ag_2CrO_4 = 1.12 \times 10^{-12}$

Answer: In order for Ag_2CrO_4 to precipitate, Q will have to exceed K_{sp}. The first thing to do is calculate Q:

The dissociation of Ag_2CrO_4 will establish the following equilibrium:

$$Ag_2CrO_4(s) \rightleftharpoons 2Ag^+(aq) + CrO_4^{2-}(aq)$$

Therefore, the ion product will be

$$Q = [Ag^+]^2[CrO_4^{2-}]$$

We need to determine the concentrations of each ion to calculate the ion product. There are a few things to keep in mind as we do this. First, when the two solutions are added together, the total volume increases to $0.10\,L + 0.10\,L = 0.20\,L$. Second, we need to determine the number of moles of each ion, and then calculate the molarity based on the new volumes.

In 0.10 L of 1.0×10^{-4} M $AgNO_3$, the number of moles of Ag^+ ions is $0.10\,L \times \left(\frac{1.0 \times 10^{-4}\ \text{mol}}{L} \right) = 1 \times 10^{-5}$ mol Ag^+ (we don't care about the nitrate)

The concentration of Ag^+ in 0.20 L of solution (the new volume) is

$$[Ag^+] = \frac{1.0 \times 10^{-5} \text{ mol}}{0.20 \text{ L}} = 5.0 \times 10^{-5} M$$

Next, we need the concentration of chromate, which we'll determine in the same way:

$$0.10 \text{ L} \times \left(\frac{2.5 \times 10^{-4} \text{ mol}}{\text{L}}\right) = 2.5 \times 10^{-5} \text{ mol CrO}_4^{2-}$$

which in 0.20 L of solution has the concentration:

$$[CrO_4^{2-}] = \frac{2.5 \times 10^{-5} \text{ mol}}{0.20 \text{ L}} = 1.25 \times 10^{-4} M$$

With both concentrations, we can calculate the ion product:

$$Q = [Ag^+]^2[CrO_4^{2-}] = (5.0 \times 10^{-5})^2(1.25 \times 10^{-4}) = 3.1 \times 10^{-13}$$

Because $Q < K_{sp}$, no precipitation will occur.

You Try It!

Will the bright yellow precipitate, PbI_2, form when 0.200 L of 0.015 M $Pb(NO_3)_2$ is mixed with 0.300 L of 0.050 M KI? K_{sp} for PbI_2 is 9.8×10^{-9}.

Answer: $Q = 5.4 \times 10^{-6}$; $Q > K_{sp}$; Yes, a precipitate will form.

FACTORS THAT AFFECT SOLUBILITY

A major factor that affects the solubility of solutes is temperature. Most substances become more soluble at higher temperatures. This is something you have probably had experience with in the past as you tried to dissolve things (that you are either going to eat or drink). There are some substances that become less soluble at higher temperatures, but they are more the exception than the rule. The three additional factors that we are going to consider in this chapter are the common-ion effect, pH, and the presence of complexing agents.

THE COMMON-ION EFFECT

You were first introduced to the common-ion effect in the last chapter on acids and bases. The basic principle behind the effect relates back to Le Châtelier's principle, which was first introduced in Chapter 12. If you recall, one aspect of Le Châtelier's principle states that an increase in the concentration of a reactant will shift the equilibrium of the system in a way that will relieve the distress, or that will help reduce the concentration of the newly added reactant. When an ionic solute dissolves, it is broken into its constituent ions. When equilibrium is established, the dissolved solute is in equilibrium with its solid. At this point, if any of the constituent ions are added, they will cause a shift in the equilibrium.

It is not necessary that these ions come from the original solute, however. For example, in a solution of silver chloride at equilibrium, if silver nitrate is added it will dissociate to generate additional silver ions. As Le Châtelier's principle predicts, the presence of these additional silver ions will drive the equilibrium to the left, causing the precipitation of silver chloride. Or, as you learned in the last section, the increase in silver ions will increase the ion product, Q, making it greater than K_{sp}. The system can only restore itself by the precipitation of silver chloride. In the sample that follows, we will look at a quantitative example of the common-ion effect.

Sample: Calculate the molar solubility of strontium sulfate, $SrSO_4$, in 0.25 M sodium sulfate, Na_2SO_4. K_{sp} for strontium sulfate is 3.44×10^{-7}.

Answer: This problem is very similar to sample 2 in the solubility section of the chapter. The only difference with this one is that the starting concentration of sulfate ion is not zero. You must also assume that because all sodium salts are highly soluble, all of the sodium sulfate has dissolved. Solving this problem will require us to determine the concentrations of the constituent ions at equilibrium. Our first step is to set up an equilibrium table. The concentration of sulfate ion is 0.25 M at the start of the table, since this is the concentration of sulfate in the sodium sulfate solution.

$SrSO_4(s) \rightleftharpoons Sr^{2+}(aq) + SO_4^{2-}(aq)$		
	$SrSO_4(s)$	Sr^{2+}	SO_4^{2-}
Start		0	0.25
Δ		$+x$	$+x$
Finish		x	$0.25 + x$

$$K_{sp} = [Sr^{2+}][SO_4^{2-}] = (x)(0.25 + x)$$

We're going to make the approximation that x will be small enough that $0.25 + x \approx 0.25$; $3.44 \times 10^{-7} = (x)(0.25)$

$$x = \frac{3.44 \times 10^{-7}}{0.25} = 1.4 \times 10^{-6} \ M$$

To help you get a feel for the common-ion effect, let's compare the molar solubility in the sodium sulfate solution with that in pure water. The equilibrium table would be similar except the initial concentration of sulfate ion would be 0, which would make the final concentration of sulfate ion x. The molar solubility would be calculated as follows:

$$K_{sp} = [Sr^{2+}][SO_4^{2-}] = (x)(x) = x^2$$

$$x = \sqrt{3.44 \times 10^{-7}} = 5.9 \times 10^{-4}$$

Notice how the solubility increases because of the absence of the additional sulfate ion.

You Try It!

Calculate the molar solubility of barium sulfate, $BaSO_4$, in 0.020 M sodium sulfate, K_2SO_4, K_{sp} for $BaSO_4$ is 1.08×10^{-10}.

Answer: $5.4 \times 10^{-9} \ M$

THE EFFECT OF pH ON SOLUBILITY

This section will integrate material from this chapter with material from the last chapter. In the last chapter, we looked at salts composed of strong and weak acids and bases. We saw that these salts have characteristic behaviors in solution. So far in this chapter, we have not considered the pH of the solutions. We're going to connect these two ideas to consider the solubilities of salts in non-neutral solutions.

Let's begin with a conceptual example by considering the salt magnesium hydroxide, $Mg(OH)_2$, which is a common ingredient in many over-the-counter antacids. Magnesium hydroxide is somewhat soluble in water, has a $K_{sp} = 5.61 \times 10^{-12}$, and maintains the following equilibrium:

$$Mg(OH)_2(s) \rightleftharpoons Mg^{2+}(aq) + 2OH^-(aq)$$

If a strong acid, such as HCl is added to the solution, the hydrogen ions will react with the hydroxide ions in solution to form water molecules. Therefore, the addition of a strong acid will decrease the concentration of hydroxide ions. The ion product, Q, will decrease. Our friend Le Châtelier would tell us that at this point the equilibrium will shift to right to compensate for the loss of the hydroxide ions. The $Mg(OH)_2$ will continue to dissociate until equilibrium is restored. If additional HCl is added to the solution, it will drive the equilibrium to the right again. If sufficient acid is added, all of the $Mg(OH)_2$ will dissolve.

This process will occur with any salt whose anion is basic. Anions that are the most basic are affected the most by changes in pH. Salts whose anions are from strong acids have virtually no basicity and will therefore be unaffected by changes in the pH.

Sample: For which of the following is pH likely to affect the solubility?

    (A) $BaSO_4$

    (B) BaF_2

    (C) $CaCO_3$

    (D)   MnS

    (E) $AuCl_3$

Answer: The criteria that must be considered for each of these is the basicity of the anion. The more basic the anion, the more pH will affect the solubility.

  (A) The sulfate ion, SO_4^{2-} is a very weak base and will not be affected much by changes in pH. However, because it is a very weak base, the solubility can be affected slightly in very strong acids.

  (B) F^- is the conjugate base of a weak acid, which means it is a fairly strong base. As a result, it will react with the excess hydrogen in an acidic solution. This will decrease the $[F^-]$, which will cause more BaF_2 to dissolve to restore equilibrium.

  (C) $CaCO_3$ will be affected by pH. CO_3^{2-} is a basic anion and can combine with two hydrogen ions. This will cause additional $CaCO_3$ to dissolve in order to restore equilibrium.

(D) S^{2-} is the conjugate base of a weak acid. It will combine with two hydrogen ions and force more MnS to dissolve.

(E) Cl^- is the conjugate base of a very strong acid and won't react with excess hydrogen ion. The solubility of $AuCl_3$ will be unaffected by pH.

You Try It!
For each of the following three pairs, select the salt whose solubility will be affected most by a change in pH.

(A) $Ca(NO_3)_2$, $Ca(OH)_2$

(B) $Mg_3(PO_4)_2$, $MgCl_2$

(C) $SrSO_4$, SrS

Answers: (A) $Ca(OH)_2$ (B) $Mg_3(PO_4)_2$ (C) SrS

COMPLEX IONS

In the last section we focused on the anions of the dissolved solutes, but in this section we will look at the cations. Metal ions can act as Lewis acids—which, as you recall, means they can be electron-pair acceptors when they are in the presence of Lewis bases (electron pair donors). One of the more common Lewis bases to interact with metal ions in this way is ammonia. These interactions are most common among the transition metals. One example of such an interaction is that of the silver ion and ammonia. Silver chloride is not very soluble in water (the K_{sp} is 1.77×10^{-10}) but is quite soluble if ammonia is added to the solution. The phenomenon can be understood by looking at the following equations:

$$AgCl(s) \rightleftharpoons Ag^+(aq) + Cl^-(aq)$$

This is the normal dissolving of silver chloride. Now, if ammonia is added, an additional equilibrium occurs:

$$Ag^+(aq) + 2NH_3(aq) \rightleftharpoons Ag(NH_3)_2^+(aq)$$

Because this second equilibrium removes silver ions from solution, it shifts the equilibrium of the first reaction to the right, causing additional AgCl to dissolve. $Ag(NH_3)_2^+$ is an example of a complex ion, which is a term used to describe an ion that forms between a metal ion and Lewis bases. While the dissolving of silver chloride is not highly favorable (as evident by the small K_{sp}), the formation of the complex ion is. The equilibrium constant used to describe the formation of a complex ion is known as the formation constant, K_f. The K_f for the formation of $Ag(NH_3)_2^+$ is 1.7×10^7 and is calculated by the expression

$$K_f = \frac{\left[Ag(NH_3)_2^+\right]}{\left[Ag^+\right]\left[NH_3\right]^2}$$

Amphoterism

If you recall from Chapter 13, the term "amphoteric" refers to a substance that can act as either an acid or a base. Many metal oxides and hydroxides that are fairly insoluble in water are quite soluble in strongly acidic and basic solutions. These materials can dissolve in both acids and bases because they are amphoteric—that is, they are capable of acting like acids or bases. One example is zinc hydroxide, $Zn(OH)_2$. Zinc hydroxide is quite insoluble in water ($K_{sp} = 3 \times 10^{-17}$). However, if placed in a strong acid, the hydroxide ion reacts with the hydrogen ion in the acid in the following way:

$$Zn(OH)_2(s) + 2H^+(aq) \rightleftharpoons Zn^{2+}(aq) + 2H_2O(l)$$

However, zinc hydroxide can also form a complex ion with hydroxide ions, making it soluble in bases, as shown in this reaction:

$$Zn(OH)_2(s) + 2OH^-(aq) \rightleftharpoons Zn(OH)_4^{2-}(aq)$$

K_f for $Zn(OH)_4^{2-}$ is 2.8×10^{15}, making this a very favorable reaction.

Miscellaneous Topics

There are two topics that are somewhat related to the material in this chapter. One of them is frequently referred to in questions, while the second only rarely pops up. The first deals with the colors of various substances; at least one multiple-choice question usually refers to it. The second topic is the formation of complexes, like the ones mentioned in the previous section, but it goes a bit beyond the subject as it is addressed here. Occasionally a question about the nomenclature of complex ions appears, so we'll address that here (for lack of a better place to put it).

Colors of Various Substances

The list below is by no means a comprehensive one, but it does list some fairly characteristic colors.

These flame tests represent the color of the flame, not the individual spectral lines.

Cation	Flame Color
Li^+	Deep red (crimson)
Na^+	Yellow
K^+	Violet
Ca^{2+}	Orange
Sr^{2+}	Red
Ba^{2+}	Green
Cu^{2+}	Blue-green
Li^+	Deep red (crimson)
Na^+	Yellow
K^+	Violet
Ca^{2+}	Orange
Sr^{2+}	Red
Ba^{2+}	Green
Cu^{2+}	Blue-green

Colors of Ions

These are some typical colors. Again this is not a comprehensive list.

Cations	Color
Cu	Green to blue (depending on anion and charge on Cu)
Fe	Yellow to red-orange (depending on anion and charge on Fe); in rare instances, can form complex ions that produce a deep blue color

Cations	Color
Co	Pink
Cr	Green
Ni	Green

Anions	
CrO_4^{2-}	Yellow
$Cr_2O_7^{2-}$	Orange

Assorted compounds	
NO_2	Brown gas; associated with reactions between metals (like copper) and nitric acid
PbI_2	Bright yellow precipitate
$Cu(NH_3)_4^{2+}$	Dark blue; produced as ammonia is added to light blue copper solutions (e.g., $CuSO_4$, $Cu(NO_3)_2$)

This list is not intended to list all compounds that have characteristic colors. These are some that are quite common and that have appeared in some form on previous AP exams.

COORDINATION COMPLEXES

Earlier in the chapter, we discussed the term complex ion, which referred to the ions formed by a metallic cation and an anion acting as a Lewis base. These Lewis bases that surround metal ions in a complex are known as **ligands**. Some common ligands are NH_3, H_2O, and CN^-. The most common metals to form complexes are the transition metals because they have many empty valence orbitals that allow them to function as Lewis Acids (accept electron pairs). In these compounds, the central metal ion and the attached ligands are written in brackets to distinguish the complex from the rest of the compound. For instance, the formula for the salt potassium hexacyanoferrate (II) is written

$$K_4[F_3(CN)_6]$$

where the complex hexacyanoferrate (II) ion, $Fe(CN)_6^{4-}$, is set aside from the potassium by brackets. In case you are wondering where the charge 4^- came from on this ion, it came by adding the charges on each constituent ion. The $Fe(CN)_6^{4-}$ ion was formed by the addition of six cyanides to an Fe^{2+} ion. The procedure for determining the charge on the entire ion (the same procedure that is used for all complex ions) can be demonstrated as follows:

$$Fe^{2+} \times 1 = +2$$
$$CN^- \times 6 = -6$$

The charge equals $+2 + (-6) = -4$

Another term you should be familiar with is the **coordination number** of the metal ion. This number refers to the total number of bonds formed with the ligands. In the $Fe(CN)_6^{4-}$ ion, iron has formed 6 bonds (one with each cyanide), so the coordination number of iron in this complex is 6.

Compounds can also be referred to by the type of ligands they contain. Many ligands, like NH_3 and Cl^-, can only form single bonds to the metallic ions. This type of ligand is referred to as a **monodentate ligand**. Other ligands, like the amine group, NH_2, can bind two times and are known as bidentate (or polydentate) ligands. Some of the more common **polydentate ligands** are known as chelating agents. These chelating agents bind to metal ions in such a way that they literally wrap around them.

NOMENCLATURE OF COORDINATION COMPLEXES

If pressed for time, you're better off skipping this section in favor of another more important section, but if you have the luxury of time, read on. The name of a coordination complex has come up on the multiple-choice exam before. There is an established set of rules for naming these compounds that has been developed by the IUPAC, and it consists of the following parts:

1. When naming salts, the name of the cation is given before the name of the anion (this is the same as the other nomenclature rules).

2. The name of the complex ion, whether it is an anion, cation, or neutral, is written as two parts that are combined into one word. The first part consists of the name of the ligand, and the second part, the name of the metal ion. If more than one of the same type of ligand appears, Greek prefixes are used to indicate the number of times the ligand occurs. A Roman numeral is used to indicate the charge on the cation. For instance, the name of the ion in the previous example, $Fe(CN)_6^{4-}$, is hexacyanoferrate (II) ion

   The prefix hexa- represents the six cyanide ligands, the anion appears before the cation, and the Roman numeral (II) in parentheses indicates the 2^+ charge on the iron ion.

3. One thing you may have noticed in the previous example is the ending –o on the end of cyano. Most anionic ligands are written with an –o ending, like chloro, bromo, cyano, and oxo. Neutral ligands are usually given the name of the molecule. A few notable exceptions to this are NH_3, known as ammine; H_2O, known as aqua; and CO, known as carbonyl.

4. You may also have noticed the term ferrate present to describe iron. This is a by-product of the old naming system that used the Latin terms for elements instead of Roman numerals to indicate their names (and charges). In this naming system, these older Latin names of elements are given an –ate ending. Most of these older forms have been discarded, except they do appear here. The Latin names for elements are responsible for the symbols that may hve been difficult for you to memorize because they don't start with the same letters as the elements common names. Some examples of these older names and their use in naming anions in complexes are seen below

Common English name	Latin name and symbol	Anion name (used in complex)
Copper	Cuprum, Cu	Cuprate
Lead	Plumbum, Pb	Plumbate
Iron	Ferrum, Fe	Ferrate
Tin	Stannum, Sn	Stannate
Gold	Aurum, Au	Aurate
Silver	Argentum, Ag	Argentate

Even when the Latin name is used, the charge still must be written in parentheses next to the anion's name.

5. In a complex ion or molecule, if more than one type of ligand appears, the order of appearance is determined alphabetically. For example, the complex ion $Pt(NH_3)_4Cl_2^{2+}$ contains two ligands, NH_3 and Cl^-. The name of the ion is

tetraamminedichloroplatinum(IV) ion

You'll notice that the ammine appears before chloro (you use the root to determine alphabetic order) because a comes before c. The prefixes tetra is used to indicate the four NH_3 ligands and di- indicates the two Cl^- ligands. Also notice the –o ending on chloro, which is not present on ammine. Finally, the Roman numeral (IV) indicates a 4+ charge on platinum. The overall charge on the ion, 2+, can be determined by adding the 4+ charge of platinum to the 2(1⁻), or 2⁻, charge of the chloride ions. If this ion complex was attached to a chloride ion, the resulting compound, $[Pt(NH_3)_4Cl_2]Cl_2$, would be called tetraamminedichloroplatinum(IV) chloride.

Sample 1: Name the following coordination compound, list the coordination number of the transition element, and determine the charge of the complex ion.

$$K_4[Mo(CN)_8]$$

Answer: The name is potassium, octacyanomolybdate(IV).

The name of the cation, potassium, is written first, followed by the anion. The complex ion is written with the ligand first, followed by the metal ion. The ligand has the Greek prefix indicating 8 and an –o ending for the cyano term. The metal ion, molybdenum, has been given the –ate ending and is followed with the Roman numeral of its charge.

The coordination number of molybdenum is 8.

The charge of the complex ion is 4^-. This is determined by the ratio of it to potassium. Potassium always has a charge of 1^+, which means that the charge on the complex ion must be 4^-. The Roman numeral for molybdenum can be determined from this number as well. The overall charge is 4^-. The cyanide ion, CN^-, has a charge of 1^-, so 8 of them would have a charge of 8^-. The charge of Mo must be 4^+ to give an overall charge of 4^-.

Sample 2: Write the formula for tetraamminesulfatochromium(III) chloride.

Answer: You need to begin dissecting this piece by piece. First, you know there is a chromium ion with a 3^+ charge in the complex. There are also two ligands, ammonia (which goes by the name ammine), NH_3, and sulfate, (which goes by sulfato), SO_4^{2-}. The tetra- before ammine indicates that there are four ammonia molecules in the complex. Because the name of the complex appears first, it must be the cation. A quick check of the individual charges of each component will determine the charge of the complex ion as well as verify its identity as a cation. We already know that chromium has a 3^+ charge (by the Roman numeral). We also know that ammonia has no charge and sulfate has a charge of 2^-. In addition, the absence of a prefix in front of the sulfato term in the name indicates there is only one sulfate ion present. Therefore, the net charge on the complex ion is $3^+ + (2^-) = 1^+$. Because it has a 1^+ charge, it will combine in a one-to-one ratio with the chloride ion, which has a 1^- charge. The formula, therefore, is

$$[Cr(NH_3)_4SO_4]Cl$$

You Try It!

(A) Determine the name of $[Cu(NH_3)_4]SO_4$.

(B) Write the formula for ammonium aquapentafluoroferrate(III).

Answers: (A) tetraamminecuprate(II) sulfate
                   (B) $(NH_4)_2[Fe(H_2O)F_5]$

Summary: Additional Equilibrium Concepts

- The equilibrium between ionic solutes and their constituent ions can be summarized using the equilibrium constant known as the solubility product constant, K_{sp}.

- Solubility, which refers to the amount of a substance that can be dissolved in solution, differs from the solubility product. K_{sp} for a substance remains constant as long as temperature is constant, while the solubility of a substance is subject to change.

- The ion product, Q, provides a quantitative description of the relationship between solute and the constituent ions at any time, regardless of whether equilibrium has been established. The relationship between Q and K_{sp} can also be used to indicate the status of the mixture (i.e., whether the solute is dissolving at a faster rate than crystals are forming).

- Three factors, other than temperature, that affect solubility are the common-ion effect, pH, and the formation of complex ions.

- The presence of salts that share a common ion to the constituent ions of a solute will affect the solubility of a solute. Because of Le Châtelier's principle, the addition of common ions shifts the equilibrium toward the formation of additional solute (solid), which decreases its solubility.

- Solubility can also be affected by pH. Salts whose anions are basic will increase in solubility in acidic solutions. This is because the anions will combine with excess hydrogen ions. According to Le Châtelier's principle, this will shift the equilibrium to the right to restore equilibrium.

- Some salts contain metal ions that can act as Lewis acids in solution. These often form complex ions when in solutions with Lewis bases like water or ammonia. In the presence of these Lewis bases, the anions form complex ions. The formation of these complex ions reduces the concentration of the anion, which will cause the equilibrium to shift right (or increase dissolving).

- The AP exam frequently adds questions about the colors of different substances. You should familiarize yourself with some of the more colorful elements and compounds.

- Complex ions combine with cations or anions to form coordination complexes. These complex ions usually consist of a transition metal ion attached to ligands. You should be familiar with the basic nomenclature for coordination complexes.

REVIEW QUESTIONS

1. What is the molar solubility of silver oxalate? (K_{sp} for $Ag_2C_2O_4$ is 5.4×10^{-12})

    (A) 1.1×10^{-4}

    (B) 1.4×10^{-4}

    (C) 1.6×10^{-6}

    (D) 1.4×10^{-12}

    (E) 5.4×10^{-12}

2. What is the final concentration of silver ions, $[Ag^+]$, in solution when 100 mL of $0.10\ M\ AgNO_3(aq)$ is mixed with 100 mL of $0.050\ M\ HCl(aq)$?

    (A) $0.00\ M$

    (B) $0.012\ M$

    (C) $0.025\ M$

    (D) $0.075\ M$

    (E) $0.10\ M$

3. If the solubility of $Fe(OH)_2$ in water is $7.7 \times 10^{-6}\ M$, what is the value of K_{sp} at this temperature?

    (A) 7.7×10^{-6}

    (B) 2.4×10^{-10}

    (C) 9.1×10^{-16}

    (D) 1.8×10^{-15}

    (E) 4.6×10^{-16}

4. The solubility of $BaCO_3$ in water is increased by which of the following?

    I.   Addition of NaOH

    II. Decreasing the pH of the solution

    III. Increasing the pH of the solution

    (A) I only

    (B) II only

    (C) III only

    (D) I and II

    (E) I and III

5. A 30 mL sample of $0.40\ M\ Pb(C_2H_3O_2)_2$ solution is added to 20 mL of $0.20\ M$ Na_2CrO_4 solution. Lead chromate precipitates out of solution. The concentration of lead (II) ion, Pb^{2+}, in solution after the lead (II) chromate precipitates is

    (A) $0.150\ M$

    (B) $0.160\ M$

    (C) $0.200\ M$

    (D) $0.240\ M$

    (E) $0.267\ M$

6. When 100 mL of 1.0 M K_2CrO_4 is mixed with 100 mL of 1.0 M $AgNO_3$, a brownish-red precipitate forms and $[Ag^+]$ becomes quite small. Of the ions remaining in solution, which of the following is the correct listing of the ions remaining in solution, in order of increasing concentration?

   (A) $[CrO_4] < [NO_3^-] < [K^+]$

   (B) $[CrO_4] < [K^+] < [NO_3^-]$

   (C) $[NO_3^-] < [CrO_4] < [K^+]$

   (D) $[K^+] < [NO_3^-] < [CrO_4]$

   (E) $[K^+] < [CrO_4] < [NO_3^-]$

7. A 1.0 L sample of an aqueous solution contains 0.20 mol of NaI and 0.20 mol of SrI_2. What is the minimum number of moles of $AgNO_3$ that must be added to the solution in order to remove all available I^- as the precipitate $AgI(s)$? (AgI is very insoluble in water.)

   (A) 0.10 mol

   (B) 0.20 mol

   (C) 0.30 mol

   (D) 0.40 mol

   (E) 0.60 mol

8. What is the molar solubility of AgCl in 3.0×10^{-2} M $AgNO_3$ solution? K_{sp} for AgCl is 1.8×10^{-10}.

   (A) 1.8×10^{-10} M

   (B) 3.0×10^{-9} M

   (C) 1.3×10^{-5} M

   (D) 6.0×10^{-9} M

   (E) 4.8×10^{-12} M

9. Which of the following will be more soluble at an acidic pH than in water?

   I. AgCl

   II. $Mg(OH)_2$

   III. $BaCO_3$

   (A) I only

   (B) II only

   (C) III only

   (D) I and II

   (E) II and III

10. When a solution of potassium chloride is vaporized in a flame, the color of the flame is

   (A) red.

   (B) yellow.

   (C) green.

   (D) violet.

   (E) orange.

11. The formula for sodium tetrahydroxoaluminate(III) is

 (A) $Na_4[Al(OH)_4]$

 (B) $Na_3[Al(OH)_4]$

 (C) $Na[Al(OH)_4]$

 (D) $Na_4Al(OH)_3$

 (E) $Na(OH)_4$

12. Silver chloride is least soluble in a 0.1 M solution of which of the following?

 (A) $FeCl_3$

 (B) $MgCl_2$

 (C) $NaCl$

 (D) H_2O

 (E) $AgNO_3$

Free Response

Question 1

In this problem, assume that the temperature remains constant at 25 °C. K_{sp} for barium sulfate, $BaSO_4$, is 1.1×10^{-10}, and K_{sp} for barium fluoride, BaF_2, is 1.8×10^{-7}.

(A) What is the molar solubility of $BaSO_4$ in pure water?

(B) What is the molar solubility of BaF_2?

(C) If an aqueous solution of $Ba(NO_3)_2$ is added to 1.0 L of a solution containing 0.05 mol F^- and 0.075 mol SO_4^{2-}, which salt will precipitate first? (Assume that the volume of the solution remains 1.0 L.)

(E) Based on your calculations in part (c), what is the concentration of Ba^{2+} in the solution when the first precipitate forms?

Question 2

The solubility of magnesium hydroxide, $Mg(OH)_2$, is 6.53×10^{-3} grams per liter at 25 °C. Assume that this temperature is maintained for all parts of the question.

(A) Write a balanced equation for the solubility equilibrium.

(B) Write the the expression for K_{sp}, and determine its value.

(C) Calculate the pH of a saturated solution of $Mg(OH)_2$.

(D) If 100 mL of 2.5×10^{-3} M $Mg(NO_3)_2$ solution is added to 100 mL of a 3.5×10^{-4} M NaOH solution, will a precipitate of $Mg(OH)_2$ form? Justify your response by using your calculated data.

ANSWERS

1. **The correct answer is (A).** First you must set up an equation for the equilibrium and set up the equilibrium expression.

$$Ag_2C_2O_4(s) \rightleftharpoons 2Ag^+(aq) + C_2O_4(aq)$$

$$K_{sp} = [Ag^+]^2[C_2O_4]$$

Next, set up an equilibrium table for the two substances:

$Ag_2C_2O_4(s) \rightleftharpoons 2Ag^+(aq) + C_2O_4(aq)$			
	$Ag_2C_2O_4$	$2Ag^+$	C_2O_4
Start		0	0
Δ		+2x	+x
Finish		2x	x

Finally, the molar solubility (x) can be calculated:

$$K_{sp} = [Ag^+]^2[C_2O_4]$$

$$5.4 \times 10^{-12} = (2x)^2(x) = 4x^3$$

$$x = \sqrt[3]{1.35 \times 10^{-12}} = 1.1 \times 10^{-4}$$

2. **The correct answer is (C).** The first assumption is that the silver chloride will precipitate out of solution. The second assumption is that there is an excess of silver ions so that there will be some left over. In order to determine this, you need to determine the amount, in moles, of each substance, and then use the balanced equation to determine what is left over.

$$Ag+(aq) + Cl–(aq) \rightleftharpoons AgCl(s)$$

To determine the number moles of Ag+ in $AgNO_3$, you can assume the number of moles of silver ions is the same as the number of moles of silver nitrate because of the 1:1 ratio in the dissociation.

$$0.100 \, L \times \frac{0.10 \, mol}{L} = 0.010 \, mol \, Ag^+$$

Next, determine the number of moles of Cl⁻, which you can also assume is the same as the number of moles of HCl:

$$0.100 \, L \times \frac{0.05 \, mol}{L} = 0.005 \, mol \, Cl^-$$

The numbers tell us that 0.005 mol of silver with react with all 0.005 mol of chloride ions to yield 0.005 mol AgCl. This will leave 0.005 mol of excess Ag^+. The final calculation is to determine what [Ag^+] is in 200 mL of solution. (Don't forget to add the volumes together.)

$$\frac{0.005 \, mol \, Ag^+}{0.200 \, L \, soln} = 0.025 \, M$$

3. **The correct answer is (D).** You are given the value of x in this problem. You need to set up an equilibrium table to determine equilibrium concentrations of each substance, and then you can substitute the given value of x to determine K_{sp}.

$Fe(OH)_2(s) \rightleftharpoons Fe^{2+}(aq) + 2OH^-(aq)$			
	$Fe(OH)_2$	Fe^{2+}	$2OH^-$
Start		0	0
Δ		$+x$	$+2x$
Finish		x	$2x$

$$K_{sp} = [Fe^{2+}][OH^-]^2 = (x)(2x)^2 = 4x^3$$

Therefore, $K_{sp} = 4(7.7 \times 10^{-6})^3 = 1.8 \times 10^{-15}$

4. **The correct answer is (B).** You should pick up that the question is seeing if you know the effects of pH on the solubility of $BaCO_3$. With this in mind, you need to consider the compound, looking in particular at the anion, CO_3. Remember, if the anion is the conjugate of a weak acid, it will be a strong base. This means it will be affected by an acidic pH because the base will combine with the H^+, driving the equilibrium to the right (more dissolving of the slightly soluble solid). Choices I and II both indicate changes in the basic direction, which won't affect the solubility (or decrease it if anything). II is the only condition that will increase the solubility of $BaCO_3$.

5. **The correct answer is (B).** This is very much like question 2. You need to determine if there is excess Pb after the precipitation.

   The amount of Pb available (each $Pb(C_2H_3O_2)_2$ releases one Pb^{2+}):

   $$0.030 \text{ L} \times \frac{0.40 \text{ mol}}{\text{L}} = 0.012 \text{ mol } Pb^{2+}$$

   The amount of CrO_4^{2-} available (each Na_2CrO_4 releases one CrO_4^{2-}):

   $$0.020 \text{ L} \times \frac{0.20 \text{ mol}}{\text{L}} = 0.004 \text{ mol } CrO_4^{2-}$$

   0.004 mol of Pb^{2+} will react with CrO_4^{2-} and precipitate out of solution, leaving the remaining 0.008 mol in solution. This 0.008 mol is in 50 mL of solution, which makes the concentration:

   $$\frac{0.008 \text{ mol}}{0.050 \text{ L}} = 0.16 \, M$$

6. **The correct answer is (A).** This doesn't require any calculations—just some logic. We'll look at some numbers to make the explanation easier, but they are not necessary to solve the problem.

   If you have 100 mL of 1.0 M K_2CrO_4, you have 0.1 mol K_2CrO_4. Using stoichiometric principles, this means you have 0.2 mol K^+ and 0.1 mol CrO_4^{2-} in solution.

   Similarly, in 100 mL of 1.0 M $AgNO_3$, you have 0.1 mol Ag^+ and 0.1 mol NO_3^-.

   The precipitate must be Ag_2CrO_4 because all potassium and nitrate salts are soluble. An important thing to notice is the formula of silver chromate. Each chromate will combine with two silver ions. Since both start out with 0.1 mol, silver is a limiting reactant. Only 0.05 mol of CrO_4^{2-} will be able to precipitate. At the end of the reaction then, there will be

   0.05 mol CrO_4^{2-}, 0.10 mol NO_3^-, and 0.20 mol K^+

7. **The correct answer is (E).** You can solve this one in your head as well, but you need to understand the nature of the problem. You have a 1.0 liter container that has 0.20 mole each of NaI and SrI_2 dissolved in it. The dissociated silver ions from silver nitrate will react with the I^- ions from the other two salts to produce the insoluble solid AgI. All you have to do is determine how many moles of iodide ions are in solution, and this will be the number of moles of silver that will be required to react with it (because AgI has a 1:1 ratio of silver to iodide).

   NaI dissociates to yield one Na^+ and one I^-. SrI_2 dissociates to yield one Sr^{2+} and *two* I^-. As a result, 0.20 mol NaI will produce 0.20 mol I^-, and 0.20 mol SrI_2 will produce 0.40 mol I^-. The total amount of I^- generated is 0.60 mol, which is the minimum amount of $AgNO_3$ required to react with it.

8. **The correct answer is (D).** This is a common–ion problem. Before you solve it, you should predict what you think the answer will be based on what you know about the common-ion effect. If you are trying to dissolve AgCl in a solution of $AgNO_3$, there will be silver ions in solution before the AgCl starts to dissolve. This will limit its ability to dissolve. We would expect a fairly small molar solubility as a result. To solve the problem, we begin by setting up an equilibrium table, keeping in mind that we are starting out with some silver ions.

$AgCl(s) \rightleftharpoons Ag^+(aq) + Cl^-(aq)$			
	AgCl	Ag^+	Cl–
Start		0.03	0
Δ		+x	+x
Finish		(0.03 + x)	x

The next step is to set up the equilibrium expression:

$K_{sp} = [Ag^+][Cl^-] = (0.03 + x)(x)$

We are going to assume that the value of x is small enough that the sum of $0.03 + x$ is approximately 0.03.

$1.8 \times 10^{-10} = 0.03x$

$x = 6 \times 10^{-9}$ M (our assumption is valid), so this is the molar solubility.

9. **The correct answer is (E).** This is another question about the effect of pH on solubility. Since the question is asking which would be more soluble at acidic pH, you should be looking for compounds whose anions are basic or are amphoteric substances. Because Cl has negligible basicity, it can be disregarded. Magnesium hydroxide has a basic anion (that will react with H^+ to form water), as does $BaCO_3$ (the carbonate ion will react with H^+). Therefore, both II and III will be more soluble at acidic pH. The solubility of AgCl is unaffected at acidic pH. AgCl is more soluble in solutions containing NH_3 because it can form complex ions with NH_3.

10. **The correct answer is (D).** You either know this or you don't. Most of the color information included in this chapter is much easier to remember if you have done the labs that show the colors. Even if you haven't, you should try to commit these to memory. The AP exam usually has one or two of these questions lurking about.

11. **The correct answer is (C).** The tetra tells you that there are four hydroxide ions (indicated by the hydroxo- term) combined with the metal aluminum. The aluminum has a charge of 3^+ (indicated by the Roman numeral). The complex ion tetrahydroxoaluminate(III) must have a charge of 1^- because the charge of aluminum is 3^+, and the charge of each hydroxide is 1^- (there are four, so that makes 4^-). This is confirmed because the term appears second in the name, indicating its status as the anion. The formula then should have one sodium ion. (The 1^+ charge of sodium balances the 1^- charge of the complex ion)

$Na[Al(OH)_4]$

12. **The correct answer is (A).** You have to consider the factors that affect solubility before you answer this one. This helps clue you in on what the question is looking for. The common-ion effect, pH, and complex ion formation are the possible items. Because four of the five compounds shown contain a common ion, this is the most likely topic the question is testing you on. If you note, the first three compounds differ by one chloride ion. What you need to remember is that the larger the amount of common ion in solution, the less soluble the salt will be. $FeCl_3$ has three moles of chloride ions per mole of $FeCl_3$. $MgCl_2$ has two moles, and NaCl has one. $AgNO_3$ also has a common ion, but only one. Water has no common ions, which means that AgCl will be the most soluble in it. AgCl is least soluble in $FeCl_3$ because the presence of the excess chloride ions in solution shifts the equilibrium to the left (toward the solid).

Free Response

Question 1

You should always try to get the "big picture" of a free-response question before answering it. It helps you to focus and to determine if all parts of the problem are related. In this problem, the only two parts that are completely related are (C) and (D). You are going to need the given information in all parts of the problem.

(A) To solve this one (and part B), you need to set up an equilibrium calculation table and solve for x.

		$BaSO_4(s) \rightleftharpoons Ba^{2+}(aq) + SO_4^{2-}(aq)$	
	$BaSO_4$	Ba^{2+}	SO_4^{2-}
Start		0	0
Δ		$+x$	$+x$
Finish		x	x

You may have recognized that when the solid dissociates into two ions that have no coefficients, the ending values will always be x and the K_{sp} expression will always come out so that $K_{sp} = x^2$. If you do recognize this, it will save you time on the multiple-choice section where you don't have to show your calculations.

$$K_{sp} = [Ba^{2+}][SO_4^{2-}] = (x)(x) = x^2$$

$$1.1 \times 10^{-10} = x^2$$

$$x = 1.0 \times 10^{-5} \, M \text{ (rounded for significant figures)}$$

(B) This requires another equilibrium calculation table.

		$BaF_2(s) \rightleftharpoons Ba^{2+}(aq) + 2F^-(aq)$	
	BaF_2	Ba^{2+}	$2F^-$
Start		0	0
Δ		$+x$	$+2x$
Finish		x	$2x$

$$K_{sp} = [Ba^{2+}][F^-]^2 = (x)(2x)^2 = 4x^3$$

$$1.8 \times 10^{-7} = 4x^3$$

$$x = \sqrt[3]{\frac{1.8 \times 10^{-7}}{4}} \quad 3.6 \times 10^{-3} \, M$$

(C) To solve this, you need to determine the minimum amount of $Ba(NO_3)_2$ that must be added to each one to cause a precipitate to form, and then you should compare these numbers. Whichever substance has the smaller number is the one that will precipitate first.

For BaF_2, the concentration of barium ions that will be required to form a precipitate is

$$K_{sp} = [Ba^{2+}][F^-]^2$$

We're given the concentration of fluoride ions, so we can use this in the expression. In addition, because the solution is 1.0 L in volume, the number of moles is equal to the molarity. Therefore, for BaF_2

$$1.8 \times 10^{-7} = [Ba^{2+}](0.05)^2$$

$$[Ba^{2+}] = \frac{1.8 \times 10^{-7}}{2.5 \times 10^{-3}} = 7.2 \times 10^{-5} \, M$$

For $BaSO_4$, the concentration of Ba required is

$$K_{sp} = [Ba^{2+}][SO_4^{2-}]$$

$$1.1 \times 10^{-10} = [Ba^{2+}](0.075)$$

$$[Ba^{2+}] = \frac{1.1 \times 10^{-10}}{0.075} = 1.5 \times 10^{-9}$$

Because $1.5 \times 10^{-9} < 7.2 \times 10^{-5}$, $BaSO_4$ will precipitate first.

(D) For part (D), we need only provide the calculation from part (C):

$$[Ba^{2+}] = \frac{1.1 \times 10^{-10}}{0.075} = 1.5 \times 10^{-9}$$

Question 2

(A) $Mg(OH)_2(s) \rightleftharpoons Mg^{2+}(aq) + 2OH^-(aq)$

(B) $K_{sp} = [Mg^{2+}][OH^-]^2$

To calculate the value of K_{sp}, we need to know the molar solubility. We can then set up an expression for K_{sp} using values from an equilibrium calculation table and substitute the molar solubility, x, into the expression.

Step 1: The molar solubility of $Mg(OH)_2$ is

$$\left(\frac{6.53 \times 10^{-3} \text{ g Mg(OH)}_2}{L} \right) \left(\frac{1 \text{ mol}}{58.32 \text{ g Mg(OH)}_2} \right) = 1.12 \times 10^{-4} \, M$$

Step 2: Determine the expression for K_{sp}:

	$Mg(OH)_2(s) \rightleftharpoons Mg^{2+}(aq) + 2OH^-(aq)$		
	$Mg(OH)_2$	Mg^{2+}	$2OH^-$
Start		0	0
Δ		$+x$	$+2x$
Finish		x	$2x$

$$K_{sp} = [Mg^{2+}][OH^-]^2 = (x)(2x)^2 = 4x^3$$

Step 3: Substitute the molar solubility for x:

$$K_{sp} = 4x^3 = 4(1.12 \times 10^{-4})^3 = 5.62 \times 10^{-12}$$

(C) We can solve this two different ways. To start either way, we use the value for the molar solubility to determine the $[OH^-]$. Once $[OH^-]$ is known, we convert it to $[H^+]$ and solve for pH. The other way is to calculate pOH and convert this to pH. Both methods are shown below:

From the equilibrium table, we know that the value of $[OH^-]$ is $2x$. Therefore, we can substitute the value of x into the expression to calculate $[OH^-]$

$$[OH^-] = 2x = 2(1.12 \times 10^{-4}) = 2.24 \times 10^{-4}$$

Using pH:

$$1.0 \times 10^{-14} = [H^+][OH^-]$$

$$1.0 \times 10^{-14} = [H^+](2.24 \times 10^{-4})$$

$$[H^+] = \frac{1.00 \times 10^{-14}}{2.24 \times 10^{-4}} = 4.46 \times 10^{-11}$$

$$pH = -\log[H^+] = -\log(4.46 \times 10^{-11}) = 10.4$$

Using pOH:

$$pOH = -\log[OH^-] = -\log(2.24 \times 10^{-4}) = 3.6$$

$$pH = 14.0 - pOH = 14.0 - 3.6 = 10.4$$

(D) This is an ion-product problem. We need to calculate Q and compare it to K_{sp}, which we calculated in part (B).

$$Q = [Mg^{2+}][OH^-]^2$$

To obtain the molar concentrations of each ion, we need to use the given information in (D).

For $[Mg^{2+}]$, each mole of $Mg(NO_3)_2$ dissociates to form 1 mole of Mg^{2+}, so

$$0.100 \text{ L} \times \frac{2.5 \times 10^{-4} \text{ mol } Mg(NO_3)_2}{0.200 \text{ L}} = 2.5 \times 10^{-4} \text{ mol } Mg(NO_3)_2$$

In 200 mL of solution, this makes the $[Mg^{2+}]$

$$[Mg^{2+}] = \frac{2.5 \times 10^{-3} \text{ mol } Mg(NO_3)_2}{0.200 \text{ L}} = 1.25 \times 10^{-3} \text{ } M$$

For $[OH^-]$, each mole of NaOH makes one mole of OH^-, so

$$0.100 \text{ L} \times \frac{3.5 \times 10^{-4} \text{ mol NaOH}}{\text{L}} = 3.5 \times 10^{-5} \text{ mol NaOH}$$

In 200 mL of solution, this will make $[OH^-]$

$$[OH^-] = \frac{3.5 \times 10^{-4} \text{ mol NaOH}}{0.200 \text{ L}} = 1.75 \times 10^{-4} \text{ } M$$

Now, you are ready to substitute these values into the expression for Q:

$$Q = [Mg^{2+}][OH^-]^2 = (1.25 \times 10^{-3})(1.75 \times 10^{-4})^2 = 3.8 \times 10^{-11}$$

Because $Q > K_{sp}$, this indicates an excess of ions in solution (compared to equilibrium). The only way to restore equilibrium is to remove the excess by allowing it to precipitate as $Mg(OH)_2$.

Kinetics

Up to this point, we have primarily studied the descriptive aspects of chemical reactions. That is, we've discussed what's occurring during reactions without much detail about the driving forces behind the reactions. The purpose of the next two chapters is to provide such detail. In this chapter, we will look at the major models that have been developed to explain the mechanisms by which reactions occur. The focus of this chapter is **kinetics**, an area of chemistry that explores the rates at which chemical reactions occur. In the first portion of the chapter, we will focus on a few techniques we use to describe or define the rate of a reaction. Once that is established, we will move our attention to the factors that affect the rate of a reaction: concentration, temperature, surface area, and the presence of a catalyst.

REACTION RATE

One thing that is very important to consider as you proceed through this chapter is that rate and other items related to rate (the rate constant or rate law) can only be determined experimentally. Balanced equations can provide us with a means to speculate about the rate of a reaction, but the only way to accurately describe factors associated with rate is to determine them experimentally. On the AP exam, you don't have the ability to perform any measurements, so all data is given to you, usually in a table.

The term *rate* is usually associated with the occurrence of something per unit of time. When you move, the speed at which you are moving is a rate, determined by the distance you have traveled divided by the time it took for you to travel that distance (e.g., miles per hour or meters per second). In a chemical reaction, rate is usually associated with the rate at which a reactant is being used up (this is usually referred to as the **rate of disappearance**) or the rate at which a product is being created (usually called the **rate of appearance**). Although there are different techniques for making these measurements, the end result is the same—you want to collect data that tracks the appearance or disappearance of a substance over a time interval.

This data is quite often placed on a graph to illustrate the progression of the reaction. Figures 15.1 and 15.2 show typical curves for the appearance and disappearance of a substance.

ROAD MAP

- *Reaction Rate*
- *Using Concentrations to Describe Rate*
- *Units and Rate Constants*
- *Determining Rate Laws*
- *Reaction Types*
- *Half-Life*
- *The Relationship between Temperature and Rate*
- *Reaction Mechanisms*
- *Rate-Determining Steps and Rate Laws*
- *The Effect of Catalysts on Reaction Rate*

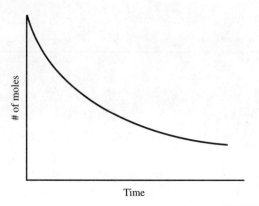

Figure 15.1: Typical curve showing the rate of appearance of a substance. Note that the rate is highest when the concentrations of reactants is the highest (at the beginning stages of the reaction).

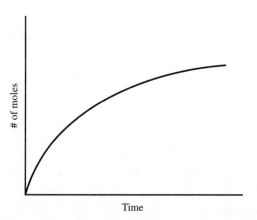

Figure 15.2: Typical curve showing the rate of disappearance of a substance. This could be superimposed over Figure 15.1 because it is showing the behavior of the reactants in the same reaction for which the product is being shown in Figure 15.1.

The graphs in Figures 15.1 and 15.2 represent the most simplistic of reactions, those in which there is a 1:1 stoichiometric relationship among reactants and products. That is, for every mole of reactant used up, there is a mole of product created. Not all reactions proceed in such a manner, but these figures at least give you an idea of how graphs can be used to display the rate of reaction. Most graphs that you will be working with—and most reaction rates—are described in terms of changing concentrations over time (as opposed to moles, as are seen in Figures 15.1 and 15.2). We will spend more time on graphs in a later section.

USING CONCENTRATIONS TO DESCRIBE RATE

Reactions are usually described in terms of changes in concentration over time. In the hypothetical reaction

$$aA + bB \rightarrow cC + dD$$

if we were going to monitor the rate of reaction, we could measure the concentration of one of the substances over time. We could use stoichiometric principles to convert the data for the other substances. However, if we collected data about one of the substances, we could then determine for various intervals of time how the concentration is changing. If we were measuring the concentration of A at 10-minute intervals, we would have a list of concentrations as well as a list of times. We could determine the rate of disappearance of A by using the equation

$$\text{Average rate} = \frac{\Delta[A]}{\Delta t}$$

(Equation 15.1)

Remember that the Greek letter delta, Δ, means "change in" a variable. For this case, the equation can be rewritten as

$$\text{Average rate} = \left(\frac{[A]_{\text{final time}} - [A]_{\text{initial time}}}{\text{final time} - \text{initial time}} \right)$$

This value is called an average because the calculation is only taking into account two measurements and nothing in between. The graph is actually curving during this time interval, which means the rate is changing. Taking a measurement of the average rate can sometimes be misleading, depending on the slope of the graph. For instance, look at Figure 15.3, which represents the rate of disappearance of a substance. If the average rate is measured between points 1 and 2, the average rate is a very good approximation of the reaction rate because the slope of the line connecting the two points is a very close fit to the curve. The slope is used because if you look at the formula for average rate, the numerator, $\Delta[A]$, represents the "rise" of the slope (in math it's often referred to as Δy), while Δt represents the "run" (or Δx in math terms). You may recall from previous course work that the "rise" divided by the "run" determines the slope of a line.

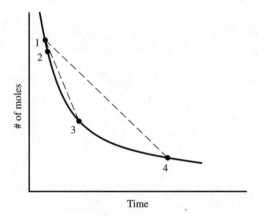

Figure 15.3

For the line connecting points 1 and 3 in Figure 15.3, you can see that the line is beginning to deviate substantially from the curve representing the reaction. The means that at any point along the dotted line (the average rate), the rate is different from the experimentally measured rate. The difference grows more significant when you look at the difference between points 1 and 4. So the average rate is much more accurate for smaller time intervals than it is for larger time intervals.

There is another way to graphically determine the rate of a reaction, and that is with the **instantaneous rate**. As the term suggests, this is the rate at a particular instance in time, as opposed to a time interval. The technique of calculating the instantaneous rate is to draw a tangent to the curved line of the graph. Figure 15.4 shows such lines drawn on the curve from Figure 15.3.

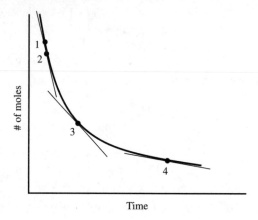

Figure 15.4

Sample: Consider the reaction $a\text{A} + b\text{B} \rightarrow c\text{C} + d\text{D}$. The concentration of C was recorded for a period of time, and some of the data is shown in the table below:

Time (s)	[C] M
2.0	0.00230
4.0	0.00275

Calculate the average rate of reaction of C during this time interval.

Answer: We are going to use the equation for average rate,

$$\text{Average rate} = \frac{\Delta[\text{C}]}{\Delta t}$$

which is the change in the concentration of C during time interval t, which can be calculated using the equation

$$\text{Average rate} = \left(\frac{[\text{C}]_{\text{final time}} - [\text{C}]_{\text{initial time}}}{\text{final time–initial time}} \right) = \frac{0.00275 - 0.00230}{4 - 2} = 2.3 \times 10^{-4} \text{ M s}^{-1}$$

You Try It!

In a different experiment, the concentration of D was measured. Determine the average rate for D based on the data shown below

Time (s)	[D] M
3.0	0.00470
7.0	0.00635

Answer: $4.1 \times 10^{-4} \text{ M s}^{-1}$

The Relationship between Reaction Rate and Stoichiometry

In the initial example in this chapter, the stoichiometric relationship between all reactants and products was one-to-one. For every mole of reactant used, a mole of product was produced. From your work in previous chapters, you know that many reactions do not follow this simple pattern (it sure would make balancing equations easier if they did, though!). How do you set up an expression for a reaction where the stoichiometric relationships are not one-to-one? If we refer to the general reaction shown below

$$aA + bB \rightarrow cC + dD$$

the reaction rates for each substance are determined using the following equalities:

(Equation 15.2)

$$\text{Rate} = -\frac{1}{a}\frac{\Delta[A]}{\Delta t} = -\frac{1}{b}\frac{\Delta[B]}{\Delta t} = \frac{1}{c}\frac{\Delta[C]}{\Delta t} = \frac{1}{d}\frac{\Delta[D]}{\Delta t}$$

You may notice the negative signs in front of the A and B expressions. This is to denote that these are rates of disappearance while C and D are rates of appearance. Although these formulas are often introduced this way to help you get a better conceptual understanding of the rate, reaction rate is usually expressed as a positive value, and the negative sign is implied (if the rate is a disappearance). You need to be able to use this expression, so we'll learn how to use it in Sample 1 and then try a calculation with it in Sample 2.

Sample 1: For the reaction $2N_2O_5(g) \rightarrow 4NO_2(g) + O_2(g)$, write the rate expression for each substance as shown in equation 15.2.

Answer: Equation 15.2, though it may look complicated, is really quite simple. Each rate consists of two parts: the first part is a stoichiometric factor (1/a, etc.), and the second part is the average rate from equation 15.1. The reason the stoichiometric factor is needed is because the rates of disappearance or appearance of each substance are related to the number of moles of each that are present. For instance, for every two moles of N_2O_5 that decompose, one mole of O_2 is produced. This means that the rate of disappearance of N_2O_5 will be $\frac{1}{2}$ the rate of appearance of oxygen. The expression for the entire equation looks like this:

$$\text{Rate} = -\frac{1}{2}\frac{\Delta\left[N_2O_5\right]}{\Delta t} = \frac{1}{4}\frac{\Delta\left[NO_2\right]}{\Delta t} = \frac{\Delta\left[O_2\right]}{\Delta t}$$

You Try It!

Write the rate expression for each substance in the following reaction:

$$2N_2O(g) \rightarrow 2N_2(g) + O_2(g)$$

Answer:

$$\text{Rate} = -\frac{1}{2}\frac{\Delta\left[N_2O_5\right]}{\Delta t} = \frac{1}{2}\frac{\Delta\left[N_2\right]}{\Delta t} = \frac{\Delta\left[O_2\right]}{\Delta t}$$

Sample 2: We'll refer to the reaction from Sample 1: $2N_2O_5(g) \rightarrow 4NO_2(g)$ $+ O_2(g)$. If, at one point, the rate of disappearance of N_2O_5 was 1.3×10^{-3} M s^{-1}, what would the rate of appearance of O_2 be at this point?

Answer: If we substitute the value 1.3×10^{-3} M s^{-1} in for the rate of disappearance of N_2O_5, we will end up with

$$-\frac{1}{2}\frac{\Delta[N_2O_5]}{\Delta t} = \frac{\Delta[O_2]}{\Delta t}$$

$$-\frac{1}{2}\left(1.3 \times 10^{-3} \ M \ s^{-1}\right) = \frac{\Delta[O_2]}{\Delta t}$$

$$\text{rate } O_2 = 6.5 \times 10^{-4}$$

Note that the negative sign was dropped. It is customarily omitted from the reaction rate. In this case, O_2 is being formed, so it would be positive anyway.

You Try it!

In the reaction $2NO(g) \rightarrow N_2(g) + O_2(g)$, the measured rate of appearance of N_2 during one experiment was 0.12 M s^{-1}. At this point, what would be the rate of disappearance of N_2O_5?

Answer: 0.24 M s^{-1}

Rate Laws

In this next section, we are going to look a little more closely at the relationships between concentration and reaction rate. We're also going to introduce some general procedures that can help you understand these relationships in almost any reaction. To begin, we will look at some data from a fictitious series of experiments in which substance A was combined with substance B to form substances C and D in a reaction that has the equation

$$A + 2B \rightarrow C + D$$

In these experiments, the amounts of A and B were carefully measured prior to their combination. The initial rates for each experiment were calculated, and all data was placed in Table 15.1.

Table 15.1			
Experiment	**Initial [A] M**	**Initial [B] M**	**Initial Rate (M s^{-1})**
1	0.10	0.10	1.3×10^{-6}
2	0.20	0.10	2.6×10^{-6}
3	0.40	0.10	5.2×10^{-6}
4	0.10	0.20	2.6×10^{-6}
5	0.20	0.40	1.04×10^{-5}

You may notice some distinct patterns in the data. For instance, in the first two experiments, the A doubled while B remained constant. The reaction rate also doubled during this period. In experiment 3, the A doubled again, and so did the reaction rate. It seems that the reaction rate is directly proportional to the concentration of A.

If you look at experiment 4, the concentration of A is back to its initial levels (experiment 1), but the concentration of B has been doubled (compared to experiment 1). This had the same effect on the rate of reaction as doubling A. Doubling B caused the reaction rate to double. It appears that the reaction rate is also directly proportional to B. We can check this assumption with the last experiment. In this experiment, the levels of A are twice what they were in experiment 1, while the levels of B are 4 times larger. If the reaction rate is directly proportional to the concentration of each reactant, we would expect the new reaction rate to be 8 times larger than the original value (2×4). Comparison of the two values reveals that it is indeed 8 times larger, validating our assumption that the concentration of each substance is directly proportional to the reaction rate.

The relationship between the concentration of reactants and the reaction rate is described by a factor known as the **reaction order**. In the previous example, the relationship between the reactants and the reaction rate was directly proportional, meaning that an increase in the concentration of one reactant caused proportionally the same increase in the rate. Doubling the concentration of a reactant doubled the rate of the reaction. This directly proportional relationship is known as a **first-order relationship**. If changing the concentration of a reactant had no effect on the reaction rate, the relationship would be described as a **zero-order relationship**. A **second-order relationship** is exponential; in other words, doubling the concentration of a reactant will increase by rate by 4. The reaction order for a particular reactant is written as an exponent next to the concentration of that reactant. For instance, because the previous reaction was first order for substance A, we could represent this symbolically as [A] (the exponent 1 is understood). If A had a zero-order or second-order relationship, the symbols would be written $[A]^0$ and $[A]^2$, respectively.

These symbols can be used to create a general expression to describe the relationships between the concentration of the reactants and the reaction rate. This expression is known as a **rate law**, and for the previous reaction it would have the form

$$\text{Rate} = k[A][B]$$

(Equation 15.3)

The variable k represents the **rate constant**. Note the order of each reactant is 1. The reaction order, which describes the order of the entire reaction, can be determined by adding the order of each reactant. For instance, in this example each reactant is first order (meaning each has an understood exponent of 1). The reaction order is the sum of the exponents, or $1+1=2$. This is a second-order reaction. Most reactions have an order of 0, 1, or 2, but some have fractional orders or larger numbers (though these are quite rare). The order of the reaction must be determined experimentally.

Unlike equilibrium expressions, the exponents have nothing to do with the coefficients in the balanced equations.

It is important that you make a distinction between the reaction rate and the rate constant. The biggest distinction is that the reaction rate depends on the concentrations of each reactant (which you can see from the formula), and it will always have the same units, usually $M\,s^{-1}$. The rate constant is not affected by concentrations. It maintains the same value as long as temperature is kept constant. The units of the rate constant will also vary according to the order of the reaction.

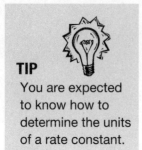

TIP

You are expected to know how to determine the units of a rate constant.

UNITS AND RATE CONSTANTS

If we were to calculate the value of units of the rate constant in the previous example, we could do so with relative ease. Beginning with the equation and rearranging it to solve for k, we obtain the expression

$$\text{Rate} = k[A][B]$$

$$k = \frac{\text{Rate}}{[A][B]}$$

Substituting units into this expression, we find

$$k = \frac{M\,s^{-1}}{(M)(M)} = \frac{M\,s^{-1}}{M^2} = M^{-1}s^{-1}$$

The units for the rate constant for this reaction are $M^{-1}s^{-1}$.

You Try It!

For each rate law, determine a) the order of each reactant, b) the overall order of the reaction, and c) the units of the rate constant, k. Assume that all reaction rates have been expressed in M s^{-1}.

    (A) rate = $k[NO]^2[O_2]$

    (B) rate = $k[O_3]^2[O_2]^{-1}$

Answers:

    (A) a) NO = second order; O_2 = first order

        b) reaction is (2+1) = third order

        c) $M^{-2}\,s^{-1}$

    (B) a) O_3 = second order; O_2 = -1 order;

        b) reaction is (2+-1) = first order

        c) s^{-1}

DETERMINING RATE LAWS

In the previous section, we used a very simple method of eyeballing the data to determine the order of the reaction (and eventually the rate law). On the AP exam, you must be able to calculate the rate law from the initial rates of reaction. The rate law that we showed in the last section can be made into a generic version that is applicable to any reaction. For a reaction where A and B are reactants (e.g., A + B → C), the rate law takes the form:

$$Rate = k[A]m[B]n$$

The exponents m and n represent the reaction order for each substance. By comparing the rates and concentrations from two different experiments, we can numerically calculate the values of m and n. In the sample problem, we will determine the rate law of a reaction based on experimental data.

Sample:

Experiment	$[A]^m$	$[B]^n$	Initial Rate M s^{-1}
1	0.20	0.20	1×10^{-3}
2	0.20	0.40	1×10^{-3}
3	0.40	0.20	4×10^{-3}

One name often used to describe this technique is the **isolation method**. The method of solution relies on one reactant being isolated. The concentrations of all reactants but one are held constant, which will allow you to cancel them in the calculation. We can use the generic rate law equation, substituting the data in for the variables. By setting up a calculation, we can try to solve for m or n.

$$Rate_{Exp\,1} = k[A]m[B]n$$

$$Rate_{Exp\,2} = k[A]m[B]n$$

If we look at the ratio of the rates of two experiments, we can usually solve the equation for either m or n. We can use experiments 1 and 2 for the first example:

$$\frac{Rate_{Exp\,2}}{Rate_{Exp\,1}} = \frac{1 \times 10^{-3}}{1 \times 10^{-3}} = 1$$

This allows us to set up the following equation:

$$\frac{Rate_{Exp\,2}}{Rate_{Exp\,1}} = \frac{k[0.20M]^m[0.40M]^n}{k[0.20M]^m[0.20M]^n} = 1$$

In this equation, we can cancel the first two terms in the numerator and denominator, leaving us with the expression

$$\frac{[0.40M]^n}{[0.20M]^n} = 1$$

Simplifying this expression gives us

$$2n = 1$$
$$n = 0$$

Anything raised to the zero power yields 1; therefore, this is a zero-order reaction for B. We can perform a similar procedure in experiments 3 and 1 to determine the reaction order for A. Since [B] is constant in experiments 3 and 1, we can cancel it.

$$\frac{\text{Rate}_{\text{Exp 3}}}{\text{Rate}_{\text{Exp 1}}} = \frac{4 \times 10^{-3}}{1 \times 10^{-3}} = 4$$

$$\frac{\text{Rate}_{\text{Exp 3}}}{\text{Rate}_{\text{Exp 1}}} = \frac{k[0.40M]^m[0.20M]^n}{k[0.20M]^m[0.20M]^n} = \frac{[0.40M]^m}{[0.20M]^m} = 4$$

$$2n = 4$$

$n = 2$; the reaction is second order for A.

The rate law can be written as: Rate = $k[A]^2[B]^0$, or Rate = $k[A]^2$

You Try It!

For the reaction $2A + B \rightarrow C$, experimental data was collected for three trials:

Experiment	[A] ^{m}	[B] ^{n}	Initial Rate M s^{-1}
1	0.40	0.20	5.5×10^{-3}
2	0.80	0.20	5.5×10^{-3}
3	0.40	0.40	2.2×10^{-2}

What is the rate law of the reaction?

Answer: Rate = $k[A]^0[B]^2$

REACTION TYPES

In this section, you will learn how to recognize, distinguish, and work with first-order and second-order reactions. The order is referring to the overall order of the reaction, not the order for one of the reactants. Remember, the overall order of the reaction is determined by adding the exponents of the individual reactants.

First-Order Reactions

Because the order is the sum of the exponents of the reactants, a first-order reaction must depend only on the concentration of a single reactant (we're going to ignore fractional exponents). An example of such a reaction might be a decomposition reaction with only one reactant. The rate law for such a reaction would be as follows:

Rate = $k[A]$, where the exponent is an implied one. In the first section of this chapter, we showed that the reaction rate for such a reaction would be calculated using the formula

$$\text{Average rate} = -\frac{\Delta[A]}{\Delta t}$$

If we put both of these equations together, we come up with

$$\text{Rate} = -\frac{\Delta[A]}{\Delta t} = k[A]$$

This expression can be transformed, using calculus, into an equation that allows us to determine the concentration of A at any time during the reaction. It is not necessary for you to be able to perform this transformation, but you should be familiar with the equation:

$$\ln\frac{[A]_t}{[A]_0} = -kt \qquad \text{or} \qquad \ln[A]t = -kt + \ln[A]_0 \qquad \text{(Equations 15.4 and 15.5)}$$

where $[A]_0$ is the concentration of A at the start of the reaction and $[A]t$ is the concentration of A at any later time, t.

You may be thinking that the equation on the left (15.4) looks familiar to you. It should, because it is nearly the same as equation 4.5 shown below

$$\ln\frac{N_t}{N_0} = -kt$$

which was used to show the decay of a radioactive isotope over time.

The other equation, equation 15.5 (which is just 15.4 rearranged), is designed to show you one of the more important features of this topic, graphical interpretation of reaction data. Equation 15.5 has the form of the slope-intercept expression in math: $y = mx + b$. If you recall, in this equation, m represents the slope of the line and b is the y-intercept. This is an expression for a straight line. One purpose of transforming the expression is to allow us to analyze it based on a straight-line graph. Compare the two graphs in Figure 15.5. The graph on the left shows a plot of the first-order decomposition of substance A over time. The y-axis lists the change in concentration over time. The parabolic curve in the left graph can be straightened by using the natural logarithm of the concentration instead of the concentration. This is a characteristic of a first-order reaction, and you should be able to recognize it. If the plot of the natural log of the concentration over time is a straight-line, the reaction must be first order.

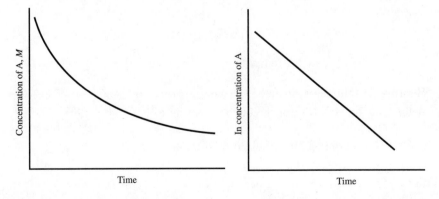

Figure 15.5

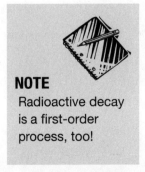

NOTE
Radioactive decay is a first-order process, too!

Sample: The first-order reaction $2N_2O_5 \rightarrow 4N_2O + O_2$ has a rate constant of 4.80×10^{-4} s^{-1} at a certain temperature. If, at this same temperature, a 2.50×10^{-3} M sample of dinitrogen pentoxide is allowed to decompose for 10.0 minutes, what will be the new concentration of N_2O_5?

Answer: Because you are solving for the concentration of N_2O_5 at time t, it is probably best to use the slope-intercept version of the formula. This equation will be set up as follows:

$$\ln[N_2O_5]_{600\,s} = -kt + \ln[N_2O_5]_0$$

$$\ln[N_2O_5]_{600\,s} = -(4.80 \times 10^{-4}\ s^{-1})(600.0\ s) + \ln(2.50 \times 10^{-3}\ M)$$

$$\ln[N_2O_5]_{600\,s} = -0.288 + (-5.991) = -6.28$$

To solve for $[N_2O_5]$, we must rearrange the equation

$$[N_2O_5] = e^{-6.28}$$

$$[N_2O_5] = 1.87 \times 10^{-3}\ M$$

You Try It!

For the reaction described in the previous sample, how long will it take for $[N_2O_5]$ to reach 1.25×10^{-3}, assuming the starting concentration is 2.50×10^{-3} M, like it was in the sample?

Answer: 1.44×10^3 s

HALF-LIFE

If you recall, back in Chapter 4 we discussed half-life in the context of the decay of radioactive nuclei. In that chapter, we defined the half-life as the amount of time it took for one half of the original sample of radioactive nuclei to decay. Because the rate of decay only depends on the amount of the radioactive sample, it is considered a first-order process. Using the same logic, we can apply the concept of half-life to first order chemical reactions as well. In this new context, the half-life is the amount of time required for the concentration of a reactant to decrease by one-half. The half-life equation 4.7 from Chapter 4 can be used to determine the half-life of a reactant:

$$t_{1/2} = \frac{0.693}{k}$$

Notice, the only factor that affects the half-life is the rate constant, k.

Sample: For the reaction in the last sample problem ($2N_2O_5 \rightarrow 4N_2O + O_2$), determine the half-life for the decomposition of N_2O_5 ($k = 4.80 \times 10^{-4}$ s^{-1}).

Answer: This is just a straight plug-and-chug.

$$t_{1/2} = \frac{0.693}{4.80 \times 10^{-4}\,s^{-1}} = 1.44 \times 10^{-3}$$

You may have noticed that this is the same answer as the last sample. If you look at the concentration values in the problem, the second concentration is one half of the first.

You Try It!

Substance X has a rate constant of 1.67×10^{-3} and decomposes in a first-order reaction. If the initial concentration of X is 4.80×10^{-2} M, how long will it take to reach a final concentration of 2.40×10^{-2} M?

Answer: 415 s $(= t_{1/2})$

Second-Order Reactions

There are different rate laws that can represent second-order reactions, but for our purposes we need not consider all of these. We can pick the easiest one, the composition of a single reactant that proceeds in a second-order reaction. In such a reaction, the rate law can be written as

$$\text{Rate} = \frac{\Delta[A]}{\Delta t} = k[A]^2 \qquad \text{(Equation 15.6)}$$

Remember, in these reactions, the rate of the reaction varies as the square of the change in concentration, so doubling the concentration will increase the rate four times.

In another transformation involving calculus (which you don't need to know), we can translate the rate expressions into a single expression that will allow us to calculate the concentration at any time during the reaction (like the expression we had for first-order reactions).

$$\frac{1}{[A]_t} = kt + \frac{1}{[A]_0} \qquad \text{(Equation 15.7)}$$

Notice again that this is written in the slope-intercept format, where the slope of the line is k once again. The differences between the equations and graphs of a second-order reaction and a first-order reaction are frequently a topic on the AP exam in some form or another.

The main difference that you must remember is that for a first-order reaction, a plot of ln [A] against t will generate a straight line, and for a second-order reaction, a plot of $1/[A]t$ against t will generate a straight line.

The half-life of a second-order reaction is also significantly different than the half-life of a first-order reaction. As equation 15.8 shows, the half-life of a second order reaction depends on the initial concentration of the reactant (for first-order reactions it does not).

$$t_{1/2} = \frac{1}{k[A]_0} \qquad \text{(Equation 15.8)}$$

THE RELATIONSHIP BETWEEN TEMPERATURE AND RATE

Temperature has a definite effect on the rate of chemical reactions. Most often, an increase in temperature corresponds to an increase in rate, although there are a small number of exceptions. One thing to keep in mind is that the rate constant is affected by changes in temperature. This is sometimes confusing to remember because it is not affected by concentrations.

Although there is a great deal of evidence to show that temperature changes affect reaction rates, there is no single theory that explains why. There are two main theories that together explain the relationships between temperature and rates. Neither theory on its own is sufficient to explain the relationship. The two theories are the collision theory and the transition state theory.

Collision Theory

The central premise behind this theory is that molecules need to crash into each other in order to collide. On many intuitive levels, this is an appealing theory. If particles must collide in order to react, then anything that increases the likelihood of collisions should increase the reaction rate. Increases in concentration, which cause increases in rate, allow more particles to come in contact or collide with each other. Increases in temperature will cause particles to move faster, which will increase the number of collisions. More collisions will lead to increased reaction rates at higher temperatures.

Neither of these ideas is disputed when trying to relate them to reaction rates. The problem with the collision theory is it is unable to explain certain relationships between temperature and rate. Some major flaws are that some reactions experience huge changes in reaction rate for relatively small changes in temperature, while others experience small changes in rate for large changes in temperature. Another problem is that only a very small percentage of collisions actually result in a reaction. These two problems raise concerns about why temperature effects are not consistent across different materials and why so few collisions result in reactions.

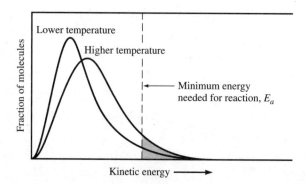

Figure 15.6

One factor that each theory shares is the view that two colliding particles will react only if their combined kinetic energies meet or exceed a threshold value known as the **activation energy** (E_a). As figure 15.6 shows, the number of particles possessing the activation energy increases as temperature increases. If the activation energy can't be achieved, the reaction won't occur. The gasoline that is in the gas tank of a parked car will sit indefinitely, despite the fact that the particles are colliding. However, if a spark energizes the same particles, they can gain sufficient activation energy to start the chemical reaction that will allow the car to drive. This combustion reaction is a highly exothermic reaction (gives off heat). If the potential energy of such a reaction is plotted against the progress of the reaction, the resulting graph looks like the graph (a) on the left in Figure 15.7. The figure illustrates a few significant points. First, since the potential energy in the graph is directly related to the transfer of kinetic energy during the collision, the graph shows that the kinetic energy must be sufficient to reach the top of the "hill" for the reaction to continue. Second, the particles that collide stick together for a brief period, forming what is known as an **activated complex**. The activated complex is a temporary species that forms as a result of the collision between particles. Its existence is temporary, so it will eventually fall apart. Finally note that potential energy drops below its original level when the products are formed. This is characteristic of an exothermic reaction, where the products are more stable than the reactants. The excess energy is released mostly as heat, though sometimes it is accompanied by light and sound.

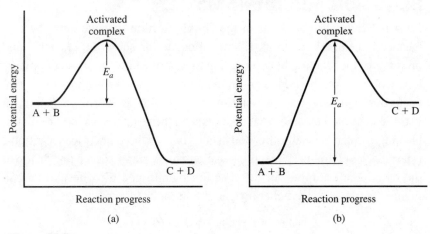

Figure 15.7

The graph (b) on the right in Figure 15.7 shows an endothermic reaction. The products of an endothermic reaction are less stable than the reactants, so the energy after the reaction occurs is higher than the energy before the reaction. Note how the activation energy is also much larger for an endothermic reaction. In a sense, you have to force reactants to do something they really don't want to do.

Transition-State Theory

Collision theory, as its name might suggest, focuses on the collisions between particles. The collisions must be frequent, and the colliding particles must have sufficient energy to form an activated complex. The transition-state theory focuses on the behavior of the activated complex. According to the transition-state theory, there are three main factors that determine if a reaction will occur:

1 The concentration of activated complexes

2. The rate at which the complexes break apart

3. The direction that the complexes fall apart (whether they break apart into the products or fall back apart as reactants)

Transition-state theory assumes that an equilibrium forms between the activated complex and the reactants. Large activation energies shift the equilibrium to favor the reactants, while smaller activation energies shift more toward the activated complex. The mathematics that comprise the transition-state theory are too complex for consideration in the AP course, but you should have a conceptual understanding of the basic premises. In the next section of the chapter, we will look more carefully at the stages that take place during the brief time between the formation of the activated complex and the formation of products.

REACTION MECHANISMS

Most reactions do not occur in the simple fashion that we describe in a balanced chemical equation. Chemical equations show the reactants and products of the reaction but do nothing to describe how the former converts to the latter. A method that is used to show the intermediate processes that occur during a reaction is a **reaction mechanism**. A reaction mechanism lists the proposed changes that take place to the reactants as the product(s) is being formed. Usually this consists of two or three chemical reactions, referred to as elementary reactions or elementary steps, shown one on top of the other. For example, in the reaction of nitrogen dioxide and carbon monoxide, the balanced chemical equation looks like this:

$$NO_2(g) + CO(g) \rightarrow NO(g) + CO_2(g)$$

While it may seem perfectly reasonable that the carbon monoxide molecule could crash into the nitrogen dioxide molecule in just the right way and steal the oxygen atom for itself. Analysis of the reaction, however, has detected the presence of the substance NO_3, which is neither a reactant nor a product of the reaction. One explanation for this finding is that the reaction proceeds in two steps:

$$\text{Step 1)} \quad NO_2 + NO_2 \rightarrow NO_3 + NO$$

$$\text{Step 2)} \quad NO_3 + CO \rightarrow NO_2 + CO_2$$

These two steps are known as the reaction mechanism for this reaction. A reaction mechanism must correctly represent the overall chemical equation if it is to be considered correct. The way either to obtain an overall equation from the elementary steps or to verify that the elementary steps are possibilities is to add the two together. In this process, all reactants are placed on the left side of the equation and all products are placed on the right side of the equation. Any substances that are found on both sides may be cancelled.

Elementary steps	$NO_2 + NO_2 \rightarrow NO_3 + NO$
	$NO_3 + CO \rightarrow NO_2 + CO_2$
Sum of steps	$\cancel{NO_2} + NO_2 + \cancel{NO_3} + CO \rightarrow \cancel{NO_3} + NO + \cancel{NO_2} + CO_2$
Overall equation	$NO_2 + CO \rightarrow NO + CO_2$

Any substance that is neither a reactant nor a product but that exists during the reaction is known as a **reaction intermediate**. The number of intermediates can vary depending on the complexity of a reaction.

In each elementary step, the number of molecules that take part in the reaction determines the **molecularity** of that step. When a single molecule is involved (this usually involves some type of rearrangement), the reaction is labeled **unimolecular**. In the previous example, each step had two molecules reacting, which makes it a **bimolecular** reaction. **Termolecular** reactions involve three molecules but are quite rare because they require the simultaneous collisions of three molecules.

You Try It!
Using the two elementary steps shown below, construct the balanced equation, and determine the molecularity of each step.

$$NO + NO \rightarrow N_2O_2$$

$$N_2O_2 + O_2 \rightarrow NO_2 + NO_2$$

Answer: $2NO + O_2 \rightarrow 2NO_2$; step 1 and 2 = bimolecular

Determining Rate Laws for Elementary Steps

While it is not possible to determine the rate law of a reaction by inspecting its balanced equation, it is possible to deduce the rate law if you know the elementary steps for the reaction or, in other words, the reaction mechanism. Knowing the molecularity of the elementary step will help you determine the rate law for that step. For example, consider the elementary step that involves the decomposition of substance A into one or more product:

$$A \rightarrow products$$

Remember, rate laws are written in terms of the concentration of the reactants. How will the rate of this reaction depend on the concentration of A? You may remember from earlier in the chapter that it will vary directly with the concentration. This is also the same form as a radioactive decay.

These reactions are first order, and the reaction rate can be summarized as

$$\text{Rate} = k[A]$$

The elementary steps in the **You Try It!** reaction that you just completed are examples of bimolecular reactions. Each step represents one of the two different types of rate laws that can be written for bimolecular elementary reactions. The first:

$$NO + NO \rightarrow N_2O_2$$

involves the collision of two identical molecules. This can be rewritten in a generic form:

$$A + A \rightarrow \text{products}$$

An increase in the concentration of A should cause a proportional increase in the number of collisions. This will create the rate law expression:

$$\text{Rate} = k[A][A] \text{ or Rate} = k[A]^2$$

The second elementary step in the example was

$$N_2O_2 + O_2 \rightarrow NO_2 + NO_2$$

In this step, the two reactant molecules are different substances. The generic equation for the rate of such a bimolecular reaction is

$$A + B \rightarrow \text{products}$$

The reaction is first-order for each reactant because the rate will be proportional to each reactants concentration, so the reaction rate expression for this type of step will be

$$\text{Rate} = k[A][B]$$

RATE-DETERMINING STEPS AND RATE LAWS

In reaction mechanisms, the different elementary steps tend to occur at different rates. Some are faster than others. The slowest step is known as the **rate-determining step** for the reaction and will determine the overall rate at which the reaction will proceed. Let's look at an analogy that you may be able to relate to.

Imagine that you are a customer at a fast-food restaurant. You arrive at a very busy time of day, and there are lines standing at each cash register. Suppose you have nothing better to do than watch what the employees are doing behind the counter. You notice that each cashier takes an order and then fills up the drinks. After placing the drinks on the counter, the cashier grabs a tray or a bag and begins collecting the food for the order. First, he picks up the burgers from a bin that is being filled up by a very anxious-looking woman who appears to be working rather quickly. Next, he walks over to the french fry area to pick up the fries for the order. There is a young man in charge of the fry area who is cooking the fries and filling up the fry bags and boxes for the cashiers. Just when your hunger has reached its breaking point, you step up to the counter and place your order with the eager cashier. He goes to get your drink, goes to the burger bin and gets your burger, walks over to the fry area, and then stops. For some reason, there are no fries ready. Within seconds, the other cashiers begin piling up around the fry station. The drive-thru is starting to back up. The fry guy is staring nervously into the fry vats, hoping he can will the fries to cook more quickly. In this example, nobody who ordered fries can be served until those fries are done. Even though the drinks can be filled quickly, the burgers are ready to go, and the cashiers are moving quickly, no one can get served until the fries are cooked. The fry station is the rate-determining step in this scenario.

In chemical reactions, the rate-determining step works in much the same way. From a conceptual standpoint, consider a reaction with two elementary steps where the first step is the slow one (the rate-determining step). The concentration of the reactants in the first step is far more important than the concentration of the additional reactants in the second step. That is because the second step can't start until the first step has been completed. In our fast food example, it's the equivalent of saying that you can't speed up the process by adding more cashiers. You can have fifty cashiers, but if there are no french fries for them to pick up, they can't do anything.

Using a reaction as an example, consider the reaction that occurs between nitrogen dioxide and fluorine. The reaction is believed to have the following elementary steps:

$$NO_2 + F_2 \xrightarrow{k_1} NO_2F + F$$

$$F + NO_2 \xrightarrow{k_2} NO_2F$$

The k_1 and k_2 written above the arrow represent the rate constant for those elementary steps, and the subscripts are used to distinguish them from the rate constant, k, for the overall reaction.

In this reaction, if the first step is the rate-determining step (slow), then as soon as F_2 reacts to form NO_2F, the F that is produced will quickly react to form another NOF. Therefore, the rate of appearance of NO_2F is directly related to the rate of disappearance of F_2. This means that the first step is considered the rate-determining step. In the previous section, we saw that a bimolecular reaction, like the elementary steps in this reaction, has a predictable rate law that will take the form

$$Rate = k_1[NO_2][F_2]$$

At this point, the rate law is just an educated guess. It must be compared with experimental data to determine if it is supported. k_1 should equal the experimentally determined rate constant, k. An important note here is that even if the experimental data matches our predicted rate law, it does not mean that our rate law is correct. If the data disagrees with ours, it does allow us to rule out our reaction mechanism, but if the data supports ours, it only allows us to know that we have produced the best explanation for the time being. For your purposes on the AP exam, what this translates to is that you should be careful how you word any responses when you are predicting the rate law from a reaction mechanism. Always reserve a little room for doubt.

Mechanisms Where the Initial Step Is Fast

What if the rate-determining step is the second step? This becomes a bit more difficult to determine because an intermediate is involved in the rate law. Because intermediates are usually quite unstable, it is difficult to predict their concentrations. If the second step is slow, then you have to assume that the first step quickly produces an intermediate. However, if the second step is slow, the intermediate may not be able to break apart to form products. What generally happens in this case is that the intermediate will fall apart into the reactants again. The reactants will reform the intermediate, and equilibrium will begin between the intermediate and the reactants. For mechanisms where a slow step is preceded by a fast one, it is assumed that equilibrium is established in the fast reaction. Let's see how this works in an example. In the reaction

$$H_2(g) + I_2(g) \rightarrow 2HI(g)$$

the experimentally determined rate law is

$$\text{Rate} = k[H_2][I_2]$$

A possible mechanism that includes a fast initial step is

$$I_2 \underset{k_{-1}}{\overset{k_1}{\rightleftharpoons}} 2I \qquad \text{(fast)}$$

$$I + I + H_2 \overset{k_2}{\rightarrow} 2HI \qquad \text{(slow)}$$

Remember, if the slow reaction is preceded by a fast one, the fast one will establish equilibrium. The rate constant of the forward reaction (k_1) is equal to the rate constant of the reverse reaction (k_{-1}). If we use the logic of the previous example, then the slow reaction will determine the rate for the overall reaction. However, if we write the rate law for this reaction, we run into a problem. The rate law for the second step is

$$\text{Rate} = k_2[I][I][H_2], \text{ or Rate} = k_2[I]^2[H_2]$$

The problem is that the reaction intermediate is present in the rate law. Because these are so unstable, they are inappropriate for rate laws. The way to get around this is to express the intermediate in terms of the initial reactant, I^2. This can be done using our assumption about the equilibrium that is established in the first step. In this equilibrium, we can say that

$$\text{Rate} = k_1[I_2] = k_{-1}[I]^2$$

If we rearrange this a bit, we can find a suitable substitute for the $[I]^2$ portion in the rate law:

$$[I]^2 = \frac{k_1}{k_{-1}}[I_2]$$

If we substitute this into the original rate law, we end up with

$$\text{Rate} = k_2 \frac{k_1}{k_{-1}} [\text{I}_2][\text{H}_2]$$

If it can be shown that $k_2 \frac{k_1}{k_{-1}}$ is equal to k, this is a reasonable reaction mechanism (experimental evidence does support this assumption).

You Try It!

The following reaction

$$2\text{NO}(g) + \text{O}_2(g) \rightarrow 2\text{NO}(g)$$

is believed to proceed by the mechanism shown below:

$$\text{NO} + \text{O}_2 \underset{k_{-1}}{\overset{k_1}{\rightleftharpoons}} \text{NO}_3 \qquad \text{(fast)}$$

$$\text{NO}_3 + \text{NO} \xrightarrow{k_2} \text{NO}_2 + \text{NO}_2 \qquad \text{(slow)}$$

Write a rate law for this reaction that is consistent with the mechanism.

Answer: Rate $= k_2 \dfrac{k_1}{k_{-1}} [\text{NO}]^2[\text{O}_2]$

THE EFFECT OF CATALYSTS ON REACTION RATE

Catalysts are substances that change the rate of a reaction without being consumed. They help the reaction to occur at a faster rate. Introductory courses often work with the decomposition of hydrogen peroxide as an example of a reaction affected by a catalyst. The decomposition, shown below, occurs very slowly under normal conditions:

$$2\text{H}_2\text{O}_2(aq) \rightarrow 2\text{H}_2\text{O}(l) + \text{O}_2(g)$$

If you sprinkle a little bit of manganese dioxide into the hydrogen peroxide, the reaction begins to proceed quite rapidly. When the reaction is complete, the manganese dioxide can be recovered intact. In biology classes, the same reaction can be performed using an enzyme (a organic catalyst that is produced in living organisms) extracted from beef liver.

The important effect of a catalyst is to help a reaction occur more quickly than it could without the catalyst. The way that a catalyst accomplishes this is to lower the activation energy of the reaction. In Figure 15.8, notice the decreased height of the curve, indicating the lowered activation energy.

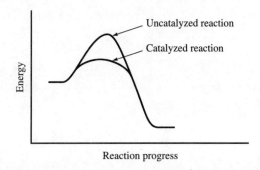

Figure 15.8

There are three different forms of catalysis. The first is **homogeneous catalysis**, in which the catalyst is in the same phase as the reactants. The decomposition of hydrogen peroxide can also be performed using a homogeneous catalyst like HBr. The bromine ions catalyze the decomposition. The second type of catalysis is shown with the use of manganese dioxide as a catalyst in the hydrogen peroxide decomposition. This type is known as **heterogeneous catalysis** because the catalyst is in a different phase than the reactants (making a heterogeneous mixture). The final type is biological, and catalysis is done with enzymes. Quite often catalysts will help bend, stretch, or orient molecules so that they can react more easily.

Summary: Kinetics

- The rate at which a reaction occurs is known as the reaction rate. This rate is typically determined by measuring the amount of one substance (either a reactant or product) over time. The reaction stoichiometry can then be used to determine the other substances that were not measured.

- The rate of a reaction is sometimes affected by the concentration of a reactant. The degree to which the reaction is affected depends on the rate law for the reaction.

- The rate law is an equation that relates the concentration of the reactants to the rate of the reaction. The rate law can only be determined experimentally and is not affected by changes in concentration.

- The reaction order determines the exact numerical relationship between the reactants and the reaction rate. There are times when the concentration of a reactant does not affect the reaction rate. Such reactants are described as zero-order for the reaction (as long as they are present, it does not matter how much there is).

- First-order reactions only depend on the concentration of a single substance. Quite often they are decomposition reactions that follow the form of a nuclear decay.

- Temperature has a definite effect on reaction rate, but the reasons for the changes are not completely understood. The two theories that describe this relationship are the collision theory and the transition-state model.

- Collision theory proposes that increases in temperature increase reaction rates by increasing the number of collisions that occur between particles and by increasing the kinetic energy that particles possess when they collide.

- Transition-state theory focuses on the rates at which particles form and are formed from activated complexes.

- Crucial to both theories is the concept of activation energy, which is the amount of energy that is required to cause substances to react.

- Catalysts are substances that increase the reaction rate without being consumed in the process. They work by decreasing the activation energy for a reaction.

- Reaction mechanisms are proposed steps that occur during a chemical reaction. By comparing proposed reaction mechanisms with experimental rate data, you can determine the rate law of a reaction.

- In reaction mechanisms of more than one step, the slowest step, known as the rate-determining step, will determine the rate law and the rate of the reaction.

REVIEW QUESTIONS

1. If a reaction, $2A + 3B \rightarrow$ products, is first-order for A and second-order for B, the rate law for the overall reaction will be written as Rate = _____.

   (A) $k[A][B]$

   (B) $k[A][D]^2$

   (C) $k[A]^2[D]^2$

   (D) $k[A]^2[D]^3$

   (E) $k[A]^2[D]$

2. The rate law for the reaction $2A + B \rightarrow C$ was found to be Rate = $k[A][B]^2$. If the concentration of B is tripled, what will happen to the rate of the reaction?

   (A) It will stay the same.

   (B) It will increase by two times.

   (C) It will increase by three times.

   (D) It will increase by six times.

   (E) It will increase by nine times.

The data table below is to be used for question 3.

Experiment	Initial $[NO_2]$ m	Initial Reaction Rate M s^{-1}
1	0.010	7.1×10^{-5}
2	0.020	28×10^{-5} M s

3. Nitrogen dioxide decomposes according to the following reaction:

   $$2NO_2(g) \rightarrow 2NO(g) + O_2(g)$$

   For the initial rate data given above, what is the value of k in the rate law?

   (A) 0.010 M

   (B) 7.1×10^{-3} s^{-1}

   (C) 3.5×10^{-3} s^{-1}

   (D) 0.71 $M^{-1}s^{-1}$

   (E) 4

   $$2H_2O_2(l) \rightarrow 2H_2O(l) + O_2(g)$$

4. Hydrogen peroxide decomposes according to the reaction above, which is first order for H_2O_2 and has a half-life 18.0 minutes. If an H_2O_2 solution that was initially 0.80 M is allowed to decompose for 72 minutes, what will the concentration be at that time?

   (A) 0.80 M

   (B) 0.40 M

   (C) 0.20 M

   (D) 0.10 M

   (E) 0.05 M

5. Which of the following would produce a linear graph for the following reaction?

$$A \rightarrow product(s)$$

   (A) mol A vs. time if the reaction is first-order for A

   (B) $\dfrac{1}{[A]}$ vs. time if the reaction is first-order for A

   (C) $\dfrac{1}{[A]^2}$ vs. time if the reaction is second-order for A

   (D) ln [A] vs. time if the reaction is first-order for A

   (E) ln [A] vs. time if the reaction is second-order for A

$$\text{Rate} = k[HCrO_4^-][HSO_3^-]^2[H^+]$$

6. In the reaction above, what is the order of the reaction with respect to H^+?

   (A) 0

   (B) 1

   (C) 2

   (D) 3

   (E) 4

$$\text{Rate} = k[NO]^2[Br_2]$$

7. What is the order for the overall reaction shown above?

   (A) Zero order

   (B) First order

   (C) Second order

   (D) Third order

   (E) Not enough information.

8. Which of the graphs below represents an exothermic reaction?

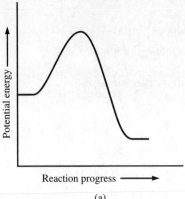

(a)

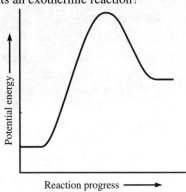

(b)

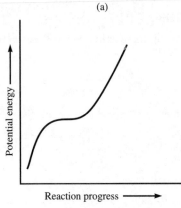

(c)

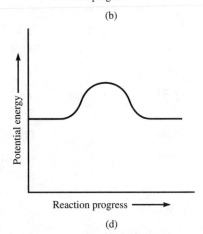

(d)

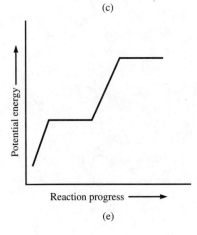

(e)

9. A catalyst does *not* affect which of the following?

   I. Activation energy

  II. Reaction rate

 III. Potential energies reactants or products

(A) I only

(B) II only

(C) III only

(D) I and II

(E) II and III

$$2A + B \rightarrow products$$

10. The rate law for the reaction above is Rate = $k[A]^2$. What effect would adding additional B have? (Assume no change in temperature or volume.)

    (A) Both the value of k and the reaction rate would decrease

    (B) Both the value of k and the reaction rate would increase

    (C) The value of k would remain constant, but the rate would decrease.

    (D) The value of k would remain constant, but the rate would increase.

    (E) Neither nor the reaction rate would change.

    Step 1) $NO(g) + Cl_2(g) \rightleftharpoons NOCl_2(g)$ (fast equilibrium)

    Step 2) $NO(g) + NOCl_2(g) \rightarrow 2NOCl(g)$ (slow)

11. Which of the following rate laws is consistent with the reaction mechanism shown above?

    (A) Rate = $k[NO][Cl_2]$

    (B) Rate = $k[NO]_2$

    (C) Rate = $k[NO][NOCl_2]$

    (D) Rate = $k[NO]^2[Cl]$

    (E) Rate = $k[NO]^2[Cl][NOCl_2]$

12. The reaction mechanism for the chlorination of trichloromethane is shown below:

    $$Cl_2(g) \underset{k_{-1}}{\overset{k_1}{\rightleftharpoons}} 2Cl(g)$$ fast

    $$Cl(g) + CHCl_3(g) \overset{k_2}{\rightarrow} HCl(g) + CCl_3(g)$$ slow

    $$Cl(g) + CCl_3(g) \overset{k_3}{\rightarrow} CCl_4(g)$$ fast

    Which of the following represents an intermediate in the reaction?

    (A) $CHCl_3$

    (B) Cl

    (C) Cl_2

    (D) CCl_4

    (E) HCl

Free Response

Question 1

A hypothetical reaction takes place according to the following equation:

$$2A + B \rightarrow 3C + 2D$$

The following rate data were obtained from three different experiments, all of which were performed at the same temperature.

Experiment	Initial $[A]m$	Initial $[B]n$	Initial rate $M\ s^{-1}$
1	0.10	0.10	0.10
2	0.20	0.10	0.40
3	0.20	0.20	0.40

(A) Determine the rate law for the reaction.

(B) Calculate the rate constant, k.

(C) Calculate the rate of the reaction when $[A] = 0.30\ M$ and $[B] = 0.30\ M$.

Question 2

The proposed mechanism for the reaction in this question is shown below:

Step 1) $\quad 2NO(g) \underset{k_{-1}}{\overset{k_1}{\rightleftharpoons}} N_2O_2(g)$ \qquad\qquad (fast)

Step 2) $\quad N_2O_2(g) + H_2(g) \overset{k_2}{\rightarrow} H_2O_2(g) + N_2(g)$ \qquad (slow)

Step 3) $\quad H_2(g) + H_2O_2(g) \underset{k_{-1}}{\overset{k_1}{\rightleftharpoons}} 2H_2O$ \qquad\qquad (fast)

(A) Write the balanced equation for this reaction.

(B) Identify the rate-determining step.

(C) Write a rate law that is most consistent with this mechanism.

(D) Based on your rate law, determine the effect of doubling the concentration of NO (while maintaining constant amounts of all other reactants) on the reaction rate.

ANSWERS

1. **The correct answer is (B).** The order tells you the exponent to place next to the concentration. Because A is first order, an understood 1 is next to [A]. B is second order, so [B] will be squared.

2. **The correct answer is (E).** Because the rate law has the concentration of B squared, the effect of tripling B will increase the rate by $(3)^2 = 9$.

3. **The correct answer is (D).** First, you must determine what the rate law should be. This is a bimolecular reaction with a single reactant. Therefore, the rate law should be Rate $= k[NO_2]^2$. Another way to solve this is to use the experimental data to determine the order of the reaction for NO_2. This technique begins with the assumption that rate $= k[NO_2]m$. You need to solve for m. You can set up an equation to solve for m:

$$\frac{\text{rate 2}}{\text{rate 1}} = \frac{28 \times 10^{-5}}{7.1 \times 10^{-5}} = \frac{k(0.020)^m}{k(0.010)^m}$$

$$4 = 2m; \, m = 2$$

Once you have the rate law, you just substitute the numbers from one of the experiments and solve for k.

$$\text{Rate} = k[NO_2]^2$$

$$k = \frac{\text{Rate}}{[NO_2]^2} = \frac{7.1 \times 10^{-5}}{(0.010)^2} = 0.71 \, M^{-1}s^{-1}$$

4. **The correct answer is (E).**

   Probably the easiest way to solve this is without an equation. If the half life is 18 minutes, then 72 minutes makes 4 half-lives. If the sample 0.80 cuts in half four times, it becomes 0.80→0.40→0.20→0.10→0.05 M.

   We also had an equation (equation 6.1) that can be rearranged to solve for H_2O_2 (instead of N, which is in the equation).

   $[H_2O_2] = [H_2O]t_{=0}(\frac{1}{2})^4$

   $[H_2O_2] = (0.8) (\frac{1}{2})^4 = 0.05 \, M$

5. **The correct answer is (D).** This is a first-order reaction with a single reactant. A graph of the concentration plotted against time would produce a curve. By plotting the natural logarithm of the concentration against the time, you can produce a straight line. This is characteristic of a first-order reaction. A similar transformation is also accomplished by taking the base 10 logarithm of the concentration.

6. **The correct answer is (B).** The order of the reaction with respect to H^+ is determined by looking at the exponent next to the $[H^+]$. Since there is none written, this means it is an understood 1, which represents first-order.

7. **The correct answer is (D).** Simply add the exponents for each concentration: $(2 + 1) = 3$

8. **The correct answer is (A).** In an exothermic reaction, the potential energy of the products will be lower than that of the reactants. The energy difference is due to the loss of energy as heat. The only graph that shows a decrease in the energy of the products is A. The other most common type of plot is B, which represents an endothermic reaction.

9. **The correct answer is (C).** A catalyst does lower the activation energy and the reaction rate. However, the initial potential energy of the reactants and the final potential energies of the products are the same with or without catalysis.

10. **The correct answer is (E).** Because B is not part of the rate law, it's concentration does not affect the rate or rate constant for the reaction (as long as some is present).

11. **The correct answer is (D).** In this reaction, the rate-determining step is the second step. The rate law should be written from this step. However, when writing the rate law:

$$Rate = k[NO][NOCl_2]$$

you enter the concentration of an intermediate, which is incorrect. You must rewrite the rate law in terms of the reactants. Therefore, you need to create an equality based on the initial equilibrium, which will allow you to substitute the reactants into the expression.

$$NO(g) + Cl_2(g) \underset{k_{-1}}{\overset{k_1}{\rightleftharpoons}} NOCl_2(g)$$

$$Rate = k_1[NO][Cl_2]$$

$$Rate = k_{-1}[NOCl_2]$$

$$k_1[NO][Cl_2] = k_{-1}[NOCl_2]$$

$$\frac{k_1}{k_{-1}}[NO][Cl_2] = [NOCl_2]$$

This can now be substituted into the rate law:

$$Rate = k_2[NO][NOCl_2]$$

$$Rate = k_2\frac{k_1}{k_{-1}}[NO][NO][Cl_2]$$

which can now be rearranged. During the rearrangement, it is assumed that $k_2\dfrac{k_1}{k_{-1}}$ is equivalent to the experimental rate law constant, k.

$$Rate = k[NO]^2[Cl]$$

12. **The correct answer is (B).** The easiest way to determine the intermediates is to write one equation with all of the reactants on one side and all of the products on the other side. For this reaction, the following equation results:

$$Cl_2(g) + Cl(g) + CHCl_3(g) + Cl(g) + CCl_3(g) \rightarrow 2Cl(g) + HCl(g) + CCl_3(g) + CCl_4(g)$$

All substances that are on both sides of the arrow can be cancelled:

$$Cl_2(g) + CHCl_3(g) \rightarrow HCl(g) + CCl_4(g)$$

The intermediates are those substances that appear in the longer, first equation but not in the balanced equation. Although CCl_3 is also an intermediate, it is not one of the choices in the question.

Free Response

Question 1

(A) The first question can be done in your head, but you may be asked to show your work, so it is useful to be able to solve the problem both ways. The quick inspection method is to look at what happens to the rate when only one substance changes. For example, in experiment 2 the concentration of A doubles while the concentration of B stays the same. The reaction rate increases by 4, which indicates the reaction is second order for A. In experiment 3, the concentration of B doubles while A remains constant. This change produces no change in reaction rate, meaning that the reaction is zero order for B. By inspection, the rate equation becomes Rate = $k[A]^2$. Using rates equations, you can also determine the rate law. This requires solving for the variables m and n in the equation:

$$\text{Rate} = k[A]m[B]n$$

To solve for m, we need to choose two experiments where B is constant. This allows us to cancel n and isolate m.

$$\frac{\text{Rate 2}}{\text{Rate 1}} = \frac{0.40\ M\ \text{s}^{-1}}{0.10\ M\ \text{s}^{-1}} = \frac{k[0.20]^m[0.10]^n}{k[0.10]^m[0.10]^n}$$

$$4 = 2m;\ 2 = m$$

The same is repeated for n:

$$\frac{\text{Rate 3}}{\text{Rate 2}} = \frac{0.40\ M\ \text{s}^{-1}}{0.10\ M\ \text{s}^{-1}} = \frac{k[0.20]^m[0.20]^n}{k[0.20]^m[0.10]^n}$$

$$1 = 2n;\ n = 0$$

Using equations, we still get Rate = $k[A]^2[B]^0$, or Rate = $k[A]^2$

(B) To calculate the rate law, we just need to substitute some data into the equation. It doesn't matter which experiment we use.

$$\text{Rate} = k[A]^2$$

$$0.10\ \text{M s}^{-1} = k(0.10\ \text{M})^2$$

$$k = \frac{0.10\ \text{M s}^{-1}}{0.01\ \text{M}^2} = 10\text{M}^{-1}\text{s}^{-1}$$

(C) Now that you have calculated k, you can substitute the values of A and B into the rate equation:

$$\text{Rate} = k[A]^2 = (10\ \text{M}^{-1}\ \text{s}^{-1})(0.3\ \text{M})^2 = 0.9\ \text{M s}^{-1}$$

Question 2

(A) To write the balanced equation, we need to write all reactants and products and cancel like substances:

$$2NO(g) + N_2O_2(g) + H_2(g) + H_2(g) + H_2O_2(g) \rightarrow N_2O_2(g) + H_2O_2(g) + N_2(g) + 2H_2O$$

After canceling all substances that appear on both sides of the arrow, the equation becomes

$$2NO(g) + 2H_2(g) \rightarrow N_2(g) + 2H_2O$$

(B) The rate-determining step is the slow one, Step 2.

(C) The rate law that is most consistent with this mechanism must be determined from Step 2, the rate-determining step. From this step, we obtain the rate law,

$$\text{Rate} = k_2[N_2O_2][H_2]$$

Unfortunately, we can't use this expression because it contains an intermediate. We need to find a suitable replacement for N_2O_2. In this case, we can obtain it from the equilibrium ion step 1. By using the equilibrium, we can solve for N_2O_2 in terms of one of the reactants, NO.

For the forward reaction: $\text{Rate} = k_1[NO]^2$;

For the reverse reaction: $\text{Rate} = k_{-1}[N_2O_2]$

The two reactions have the same rate, so they are equal to each other. You can set up the equality and then rewrite the expression in terms of $[N_2O_2]$.

$$k_1[NO]_2 = k_{-1}[N_2O_2]$$

$$[N_2O_2] = \frac{k_1}{k_{-1}}[NO]^2$$

This can be placed into the rate equation instead of N_2O_2:

$$\text{Rate} = k_2[N_2O_2][H_2]$$

$$\text{Rate} = k_2\frac{k_1}{k_{-1}}[NO]^2[H_2]$$

If $k_2\dfrac{k_1}{k_{-1}}$ is assumed to be equivalent to the overall rate constant, k, the expression can then become:

$$\text{Rate} = k[NO]^2[H_2]$$

(D) Because the reaction is second-order for NO, doubling the concentration of NO will increase the rate of reaction four times ($2^2 = 4$).

Thermodynamics

One aspect of chemical behavior that we have not looked at in much detail is the relationship among the energies of reactants, products, and reactions. Near the end of Chapter 15, you read about activation energy and how reactants must meet or exceed that threshold value before a reaction can occur. In this chapter, we will look more closely at the energy interactions between chemical reactions and the surrounding environment. Although these interactions can be quite complex, there are some basic patterns that you can learn that will allow you to make accurate predictions about chemical behaviors.

INTRODUCTION

In this chapter, there is some terminology that must be clear before we begin. The first term is the word **system**. The universe is a very large place and it would be impossible—and a bit ridiculous—to describe all energy changes in terms of the universe. If we are describing a chemical reaction that is occurring in a beaker, it is useful to be able to restrict our attention to the activities within the beaker without having to qualify our comments by including everything outside the beaker. If the beaker contains a silver nitrate solution reacting with a zinc strip, the beaker, the solution, and the zinc make up all that we are really interested in. This specific place or portion of the universe that we are setting aside for observation is the system. Everything else is considered the surroundings. This particular system represents an **open system** because it is open to the rest of the atmosphere. As such, the contents of the system are free to interact with the surroundings, and vice-versa. The most common of these interactions is the pressure exerted by the atmosphere on the system. Open systems exist at atmospheric pressure and are affected by the temperature of the surroundings. **Closed systems** are physically isolated from the surroundings. A stoppered test tube or a sealed flask represent closed systems. Most of the lab work that you do as part of the AP course takes place in an open system.

The next term that is used or implied throughout this chapter is **state function**. A state function is a property of a system that is only related to its current conditions—it is not concerned with how it got to be at those conditions. An example would be a beaker of water at 50 °C. The beaker of water possesses a certain temperature, volume, and energy under these conditions. It does not matter if it was once filled with ice and reached 50 °C by being warmed or if it was once boiling and reached 50 °C by being cooled.

ROAD MAP

- *Introduction*
- *The First Law of Thermodynamics*
- *Enthalpy*
- *Thermochemical Equations*
- *Hess's Law*
- *Spontaneity*
- *Entropy*
- *The Second Law of Thermodynamics*
- *Gibbs Free Energy*

The state functions, among which are pressure, volume, temperature, energy, and enthalpy, simply describe the substance as it is at a particular moment.

THE FIRST LAW OF THERMODYNAMICS

The first law of thermodynamics is one of the most fundamental premises in science. Also known as the *law of conservation of energy*, it states that energy can neither be created nor destroyed—it is conserved. An important thing to remember is that this applies to the universe, not a particular system. Energy can be lost or gained by a system, but the law of conservation of energy tells us that it doesn't just appear or disappear. It is transferred from one object to another in any number of forms. Any system, therefore, will gain and lose energy from the surrounding environment.

The energy of a system consists of the energies of all components in the system at all levels, including the atomic level. There are too many energy-related factors to consider in a system, so the energy of a system can't be measured directly. We can, however, measure changes in the energy, which will give us an indirect look at the initial and final energies. The energy change in the system is defined as ΔE, which is calculated using the equation:

(Equation 16.1)

$$\Delta E = E_{final} - E_{initial}$$

(In future problems, we will use the symbols "*f*" and "*i*" to represent final and initial.)

Energy must be defined as having a direction as well as an amount. This will be true for all of the measurements we discuss in this chapter. Direction is necessary to understand whether energy is being gained or lost by the system. A positive change in energy, ΔE, indicates energy is gained by the system, while a negative ΔE shows an energy loss. Energy exchanges with the environment are defined in terms of heat, q, and work, w. The energy of a system will increase as heat is added and will decrease as heat is lost. Likewise, work done on a system will increase its energy, while work done by a system will decrease its energy. The relationship between energy, heat, and work can be summarized in equation 16.2, shown below:

(Equation 16.2)

$$\Delta E = q + w$$

Like E, q and w have signs associated with their directions. The value of q is positive when heat is being added to the system and negative when heat is being lost. The value of w is positive when work is done on the system and negative when work is being done by the system. The sign of ΔE will depend on the signs of q and w.

ENTHALPY

Because the systems that you are working with are under fairly standard conditions, you can ignore the effects of work on the system. This means that the changes in energy will be related to heat. The heat that is gained or lost by a system is defined as the **enthalpy** of the system. Enthalpy is a state function and is defined by the symbol H. Like energy, enthalpy can't be measured directly. It is understood in terms of changes in enthalpy, ΔH. The change in enthalpy, ΔH, at constant pressure, can be defined as:

$$\Delta H = H_f - H_i = q_p$$

(Equation 16.3)

where qp is the heat associated with constant pressure. When pressure changes, work has to be considered, which makes things a bit more complicated. You are not responsible for knowing about this special situation. The sign of ΔH also relates to the direction of heat transfer. A positive value of ΔH indicates that the system has gained heat from the surroundings. We have previously described this as being an **endothermic** process. A negative value of ΔH indicates the system has lost heat to the surroundings, which is an **exothermic** process.

THERMOCHEMICAL EQUATIONS

A thermochemical equation must be balanced, include all states of each reactant and product, and list the enthalpy for the reaction. An example of such a reaction is shown below:

$$N_2(g) + 3H_2(g) \rightarrow 2NH_3(g); \ \Delta H = -91.8 \text{ kJ}$$

There are reasons for the specific criteria in the design of this equation. The states of matter must be specified because, as you may recall, a certain amount of heat may be required or lost by reactants and/or products if they change state in the course of a reaction. Second, the equation must be balanced because enthalpy values for equations vary according to the number of moles of a substance. That is, the value of ΔH changes proportionally to the coefficients in a balanced equation. If you combine twice the amount of reactants, the enthalpy will be twice as great. This also allows you to place fractional coefficients in front of substances to simplify problems.

A final assumption of thermochemical equations is that when you reverse the direction of a chemical reaction, you only change the sign of the enthalpy. For example, the synthesis of ammonia is an exothermic process that releases 91.8 kJ of heat. If you reverse the direction to show the decomposition of ammonia, the reaction becomes endothermic:

$$2NH_3(g) \rightarrow N_2(g) + 3H_2(g); \ \Delta H = +91.8 \text{ kJ}$$

Sample: The complete combustion of butane gas, C_4H_{10}, in oxygen gas, O_2, produces CO_2 and H_2O. It is a highly exothermic process releasing 2845 kJ of heat per mole of butane. Write the balanced thermochemical equation, using all whole-number coefficients. Also, determine the enthalpy change in burning 50.0 g of butane gas.

Answer:

$$2C_4H_{10}(g) + 13O_2(g) \rightarrow 8CO_2(g) + 10H_2O(g); \ \Delta H = -5690 \text{ kJ}$$

The enthalpy has to be negative because the heat is given off in the reaction. The quantity has to be doubled because the original value is for one mole of butane. Many times, fractional coefficients are used to simplify the equations. For example, the same reaction can be rewritten as:

$$C_4H_{10}(g) + \frac{13}{2}O_2(g) \rightarrow 4CO_2(g) + 5H_2O(g); \quad \Delta H = -2845 \text{ kJ}$$

For the second part of this question, you know that the enthalpy change for one mole of butane is –2845 kJ. All you need to do is determine what fraction of a mole 50.0 g is and reduce the enthalpy by that amount:

$$50.0 \text{ g} \times \frac{1 \text{ mol}}{58.14 \text{ g}} = 0.86$$

The enthalpy for 50.0 g is $0.86 \times -2845 \text{ kJ} = -2447 \text{ kJ}$

Measuring the Heat of Reaction

Enthalpy changes, like the ones we've just finished looking at, can be determined experimentally. We have described enthalpies in terms of energy interactions between a system and the surroundings. Enthalpy changes can be experimentally determined by measuring the effects that a substance has on its surroundings as well as the effects of the surroundings on the substance. In this section, we will look at how these changes are measured.

Thermochemical measurements are based on the relationships between heat and temperature. The measurement that relates to the two is **heat capacity,** defined as the amount of heat that is required to raise the temperature of a substance 1 °C. (The amount of substance is sometimes expressed in moles or in grams.) The heat capacity of a mole of a substance is known as the **molar heat capacity**, while the heat capacity for gram values of a substance are known as **specific heat capacities**. The **specific heat** of a substance is the amount of heat required to raise 1 gram of the substance 1 °C. The formula that is used to calculate specific heat is

(Equation 16.4)
$$q = m\,s\,\Delta T$$

where q is the heat required, m is the number of grams of the substance, s is the specific heat, and ΔT is the difference between the final temperature and the initial temperature. If you examine the equation, you will see that if you add equal amounts of heat to equivalent masses of different materials, the change in temperature will be inversely related to the specific heat. If a substance has a small specific heat, it will only take a small amount of heat to produce a large change in temperature. Likewise, a substance with a large specific heat requires a large amount of heat to produce a similar change in temperature. Water has one of the highest specific heats at 4.18 J/g °C; copper, by comparison, is 0.384 J/g °C. To help you visualize this concept, imagine a cup of water sitting in the midday sun on a hot summer day. Next to it, picture an equivalent mass of copper. Now imagine picking up the piece of copper or sticking your finger in the water. The copper will be much hotter because the addition of about the same amount of heat produced a much larger temperature change (due to the lower specific heat).

The typical way to measure the heat released during a reaction is to measure the temperature change of the surroundings. This can be accomplished by using a device known as a **calorimeter**. The purpose of a calorimeter is to create a closed system in which to perform the reaction. The closed system allows the heat to be transferred entirely from the reactants to the surroundings without interference from the outside environment. Any device that insulates the reaction from the outside environment can serve as a calorimeter. The most basic type consists of a styrofoam coffee cup, while more sophisticated calorimeters are used for more accurate work.

NOTE
Sometimes the variable c is used in place of s in heat capacity equations.

The premise behind the function of the calorimeter is that any heat released during a chemical reaction will be lost to the surroundings. This gain of heat by the surroundings produces a temperature change in the surroundings. We can use the increase in temperature as a way to detect the enthalpy of the reaction. To help you understand the concept of this process, we'll consider a very simple example.

Consider a coffee-cup calorimeter filled with 250 g of distilled water at room temperature (25 °C). Now, let's say you take a 5.00 g piece of iron that has been heated to 100 °C by placing it in a container of boiling water for an extended period of time. If you place the iron into the room temperature water, you can probably imagine that the temperature of the iron will cool down while the temperature of the water will increase. The increase in the water's temperature and decrease in the iron's temperature are directly related to the transfer of heat from the iron to the water. The two will not stop changing temperature until they have both reached the same temperature. If the final temperature of the water is 25.2 °C, what is the specific heat of the unknown metal? The specific heat of water is 4.18 J/g °C.

The heat lost by the iron will equal the heat gained by the water, so we can use the specific heat equation to solve the problem.

$$q_m = m_m \, s_m \, \Delta T_m$$

$$q_{H_2O} = m_{H_2O} \, s_{H_2O} \, \Delta T_{H_2O}$$

Since $q_m = q_{H_2O}$ we can make these two equations equal to each other and solve them:

$$mm \; sm \; \Delta Tm = m_{H_2O} \, s_{H_2O} \, \Delta T_{H_2O}$$

$$(5.0 \text{ g})(s_m)(25.2 \text{ °C} - 100 \text{ °C}) = (250 \text{ g})(4.18 \text{ J/g °C})(25.2 \text{ °C} - 25.0 \text{ °C})$$

$$s_m = \frac{209 \text{ J}}{374 \text{ g °C}} = 0.559 \text{ J g °C}$$

In this second type of sample, the enthalpy of a reaction can be determined from the heat of the reaction, which will take place at constant atmospheric pressure.

Sample 2: In this problem, 50.0 mL of 0.100 M AgNO$_3$ and 50.0 mL of 0.100 M HCl are mixed together. The solid silver chloride will form according to the reaction shown below:

$$Ag^+(aq) + Cl^-(aq) \rightarrow AgCl(s)$$

The initial temperature of the solution was 25.0 °C, and the final temperature was 25.8 °C. Determine the enthalpy, in kJ/mol, for the formation of silver chloride. The volume of the final solution was 100 mL, and it had a density of 1.00 g/mL. The specific heat of water is 4.18 J/g °C.

Answer: The temperature change of the solution is determined by the amount of heat lost in the reaction. Using the formula for specific heat, we can determine the heat gained by the solution. The mass of the solution must be calculated from the density:

$$100 \text{ mL} \times \frac{100 \text{ g}}{1 \text{ mL}} = 100 \text{ g}$$

$$q = m \, s \, \Delta T$$

$$q = (100. \text{ g})(4.18 \text{ J/g °C})(25.8 \text{ °C} - 25.0 \text{ °C}) = 334.4 \text{ J}$$

This number represents the amount of heat gained by the water. The problem is asking for the enthalpy in kJ/mol. To convert to this answer, we need to determine the molar quantities of each substance.

$$50 \text{ mL of } 0.100 \text{ M AgNO}_3 = 0.050 \text{ L} \times \frac{0.100 \text{ mol}}{1 \text{ L}} = 5 \times 10^{-3} \text{ mol AgNO}_3$$

$$50 \text{ mL of } 0.100 \text{ M HCl} = 0.050 \text{ L} \times \frac{0.100 \text{ mol}}{1 \text{ L}} = 5 \times 10^{-3} \text{ mol HCl}$$

These two will combine to produce 5×10^{-3} mol AgCl. Therefore, we can convert the heat given in J to kJ/mol using the following procedure:

$$\frac{(334.4 \text{J})(1 \text{kJ} / 1000 \text{J})}{5 \times 10^{-3} \text{ mol AgCl}} = 66.9 \text{ kJ mol}^{-1}$$

Because the formation of silver chloride is exothermic (it caused a temperature increase in the solution), the sign must be changed to negative $q = \Delta H = -66.9$ kJ mol^{-1}

You Try It!

A 2.50 kg piece of copper metal is heated from 25 °C to 225 °C. How much heat, in kJ, is absorbed by the copper? The specific heat of copper is 0.384 J/g °C.

Answer: $q = 192$ kJ

HESS'S LAW

Hess's law is an extremely useful principle that helps us to determine the enthalpies of reaction for nearly any combination of materials. It states that for reactions that occur in different steps, the enthalpy of reaction is equal to the sum of the enthalpies for each step. Hess's law will allow us to calculate the enthalpy of reaction by using information about each reactant. In an example, let's consider the complete combustion of ethanol, C_2H_5OH, which is shown in the equation below:

$$C_2H_5OH(l) + 3O_2(g) \rightarrow 2CO_2(g) + 3H_2O(l)$$

If we want to determine the heat of reaction, where do we even begin? The easiest place is to look at a measurement known as the **standard enthalpy of formation**, $\Delta H°f$. This is based on two different units, the **enthalpy of formation**, ΔHf, which represents the enthalpy change that occurs when a compound is formed from its constituent elements, and the **standard enthalpy of reaction**, $\Delta H°$, which is the enthalpy for a reaction when all reactants and products are in their standard state (the state they exist in at 25 °C and 1 atm). The standard enthalpy of formation is 1 mole of a compound from its constituent elements in their standard states. Enthalpies of formation can be found in many different reference books. Let's take a look at how we can use enthalpies of formation to determine the enthalpy of reaction for the combustion of ethanol.

There are four different substances in the equation: ethanol, oxygen, carbon dioxide, and water. We can use the heats of formation for each of these four substances to determine the heat of reaction for the combustion. An important thing to remember is that the heats of formation represent the energies of formation of a substance. For ethanol, the equation and subsequent heat of formation is

$$2C(graphite) + 3H_2(g) + \tfrac{1}{2}O_2(g) \rightarrow C_2H_5OH(l); \quad \Delta H°f = -277.7 \text{ kJ}$$

In the combustion reaction, however, ethanol is being broken apart, not put together. Earlier in the chapter we learned an easy way around this. All we have to do is turn the reaction around in the other direction and reverse the sign of the enthalpy. Therefore, by switching the direction we obtain the equation:

$$C_2H_5OH(l) \rightarrow 2C(graphite) + 3H_2(g) + \tfrac{1}{2}O_2(g) \quad \Delta H°f = +277.7 \text{ kJ}$$

A second consideration is the other reactant oxygen, O_2. The enthalpy of formation for any element in its most stable state is zero. Therefore, we can disregard any elements in their most stable standard state.

The final consideration is that heats of formation are listed for quantities of one mole. In the balanced equation for this reaction, not all substances are present in quantities of one mole. As a result, the enthalpies of formation will have to be multiplied to account for the differences. Using Hess's law, we can now combine the heats of formation for the three substances into one large equation:

$$C_2H_5OH(l) \rightarrow 2C(s) + 3H_2(g) + O_2(g) \qquad \Delta H_1 = -\Delta H°f[C_2H_5OH(l)]$$
$$+ 2C(s) + 2O_2(g) \rightarrow 2CO_2(g) \qquad \Delta H_2 = 2\Delta H°f[CO_2(g)]$$
$$+ 3H_2(g) + \frac{3}{2}O_2(g) \rightarrow 3H_2O(l) \qquad \Delta H_2 = 3\Delta H°f[H_2O(l)]$$

$$C_2H_5OH(l) + 3O_2(g) \rightarrow 2CO_2(g) + 3H_2O(l) \qquad \Delta H°_{rxn} = \Delta H_1 + \Delta H_2 + \Delta H_3$$

We can substitute the values from a table of standard enthalpies of formation to determine the heat of reaction.

$$\Delta H°_{rxn} = \Delta H_1 + \Delta H_2 + \Delta H_3 =$$

$$-\Delta H°_f[C_2H_5OH(l)] + 2\Delta H°_f[CO_2(g)] + 3\Delta H°_f[H_2O(l)] =$$

$$-(-277.7 \text{ kJ}) + 2(-393.5 \text{ kJ}) + 3(-282.8 \text{ kJ}) = -1358 \text{ kJ}$$

You Try It!

Determine the standard enthalpy of reaction for the combustion of hydrogen sulfide gas, which proceeds according to the reaction shown below:

$$2H_2S(g) + 3O_2(g) \rightarrow 2H_2O(l) + 2SO_2(g)$$

The standard enthalpies for the constituents are as follows:

Formula	$\Delta H°_f$ (kJ/mol)
$H_2S(g)$	−20
$H_2O(l)$	−285.8
$SO_2(g)$	−296.8

Answer: −1125 kJ

The general equation that describes this process is

(Equation 16.5)

$$\Delta H°_{rxn} = n\Delta H°_f(\text{products}) - m\Delta H°_f(\text{reactants})$$

where n and m represent the stoichiometric coefficients from the balanced equation.

SPONTANEITY

In the next portion of the chapter we are going to consider factors that determine the spontaneity of events. In the chemical context, the term spontaneous refers to events that will occur on their own, in a particular direction, and with no additional energy requirement. If a hot piece of metal is placed on a table, the metal will slowly cool off and its surroundings will warm up. When the piece of metal has cooled completely, it will be the same temperature as the surroundings. Reaching this temperature was a spontaneous occurrence, but the piece of metal will not spontaneously get hot again. It can be made to get hot again, but this requires that work be done on it (energy must be added). Chemical reactions can occur spontaneously as well. Previously we looked at the addition of lead (II) nitrate solution to potassium iodide solution. When the two are mixed, the yellow precipitate, lead (II) iodide, forms without anything extra being done to the mixture. The reaction occurs spontaneously. It does not reverse itself and become two clear solutions of potassium iodide and lead (II) nitrate again.

Chemical reactions, like the metathesis reaction that produces lead (II) iodide, can occur spontaneously, just like physical processes. It was once believed that only exothermic processes occurred spontaneously; however, it has been shown that many endothermic reactions can occur spontaneously as well. Another factor that must be considered when determining the spontaneity of a reaction is entropy.

ENTROPY

Entropy describes the randomness or disorder of a system. When a system becomes more disordered, its entropy increases. For example, when water evaporates, it changes from a liquid state, in which the particles are relatively close together and whose motion is somewhat restricted, to a gaseous state, in which the particles are far apart and motion is completely random. The arrangements of the particles have become more random, which means that the entropy has increased. Increases in entropy result in positive entropy values; decreases in entropy result in negative changes. Entropy remains constant, at zero, for some processes that are considered reversible processes. Reversible processes are at equilibrium and do not move spontaneously in any particular direction. An example would be the equilibrium of water at the melting point, 0 °C. At this temperature, water can either freeze and become solid or melt and become liquid. Neither process is favored over the other. The water molecules that join together in the solid state can just as easily fall apart and become liquid again. If this equilibrium mixture is placed in a 25 °C room, the process will spontaneously proceed in the liquid direction, and melting will occur. The process is no longer reversible, and the water will never freeze.

THE SECOND LAW OF THERMODYNAMICS

The **second law of thermodynamics** states that for all spontaneous processes the entropy of the universe will always increase. This is often misunderstood to mean that the entropy of all parts of the system will increase. For example, if a small container of water is placed into a freezer, it will spontaneously freeze. Although the entropy of the water in the container decreased, a number of processes had to occur for that change to take place. The processes that occurred in the freezer that allowed the water to freeze (such as the movement of the compressor, the evaporation and condensation of the refrigerant, and the warming of the air around the container), all combine to produce a net increase in the entropy of the universe.

At the molecular level, entropy is often described in terms of the motion of particles within a system. The motion can involve the entire particle moving about (translational motion), the vibrating of atoms within a molecule (vibrational motion), or the rotation of entire molecules of atoms within a molecule (rotational motion). Increases in motion are associated with higher entropy values. The **third law of thermodynamics** states that the entropy of a pure solid at absolute zero is zero.

There are a few general trends about entropy that you should become familiar with. The AP exam will occasionally ask you to pick, from a list, the substances or reactions that have the highest entropy. The general processes that are associated with increases in entropy include

(a) When a solid melts (more motion is possible)

(b) When a solid dissolves in solution (solute breaks apart and can move about more freely)

(c) When a solid or liquid becomes a gas (more motion)

(d) When a gaseous chemical reaction produces more molecules (more randomly moving particles)

(e) When the temperature of a substance increases (more motion)

Calculating Entropy Changes

Like enthalpy, entropy can't be measured directly. It is possible to measure changes in the enthalpy of a system, which allows you to better understand the entropy of a system under specific conditions. The entropy values for one mole of a substance are known as standard molar entropies, $S°$. The entropy change in a chemical reaction can be calculated using the equation:

$$\Delta S° = n\Delta S°(\text{products}) - m\Delta S°(\text{reactants})$$

Sample: Calculate the entropy change for the reaction shown below (assume that the reaction occurs at 25 °C).

$$2SO_2(g) + O_2(g) \rightarrow 2SO_3(g)$$

The standard molar entropy value for the substances in the reaction are $SO_2(g) = 248.1$ J K^{-1}; $SO_3(g) = 256.7$ J K^{-1}; $O_2(g) = 205.0$ J K^{-1}.

Answer: You need to begin with equation 18.6.

(Equation 16.6)
$$\Delta S° = n\Delta S°(\text{products}) - m\Delta S°(\text{reactants})$$

$$\Delta S°_{rxn} = 2\Delta S°(SO_3) - [2\Delta S°(SO_2) + \Delta S°(O_2)]$$

$$\Delta S°_{rxn} = 2\ (256.7\ \text{J K}^{-1}) - [2(248.1\ \text{J K}^{-1}) + (205.0\ \text{J K}^{-1})]$$

$$\Delta S°_{rxn} = 513.4\ \text{J K}^{-1} - [496.2\ \text{J K}^{-1} + 205.0\ \text{J K}^{-1}]$$

$$\Delta S°_{rxn} = 513.4\ \text{J K}^{-1} - 701.2\ \text{J K}^{-1} = -187.8\ \text{J K}^{-1}$$

The negative value tells you that this is a decrease in entropy, which is predicted because this is a gaseous reaction in which the number of moles of particles decreases from 3 to 2.

You Try It!

Calculate the entropy change, $\Delta S°$, for the reaction shown below:

$$2H_2(g) + O_2(g) \rightarrow H_2O(l)$$

The standard molar entropy values are $H_2(g) = 130.6$ J K^{-1}; $O_2(g) = 205.0$ J K^{-1}; $H_2O(l) = 69.9$ J K^{-1}

Answer: −326.4 J K^{-1}

GIBBS FREE ENERGY

Gibbs free energy, also known as free energy, provides a way to predict the spontaneity of a reaction using a combination of the enthalpy and entropy of a reaction. Free energy is defined as

$$G = H - TS$$

where T is the absolute temperature. If temperature is constant, the free energy change, ΔG, for a reaction is determined by the following equation:

$$\Delta G = \Delta H - T\Delta S$$ (Equation 16.7)

The value of ΔG will tell us if the reaction is spontaneous. There are three possible values for ΔG:

    $\Delta G < 0$ The forward reaction is spontaneous.

    $\Delta G = 0$ The reaction is at equilibrium.

    $\Delta G > 0$ The forward reaction is nonspontaneous, but the reverse reaction is spontaneous.

    Since we already have tables of standard enthalpies and standard entropies, we can substitute these values into the free energy equation and determine the standard free energies of formation for substances. The standard free energies of formation tell you if a substance will form spontaneously if the constituent atoms are combined. The formula to determine the standard free energy change for a reaction is the same as the equation for the enthalpy change (except G's are substituted for the H's):

$$\Delta G° = n\Delta G°_f(\text{products}) - m\Delta G°_f(\text{reactants})$$ (Equation 16.8)

Sample: Calculate the standard free energy change for the complete combustion of methane, CH_4, at 25 °C.

Answer:

$$CH_4(g) + 2O_2(g) \rightarrow CO_2(g) + 2H_2O(l)$$

The standard free energies, $\Delta G°$, for the reactants and products are $CH_4(g)$ = –50.8 kJ mol^{-1} + $2O_2(g)$ = 0 (free energies for all elements in their most stable form are zero) $CO_2(g)$ = –394.4 kJ mol^{-1} $2H_2O(l)$ = –237.2 kJ mol^{-1}

    $\Delta G° = n\Delta G°_f(\text{products}) - m\Delta G°_f(\text{reactants})$

    $\Delta G° = [\Delta G°_f(CO_2) + 2\Delta G°_f(H_2O)] - [\Delta G°_f(CH_4) + 2\Delta G°_f(O_2)]$

    $\Delta G° = [(-394.4\ \text{kJ}) + 2(-237.2\ \text{kJ})] - [(-50.8\ \text{kJ}) + 2(0)]$

    $\Delta G° = (-868.8\ \text{kJ}) - (-50.8\ \text{kJ}) = -818.0\ \text{kJ}$

This reaction is spontaneous.

You Try It!

Calculate $\Delta G°$ for the reaction of aluminum with iron (III) oxide.

$$2Al(s) + Fe_2O_3(s) \rightarrow Al_2O_3(s) + 2Fe(s)$$

The standard free energies, $DG°$, for the reactants and products are: $Al(s)$ = 0; $Fe_2O_3(s)$ = –740.98 kJ mol^{-1}; $Al_2O_3(s)$ = –1576.5 kJ mol^{-1}; $Fe(s)$ = 0

Answer: –835.5 kJ

Once you begin to get a feel for the enthalpy and entropy concepts, you'll probably learn to eyeball a reaction and tell whether or not it will proceed spontaneously. There are some patterns that you can study to help you remember the different possible relationships between enthalpy, entropy, and free energy. You can learn these conceptually or from a mathematical perspective. All of the relationships are based on equation 16.7.

$$\Delta G = \Delta H - T\Delta S$$

There are two conditions that always produce the same result, while two will vary according to temperature. If a reaction is exothermic, the potential energy of the reactants is greater than the potential energy of the products (which means the products are more stable). If entropy is positive, the reaction is creating more disorder. Both of these conditions are favorable, so if a reaction has both a negative enthalpy (exothermic) and a positive entropy (more disordered) it will always be spontaneous (have a negative free energy). The opposite is also true: if a reaction is endothermic (positive enthalpy) and has a negative entropy (becoming more ordered), the free energy will always be positive (the reaction will not be spontaneous).

Both of these ideas can be understood mathematically from equation 16.7. If ΔH is negative and ΔS is positive, the value of ΔG will stay negative (a negative minus a positive becomes more negative). If ΔH is positive and ΔS is negative, ΔG has to be positive (a positive minus a negative becomes more positive).

The other two conditions are dependent on temperature. For example, assume the reaction is exothermic (ΔH will have a negative value). If the expression $T\Delta S$ becomes sufficiently negative, ΔG will have a positive value. In order for the expression to become more negative, ΔS must be negative, and T must be large. So, for the condition where a reaction is exothermic and is becoming more ordered, the reaction will tend to be spontaneous at lower temperatures but nonspontaneous at higher temperatures. For the opposite condition, the opposite is true. If a reaction is endothermic, ΔH will be positive. If $T\Delta S$ is positive and small, the free energy will remain positive (and the reaction nonspontaneous), but as $T\Delta S$ becomes positive and larger, the free energy may become negative (and the reaction spontaneous). These relationships are summarized in Table 16.1.

Table 16.1

ΔH	ΔS	ΔG
−	+	Always negative (spontaneous)
+	−	Always positive (nonspontaneous)
−	−	Negative (spontaneous) at low temperature, but positive (nonspontaneous) at higher temperatures.
+	+	Positive (nonspontaneous) at low temperatures, but negative (spontaneous) at higher temperatures.

Sample: Predict the effect of increasing temperature on the spontaneity of the reaction below:

$$2N_2O_5(g) \rightarrow 4NO_2(g) + O_2(g)$$

Answer: This is a reaction that takes place in the gaseous state. There are 2 moles of gas particles on the left side of the equation and 5 moles of gas particles on the right side. The value of $\Delta S°$ will therefore be positive. As a result, the expression $-T\Delta S$ is negative and becomes increasingly larger as the temperature increases. At higher temperatures, this reaction has a better chance of being spontaneous. If the reaction is exothermic, the reaction will be spontaneous regardless of temperature.

You Try It!

Predict the effect of increasing temperature on the spontaneity of the reaction below:

$$N_2(g) + 3H_2(g) \rightarrow 2NH_3(g)$$

Answer: Because ΔS is negative, the term $-T\Delta S$ is positive. As the temperature increases, $-T\Delta S$ gets more positive making the reaction less spontaneous. If the reaction is endothermic, it will not be spontaneous at any temperatures; if the reaction is exothermic, it can be spontaneous at lower temperatures.

Free Energy at Nonstandard Conditions

When the reaction conditions are not standard, a new expression allows us to calculate the free energy. This equation, 16.9, is shown below:

$$\Delta G = \Delta G° + RT \ln Q \qquad \text{(Equation 16.9)}$$

where R is the ideal gas constant (8.314 J mol^{-1}K^{-1}), T is the absolute temperature, and Q is the reaction quotient (Chapter 12). If you recall, when a reaction is at equilibrium, $Q = K$ (the equilibrium constant) and $\Delta G = 0$. As a result, when a reaction is at equilibrium, equation 16.9 can be changed to:

$$\Delta G° = -RT \ln K \qquad \text{(Equation 16.10)}$$

Summary: Thermodynamics

(a) A system is a term used to describe a discrete region of space that is set off in some way from the surroundings. Open systems can exchange matter and/or energy with the surroundings; closed systems can only exchange energy.

(b) A state function is any property of a system that is only related to its physical state at any particular time. Some examples of state functions are *P, V, T, E, H, S*, and *G*.

(c) The first law of thermodynamics is the same as the law of conservation of energy, which states that matter is neither created nor destroyed in the universe.

(d) The energy of a system is determined by the amount of heat put into or lost from a system and the amount of work either done on or by the system.

(e) Enthalpy is a measure of the heat gained or lost by a system. When no work is done on or by a system, energy and enthalpy are equal.

(f) A thermochemical equation shows a balanced chemical equation and the enthalpy of the reaction.

(g) Endothermic reactions, which require the addition of heat, have a positive enthalpy value.

(h) Exothermic reactions, which give off heat, have a negative enthalpy value.

(i) The heat capacity of an object is the amount of heat needed to raise the temperature by 1 °C. Sometimes the units are described as the energy required to raise the temperature by 1 K. Understand that a difference of 1 Kelvin is the same as a difference of 1 °C.

(j) The specific heat of a substance describes the energy required to raise the temperature of 1 gram of a substance by 1 K (or 1 °C).

(k) A calorimeter is a device that insulates a reaction from the external environment. It can be used to measure heats of reaction.

(l) Hess's law is a useful technique that allows us to determine the heat of reaction for an unknown reaction through manipulation.

(m) Standard units apply to systems that are at standard (normal) conditions. Standard conditions include such conditions as 25 °C (room temperature) and 1 atm (atmospheric pressure at sea level).

(n) Spontaneous events occur on their own without any additional energy requirements than are present in the surroundings.

(o) Entropy is a measure of the disorder of a system. A positive value of entropy, *S*, refers to an increase in entropy, while a negative value of *S* describes a decrease in entropy.

(p) The second law of thermodynamics states that the entropy of the universe is always increasing. Even if a particular system is decreasing in entropy, it can only do so at the expense of the surroundings (which must be increasing in entropy).

(q) Gibbs free energy describes the spontaneity of chemical reactions in terms of enthalpy, entropy, and temperature. Negative values signify a spontaneous reaction, while positive values are nonspontaneous. A free energy of zero denotes equilibrium conditions.

REVIEW QUESTIONS

1. When a system experiences the following two conditions, the ΔE is always negative.

   (A) Absorbs heat and does work

   (B) Absorbs heat and has work done on it

   (C) Releases heat and does work

   (D) Releases heat and has work done on it

   (E) Because energy is always conserved, ΔE is always 0.

2. The specific heat of lead metal, Pb, is 0.127 J g^{-1} °C^{-1}. How many joules of heat would be required to raise the temperature of a 5.00 g sample from 25 °C to 35 °C?

   (A) 2.5×10^{-3}

   (B) 0.127

   (C) 6.4

   (D) 16.1

   (E) 394

$$CH_4(g) + 2O_2(g) \rightarrow CO_2(g) + 2H_2O(g)$$

3. For the complete combustion of methane gas, CH_4, represented above, ΔH is − 802 kJ. What is the value of ΔH if the combustion produced liquid water $H_2O(l)$, rather than water vapor $H_2O(g)$? (ΔH for the phase change $H_2O(g) \rightarrow H_2O(l)$ is −44 kJ mol^{-1}.)

   (A) −714 kJ

   (B) −758 kJ

   (C) −802 kJ

   (D) −846 kJ

   (E) −890 kJ

Substance	$\Delta H°f$ (kJ mol^{-1})
NO(g)	90.37
O_2(g)	0
NO_2(g)	33.84

4. Use the information shown above to determine the standard enthalpy change for the formation of nitrogen dioxide shown in the reaction below

$$2NO(g) + O_2(g) \rightarrow 2NO_2(g)$$

   (A) −113.06

   (B) −56.53

   (C) 56.53

   (D) 90.37

   (E) 124.21

$$C_2H_4(g) + 6F_2(g) \rightarrow 2CF_4(g) + 4HF(g)$$

5. For the equation shown above, which material in the reaction has a $\Delta H°_f = 0$?

   (A) C_2H_4

   (B) F_2

   (C) CF_4

   (D) HF

   (E) None; all substances have nonzero values for $\Delta H°_f$.

6. For which of the following processes would ΔS have a negative value?

   I. $CaCO_3(s) \rightarrow CaO(s) + CO_2(g)$

   II. $H^+(aq) + Cl^-(aq) \rightarrow HCl(s)$

   III. $N_2(g) + 3H_2(g) \rightarrow 2NH_3(g)$

   (A) I only

   (B) II only

   (C) III only

   (D) II and III only

   (E) I, II, and III

7. When solid ammonium nitrate is placed into a flask of room temperature water and swirled, the solid dissolves and the flask gets noticeably colder. What conclusions can you make about the values of ΔH and ΔS for this process?

   (A) ΔH is negative, and ΔS is negative.

   (B) ΔH is negative, and ΔS is positive.

   (C) ΔH is positive, and ΔS is negative.

   (D) ΔH is positive, and ΔS is positive.

   (E) Not enough information is provided to make a valid conclusion.

8. Which of the following reactions involves the largest increase in entropy?

   (A) $AgNO_3(aq) + HCl(aq) \rightarrow AgCl(s) + HNO_3(aq)$

   (B) $N_2(g) + O_2(g) \rightarrow 2NO(g)$

   (C) $2NO(g) + O_2(g) \rightarrow 2NO_2(g)$

   (D) $2KClO_3(s) \rightarrow 2KCl(s) + 3O_2(g)$

   (E) $2SO_2(g) + O_2(g) \rightarrow 2SO_3(g)$

9. A reaction is spontaneous only at high temperatures. The signs of $\Delta H°$ and $\Delta S°$ must be

   (A) $\Delta H° = +$, $\Delta S° = +$

   (B) $\Delta H° = +$, $\Delta S° = -$

   (C) $\Delta H° = -$, $\Delta S° = +$

   (D) $\Delta H° = -$, $\Delta S° = -$

   (E) You can't answer this without knowing the free energy.

Substance	$\Delta S°$ (J mol^{-1} K^{-1})
$N_2(g)$	191.5
$H_2(g)$	130.6
$NH_3(g)$	192.5

10. Based on the information above, what is the $\Delta S°$ for the reaction shown below?

$$N_2(g) + 3H_2(g) \rightarrow 2NH_3(g)$$

(A) -129.6 J K^{-1}

(B) -198.3 J K^{-1}

(C) 192.5 J K^{-1}

(D) 585.3 J K^{-1}

(E) 968.3 J K^{-1}

$$N_2 + O_2 \rightarrow N_2O$$

11. The reaction indicated above is thermodynamically nonspontaneous at 298 K, but becomes spontaneous at higher temperatures. Which of the following is true at 298 K?

	ΔG	ΔH	ΔS
(A)	+	+	+
(B)	−	−	−
(C)	−	−	+
(D)	−	+	−
(E)	+	+	−

12. If the free energy, $\Delta G°$, for a reaction is negative, what must the value of the equilibrium constant, K, be for that reaction?

(A) $K > 1$

(B) $K < 1$

(C) $K = 1$

(D) $K = 0$

(E) K and $\Delta G°$ are not related.

Free Response

Question 1

Acetylene gas, C_2H_2, is used in gas welding procedures and is a very important commercial gas. Use the data below to answer the following questions about the combustion of acetylene gas.

Substance	$\Delta H°_f$ (kJ mol^{-1})	$S°$ (J mol^{-1} K^{-1})
$C_2H_2(g)$	227	200.9
$O_2(g)$	0	205.0
$CO_2(g)$	–393.5	213.7
$H_2O(l)$	–285.8	69.9

Use the data above to answer the questions that follow. Assume all reactions occur at 25 °C.

(A) Write a complete balanced chemical equation for the combustion of acetylene, C_2H_2. Assume that $CO_2(g)$ and $H_2O(l)$ are the only products.

(B) Calculate the standard enthalpy change, $\Delta H°$, for the combustion of acetylene.

(C) Calculate the standard entropy change, $\Delta S°$, for the combustion of acetylene gas.

(D) Determine the value of $\Delta G°$ for the reaction.

(E) If 1 mol of C_2H_2 is burned and all of the evolved heat is used to heat a 6.00 kg of pure water, what will the temperature change of the water be? The specific heat of water is 4.18 J g^{-1} K^{-1}.

Question 2

(A) An ice cube is placed in a flask at room temperature and allowed to sit until the temperature of the water in the flask has reached room temperature. Describe the changes in enthalpy, entropy free energy, and temperature that occur during the time interval.

(B) 40.0 g of sodium hydroxide pellets are added to 500 mL of water, and most of it dissolves very quickly. The temperature of the system increases. Describe the changes in enthalpy, entropy, and free energy during this process.

(C) Commercial instant ice packs are available that contain a mixture of ammonium nitrate and water separated by a barrier. When the ice pack is twisted, the barrier breaks and the two substances mix. The temperature rapidly decreases as the ammonium nitrate dissolves in the water. Describe the changes in enthalpy, entropy, and free energy during this process.

ANSWERS

1. **The correct answer is (C).** ΔE is determined by the sum of the heat and work $(q + w)$. The system loses energy when it releases heat or does work. When the system gains heat or has work done on it, it gains energy. Losses of energy are shown as negative energy values and gains are expressed using positive values. The only way to guarantee the ΔE will be negative is to release heat and do work.

2. **The correct answer is (C).** In this problem you need to use the equation 16.4:

$$q = m \, s \, \Delta T$$

You will need to solve for q by substituting the given information:

$$q = (5.00 \text{ g})(0.127 \text{ J g}{-1} \text{ }^\circ\text{C}^{-1})(35 \text{ }^\circ\text{C} - 25 \text{ }^\circ\text{C}) = 6.4$$

3. **The correct answer is (E).** In this problem the enthalpy of reaction has already been determined. The only step, therefore, is to determine the effect of the additional heat loss of 44 kJ mol^{-1} as the water condenses. For each mole of gaseous water vapor, an additional 44 kJ of heat will be lost. Because the balanced equation shows two moles of water vapor, the total released during condensation is 88 kJ. Therefore, the total heat loss in the reaction will be –802 kJ + (–88 kJ) = –890 kJ.

4. **The correct answer is (A).** This question requires the use of equation 16.5:

$$\Delta H^\circ_{rxn} = n\Delta H^\circ_f(\text{products}) - m\Delta H^\circ_f(\text{reactants})$$
$$\Delta H^\circ_{rxn} = [(2)(33.84 \text{ kJ}] - [(2)(90.37 \text{ kJ}) + 0] = -113.06 \text{ kJ}$$

5. **The correct answer is (B).** All elements in their most stable form have a $\Delta H^\circ_f = 0$

6. **The correct answer is (D).** A negative value for ΔS means that a substance is decreasing in entropy, or becoming more organized. In I, a solid is forming a solid and a gas. The conversion from solid or liquid to gas always increases entropy. In II, ions in solution are much more free to move randomly about than ions packed in a solid crystalline lattice. Therefore II experiences a decrease in entropy. In III, the reaction reduces the number of gas particles, which decreases the entropy. Both II and III decrease the entropy, making it more negative.

7. **The correct answer is (D).** There are two different events that need to be considered here—the enthalpy and entropy. As far as the enthalpy goes, the decrease in temperature indicates an endothermic process (heat is being removed from the surroundings to energize the process). Endothermic processes have positive values for ΔH. The next consideration is the entropy. The solid is dissolving in the water, which means that the dissolved ions have much more freedom or rotation than their crystallized counterparts. Therefore, the dissolving increases the entropy of the ammonium nitrate, making ΔS more positive.

8. **The correct answer is (D).** One of the major things to look for on a question like this is the number of reactants and product particles and their states. The largest entropy changes will be associated with transformations from solids or liquids to gases. In the event that several choices lists gases as reactants and/or products, look for the number of moles of each. An increase in the number of moles of gas increases the entropy, while a decrease in the number of moles signals a decrease in the entropy.

9. **The correct answer is (A).** There are two ways to work this problem. The first is to memorize the different possible combinations of ΔH and ΔS and the corresponding values of ΔG. There is so much material that has to be memorized already that this may not be the best approach. The more efficient approach is to use the equation $\Delta G° = \Delta H° - T\Delta S°$. By substituting various values into the equation, you can determine the sign of $\Delta G°$ (remember, negative indicates spontaneous, while positive is nonspontaneous). At high temperatures, the value of $T\Delta S°$ becomes large enough to make $\Delta G°$ negative.

10. **The correct answer is (B).** To calculate $\Delta S°$, you need to use equation 16.6 and the given values:

$$\Delta S°_{rxn} = n\Delta S°(\text{products}) - m\Delta S°(\text{reactants})$$

$$\Delta S° = [(2)(192.5 \text{ J K}^{-1})] - [(1)(191.5 \text{ J K}^{-1}) + (3)(130.6 \text{ J K}^{-1})] = -198.3 \text{ J K}^{-1}$$

11. **The correct answer is (A).** This is just a variation of question 9. The reaction has a positive enthalpy and entropy at all temperatures (just like question 9). What will vary according to the temperature is the free energy. Because the problem tells you that the reaction is nonspontaneous at 298, it has to have a positive value (since a negative free energy indicates a spontaneous reaction).

12. **The correct answer is (A).** There are two ways to do this one. One solution is more mathematical and involves the use of equation 18.10, $\Delta G = -RT \ln K$. ΔG can only be negative if $\ln K$ is a positive value. Any value less than 1 produces a negative natural logarithm, and a value of 1 produces a natural log of 0. Therefore, only when $K > 1$ can you have a negative ΔG. The other way to solve this is to use the conceptual idea that a spontaneous reaction will favor the products. Therefore, K is greater than 1 for a spontaneous reaction.

Free Response

Question 1

(A) $2C_2H_2(g) + 5O_2(g) \rightarrow 4CO_2(g) + 2H_2O(l)$

(B) 2600 kJ. You need to use equation 16.5 to solve part (B). To simplify things, we will solve the equation for the combustion of 1 mole of acetylene. This can be accomplished using the balanced equation:

$$C_2H_2(g) + \frac{5}{2}O_2(g) \rightarrow 2CO_2(g) + H_2O(l)$$

$$\Delta H°_{rxn} = n\Delta H°_f(\text{products}) - m\Delta H°_f(\text{reactants})$$

$$\Delta H° = [(2)(-393.5 \text{ kJ}) + (1)(-285.8 \text{ kJ})] - [(1)(227 \text{ kJ}) + 0] = (-1072.8 \text{ kJ}) - (227 \text{ kJ}) = -1300 \text{ kJ}$$

Because this is determined for 1 mole of acetylene, this can also be written 1300 kJ mol^{-1}.

(C) To calculate the standard entropy change, use equation 18.6:

$$\Delta S°_{rxn} = n\Delta S°(\text{products}) - m\Delta S°(\text{reactants})$$

$$\Delta S° = \Delta H° =$$
$$[(2)(213.7 \text{ J K}^{-1}) + (1)(69.9 \text{ J K}^{-1})] - [(1)(200.9 \text{ J K}^{-1}) + (5/2)(205.0 \text{ J K}^{-1})] = (497.3 \text{ J K}^{-1}) - (713.8 \text{ J K}^{-1}) = -216 \text{ J K}^{-1}$$

You have to remember that elements have zero values for ΔH and ΔG, but not for ΔS.

(D) To solve for $\Delta G°$, you need to use equation 16.7:

$$\Delta G = \Delta H - T\Delta S$$

$$\Delta G = -1300 \text{ kJ} - (298 \text{ K})(-216 \text{ J K}^{-1})(1 \text{ kJ} / 10^3 \text{ J}) = -1300 \text{ kJ} + 64.4 \text{ kJ} = -1236 \text{ kJ}$$

From the answer, you know that the reaction is not spontaneous at room temperature. Some logic will help you to validate this: Most gases require that you add energy (e.g., a spark, a match) before they will react with oxygen.

(E) This is a specific heat problem. The first thing that you need to do is determine the amount of heat that will be generated from the combustion of 1 mol of C_2H_2. Because no heat is lost in the heating of the water, you can assume that the heat lost by the acetylene will be equal to the heat gained by the water. This heat will be used to determine the temperature increase of the water.

$$\Delta H = (1 \text{ mol } C_2H_2)(-1300 \text{ kJ mol}^{-1}) = -1300 \text{ kJ}$$

This amount of heat will be the heat, q, used in equation 16.4. However, because the heat lost by the acetylene will equal the heat gained by the water, the value of q will need to be changed to positive in equation 16.4:

$$q = m s \Delta T$$

$$1.30 \times 10^6 \text{ J} = (6000 \text{ g H}_2\text{O})(4.18 \text{ J g}^{-1} \text{ K}^{-1}) \Delta T$$

$\Delta T = 51.8 \text{ K} = 51.8 °C$ (since a change of 1 K = 1 °C, ΔT will produce the same value for K or °C).

Question 2

(A) The ice cube will not melt unless heat is added. Therefore, ΔH is positive, denoting an endothermic process. Liquid water has more freedom of movement and therefore will possess a greater entropy, so ΔS will be positive. This process occurs spontaneously, so ΔG must be negative. The temperature increases during this transformation.

(B) The amounts are really meaningless in this problem. The key pieces of information are the words dissolved and that the temperature increases. Because the temperature of the system increases, the dissolving must be an exothermic process, meaning that $\Delta H < 0$. The sodium hydroxide dissolves in solution, meaning that the crystalline lattice breaks apart into solvated ions. This is a much less orderly formation, which means the entropy has increased. Therefore, $\Delta S > 0$ in this process. Because the dissolving occurs spontaneously, ΔG must be negative.

(C) Because the temperature decreases, the process is endothermic. Therefore, $\Delta H > 0$. The ammonium nitrate dissolves in the water so the entropy increases ($\Delta S > 0$). The process occurs spontaneously, which means that ΔG must be negative.

Chapter

Electrochemistry

You had a brief introduction to the topic of electrochemistry in Chapter 10 when you reviewed the oxidation-reduction process in which reactions occur by the transfer of electrons. One of the procedures you looked at was the half-reaction method of balancing redox equations. In this chapter, we will be looking at the oxidation and reduction process in even more depth.

REVIEW OF OXIDATION AND REDUCTION

Oxidation and reduction reactions, also known as redox reactions, involve the transfer of electrons from one substance that is being oxidized (losing electrons) to another that is being reduced (gaining electrons). A very common example of a redox reaction, one that you may very well have done in the lab, is the reaction that occurs when you place clean, iron nails into a copper sulfate solution. In this reaction, shown below, iron is oxidized and copper is reduced:

$$Fe(s) + Cu^{2+}(aq) \rightarrow Cu(s) + Fe^{2+}(aq)$$

Two electrons are removed from iron by the copper ion. The iron, now an ion, moves into the solution, while copper, now a solid, forms on the surface of the nail. This process can be summarized using redox half-reactions (Chapter 10), such as the one shown here:

Oxidation: $Fe \rightarrow Fe^{2+} + 2e^-$

Reduction: $Cu^{2+} + 2e^- \rightarrow Cu$

The half-reaction shows the transfer of the electrons that occurs in the reaction.

VOLTAIC CELLS

A **voltaic cell** (also known as a *galvanic cell*) is a device that allows for the transfer of electrons (in a redox reaction) to be completed in a separate pathway from the reaction mixtures. In a voltaic cell, the two half-reactions are physically separated from each other by placing them into two separate reaction vessels. The electrons are transferred from one vessel to the other by a connecting wire (see Figure 17.1). In voltaic cells, the reactions in each vessel must be spontaneous. In figure 17.1, in the reaction on the left, a zinc strip is placed in a zinc sulfate solution, where zinc from the strip replaces zinc in solution ($Zn \rightarrow Zn^{2+} + 2e^-$). In the reaction vessel on the left, the zinc

ROAD MAP

- *Review of Oxidation and Reduction*
- *Voltaic Cells*
- *The Relationship between emf and Free Energy*
- *The Nernst Equation*
- *Electrolysis*
- *Faraday's Laws*

strip will lose mass over time. Electrons create an electric potential difference across the wire, which is also known as a voltage. The voltage across the wire will allow electrons to be forced from the zinc strip, across the wire, to the copper strip. However, an electric current cannot be established until the circuit is completed.

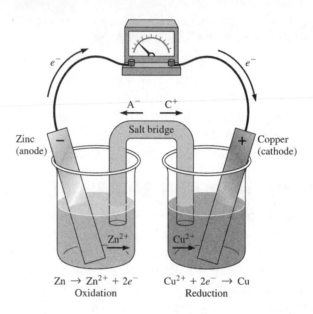

Figure 17.1

The circuit can be completed in a couple of difference ways, but in Figure 17.1, the circuit is completed by the use of a **salt bridge**. The salt bridge is an inverted U-tube into which a gel that contains a dissolved salt is placed. The gel is needed so the salt solution won't run into the reaction vessels. In Figure 17.1, the anion in the salt bridge is labeled as "A⁻" and the cation as "C⁺". The salt bridge allows ions to pass from one vessel to the other so that the reaction can proceed. The positive ions (Zn^{2+}, Cu^{2+}, and C^+) move toward the copper strip, while the negative ions (SO_4^{2-}, A^-) move toward the zinc strip.

The force that allows a current to travel through wire is **voltage**. An electrical current can flow when there is a difference in electrical potential (voltage) from one location to another (this is created by a potential energy whose origins are electrostatic forces between charged particles). There is a fairly good analogy that can help you understand the idea of electric potential and the flow of electrons. If you were to turn on a water spigot on which a closed-up garden hose had been placed, the hose would fill up, but no water would flow. At this point, there is a water pressure that has built up inside the hose, but because there is nowhere for the water to exit, the pressure stays built up in the hose. The pressure at one end of the hose is no different from the pressure at the other end of the hose, and as a result, nothing happens. If you unplug the end of the garden hose, suddenly there is a difference in pressure between the ends. This difference allows the water to flow from the end where the pressure is highest to the end where it is lowest. Electrons will move from an area of high electrical potential (voltage) to an area of low electrical potential. Moving electrons allow current to flow.

Another important part of the water analogy is that the water that initially comes out of the hose is not the water that is coming out of the spigot. Instead, it is water that is being pushed out of the end of the hose by the pressure exerted by the water at the spigot-end of the hose. In a similar fashion, the electrons that are entering the copper strip are not the electrons that were leaving the zinc strip. The electrons in the zinc strip create a "pressure" (voltage) that forces electrons in the wire to move onto the copper strip.

It is easy to think that the electrons that are being created in the zinc vessel are the same electrons that are reducing copper in the copper vessel, but this is not the case. The electrons in the zinc vessel are helping to create the voltage that will allow electrons in the wire and/or copper strip to reduce the copper ions. Another concept that may seem strange to you is the idea of current. Current is actually said to move in the direction opposite the flow of electrons. The current in this circuit is actually moving from the copper vessel to the zinc vessel. On the AP Chemistry exam, you do not need to know any of these details. What you are accountable for is understanding the basic workings of a voltaic cell, what voltage is, and the nature of the reactions that are occurring on the vessels. The more complicated ideas of current and movements of electrons are more thoroughly discussed in physics classes.

There are several terms you should be familiar with for voltaic cells. First, the voltage that is impressed across the circuit (that is, the difference in electrical potential between the zinc strip and the copper strip) is known as the **cell voltage**, which is also occasionally called the *cell potential* or the *electromotive force*, EMF. The copper electrode, because it becomes negatively charged and attracts cations, is known as the **cathode**. The zinc electrode becomes positively charged and is known as the **anode**. You are expected to know which part of the reaction takes place at the cathode and which place takes place at the anode. These can sometimes be difficult to remember, so a simple mnemonic device can help you distinguish between the two. *O*xidation occurs at the *A*node (note how each term starts with a vowel), and *R*eduction occurs at the *C*athode (note how each term starts with a consonant).

To summarize voltaic cells, let's review the components that create the cell. First, you need two half-cells, each of which contains an electrode immersed in an electrolytic solution (typically containing the cation of the metal in the electrode). A spontaneous reaction must occur between the electrode and the solution. A wire connects the two electrodes and will allow the external flow of electrons from the anode to the cathode. In figure 17.1, a voltmeter is shown as part of the circuit between the two electrodes. This is not a necessary part of the circuit—it is simply there to measure the voltage across the circuit. The salt bridge completes the electric circuit and allows the flow of cations and anions between the two half-reactions. Sometimes a porous disc is used in place of a salt bridge. The driving force for the current is the difference in potential energies between the two half-cells.

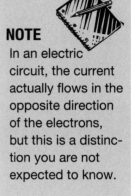

NOTE
In an electric circuit, the current actually flows in the opposite direction of the electrons, but this is a distinction you are not expected to know.

Cell Potentials and the Reduction Potential

The voltage (or electrical potential) across the circuit is described as the **cell voltage** and defined by the symbol E_{cell}. When the half-cells contain 1 M solutions at 25 °C and 1 atm pressure, the cell voltage is called the **standard cell voltage** or *standard emf* and is labeled as $E°_{cell}$. The cell voltage is determined by the difference between the two electrode potentials. The cell voltage is determined according to equation 17.1 below:

(Equation 17.1)

$$E°_{cell} = E°_{ox} + E°_{red}$$

The subscript "ox" is short for oxidation potential, which is the ability of the anode to produce electrons (through the oxidation half-reaction), and the subscript "red" is short for reduction potential, which is the ability of the reduction half-reaction to gain electrons at the cathode.

You have probably worked with tables of standard reduction potentials before. These tables provide the reduction potentials of various substances. It describes an oxidized species's ability to gain electrons in a reduction half-reaction (like copper in the voltaic cell example). According to this definition, we can use a value from the table to represent the $E°_{red}$ in the expression above, but how do you find the $E°_{ox}$?

Very conveniently, the oxidation potential is the reverse of the reduction potential. For example, consider the oxidation of zinc in our previous example:

$$Zn \rightarrow Zn^{2+} + 2e^-$$

In its reduction, the zinc ion will need to gain 2 electrons, making the reduction of zinc exactly opposite the oxidation:

$$Zn^{2+} + 2e^- \rightarrow Zn$$

Because oxidation is simply the opposite of reduction, it is only necessary to create a table of one of the values. By convention, the reduction potential is used in tables, and the values are typically given for the standard reduction potential, $E°$, also written $E°_{red}$, in units of volts, V. Because oxidation takes place at the anode, this is the value that will need to be reversed (since oxidation potential = –reduction potential). Therefore, we can rearrange equation 17.1 so we can use values from the reduction potential tables:

(Equation 17.2)

$$E_{cell} = E_{cathode} - E_{anode}$$

From a conceptual perspective, the size of the reduction potential helps to illustrate a substance's tendency to be reduced. A large (more positive) value for the reduction potential indicates that a species will be more easily reduced (the oxidized species will gain electrons). The more positive the value, the more likely the substance will gain electrons. If you remember back, this means that the substance will have to take those electrons from another substance. Therefore, the more likely a substance is to gain electrons, the more likely it is to take them from another substance. The term to describe a substance that removes the electrons from another (oxidizes it) is an **oxidizing agent**.

Large negative values indicate that the substance is more easily oxidized (will lose electrons). Because this oxidation will require another substance to be reduced, the oxidized substance is known as a **reducing agent**. The substances with the most negative reduction potentials are the best reducing agents. Lithium is the most easily oxidized substance (and therefore the best reducing agent), and fluorine is the most difficult substance to oxidize (and as a result is the best oxidizing agent). This is consistent with what you learned about the electronegativity and ionization energy values for these substances (Chapters 3 and 5).

Sample: Which is the better oxidizing agent, $Cl_2(aq)$ or $Fe^{3+}(aq)$? Which is the best reducing agent, $Al(s)$ or $Cu(s)$?

Answer: The best oxidizing agent will be the substance that is the easiest to reduce (has the most positive reduction potential). To determine the reduction potential of these two species, you need to locate the half-reaction that shows each as the reactant. Chapter 1 has a table of standard reduction potentials that you can use for this question. The values for Cl_2 and Fe^{3+} are

$$Cl_2(g) + 2e^- \rightarrow 2Cl^- \qquad 1.36 \text{ V}$$

$$Fe^{3+}(aq) + e^- \qquad 0.77 \text{ V}$$

Since Cl_2 has the largest (most positive) value, it is the best oxidizing agent.

On the second question, the best reducing agent is the substance that is most easily oxidized (thereby reducing the other substance it comes into contact with). Therefore, the best reducing agents will have the most negative reduction potentials. If we consult the table, we find that:

$$Al^{3+}(aq) + 3e^- \rightarrow Al \qquad -1.66 \text{ V}$$

$$Cu^{2+}(aq) + 2e^- \rightarrow Cu \qquad 0.34 \text{ V}$$

Cu^{2+} was chosen because it is the most common form of copper ion in solution. Regardless of which copper had been chosen, however, aluminum is clearly more negative and therefore a better reducing agent.

You Try It!
A. Between $Zn^{2+}(aq)$ and $Pb^{2+}(aq)$, which is the best oxidizing agent?
B. Between $Ag(s)$ and $Au(s)$, which is the best reducing agent?

Answers: A. $Pb^{2+}(aq)$ B. $Ag(s)$

Sample: A voltaic cell is created with two half cells. In the first half cell, a copper electrode is placed in a $1.0 M$ $Cu(NO_3)_2$ solution. In the second half cell, a tin electrode is placed in a solution of $1.0 M$ $Sn(NO_3)_2$. A salt bridge is placed between the two half cells to complete the circuit. Assume tin is the anode. Calculate the cell voltage of the voltaic cell.

Answer: To solve this, we need to use equation 17.2, along with the reduction potentials of the two materials.

$$E_{cell} = E_{cathode} - E_{anode}$$

We are told that tin is the anode, so we can set up the equation so that:

$$E_{cell} = E_{Cu} - E_{Sn}$$

Looking up the reduction potentials, we determine that:

$$Cu^{2+}(aq) + 2e^- \rightarrow Cu \qquad 0.34 \text{ V}$$

$$Sn^{2+}(aq) + 2e^- \rightarrow Sn \qquad -0.14 \text{ V}$$

Substituting these values into equation 17.2, we determine that:

$$E_{cell} = 0.34 - (-0.14) = 0.48 \text{ V}$$

Summary of Voltaic Cells

The difference between the cathode and anode represents the difference in potential energies. Because oxidation occurs at the anode and reduction occurs at the cathode, the substance in the cell that is highest (most positive) on the chart of reduction potentials will be the cathode. That's how you can determine the anode and cathode if you are not given that information.

If a voltaic cell is to run spontaneously, the reduction potential at the cathode must be higher (more positive) than the reduction potential at the anode. This will allow the reaction at the anode to proceed as an oxidation (rather than a reduction). The greater the difference in potentials between the cathode and anode, the greater the cell voltage. E or $E°$ will be positive for spontaneous processes and negative for nonspontaneous ones.

You Try It!

In a voltaic cell, a zinc electrode is placed in a solution that is $1.0\,M$ for Zn^{2+}, while a copper electrode is placed in a $1.0\,M\,Cu^{2+}$ solution. Calculate the cell potential for the voltaic cell. (Assume a salt bridge is in place.)

Answer: 1.10 V

The Activity Series of Metals

If you recall, in Chapter 10 we described the activity series for metals. This list helps predict the behavior of metals in chemical reactions (particularly replacement reactions). Based upon the activity series of metals, if a material is higher than another on the list, it can replace the metal below it. What that really means is that the metal below it exists as a cation, and the other metal is giving it electrons or reducing it. Therefore, if a metal is a better reducing agent than another, it will replace the other substance (by reducing its cation). Therefore, if we consider placing a magnesium strip in a solution of nickel (II) nitrate, we would expect to the reaction to proceed as:

$$Mg(s) + Ni(NO_3)_2(aq) \rightarrow Mg(NO_3)_2(aq) + Ni(s)$$

Or, more simply put:

$$Mg(s) + Ni^{2+}(aq) \rightarrow Mg^{2+}(aq) + Ni(s)$$

If you wanted to determine the standard emf for this reaction, it will be calculated as:

$$E_{cell} = E_{cathode} - E_{anode} = E^{\circ}_{Ni} - E^{\circ}_{Mg} = -0.25V - (-2.37V) = 2.12 \text{ V}$$

THE RELATIONSHIP BETWEEN emf AND FREE ENERGY

In Chapter 16, we showed the relationship between free energy and the spontaneity of a reaction. If you recall, a negative value for ΔG indicated a spontaneous reaction. In the last section, we saw that a positive cell voltage, or emf, indicates a spontaneous process. The free energy and emf can be related in equation 17.3, which states

$$\Delta G = -nFE$$

(Equation 17.3)

(where n is the number of moles of electrons transferred and F is Faraday's constant, 96, 500 J V^{-1} $mol^{-1}e^{-}$).

Because n and F are both positive, a positive cell emf (spontaneous reaction) will produce a negative ΔG (spontaneous reaction). On the AP exam, the symbol for Faraday's constant is written as $\mathcal{F}$.

Sample: Calculate the standard free-energy change for the reaction shown below:

$$Zn(s) + 2Ag^{+}(aq) \rightarrow Zn^{2+}(aq) + 2Ag(s)$$

Answer: To solve the problem we need to know the values for n and E. Let's begin by looking at E. Zinc is the anode in this reaction, and silver is the cathode. You can tell this in two ways: the first is that the reduction potential for silver is more positive than zinc, and second because silver is being reduced in the reaction. Knowing this, we can use equation 19.2 to determine E.

$$E_{cell} = E_{cathode} - E_{anode} = E^{\circ}_{Ag} - E^{\circ}_{Zn} = 0.80V - (-0.76V) = 1.56V$$

We already know that this will occur spontaneously because of the positive value for E. In the reaction, two electrons are transferred from Zn to $2Ag^{+}$, which is evident from the half reactions shown below:

$$Zn(s) \rightarrow Zn^{2+}(aq) + 2e^{-}(s)$$

$$2Ag^{+}(aq) + 2e^{-} \rightarrow 2Ag(s)$$

Because the value of n is 2, we are ready to substitute our data into equation 17.3:

$$\Delta G = -nFE$$

$\Delta G = -(2)(1.56V)(96,500 \text{ J } V^{-1} mol^{-1}e^{-}) = -3.01\times10^{5}$ J. Because free energies are given in kJ mol^{-1}, we can convert out answer to kilojoules:

$$-3.01 \times 10^{5} \text{ J} = -301 \text{ kJ}$$

You Try It!
Calculate the standard free-energy change for the reaction shown below:

$Cu^{2+}(aq) + Fe(s) \rightarrow Cu(s) + Fe^{2+}(aq)$

Answer: –151 kJ

THE NERNST EQUATION

In the examples used so far, we have only considered cases where the concentration of the solutions in each half-cell was 1.0 M. However, the concentration of the reactants and products in the half-cells does affect the emf. We just finished showing how free energy and emf are related. In the last chapter, we saw how the concentrations of reactants and products affect the free energy in equation 16.9:

$$\Delta G = \Delta G^\circ + RT \ln Q$$

By combining this equation with equation 17.3, $\Delta G = -nFE$, we come up with a new expression,

$$-nFE = (-nFE)^\circ + RT \ln Q$$

If this equation is rearranged to solve for E, it becomes the Nernst equation,

(Equation 17.4)
$$E = E^\circ - \frac{RT}{nF} \ln Q$$

This expression can also be written using the base 10 logarithm as opposed to the natural logarithm. In this form, the equation reads

(Equation 17.5)
$$E = E^\circ - \frac{2.303RT}{nF} \log Q$$

Because R and F are constants, the expression can be simplified if the reaction takes place at standard temperature (remember, you have to use the absolute temperature in this expression, so standard temperature is 298 K). The simplification is shown below:

$$\frac{2.303RT}{nF} = \frac{2.303(8.31 \text{ J mol}^{-1} \text{ K}^{-1})(298 \text{ K})}{n(96,500 \text{ J V}^{-1} \text{ mol}^{-1} e^-)} = \frac{0.0592}{n}$$

If this is substituted into equation 19.5, at standard temperature, the equation becomes

(Equation 17.6)
$$E = E^\circ - \frac{0.0592}{n} \log Q *$$

In the **You Try It!** from the voltaic cells section, you looked at the reaction below:

$$Zn(s) + Cu^{2+}(aq) \rightarrow Zn^{2+}(aq) + Cu(s)$$

(where each solution began at 1.0 M concentration).

---

* If you actually try to perform the calculation shown, you will obtain 0.0591/n, rather than 0.0592/n. The actual value is obtained using the non-rounded values for each number (2.303)(8.314)(298.15)/ (96485) = 0.0592

In that problem, the emf was calculated at 1.10 V. Let's use the Nernst equation to determine what would happen if we used a concentration of 0.1 M Cu^{2+} solution instead of 1.0 M.

To start with, the reaction quotient, Q, will only contain the concentrations of the ions, since the neutral atoms are both in the solid state. Therefore, Q will be:

$$Q = \frac{\left[Zn^{2+}\right]}{\left[Cu^{2+}\right]} = \frac{1.0M}{0.10M}$$

Substituting this into the simplified Nernst equation, equation 19.6, we obtain

$$E = E° - \frac{0.0592}{n}\log Q = 1.10\ V - \frac{0.0592\ V}{2}\log\left(\frac{1.0M}{0.10M}\right)$$

$$E = 1.10\ V - [(0.0296\ V)(1)] = 1.07\ V$$

ELECTROLYSIS

So far, we've focused our attention on voltaic cells, which rely on spontaneous chemical reactions to drive them. In this section, we will look more closely at a different type of cell—one that requires electrical energy from an external source to allow a nonspontaneous reaction to occur. This new type of reaction is known as electrolysis, and it takes place in an electrolytic cell.

An electrolytic cell is similar to a voltaic cell, but there are some slight differences. One of the first differences is the source of electrons. In the voltaic cell, the source of the electrons is the spontaneous oxidation that occurs at the anode. Because no spontaneous reactions occur in an electrolytic cell, the source of electrons is a dc (direct current) power supply. The power supply forces electrons to the cathode rather than the potential of the half-reactions. The cathode in an electrolytic cell acquires a negative charge (which is opposite from a voltaic cell) because electrons are being forced onto it, while the anode takes on a positive charge (which is opposite from a voltaic cell) because electrons are being removed from it by the power supply.

The electrodes in an electrolytic cell are placed in a container with either a solution or a molten salt. The important feature is that there are ions available to interact at the electrodes. Even though the signs on the electrodes are reversed, the same process occurs at each. Oxidation still occurs at the anode as the anion in the cell is attracted to it and will lose its electron(s) there. For example, in a cell containing molten sodium chloride, the Cl^- ions will be attracted to the anion and be oxidized at the electrode. The neutral chlorine atoms will react to form chlorine gas, which bubbles out of the cell. The sodium ions will be attracted to the cathode, where they will be reduced. As the electrons are added to the sodium ions, the sodium will begin to "plate out" on the electrode. That is, the metal begins to form on the electrode. In this particular example, an aqueous solution of sodium chloride would not form sodium and chlorine because the water would be attracted to the electrodes before the two ions.

Because the reaction in an electrolytic cell is nonspontaneous, a certain amount of voltage must be applied across the circuit to cause the reaction to occur. The minimum voltage required to force the reaction is determined using equation 17.2. For example, if an electrolytic cell contains molten $MgCl_2$, we can determine the minimum emf for the cell. To begin, we need the half-reactions and reduction potentials of each substance.

$$\text{Cathode:} \quad Mg^{2+}(l) + 2e^- \rightarrow Mg(s) \quad E^\circ_{red} = -2.37$$

$$\text{Anode:} \quad 2Cl^-(l) \rightarrow Cl_2(g) + 2e^- \quad E^\circ_{red} = 1.36$$

These values are then used to determine the minimum emf:

$$E_{cell} = E_{cathode} - E_{anode} = E^\circ_{Mg} - E^\circ_{Cl} = -2.37 \text{ V} - 1.36 \text{ V} = -3.73 \text{ V}$$

You Try It!

What is the minimum emf required for the electrolytic cell containing molten KCl?

Answer: -4.28 V

Special Considerations for Aqueous Solutions

In the last section, we looked at an electrolytic cell containing molten NaCl. Very high temperatures are needed to melt sodium chloride, so you might ask, "Why can't we just dissolve it in water and do the same thing?" Before answering that question, you may wish to consider a procedure that you may have seen demonstrated for you (or even performed) in an introductory class—the electrolysis of water. Water can also be separated into hydrogen and oxygen gas at the electrodes of an electrolytic cell. The question must now be reconsidered: If you dissolve salt in water and place it in an electrolytic cell, which of the following will collect at the electrodes: sodium and chlorine or hydrogen and oxygen?

The first step to answering this question is to determine from which electrode the hydrogen and oxygen will be liberated. The cathode will attract the hydrogen ions (which are positively charge), while oxygen is created at the anode. The next consideration must be which substance will react at each electrode.

At the cathode, two different reactions are possible:

$$2H_2O(l) + 2e^- \rightarrow H_2(g) + 2OH^-(aq) \quad E^\circ_{red} = -0.83 \text{ V}$$

$$Na^+(aq) + e^- \rightarrow Na(s) \quad E^\circ_{red} = -2.71 \text{ V}$$

Earlier, we said that the more positive the reduction potential, the more likely the reduction would be. Since the first value is more positive, hydrogen gas, H_2, is more likely to be produced at the cathode. Now let's take a look at the anode to see which is more likely to be oxidized there.

$$2Cl^-(aq) \rightarrow Cl_2(g) + 2e^- \qquad E°_{red} = 1.36 \text{ V}$$

$$2H_2O(l) \rightarrow 4H^+(aq) + O_2(g) + 4e^- \qquad E°_{red} = 1.23 \text{ V}$$

The oxidation of water is slightly favored at the anode, but the values are quite close to each other. If any extra voltage is applied, it is likely that chlorine gas will form at the anode. The difference between sodium and hydrogen, however, is so large that sodium will not be produced. The only way to produce the pure sodium is in an electrolytic cell with molten sodium chloride (or some other similar salt).

You Try It!

If aqueous $MgCl_2$ is placed in an electrolytic cell, what will the products be?

Answer: Cathode: $H_2(g)$; Anode: $O_2(g)$, or $Cl_2(g)$

Purification of Metals by Electrolysis

In the section on voltaic cells, we saw that the anode lost mass over time (as the metals were oxidized and went into solution), while the cathode gained mass over time (as the cations were reduced and plated on the surface. The voltaic cell, however, requires spontaneous reactions in each half-cell, which limits the types of electrodes that can be used. In an electrolytic cell, because we are adding electric current to the cathode and the anode, we can force nonspontaneous reactions to occur. In some cases, this allows us to use electrolysis for purposes other than separating a molten compound or aqueous solution. One of the more common alternate uses is the purification of different metals.

When electrolysis is used to purify a metal, like copper the electrolytic cell is set up with a pure cathode and an impure anode. When current is applied to the cell, the impure anode will begin to break apart as: a) copper ions are oxidized and enter solution, b) other reactive ions are oxidized and enter solution, or c) other nonreactive ions simply fall off the decomposing anode to the bottom of the reaction vessel. The copper ions will plate out on the pure copper cathode, thus creating a larger, pure copper cathode.

A similar technique is used to perform "electroplating." This technique allows a thin coat of metal to be plated on the surface of another to improve appearance, resist corrosion, or, in the case of jewelry, save money on precious metals. In this technique, the metal to be plated is made a cathode in an electrolytic cell with a molten metal or metallic salts.

FARADAY'S LAWS

In the 1830s, Michael Faraday determined what are now known as Faraday's laws. They have been revised to be consistent with modern atomic theory (which was in its infancy in his day). Faraday's laws are as follows:

1. If the same quantity of electricity is passed through a cell, it will always lead to the same amount of chemical change for a given reaction. The weight of an element that is deposited or liberated at an electrode is proportional to the amount of electricity that is passed through.

2. 96,500 coulombs of electricity are required to deposit or liberate 1 mole of a substance that gains or loses 1 electron during the cell reaction. For every n electrons involved in a reaction, 96,500 n coulombs of electricity are required to liberate a mole of product.

The quantity 96,500 coulombs (96,485 is the number actually used, but the AP exam and many texts round it to 96,500) was introduced earlier in the chapter as Faraday's constant, where its units were given as J V^{-1} $mol^{-1}e^-$. The origins of this unit may help you understand it more clearly. In Faraday's laws, he uses an amount required to deposit or liberate one mole of a substance that gains or loses one electron during the reaction. That is equivalent to saying 1 mole of electrons are deposited or liberated. Robert Millikan later determined that the charge of a single electron is $1.60217733 \times 10^{-19}$ coulombs (coulomb is the SI unit of charge). It was also later learned that one mole of anything is 6.0221367×10^{23} particles. If you release one mole of electrons, that would be 6.0221367×10^{23} electrons. If the charge on each electron is $1.60217733 \times 10^{-19}$ coulombs, then the total amount of charge belonging to 1 mole of electrons is $(6.0221367 \times 10^{23})(1.60217733 \times 10^{-19}$ C$) = 96,485$ coulombs. Therefore, part two of Faraday's law says that 96, 500 coulombs /mole of electrons. Because a volt is defined as one Joule per Coulomb, the expression 1 C = 1 J V^{-1} is substituted into Faraday's constant for Coulombs. Therefore, 96,500 is not some magic number—it's just the charge of one mole of electrons! To make things easier, this quantity of charge is often referred to as a single unit, the Faraday, $\mathcal{F}$. 1 Faraday of charge = 96,500 coulombs.

Quantitative Treatment of Faraday's Laws

A fairly common type of question on the AP exam will ask you to determine how much metal can be collected on the cathode (plated out) for a certain amount of charge added. This is a direct application of Faraday's laws, and we'll examine this type of problem in this section.

The conceptual treatment of this topic is rather simple. In the previous sections, we looked at the number of electrons that are required to complete an electrolytic process. This was accomplished through the stoichiometry of the half-reactions. For instance, in the half-reaction

$$Cu^{2+}(l) + 2e^- \rightarrow Cu(s)$$

you can see that for each mole of copper ions that is reduced at the cathode, two moles of electrons are required. That means 2 faradays of charge are required to complete this process. If we were talking about a substance like sodium, only one faraday would be required:

$$Na^+(l) + e^- \rightarrow Na(s)$$

That's all there is to it. Problems are made more difficult by giving you information such as lengths of time or fractions of faradays or by asking for quantities in grams instead of moles. Each of these permutations just adds another layer of conversion into the problem, but you should always keep in mind Faraday's laws as a means of doing a quick check on your work.

One of the first things you need to know is the relationship between current and electrical charge. Electric current is a measurement of the rate of charge flow. It measures the amount of charge that passes a given point in a given amount of time. The SI unit of current is the **ampere**, abbreviated **A**, and is commonly shortened to the word *amp*. One ampere is described by the flow of one coulomb of charge per second. The formula for current is seen in equation 17.7:

$$I = \frac{q}{t}$$

(Equation 17.7)

(where I is the symbol for current, and q is the symbol for charge).

If units are substituted into the expression, the formula becomes:

$$\text{Amperes} = \frac{\text{Coulombs}}{\text{second}} \text{ or } A = \frac{C}{s}$$

This equation can be rearranged as necessary. We can demonstrate how these ideas are used in a sample problem.

Sample: 10.0 amperes of current is passed through an electrolytic cell filled with molten lithium chloride, LiCl, for 500 s. How many grams of lithium are collected at the cathode?

Answer: Remember, for every 9.65×10^4 coulombs of charge, one mole of electrons can be used to reduce lithium at the cathode. Because the lithium ion only needs one electron, we will only need 9.65×10^4 coulombs per mole of lithium. We just need to figure out how many coulombs of charge have are applied. This will tell us what fraction of a mole we can reduce, which we can easily convert to grams. This process can be summarized into four basic steps:

1. Determine the amount of charge, in coulombs, that pass through the cell.

2. Using Faraday's constant, determine the number of moles of electrons that is equivalent to 5000C.

3. Using a half-reaction, determine the number of moles of the substance that can be reduced by the moles of electrons from number 2.

4. Convert the moles of the substance to grams.

Using our steps, we can begin to solve the problem:

1. Determine the amount of charge, in coulombs, that pass through the cell.

   In this problem, you are told that 10 amperes pass through in 500 s. This is a total of 5000 C. This can be shown mathematically using equation 17.7:

$$q = It$$

$$q = (10 \text{ A})(500 \text{ s}) = 5000 \text{ C}$$

2. Using Faraday's constant, determine the number of moles of electrons that is equivalent to 5000 C.

$$5000 \text{ C} \times \frac{1 \text{ mol } e^-}{9.65 \times 10^4 \, C} = 0.051813 \text{ mol } e^-$$

   (extra digits to minimize rounding errors)

3. Using a half-reaction, determine the number of moles of the substance that can be reduced by 0.051813 moles of electrons.

$$Li^+(l) + e^- \rightarrow Li(s)$$

$$0.051813 \text{ mol } e^- \times \frac{1 \text{ mol Li}}{1 \text{ mol } e^-} = 0.051813 \text{ mol Li ions can be reduced.}$$

4. Convert 0.051813 moles to grams of lithium.

$$0.051813 \text{ mol Li} \times \frac{6.941 \text{ g Li}}{1 \text{ mol Li}} = 0.360 \text{ g Li}$$

You Try It!
If 3.0 A of current is passed through an electrolytic cell containing a concentrated $CuSO_4$ solution for 2.0 hours, how many grams of copper metal can be collected at the cathode?

Answer: 7.11 g Cu
A similar variation requires that you determine how long it will take to plate out a certain quantity of a substance. The process is very similar, except that it is worked in reverse. We'll examine this type of problem in the next sample.

Sample: 2.65 g of silver are collected at the cathode in an electrolytic cell filled with aqueous silver nitrate. How long did it take to collect this much silver if a constant current of 0.25 A was applied?

Answer: The procedure is very similar to the previous problem. In this problem, you already know how many grams of silver were collected. By working backwards, you can determine how many moles of silver this is. From the half-reaction, you can determine how many moles of electrons would have been required to reduce the silver at the cathode. Faraday's constant can be used to convert the number of moles of electrons to coulombs, amps, or seconds.

The first step is to determine the number of moles in 2.65 g of silver:

$$2.65 \text{ g Ag} \times \frac{1 \text{ mol Ag}}{107.87 \text{ g Ag}} = 0.02457 \text{ mol Ag}$$

We can use the half-reaction to determine the number of electrons required to reduce 0.02457 mol Ag.

$$Ag^+(aq) + e^- \rightarrow Ag(s)$$

$$0.02457 \text{ mol Ag} \times \frac{1 \text{ mol } e^{-1}}{1 \text{ mol Ag}} = 0.02457 \text{ mol } e^-$$

Next, we use Faraday's constant to convert the moles of electrons to coulombs:

$$0.02457 \text{ mol } e^- \times \frac{9.65 \times 10^4 \text{ C}}{1 \text{ mol } e^{-1}} = 2371.0 \text{ C}$$

In this step, we will use equation 17.7 to determine the time:

$$I = \frac{q}{t} \text{, rearranged to solve for } t \text{ is } t = \frac{q}{I}$$

$$t = \frac{2371.0 \text{ C}}{0.25 \text{ A}} = 9484 \text{ s or } 158 \text{ min}$$

You Try It!

How long does 4.00 A have to be applied to an electrolytic cell containing aqueous silver nitrate to collect 9.5 g of silver at the cathode?

Answer: 2.13 s or 35.5 min

Summary: Electrochemistry

- Half-reactions are a way to show the transfer of electrons that occurs during oxidation-reduction (redox) reactions.

- A voltaic, or galvanic, cell allows the oxidation and reduction of substances to be physically separated. This is accomplished by allowing the electrons to pass from one location to the other by way of an external path (such as a wire). The circuit in a voltaic cell must be completed using a salt bridge or another porous barrier that allows for the transfer of anions between the two half-cells.

- A voltage is created when there is a difference in electrical potential energy between two locations. A voltage allows current to flow from one location to another.

- In a voltaic cell, oxidation takes place at the anode and reduction occurs at the cathode. The anode is positively charged, while the cathode is negatively charged.

- The standard reduction potentials of the two half-cells can be used to determine the cell voltage (also known as cell potential or emf).

- An oxidizing agent is a substance that removes electrons from another substance, while a reducing agent adds electrons. Materials that are good oxidizing agents have the most positive reduction potentials, while good reducing agents have the most negative reduction potentials.

- Voltaic cells can only be created when each half-cell contains a reaction that occurs spontaneously. Because of this, cell voltage and free energy can be related (using equation 17.3).

- The Nernst equation (equation 17.4) can be used to relate the cell potential to the concentration of the solutions in each half-cell.

- Electrolytic cells can be created to separate materials. Unlike the reactions in voltaic cells, the reactions in electrolytic cells are nonspontaneous. In an electrolytic cell, a voltage is applied using a power supply.

- In an electrolytic cell, the anode is positively charged and the cathode is negatively charged.

- When aqueous solutions are placed in electrolytic cells, the collection of the solute at the cathode and anode may be affected by the presence of hydrogen and hydroxide ions in the solution.

- Faraday's laws can be used to determine the amount of a substance that can be collected at an electrode. In addition, Faraday's laws can determine the amount of current that must be supplied to an electrolytic cell.

REVIEW QUESTIONS

1. Which of the following will be the best oxidizing agent?

   (A) Cl_2

   (B) Fe

   (C) Na

   (D) Na^+

   (E) F^-

2. A piece of copper metal is placed into solutions containing each of the following three cations. Which ion will be reduced by the copper metal?

   I. Sn^{2+}

   II. Zn^{2+}

   III. Ag^+

   (A) I only

   (B) II only

   (C) III only

   (D) I and II

   (E) I, II, and III

3. When molten $CaCl_2$ is electrolyzed, the calcium metal collects at the _____ charged electrode, which is called the _____, and the chlorine is given off at the _____ charged electrode, which is known as the _____.

   (A) positively, anode, negatively, cathode

   (B) positively, cathode, negatively, anode

   (C) negatively, anode, positively, cathode

   (D) negatively, cathode, positively, anode

   (E) positively, electrolyte, negatively, emf

4. If 0.500 A of current is applied for 1.50 h to an electrolytic cell containing molten lithium chloride, how many grams of lithium would be deposited on the cathode?

   (A) 0.388 g

   (B) 0.194 g

   (C) 0.097 g

   (D) 0.050 g

   (E) 5.4×10^{-5} g

5. The reduction of 3.00 moles of Ca^{2+} to Ca would require how many coulombs?

   (A) 6.22×10^{-5} C

   (B) 3.22×10^4 C

   (C) 1.61×10^4 C

   (D) 2.90×10^5 C

   (E) 5.79×10^5 C

6. A voltaic cell is created with one half–cell consisting of a copper electrode immersed in 1.0 M $CuSO_4$ solution and the other half cell consisting of a lead electrode immersed in a 1.0 M $Pb(NO_3)_2$ solution. Each half–cell is maintained at 25 °C. What is the cell potential, in volts?

   (A) 0.47 V

   (B) 0.21 V

   (C) –0.21 V

   (D) –0.47 V

   (E) 2.50 V

$$Ag^+(aq) + Fe^{2+}(aq) \rightarrow Ag(s) + Fe^{3+}(aq)$$

7. For the reaction above, what is the equilibrium constant at 25 °C?

   (A) 1.0

   (B) 1.6

   (C) 3.2

   (D) 6.4

   (E) 10.0

8. If a current of 15.0 A is applied to a solution of Cr^{3+} ions, how long will it take to plate out 1.86 g of chromium metal?

   (A) 3.83 minutes

   (B) 5.7 minutes

   (C) 11.5 minutes

   (D) 35.0 minutes

   (E) 690 minutes

9. A voltaic cell is set up with two half-cells. In the first half-cell, a silver electrode is placed in an aqueous solution containing Ag^+ ions. In the second half-cell, a nickel electrode is placed in an aqueous solution containing Ni^{2+} ions. The silver electrode is the _____ and has a _____ charge.

   (A) cathode, positive

   (B) cathode, negative

   (C) anode, positive

   (D) anode, negative

   (E) salt bridge, positive and negative

10. A voltaic cell contains one half-cell with a zinc electrode in a $Zn^{2+}(aq)$ solution and a copper electrode in a $Cu^{2+}(aq)$ solution. At standard condition, $E° = 1.10$ V. Which condition below would cause the cell potential to be greater than 1.10 V?

   (A) 1.0 M $Zn^{2+}(aq)$, 1.0 M $Cu^{2+}(aq)$

   (B) 5.0 M $Zn^{2+}(aq)$, 5.0 M $Cu^{2+}(aq)$

   (C) 5.0 M $Zn^{2+}(aq)$, 1.0 M $Cu^{2+}(aq)$

   (D) 0.5 M $Zn^{2+}(aq)$, 0.5 M $Cu^{2+}(aq)$

   (E) 0.1 M $Zn^{2+}(aq)$, 1.0 M $Cu^{2+}(aq)$

11. What is the standard free energy change ($\Delta G°$) for the reaction shown below?

$$Fe^{3+}(aq) + Ag(s) \rightarrow Fe^{2+}(aq) + Ag^+(aq)$$

(A) −2.5 kJ

(B) 2.9 kJ

(C) 8.7 kJ

(D) 10.0 kJ

(E) 29 kJ

12. An electrolytic cell contains molten $CuBr_2$. What is the minimum voltage that must be applied to begin electrolysis?

(A) 0.17 V

(B) 0.34 V

(C) 0.73 V

(D) 1.07 V

(E) 1.41 V

Free Response

Question 1

A voltaic cell is created using a zinc electrode immersed in a 1.0 M solution of Zn^{2+} ions and a silver electrode immersed in a solution of 1.0 M Ag^+ ions. The two electrodes are connected with a wire, and a salt bridge is placed between the two half-cells. The temperature of the cells is 25 °C.

(A) Write the balanced half-reactions that are occurring at the cathode and the anode.

(B) Calculate the standard cell voltage for the cell.

(C) Calculate $\Delta G°$ for the cell.

(D) How will the voltage be affected if 2.5 g of KCl is added to each half cell? Justify your response.

Question 2

An electrolytic cell contains molten NaCl.

(A) Gas is seen bubbling at one of the electrodes. Is this the cathode or anode? Explain.

(B) If a current of 0.5 A is applied to the cell for 30 minutes, how many grams of sodium metal will be collected?

(C) If the current is raised to 5.0 A, how long will it have to be applied to produced 10.0 g of sodium metal?

(D) If the molten NaCl is replaced by an 1.0 M aqueous sodium chloride solution, how much sodium can be collected if a current of 1.0 A is applied for 1 hour?

ANSWERS

1. **The correct answer is (A).** An oxidizing agent is a substance that oxidizes another substance (by removing electrons). Therefore, it must be a substance that has a strong attraction for electrons. One way to think of this is to consider the most electronegative substance. The fluoride ion has been thrown in as a distracter, but because it is an ion, it already has the noble gas configuration. Chlorine is the most electronegative substance left. Another way to think of this is by looking at the chart of standard reduction potentials. The substances closest to the top are the best reducing agents while those at the bottom are the best oxidizing agents.

2. **The correct answer is (C).** You can answer this by looking at the table of standard reduction potentials. Silver is the only substance that is below copper.

3. **The correct answer is (D).** Molten $CaCl_2$ consists of Ca^{2+} and Cl^- ions. Calcium ions will be attracted to the negatively charged electrode. In an electrolytic cell, the negatively charged electrode that attracts cations is known as the cathode. Anions are attracted to the positive anode.

4. **The correct answer is (B).** You need to use equation 17.7 for this problem. In the equation

$$I = \frac{q}{t}$$

$$0.500 \text{ A} = \frac{q}{(1.50 \text{ h})(60 \text{ min} / \text{h})(60 \text{ s} / \text{min})}$$

$$q = 2700 \text{ C}$$

Using Faraday's laws, we can convert this to moles of electrons:

$$2700 \text{ C} \times \frac{1 \text{ mol } e^{-1}}{9.65 \times 10^4 \text{ C}} = 0.0280 \text{ mol } e^-$$

Because each mole of lithium ions requires 1 mole of electrons,

$$Li^+(l) + e^- \rightarrow Li(s)$$

$$0.0280 \text{ mol } e^- \times \frac{1 \text{ mol Li}}{1 \text{ mol } e^{-1}} = 0.0280 \text{ mol Li}$$

Finally, convert the moles to grams:

$$0.0280 \text{ mol Li} \times \frac{6.941 \text{ g}}{1 \text{ mol Li}} = 0.194 \text{ g}$$

5. **The correct answer is (E).** In this problem, you simply need to determine how many moles of electrons will be needed to accomplish this, and then convert this to coulombs (using Faraday's constant).

Each mole of Ca^{2+} ions requires $2 \, e^-$, as can be seen in the half-reaction:

$$Ca^{2+} + 2e^- \rightarrow Ca$$

Therefore, 3.00 moles of Ca^{2+} will require 6.00 moles of electrons. When this is converted to coulombs, the result yields the following answer:

$$6.00 \text{ mol } e^- \times \frac{9.65 \times 10^4 \text{ C}}{1 \text{ mol } e^{-1}} = 5.79 \; 10^5 \text{ C}$$

6. **The correct answer is (A).** Because each solution is present at 1.0 M concentrations, we can use equation 17.2. First, we need to determine which electrode is the cathode and which is the anode. The substance with the most negative reduction potential will be the anode and the most positive reduction potential will be the cathode. Lead has a reduction potential of –0.13, while copper has a value of 0.34. Therefore, lead will be the anode and copper will be the cathode. By looking at the half-reactions, we see that the anode can supply the cathode with all necessary electrons.

$$\text{Anode: } Pb^{2+}(aq) + 2e^- \rightarrow Pb(s) \qquad E° = -0.13 \text{ V}$$

$$\text{Cathode: } Cu^{2+}(aq) + 2e^- \rightarrow Cu(s) \qquad E° = 0.34 \text{ V}$$

Substituting these values into equation 17.2, we obtain:

$$E_{cell} = E_{cathode} - E_{anode}$$
$$E° = 0.34 \text{ V} - (-0.13 \text{ V}) = 0.47 \text{ V}$$

7. **The correct answer is (C).** When solving problems that require the equilibrium constant, you need to use the Nernst equation:

$$E = E° - \frac{0.0592}{n} \log Q$$

We can rearrange the equation to determine the equilibrium constant (when $Q = K$). Under the new equation:

$$E° = \frac{0.0592 \text{ V}}{n} \log K$$

To solve for K, we will need to know $E°$. We can obtain this from the half-reactions.

In the equation, silver is being reduced and iron is being oxidized. The half-reactions would be set up as follows:

$$\text{Oxidation: } Fe^{2+}(aq) \rightarrow Fe^{3+}(aq) + e^-$$

Because this is an oxidation, we will need to reverse the equation to use the value of the reduction potential:

$$Fe^{3+}(aq) + e^- \rightarrow Fe^{2+}(aq) \qquad E° = 0.77 \text{ V}$$

The oxidation will have a value of –0.77 V

$$\text{Reduction: } Ag^+(aq) + e^- \rightarrow Ag(s) \qquad E° = 0.80$$

$$E°_{cell} = E°_{ox} + E°_{red} = -0.77 \text{ V} + 0.80 \text{ V} = 0.03 \text{ V}$$

This value can be substituted into our equation, along with a value of $n=1$ (because only one mole of electrons is transferred):

$$E° = \frac{0.0592 \text{ V}}{n} \log K$$

$$0.03 \text{ V} = \frac{0.0592 \text{ V}}{1} \log K$$

$$\log K = 0.5068$$

$$K = 10^{0.5068} = 3.21$$

8. **The correct answer is (C).** First, we need to determine how many moles of chromium are in 1.86 g of chromium. Once we know this, we can determine the number of moles of electrons that were required to reduce that number of moles, which will allow us to solve the rest of the problem.

$$1.86 \text{ g Cr} \times \frac{1 \text{ mol Cr}}{52.00 \text{ g Cr}} = 0.035769 \text{ mol (extra digits to avoid error)}$$

The half-reaction tells us that each mole of chromium ions requires 3 electrons:

$$Cr^{3+}(aq) + 3e^- \rightarrow Cr(s)$$

Therefore, we need to use Faraday's constant to determine the amount of charge required to reduce this quantity of chromium ions:

$$0.035769 \text{ mol Cr}^{3+} \text{ ions} \times \left(\frac{3 \text{ mol } e^{-1}}{1 \text{ mol Cr}^{3+}} \right) \left(\frac{9.65 \times 10^4 \text{ C}}{1 \text{ mol } e^{-1}} \right) = 10355.13 \text{ C}$$

To finish the calculation, use equation 17.7 to solve for t:

$$I = \frac{q}{t}$$

$$t = \frac{q}{I} = \frac{10355.13 \text{ C}}{15.0 \text{ A}} = 690.3 \text{ s}$$

Converting to minutes, we find that

$$690.3 \text{ s} \times \frac{1 \text{ min}}{60 \text{ s}} = 11.5 \text{ min}$$

9. **The correct answer is (A).** In a voltaic cell, the substance with the most positive reduction potential will be the cathode. Ag^+ has a value of 0.80 V, and Ni^{2+} has a value of –0.25 V. That would make the silver electrode the cathode. In a voltaic cell, the cathode always has a positive charge.

10. **The correct answer is (E).** By examining equation 17.6, with the variable substituted in,

$$E = E° - \frac{0.0592}{n} \log Q = 1.10 \text{ V} - \frac{0.0592 \text{ V}}{2} \log \frac{\left[Zn^{2+} \right]}{\left[Cu^{2+} \right]}$$

we see that the only way to have a value greater than 1.10 V is if

$$\frac{0.0592 \text{ V}}{2} \log \frac{\left[Zn^{2+} \right]}{\left[Cu^{2+} \right]}$$

produces a negative value. This can only happen when the $[Zn^{2+}]$ is less than the $[Cu^{2+}]$. This is only true for choice (E).

11. **The correct answer is (B).** Equations 17.2 and 17.3 will be needed to solve this problem. First, the value of E must be determined. It can then be used in equation 17.3. The first step, therefore, is to calculate E:

$$E^\circ_{cell} = E^\circ_{ox} + E^\circ_{red}$$

By using the same procedures as in problem 7, we find that

$$E^\circ_{cell} = -E^\circ_{Ag} + E^\circ_{Fe} = -(0.80 \text{ V}) + (0.77 \text{ V}) = -0.03 \text{ V}$$

We can now substitute this value into equation 17.3:

$$\Delta G = -nFE = -(1 \text{ mol } e^-)(96{,}500 \text{ J V}^{-1} \text{ mol}^{-1} e^-)(-0.03 \text{ V}) = 2895 \text{ J}$$

$$\Delta G = 2.9 \text{ kJ}$$

12. **The correct answer is (C).** In an electrolytic cell, the reactions are nonspontaneous and will only occur if a certain amount of voltage is applied. This can be calculated using the equation

$$E_{cell} = E_{cathode} - E_{anode}$$

which for this cell will be

$$E_{cell} = E^\circ_{Cu} - E^\circ_{Br} = 0.34 \text{ V} - (1.07) = -0.73 \text{ V}$$

Therefore, the cell requires 0.73 V to begin electrolysis.

Free Response

Question 1

(A) The cathode and anode can be determined by the reduction potentials of each substance. The substance with the most positive reduction potential will be the cathode. Therefore, in this reaction, Ag is the cathode and Zn is the anode. The half reactions, therefore, will be as follows:

$$\text{Oxidation: } Zn(s) \rightarrow Zn^{2+}(aq) + 2e^-$$

$$\text{Reduction: } 2Ag^+(aq) + 2e^- \rightarrow 2Ag(s)$$

(B) The standard cell voltage for the cell will be

$$E_{cell} = E_{cathode} - E_{anode} = (0.80 \text{ V} - (-0.76)) = 1.56 \text{ V}$$

(C) To solve for ΔG°, we will use equation 17.3:

$$\Delta G = -nFE$$

where n will equal 2 because 2 moles of electrons are needed to reduce the silver:

$$\Delta G = -(2 \text{ mol } e^-)(96{,}500 \text{ J V}^{-1} \text{ mol}^{-1} e^-)(1.56 \text{ V}) = -301 \text{ kJ}$$

(D) In the zinc cell, the addition of KCl will have no effect, but in the silver cell, the addition of KCl will cause the formation of the precipitate AgCl(s). This will decrease the amount of available Ag^+ and therefore decrease the voltage.

Question 2

(A) The bubbling gas must be chlorine gas. Therefore, the reaction that must be occurring at the electrode is

$$2Cl^- \rightarrow Cl_2(g) + 2e^-$$

Since this is an oxidation, it must be the anode. In electrolytic cells, the anode is positively charged and will therefore attract anions.

(B) If 0.5 A is applied for 30 minutes, it means the total charge applied is

$$q = It$$

$$q = (0.5 \text{ A})(30 \text{ min})(60 \text{ s/1 min}) = 900 \text{ C}$$

This value can be used to determine the number of moles of electrons that will be supplied:

$$900 \text{ C} \times \frac{1 \text{ mol } e^{-1}}{9.65 \times 10^4 \text{ C}} = 9.33 \times 10^{-3} \, e^-$$

Because the reduction of each mole of sodium ions requires one mole of electrons, the number of moles of sodium ions will also equal 9.33×10^{-3}. If this is converted to grams, the total amount of sodium equals

$$9.33 \times 10^{-3} \text{ mol Na} \times \frac{22.99 \text{ g Na}}{1 \text{ mol Na}} = 0.214 \text{ g Na}$$

(C) This problem must be solved in the reverse order of (b). The 10.0 g of Na must be converted to moles of electrons, and then to coulombs. The charge can then be used to solve for t.

$$10.0 \text{ g Na} \times \frac{1 \text{ mol Na}}{22.99 \text{ g Na}} = 0.435 \text{ mol Na}$$

Each mole of sodium atoms was generated with one mole of electrons, so the amount of electrons required is also equal to 0.435 e^-.

This can be converted to coulombs using Faraday's constant:

$$0.435 \text{ mol } e^- \times \frac{9.65 \times 10^4 \text{ C}}{1 \text{ mol } e^{-1}} = 41977.5 \text{ C}$$

This value is then used to determine t:

$$t = \frac{q}{I} = \frac{41977.5 \text{ C}}{5.0 \text{ A}} = 8395.5 \text{ s} = 140 \text{ min}$$

(D) In aqueous sodium chloride, sodium is no longer collected at the cathode. Because hydrogen is much more readily reduced than hydrogen, hydrogen gas will collect at the cathode. Therefore, no sodium will be collected.

Organic Chemistry

This topic will be treated differently from the others in the book. The main reason is that the AP exam has almost no questions that deal strictly with the topic. In many of the previous chapters, organic compounds have been discussed among the inorganic compounds (e.g., acid-base equilibria, chemical bonding, intermolecular forces), but no specific knowledge is needed to distinguish the organic compounds from the inorganic compounds. The only topics unique to organic chemistry that are covered on the AP exam are nomenclature and structure. There are usually only one or two multiple-choice questions devoted to this topic, so it is unnecessary to have end-of-chapter questions and practice essays.

The structures and nomenclature of organic chemistry are all based on the carbon and hydrogen skeleton, known as a **hydrocarbon**. Different arrangements of carbon and hydrogen atoms, as well as the addition of other atoms or groups of atoms, allow a wide diversity in the number and types of organic compounds. In this chapter, we will proceed from the most basic hydrocarbons to more complex arrangements.

ALKANES

The **alkanes** are the most basic type of hydrocarbon compound, containing only carbon and hydrogen. All bonds in alkane molecules are single, covalent bonds. Carbon atoms can form four bonds in any combination (i.e., four single bonds, one double bond and two single bonds). Alkanes, also known as saturated hydrocarbons, contain all single bonds. Each carbon atom is bonded to at least one other carbon atom, and the remaining bonds are all single bonds with hydrogen. The smallest alkane is methane, CH_4, which is composed of one carbon atom bonded with single bonds to four hydrogen atoms.

When an alkane contains two or more carbon atoms, the carbon atoms will begin bonding to each other. The resulting structures are known as hydrocarbon chains because of the way the carbon atoms "link" together. There are two types of hydrocarbon chains that can form—**straight-chain** and **branched-chain** hydrocarbons. In a straight chain, the carbon atoms at the end of the molecule are bonded to one carbon and three hydrocarbons (shown as a $-CH_3$ group). The central carbon atoms are bonded to two carbon atoms and two hydrogen atoms ($-CH_2-$). The empirical formula for all alkanes is C_nH_{2n+2}. The names of all alkanes end in *–ane*. Some examples are the ethane molecule, C_2H_6, and propane, C_3H_8. Table 18.1 shows the names of the alkanes with up to 10 carbon atoms.

Table 18.1		
Molecular Formula	**Structural Formula**	**Name**
CH_4	CH_4	Methane
C_2H_6	CH_3CH_3	Ethane
C_3H_8	$CH_3CH_2CH_3$	Propane
C_4H_{10}	$CH_3(CH_2)_2CH_3$	Butane
C_5H_{12}	$CH_3(CH_2)_3CH_3$	Pentane
C_6H_{14}	$CH_3(CH_2)_4CH_3$	Hexane
C_7H_{16}	$CH_3(CH_2)_5CH_3$	Heptane
C_8H_{18}	$CH_3(CH_2)_6CH_3$	Octane
C_9H_{20}	$CH_3(CH_2)_7CH_3$	Nonane
$C_{10}H_{22}$	$CH_3(CH_2)_8CH_3$	Decane

There are several different ways to describe organic compounds. The figure below shows five of the most basic types of formulas, both molecular and structural, that are used to describe organic compounds.

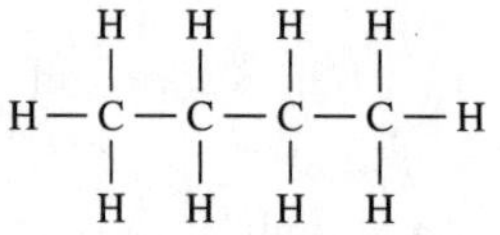

Lewis structure

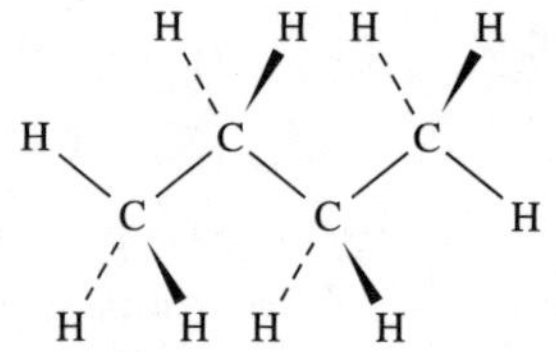

Structural Diagram

Branched-Chain Hydrocarbons

So far, we have just looked at hydrocarbons that are straight chains. There are many compounds where central carbon atoms are bonded to three or four carbon atoms or other non-hydrogen atoms. For branched-chain hydrocarbons, there are special procedures for naming compounds. To start with, we will only consider saturated hydrocarbons. Once you understand some of the basic rules of nomenclature, we can begin to look at unsaturated hydrocarbons and atoms other than carbon and hydrogen.

In branched-chain hydrocarbons, the branches occur when a carbon atom replaces a hydrogen atom bonded to a central carbon atom. If a carbon atom replaces hydrogen on either of the end carbon atoms, the chain simply increases in length by one rather than branching. In this example, the carbon that adds on to the middle of the chain is known as an alkyl group. **Alkyl** groups are alkanes that are missing a hydrogen atom and can therefore bond to another substance. For example, when the molecule methane, CH_4, loses one hydrogen atom, it becomes CH_3-, known as a methyl group. Note, the *–ane* ending of the alkane is replaced with a *–yl* ending in the alkyl group. The methyl group can bond to a carbon in another hydrocarbon chain. Ethane, C_2H_6, becomes an ethyl group when it loses a hydrogen atom.

One difficulty that branches present is the possibility of the formation of **isomers**, molecules that have the same molecular formula but different structures. In figure 18.2, note how the molecules butane and 2-methylpropane have the same molecular formulas but different structures and properties.

$$CH_3CH_2CH_2CH_3$$
n-butane

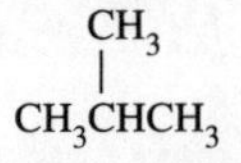

$$\overset{\displaystyle CH_3}{\underset{\displaystyle \,}{\overset{\displaystyle |}{CH_3CHCH_3}}}$$
2-methylpropane

For example, butane has a boiling point of –0.5 °C, while 2-methylpropane's boiling point is –11.7 °C. Only hydrocarbon chains with at least four carbon atoms are capable of forming a branch. Because there must be a way to distinguish isomers, the nomenclature must take these into account. The following are general rules for naming branched-chain alkanes:

- Locate the longest, straight hydrocarbon chain in the molecule. This is the main part of the name of the molecule. The names of any branches will be added onto this. Numbers are assigned to each carbon atom beginning with the carbon atom closest to the substituent.

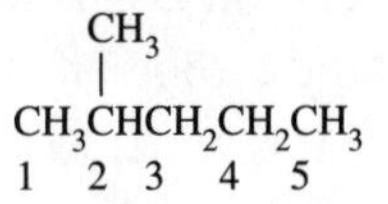

$$\overset{\displaystyle CH_3}{\overset{\displaystyle |}{CH_3CHCH_2CH_2CH_3}}$$
1 2 3 4 5
2-methylpentane
(not 4-methylpentane)

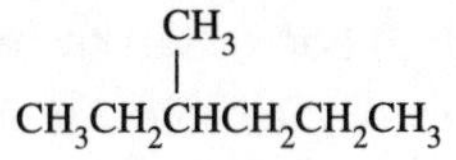

$$\overset{\displaystyle CH_3}{\overset{\displaystyle |}{CH_3CH_2CHCH_2CH_2CH_3}}$$
3-methylhexane
(not 4-methylhexane)

- If more than one group is attached, a Greek prefix is used to designate the number of groups. Each group will still be assigned a number. The numbers should be followed by a hyphen and the name of the molecule.

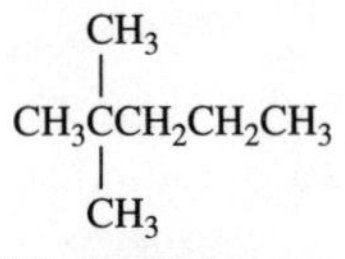

$$\overset{\displaystyle CH_3}{\underset{\displaystyle CH_3}{\overset{\displaystyle |}{\underset{\displaystyle |}{CH_3CCH_2CH_2CH_3}}}}$$
2,2-dimethylpentane
(not 2-dimethylpentane)

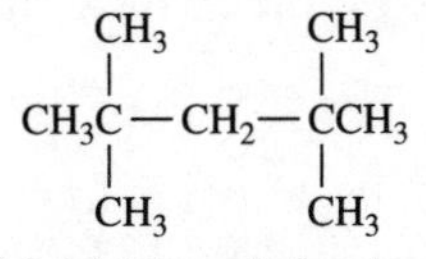

$$\overset{\displaystyle CH_3 \qquad CH_3}{\underset{\displaystyle CH_3 \qquad CH_3}{\overset{\displaystyle | \qquad\quad |}{\underset{\displaystyle | \qquad\quad |}{CH_3C-CH_2-CCH_3}}}}$$
2,2,4,4-tetramethylpentane

• When two or more groups are attached, the longest chain is numbered so that the series of numbers for all groups is lowest. Each number should be separated by a comma, and the last number should be followed by a hyphen.

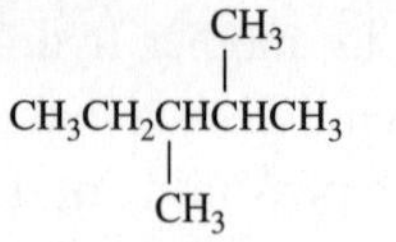

$$CH_3CH_2CHCHCH_3$$
with CH_3 attached above and CH_3 attached below

2,3-dimethylpentane
(not 3,4-dimethylpentane)

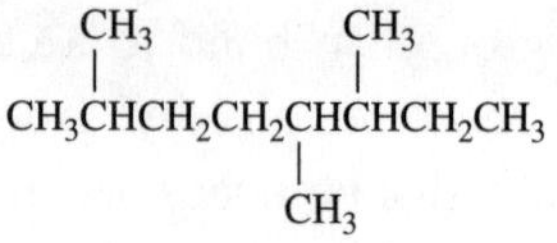

$$CH_3CHCH_2CH_2CHCHCH_2CH_3$$
with CH_3 attached above (two places) and CH_3 attached below

2,5,6-trimethyloctane
(not 3,4,7-trimethyloctane)

• When more than one type of substituent is present, they are listed in alphabetical order, with numbers designating the location of each group.

3-ethyl-2 methylhexane

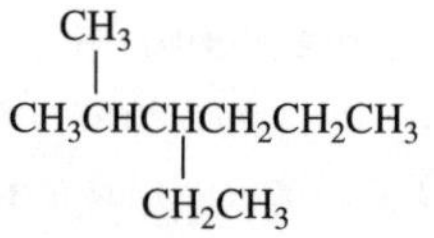

$$CH_3CHCHCH_2CH_2CH_3$$
with CH_3 attached above and CH_2CH_3 attached below

Sample 1: Name the molecule shown below.

$$CH_3CH_2CH_2CHCHCH_3$$
with CH_3 attached above and CH_3 attached below

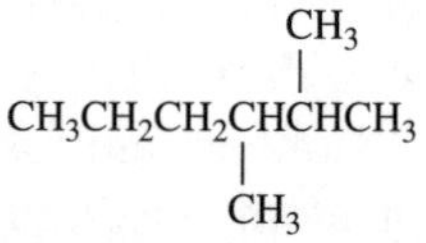

Answer: Step 1: The longest chain is six carbon atoms long, making it a hexane molecule. It could start from either the carbon on the far right or the one above the rest of the molecule. Because it is easier to work in a straight line, we will count from one to six, moving from right to left.

Steps 2 and 3: The two groups are methyl groups and are attached at carbons 2 and 3. The numbers must go from right to left since going from left to right would result in the larger numbers 4 and 5. The prefix *di-* will be used since there are two methyl groups attached. Step 4 is not necessary because the two substituent groups are the same.

The name is 2,3-dimethylhexane.

You Try It!

Name the molecule shown below.

$$CH_3CHCHCHCH_3$$
with CH_3 attached above (middle) and CH_3, CH_3 attached below

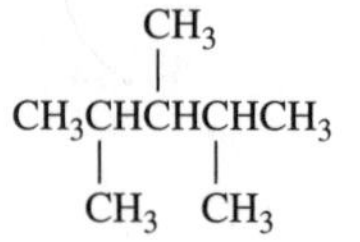

Answer: 2,3,4-trimethylpentane

Sample 2: Draw a structural formula for 2,2,3-trimethylpentane.

Answer: First you need to draw a 5-carbon chain since the molecule is called pentane. Onto the 5-carbon chain, you need to attach 3 methyl groups (you know this from the prefix *tri-*). The locations of each of the three methyl groups are two on carbon 2 and one on carbon 3. The molecule will look like:

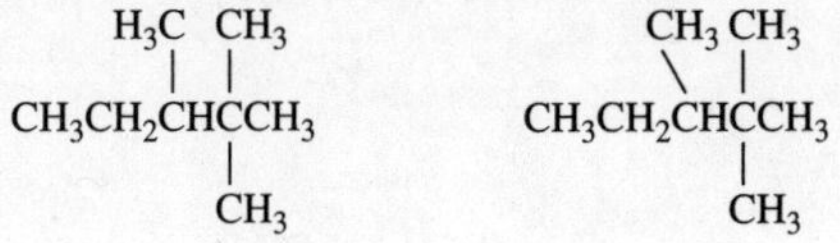

$$
\begin{array}{cc}
\text{H}_3\text{C}\ \ \text{CH}_3 & \text{CH}_3\ \text{CH}_3 \\
|\ \ \ \ | & \ \ \ \diagdown\ \ | \\
\text{CH}_3\text{CH}_2\text{CHCCH}_3 & \text{CH}_3\text{CH}_2\text{CHCCH}_3 \\
|\ \ & |\ \ \\
\text{CH}_3 & \text{CH}_3
\end{array}
$$

You Try It!
Draw a structural formula for 3-ethyl-2-methylpentane.

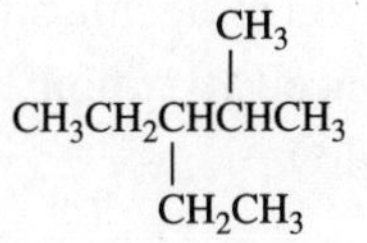

$$
\begin{array}{c}
\text{CH}_3 \\
| \\
\text{CH}_3\text{CH}_2\text{CHCHCH}_3 \\
| \\
\text{CH}_2\text{CH}_3
\end{array}
$$

Cycloalkanes

In addition to branched chains, alkanes can also form rings. The two terminal carbons bond together to complete a ring. The nomenclature is very similar except the prefix *cyclo-* is added before the name of the alkane. For instance, when the two terminal carbon atoms in hexane connect together, a six-sided ring is formed, called **cyclohexane**. A five-sided ring would be called **cyclopentane**. Each of these molecules is shown below:

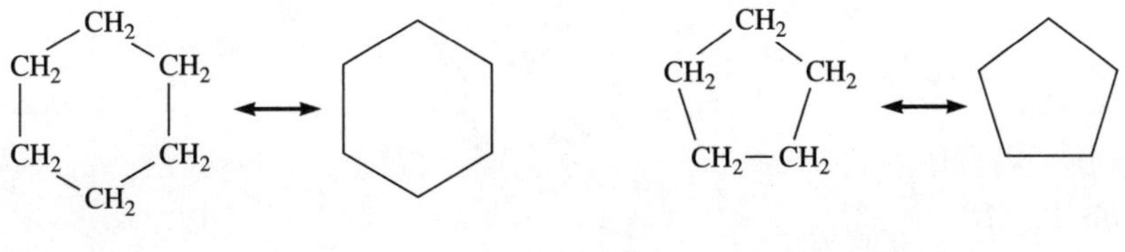

ISOMERS

In the previous section, we mentioned that different molecules, isomers, can have the same molecular formula but have a different structure. Butane, C_4H_{10}, we saw has two isomers—butane (also known as *n*-butane) and 2-methylpropane. As molecules get longer, more and more isomers become possible. In the first sample, we will consider the number of isomers of pentane.

Sample: Determine the number of isomers of pentane, and draw each isomer's structure.

Answer: The number of possible isomers begins to increase dramatically with the addition of more carbon atoms. While C_5 has only three isomers, C_{10} has 75. To answer this question, the first thing we will need to do is draw the straight chain first. The first isomer is the straight chain, called n-pentane, shown below.

n-pentane

$CH_3CH_2CH_2CH_2CH_3$

After that, small groups of atoms should be removed from the end of the molecule and placed at other locations. You should begin by removing a methyl group from the end of the molecule and placing it somewhere in the middle. If a methyl group is placed at carbon 2, the compound now becomes 2-methylbutane, as shown below:

2-methylbutane

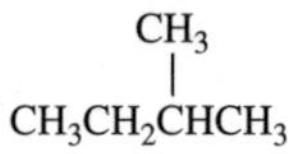

CH_3
|
$CH_3CH_2CHCH_3$

Note, that if you move the methyl group to carbon 3, the carbon atoms would have to be numbered from the opposite end, making it in position 2 again. This would not change its structure. So, the next thing to do is try to bring another methyl group from the other end of the molecule. Doing so produces 2,2-dimethylpropane, the third C_5H_{12} isomer, shown below:

2,2-dimethylpropane

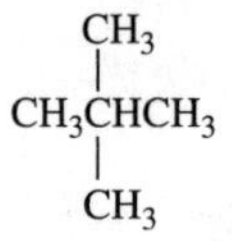

CH_3
|
CH_3CHCH_3
|
CH_3

You Try It!
Draw and name the 5 isomers of C_6H_{14}.

Answer:

$CH_3CH_2CH_2CH_2CH_2CH_3$	$CH_3CH_2CH_2CHCH_3$ | CH_3	$CH_3CH_2CHCH_2CH_3$ | CH_3
n-hexane	2-methylpentane	3-methylpentane

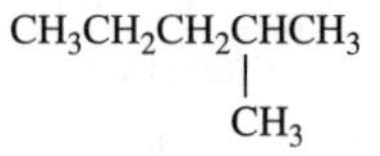

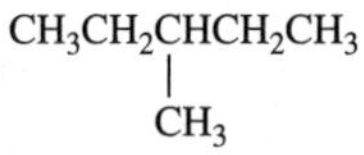

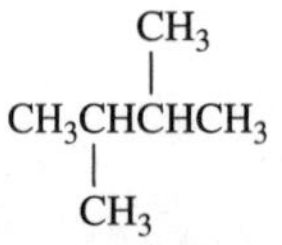

CH_3 | $CH_3CHCHCH_3$ | CH_3	CH_3 | $CH_3CH_2CCH_3$ | CH_3
2,3-dimethylbutane	2,2-dimethylbutane

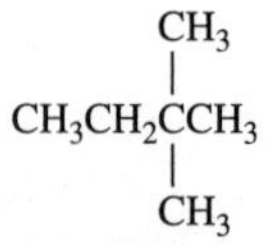

UNSATURATED HYDROCARBONS
Alkenes

Alkenes are hydrocarbons containing at least one double bond. For alkenes with only one double bond, the empirical formula is CnH_2n. The names for all alkenes end with *–ene*. The naming system on alkenes is the same as alkanes, with the exception of the *–ene* ending. For example, the two-carbon alkane, C_2H_6, is called ethane, while the two-carbon alkene, C_2H_4, is called ethene.

For alkenes longer than 3 carbons, the double bond can be in different places in the molecule. Writing a number before the name of the alkene identifies the location of the bond. The number represents the bond number in the molecule, rather than the carbon number. The bond between carbons 1 and 2 is labeled "1," the bond between carbons 2 and 3 is labeled "2," and so on. If more than one double bond is found, a prefix is used to show how many are present and numbers are given to each one. The following figure shows two different possible structures of pentenes:

$$CH_2 = CH - CH_2CH_2CH_3 \qquad CH_2 = CH - CH = CHCH_3$$

1-pentene   1,3-pentadiene

In addition to the locations of the double bonds, another difference of alkenes is the molecule's inability to rotate at the double bond. With alkanes, when substituent groups attach to a carbon, the molecule can rotate around the C-C bonds in response to electron-electron repulsions. Because the double bond in the alkene is composed of both sigma and pi bonds, the molecule can't rotate around the double bond (see Chapter 6). What this means for alkenes is that the molecule can have different structural orientations around the double bond. These different orientations allow a new kind of isomerism, known as **geometrical isomerism**. When the non-hydrogen parts of the molecule are on the same side of the molecule, the term *cis-* is placed in front of the name. When the non-hydrogen parts are placed on opposite sides of the molecule, the term *trans-* is placed in front of the name. In the previous section, you saw that the alkane butane has only two isomers. Because of geometrical isomerism, butene has four isomers, shown below:

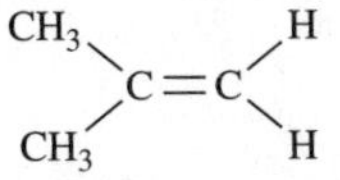

2-methylpropene

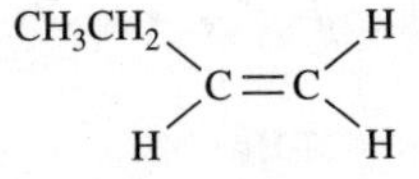

1-butene

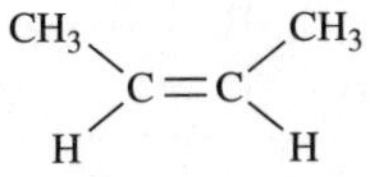

cis-2-butene

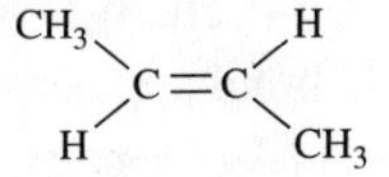

trans-2-butene

Sample: Name the compound shown below.

$$CH_3CH(CH_3)—C(H)=C(CH_3)(H)$$

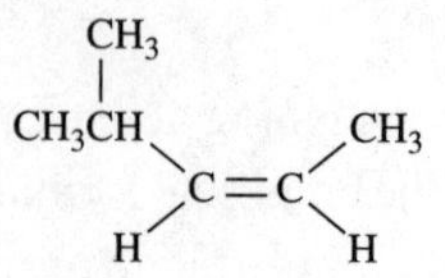

Answer: First, notice that the longest carbon chain is 5 carbons long, making this pentene. In numbering the chain, the numbering should start so that the double bond is given the lowest possible number. In this case, that means numbering right to left, which places the bond at position 2. The next thing to do is identify the substituent group on the chain. A methyl group is located on carbon 4. Finally, the position of the groups along the double bond places the non-hydrogen groups on the same side of the bond, making this a *cis*-configuration. Putting all of this information together, we come up with the term:

cis-4-methyl-2-pentene

You Try It!
Name the molecule shown below.

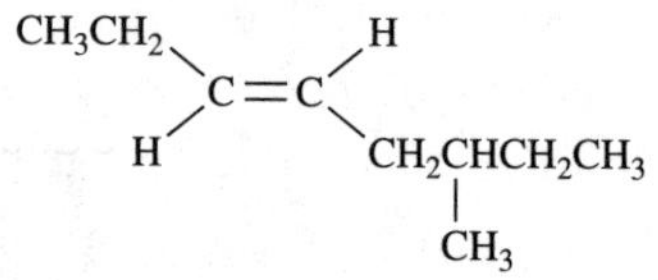

$$CH_3CH_2—C(H)=C(H)—CH_2CHCH_2CH_3 | CH_3$$

Answer: trans-6-methyl-3-octene

Alkynes

Alkynes are hydrocarbons containing at least one triple bond. The empirical formula for alkynes is C_nH_{2n-2}, and the names end in *–yne*. For example, the two carbon alkyne has the formula C_2H_2, and is known as ethyne.

The naming system for alkynes is the same as for alkenes, except that alkynes do not have geometrical isomers. The triple bond only allows a single group to extend off of the carbon atoms attached by a triple bond, so no *cis-* or *trans-* isomers are possible.

Sample: Name the compound shown below.

$$CH_3C≡CCH_3$$

Answer: The longest chain is 4 carbon atoms long, so it will be called butyne. The triple bond appears at position 2 in the molecule, so the name of this compound is 2-butyne.

You Try It!
Name the compound shown below.

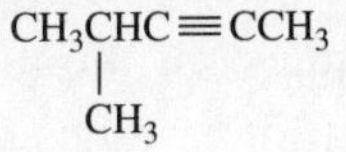

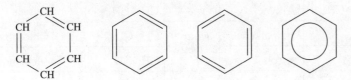

Answer: 4-methyl-2-pentyne

Aromatic Hydrocarbons

Aromatic hydrocarbons are cyclic, planar compounds containing delocalized electrons. The delocalization of the electrons in the pi orbitals makes these very stable structures. The most common aromatic hydrocarbon is C_6H_6, benzene. The structure of benzene is shown below:

There are two important things in the diagrams. First, you see the shorthand notation for hydrocarbon chains, which are bent lines. Each bend represents a C-C-C bond. Each point is understood to represent C-H bonds. In the case of the benzene ring, because there are double bonds present, each point represents a CH grouping (as opposed to a CH_2 group for a hydrocarbon chain with all single bonds). The second important feature is the representation of the resonance structures. Because the electrons in the benzene ring are delocalized, (see resonance in Chapter 6), the figure is usually drawn with a circle in the center, which represents the delocalization of the pi electrons in the benzene ring.

Additions to Alkenes and Alkynes

The double and triple bonds in hydrocarbon chains are very reactive. Halogens readily react with the carbon atoms by forming bonds with the electrons in the pi orbitals of the double (or triple) bond.

FUNCTIONAL GROUPS

There are certain reactive sites in organic compounds known as functional groups. Functional groups are specific combinations of atoms that undergo characteristic reactions regardless of the molecule in which they appear. Because the functional group determines the reactivity of organic molecules, molecules are usually classified according to the functional group they contain. Table 18.2 contains a list of the common functional groups.

Table 18.2

Functional Group	Type of Compound	Suffix/prefix	Sample	Name
$CH_2=CH_2$	Alkene	-ene	$CH_2=CH_2$	Ethene
$CH\equiv CH$	Alkyne	-yne	$CH\equiv CH$	Ethyne
R-X	Haloalkene	Halo-	CH_3-Cl	Chloromethane
R-OH	Alcohol	-ol	CH_3-OH	Methanol
R-O-R´	Ether	Ether	CH_3-O-CH_3	Dimethyl ether
R-COH	Aldehyde	-al	CH_3-COH	Ethanal
R-CO-R´	Ketone	-one	CH_3-CO-CH_3	2-propanone
R-COOH	Carboxylic acid	-oic acid	CH_3CH_2-COOH	Propanoic acid
R-COO-R´	Ester	-oate	CH_3-COO-CH_2CH_3	Ethyl ethanoate
R_3N	Amine	-amine	CH_3-NH_2	Methylamine (methanamine)
R-CO-NR´$_2$	Amide	-amide	CH_3CH_2-CO-NH_2	Propanamide

Alcohols (R-OH)

The polar hydroxyl group (-OH) present in alcohols makes alcohols more soluble in polar solvents than other hydrocarbons and also increases the boiling temperature of these compounds (because of increased hydrogen bonding). The boiling temperatures of alcohols are much higher than the boiling temperatures of the alkanes to which they are attached.

When naming alcohols, the ending of the hydrocarbon is removed and the suffix -ol is used instead. For example, when a hydroxyl group attaches to an ethane molecule, CH_3CH_3, the resulting alcohol, CH_3CH_2OH, is known as ethanol.

Ethers (R-O-R´)

Ethers are formed from condensation reactions (result in the formation of water) between two alcohols. The main function of ethers is their use as solvents. Ethers are named by placing the names of the two R groups (R and

R´) before the word ether. The R groups should be listed in alphabetical order if they are two different groups.

Aldehydes (R-COH)

Aldehydes contain a **carbonyl** group (C=O) to which at least one hydrogen atom is attached. The suffix –al is placed on the end of the name of aldehydes. For example, the molecule CH_3CH_2COH is known as propanal. Aldehydes must have the carbonyl on the last carbon on the chain (in order to have the hydrogen atom attached to the carbon). As a result, there is no need for the use of numbers to distinguish the position of the carbonyl group.

Ketones (R-CO-R´)

Ketones have the carbonyl group attached to an interior carbon atom of an organic compound. The carbonyl group gives the molecular polarity, thus many ketones are used as solvents. In the naming of ketones, you need to replace the ending of the molecule with the suffix –one. A number is used to indicate the position of the carbonyl group in the molecule.

Carboxylic Acids (R-COOH)

The functional group in these organic acids is the carboxyl group (COOH). These weak acids are very common and dissociate in solution to yield a negatively-charged COO^- group and a H^+ ion. The naming system for carboxylic acids is to use name of the molecule but to replace the ending with –oic acid.

Esters (R-COO-R´)

Esters are formed from the condensation reaction of carboxylic acid and an alcohol. In this reaction, the hydrocarbon group left behind when the alcohol lost the OH- group replaces the hydrogen of the carboxylic acid. Esters are usually sweet-smelling substances and are used in soap making. When naming esters, the first thing is to use the name of the group derived from the alcohol followed by the name of the name of the group derived from the acid, ending with –oate.

Amines (R₃N)

Amines are organic bases. In the generic formula, R_3N, the R groups can be hydrocarbon groups or hydrogen atoms. The naming system uses the names of the hydrocarbon groups followed by the term amine, written as a single word.

Amides (RCO-NR´₂)

Amides are formed when amines undergo a condensation reaction with a carboxylic acid. During the process of protein synthesis, this condensation reaction is responsible for the linkages between huge numbers of amino acids (which contain an amine group and a carboxylic acid). When naming amides, the root of the carboxylic acid (minus the –*oic acid*) is attached to the term *amide* to form a single word.

You Try It!

Name each of the following compounds, and identify the functional group in each.

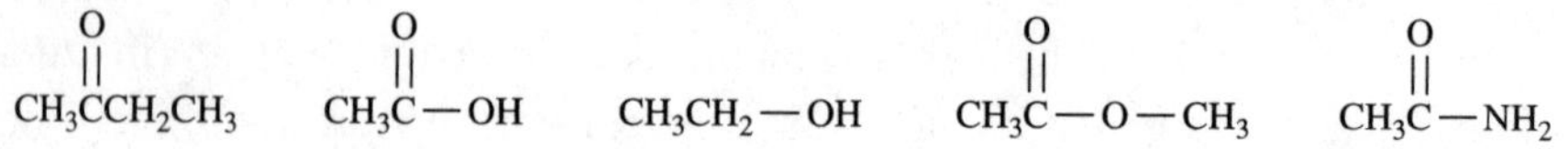

$$\underset{\text{(a)}}{CH_3CCH_2CH_3}\overset{\overset{O}{\|}}{} \qquad \underset{\text{(b)}}{CH_3C-OH}\overset{\overset{O}{\|}}{} \qquad \underset{\text{(c)}}{CH_3CH_2-OH} \qquad \underset{\text{(d)}}{CH_3C-O-CH_3}\overset{\overset{O}{\|}}{} \qquad \underset{\text{(e)}}{CH_3C-NH_2}\overset{\overset{O}{\|}}{}$$

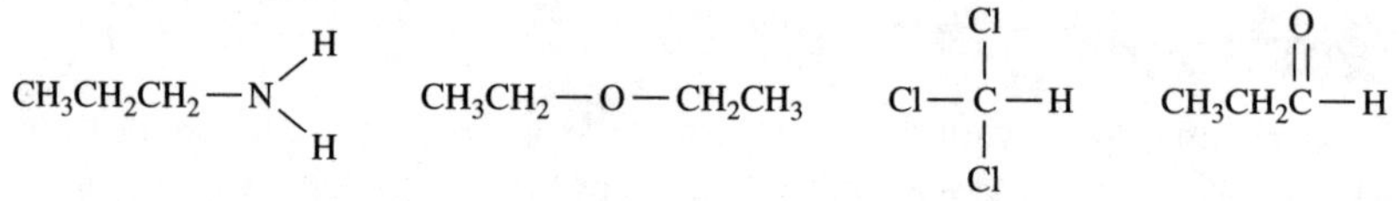

$$\underset{\text{(f)}}{CH_3CH_2CH_2-N\overset{\diagup H}{\diagdown_{H}}} \qquad \underset{\text{(g)}}{CH_3CH_2-O-CH_2CH_3} \qquad \underset{\text{(h)}}{Cl-\overset{\overset{Cl}{|}}{\underset{\underset{Cl}{|}}{C}}-H} \qquad \underset{\text{(i)}}{CH_3CH_2C-H}\overset{\overset{O}{\|}}{}$$

Answers:

    (a) 2-Butanone; ketone

    (b) Ethanoic acid; carboxylic acid

    (c) Ethanol; alcohol

    (d) Methyl ethanoate; ester

    (e) Ethanamide; amide

    (f) Propylamine; amine

    (g) Diethyl ether; ether

    (h) Trichloromethane; haloalkane

    (i) Propanal; aldehyde

Summary: Organic Chemistry

- The basic structural unit for all organic compounds is the hydrocarbon backbone, consisting of a carbon atom bonded to hydrogen atoms.

- A carbon atom can form four bonds, which can be any combination of single, double, or triple bonds.

- Alkanes are hydrocarbon compounds that contain all single bonds. The basic formula for all alkanes is C_nH_{2n+2}.

- Alkanes can be either straight-chain or branched-chain. In straight-chain hydrocarbons, the carbon atoms on the end of the chain bond to only a single carbon atom and carbon atoms in the middle of the chain bond to only two carbon atoms, one on each side. In branched-chain hydrocarbons, the central carbon atoms bond to additional carbon atoms.

- The branched-chain structures allow more than one molecule to have the same molecular formula, while having a different molecular structure. Molecules with these characteristics are known as isomers.

- Hydrocarbons with single carbon-carbon bonds are known as saturated, while those containing double or triple bonds between carbon atoms are known as unsaturated.

- Alkenes are unsaturated hydrocarbons that contain at least one carbon-carbon double bond.

- Alkenes are not free to rotate around the double bond. As a result, alkenes can form isomers based on the types of substituent groups attached to them as well as the orientation of the molecule on either side of the double bond. When isomers form because of these differences in orientation, they are known as geometrical isomers.

- Alkynes contain triple bonds. Although they are also not able to rotate about the triple bond, they don't form geometrical isomers because the molecule has 180° bond angles at either end of the triple bond.

- Aromatic hydrocarbons are cyclic compounds with delocalized electrons. They are very stable structures and are found as either the root or the substituent in many organic compounds.

- Functional groups are special reactive sites that are located within organic compounds that give them characteristic properties. You should be able to recognize and identify each of the functional groups listed in Table 18.2.

Practice Tests

PART
IV

PREVIEW

Practice Test 1

Practice Test 2

Practice Test 1
Answer Sheet

If a section has fewer questions than answer ovals, leave the extra ovals blank.

SECTION I

1. Ⓐ Ⓑ Ⓒ Ⓓ Ⓔ   16. Ⓐ Ⓑ Ⓒ Ⓓ Ⓔ   31. Ⓐ Ⓑ Ⓒ Ⓓ Ⓔ   46. Ⓐ Ⓑ Ⓒ Ⓓ Ⓔ   61. Ⓐ Ⓑ Ⓒ Ⓓ Ⓔ

2. Ⓐ Ⓑ Ⓒ Ⓓ Ⓔ   17. Ⓐ Ⓑ Ⓒ Ⓓ Ⓔ   32. Ⓐ Ⓑ Ⓒ Ⓓ Ⓔ   47. Ⓐ Ⓑ Ⓒ Ⓓ Ⓔ   62. Ⓐ Ⓑ Ⓒ Ⓓ Ⓔ

3. Ⓐ Ⓑ Ⓒ Ⓓ Ⓔ   18. Ⓐ Ⓑ Ⓒ Ⓓ Ⓔ   33. Ⓐ Ⓑ Ⓒ Ⓓ Ⓔ   48. Ⓐ Ⓑ Ⓒ Ⓓ Ⓔ   63. Ⓐ Ⓑ Ⓒ Ⓓ Ⓔ

4. Ⓐ Ⓑ Ⓒ Ⓓ Ⓔ   19. Ⓐ Ⓑ Ⓒ Ⓓ Ⓔ   34. Ⓐ Ⓑ Ⓒ Ⓓ Ⓔ   49. Ⓐ Ⓑ Ⓒ Ⓓ Ⓔ   64. Ⓐ Ⓑ Ⓒ Ⓓ Ⓔ

5. Ⓐ Ⓑ Ⓒ Ⓓ Ⓔ   20. Ⓐ Ⓑ Ⓒ Ⓓ Ⓔ   35. Ⓐ Ⓑ Ⓒ Ⓓ Ⓔ   50. Ⓐ Ⓑ Ⓒ Ⓓ Ⓔ   65. Ⓐ Ⓑ Ⓒ Ⓓ Ⓔ

6. Ⓐ Ⓑ Ⓒ Ⓓ Ⓔ   21. Ⓐ Ⓑ Ⓒ Ⓓ Ⓔ   36. Ⓐ Ⓑ Ⓒ Ⓓ Ⓔ   51. Ⓐ Ⓑ Ⓒ Ⓓ Ⓔ   66. Ⓐ Ⓑ Ⓒ Ⓓ Ⓔ

7. Ⓐ Ⓑ Ⓒ Ⓓ Ⓔ   22. Ⓐ Ⓑ Ⓒ Ⓓ Ⓔ   37. Ⓐ Ⓑ Ⓒ Ⓓ Ⓔ   52. Ⓐ Ⓑ Ⓒ Ⓓ Ⓔ   67. Ⓐ Ⓑ Ⓒ Ⓓ Ⓔ

8. Ⓐ Ⓑ Ⓒ Ⓓ Ⓔ   23. Ⓐ Ⓑ Ⓒ Ⓓ Ⓔ   38. Ⓐ Ⓑ Ⓒ Ⓓ Ⓔ   53. Ⓐ Ⓑ Ⓒ Ⓓ Ⓔ   68. Ⓐ Ⓑ Ⓒ Ⓓ Ⓔ

9. Ⓐ Ⓑ Ⓒ Ⓓ Ⓔ   24. Ⓐ Ⓑ Ⓒ Ⓓ Ⓔ   39. Ⓐ Ⓑ Ⓒ Ⓓ Ⓔ   54. Ⓐ Ⓑ Ⓒ Ⓓ Ⓔ   69. Ⓐ Ⓑ Ⓒ Ⓓ Ⓔ

10. Ⓐ Ⓑ Ⓒ Ⓓ Ⓔ   25. Ⓐ Ⓑ Ⓒ Ⓓ Ⓔ   40. Ⓐ Ⓑ Ⓒ Ⓓ Ⓔ   55. Ⓐ Ⓑ Ⓒ Ⓓ Ⓔ   70. Ⓐ Ⓑ Ⓒ Ⓓ Ⓔ

11. Ⓐ Ⓑ Ⓒ Ⓓ Ⓔ   26. Ⓐ Ⓑ Ⓒ Ⓓ Ⓔ   41. Ⓐ Ⓑ Ⓒ Ⓓ Ⓔ   56. Ⓐ Ⓑ Ⓒ Ⓓ Ⓔ   71. Ⓐ Ⓑ Ⓒ Ⓓ Ⓔ

12. Ⓐ Ⓑ Ⓒ Ⓓ Ⓔ   27. Ⓐ Ⓑ Ⓒ Ⓓ Ⓔ   42. Ⓐ Ⓑ Ⓒ Ⓓ Ⓔ   57. Ⓐ Ⓑ Ⓒ Ⓓ Ⓔ   72. Ⓐ Ⓑ Ⓒ Ⓓ Ⓔ

13. Ⓐ Ⓑ Ⓒ Ⓓ Ⓔ   28. Ⓐ Ⓑ Ⓒ Ⓓ Ⓔ   43. Ⓐ Ⓑ Ⓒ Ⓓ Ⓔ   58. Ⓐ Ⓑ Ⓒ Ⓓ Ⓔ   73. Ⓐ Ⓑ Ⓒ Ⓓ Ⓔ

14. Ⓐ Ⓑ Ⓒ Ⓓ Ⓔ   29. Ⓐ Ⓑ Ⓒ Ⓓ Ⓔ   44. Ⓐ Ⓑ Ⓒ Ⓓ Ⓔ   59. Ⓐ Ⓑ Ⓒ Ⓓ Ⓔ   74. Ⓐ Ⓑ Ⓒ Ⓓ Ⓔ

15. Ⓐ Ⓑ Ⓒ Ⓓ Ⓔ   30. Ⓐ Ⓑ Ⓒ Ⓓ Ⓔ   45. Ⓐ Ⓑ Ⓒ Ⓓ Ⓔ   60. Ⓐ Ⓑ Ⓒ Ⓓ Ⓔ   75. Ⓐ Ⓑ Ⓒ Ⓓ Ⓔ

Practice Test 1

SECTION I

Time—1 Hour and 30 Minutes

NO CALCULATORS MAY BE USED WITH SECTION I.

Note: For all questions, assume that the temperature is 298 K, the pressure is 1.00 atmosphere, and solutions are aqueous unless otherwise specified.

Throughout the test, the following symbols have the definitions specified unless otherwise noted.

T = temperature	M = molar
P = pressure	m = molal
V = volume	L, mL = liter(s), milliliter(s)
S = entropy	g = gram(s)
H = enthalpy	nm = nanometer(s)
G = free energy	atm = atmosphere(s)
R = molar gas constant	J, kJ = joule(s), kilojoule(s)
n = number of moles	v = volt(s)
	mol = mole(s)

Directions: Each set of lettered choices below refers to the numbered statements immediately following it. Select the one lettered choice that best fits each statement and then fill in the corresponding oval on the answer sheet. A choice may be used once, more than once, or not at all in each set.

Questions 1–4 refer to the orbital diagrams shown below:

(A) [↑↓] [↑↑] [↑][ ][ ]

(B) [↑↓] [↑↓] [↑↓][ ][ ]

(C) [↑↓] [↑↓] [↑↓][↑↓][↑↓]

(D) [ ] [ ] [↑][ ][ ]

(E) [↑↓] [↑↓] [↑][ ][ ]

1. Represents a nonreactive atom

2. Represents a violation of the Pauli Exclusion Principle

3. Represents a violation of Hund's Rule

4. Represents an atom in an excited state

Use these answers for questions 5–8.

(A) Hydrogen bonding

(B) Resonance (delocalization)

(C) Ionic bonding

(D) Hybridized orbitals

(E) Dispersion forces

5. Explains why methane has a boiling point of -161 °C and octane has a boiling point of 125.6 °C

6. Explains why benzene, which mathematically should have three double bonds and three single bonds, actually has 6 bonds of identical length

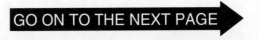

GO ON TO THE NEXT PAGE

7. Is used to explain the fact that the four bonds in methane are equivalent

8. Explains why the boiling point of helium is −269 °C and the boiling point for xenon is −108 °C

Questions 9–11 refer to the phase diagram of a pure substance, shown below.

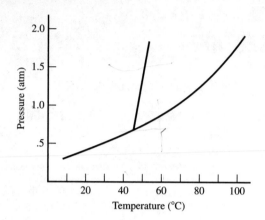

(A) Freezing

(B) Melting

(C) Sublimation

(D) Condensation

(E) Vaporization

9. If the temperature increases from 40 °C to 60 °C at a pressure of 1.5 atm, which process is occurring?

10. If the temperature increases from 20 °C to 60 °C at a pressure of 0.5 atm, which process is occurring?

11. If the pressure increases from 0.5 atm to 1.0 atm at 60 °C, which process is occurring?

Directions: Each of the questions or incomplete statements below is followed by five answers or completions. Select the one that is best in each case and then fill in the corresponding oval on the answer sheet.

12. Which of the following is the safest and most effective procedure to treat a base spill onto skin?

   (A) Dry the affected area with paper towels.

   (B) Flush the area with a dilute solution of HCl.

   (C) Flush the affected area with water and then with a dilute NaOH solution.

   (D) Flush the affected area with water and then with a dilute $NaHCO_3$ solution.

   (E) Flush the affected area with water and then with a dilute vinegar solution.

13. Which of the following has an optical isomer?

   (A) CH_3
        |
   $CH_3—C—OH$
        |
        CH_3

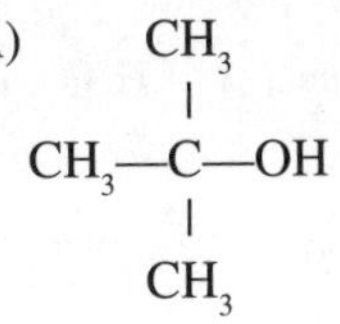

   (B) Br
        |
   $CH_3—CH_2—C—CH_3$
        |
        CH_3

   (C) CH_2
                    ‖
   $CH_3CH_2CH_2—C—OH$

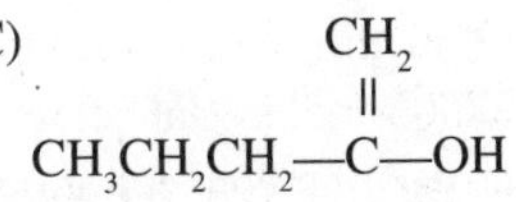

   (D) NH_2
              |
   $CH_3CH_2—C—CH_2OH$
              |
             CH_3

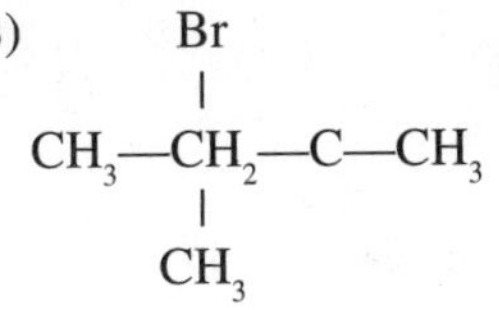

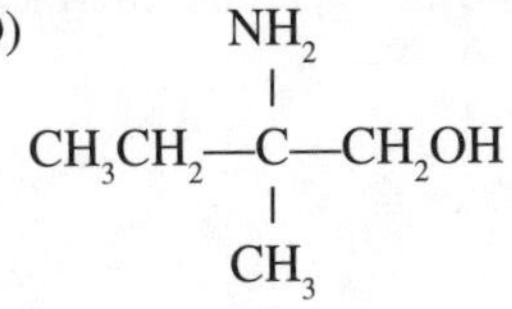

   (E) CH_3
        |
   $CH_3—C—CH_3$
        |
        CH_3

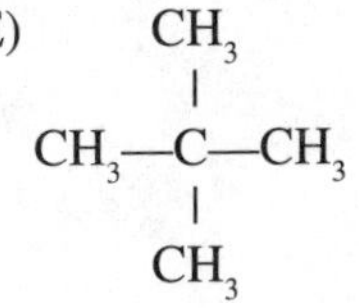

14. What was the key finding in Rutherford's famous "gold-foil" experiment?

   (A) Electrons orbit the nucleus in concentric rings.

   (B) All neutrons are located in a central nucleus.

   (C) Most of the mass of an atom is located in a central, dense core.

   (D) Atoms are composed of positively and negatively charge particles.

   (E) Alpha particles are attracted to a negatively charged plate.

15. Which of the following reactions is possible at the anode of a galvanic cell?

   (A) $Zn \rightarrow Zn^{2+} + 2e^-$

   (B) $Zn^{2+} + 2e^- \rightarrow Zn$

   (C) $Ag^+ + e^- \rightarrow Ag$

   (D) $Mg + Ag^+ \rightarrow Mg^{2+} + Ag$

   (E) $Pb^{2+} + 2I^- \rightarrow PbI_2$

16. What is the final concentration of lead ions, $[Pb^{2+}]$, in solution when 100 mL of 0.10 M $PbCl_2$(aq) is mixed with 100 mL of 0.050 M H_2SO_4(aq)?

   (A) 0.005 M

   (B) 0.012 M

   (C) 0.025 M

   (D) 0.250 M

   (E) 0.10 M

GO ON TO THE NEXT PAGE

$N_2(g) + 3H_2(g) \rightleftharpoons 2NH_3(g)$
$\Delta H° = -92$ kJ

17. Which of the following changes would cause a decrease in the equilibrium constant, K_{eq}, for the reaction shown above?

(A) Decrease the temperature

(B) Increase the temperature

(C) Increase the pressure of the reaction vessel by decreasing the volume

(D) The addition of nitrogen gas to the reaction vessel

(E) The addition of argon gas to the reaction vessel

$$^{53}_{23}V \rightarrow ^{0}_{-1}e + \underline{\hspace{1.5cm}}$$

18. In the nuclear equation shown above, what is the missing product?

(A) $^{49}_{21}Sc$

(B) $^{53}_{22}Ti$

(C) $^{55}_{23}V$

(D) $^{51}_{22}Ti$

(E) $^{53}_{24}Cr$

19. In a 1.0 L sample of 0.01 M potassium sulfate, K_2SO_4, what is the minimum number of moles of calcium chloride, $CaCl_2$, that can be added to the solution before the precipitate calcium sulfate forms? Assume that the addition of calcium chloride has a negligible effect on the total volume of the solution. K_{sp} for $CaSO_4 = 2.4 \times 10^{-5}$

(A) 2.4×10^{-5} mol

(B) 1.2×10^{-5} mol

(C) 2.4×10^{-3} mol

(D) 1.2×10^{-3} mol

(E) 0.01 mol

20. Which of the following combinations of quantum numbers (n, l, ml, ms) is not allowed?

(A) $1, 1, 0, \frac{1}{2}$

(B) $3, 0, 0, -\frac{1}{2}$

(C) $2, 1, -1, \frac{1}{2}$

(D) $4, 3, -2, -\frac{1}{2}$

(E) $4, 2, 0, \frac{1}{2}$

21. What would happen to the average kinetic energy of the molecules of a gas sample if the temperature of the sample increased from 20°C to 40°C?

(A) It would double.

(B) It would increase.

(C) It would decrease.

(D) It would become half its value.

(E) Two of the above.

22. As the bond order of a bond increases, its bond energy _____ and its bond length _____.

(A) increases, increases

(B) decreases, decreases

(C) increases, decreases

(D) decreases, increases

(E) is unaffected, increases

23. At normal atmospheric pressure and a temperature of 0°C, which phase(s) of H_2O can exist?

(A) Ice and water

(B) Ice and water vapor

(C) Water only

(D) Water vapor only

(E) Ice only

24. Commercial vinegar was titrated with NaOH solution to determine the content of acetic acid, $HC_2H_3O_2$. For 20.0 milliliters of the vinegar, 36.0 milliliters of 0.500-molar NaOH solution was required. What was the concentration of acetic acid in the vinegar assuming no other acid was present?

(A) 1.80 M

(B) 0.900 M

(C) 0.750 M

(D) 0.450 M

(E) 0.028 M

25. Based on the data below for a reaction in which A and B react to form C, what is the rate law for the reaction?

[A] (mol L^{-1})	[B] (mol L^{-1})	Initial Rate of Formation of C (mol L^{-1} s^{-1})
0.2	0.2	0.50
0.4	0.2	2.00
0.8	0.2	8.00
0.2	0.4	1.00
0.2	0.8	2.00

(A) Rate = k[A][B]

(B) Rate = k[A]^2[B]

(C) Rate = k[A][B]^2

(D) Rate = k[A]^2[B]^2

(E) Rate = k[A]^3

26. In which of the following reactions does the H$_2$PO$_4^-$ ion act as an acid?

(I) $H_3PO_4 + H_2O \rightarrow H_3O^+ + H_2PO_4^-$

(II) $H_2PO_4^- + H_2O \rightarrow H_3O^+ + HPO_4^{2-}$

(III) $H_2PO_4^- + OH^- \rightarrow H_3PO_4 + O^{2-}$

(A) I only

(B) II only

(C) III only

(D) I and II

(E) I and III

Questions 27 and 28 refer to the following diagram:

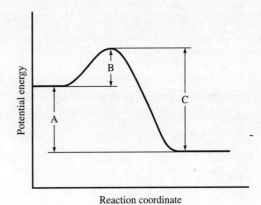

I.   A

II. B

III. C

27. Which will be affected by the addition of a catalyst?

(A) I only

(B) II only

(C) III only

(D) I and II

(E) II and III

28. The reaction shown in the graph is a _____ reaction.

(A) first-order

(B) catalyzed

(C) endothermic

(D) exothermic

(E) primary

GO ON TO THE NEXT PAGE

Ionization Energies for element X (kJ mol^{-1})				
First	Second	Third	Fourth	Fifth
801	2427	3660	25024	32827

29. The ionization energies for element X are listed in the table above. On the basis of the data, which of the following is element X most likely to be?

    (A) Li
    (B) Be
    (C) B
    (D) C
    (E) N

30. When solid sodium hydroxide, NaOH(s), is added to water at 25 °C, it dissolves and the temperature of the solution increases. Which of the following is true for the values of ΔH and ΔS for the dissolving process?

	ΔH	ΔS
(A)	+	+
(B)	+	–
(C)	0	0
(D)	–	–
(E)	–	+

31. Copper is electroplated from CuSO$_4$ solution. A constant current of 10.00 amps is applied by an external power supply for exactly 75.0 minutes. How many grams of copper can be plated out during this time interval? The atomic mass of copper is 63.55.

    (A) 3.67×10^{-3} g
    (B) 0.247 g
    (C) 7.4 g
    (D) 14.8 g
    (E) 29.6 g

Question 32 refers to the following standard heats of formation, $\Delta H°f$:

$$\Delta H°f\, P_4O_{10}(s) = -3110 \text{ kJ/mol}$$
$$\Delta H°f\, H_2O(l) = -286 \text{ kJ/mol}$$
$$\Delta H°f\, H_3PO_4(s) = -1279 \text{ kJ/mol}$$

32. Given the standard heats of formation shown above, calculate the change in enthalpy for the following process:

    $$P_4O_{10}(s) + 6\, H_2O(l) \rightarrow 4\, H_3PO_4(s)$$

    (A) –290 kJ
    (B) –1128 kJ
    (C) –2117 kJ
    (D) –3547 kJ
    (E) –4675 kJ

33. Types of hybridization exhibited by the C atoms in acetylene, C$_2$H$_2$, include which of the following?

    I.   sp
    II. sp^2
    III. sp^3

    (A) I only
    (B) II only
    (C) III only
    (D) I and II
    (E) I and III

34. The nuclide $^{12}_{7}$N is unstable. What type of radioactive decay would be expected?

    (A) β^-
    (B) β^+
    (C) ϕ
    (D) α
    (E) $^1_0$n

35. What volume of 0.500 M NaOH is required to neutralize 25.0 mL of 1.2 M H$_2$SO$_4$? (Assume complete ionization of the acid.)

    (A) 60 mL
    (B) 90 mL
    (C) 100 mL
    (D) 120 mL
    (E) 180 mL

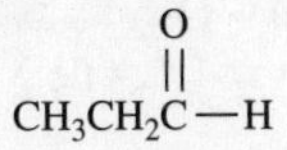

$$\underset{\substack{| \\ CH_3CH_2C-H}}{\overset{\overset{O}{||}}{}}$$

36. The organic compound represented above is an example of

(A) an organic acid.

(B) an alcohol.

(C) an ether.

(D) an aldehyde.

(E) a ketone.

37. The pH of a 1.0 M sodium acetate solution is

(A) 7.0

(B) greater than 7.0

(C) less than 7.0

(D) 0

(E) impossible to predict

$$C_2H_4(g) + 3O_2(g) \rightarrow 2CO_2(g) + 2H_2O(l)$$

38. When 200.0 g of ethylene (C_2H_4) burns in oxygen to give carbon dioxide and water, how many grams of CO_2 are formed?

(A) 200 g

(B) 255 g

(C) 314 g

(D) 400 g

(E) 628 g

Question 39 refers to the phase diagram for a pure substance shown below:

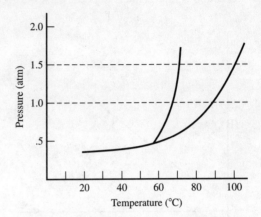

39. The normal boiling point for the substance represented in the phase diagram above is

(A) 33 °C

(B) 35 °C

(C) 44 °C

(D) 50 °C

(E) 28 °C

40. Which of the following solid salts should be more soluble in 1.0 M NH_3 than in water?

(A) Na_2CO_3

(B) KCl

(C) AgBr

(D) KNO_3

(E) NaBr

GO ON TO THE NEXT PAGE

41. In the graph below, which shows the relationship between concentration and time, what type of reaction is represented?

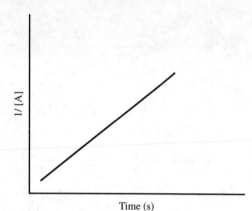

Time (s)

(A) Zero order

(B) First order

(C) Second order

(D) Third order

(E) The graph does not represent any type of reaction.

42. What is the molar solubility of $PbSO_4$ in water at 25 °C (K_{sp} for $PbSO_4$ is 1.3×10^{-8})?

(A) 1.1×10^{-4} M

(B) 2.2×10^{-4} M

(C) 5.1×10^{-5} M

(D) 1.3×10^{-8} M

(E) 1.3×10^{-6} M

43. $\frac{PV}{nRT}$ will be less than 1 for a real gas where

(A) the gas molecules are large enough to occupy a large amount of space.

(B) there is a large sample of very fast moving particles.

(C) the gas molecules have a very small molar mass.

(D) the gas molecules are attracted to each other.

(E) the gas molecules are repelled from each other.

$$2CO(g) + O_2(g) \rightleftharpoons 2CO_2(g)$$
$$\Delta H° = -514.2 \text{ kJ}$$

44. In the above reaction, which factors will cause the equilibrium to shift to the right?

I. An increase in volume

II. An increase in temperature

III. Removal of CO_2

(A) I only

(B) II only

(C) III only

(D) I and II only

(E) II and III only

45. If the temperature of a solution changes, which measure of concentration will change?

(A) Mass percent

(B) Mole fraction

(C) Molality

(D) Molarity

(E) None of these measures will change.

46. The pH of a 0.100 M solution of an aqueous weak acid (HA) is 4.00. The K_a for the weak acid is

(A) 1.0×10^{-4}

(B) 4.0×10^{-4}

(C) 1.0×10^{-7}

(D) 1.0×10^{-8}

(E) 4.0×10^{-8}

47. Equal numbers of moles of the gases Cl_2, NO_2, and CH_4 are placed into an evacuated vessel equipped with a valve. The valve has a very small hold, similar to the size of a pinhole. If the valve is opened for a brief period of time and then closed, which will be true of the partial pressures of the gases remaining in the flask?

(A) $P_{Cl_2} < P_{NO_2} < P_{CH_4}$

(B) $P_{NO_2} < P_{CH_4} < P_{Cl_2}$

(C) $P_{CH_4} < P_{Cl_2} < P_{NO_2}$

(D) $P_{NO_2} < P_{Cl_2} < P_{CH_4}$

(E) $P_{CH_4} < P_{NO_2} < P_{Cl_2}$

48. Liquid A and liquid B form a solution that behaves ideally according to Raoult's law. The vapor pressures of the pure substances A and B are 75 mm Hg and 25 mm Hg, respectively. Determine the vapor pressure over the solution if 1.50 moles of liquid A is added to 5.50 moles of liquid B.

(A) 30.0 mm Hg

(B) 35.7 mm Hg

(C) 71.4 mm Hg

(D) 125 mm Hg

(E) 250 mm Hg

49. How many grams are in a 6.94-mol sample of sodium hydroxide?

(A) 40.0 g

(B) 278 g

(C) 169 g

(D) 131 g

(E) 34.2 g

$$2C(s) + O_2(g) \rightarrow 2CO(g)$$

50. 1.2 mol of O_2 and 3.50 mol of solid C are placed in a 2.00 L evacuated vessel at 25 °C. If the carbon and oxygen react completely to form $CO(g)$, what will the final pressure be in the container?

(A) 1.2 atm

(B) 14.7 atm

(C) 20.0 atm

(D) 29.4 atm

(E) 42.8 atm

51. An unknown substance is placed into a hot flame. The color of the flame is a bright red. Which of the following substances is most likely to be the unknown?

(A) $Cu(NO_3)_2$

(B) NaCl

(C) KCl

(D) LiCl

(E) $Ba(NO_3)_2$

52. Vitamin C is composed of 40.9% C, 4.58% H, and 54.52% O by mass. If the molar mass of vitamin C is 176.1, what is the molecular formula?

(A) $C_2H_3O_2$

(B) $C_3H_4O_3$

(C) $C_4H_6O_4$

(D) $C_6H_8O_6$

(E) $C_4H_{10}O_3$

53. A molecule or an ion is a Lewis base if it

(A) accepts a proton from water.

(B) accepts a pair of electrons to form a bond.

(C) donates a pair of electrons to form a bond.

(D) donates a proton to water.

(E) donates a hydroxide ion in solution.

$$2NO + O_2 \rightleftharpoons 2NO_2$$

54. In an experiment, the gases above are allowed to establish equilibrium at 25 °C. If $[NO] = [O_2] = 2.0 \times 10^{-6}$ M, how would you set up the equation to determine $[NO_2]$?

(A) $4.0 \times 10^{13} = \dfrac{\left[NO_2\right]}{\left[2.0 \times 10^{-6}\right]\left[2.0 \times 10^{-6}\right]}$

(B) $4.0 \times 10^{13} = \dfrac{\left[NO_2\right]^2}{\left[2.0 \times 10^{-6}\right]^2\left[2.0 \times 10^{-6}\right]}$

(C) $4.0 \times 10^{13} = \dfrac{\left[NO_2\right]}{\left[2.0 \times 10^{-6}\right]^2}$

(D) $2.0 \times 10^{-6} = \dfrac{\left[NO_2\right]^2}{\left[4.0 \times 10^{13}\right]^2\left[4.0 \times 10^{13}\right]}$

(E) $4.0 \times 10^{13} = \dfrac{\left[2.0 \times 10^{-6}\right]^2\left[2.0 \times 10^{-6}\right]}{\left[NO_2\right]^2}$

GO ON TO THE NEXT PAGE

55. If an open container of salt solution is left out for an extended period of time in a room where temperature and pressure are constant, the vapor pressure of the solution will

(A) increase over time.

(B) decrease over time.

(C) remain constant at all times

(D) be zero since the container is open.

(E) increase for a period of time and then sharply decrease.

$$Ca(OH)_2(aq) + 2HNO_3(aq) \rightarrow Ca(NO_3)_2(aq) + 2H_2O(l)$$

56. How many grams of $Ca(NO_3)_2$ can be produced by reacting excess HNO_3 with 7.40 g of $Ca(OH)_2$?

(A) 10.2 g

(B) 16.4 g

(C) 32.8 g

(D) 8.22 g

(E) 7.40 g

57. Which of the following substances would you expect to have the lowest boiling point?

(A) Diamond

(B) Ammonia, NH_3

(C) Sodium acetate, $NaC_2H_3O_2$

(D) Glycerine, $C_3H_5(OH)_3$

(E) Silver

58. Which substance(s) listed below would form basic solutions?

(I) NH_4Cl

(II) K_2CO_3

(III) NaF

(A) I only

(B) II only

(C) III only

(D) I and II

(E) II and III

59. 50.0 g of an unknown substance is heated to 98.0 °C and then placed in a calorimeter containing 100.0 g of water (c = 4.18 J/g °C) at 20.91 °C. The final temperature of the mixture is 23.0 °C. Which metal was used?

(A) Aluminum (c = 0.90 J/g°C)

(B) Iron (c = 0.45 J/g°C)

(C) Copper (c = 0.38 J/g°C)

(D) Lead (c = 0.13 J/g°C)

(E) Silver (c = 0.23 J/g°C)

$$C(s) + CO_2(g) \rightleftharpoons 2CO(g)$$

60. In the reaction shown above, the value of K_p is 167.5 at a temperature of 1273 K. If the P_{CO_2} at this temperature is 0.10 atm, what will the P_{CO} be?

(A) 0.1 atm

(B) 4.1 atm

(C) 12.9 atm

(D) 16.7 atm

(E) 53.0 atm

61. 0.05 mol of solid $HgCl_2$ is vaporized in a 1.00 L evacuated flask at 680 K. What is the pressure inside the flask? (The value of the gas constant, R, is 0.0821 L atm mol^{-1} K^{-1}.)

(A) 0.05 atm

(B) 1.00 atm

(C) 2.0 atm

(D) 2.8 atm

(E) 3.2 atm

62. The volume of distilled water that should be added to 10.0 mL of 12.0 M HCl(aq) in order to prepare a 1.00 M HCl(aq) solution is approximately

(A) 50.0 mL

(B) 60.0 mL

(C) 100 mL

(D) 110 mL

(E) 120 mL

63. If $G° > 0$ for a reaction, which of the following statements about the equilibrium constant, K, is true?

(A) $K = 0$

(B) $K > 1$

(C) $K < 1$

(D) $K = 1$

(E) $K = G°$

64. How many of the following molecules have all of their atoms in the same plane?

CH_2CH_2 F_2O H_2CO NH_3 CO_2 $BeCl_2$ H_2O_2

(A) 3

(B) 4

(C) 5

(D) 6

(E) 7

65. What is the coefficient for water when the equation below is balanced?

$$\_As(OH)_3\ (s) + \_H_2SO_4\ (aq) \rightarrow$$
$$\_As_2(SO_4)_3(aq) + \_H_2O(l)$$

(A) 1

(B) 2

(C) 4

(D) 6

(E) 12

66. In a voltaic cell, one half cell contains a cobalt electrode immersed in a $1.0\,M\,Co^{2+}$ solution. In the other half cell, a lead electrode is immersed in a 1.0 $M\,Pb^{2+}$ solution. The value for $E°$ is 0.15 V in this cell. In a similar voltaic cell, a cobalt electrode is immersed in a $0.0010\,M\,Co^{2+}$ solution and a lead electrode is immersed in a $0.10\,M\,Pb^{2+}$ solution. Which statement below accurately describes the second voltaic cell?

$$Co^{2+} + 2e^- \rightarrow Co \quad E° = -0.28\ V$$
$$Pb^{2+} + 2e^- \rightarrow Pb \quad E° = -0.13\ V$$

(A) The cell will have a lower E.

(B) The cell will have a higher E.

(C) The cell will have an identical E, since E is unaffected by concentration.

(D) Cobalt will become the cathode.

(E) The cathode will dissolve.

Refer to the data below to answer question 67.

$$C_2H_6(g) \rightarrow C_2H_4(g) + H_2(g);\ H° = 137\ kJ;$$
$$S° = 120\ J/K$$

67. Based on the data above, the reaction will be

(A) spontaneous at all temperatures.

(B) spontaneous at high temperatures.

(C) spontaneous only at low temperatures.

(D) nonspontaneous at all temperatures.

(E) nonspontaneous at high temperatures.

68. Which of the following molecules has a dipole moment?

(A) BCl_3

(B) CO_2

(C) PCl_3

(D) Cl_2

(E) N_2

69. Which of the following solutions has the lowest freezing point?

(A) $0.10\ m\ C_6H_{12}O_6$, glucose

(B) $0.10\ m\ CoI_2$

(C) $0.10\ m\ ZnSO_4$

(D) $0.10\ m\ NaI$

(E) $0.10\ m\ AlI_3$

70. What is the pH of a solution prepared by mixing 50 mL of 0.125 M KOH with 0.050 L of 0.125 M HCl?

(A) 4.0

(B) 5.7

(C) 6.3

(D) 7.0

(E) 8.1

71. What volume of 18.0 M sulfuric acid must be used to prepare 15.5 L of 0.195 M H_2SO_4?

(A) 168 mL

(B) 0.336 L

(C) 92.3 mL

(D) 226 mL

(E) 125 mL

GO ON TO THE NEXT PAGE

72. A large, old car bumper is going to be chrome plated. This can be accomplished using an electrolytic cell where the bumper will act as a cathode in an acidic dichromate, $Cr_2O_7^{2-}$, solution. If the current is 20.0 amperes, how long will it take to deposit 100 grams of $Cr(s)$ onto the bumper? The atomic mass of Cr is 52.00; 1 faraday = 96,500 coulombs.

    (A) 15.5 h
    (B) 1.29 days
    (C) 309 min
    (D) 76.3 s
    (E) 5.3 days

73. The correct name for the compound $[Co(NH_3)_6]Cl_3$ is

    (A) cobalt (III) hexammine chloride.
    (B) hexamminecobalt chloride (III).
    (C) hexamminecobalt (III) chloride.
    (D) hexamminecobalt trichloride.
    (E) hexamminecobalt (VI) chloride.

74. Calculate the pH of a solution that is 0.2 M in acetic acid ($K_a = 1.8 \times 10^{-5}$) and 0.2 M in sodium acetate.

    (A) 4.7
    (B) 9.3
    (C) 7.0
    (D) 5.4
    (E) 8.6

75. Which of the following solutions would be orange?

    (A) $KMnO_4$
    (B) $Ni(NO_3)_2$
    (C) $CuCl_2$
    (D) $K_2Cr_2O_7$
    (E) Na_2CrO_4

STOP

END OF SECTION I. IF YOU HAVE ANY TIME LEFT, GO OVER YOUR WORK IN THIS SECTION ONLY. DO NOT WORK IN ANY OTHER SECTION OF THE TEST.

SECTION II REFERENCE INFORMATION

1A 1																	8A 18
1 **H** 1.0079	2A 2											3A 13	4A 14	5A 15	6A 16	7A 17	2 **He** 4.0026
3 **Li** 6.941	4 **Be** 9.012											5 **B** 10.811	6 **C** 12.011	7 **N** 14.007	8 **O** 16.00	9 **F** 19.00	10 **Ne** 20.179
11 **Na** 22.99	12 **Mg** 24.30	3B 3	4B 4	5B 5	6B 6	7B 7		8B 9	10	1B 11	2B 12	13 **Al** 26.98	14 **Si** 28.09	15 **P** 30.974	16 **S** 32.06	17 **Cl** 35.453	18 **Ar** 39.948
19 **K** 39.10	20 **Ca** 40.08	21 **Sc** 44.96	22 **Ti** 47.90	23 **V** 50.94	24 **Cr** 52.00	25 **Mn** 54.938	26 **Fe** 55.85	27 **Co** 58.93	28 **Ni** 58.69	29 **Cu** 63.55	30 **Zn** 65.39	31 **Ga** 69.72	32 **Ge** 72.59	33 **As** 74.92	34 **Se** 78.96	35 **Br** 79.90	36 **Kr** 83.80
37 **Rb** 85.47	38 **Sr** 87.62	39 **Y** 88.91	40 **Zr** 91.22	41 **Nb** 92.91	42 **Mo** 95.94	43 **Tc** (98)	44 **Ru** 101.1	45 **Rh** 102.91	46 **Pd** 106.42	47 **Ag** 107.87	48 **Cd** 112.41	49 **In** 114.82	50 **Sn** 118.71	51 **Sb** 121.75	52 **Te** 127.60	53 **I** 126.91	54 **Xe** 131.29
55 **Cs** 132.91	56 **Ba** 137.33	57 **La** 138.91	72 **Hf** 178.49	73 **Ta** 180.95	74 **W** 183.85	75 **Re** 186.21	76 **Os** 190.2	77 **Ir** 192.2	78 **Pt** 195.08	79 **Au** 196.97	80 **Hg** 200.59	81 **Tl** 204.38	82 **Pb** 207.2	83 **Bi** 208.98	84 **Po** (209)	85 **At** (210)	86 **Rn** (222)
87 **Fr** (223)	88 **Ra** 226.02	89 **Ac** 227.03	104 **Unq** (261)	105 **Unp** (262)	106 **Unh** (263)	107 **Uns** (264)	108 **Uno** (265)	109 **Une** (266)									

	58 **Ce** 140.12	59 **Pr** 140.91	60 **Nd** 144.24	61 **Pm** (145)	62 **Sm** 150.4	63 **Eu** 151.97	64 **Gd** 157.25	65 **Tb** 158.93	66 **Dy** 162.50	67 **Ho** 164.93	68 **Er** 167.26	69 **Tm** 168.93	70 **Yb** 173.04	71 **Lu** 174.97
Lanthanide series														
Actinide series	90 **Th** 232.04	91 **Pa** 231.04	92 **U** 238.03	93 **Np** 237.05	94 **Pu** (244)	95 **Am** (243)	96 **Cm** (247)	97 **Bk** (247)	98 **Cf** (251)	99 **Es** (252)	100 **Fm** (257)	101 **Md** (258)	102 **No** (259)	103 **Lr** (260)

STANDARD REDUCTION POTENTIALS IN AQUEOUS SOLUTION AT 25°C

Half-reaction E((V)

$Li^+ + e^-$	$\rightarrow$	$Li(s)$	-3.05
$Cs^+ + e^-$	$\rightarrow$	$Cs(s)$	-2.92
$K^+ + e^-$	$\rightarrow$	$K(s)$	-2.92
$Rb^+ + e^-$	$\rightarrow$	$Rb(s)$	-2.92
$Ba^{2+} + 2e$	$\rightarrow$	$Ba(s)$	-2.90
$Sr^{2+} + 2e^-$	$\rightarrow$	$Sr(s)$	-2.89
$Ca^{2+} + 2e^-$	$\rightarrow$	$Ca(s)$	-2.87
$Na^+ + e^-$	$\rightarrow$	$Na(s)$	-2.71
$Mg^{2+} 2e^-$	$\rightarrow$	$Mg(s)$	-2.37
$Be^{2+} + 2e^-$	$\rightarrow$	$Be(s)$	-1.70
$Al^{3+} + 3e^-$	$\rightarrow$	$Al(s)$	-1.66
$Mn^{2+} + 2e^-$	$\rightarrow$	$Mn(s)$	-1.18
$Zn^{2+} + 2e^-$	$\rightarrow$	$Zn(s)$	-0.76
$Cr^{3+} + 3e^-$	$\rightarrow$	$Cr(s)$	-0.74
$Fe^{2+} + 2e^-$	$\rightarrow$	$Fe(s)$	-0.44
$Cr^{3+} + e^-$	$\rightarrow$	Cr^{2+}	-0.41
$Cd^{2+} + 2e^-$	$\rightarrow$	$Cd(s)$	-0.40
$Tl^+ + e^-$	$\rightarrow$	$Tl(s)$	-0.34
$Co^{2+} + 2e^-$	$\rightarrow$	$Co(s)$	-0.28
$Ni^{2+} + 2e^-$	$\rightarrow$	$Ni(s)$	-0.25
$Sn^{2+} + 2e^-$	$\rightarrow$	$Sn(s)$	-0.14
$Pb^{2+} + 2e^-$	$\rightarrow$	$Pb(s)$	-0.13
$2H^+ + 2e^-$	$\rightarrow$	$H_2(g)$	0.00
$S(s) + 2H+ + 2e^-$	$\rightarrow$	$H_2S(g)$	0.14
$Sn^{4+} + 2e^-$	$\rightarrow$	Sn^{2+}	0.15
$Cu^{2+} + e^-$	$\rightarrow$	Cu^+	0.15
$Cu^{2+} + 2e^-$	$\rightarrow$	$Cu(s)$	0.34
$Cu^+ + e^-$	$\rightarrow$	$Cu(s)$	0.52
$I_2(s) + 2e^-$	$\rightarrow$	$2I^-$	0.53
$Fe^{3+} + e^-$	$\rightarrow$	Fe^{2+}	0.77
$Hg_2^{2+} + 2e^-$	$\rightarrow$	$2 Hg(l)$	0.79
$Ag^+ + e^-$	$\rightarrow$	$Ag(s)$	0.80
$Hg^{2+} + 2e^-$	$\rightarrow$	$Hg(l)$	0.85
$2Hg^{2+} + 2e^-$	$\rightarrow$	Hg_2^{2+}	0.92
$Br_2(l) + 2e^-$	$\rightarrow$	$2Br^-$	1.07
$O_2(g) + 4H^+ + 4e^-$	$\rightarrow$	$2H_2O(l)$	1.23
$Cl_2(g) + 2e^-$	$\rightarrow$	$2Cl^-$	1.36
$Au^{3+} + 3e^-$	$\rightarrow$	$Au(s)$	1.50
$Co^{3+} + e^-$	$\rightarrow$	Co^{2+}	1.82
$F_2(g) + 2e^-$	$\rightarrow$	$2F^-$	2.87

ATOMIC STRUCTURE

$\Delta E = h\nu$

$c = \lambda\nu$

$\lambda = \dfrac{h}{mv}$

$p = mv$

$En = \dfrac{-2.178 \times 10^{-18}}{n^2} \text{ joule}$

EQUILIBRIUM

$K_a = \dfrac{\left[H^+ \right]\left[A^- \right]}{\left[HA \right]}$

$K_b = \dfrac{\left[OH^- \right]\left[HB^+ \right]}{\left[B \right]}$

$K_w = [OH^-][H^+] = 1.0 \times 10^{-14} \text{ at } 25\ ^\circ C$

$\qquad = K_a \times K_b$

$pH = -\log[H^+],\ pOH = -\log[OH^-]$

$14 = pH + pOH$

$pH = pK_a + \log\dfrac{\left[A- \right]}{\left[HA \right]}$

$pOH = pK_b + \log\dfrac{\left[HB^+ \right]}{\left[B \right]}$

$pK_a = -\log K_a,\ pK_b = -\log K_b$

$K_p = K_c(RT)^{\Delta n}$

Where Δn = moles product gas – moles reactant gas

THERMOCHEMISTRY

$$\Delta S° = \sum S° \text{ products} - \sum S° \text{ reactants}$$

$$\Delta H° = \sum H°_f \text{ products} - \sum H°_f \text{ reactants}$$

$$\Delta G° = \sum \Delta G°_f \text{ products} - \sum G°_f \text{ reactants}$$

$$\Delta G° = \Delta H° - T\,\Delta S°$$

$$= -RT \ln K = -2.303\,RT \log K$$

$$= -n\,\mathfrak{F}\,E°$$

$$\Delta G = \Delta G° + RT \ln Q = \Delta G° + 2.303 RT \log Q$$

$$q = mc\Delta T$$

$$Cp = \frac{\Delta H}{\Delta T}$$

E = energy

ν = frequency

λ = wavelength

p = momentum

v = velocity

n = principal quantum number

m = mass

Speed of light, $c = 3.0 \times 10^8 \text{ m s}^{-1}$

Planck's constant, $h = 6.63 \times 10^{-34} \text{ J s}$

Boltzmann's constant, $k = 1.38 \times 10^{-23} \text{ J K}^{-1}$

Avogadro's number $= 6.022 \times 10^{23}$ molecules mol^{-1}

Electron charge, $e = -1.602 \times 10^{-19}$ coulomb

1 electron volt per atom = 96.5 kJ mol^{-1}

EQUILIBRIUM CONSTANTS

K_a (weak acid)

K_b (weak base)

K_w (water)

K_p (gas pressure)

K_c (molar concentrations)

$S°$ = standard entropy

$H°$ = standard enthalpy

$G°$ = standard free energy

$E°$ = standard reduction potential

T = temperature

n = moles

m = mass

q = heat

c = specific heat capacity

C_p = molar heat capacity at constant pressure

1 faraday, $\mathcal{F}$ = 96,500 coulombs

P = pressure

V = volume

T = temperature

n = number of moles

D = density

m = mass

v = velocity

u_{rms} = root-mean-square speed

KE = kinetic energy

r = rate of effusion

M = molar mass

π = osmotic pressure

i = van't Hoff factor

K_f = molal freezing-point depression constant

K_b = molal boiling-point elevation constant

Q = reaction quotient

I = current amperes

q = charge (coulombs)

t = time (seconds)

$E°$ = standard reduction potential

K = equilibrium constant

Gas constant, R = 8.31 J mol^{-1}K^{-1}

            = 0.0821 L atm mol^{-1} K^{-1}

            = 8.31 volt coulomb mol^{-1} K^{-1}

Boltzmann's constant, k = 1.38×10^{-23} J K^{-1}

K_f for H_2O = 1.86 K kg mol^{-1}

K_b for H_2O = 0.512 K kg mol^{-1}

STP = 0.000 °C and 1.000 atm

Faraday's constant, $\mathcal{F}$ = 96,500 coulombs per mole of electrons

GASES, LIQUIDS, AND SOLUTIONS

$$PV = nRT$$

$$\left(P + \frac{n^2 a}{V^2}\right)(V - nb) = nRT$$

$$PA = P_{total} \times XA, \text{ where } XA = \frac{\text{moles A}}{\text{total moles}}$$

$$P_{total} = PA + PB + PC + \ldots$$

$$n = \frac{m}{M}$$

$$K = {}^\circ C + 273$$

$$\frac{P_1 V_1}{T_1} = \frac{P_2 V_2}{T_2}$$

$$D = \frac{m}{V}$$

$$u_{rms} = \sqrt{\frac{3kT}{m}} = \sqrt{\frac{3RT}{M}}$$

$$KE \text{ per molecule} = \frac{1}{2} mv^2$$

$$KE \text{ per mole} = \frac{3}{2} RTn$$

$$\frac{r_1}{r_2} = \sqrt{\frac{M_2}{M_1}}$$

molarity, M = moles solute per liter solution

molality = moles solute per kilogram solvent

$$\Delta T_f = iK_f \times \text{molality}$$
$$\Delta T_b = iK_b \times \text{molality}$$

$$\pi = \frac{nRT}{V} i$$

OXIDATION-REDUCTION; ELECTROCHEMISTRY

$$Q = \frac{[C]^c [D]^d}{[A]^a [B]^b}, \text{ where } aA + bB \rightarrow cC + dD$$

$$I = \frac{q}{t}$$

$$E_{cell} = E^\circ_{cell} - \frac{RT}{n\mathcal{F}} \ln Q$$

$$= E^\circ_{cell} - \frac{0.0592}{n} \log Q \text{ at } 25^\circ C$$

$$\log K = \frac{nE^\circ}{0.0592}$$

SECTION II
Time—90 Minutes

Part A
Time—40 Minutes

YOU MAY USE YOUR CALCULATOR FOR PART A.

Directions: CLEARLY SHOW THE METHOD USED AND STEPS INVOLVED IN ARRIVING AT YOUR ANSWERS. It is to your advantage to do this because you may earn partial credit if you do, and you will receive little or no credit if you do not. Attention should be paid to significant figures.

Answer Question 1 below. The Section II weighting for this question is 20 percent. Write all of your answers in the space provided following each question.

1. The solubility of calcium oxalate, CaC_2O_4, is 6.1×10^{-3} g per liter at 25 °C.

   (a) Determine the molar solubility of CaC_2O_4 at 25 °C.

   (b) Write a balanced equation for the solubility equilibrium.

   (c) Write the expression for the solubility product constant, K_{sp}, and calculate its value.

   (d) If CaC_2O_4 is placed in a 0.10 M $CaCl_2$ solution, how will this affect the molar solubility? Explain, and show calculations to support your answer.

   (e) If 50.0 mL of 0.0025 M $CaCl_2$ is added to 50.0 mL of 1.0×10^{-5} M $Na_2C_2O_4$, will any calcium oxalate precipitate?

GO ON TO THE NEXT PAGE

Directions: Answer EITHER Question 2 OR Question 3. Only one of these questions will be graded. If you start both questions, make sure you cross out the one you do not want scored. The Section II weight for the question you choose is 20 percent.

---

2. $I_2(g) + Br_2(g) \rightleftharpoons 2IBr(g)$

0.0015 mol each of I_2 and Br_2 were placed into an evacuated 5.0 L vessel at 150 °C. The contents are allowed to come to equilibrium at this temperature, and the equilibrium constant K_c is measured at 1.2×10^2.

   (a) Write the equilibrium expression, K_c, for this reaction.

   (b) Calculate the equilibrium composition of the mixture at 150 °C.

   (c) Calculate the value of K_p at this same temperature.

   (d) What effect would adding 0.05 mol of I_2 have on the mixture at equilibrium? Explain.

3. $2SO_2(g) + O_2(g) \rightarrow 2SO_3(g)$

Substance	$\Delta H°f$ (kJ/mol)	S° (J/K • mol)
$SO_2(g)$	-297	248
$SO_3(g)$	-396	257
$O_2(g)$	0	205

The reaction, shown above, is carried out at 25 °C and 1 atm pressure.

   (a) Calculate the value of the standard enthalpy change, $\Delta H°$.

   (b) Calculate the value of the standard entropy change, $\Delta S°$.

   (c) Calculate the value of the standard free energy change, $\Delta G°$.

   (d) Discuss whether at this temperature the reaction is

       (i)   endothermic or exothermic.

       (ii) increasing or decreasing in entropy.

       (iii) spontaneous or nonspontaneous.

Part B
Time—50 minutes

YOU MAY NOT USE CALCULATORS WITH PART B.

Directions: Answer Question 4 below. The Section II score weighting for this question is 15 percent.

4. Write the formulas to show the reactants and products for FIVE of the eight equations written below. Answers to more than five responses will not be scored, so be sure to cross out any incomplete responses. Assume that each reaction occurs. Also assume that all solutions are aqueous unless otherwise stated. If substances are extensively ionized in solution, be sure to represent them as such. Omit formulas for ions or molecules that are unchanged during the reaction. Equations need not be balanced.

Example: A strip of magnesium is added to a solution of silver nitrate.

Answer: $Mg + Ag^+ \rightarrow Mg^{2+} + Ag$

(a) Ethanol and formic acid (methanoic acid) are mixed and gently heated.

(b) Solid ammonium carbonate is heated.

(c) A solution of potassium iodide is electrolyzed.

(d) Sodium metal is added to water.

(e) A strip of copper is submerged in dilute nitric acid.

(f) Chlorine gas is bubbled into a solution of potassium iodide.

(g) Equal volumes of 0.1 M sulfuric acid and 0.1 M potassium hydroxide are mixed.

(h) Ethanol is completely burned in air.

GO ON TO THE NEXT PAGE

Directions: For the remainder of the exam, your responses will be graded according to their accuracy and relevancy. Your responses should be well organized and presented in a clear, concise manner. Brief, specific answers are preferable to longer, general responses. You may use any examples or equations if they are appropriate.

Answer BOTH Question 5 on this page AND Question 6 on the next page. Both of these questions are required and each will be graded. The weighting of these two questions in Section II is 30 percent (15 percent each).

5. $2SO_3(g) \rightleftharpoons 2SO_2(g) + O_2(g) \; \Delta H° = 197 \text{ kJ}$

For the reaction shown above, describe the changes that will occur to the number of moles of SO_3 under the following conditions:

(a) Additional oxygen is added to the reaction vessel.

(b) The pressure in the reaction vessel is decreased by increasing its volume.

(c) The pressure is increased by the addition of helium gas.

(d) The temperature is increased.

(e) Oxygen gas is removed.

6. A student performed a titration of a weak, monoprotic acid, HA, with a sodium hydroxide, NaOH, solution.

(a) On the graph that is provided, sketch an approximate representation of the titration curve for the experiment. On the curve, label the equivalence point.

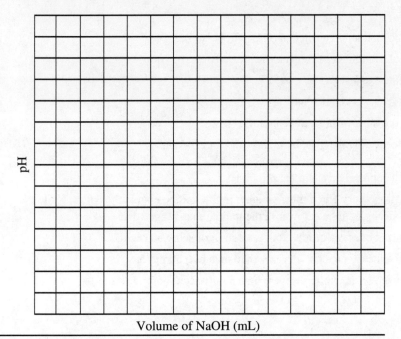

pH

Volume of NaOH (mL)

(b) Discuss at least two ways in which the sketch in (a) differs from the plot that would result from the titration of a strong, monoprotic, like HCl.

(c) The student has a choice between the two indicators: methyl red (pH range 4.8 – 6.0) or phenolphthalein (pH range = 8.2 – 10.0). Which should she choose? Justify your response.

(d) While the student was performing her first trial, she dispensed 50.0 mL of titrant (base) from her buret (the maximum), but her analyte (acid) still had not changed color. What is the most likely source of her error (assume that she did put an indicator in the analyte)?

GO ON TO THE NEXT PAGE

Directions: Answer EITHER Question 7 OR Question 8. Only one of the two questions will be graded. If you start both questions, make sure you cross out the one you don't want to be scored. The Section II weighting of the question you answer is 15 percent.

7. Two identical sealed 1.0 L containers are filled at STP with N_2 and SF_6.

   (a) Which gas has the greatest number of molecules?

   (b) Which gas has the greatest density?

   (c) Which has the highest average kinetic energy?

   (d) Which would deviate the most from ideal behavior?

   (e) If a pinhole leak was formed, which has the highest rate of effusion?

8. Answer the following using appropriate chemical principles.

   (a) The meniscus in a small mercury-filled tube is higher in the middle than at the edges, while the meniscus in a small water filled tube is lower in the middle than at the edges.

   (b) Solid salt crystals won't conduct electricity, but a solution of salt water will.

   (c) Water evaporates more quickly on a hot, dry day than on a hot, humid day.

   (d) A burn from steam is usually much more severe than a burn from boiling water.

STOP

END OF SECTION II. IF YOU HAVE ANY TIME LEFT, GO OVER YOUR WORK IN THIS SECTION ONLY. DO NOT WORK IN ANY OTHER SECTION OF THE TEST.

ANSWERS AND EXPLANATIONS

Section I

1. **The correct answer is (C).** The orbital diagram in choice (C) shows filled s and p sublevels, which are characteristic of the nonreactive noble gases.

2. **The correct answer is (A).** In choice (A), two electrons in the same orbital have like spins, which is not allowed by the Pauli Exclusion Principle (they must have opposite spins).

3. **The correct answer is (B).** The second electron in the p orbital should go into a different orbital. According to Hund's rule, all orbitals should fill with a single electron (each having like spins) prior to a second electron entering any orbital.

4. **The correct answer is (D).** The only way a single electron could be in an orbital that is of higher energy than an unoccupied orbital is if it is excited.

5. **The correct answer is (E).** Octane is a much larger molecule allowing for a greater number of interactions between the molecules. This attractive force is sufficient to allow octane to remain in the liquid state at higher temperatures.

6. **The correct answer is (B).** The identical bond lengths in each carbon-carbon bond in the benzene ring shows that all bonds are identical. This contradicts the model that would show three double bonds and three single bonds. If that model were correct, the double bonds would be shorter than the single bonds. The logical conclusion is that the electrons delocalize and spread around the entire ring so that all are shared equally.

7. **The correct answer is (D).** According to electron configuration of carbon, the carbon atom should have two electrons in the $2s$ orbital and one in each of the two $2p$ orbitals. The four carbon-hydrogen bonds in methane should be different because of the different orbitals, yet experimental evidence shows them to be the same. The solution is that one of the $2s$ electrons is raised to a p orbital, and the result is the formation of four identical hybridized sp^3 orbitals.

8. **The correct answer is (E).** Since He and Xe are both single atoms, the only intermolecular forces that can act between them are dispersion forces. Because xenon is a much larger atom, it has a larger electron density that can lead to a greater fluctuation in charge distribution, causing larger dispersion forces.

9. **The correct answer is (B).** Following the chart, the transition from 40 to 60 degrees at the constant pressure of 1.5 atm moves from solid to liquid, which is indicative of melting.

10. **The correct answer is (C).** At the low pressure listed in the problem, the change in temperature moves the substance from the solid state to the gaseous state, otherwise known as sublimation.

11. **The correct answer is (D).** This process varies the pressure while maintaining constant temperature. This causes a change from a gas to a liquid, otherwise known as condensation.

12. **The correct answer is (E).** A base spill should be treated with large amounts of water. Although water will dilute the base, a weak acid will more quickly neutralize the base and should, therefore, be used. If a strong acid is used, it could quickly neutralize the base, but if too much is used, the effects could be as harmful, or more harmful, than the base. A weak acid won't be harmful if too much is used.

13. **The correct answer is (D).** Optical isomers are non-superimposable mirror images. In the final example (choice D), all four groups are different and the molecular structure does not allow for the mirror images to be superimposed.

14. **The correct answer is (C).** The unexpected and significant finding in Rutherford's "gold foil" experiment was that the alpha particles were deflected as they passed through the foil. Had Thomson's model of the atom been correct, it was predicted that the alpha particle should pass through unhindered. This finding led him to conclude that there must be a very dense, positively charged (repels the positively charged alpha particle) core, which is now known as the nucleus. Although choice (B) mentions the nucleus, it also mentions neutrons, which weren't discovered until much later.

15. The correct answer is (A). The anode in a galvanic (voltaic) cell is where oxidation occurs. Choice (A) is the only example of an oxidation that could occur in a half-cell (Zinc is losing electrons).

16. The correct answer is (C). In this problem, you hopefully recognized that lead and sulfate will form a precipitate. What that means is that when the two substances combine, the precipitate will fall out of solution, leaving behind a certain amount of lead ions. Solving the problem requires you to determine the quantity of precipitate that can form (from the stoichiometric ratios) and then see if there is any lead left over.

Step 1: Determine how much lead is present in 100 mL of $PbCl_2$.

$$0.100 \text{ L} \times 0.1 \text{ } M \text{ } PbCl_2 = 0.01 \text{ mol } PbCl_2$$

Step 2: Use the stoichiometric ratios to determine how much $PbCl_2$ is required to completely react with H_2SO_4:

$$0.1 \text{ L} \times 0.050 \text{ } M \text{ } H_2SO_4 = 5 \times 10^{-3} \text{ mol } H_2SO_4$$

If an equation is written to show the formation of the precipitate,

$$Pb^{2+}(aq) + SO_4^{2-}(aq) \rightarrow PbSO_4(s)$$

you can see that only one mole of lead ions is required for each mole of sulfate. As a result, 0.005 mol of $PbCl_2$ will react with the 0.005 mol H_2SO_4 to yield 0.005 mol $PbSO_4$. That leaves 0.005 mol Pb^{2+} ions left over.

Because the problem is asking for the concentration of Pb^{2+}, you need to divide the number of moles by the volume, in this case 200 mL. Therefore, the solution will be

$$\frac{0.005 \text{ mol } PbSO_4}{0.200 \text{ L}} = 0.025 \text{ } M$$

17. The correct answer is (B). Because the reaction is exothermic, an increase in temperature will cause the equilibrium to shift to the left, reducing the value of K_{eq}. All of the other changes will cause a shift to the right (which increases the value of K_{eq}).

18. The correct answer is (E). In the beta decay shown, vanadium–53 will convert a neutron to a proton and a beta particle. The proton will increase the atomic number by 1, while maintaining a constant mass number. The new element, therefore, is chromium–53.

19. The correct answer is (C). To solve this, you need to use the K_{sp} expression for $CaSO_4$.

$$K_{sp} = [Ca^{2+}][SO_4^{2-}]$$

From the given information in the problem we can calculate the concentration of sulfate ion in solution. Once that has been determined, you can use the given K_{sp} to solve for $[Ca^{2+}]$.

$$0.01 \text{ } M \text{ } K_2SO_4 \times 1.0 \text{ L} = 0.01 \text{ mol } K_2SO_4$$

$$0.01 \text{ mol } K_2SO_4 \times \frac{1 \text{ mol } SO_4^{2-}}{1 \text{ mol } K_2SO_4} = 0.01 \text{ mol } SO_4^{2-}$$

$$\frac{0.01 \text{ mol } SO_4^{2-}}{1.0 \text{ L soln}} = 0.01 \text{ } M \text{ } SO_4^{2-}$$

$$K_{sp} = [Ca^{2+}][SO_4^{2-}]$$

$$2.4 \times 10^{-5} = [Ca^{2+}] (0.01 \text{ M } SO_4^{2-})$$

$$[Ca^{2+}] = 2.4 \times 10^{-3} \text{ } M$$

In 1.0 L of solution, this amounts to 2.4×10^{-3} mol Ca^{2+}, which can be found in 2.4×10^{-3} mol $CaCl_2$ (since each mole of $CaCl_2$ yields one mole of Ca^{2+}).

20. The correct answer is (A). The values for the l quantum number can only go as high as $n-1$, meaning l can't have a value of 1 when $n = 1$. An l value of 1 corresponds to a p orbital, which is not found in the first energy level.

21. The correct answer is (B). Be careful not to fall for questions like this one. The temperature gives the initial impression that it has doubled. Doubling the temperature will cause pressure and kinetic energy to double. However, careful observation will show that the absolute temperature is not doubling. The absolute temperature is only changing from 293 K to 313 K. Therefore, the average kinetic energy will increase, but it won't double.

22. The correct answer is (C). Bond order is the number of pairs of electrons shared between two atoms. Increasing the number of pairs of electrons being shared between atoms will increase the attractive force between the two atoms, which will cause a corresponding increase in the amount of energy required to break apart the atoms. This has the effect of pulling the atoms closer together (decreasing the bond length).

23. The correct answer is (A). Under normal atmospheric pressure, water can only exist as only liquid or solid at 0 °. If the pressure is manipulated, water can also exist as a gas, but that is not required in this problem.

24. **The correct answer is (B).** From a conceptual perspective, remember that to neutralize an acid you must add enough strong base so that all of the hydrogen (hydronium) ions in the acid combine with the hydroxide ions of the base to form water. Therefore, if you determine the number of moles of hydroxide ions you add to the mixture during the titration, this should equal the number of moles of acid when the solution is neutral.

The number of moles of base required for the neutralization was

$$0.036 \text{ L} \times 0.500 \ \frac{\text{mol}}{\text{L}} = 0.018 \text{ mol NaOH}$$

Because acetic acid is monoprotic, this is how many moles of acetic acid must be present in the 20 mL sample. To determine the molarity of the sample, we can use the molarity equation:

$$M = \frac{0.018 \text{ mol}}{0.020 \text{ L}} = 0.900 \ M$$

25. **The correct answer is (B).** In each of the first three measurements, when the concentration of A is doubled while B is held constant, the initial rate increases by four times (2^2). This leads to the $[A]^2$ expression. In the last two pieces of data, the concentration of B is doubled while A is held constant. This causes a doubling in the initial rate, meaning the reaction is first order for B.

26. **The correct answer is (B).** In equation II, $H_2PO_4^-$ donates a proton, making it an acid. In equations I and III, it is receiving a proton, making it a base.

27. **The correct answer is (E).** One of the more important things to remember about catalysts is that they do not reduce the energy change between reactants and products (labeled A in the diagram). A catalyst helps to provide a pathway with reduced activation energy. This will lower the heights of B and C on the chart.

28. **The correct answer is (D).** The reaction is exothermic because the energy of the products is lower than the energy of the reactants. This loss of energy is in the form of heat.

29. **The correct answer is (C).** There is an enormous gap between the third and fourth energy levels, meaning that the third electron was significantly easier to remove than the fourth. This is characteristic of an element in Group III because the fourth electron needs to come from a lower energy level. In addition, the removal of the three previous electrons leaves the nucleus with extra protons, leading to a very high effective nuclear charge on the fourth electron. Finally, the first three electrons are more shielded than the fourth electron since they are in a higher energy level.

30. **The correct answer is (E).** Dissolving increases the entropy of a substance because the particles are moving farther apart, and hence have more freedom of random motion. An increase in temperature is indicative of an exothermic process. Hence, H will be negative and S will be positive.

31. **The correct answer is (D).** In this problem you need to determine how many moles of electrons are produced. From this you can determine how many moles of copper can be reduced at the cathode.

$$10 \text{ A} \times \left(\frac{1 \text{C}}{1 \text{A} - \text{s}} \right) \times 75 \ \text{min} \times \left(\frac{60 \text{ s}}{1 \text{ min}} \right) = 4.50 \times 10^4 \text{ C}$$

$$4.50 \times 10^4 \text{ C} \times \frac{1 \text{ mol } e^-}{96\,500} = 0.4663 \text{ mol } e^-$$

$$0.4663 \text{ mol } e^- \times \left(\frac{1 \text{ mol Cu}}{2 \text{ mol } e^-} \right)\left(\frac{63.55 \text{ g}}{1 \text{ mol Cu}} \right) = 14.8 \text{ g Cu}$$

32. **The correct answer is (A).** In order to determine the enthalpy change for the reaction, you need to use Hess's law:

$\Delta H°rxn = \Sigma n\Delta H°f(\text{products}) - \Sigma \ m\Delta H°f(\text{reactants})$

$\Delta H°f P_4O_{10}(s) = -3110 \text{ kJ/mol}$

$\Delta H°f H_2O(l) = -286 \text{ kJ/mol}$

$\Delta H°f H_3PO_4(s) = -1279 \text{ kJ/mol}$

The solution is obtained by substituting the given values into the equation:

$= 4(H_3PO_4) - [P_4O_{10} + 6(H_2O)]$

$= 4(-1279) - [-3110 + 6(-286)] = -290 \text{ kJ}$

33. **The correct answer is (A).** In the acetylene molecule, one electron in the $2s$ orbital of carbon is promoted to the unoccupied $2p$ orbital. The $2s$ and one of the $2p$ orbitals hybridize to form two sp hybrid orbitals, which will form the C–H bond and the σ C–C bond. The two π bonds between the C atoms are formed by the two unhybridized p orbitals from each carbon.

34. **The correct answer is (B).** The most obvious feature to note about the isotope shown is that the number of neutrons is less than the number of protons. The most likely decay, therefore, is one that will increase the number of neutrons and

decrease the number of protons. In a positron emission, a proton is converted to a neutron and a positron. This has the effect of decreasing the atomic number by one while maintaining the same mass number. In this case, nitrogen–13 becomes carbon–13, which now has more neutrons than protons.

35. **The correct answer is (D).** This problem is another neutralization problem, but this time the acid is a diprotic acid. As a result, each mole of H_2SO_4 will yield two moles of hydrogen ions. The calculation is as follows:

Moles of H_2SO_4 in 25 mL of 1.2 M H_2SO_4

$$0.025 \text{ L} \times 1.2 \frac{\text{mol}}{\text{L}} = 0.03 \text{ mol } H_2SO_4$$

Therefore, there will be 0.06 mol H^+. To neutralize this will require 0.06 mol OH^-. To finish the problem,

$$\frac{0.06 \text{ mol}}{X \text{ L}} = 0.5 \text{ } M; X = 0.120 \text{ L or } 120 \text{ mL}$$

36. **The correct answer is (D).** The key to identifying an aldehyde is the carbonyl group on the last carbon atom.

37. **The correct answer is (B).** This is a salt produced from the cation of a strong base and the anion of a weak acid. Sodium therefore, is a very weak acid, but acetate is a strong base. Remember, the conjugate base of a weak acid is strong. The acetate ion will hydrolyze to form hydroxide ions.

38. **The correct answer is (E).** This is a mass–to–mass conversion. The solution is as follows:

$$C_2H_4(g) + 3O_2(g) \rightarrow 2CO_2(g) + 2H_2O(l)$$

$$200. \text{ g } C_2H_4 \times \left(\frac{1 \text{ mol } C_2H_4}{28.01 \text{ g}}\right)\left(\frac{2 \text{ mol } CO_2}{1 \text{ mol } C_2H_4}\right) \times$$

$$\left(\frac{44.01 \text{ g } CO_2}{1 \text{ mol } CO_2}\right) = 628 \text{ g}$$

39. **The correct answer is (C).** The normal boiling point is determined by the temperature where the liquid-gas line (on the phase diagram) is crossed by the 1.0 atm mark.

40. **The correct answer is (C).** The solubility equilibrium of AgBr is shown below:

$$AgBr(s) \rightleftharpoons Ag^+(aq) + Br^-(aq)$$

In the presence of NH_3, the silver ion, Ag^+, forms the complex ion $Ag(NH_3)^{2+}$. When this ion forms, it removes silver ions from the solution, thus driving the equilibrium reaction to the right.

41. **The correct answer is (C).** This is one you should probably commit to memory. First-order reactions can be transformed to straight-line graphs if the natural log of the concentration of the reactant is plotted against time. Second-order reactions, like the one represented in the graph for this question, are transformed to straight-line graphs by plotting the reciprocal of the concentration.

42. **The correct answer is (A).** In this question, you just need to set up the equilibrium expression for lead (II) sulfate, which is

$$K_{sp} = [Pb^{2+}][SO_4^{2-}]$$

By determining the concentrations of lead and sulfate at equilibrium, we can tell how much of it is soluble.

$$\text{Let } x = [Pb^{2+}] = [SO_4^{2-}]$$
$$K_{sp} = x^2$$
$$1.3 \times 10^{-8} = x^2$$

$$\sqrt{1.3 \times 10^{-18}} = x = 1.1 \times 10^{-4} \text{ M}$$

43. **The correct answer is (D).** The attractions between gas particles will cause them to exert less force on the walls of the container, thereby exerting less pressure. This will decrease the value of the numerator of the fraction, thereby making the result less than 1.

44. **The correct answer is (C).** In the reaction shown, an increase in volume will cause a decrease in pressure. This favors the reaction to the left because there are more moles of gas. Because the reaction is exothermic, an increase in temperature will also drive the reaction to the left. Removing CO_2 will cause the reaction to shift right to replace the removed gas. Therefore, choice (C) is the only possible answer.

45. **The correct answer is (D).** Choices (A), (B), and (C) are all based on weights, which do not change with changes in temperature. Molarity on the other hand is a concentration unit comparing mass per unit of volume. Because volume is affected by changes in temperature, molarity will be affected by temperature increase.

46. The correct answer is (C). In order to solve for the K_a, you will need to use the expression taken from the dissociation of HA:

$$HA \rightleftharpoons H^+ + A^-$$

$$K_a = \frac{[H^+][A^-]}{[HA]}$$

47. The correct answer is (E). In this problem, you need to remember that lighter gases effuse more quickly than heavier gases. That means that CH_4 will effuse most quickly, followed by NO_2, and finally Cl_2. That means that after the time period, more CH_4 will have effused than NO_2. Cl_2 will have effused the least, so it will be the most plentiful in the flask. Since partial pressures are proportional to mole fractions, the most plentiful gas will also exert the greatest partial pressure.

48. The correct answer is (B). The total pressure can be determined using the equation below:

$$P_{total} = P_A + P_B = X_A P^o_A + X_B P^o_B$$

$$P_{total} = \left(\frac{1.50 \text{ mol}}{7.0 \text{ mol}}\right)(75 \text{ mm Hg}) +$$

$$\left(\frac{5.50 \text{ mol}}{7.0 \text{ mol}}\right)(25 \text{ mm Hg}) = 35.7 \text{ mm Hg}$$

49. The correct answer is (B). This is a standard mole–to–gram conversion using the molar mass of the substance:

$$6.94 \text{ mol NaOH} \times \frac{40.0 \text{ g NaOH}}{1 \text{ mol NaOH}} = 278 \text{ g}$$

50. The correct answer is (D). There are a few things to look out for in this problem. First the temperature is given in degrees Celsius (so it must be converted). The second is the stoichiometry. The balanced equation states that two moles of carbon are needed for each mole of oxygen. In the problem, the amount of carbon given is an excess since the 1.20 mol of O_2 will only require 2.40 mol of C. It is very important, then, to not use the 3.50 mol value in the calculation. The number of moles of CO that are produced will be twice that of the oxygen that is used. Because 1.2 moles of oxygen are consumed, 2.4 mol of CO will be produced. With this out of the way, we can use the ideal gas law to solve for P:

$$P = \frac{nRT}{V}$$

$$= \frac{(2.4 \text{ mol CO}) (0.0821 \text{ L atm mol}^{-1}\text{K}^{-1}) (298 \text{ K})}{2.00 \text{ L}}$$

$$= 29.4 \text{ atm}$$

51. The correct answer is (D). Lithium salts burn bright red in flame tests. Strontium does also, but it is not listed as a choice.

52. The correct answer is (D). First, the percentages should be used to determine the empirical formula of vitamin C. The empirical formula can then be compared to the molecular formula, and any adjustments can be made at that time.

Because percents are given instead of moles or grams, assume a 100 g sample to simplify the problem:

$$40.9 \text{ g C} \times \frac{1 \text{ mol C}}{12.011 \text{ g C}} = 3.41 \text{ mol C}$$

$$4.58 \text{ g H} \times \frac{1 \text{ mol H}}{1.01 \text{ g H}} = 4.53 \text{ mol H}$$

$$54.52 \text{ g O} \times \frac{1 \text{ mol O}}{16.00 \text{ g O}} = 3.41 \text{ mol O}$$

In the next step, each is to be divided by the smallest number of moles (3.41):

$$C = \frac{3.41}{3.41} = 1.00$$

$$H = \frac{4.53}{3.41} = 1.33$$

$$O = \frac{3.41}{3.41} = 1.00$$

In order to make this work, you will need to multiply every value by 3. Therefore, the empirical formula for the compound will be

$$C_3H_4O_3$$

The formula weight for this compound is 88.1 g. Because this is exactly one half of the molecular weight, the subscripts for all substances in the empirical formula must be multiplied by 2:

$$C_6H_8O_6 = \text{vitamin C (ascorbic acid)}$$

53. The correct answer is (C). This is simply the definition of Lewis acids and bases. Lewis acids accept a pair of electrons while Lewis bases donate a pair of electrons.

54. The correct answer is (B). This is a matter of remembering the proper procedures for writing an equilibrium constant. In the expression, the product(s) is the numerator and the reactant(s) is the denominator. The coefficients for each should become exponents. Therefore in the reaction shown, the equilibrium expression should be

$$K = \frac{\left[NO_2\right]^2}{\left[NO\right]^2\left[O_2\right]}$$

Choice (B) represents this with the given information substituted in.

55. The correct answer is (B). As the salt solution sits out, water will continue to evaporate while the amount of solute will remain constant. As a result, the concentration of the solution continues to increase over time. This causes the vapor pressure to decrease over time.

56. The correct answer is (B). A mass-to-mass conversion. The solution is as follows:

$$Ca(OH)_2(aq) + 2HNO_3(aq) \rightarrow Ca(NO_3)_2(aq) + 2H_2O(l)$$

$$7.40 \text{ g Ca(OH)}_2 \left(\frac{1 \text{ mol Ca(OH)}_2}{74.1 \text{ g}}\right) \times$$

$$\left(\frac{1 \text{ mol Ca(NO}_3)_2}{1 \text{ mol Ca(OH)}_2}\right)\left(\frac{164.1 \text{ g Ca(NO}_3)_2}{1 \text{ mol Ca(NO}_3)_2}\right)$$

$$= 16.4 \text{ g}$$

57. The correct answer is (B). NH_3 has the weakest intermolecular forces of the other molecules. Diamond exists in a covalent network bond, sodium acetate is an ionic compound, and glycerine contains several C–O and O–H bonds (which allow hydrogen bonding). Silver has metallic bonds while ammonia, NH_3, is only held together by fairly weak hydrogen bonds (the N–H bond is not very polar).

58. The correct answer is (E). NH_4Cl is a salt formed from a weak base (NH_3) and a strong acid (HCl). It will hydrolyze to form an acidic solution. The other two substances, NaF and K_2CO_3, are salts of strong bases and weak acids. As a result, the conjugates, F^- and CO_3^-, will hydrolyze to form basic solutions.

59. The correct answer is (E). This problem requires the use of the formula for determining the specific heat of a substance. You also have to remember that the amount of heat lost by the object as it cools will

be the same as the amount of heat gained by the water. First, we can determine the amount of heat gained by the water:

$$q = mCp\Delta T = (100.0 \text{ g})(4.18 \text{ J/g } °C)(2.09 \text{ °C})$$

$$= 873.6 \text{ J}$$

Knowing this, we can assume that it is the same as the amount of heat that was lost by the unknown metal. We can determine the specific heat of the metal using the formula below:

$$C_p = \frac{q}{m\Delta T} = \frac{873.6 \text{ J}}{(50.0 \text{ g})(75°C)} = 0.23 \text{ J/g°C}$$

60. The correct answer is (B). An important consideration when you set this problem up is to remember that C is a solid and should not be entered into the equilibrium constant expression. As a result, the expression for K_p should be written as:

$$K_p = \frac{(P_{CO})^2}{(P_{CO_2})}$$

The other important thing to remember is to square the value of P_{CO} because of the coefficient of it has in the balanced equation. Substituting the value of K and the value of P_{CO_2} into the equation, we find that:

$$167.5 = \frac{(P_{CO})^2}{0.10 \text{ atm}}$$

$$P_{CO} = \sqrt{16.75} = 4.1$$

61. The correct answer is (D).

This problem requires the use of the ideal gas equation, $PV = nRT$. You are given all but P, so the problem can be set up as:

$$P = \frac{nRT}{V}$$

$$= \frac{(0.05 \text{ mol})(0.0821 \text{ L atm mol}^{-1}\text{K}^{-1})(680 \text{ K})}{1.00 \text{ L}}$$

$$= 2.8 \text{ atm}$$

62. The correct answer is (D). This is a dilution problem. In order to solve it, you need to use a modified version of the molarity equation. You know the molarity and the volume of the original solution, which means you can determine the number of moles of HCl in the original 10.0 mL. This is done using the calculation:

$$0.010 \text{ L} \times 12.0 \ \frac{\text{mol}}{\text{L}} = 0.12 \text{ mol HCl}$$

You need to add enough water so that the TOTAL volume (the 10 mL you started with plus what you added) is sufficient to create a molarity of 1.00 M.

$$Vf \times 1.00 \ \frac{\text{mol}}{\text{L}} = 0.12 \text{ mol HCl}$$

$Vf = 0.120$ L, meaning that 110 mL must be added to the 10 mL you started with to give a new volume of 120 mL (0.120 L). The shortcut formula that can be used to solve this type of problem is:

$$M_1 V_1 = M_2 V_2$$

Where the subscripts 1 and 2 represent the initial and final states.

63. **The correct answer is (C).** To determine the correct answer you need to use the relationship

$$\Delta G^\circ = -RT \ln K \text{ or } \Delta G^\circ = -2.303 \ RT \log K$$

For this step, you need to recall that the when K is greater than 1, log K (or ln$K$) is positive, and therefore ΔG° is negative. When K is less than 1, log K (ln K) is negative, and ΔG° is positive. So, when K is less than 1, the value of ΔG° will be positive.

64. **The correct answer is (C).** Of the seven choices, three are very easy to identify—the molecules with only three atoms in them. A molecule with three atoms must exist in a single plane. The next are a bit trickier. Ethylene (ethene), because of the pi bond between the carbon atoms, is locked into a rigid structure that is in a single plane. In the remaining structures, the lone pair electrons in ammonia, NH_3, push the hydrogen atoms into a pyramidal geometry. The C=O double bond in formaldehyde (methanal) locks the molecule in a planar configuration. The hydrogen peroxide molecule is the most difficult to identify. It forms a rather strange structure known as a skew-chain, which is not planar but rather bends into two planes. So, there are five different molecules among the choices that have all atoms in the same plane.

65. **The correct answer is (D).** The balanced equation, which balanced rather easily if you start with the polyatomic ion sulfate, is

2 As(OH)$_3$ (s) + 3 H$_2$SO$_4$ (aq) →
As$_2$(SO$_4$)$_3$(aq) + 6 H$_2$O(l)

66. **The correct answer is (B).** This problem requires the use of the Nernst equation (or at least its application). However, before you can solve the

equation, you need to know which electrode is the cathode and which is the anode. Remember, the substance with the most negative reduction potential is the most easily oxidized, making it the anode. In this problem, lead is the anode and cobalt the cathode. The emf of the second cell can be determined by

$$\begin{aligned} E &= E^\circ - \frac{0.0592}{n} \log Q \\ &= 0.15 \text{ V} - \left(\frac{0.0592}{2}\right) \times \log\left(\frac{0.001}{0.10}\right) \\ &= 0.21 \text{ V} \end{aligned}$$

You won't have a calculator to figure this out, but with a little logic you can still get the answer. Remember that the logarithm of a number less than 1 will be negative. Therefore, in the equation, you will be subtracting a negative number (which is the same as adding a positive). This will produce a result that is larger than the original voltage, which, in this case, is all the answer requires you to know.

67. **The correct answer is (B).** For this problem, refer to the equation:

$$\Delta G = \Delta H - T\Delta S$$

A negative G indicates a spontaneous reaction. If you substitute the values of ΔH and ΔS in the equation,

$$\Delta G = 1.37 \times 10^3 \text{ J} - T(120 \text{ J/K})$$

you can see that ΔG can only be negative when T is a large value.

68. **The correct answer is (C).** Bond dipoles can be treated as vector quantities or quantities with both a magnitude and a direction. Symmetric molecules, such as CO_2 and BCl_3, have vectors that cancel each other out (as do the equal and opposite attractions between the diatomic Cl_2). Only PCl_3, with its trigonal pyramidal shape, displays a net force or dipole moment.

69. **The correct answer is (E).** In this problem, you have to consider the van't Hoff factor for each solute. This is because as the number of ions in solution increases, the freezing point of the solution will decrease. Therefore, the solute that dissociates into the largest number of ions will produce the largest freezing point depression. In this problem, AlI_3 produces four ions, more than any other choice.

70. The correct answer is (D). If you're thinking quickly, you will realize the simplicity of this problem. First of all, 0.050 L is the same thing as 50 mL. Because of this, you have equal volumes of solutions with identical molarities. That means the number of moles of hydrogen ions in the acidic solution will equal the number of moles of hydroxide ions in the basic solution. As a result, the two solutions will completely neutralize one another, resulting in a solution with pH 7.0. No calculation is necessary.

71. The correct answer is (A). This problem can be solved by determing the volume where the number of moles will be equal in the two solutions. This is accomplished using the equation:

$$M_1V_1 = M_2V_2$$
$$(18.0\ M)(V_1) = (15.5\ L)(0.195\ M)$$
$$V_1 = 0.168\ L = 168\ mL$$

72. The correct answer is (A). To solve this problem we need to determine how many moles of electrons will be required to produce 100.0 g of chromium atoms (from the reduction of chromium ions). Once we know this, we can determine how long the 20.0 A current needs to flow.

$$100.0\ g\ Cr \times \frac{1\ mol}{52.00\ g} = 1.923\ mol\ Cr$$

The oxidation state of the chromium ions in the dichromate ions is +6, so six moles of electrons will be required to reduce 1 mole of Cr^{6+} ions.

$$1.923\ mol\ Cr \times \frac{6\ mol\ e^-}{1\ mol\ Cr} = 11.54\ mol\ e^-$$

$$11.54\ mol\ e^- \times \frac{96500\ C}{1\ mol\ e^-} = 1.114 \times 10^6\ C$$

$$5.567 \times 10^5\ C \times \left(\frac{1A-s}{1C}\right)\left(\frac{1}{20A}\right) = 5.570 \times 10^4\ s$$

$$5.570 \times 10^4\ s \times \left(\frac{1\ min}{60\ s}\right)\left(\frac{1\ hr}{60\ min}\right) = 15.5\ hr$$

73. The correct answer is (C). If you remember from chapter 16, the name of the ligand (NH_3 in this case) comes first preceded by a prefix indicating the number of times the ligand occurs. This is followed by the name of the metal ion, whose charge is indicated by a Roman numeral. Finally, the name of the anion is listed.

74. The correct answer is (A). This problem is an example of the common-ion effect. The weak acetic acid ionizes in water according to the following equation:

$$HC_2H_3O_2 \rightleftharpoons H^+ + C_2H_3O_2^-$$

Because this is in equilibrium, it will be disturbed by the presence of the acetate ion, donated by the sodium acetate. Sodium will not affect the equilibrium. The next step is to set up an equilibrium table, taking into account the initial presence of acetate ion.

	$HC_2H_3O_2$	H^+	$C_2H_3O_2^-$
Start	0.20	0	0.20
Δ	$-x$	$+x$	$+x$
Finish	$0.20 - x$	x	$0.20 + x$

The expression for K_a, then becomes

$$K_a = \frac{\left[H^+\right]\left[C_2H_3O_2^-\right]}{\left[HC_2H_3O_2\right]} = \frac{(x)(0.20+x)}{(0.20-x)}$$

It must be assumed that x is very small relative to 0.20 (we can check this later), so we can rewrite the expression as

$$K_a = 1.8 \times 10^{-5} = \frac{(x)(0.20)}{(0.20)} = x$$
$$1.8 \times 10^{-5} = x$$

Our assumption about x being much smaller than 0.20 is supported, so we can solve the problem.

$$[H+] = 1.8 \times 10^{-5}\ M$$
$$pH = -\log[1.8 \times 10^{-5}] = 4.7$$

You won't be able to use a calculator on the multiple-choice questions, but your familiarity with logarithms can help you here. You should know that the $-\log(1.0 \times 10^{-5})$ is 5. Concentrations higher than this will produce a pH lower than 5.0 and concentrations lower than this will produce a pH higher than 5.0. Since $1.8 \times 10^{-5} > 1.0 \times 10^{-5}$, you can rule out the other possible answer, choice (D), which is 5.4.

75. The correct answer is (D). Only experience with these chemicals, either through actual lab experience or demonstrations, will help you answer questions like these. The dichromate ion has a characteristic orange color. Na_2CrO_4 is yellow, $KmnO_4$ is purple, $Ni(NO_3)_2$ is green, and $CuCl_2$ is blue-green.

Section II

1. (a) If 6.1×10^{-3} g CaC_2O_4 can be dissolved per liter of solution, then determining the molar solubility of the substance simply requires that you convert this value to the number of moles per liter:

$$6.1 \times 10^{-3} \text{ g } CaC_2O_4 \times \frac{1 \text{ mol } CaC_2O_4}{128.1 \text{ g } CaC_2O_4}$$

$$= 4.8 \times 10^{-5} \text{ mol per liter.}$$

(b) The solubility equilibrium is based on the following equation:

$$CaC_2O_4(s) \rightleftharpoons Ca^{2+}(aq) + C_2O_4^{2-}(aq)$$

(c) K_{sp} can be calculated based on the following:

$$K_{sp} = [Ca^{2+}][C_2O_4^{2-}]$$

where the concentrations used in the equation will be obtained from (a). While this step is probably one that you can do in your head, we'll go through it just to make sure you are following the correct procedure. The next step is to set up an equilibrium table:

	CaC_2O_4	Ca^{2+}	$C_2O_4^{2-}$
Start		0	0
Δ		$+4.8 \times 10^{-5}$	$+4.8 \times 10^{-5}$
Finish		4.8×10^{-5}	4.8×10^{-5}

$$K_{sp} = [Ca^{2+}][C_2O_4^{2-}] = (4.8 \times 10^{-5})(4.8 \times 10^{-5})$$

$$= 2.3 \times 10^{-9}$$

(d) In this problem, calcium oxalate is being placed into a solution that contains a common ion. Any calculations related to solubility will have to take this into account. In this case, the equilibrium concentrations of the substances will be affected by the initial presence of calcium ions in solution (the calcium from calcium chloride will suppress the dissolving of some of the calcium oxalate). To determine the extent of this effect we must observe the solubility equilibrium expression using the modified concentration data:

	CaC_2O_4	Ca^{2+}	$C_2O_4^{2-}$
Start		0.10	0
Δ		$+x$	$+x$
Finish		$0.10 + x$	x

At this point, we can use the value of K_{sp} that was calculated in part (c) to set up the expression that will solve for x, the molar solubility:

$$K_{sp} = [Ca^{2+}][C_2O_4^{2-}]$$

$$2.3 \times 10^{-9} = (0.10 + x)x$$

At this point, we will make the assumption that x is quite small compared to 0.10 and, as a result, will not be included in that portion of the calculation. Therefore:

$$2.3 \times 10^{-9} = 0.10x$$

$$x = 2.3 \times 10^{-8} M$$

By comparison, this number is much smaller than the value for dissolving in pure substances. In addition, our assumption that x was much smaller than 0.10 has been supported.

(e) This problem calls for the use of the ion product. If we calculate the ion product, we can then compare it to K_{sp} for the substance. If it is less than K_{sp}, precipitation will not occur. If it exceeds K_{sp}, then precipitation will occur.

Because we are given volumes, we need to determine the concentrations in the final mixture. This will be accomplished by determining how many moles are in the original solution and then using the combined volumes of the two solutions to calculate the new concentration.

The number of moles in 50.0 mL of 0.0025 M $CaCl_2$ is

$$0.050 \text{ L} \times \frac{0.0025 \text{ mol } CaCl_2}{1 \text{ L } CaCl_2}$$

$$= 1.25 \times 10^{-4} \text{ mol } CaCl_2$$

Because the dissociation of $CaCl_2$ yields one mole of Ca^{2+} for every mole of $CaCl_2$, we can say that we have 1.25×10^{-4} mol Ca^{2+}.

Next, we need to find the number of moles of oxalate ions.

$$0.050 \text{ L } Na_2C_2O_4 \times \frac{1.0 \times 10^{-5} \text{ mol } Na_2C_2O_4}{1 L \text{ } Na_2C_2O_4}$$

$$= 5.0 \times 10^{-7} \text{ mol } Na_2C_2O_4$$

Because each mole of $Na_2C_2O_4$ yields one mole of $C_2O_4^{2-}$ ions, we can say that we have 5.0×10^{-7} mol $C_2O_4^{2-}$ ions.

Before we can use these quantities in the ion product expression, we will have to convert them to molarities. We need to make sure we are using the combined volume of the two solutions to determine the molarity in the final mixture.

$$[Ca^{2+}] = \frac{125 \times 10^{-4} \text{ mol}}{0.100 \text{L}} = 1.25 \times 10^{-3} \text{ M}$$

$$[C_2O_4^{2-}] = \frac{5 \times 10^{-7} \text{ mol}}{0.100 \text{L}} = 5.0 \times 10^{-6} \text{ M}$$

At this point, we are ready to calculate Q:

$Q = [Ca^{2+}][C_2O_4^{2-}]$

$= [1.25 \times 10^{-3} M][5.0 \times 10^{-6} M] = 6.25 \times 10^{-9}$

Because $Q > K_{sp}$, we expect that CaC_2O_4 will precipitate.

2. **(a)** The equilibrium expression, K_c, can be written as:

$$K_c = \frac{[IBr]^2}{[I_2][Br_2]}$$

(b) This process will require a few steps. In the first, we need to determine the concentration of each substance when they were first put in the flask. This is obtained by:

$$M = \frac{0.0015 \text{ mol}}{5.00 \text{ L}} = 3.0 \times 10^{-4} \text{ M}$$

Once this is known, we can set up an equilibrium calculation table to determine the concentrations of the substances at equilibrium:

	I$_2$	Br$_2$	2IBr
Start	3.0×10^{-4}	3.0×10^{-4}	0
Δ	$-x$	$-x$	$+2x$
Finish	$(3.0 \times 10^{-4}) - x$	$(3.0 \times 10^{-4}) - x$	$2x$

These values can now be placed into the equilibrium constant expression from (a):

$$K_c = \frac{[IBr]^2}{[I_2][Br_2]}$$

$$1.2 \times 10^2 = \frac{(2x)^2}{(3.0 \times 10^{-4} - x)(3.0 \times 10^{-4} - x)}$$

To simplify what could be a rather messy problem, we can take the square root of each side of the equation:

$$\sqrt{1.2 \times 10^2} = \sqrt{\frac{(2x)^2}{(3.0 \times 10^{-4} - x)(3.0 \times 10^{-4} - x)}}$$

$$10.95 = \frac{(2x)}{3.0 \times 10^{-4}}$$

We can now rearrange this equation and solve for x:

$$(3.0 \times 10^{-4} - x) = \frac{2x}{10.95} = 0.183x$$

$$3.0 \times 10^{-4} = 1.183x$$

$$\frac{3.0 \times 10^{-4}}{1.183} = x = 2.54 \times 10^{-4} \text{ M}$$

Now that we know the value of x, we can substitute it back into the values shown in the equilibrium table to solve the problem.

$[I_2] = [Br_2] = (3.0 \times 10^{-4} - 2.54 \times 10^{-4})$

$= 4.6 \times 10^{-5}$

$[IBr] = 2x = 2(2.54 \times 10^{-4}) = 5.1 \times 10^{-4}$

(c) To solve this problem, you need to use the value for K_c and the formula:

$$K_p = K_c(RT)\Delta n$$

For this reaction, Δn = moles products – moles reactants = 2–2 = 0. Since $\Delta n = 0$, then $Kp = Kc$ for this reaction.

(d) If 0.05 mol I$_2$ are added to the vessel, the equilibrium will shift to the right (the formation of 2IBr) to alleviate the stress.

3. **(a)** In order to solve this problem, you need to use the given information in this formula:

$\Delta H°rxn = \Sigma n\Delta H°f(\text{products}) - \Sigma m\Delta H°f(\text{reactants})$

Substituting the data, we get

$\Delta H° = 2(SO_3) - [2(SO_2) + O_2]$

$= 2 \text{ mol}(-396 \text{ kJ/mol}) - [2 \text{ mol}(-297 \text{ kJ/mol}) + 0)]$

$= -792 \text{ kJ} + 594 \text{ kJ}$

$= -198 \text{ kJ}$

(b) For this problem, you need to use the equation below:

$\Delta S° = \Sigma n\Delta S°(\text{products}) - \Sigma m\Delta S°(\text{reactants}$

$\Delta S° = 2(SO_3) - [2(SO_2) + O_2]$

$\Delta S° = 2 \text{ mol}(257 \text{ J/K} \bullet \text{mol}) -$

$[2 \text{ mol}(248 \text{ J/K} \bullet \text{mol}) + 1\text{mol}(205 \text{ J/K} \bullet \text{mol})]$

$\Delta S° = 514 \text{ J/K} - 701 \text{ J/K} = -187 \text{ J/K}$

(c) In this portion, you don't need to use the standard free energy values. You have already calculated entropy and enthalpy, so the equation to use is

$$\Delta G° = \Delta H° - T\Delta S°$$

$$\Delta G° = -198 \text{ kJ} - [(298 \text{ K})(-187 \text{ J/K})\left(\frac{1 \text{ kJ}}{1000 \text{ J}}\right)]$$

$$= -198 \text{ kJ} + 55.7 \text{ kJ} = -142 \text{ kJ}$$

(d)

i) The reaction is exothermic, which you can tell by the negative value of $\Delta H°$.

ii) The reaction is decreasing in entropy. This is consistent with the fact that you are starting with 3 moles of gas and decreasing to 2 moles of gas.

iii) The process is spontaneous, which you can tell by the negative value for $\Delta G°$.

4. (a) $C_2H_5OH + HCOOH \rightarrow HCOOC_2H_5 + H_2O$

In this condensation reaction, the alcohol ethanol reacts with methanoic acid to yield the ester ethyl methanoate and water (which is always produced in condensation reactions).

(b) $(NH_4)_2CO_3 \rightarrow H_2O + CO_2 + NH_3$

This is a decomposition reaction that is very frequently referred to and/or performed in introductory classes.

(c) $I^- + H_2O \rightarrow I_2 + H_2 + OH^-$

This is an electrolysis of an aqueous solution. When you get a problem like this, you need to be aware that water can be electrolyzed. In this case it is because water is more easily reduced than potassium. Because the water is reduced to yield hydrogen gas, the hydroxide ions will be left behind in solution.

(d) $Na + H_2O \rightarrow Na^+ + OH^- + H_2$

Sodium is a better reducing agent than hydrogen. As a result, when sodium metal is placed in water, it is oxidized, yielding hydrogen gas and a sodium hydroxide solution.

(e) $Cu + H^+ + NO_3^- \rightarrow Cu^{2+} + NO + H_2O$

This is a tricky one. One of the key clues in the problem was the term *dilute* in reference to nitric acid. This outcome is different from the outcome with concentrated nitric acid. When concentrated acid is used, the nitrate ion is reduced to NO_2, but with the dilute acid, it is reduced to NO. Hydrogen facilitates in the reaction but does not form a gas (it is used to form water).

(f) $Cl_2 + I^- \rightarrow I_2 + Cl^-$

Cl_2 oxidizes iodide to yield chloride ions and iodine. With the halogens, fluorine is the most powerful oxidizing agent, and each element going down the group becomes less powerful. As a result, a halogen can oxidize the halogens below it in a replacement reaction.

(g) $H^+ + OH^- \rightarrow H_2O$

This is a classic neutralization reaction of a strong acid combined with a strong base.

(h) $C_2H_5OH + O_2 \rightarrow CO_2 + H_2O$
(CO if O_2 is not in excess)

This is a typical combustion reaction. The reaction shown is a complete combustion reaction, which assumes an excess of O_2. If O_2 is not considered in excess then CO would also be a product.

5. (a) According to Le Châtelier's principle, the addition of oxygen gas will force the reaction to the left; therefore, there will be an increase in SO_3.

(b) If the pressure is reduced by increasing the volume, the reaction will shift to the right. This will create more gas particles to compensate for the decrease in pressure. The shift to the right will cause a decrease in SO_3.

(c) The addition of an inert gas, like helium, will have no effect on the equilibrium mixture. Although the inert gas increases the overall pressure in the container, it does not affect the concentrations or partial pressures of the individual gases. As a result, the amount of SO_3 will remain constant.

(d) The reaction is endothermic (as evident from the positive value of ΔH). Therefore, if the reaction mixture is heated, the equilibrium will shift to the right, decreasing the amount of SO_3.

(e) If oxygen gas is removed, the equilibrium will shift to the right to create more. This will cause a decrease in the amount of SO_3.

6. (a)

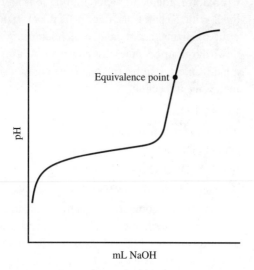

pH

mL NaOH

Equivalence point

(b) One of the biggest differences is the steepness of the curve around the equivalence point. Strong acids experience a very large increase in pH with a relatively small addition of base.

One other difference is the location of the equivalence point. For strong acids, the equivalence point is located at 7.0, but for weaker acids, this equivalence point is at a higher pH.

(c) Strong acid, strong base titrations are much more forgiving on your choice of indicator. The reason for this is because of the large change in pH with a relatively small addition of base near the equivalence point. The difference in base volume required to change from pH 4 to pH 10 is relatively small. Therefore, a variety of indicators can be used with reasonably small errors.

With a weak acid, strong base titration like this one, the situation is more critical for two reasons. First, the pH changes a bit more gradually than with strong acid titrations. As a result, an indicator like methyl red will change color well before the equivalence point is reached.

The second reason the indicator choice is critical is really an extension of the first reason. For weak acids, the pH at the equivalence is greater than 7.0. Because the pH changes gradually and because the pH is greater than 7, it is important to select an indicator, like phenolphthalein, that will change color in a range of pH values between 8 and 10.

(d) The most likely source of the error is a problem with the concentration of the titrant. If the base is too dilute, the volume that must be added (to supply enough hydroxide ions) must be increased—so much so that it can exceed the volume of the buret. It is important to perform some approximate calculations prior to a titration to assure that an adequate concentration of base is used.

7. (a) The number of molecules in each vessel is the same. This is consistent with Avogadro's hypothesis since both gases are in equal size containers at the same temperature. Each container will have the same number of moles of gas in it and, therefore, the same number of molecules.

(b) Because each container has the same number of particles in it and since the SF_6 molecules are much heavier than the N_2 molecules, the density of the SF_6 will be higher than that of N_2.

(c) The average kinetic energy of the particles is determined by the temperature, which in this case is the same. Therefore, the average kinetic energies will be the same.

(d) SF_6 is going to deviate the most from ideal behavior because of its large size. Not only does it have a large volume, but it will experience more intermolecular attractions than N_2.

(e) The rate of effusion, per Graham's law, is inversely related to the mass of the particles. The larger the particle, the slower the rate of effusion. Therefore, nitrogen will have a higher rate of effusion because of its smaller molecular mass.

8. (a) The main principle here is the difference between adhesive and cohesive forces. Adhesive forces, or the forces between a substance and a surface, are responsible for the attraction between the molecules of water (or mercury) and the glass. Cohesive forces are the forces between the water molecules or the mercury molecules.

For water, the adhesive force that attracts water to the glass is greater than the cohesive force holding the water molecules together. As a result, the molecules on the edge of the glass cling to the glass while the water molecules in the middle hang down to form the meniscus.

For mercury, the cohesive forces between mercury particles are greater than the adhesive forces holding mercury to the glass. As a result, the inward-directed cohesion, which is disproportionate on the surface of the liquid, causes the downward curvature at the edges of the mercury.

(b) In a salt crystal, the sodium and chloride ions as well as their electrons are locked in a rigid crystalline lattice. The electrons that are in the crystal are localized around specific atoms. These electrons are tightly bound to each ion inside the rigid structure and, as a result, are not free to move about. Salt crystals do not conduct electricity.

However, when dissolved, the individual component ions separate and move freely about in solution. This free movement of charged particles provides the basis for the conductivity of ionic substances in solution.

(c) When it is humid, there is a larger amount of water vapor in the air. This larger amount of water vapor causes more particles to re-enter the liquid phase from the gaseous phase. This will decrease the net change of particles from the liquid to the gaseous phase, which is when cooling occurs. On a dry day, there is a greater net flow of molecules from the liquid to the gaseous phase and, hence, a greater cooling effect.

(d) Steam burns are usually more severe than burns from boiling water for two reasons. First, steam can exist at temperatures greater than 100 °C. Second, and most important, the heat of vaporization of water, which is rather substantial, is released as the water changes from the gaseous phase to the liquid phase.

Practice Test 2
Answer Sheet

If a section has fewer questions than answer ovals, leave the extra ovals blank.

SECTION I

1. Ⓐ Ⓑ Ⓒ Ⓓ Ⓔ   16. Ⓐ Ⓑ Ⓒ Ⓓ Ⓔ   31. Ⓐ Ⓑ Ⓒ Ⓓ Ⓔ   46. Ⓐ Ⓑ Ⓒ Ⓓ Ⓔ   61. Ⓐ Ⓑ Ⓒ Ⓓ Ⓔ

2. Ⓐ Ⓑ Ⓒ Ⓓ Ⓔ   17. Ⓐ Ⓑ Ⓒ Ⓓ Ⓔ   32. Ⓐ Ⓑ Ⓒ Ⓓ Ⓔ   47. Ⓐ Ⓑ Ⓒ Ⓓ Ⓔ   62. Ⓐ Ⓑ Ⓒ Ⓓ Ⓔ

3. Ⓐ Ⓑ Ⓒ Ⓓ Ⓔ   18. Ⓐ Ⓑ Ⓒ Ⓓ Ⓔ   33. Ⓐ Ⓑ Ⓒ Ⓓ Ⓔ   48. Ⓐ Ⓑ Ⓒ Ⓓ Ⓔ   63. Ⓐ Ⓑ Ⓒ Ⓓ Ⓔ

4. Ⓐ Ⓑ Ⓒ Ⓓ Ⓔ   19. Ⓐ Ⓑ Ⓒ Ⓓ Ⓔ   34. Ⓐ Ⓑ Ⓒ Ⓓ Ⓔ   49. Ⓐ Ⓑ Ⓒ Ⓓ Ⓔ   64. Ⓐ Ⓑ Ⓒ Ⓓ Ⓔ

5. Ⓐ Ⓑ Ⓒ Ⓓ Ⓔ   20. Ⓐ Ⓑ Ⓒ Ⓓ Ⓔ   35. Ⓐ Ⓑ Ⓒ Ⓓ Ⓔ   50. Ⓐ Ⓑ Ⓒ Ⓓ Ⓔ   65. Ⓐ Ⓑ Ⓒ Ⓓ Ⓔ

6. Ⓐ Ⓑ Ⓒ Ⓓ Ⓔ   21. Ⓐ Ⓑ Ⓒ Ⓓ Ⓔ   36. Ⓐ Ⓑ Ⓒ Ⓓ Ⓔ   51. Ⓐ Ⓑ Ⓒ Ⓓ Ⓔ   66. Ⓐ Ⓑ Ⓒ Ⓓ Ⓔ

7. Ⓐ Ⓑ Ⓒ Ⓓ Ⓔ   22. Ⓐ Ⓑ Ⓒ Ⓓ Ⓔ   37. Ⓐ Ⓑ Ⓒ Ⓓ Ⓔ   52. Ⓐ Ⓑ Ⓒ Ⓓ Ⓔ   67. Ⓐ Ⓑ Ⓒ Ⓓ Ⓔ

8. Ⓐ Ⓑ Ⓒ Ⓓ Ⓔ   23. Ⓐ Ⓑ Ⓒ Ⓓ Ⓔ   38. Ⓐ Ⓑ Ⓒ Ⓓ Ⓔ   53. Ⓐ Ⓑ Ⓒ Ⓓ Ⓔ   68. Ⓐ Ⓑ Ⓒ Ⓓ Ⓔ

9. Ⓐ Ⓑ Ⓒ Ⓓ Ⓔ   24. Ⓐ Ⓑ Ⓒ Ⓓ Ⓔ   39. Ⓐ Ⓑ Ⓒ Ⓓ Ⓔ   54. Ⓐ Ⓑ Ⓒ Ⓓ Ⓔ   69. Ⓐ Ⓑ Ⓒ Ⓓ Ⓔ

10. Ⓐ Ⓑ Ⓒ Ⓓ Ⓔ   25. Ⓐ Ⓑ Ⓒ Ⓓ Ⓔ   40. Ⓐ Ⓑ Ⓒ Ⓓ Ⓔ   55. Ⓐ Ⓑ Ⓒ Ⓓ Ⓔ   70. Ⓐ Ⓑ Ⓒ Ⓓ Ⓔ

11. Ⓐ Ⓑ Ⓒ Ⓓ Ⓔ   26. Ⓐ Ⓑ Ⓒ Ⓓ Ⓔ   41. Ⓐ Ⓑ Ⓒ Ⓓ Ⓔ   56. Ⓐ Ⓑ Ⓒ Ⓓ Ⓔ   71. Ⓐ Ⓑ Ⓒ Ⓓ Ⓔ

12. Ⓐ Ⓑ Ⓒ Ⓓ Ⓔ   27. Ⓐ Ⓑ Ⓒ Ⓓ Ⓔ   42. Ⓐ Ⓑ Ⓒ Ⓓ Ⓔ   57. Ⓐ Ⓑ Ⓒ Ⓓ Ⓔ   72. Ⓐ Ⓑ Ⓒ Ⓓ Ⓔ

13. Ⓐ Ⓑ Ⓒ Ⓓ Ⓔ   28. Ⓐ Ⓑ Ⓒ Ⓓ Ⓔ   43. Ⓐ Ⓑ Ⓒ Ⓓ Ⓔ   58. Ⓐ Ⓑ Ⓒ Ⓓ Ⓔ   73. Ⓐ Ⓑ Ⓒ Ⓓ Ⓔ

14. Ⓐ Ⓑ Ⓒ Ⓓ Ⓔ   29. Ⓐ Ⓑ Ⓒ Ⓓ Ⓔ   44. Ⓐ Ⓑ Ⓒ Ⓓ Ⓔ   59. Ⓐ Ⓑ Ⓒ Ⓓ Ⓔ   74. Ⓐ Ⓑ Ⓒ Ⓓ Ⓔ

15. Ⓐ Ⓑ Ⓒ Ⓓ Ⓔ   30. Ⓐ Ⓑ Ⓒ Ⓓ Ⓔ   45. Ⓐ Ⓑ Ⓒ Ⓓ Ⓔ   60. Ⓐ Ⓑ Ⓒ Ⓓ Ⓔ   75. Ⓐ Ⓑ Ⓒ Ⓓ Ⓔ

Practice Test 2

SECTION I

Time—1 Hour and 30 Minutes

NO CALCULATORS MAY BE USED WITH SECTION I.

Note: For all questions, assume that the temperature is 298 K, the pressure is 1.00 atmosphere, and solutions are aqueous unless otherwise specified.

Throughout the test, the following symbols have the definitions specified unless otherwise noted.

T = temperature	*M* = molar
P = pressure	*m* = molal
V = volume	L, mL = liter(s), milliliter(s)
S = entropy	g = gram(s)
H = enthalpy	nm = nanometer(s)
G = free energy	atm = atmosphere(s)
R = molar gas constant	J, kJ = joule(s), kilojoule(s)
n = number of moles	v = volt(s)
	mol = mole(s)

Directions: Each set of lettered choices below refers to the numbered statements immediately following it. Select the one lettered choice that best fits each statement and then fill in the corresponding oval on the answer sheet. A choice may be used once, more than once, or not at all in each set.

Questions 1–3 refer to the choices below:

(A) Heisenberg uncertainty principle

(B) Schrödinger equation

(C) Hund's rule

(D) X-ray diffraction

(E) Photoelectric effect

1. Can be used to predict the paramagnetism of certain elements

2. Predicts that it is impossible to simultaneously know both the location and momentum of an electron

3. Predicts the locations and orientations of atomic orbitals

Use these answers for questions 4–6:

(A) Arrhenius acid

(B) Brønsted-Lowry acid

(C) Brønsted-Lowry base

(D) Lewis acid

(E) Lewis base

4. BF_3 in the reaction: $BF_3 + F^- \rightarrow BF_4$

5. CN^- in the reaction: $Cu^{2+}(aq) + 4CN^-(aq) \rightarrow Cu(CN)_4^{2-}(aq)$

6. H_2O in the reaction: $HC_2H_3O_2(aq) + H_2O(aq) \rightarrow C_2H_3O_2^-(aq) + H_3O^+(aq)$

GO ON TO THE NEXT PAGE

Questions 7–9 refer to the choices below:

(A) N

(B) Cl

(C) Ne

(D) Mg

(E) Rb

7. Which element is the most electronegative?

8. Which element has the most possible oxidation states?

9. Which element has the smallest first ionization energy?

Directions: Each of the questions or incomplete statements below is followed by five answers or completions. Select the one that is best in each case and then fill in the corresponding oval on the answer sheet.

10. About how many milliliters of 6.0-molar HCl must be diluted to obtain 1.0 liter of 2.5-molar HCl?

(A) 133 mL

(B) 250 mL

(C) 400 mL

(D) 420 mL

(E) 840 mL

11. Which of the following is most likely to be a solid at room temperature?

(A) Na_2S

(B) HF

(C) NH_3

(D) N_2

(E) H_2

12. The K_{sp} of $Al(OH)_3$ is 2×10^{-32}. At what pH will a $0.2\ M\ Al^{3+}$ solution begin to show precipitation of $Al(OH)_3$?

(A) $-\log\left(\dfrac{1 \times 10^{-14}}{\sqrt[3]{1.0 \times 10^{-31}}}\right)$

(B) $-\log\sqrt[3]{1.0 \times 10^{-31}}$

(C) $-\log\left(\dfrac{1 \times 10^{-14}}{\sqrt[3]{2.0 \times 10^{-32}}}\right)$

(D) $-\log\sqrt[3]{2.0 \times 10^{-32}}$

(E) $-\log\left(\dfrac{1 \times 10^{-14}}{2.0 \times 10^{-32}}\right)$

13. Which of the following represents a pair of isotopes of the same element?

		Atomic number	Mass number
(A)	I.	92	208
	II.	92	211
(B)	I.	45	106
	II.	92	206
(C)	I.	92	238
	II.	89	235
(D)	I.	92	233
	II.	89	233
(E)	I.	7	15
	II.	8	16

14. The melting point of MgS is higher than that of KCl. Which of the following observations can explain this?

I. Mg^{2+} has a greater positive charge than K^+

II. S^{2-} has a greater negative charge than Cl^-

III. S^{2-} has a smaller radius than Cl^-

(A) III only

(B) II and III only

(C) I and III only

(D) I and II only

(E) I, II, and III

15. Which choice shows the correct arrangement of the acids in order of increasing acid strength?

(A) $HClO_4$, $HClO_3$, $HClO_2$, $HClO$

(B) $HClO_4$, $HClO$, $HClO_3$, $HClO_2$

(C) $HClO$, $HClO_2$, $HClO_3$, $HClO_4$

(D) $HClO_3$, $HClO$, $HClO_4$, $HClO_2$

(E) More information is needed to answer the question.

16. The half-life of $^{90}_{38}Sr$ is 28 years. How long will it take for a given sample of $^{90}_{38}Sr$ to be 87.5% decomposed?

(A) 8.75 half-lives

(B) 3.5 years

(C) 84 years

(D) 24.5 years

(E) 2.2×10^4 years

17. Which one of the following reactions would have a positive value for $\Delta S°$?

(A) $Ba(OH)_2(s) + CO_2(g) \rightarrow BaCO_3(s) + H_2O(l)$

(B) $N_2(g) + 3H_2(g) \rightarrow 2NH_3(g)$

(C) $2SO_3(g) \rightarrow 2SO_2(g) + O_2(g)$

(D) $AgNO_3(aq) + HCl(aq) \rightarrow AgCl(s) + HNO_3(aq)$

(E) $2NO_2(g) \rightarrow N_2O_4(g)$

18. In the molecule SF_6, what is the hybridization of S?

(A) sp

(B) sp^2

(C) sp^3

(D) dsp^3

(E) d^2sp^3

19. Which of the following species cannot function as an oxidizing agent?

(A) $S(s)$

(B) $NO_3^-(aq)$

(C) $Cr_2O_7^{2-}(aq)$

(D) $I^-(aq)$

(E) $MnO_4^-(aq)$

20. Which of the following processes must exist in equilibrium with the evaporation process when a measurement of vapor pressure is made?

(A) Fusion

(B) Vaporization

(C) Sublimation

(D) Boiling

(E) Condensation

GO ON TO THE NEXT PAGE

$$2CO_2(g) \rightleftharpoons 2CO(g) + O_2(g)$$
$$\Delta H° = -514 \text{ kJ}$$

21. The equilibrium constant will be the highest when the reaction above is carried out at

(A) low temperature and low pressure.

(B) low temperature and high pressure.

(C) high temperature and high pressure.

(D) high temperature and low pressure.

(E) any temperature or pressure; neither affect the reaction.

22. Which of the following solid salts is more soluble in 1.0 M H$^+$ than in pure water?

(A) NaCl

(B) CaCO$_3$

(C) KCl

(D) AgCl

(E) KNO$_3$

23. Which of the following is a conjugate acid/base pair?

(A) H$_3$O$^+$ and OH$^-$

(B) HCl and OCl$^-$

(C) NH$_4^+$ / NH$_3$

(D) H$_2$SO$_4$ / SO$_4^{2-}$

(E) HClO$_4$ and ClO$_4^-$

24. Place the elements S, Cl, and F in order of increasing atomic radius.

(A) S, Cl, F

(B) S, F, Cl

(C) F, Cl, S

(D) F, S, Cl

(E) Cl, F, S

$$3H_2(g) + N_2(g) \rightleftharpoons 2NH_3(g)$$

25. If 2.00 mol H$_2$, 1.00 mol N$_2$, and 2.00 mol NH$_3$ are placed into a 1.00 L evacuated flask. How will the reaction above proceed if K_c = 0.105 at this temperature?

(A) The reaction must proceed from right to left.

(B) The reaction must proceed from left to right.

(C) The reaction is already at equilibrium, so no net movement will occur.

(D) The reaction cannot establish equilibrium at this temperature.

(E) The reaction will proceed from left to right until 2.23 mol NH$_3$ have been produced.

26. A gas sample is heated from $-23.0°C$ to $57.0°C$, and the volume is increased from 2.00 L to 4.00 L. If the initial pressure is 0.125 atm, which of the following calculations will yield the correct final pressure?

(A) $\dfrac{(0.125)(2.00)(-23.0)}{(57)(4.00)}$

(B) $\dfrac{(57)(4.00)}{(0.125)(2.00)(-23.0)}$

(C) $\dfrac{(0.125)(2.00)(330)}{(250)(4.00)}$

(D) $\dfrac{(250)(4.00)}{(0.125)(2.00)(330)}$

(E) $\dfrac{(0.125)(4.00)(2.00)}{(250)(330)}$

27. A 0.10-molar solution of a weak monoprotic acid, HA, has a pH of 4.00. The ionization constant of this acid is

(A) 5.0×10^{-7}

(B) 1.0×10^{-7}

(C) 5.0×10^{-6}

(D) 1.0×10^{-6}

(E) 5.0×10^{-6}

$$\text{Rate} = k[NO]^2[Cl_2]$$

28. What is the order of the reaction with respect to nitric oxide, NO?

(A) 0

(B) 1

(C) 2

(D) 3

(E) 4

$$Mg + 2H_2O \rightarrow Mg(OH)_2 + H_2$$

29. What mass of hydrogen can be produced by reaction of 4.73 g of magnesium with 1.83 g of water?

(A) 0.103 g

(B) 0.0162 g

(C) 0.0485 g

(D) 0.219 g

(E) 3.20 g

30. H_2S is a gas at room temperature while H_2O is a liquid. What can explain this difference?

(A) H_2O is amphoteric.

(B) H_2S is flammable.

(C) H_2O molecules have smaller dipole moments than H_2S.

(D) H_2S is a heavier molecule.

(E) The greater electronegativity of O allows more hydrogen bonding.

31. A voltaic cell is designed with a copper electrode immersed in 1.0 M copper (II) sulfate solution, $CuSO_4$(aq), and a lead electrode immersed in 1.0 M lead (II) nitrate solution, $Pb(NO_3)_2$(aq) at 25 °C. Given the standard reduction potentials shown below, determine the potential of the cell in volts.

$$Pb^{2+} + 2e^- \rightarrow Pb \qquad E° = -0.13 \text{ V}$$
$$Cu^{2+} + 2e^- \rightarrow Cu \qquad E° = +0.34 \text{ V}$$

(A) 0.47 V

(B) 0.92 V

(C) 0.22 V

(D) 0.58 V

(E) 0.17 V

32. Which of the following is the least soluble?

(A) $CaSO_4$ $\qquad K_{sp} = 9.1\ 10^{-6}$

(B) BaF_2 $\qquad K_{sp} = 1.0\ 10^{-6}$

(C) $NiCO_3$ $\qquad K_{sp} = 6.6\ 10^{-14}$

(D) $CaCrO_4$ $\qquad K_{sp} = 7.1\ 10^{-4}$

(E) $Sn(OH)_2$ $\qquad K_{sp} = 1.4\ 10^{-28}$

33. Which of the following has an incomplete octet in its Lewis structure?

(A) SO_2

(B) ICl

(C) CO_2

(D) F_2

(E) NO

34. How many milliliters of 0.20 M KOH are needed to completely neutralize 20 mL of 0.10 M H_3PO_4?

(A) 3.0 mL

(B) 10 mL

(C) 20 mL

(D) 30 mL

(E) 60 mL

35. If $^{214}_{82}Pb$ undergoes a beta decay and the product of this decay undergoes another beta decay, which nuclide is produced?

(A) $^{212}_{82}Bi$

(B) $^{214}_{82}Pb$

(C) $^{214}_{84}Po$

(D) $^{212}_{83}Bi$

(E) $^{206}_{82}Pb$

$$Zn(s) + 2HCl(aq) \rightarrow ZnCl_2(aq) + H_2(g)$$

36. If 32.7 g of Zn are allowed to react completely with an excess of HCl, how many liters of hydrogen gas, H_2, will be produced?

(A) 5.6 L

(B) 11.2 L

(C) 22.4 L

(D) 33.6 L

(E) 44.8 L

GO ON TO THE NEXT PAGE

37. Nickel is electroplated from a $NiSO_4$ solution. If a constant current of 5.00 amp is applied to a $NiSO_4$ solution, how long will it take to deposit 100.0 g of Ni?

    (A) 1.22 s

    (B) 57.2 s

    (C) 62.9 min

    (D) 18.3 h

    (E) 2.41 days

38. An ice cube melts at room temperature and atmospheric pressure. Which statement below correctly describes the thermodynamic properties of this process?

	ΔH	ΔS	ΔG
(A)	–	+	+
(B)	–	–	+
(C)	+	–	–
(D)	+	+	+
(E)	+	+	–

39. Which of the ions below has the largest ionic radius?

    (A) Li

    (B) Be

    (C) F

    (D) Cl

    (E) Br

40. The compound below is an example of which of the following?

$$\underset{CH_3CH_2CH_2}{}\overset{\overset{\textstyle O}{\|}}{C}-O-CH_3$$

    (A) Aldehyde

    (B) Ester

    (C) Amine

    (D) Ketone

    (E) Ether

$$PCl_5(g) \rightleftharpoons PCl_3(g) + Cl_2(g)$$

41. In the reaction above, assume that 0.75 mol of PCl_5 is placed in a 1.0 L reaction vessel. At equilibrium, the 0.65 mol of PCl_5 is present. What is K_c?

    (A) 65

    (B) 6.5

    (C) 0.10

    (D) 0.15

    (E) 0.015

42. Solid barium nitrate, $Ba(NO_3)_2$, gradually dissolved in a $1.0 \times 10^{-4}\,M\,Na_2CO_3$ solution. At what Ba^{2+} concentration will a precipitate begin to form? (K_{sp} for $BaCO_3 = 5.1 \times 10^{-9}$)

    (A) $4.1 \leftarrow 10^{-5}\,M$

    (B) $8.1 \leftarrow 10^{-5}\,M$

    (C) $5.1 \leftarrow 10^{-5}\,M$

    (D) $1.2 \leftarrow 10^{-6}\,M$

    (E) $8.1 \leftarrow 10^{-8}\,M$

43. Which of the following is an isomer of n-hexane?

    (A) 2,3-dimethylbutane

    (B) 2-methylbutane

    (C) 2,2-dimethylpropane

    (D) 2,3-dimethylpentane

    (E) 3-ethyl-2-methylpentane

44. A crystal of NaCl is

    (A) soft, low melting, and a good electrical conductor.

    (B) hard, high melting, and a good electrical conductor.

    (C) soft, low melting, and a poor electrical conductor.

    (D) hard, high melting, and a poor electrical conductor.

    (E) soft, high melting, and a poor electrical conductor.

45. A voltaic cell is set up at standard temperature with a zinc electrode placed in a 0.5 M solution of Zn^{2+}. The other cell contains a copper electrode immersed in a 0.5 M solution of Cu2+. What will happen to the cell emf if the copper solution is increased in concentration from 0.5 M to 5.0 M?

(A) emf will increase.

(B) emf will decrease.

(C) emf will experience a rapid decrease followed by a steady increase.

(D) emf will only change if the zinc solution is changed.

(E) emf is unaffected.

46. Several pieces of mossy zinc are added to hydrochloric acid in a filter flask fitted with a piece of rubber tubing. The rubber tubing is submerged under water so that the gas can be bubbled through the water and collected in a gas-collection tube. After a certain amount of hydrogen gas had been collected, the pressure in the gas collection tube is 300 mm Hg and the temperature is 20.0°C. If the vapor pressure of water at this temperature is 18 mm Hg, what is the pressure of the hydrogen gas?

(A) 318 mm Hg

(B) 282 mm Hg

(C) 320 mm Hg

(D) 300 mm Hg

(E) 18 mm Hg

47. Generally the vapor pressure of a liquid is related to

I. the amount of liquid.

II. temperature.

III. intermolecular forces.

(A) I only

(B) II only

(C) III only

(D) I and II only

(E) II and III only

48. The molar solubility of $BaCO_3$ ($K_{sp} = 1.6 \times 10^{-9}$) in 0.10 M $BaCl_2$ solution is

(A) 1.6×10^{-10}

(B) 4.0×10^{-5}

(C) 7.4×10^{-4}

(D) 0.10

(E) 1.6×10^{-8}

49. Each of the following can act as both a Brønsted acid and a Brønsted base EXCEPT

(A) HSO_4^-

(B) $H_2PO_4^-$

(C) NH_4^+

(D) H_2O

(E) HCO_3^-

50. Which of the following violates the octet rule?

(A) NF_3

(B) IF_3

(C) PF_3

(D) SbF_3

(E) AsF_3

51. The molality of the magnesium sulfate in a 1.0 M $MgSO_4$ solution can be determined using the

(A) temperature of the solution.

(B) K_{sp} for $MgSO_4$.

(C) volume of the solution.

(D) ion-product.

(E) density of the solution.

GO ON TO THE NEXT PAGE

52. A lab instructor is preparing 5.00 liters of a 0.100-molar $Pb(NO_3)_2$ (molecular weight 331) solution. She should weigh out

    (A) 165.5 g of $Pb(NO_3)_2$ and add 5.00 kg of H_2O.

    (B) 165.5 g of $Pb(NO_3)_2$ and add H_2O until the solution has a volume of 5.00 liters.

    (C) 33.1 g of $Pb(NO_3)_2$ and add H_2O until the solution has a volume of 5.00 liters.

    (D) 331 g of $Pb(NO_3)_2$ and add 5.00 liters of H_2O.

    (E) 165.5 g of $Pb(NO_3)_2$ and add 5.00 liters of H_2O.

53. Which of the following aqueous solutions has the highest boiling point?

    (A) 0.10 M NaCl

    (B) 0.10 M NH_4NO_3

    (C) 0.10 M NH_4Cl

    (D) 0.10 M HCl

    (E) 0.10 M Na_2SO_4

54. A 2.00-liter sample of argon gas at 77 °C and 720 mm Hg is heated until it occupies a volume of 4.00 liters. During the expansion, the pressure is constant. What is the temperature of the gas after it has expanded?

    (A) 154 °C

    (B) 308 °C

    (C) 427 °C

    (D) 700 °C

    (E) 720. °C

55. $2NO \underset{k_{-1}}{\overset{k_1}{\rightleftharpoons}} N_2O_2$ (fast equilibrium)

    $N_2O_2 + H_2 \overset{k_2}{\rightarrow} N_2O + H_2O$ (slow)

    $N_2O + H_2 \overset{k_3}{\rightarrow} N_2 + H_2O$ (fast)

    Nitric oxide, NO, can be reduced by hydrogen gas to yield nitrogen gas and water vapor. The decomposition is believed to occur according to the reaction mechanism shown above. The rate law for the reaction that is consistent with this mechanism is given by which of the following?

    (A) Rate = $k[NO]^2$

    (B) Rate = $k[NO]^2[N_2O_2]$

    (C) Rate = $k[N_2O_2][H_2]$

    (D) Rate = $k[NO]^2[H_2]$

    (E) Rate = $k[N_2O][H_2]$

56. The normal boiling point of liquid X is less than that of Y, which is less than that of Z. Which of the following is the correct order of increasing vapor pressure of the three liquids at STP?

    (A) X, Y, Z

    (B) Z, Y, X

    (C) Y, X, Z

    (D) X, Z, Y

    (E) Y, Z, X

$$C(s) + H_2O(g) \rightarrow CO(g) + H_2(g)$$
$$\Delta G° = 91.2 \text{ kJ}; \Delta S° = 135 \text{ J}$$

57. What is the value of $\Delta H°$ for the reaction shown above at 25 °C?

    (A) 40.3 kJ

    (B) 226 kJ

    (C) 91.3 kJ

    (D) 131.4 kJ

    (E) 25.7 kJ

58. In the molecule $NaAsO_3$, what is the oxidation number of As?

(A) 1

(B) 2

(C) 3

(D) 4

(E) 5

59. A solution containing 292 g of $Mg(NO_3)_2$ per liter (of solution) has a density of 1.108 g/mL. The molality of the solution is

(A) 2.00 m

(B) 2.41 m

(C) 5.50 m

(D) 6.39 m

(E) 11.08 m

Ionization energies for unknown element Q (kJ/mol)		
First	Second	Third
520	7298	11815

60. Which element below is most likely to be element Q?

(A) Li

(B) Ca

(C) Al

(D) F

(E) Ba

61. Carbonated beverages get their "fizz" from carbon dioxide that is dissolved in water. Under which conditions is it possible to dissolve the most carbon dioxide in water?

(A) High pressure, high temperature

(B) High pressure, low temperature

(C) Low pressure, high temperature

(D) Low pressure, low temperature

(E) A vacuum, high temperature

62. Determine the molecular formula of a compound that contains 40.0% C, 6.71% H, 53.29% O and has a molecular mass of 60.05.

(A) $C_2H_4O_2$

(B) CH_2O

(C) $C_2H_3O_4$

(D) $C_2H_2O_4$

(E) $C_4H_8O_4$

63. A gaseous mixture containing 1.5 mol Ne and 4.5 mol NO_2 has a total pressure of 8.0 atm. What is the partial pressure of NO_2?

(A) 1.5 atm

(B) 2.7 atm

(C) 4.5 atm

(D) 6.0 atm

(E) 8.0 atm

64. In the compound Mn_2O_7, what is the oxidation number of manganese?

(A) +2

(B) +3

(C) +5

(D) +7

(E) +8

$$Si(s) + 2Cl_2(g) \rightarrow SiCl_4(l)$$

65. If 3.84 mol Cl_2 react with an excess of Si, how many moles of $SiCl_4$ will be produced?

(A) 0.96 mol

(B) 1.92 mol

(C) 3.84 mol

(D) 4.00 mol

(E) 5.72 mol

GO ON TO THE NEXT PAGE

66. $CO(g) + NO_2(g) \rightarrow CO_2(g) + NO(g)$

For the reaction represented above, the experimental rate law is given as follows:

$$Rate = k[NO_2]^2$$

If additional CO gas is added to the reaction vessel, while temperature remains constant, which of the following is true?

(A) Both the reaction rate and k increase.

(B) Both the reaction rate and k decrease.

(C) Both the reaction rate and k remain the same.

(D) The reaction rate increases but k remains the same.

(E) The reaction rate decreases but k remains the same.

$$N_2(g) + O_2(g) \rightleftharpoons 2NO$$

67. In the formation of NO (shown above), what effect will the addition of a catalyst have on the equilibrium constant, K_{eq}, for the reaction. Assume temperature and pressure remain constant.

(A) A catalyst will increase K_{eq}.

(B) A catalyst will decreases K_{eq}.

(C) A catalyst will have no effect on K_{eq}.

(D) A catalyst will first increase K_{eq}, until the reaction slows, then K_{eq} will decrease.

(E) A catalyst will cause a dramatic increase in K_{eq}.

68. Which of the following is predicted to have a square planar molecular structure?

(A) $TeBr_4$

(B) BrF_3

(C) IF_5

(D) XeF_4

(E) SCl_2

69. Which of the following pairs would make an effective buffer solution?

(A) $HCl / NaCl$

(B) KOH / K_2SO_4

(C) $HClO_4 / NaClO_4$

(D) $NaHCO_3 / Na_2CO_3$

(E) HCl / NH_4Cl

70. A 100.0-g sample of water at 25.0°C is mixed with 100.0 g of a certain metal at 100.0°C. After thermal equilibrium is established, the final temperature of the mixture is 30.0°C. What is the specific heat of the metal, assuming it is constant over the temperature range concerned? The specific heat of water is 4.18 J/g°C.

(A) 0.30 J/g°C

(B) 0.60 J/g°C

(C) 0.90 J/g°C

(D) 0.030 J/g°C

(E) 2.21 J/g°C

$$\dots NH_3(g) + \dots O_2(g) \rightarrow \dots NO(g) + \dots H_2O$$

71. If the equation above is balanced, the coefficient before the O_2 will be

(A) 1

(B) 2

(C) 3

(D) 5

(E) 8

72. A sample of nitrogen gas is placed into a closed container. The volume is held constant while the temperature is increased from 200 K to 400 K. Given these conditions, which of the choices below is true?

(A) The density of the gas doubles.

(B) The pressure of the gas doubles.

(C) The average velocity of the gas molecules doubles.

(D) The number of nitrogen gas molecules increases.

(E) The potential energy of the gas molecules doubles.

73.
$$2A + B \rightarrow C$$

The data below corresponds to the reaction shown above.

Experiment	Initial [A]	Initial [B]	Initial Rate
1	0.010	0.025	0.015
2	0.020	0.050	0.060
3	0.040	0.050	0.060
4	0.040	0.075	0.135

Which rate law best describes the data?

(A) Rate = $k[B]^2$

(B) Rate = $k[A]^2$

(C) Rate = $k[A][B]$

(D) Rate = $k[A]^2[B]$

(E) Rate = $k[A][B]^2$

$$3Mg + N_2 \rightarrow Mg_3N_2$$

74. What mass of magnesium nitride can be made from reaction of 1.22 g of magnesium with excess nitrogen?

(A) 1.69 g

(B) 15.2 g

(C) 5.07 g

(D) 5.02 g

(E) 0.592 g

75. Which of the following must be true for a reaction that proceeds spontaneously from initial standard state conditions?

(A) $\Delta G° > 0$ and $K_{eq} > 1$

(B) $\Delta G° > 0$ and $K_{eq} < 1$

(C) $\Delta G° < 0$ and $K_{eq} > 1$

(D) $\Delta G° < 0$ and $K_{eq} < 1$

(E) $\Delta G° = 0$ and $K_{eq} = 1$

STOP

END OF SECTION I. IF YOU HAVE ANY TIME LEFT, GO OVER YOUR WORK IN THIS SECTION ONLY. DO NOT WORK IN ANY OTHER SECTION OF THE TEST.

SECTION II REFERENCE INFORMATION

1A 1																	8A 18
1 **H** 1.0079	2A 2											3A 13	4A 14	5A 15	6A 16	7A 17	2 **He** 4.0026
3 **Li** 6.941	4 **Be** 9.012											5 **B** 10.811	6 **C** 12.011	7 **N** 14.007	8 **O** 16.00	9 **F** 19.00	10 **Ne** 20.179
11 **Na** 22.99	12 **Mg** 24.30	3B 3	4B 4	5B 5	6B 6	7B 7	8B 8	9	10	1B 11	2B 12	13 **Al** 26.98	14 **Si** 28.09	15 **P** 30.974	16 **S** 32.06	17 **Cl** 35.453	18 **Ar** 39.948
19 **K** 39.10	20 **Ca** 40.08	21 **Sc** 44.96	22 **Ti** 47.90	23 **V** 50.94	24 **Cr** 52.00	25 **Mn** 54.938	26 **Fe** 55.85	27 **Co** 58.93	28 **Ni** 58.69	29 **Cu** 63.55	30 **Zn** 65.39	31 **Ga** 69.72	32 **Ge** 72.59	33 **As** 74.92	34 **Se** 78.96	35 **Br** 79.90	36 **Kr** 83.80
37 **Rb** 85.47	38 **Sr** 87.62	39 **Y** 88.91	40 **Zr** 91.22	41 **Nb** 92.91	42 **Mo** 95.94	43 **Tc** (98)	44 **Ru** 101.1	45 **Rh** 102.91	46 **Pd** 106.42	47 **Ag** 107.87	48 **Cd** 112.41	49 **In** 114.82	50 **Sn** 118.71	51 **Sb** 121.75	52 **Te** 127.60	53 **I** 126.91	54 **Xe** 131.29
55 **Cs** 132.91	56 **Ba** 137.33	57 **La** 138.91	72 **Hf** 178.49	73 **Ta** 180.95	74 **W** 183.85	75 **Re** 186.21	76 **Os** 190.2	77 **Ir** 192.2	78 **Pt** 195.08	79 **Au** 196.97	80 **Hg** 200.59	81 **Tl** 204.38	82 **Pb** 207.2	83 **Bi** 208.98	84 **Po** (209)	85 **At** (210)	86 **Rn** (222)
87 **Fr** (223)	88 **Ra** 226.02	89 **Ac** 227.03	104 **Unq** (261)	105 **Unp** (262)	106 **Unh** (263)	107 **Uns** (264)	108 **Uno** (265)	109 **Une** (266)									

	58 **Ce** 140.12	59 **Pr** 140.91	60 **Nd** 144.24	61 **Pm** (145)	62 **Sm** 150.4	63 **Eu** 151.97	64 **Gd** 157.25	65 **Tb** 158.93	66 **Dy** 162.50	67 **Ho** 164.93	68 **Er** 167.26	69 **Tm** 168.93	70 **Yb** 173.04	71 **Lu** 174.97
Lanthanide series														
Actinide series	90 **Th** 232.04	91 **Pa** 231.04	92 **U** 238.03	93 **Np** 237.05	94 **Pu** (244)	95 **Am** (243)	96 **Cm** (247)	97 **Bk** (247)	98 **Cf** (251)	99 **Es** (252)	100 **Fm** (257)	101 **Md** (258)	102 **No** (259)	103 **Lr** (260)

STANDARD REDUCTION POTENTIALS IN AQUEOUS SOLUTION AT 25°C

Half-reaction E((V)

$Li^+ + e^-$	$\rightarrow$	$Li(s)$	-3.05
$Cs^+ + e^-$	$\rightarrow$	$Cs(s)$	-2.92
$K^+ + e^-$	$\rightarrow$	$K(s)$	-2.92
$Rb^+ + e^-$	$\rightarrow$	$Rb(s)$	-2.92
$Ba^{2+} + 2e$	$\rightarrow$	$Ba(s)$	-2.90
$Sr^{2+} + 2e^-$	$\rightarrow$	$Sr(s)$	-2.89
$Ca^{2+} + 2e^-$	$\rightarrow$	$Ca(s)$	-2.87
$Na^+ + e^-$	$\rightarrow$	$Na(s)$	-2.71
$Mg^{2+}\ 2e^-$	$\rightarrow$	$Mg(s)$	-2.37
$Be^{2+} + 2e^-$	$\rightarrow$	$Be(s)$	-1.70
$Al^{3+} + 3e^-$	$\rightarrow$	$Al(s)$	-1.66
$Mn^{2+} + 2e^-$	$\rightarrow$	$Mn(s)$	-1.18
$Zn^{2+} + 2e^-$	$\rightarrow$	$Zn(s)$	-0.76
$Cr^{3+} + 3e^-$	$\rightarrow$	$Cr(s)$	-0.74
$Fe^{2+} + 2e^-$	$\rightarrow$	$Fe(s)$	-0.44
$Cr^{3+} + e^-$	$\rightarrow$	Cr^{2+}	-0.41
$Cd^{2+} + 2e^-$	$\rightarrow$	$Cd(s)$	-0.40
$Tl^+ + e^-$	$\rightarrow$	$Tl(s)$	-0.34
$Co^{2+} + 2e^-$	$\rightarrow$	$Co(s)$	-0.28
$Ni^{2+} + 2e^-$	$\rightarrow$	$Ni(s)$	-0.25
$Sn^{2+} + 2e^-$	$\rightarrow$	$Sn(s)$	-0.14
$Pb^{2+} + 2e^-$	$\rightarrow$	$Pb(s)$	-0.13
$2H^+ + 2e^-$	$\rightarrow$	$H_2(g)$	0.00
$S^{(s)} + 2H+ + 2e^-$	$\rightarrow$	$H_2S(g)$	0.14
$Sn^{4+} + 2e^-$	$\rightarrow$	Sn^{2+}	0.15
$Cu^{2+} + e^-$	$\rightarrow$	Cu^+	0.15
$Cu^{2+} + 2e^-$	$\rightarrow$	$Cu(s)$	0.34
$Cu^+ + e^-$	$\rightarrow$	$Cu(s)$	0.52
$I_2(s) + 2e^-$	$\rightarrow$	$2I^-$	0.53
$Fe^{3+} + e^-$	$\rightarrow$	Fe^{2+}	0.77
$Hg_2^{2+} + 2e^-$	$\rightarrow$	$2\ Hg(l)$	0.79
$Ag^+ + e^-$	$\rightarrow$	$Ag(s)$	0.80
$Hg^{2+} + 2e^-$	$\rightarrow$	$Hg(l)$	0.85
$2Hg^{2+} + 2e^-$	$\rightarrow$	Hg_2^{2+}	0.92
$Br_2(l) + 2e^-$	$\rightarrow$	$2Br^-$	1.07
$O_2(g) + 4H^+ + 4e^-$	$\rightarrow$	$2H_2O(l)$	1.23
$Cl_2(g) + 2e^-$	$\rightarrow$	$2Cl^-$	1.36
$Au^{3+} + 3e^-$	$\rightarrow$	$Au(s)$	1.50
$Co^{3+} + e^-$	$\rightarrow$	Co^{2+}	1.82
$F_2(g) + 2e^-$	$\rightarrow$	$2F^-$	2.87

ATOMIC STRUCTURE

$\Delta E = h\nu$

$c = \lambda\nu$

$\lambda = \dfrac{h}{mv}$

$p = mv$

$En = \dfrac{-2.178 \times 10^{-18}}{n^2}$ joule

EQUILIBRIUM

$K_a = \dfrac{\left[H^+\right]\left[A^-\right]}{\left[HA\right]}$

$K_b = \dfrac{\left[OH^-\right]\left[HB^+\right]}{\left[B\right]}$

$K_w = [OH^-][H^+] = 1.0 \times 10^{-14}$ at 25 °C

$\quad = K_a \times K_b$

$pH = -\log[H^+], \ pOH = -\log[OH^-]$

$14 = pH + pOH$

$pH = pK_a + \log\dfrac{\left[A-\right]}{\left[HA\right]}$

$pOH = pK_b + \log\dfrac{\left[HB^+\right]}{\left[B\right]}$

$pK_a = -\log K_a, \ pK_b = -\log K_b$

$K_p = K_c(RT)^{\Delta n}$

Where Δn = moles product gas – moles reactant gas

THERMOCHEMISTRY

$\Delta S° = \sum S°$ products $- \sum S°$ reactants

$\Delta H° = \sum H°_f$ products $- \sum H°_f$ reactants

$\Delta G° = \sum \Delta G°_f$ products $- \sum G°_f$ reactants

$\Delta G° = \Delta H° - T \Delta S°$

$\quad = -RT \ln K = -2.303 \, RT \log K$

$\quad = -n \, \mathcal{F} \, E°$

$\Delta G = \Delta G° + RT \ln Q = \Delta G° + 2.303 RT \log Q$

$q = mc\Delta T$

$Cp = \dfrac{\Delta H}{\Delta T}$

$\quad E$ = energy

$\quad \nu$ = frequency

$\quad \lambda$ = wavelength

$\quad p$ = momentum

$\quad v$ = velocity

$\quad n$ = principal quantum number

$\quad m$ = mass

Speed of light, $c = 3.0 \times 10^8$ m s^{-1}

Planck's constant, $h = 6.63 \times 10^{-34}$ J s

Boltzmann's constant, $k = 1.38 \times 10^{-23}$ J K^{-1}

Avogadro's number $= 6.022 \times 10^{23}$ molecules mol^{-1}

Electron charge, $e = -1.602 \times 10^{-19}$ coulomb

1 electron volt per atom $= 96.5$ kJ mol^{-1}

EQUILIBRIUM CONSTANTS

K_a (weak acid)

K_b (weak base)

K_w (water)

K_p (gas pressure)

K_c (molar concentrations)

$S°$ = standard entropy

$H°$ = standard enthalpy

$G°$ = standard free energy

$E°$ = standard reduction potential

T = temperature

n = moles

m = mass

q = heat

c = specific heat capacity

C_p = molar heat capacity at constant pressure

1 faraday, $\mathcal{F}$ = 96,500 coulombs

P = pressure

V = volume

T = temperature

n = number of moles

D = density

m = mass

v = velocity

u_{rms} = root-mean-square speed

KE = kinetic energy

r = rate of effusion

M = molar mass

π = osmotic pressure

i = van't Hoff factor

K_f = molal freezing-point depression constant

K_b = molal boiling-point elevation constant

Q = reaction quotient

I = current amperes

q = charge (coulombs)

t = time (seconds)

$E°$ = standard reduction potential

K = equilibrium constant

Gas constant, $R = 8.31$ J mol^{-1}K^{-1}

$\qquad = 0.0821$ L atm mol^{-1} K^{-1}

$\qquad = 8.31$ volt coulomb mol^{-1} K^{-1}

Boltzmann's constant, k $= 1.38 \times 10^{-23}$ J K^{-1}

K_f for $H_2O = 1.86$ K kg mol^{-1}

K_b for $H_2O = 0.512$ K kg mol^{-1}

STP = 0.000 °C and 1.000 atm

Faraday's constant, $\mathcal{F}$ = 96,500 coulombs per mole of electrons

GASES, LIQUIDS, AND SOLUTIONS

$PV = nRT$

$\left(P + \dfrac{n^2 a}{V^2}\right)(V - nb) = nRT$

$PA = P_{\text{total}} \times XA$, where $XA = \dfrac{\text{moles A}}{\text{total moles}}$

$P_{\text{total}} = PA + PB + PC + \ldots$

$n = \dfrac{m}{M}$

$K = {}^{\circ}C + 273$

$\dfrac{P_1 V_1}{T_1} = \dfrac{P_2 V_2}{T_2}$

$D = \dfrac{m}{V}$

$u_{rms} = \sqrt{\dfrac{3kT}{m}} = \sqrt{\dfrac{3RT}{M}}$

KE per molecule $= \dfrac{1}{2} mv^2$

KE per mole $= \dfrac{3}{2} RTn$

$\dfrac{r_1}{r_2} = \sqrt{\dfrac{M_2}{M_1}}$

molarity, M = moles solute per liter solution

molality = moles solute per kilogram solvent

$\Delta T_f = iK_f \times$ molality

$\Delta T_b = iK_b \times$ molality

$\pi = \dfrac{nRT}{V} i$

OXIDATION-REDUCTION; ELECTROCHEMISTRY

$Q = \dfrac{[\text{C}]^c [\text{D}]^d}{[\text{A}]^a [\text{B}]^b}$, where $aA + bB \rightarrow cC + dD$

$I = \dfrac{q}{t}$

$E_{cell} = E_{cell}^{\circ} - \dfrac{RT}{n\mathcal{F}} \ln Q$

$\phantom{E_{cell}} = E_{cell}^{\circ} - \dfrac{0.0592}{n} \log Q$ at 25°C

$\log K = \dfrac{nE^{\circ}}{0.0592}$

SECTION II
Total time—90 Minutes

Part A
Time—40 Minutes

YOU MAY USE YOUR CALCULATOR FOR PART A.

> **Directions:** CLEARLY SHOW THE METHOD USED AND STEPS INVOLVED IN ARRIVING AT YOUR ANSWERS. It is to your advantage to do this because you may earn partial credit if you do and you will receive little or no credit if you do not. Attention should be paid to significant figures.
>
> Write all of your answers in the space provided following each question. Answer Question 1 below. The Section II weighting for this question is 20 percent.

1. In water, propanoic acid, $HC_3H_5O_2$, is a weak acid with an equilibrium constant, K_a, equal to 1.3×10^{-5}.

   (a) Write the equilibrium expression, K_a, for propanoic acid.

   (b) Calculate the pH of a 0.100 M solution of propanoic acid.

   (c) Calculate the pH of a 0.100 M solution of sodium propanoate, $NaC_3H_5O_2$.

   (d) Calculate the pH of a mixture made by combining equal volumes of 0.100 M propanoic acid and 0.100 M sodium propanoate.

Directions: Answer EITHER Question 2 OR Question 3. Only one of these questions will be graded. If you start both questions, make sure you cross out the one you do not want scored. The Section II weight for the question you choose is 20%.

2. $$2NO(g) + Cl_2(g) \rightarrow 2NOCl(g)$$

Experiment	Initial p_{NO} (atm)	Initial p_{Cl_2} (atm)	Initial Rate (atm s^{-1})
1	0.50	0.50	5.0×10^{-3}
2	1.0	1.0	4.0×10^{-2}
3	0.50	1.0	1.0×10^{-2}
4	0.75	1.25	???

Use the rate data for the reaction above to answer the following questions.

(a) Write the rate equation based on the experimental data.

(b) What is the order of the reaction for NO, Cl_2, and overall? Justify each response.

(c) Calculate the rate constant, k, for this reaction.

(d) Determine the missing initial rate in experiment 4.

3. An electrolytic cell contains molten $ZnCl_2$. The zinc chloride is electrolyzed by passing a current of 3.0 A through the cell for a certain length of time. During this process, 24.5 g of Zn are deposited on the cathode.

(a) Write the chemical equation for the reaction at the cathode.

(b) Write the chemical equation for the reaction at the anode.

(c) How long does the process take?

(d) What weight of chlorine gas bubbles are released at the anode?

GO ON TO THE NEXT PAGE

Part B
Time—50 Minutes

YOU MAY NOT USE CALCULATORS WITH PART B.

Directions: Answer Question 4 below. The Section II score weighting for this question is 15 percent.

4. Write the formulas to show the reactants and products for FIVE of the eight equations written below. Answers to more than five responses will not be scored, so be sure to cross out any incomplete responses. Assume that each reaction occurs. Also assume that all solutions are aqueous unless otherwise stated. If substances are extensively ionized in solution, be sure to represent them as such. Omit formulas for ions or molecules that are unchanged during the reaction. Equations need not be balanced.

Example: A strip of magnesium is added to a solution of silver nitrate.

Answer: $Mg + Ag^+ \rightarrow Mg^{2+} + Ag$

(a) Solid lead sulfide is heated strongly in air (roasted).

(b) Solid potassium chlorate is heated in the presence of manganese dioxide as a catalyst.

(c) A solution of silver nitrate is added to a solution of potassium chloride.

(d) A piece of magnesium metal is added to a solution of iron (II) chloride.

(e) A solution of tin(II) chloride is added to an acidified solution of potassium permanganate.

(f) Hydrogen sulfide gas is bubbled through a solution of cadmium nitrate.

(g) Propanol is burned completely in air.

(h) Samples of boron trichloride gas and ammonia gas are mixed.

Directions: For the remainder of the exam, your responses will be graded according to their accuracy and relevancy. Your responses should be well organized and presented in a very clear, concise manner. Brief, specific answers are preferable to longer, general responses. You may use any examples or equations if it is appropriate.

Answer BOTH Question 5 AND Question 6. Both of these questions are required and each will be graded. The weighting of these two questions in Section II is 30 percent (15 percent each).

5. You are to determine the molar mass of a volatile liquid using the vapor density method. Assume you have the following equipment available to you:

Hot water bath	Accurate balance	Thermometer	Barometer
Aluminum foil	Straight pin	Unknown liquid	125 mL Erlenmeyer flask
Clamp	Ring stand	Graduated cylinder	

    (a) Describe the procedures you would use to set up the equipment and perform the experiment.

    (b) List the measurements you would need to take.

    (c) Show the set up of the calculation of the molecular mass (not necessary to calculate).

    (d) Describe the effects on the calculated molecular mass if the liquid was not completely vaporized.

    (e) Show the setup for the calculation of the percent error if your results were 130 g/mol and the accepted value was 125.5 g/mol

6. Explain each of the following observations using principles of atomic structure and/or bonding.

    (a) Rubidium has a lower 1st ionization energy than sodium.

    (b) The ionic radius of P is larger than S.

    (c) Magnesium atoms (atomic number 12) are larger than chlorine atoms (atomic number 17).

    (d) There is a large increase between the 2nd and 3rd ionization energies of magnesium.

GO ON TO THE NEXT PAGE

Directions: Answer EITHER Question 7 OR Question 8. Only one of the two questions will be graded. If you start both questions, make sure you cross out the one you don't want to be scored. The Section II weighting of the question you answer is 15 percent.

7. Sulfur dioxide has a normal freezing point and boiling point of $-72.7\,°C$ and $-10.0\,°C$, respectively. The triple point is $-75.5\,°C$ and 1.65×10^{-3} atm. The critical point of sulfur dioxide is $157\,°C$ and 78 atm.

   (a) Draw a rough sketch of a phase diagram for SO_2, and include labels. Note: the drawing does not need to be to scale.

   (b) Describe the changes that would take place if the pressure on the gas changed from 1.50×10^{-3} atm to 20 atm at $-20\,°C$.

   (c) If the temperature of SO_2 is decreased from -50.0 C to -70.0 C at a constant pressure of 1 atm, what changes can be expected?

   (d) Does the density of the liquid increase or decrease as pressure is increased? Provide a justification for your response.

8. Answer each of the following using appropriate chemical principles.

   (a) When ice at the freezing temperature is compressed, it liquefies, while CO_2, when compressed, solidifies.

   (b) Rock salt mixed with ice is used as a freezing mixture in home ice cream makers. The slushy salt-ice mixture remains fluid at temperatures well below $0\,°C$.

   (c) Helium balloons deflate more rapidly than the same size balloons filled with air.

   (d) Ice cubes can appear cloudy because of dissolved gases that are present at freezing. To make clear ice cubes, it is preferable to use hot water over cold.

STOP

> END OF SECTION II. IF YOU HAVE ANY TIME LEFT, GO OVER YOUR WORK IN THIS SECTION ONLY. DO NOT WORK IN ANY OTHER SECTION OF THE TEST.

ANSWERS AND EXPLANATIONS

Section I

1. **The correct answer is (C).** Paramagnetism can be seen in atoms with unpaired electrons. Hund's rule allows us to predict the pairing of electrons in atomic orbitals, and therefore, the magnetic properties of the atom.

2. **The correct answer is (A).** This statement is pretty much a paraphrase of Heisenberg's principle, which eventually led to the quantum model of the atom, based on probabilities of finding electrons in certain regions.

3. **The correct answer is (B).** The Schrödinger equation allows us to narrow down the places most likely to find electrons in an atom. These locations are a variety of orbitals.

4. **The correct answer is (D).** BF_3, with its incomplete octet, is capable of accepting a pair of electrons from F^- to form a covalent bond. Electron pair acceptors are Lewis acids

5. **The correct answer is (E).** CN^- is donating a pair of electrons in the formation of the complex ion. Electron pair donors are Lewis bases.

6. **The correct answer is (E).** H_2O accepts a proton from $HC_2H_3O_2$. Proton acceptors are Brønsted–Lowry bases. Water can act as a Brønsted–Lowry acid or base, but in this reaction it is a base.

7. **The correct answer is (B).** Electronegativity is the measure of the strength of the attraction an atom has for the electrons of another atom in a chemical bond. Atoms with the highest electronegativities are those with the largest effective nuclear charge and the smallest amount of shielding. While neon seems to match this description, it is unable to form chemical bonds and therefore has no electronegativity. The halogen chlorine is the next best candidate.

8. **The correct answer is (A).** This is one of those "you either know it, or you don't" questions. If you stop to think of the variety of molecules nitrogen forms even with oxygen, it should be apparent that no other molecule in the list has such a large variety of oxidation states.

9. **The correct answer is (E).** Ionization energy, the energy required to remove an outer electron from an atom, varies much the same as electronegativity. As the amount of shielding increases, the ionization energy decreases (the shielding weakens the attraction between the nucleus and the outermost electrons). As the effective nuclear charge increases, the ionization energy increases (higher effective nuclear charge means a stronger attraction between the nucleus and the electrons). Therefore, the elements with the smallest ionization energies will be those with the most shielding and the smallest effective nuclear charges. Rubidium, a Group IA element in period 5 is the most suitable candidate among the other choices.

10. **The correct answer is (D).** In this problem, you know that in the final solution, there are 2.5 moles of HCl present in the 1.00 L of solution. That means that there must have always been 2.5 moles of HCl present. To determine the volume of 6.0 M HCl that would contain 2.5 mol HCl, we need to use the molarity equation:

$$M = \frac{\text{moles solute}}{\text{Liters soln}}$$

$$6.0\ M = \frac{2.5\ \text{mol HCl}}{\text{Liters soln}}$$

To solve for the volume, we can use the equation:

$$V = \frac{2.5\ \text{mol}}{6.0\ \text{M}}$$

Solving for V, we obtain 0.417 L. In milliliters this is closest to 420 mL.

11. **The correct answer is (A).** This question is checking your ability to determine the presence and strengths of intermolecular forces. Two of the choices are elements—(D) and (E)—which only exert dispersion forces. They will have very low boiling temperatures. The next two—(B) and (C)—experience hydrogen bonding, which will generally produce higher boiling temperatures than dispersion forces. Finally, the correct choice, (A), is an ionic compound. Ionic bonds are much stronger than any of the intermolecular forces, so Na_2S will have the highest melting/boiling point.

12. **The correct answer is (A).** The minimum amount of hydroxide ion that must be present to cause the precipitation of $Al(OH)_3$ can be calculated from the equilibrium expression.

$$K_{sp} = 2.0 \times 10^{-32} = [Al^{3+}][OH^-]^3 = (0.2)(x)^3$$

$$x^3 = \frac{2.0 \times 10^{-32}}{0.2} = 1.0 \times 10^{-31}$$

$$x = \sqrt[3]{1.0 \times 10^{-31}}$$

At this point, you know that $[OH^-] = \sqrt[3]{1.0 \times 10^{-31}}$. In order to calculate the pH, you need to determine the $[H^+]$, which is done with the calculation

$$\left[H^+\right] \frac{-1 \times 10^{-14}}{\left[OH-\right]} = \left(\frac{-1 \times 10^{-14}}{\sqrt[3]{1.0 \times 10^{-31}}}\right)$$

Because $pH = -\log[H^+]$, we can say that the pH at which precipitation will begin is

$$pH = -\log\left(\frac{-1 \times 10^{-14}}{\sqrt[3]{1.0 \times 10^{-31}}}\right)$$

13. **The correct answer is (A).** Isotopes of an element must have the same atomic number (number of protons), but a different mass number (which, for atoms with the same atomic number means they have a different number of neutrons). The only pair that has the same number of protons but different numbers of neutrons is choice (A).

14. **The correct answer is (D).** Both substances are ionic solids. The difference in melting points will be due to the differences in lattice energies. The total number of charges in the atom affects lattice energies. Since choices I and II both deal with these differences, they are the correct explanations. III describes ionic radius, which does not determine the lattice energy.

15. **The correct answer is (C).** The general trend for oxoacids is that the greater the number of oxygen atoms, the greater the strength of the acid.

16. **The correct answer is (C).** 87.5% decomposed is the same thing as saying that strontium–90 has undergone three half–lives (50% decomposes in the first; half of that, or 25% in the second, and half of that again, 12.5% decomposes in the third). Once that has been determined, the problem can be solved by multiplying the half-life by the number of half-lives:

$$\frac{28 \text{ years}}{1 \text{ half} - \text{life}} \times 3 \text{ half-lives} = 84 \text{ years}$$

17. **The correct answer is (C).** A positive value of S represents an increase in entropy. In choice (C), the number of moles of gas particles increases from 2 mol to 3 mol, an overall increase. This will create more disorder, and hence an increase in entropy.

18. **The correct answer is (E).** There are two ways to approach this. The first is to simply have memorized that when 6 electron pairs are found around a central atom, the hybridization has to be d^2sp^3. The other way is to consider the orbital diagram of sulfur: Unhybridized S atom

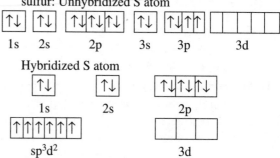

The sulfur atom, because it has empty d orbitals, can promote one $3p$ and one $3s$ electron to yield the 6 sp^3d^2 (d^2sp^3) hybridized orbitals.

19. **The correct answer is (D).** Oxidizing agents are substances that are capable of oxidizing other substances. Oxidation is the loss of electrons, which means that an oxidizing agent takes electrons away from other atoms. Only elemental iodine, I_2, acts as an oxidizing agent ($I_2 + 2e^- \rightarrow 2I^-$).

20. **The correct answer is (E).** Vapor pressure is measured when the rates of evaporation and condensation are in equilibrium.

21. **The correct answer is (A).** The reaction is exothermic, which means that a decrease in temperature will cause a shift to the right. The right side of the equation also has more moles of gas particles than the left side. This means that in low-pressure situations, the reaction will shift to the right. Therefore, under low temperature and pressure conditions, the reaction will shift to the right, raising the value of K_{eq}.

22. **The correct answer is (B).** The CO_3^{2-} ion will form an equilibrium with H^+ as shown below:

$$CO_3^{2-} + H^+ \rightleftharpoons HCO_3^-$$

Using Le Châtelier's principle, we know that if we remove CO_3^{2-} (by forming HCO_3^-), we will drive the solubility equilibrium of $CaCO_3$ to the right.

$$CaCO_3 \rightleftharpoons Ca^{2+} + CO_3^{2-}$$

23. The correct answer is (C). Conjugate acid/base pairs must be related by the loss and subsequent gain of a proton. Choice (C) is the only choice in which the loss of a single proton yields that conjugate.

24. The correct answer is (C). Atomic radius decreases moving from left to right across a period, and increases moving top to bottom down a group. Fluorine is above chlorine, so it must be smaller than chlorine. Chlorine is to the right of sulfur, meaning that it must be smaller than sulfur. Therefore, fluorine is the smallest atom, followed by chlorine, which is larger, and sulfur, which is the largest.

25. The correct answer is (A). In this problem, you will be comparing Q to K_c. From your comparison, you will determine the direction of the reaction. The calculation of Q will proceed as follows:

$$Q = \frac{\left[NH_3\right]^2}{\left[H_2\right]^3\left[N_2\right]}$$

$$= \frac{(2.00\ M\ NH_3)^2}{(2.00\ M\ H_2)^3(1.00\ M\ N_2)}$$

$$= \frac{4.00}{8.00}$$

$$= 0.5$$

The value of Q is greater than K_c, indicating that there is too much product at this stage. To achieve equilibrium (where $K_c = 0.105$), the reaction will have to proceed toward the left.

26. The correct answer is (C). This is a combined gas law problem involving pressure, volume, and temperature. One very important thing to remember is that in all gas law problems, the temperature must be the absolute temperature. Once that is established, the equation must be set up to solve for the final pressure.

$$\frac{P_1V_1}{T_1} = \frac{P_2V_2}{T_2}$$

Isolating P_2, you end up with the equation:

$$\frac{P_1V_1T_2}{T_1V_2} = P_2$$

27. The correct answer is (B). You must start this problem by setting up the equation for K_a.

$$K_a = \frac{\left[H^+\right]\left[A^-\right]}{\left[HA\right]}$$

In order to solve for K_a, we can't have any unknowns on the right side of the equation. Careful inspection lets us know that we don't. We know the pH of the solution, which means that we know the hydrogen ion concentration. In addition, because it is a monoprotic acid, we know that the concentration of A^- will be equal to the hydrogen ion concentration. We are given the initial concentration of HA so we can use that to help solve the problem.

	HA	H^+	A^-
Start	0.10	0	0
Δ	$-x$	$+x$	$+x$
Finish	$0.10-x$	x	x

Before substituting any numbers into the K_a equation, we can determine the hydrogen ion concentration.

$$[H^+] = 10^{-pH} = 10^{-4}$$

Since $[H^+] = [A^-]$,

$$K_a = \frac{\left[H^+\right]\left[A^-\right]}{\left[HA\right]} = \frac{\left(1 \times 10^{-4}\right)\left(1 \times 10^{-4}\right)}{0.10}$$

$$= 1.0 \times 10^{-7}$$

28. The correct answer is (C). The superscript number next to the concentration of NO ($[NO]^2$) indicates the order of the reaction. Since the superscript is a two, this indicates that the order with respect to NO is second.

29. The correct answer is (A). When you see two masses in a stoichiometry problem, you should be alerted that you are dealing with a limiting reactant problem. This problem will have two stages—the first is to determine the limiting reactant, and the second to determine the mass of the hydrogen gas. Before we do anything, we need to see the balanced equation for the reaction:

$$Mg(s) + 2H_2O(l) \rightarrow Mg(OH)_2(aq) + H_2(g)$$

With this established, we can begin to determine which reactant is the limiting reactant.

$$4.73 \text{ g Mg} \times \frac{1 \text{ mol Mg}}{24.30 \text{ g Mg}} = 0.195 \text{ mol Mg}$$

$$1.83 \text{ g H}_2\text{O} \times \frac{1 \text{ mol H}_2\text{O}}{18.02 \text{ g H}_2\text{O}} = 0.102 \text{ mol H}_2\text{O}$$

From the balanced equation we can see that we need two moles of H_2O for every one mole of Mg. In the present amounts the ratios are nearly reverse (there is nearly twice as much magnesium). This means that water is the limiting reactant. Because of this, we can now solve the problem using the number of moles of water present as a starting point:

$$(0.102 \text{ mol H}_2\text{O})\left(\frac{1 \text{ mol H}_2}{2 \text{ mol H}_2\text{O}}\right)\left(\frac{2.02 \text{ g H}_2}{1 \text{ mol 2H}_2}\right)$$
$$= 0.103 \text{ g}$$

30. **The correct answer is (E).** O is far more electronegative than S. As a result, the bonds in H_2O are far more polar than those in H_2S. This greater polarity allows for greater hydrogen bonding in water, and subsequently a higher boiling temperature.

31. **The correct answer is (A).** First thing you need to do is determine which material is the cathode and which is the anode. Remember that the anode is always the material with more negative reduction potential. In this case, lead is the anode and copper is the cathode. Once this has been established, you can determine the reduction potential of the cell using the formula:

$$E_{cell} = E_{cathode} - E_{anode} = 0.34 \text{ V} - (-.13 \text{ V}) = 0.47 \text{ V}$$

32. **The correct answer is (E).** In this question you are really just showing that you can interpret the solubility product constant expression, K_{sp}. Since the value of K_{sp} is the product of the concentrations of the anion and cation in solution, smaller values of K_{sp} indicate smaller concentrations of dissociated ions. This means that less of the solid has dissolved. $Sn(OH)_2$ has, by far, the smallest value for K_{sp}, and is therefore the least soluble.

33. **The correct answer is (E).** With a double bond between N and O, oxygen has an octet, however, nitrogen only possesses seven electrons. The octet rule can't be satisfied for NO.

34. **The correct answer is (D).** The first thing to notice here is that H_3PO_4 is a polyprotic acid. Each mole will yield three moles of H^+ ions. In 0.020 L of 0.10 M solution, there are 2.0×10^{-3} moles of H_3PO_4. After complete dissociation, this will yield 6.0×10^{-3} moles of H^+ ions. In order to neutralize this much H^+, you will need 6.0×10^{-3} moles / 0.20 M = 0.03 L KOH, or 30 mL.

35. **The correct answer is (C).** Beta decay occurs when a neutron breaks down to form a proton and a beta particle (electron). This will cause the atomic number to increase by one, and the mass number remains constant. In the first beta decay, lead-214 becomes bismuth–214. The second beta decay converts bismuth–214 to polonium-214, as shown below:

$$^{214}_{82}\text{Pb} \rightarrow \ ^{214}_{83}\text{Bi} + \ ^{0}_{-1}e^-$$
$$^{214}_{83}\text{Bi} \rightarrow \ ^{214}_{84}\text{Po} + \ ^{0}_{-1}e^-$$

36. **The correct answer is (B).** This is a grams to liters stoichiometric conversion. The conversion factor of 22.4 L per mole of gas will be used in the final portion.

$$32.7 \text{ g Zn} \times \left(\frac{1 \text{ mol Zn}}{65.39 \text{ g Zn}}\right)\left(\frac{1 \text{mol H}_2}{1 \text{ mol Zn}}\right)\left(\frac{22.4 \text{ L H}_2}{1 \text{ mol H}_2}\right)$$
$$= 11.2 \text{ L H}_2$$

37. **The correct answer is (D).** To solve this, first we need to determine how many moles of electrons will be required to reduce the 100.0 g of Ni. Once we know that, we can use the current to determine the time.

$$100.0 \text{ g Ni} \times \frac{1 \text{ mol Ni}}{58.69 \text{ g Ni}} = 1.704 \text{ mol Ni}$$

The next step is to determine how many moles of electrons will be required and then how many coulombs of charge.

$$1.704 \text{ mol Ni} \times \frac{2 \text{ mol } e-}{1 \text{ mol Ni}} = 3.408 \text{ mol e}^-$$

$$3.408 \text{ mol e}^- \times \frac{96\,500 \text{ C}}{1 \text{ mol } e-} = 3.289 \times 10^5 \text{ C}$$

Because charge = current × time, we can rearrange the equation to solve for time:

$$\frac{3.289 \times 10^5 \text{C}}{5.00 \text{A}} = 6.578 \times 10^4 \text{ s}$$

$$6.578 \times 10^4 \text{ s} \times \left(\frac{1 \text{ min}}{60 \text{ s}}\right)\left(\frac{1 \text{ hr}}{60 \text{ min}}\right) = 18.3 \text{ hr}$$

38. The correct answer is (E). You need to consider the answers to three questions while working through this one. First of all, if an ice cube sits out at room temperature, is heat required to melt it? If so, the process is endothermic (and $\Delta H°$ will be positive). The second question, is the water more disordered than the ice? If so, the process increases the entropy (which will be positive). The final question, is the process spontaneous? If so, the free energy is negative.

39. The correct answer is (E). Ionic radii are a little more difficult to judge than atomic radii because they vary within a period. There are certain trends that you can remember, however. For cations (mostly we look at groups IA, and IIA, and sometimes IIIA), the ionic radius decreases from left to right in a period, and increases going top to bottom. The reason for the decrease in size going across a period is that the atom loses all of its outer electrons. Because the atoms have not lost their protons, the effective nuclear charge is rather high on the remaining electrons. For anions, the reverse is true. As the atoms gain electrons, the ions become larger than the neutral atom because the additional electrons are being attracted by the same number of protons as the neutral atom. In this question, three of the atoms are in the same period, and the other two are in the same group. Br has been chosen because it is the farthest down the list.

40. The correct answer is (B). Esters have the characteristic R-COOR structure similar to this one.

41. The correct answer is (E). You need to set up an equilibrium table to solve this problem. Because the reaction takes place in a 1.0 L vessel, you can assume that the number of moles and the molarity are equivalent.

	PCl_5	PCl_3	Cl_2
Start	0.75	0	0
Δ	−0.10	+0.10	+0.10
Finish	0.65	0.10	0.10

The decrease in PCl_5 can be assumed to be the same as the increase in the other two gases since the stoichiometric ratios of each is 1:1. Now that you have the values for the concentration of each substance, you can solve for K_c:

$$K_c = \frac{[PCl_3][Cl_2]}{[PCl_5]} = \frac{(0.10)(0.10)}{(0.65)} = 0.015$$

42. The correct answer is (C). In this problem, you will need to use the K_{sp} equation for barium carbonate, substituting the given value for K_{sp} as well as the concentration of carbonate ion in the sodium carbonate solution. By using these two values, you can solve for the unknown concentration of barium ions. Because barium nitrate will only release one mole of barium ions per mole of barium nitrate, the required concentration of barium ions will equal the required concentration of barium nitrate.

$$K_{sp} = 5.1 \times 10^{-9} = [Ba^{2+}][CO_3^{2-}] = (x)(1\times10^{-4})$$

$$x = \frac{5.1\times10^{-9}}{1\times10^{-4}} = 5.1 \times 10^{-5}$$

43. The correct answer is (A). Isomers have the same molecular formulas. An isomer of n–hexane would need to have a formula C_6H_{14}. Without even drawing the structures, you should be able to determine that no choice other than (A) has six carbons. A closer inspection of choice (A) should let you know that the molecule does in fact also have the formula C_6H_{14}.

44. The correct answer is (D). Sodium chloride is a typical example of an ionic compound, giving it several unique characteristics. The melting point is high, due to the very strong electrostatic attractions binding the ions into a rigid crystalline lattice. Because of the rigidity of the crystalline lattice, ionic salts are hard. One thing that is not mentioned in the problem, but is worth remembering, is that ionic salts also tend to be brittle because of the various planes that exist within the crystalline lattice (the crystal can break along these planes). Finally, ionic salts are poor conductors of electricity because the electrons are localized about individual atoms. In solution, or in a molten state, when individual ions are free to move about, ionic compounds make good conductors.

45. The correct answer is (A). This question is a conceptual application of the Nernst Equation. The Nernst equation is used to determine the impact of differences in concentration on cell emf. The equation takes the form:

$$E = E° - \frac{0.0592}{n} \log Q$$

The value of Q depends on the concentration of the substances in the reaction. For this reaction, Q will be set up as

$$Q = \frac{[Zn^{2+}]}{[Cu^{2+}]} = \frac{0.50\,M}{5.0\,M} = 0.1$$

A little quick reminder about logarithms here: the logarithm of a number less than 1 is negative. Numbers greater than 1 are positive. Therefore, you should be able to see that as the concentration of the substance at the anode becomes less than the concentration of the substance at the cathode, the value of Q will decrease. When the value of the concentration of the substance at the anode is greater than the concentration of the substance at the cathode, the value of Q will increase.

If you look at the effect this has on the overall equation, when the value of log Q is negative, the value of $\frac{0.0592}{n}$ log Q will be added to the cell voltage. In other words, it increases over standard conditions. When the value of log Q is positive, the value of $\frac{0.0592}{n}$ log Q will be subtracted from the cell voltage. In other words, it decreases over standard conditions.

In summary, when the concentration of the substance at the anode is greater than the concentration at the cathode, the cell emf decreases. When the value of the concentration at the anode is lower than the concentration at the cathode, cell emf increases.

46. The correct answer is (B). What you need to remember in this problem is that the sum of the partial pressures in a system will equal the total pressure. In addition, you need to remember that when you collect a gas over a liquid, you need to take into account the vapor pressure of the liquid as part of the total pressure. Therefore, of the 300 mm Hg total pressure, 18 mm Hg of that is due to the vapor pressure of water at this temperature. That leaves the remainder from hydrogen.

47. The correct answer is (E). An increased temperature will cause an increase in the numbers of particles that possess enough kinetic energy to escape from the liquid to the gaseous phase. Intermolecular forces are also a key determinant as to how much energy a particle must have to be able to escape from the liquid to the gaseous phase. The amount of liquid, however, is not a determining factor in vapor pressure, as the numbers of particles that change phase are going to be proportional to the increase in sample size.

48. The correct answer is (E). We can set up an equilibrium table to determine the molar solubility of $BaCO_3$. Keep in mind that there are 0.1 mol Ba^{2+} ions already in solution from the $BaCl_2$.

	$BaCO_3$	Ba^{2+}	CO_3^{2-}
Start		0.1	0
Δ		+x	+x
Finish		0.1 + x	x

At this point, we will assume that the value of x is significantly smaller than the value 0.1, which means the equilibrium expression will be

$$K_{sp} = [Ba^{2+}][CO_3^{2-}]$$
$$1.6 \times 10^{-9} = (0.1)(x)$$
$$1.6 \times 10^{-8} = x$$

Our assumption about x is correct, so we can keep this answer.

49. The correct answer is (C). With the exception of choice (C), all of the substances can either donate a proton, or accept one. NH_4^+ can only lose an electron. It cannot gain one, so it is only a Brønsted-Lowry acid.

50. The correct answer is (B). N, P, As, and Sb are all group V elements that can form three single bonds with fluorine to yield an octet. Iodine, a group VII element, according to the octet rule, should only be able to combine with one fluorine atom. Combining with 3 is a violation of the octet rule.

51. The correct answer is (E). You should be very clear on the differences between molarity and molality. Molality is the measure of the number of moles of solute dissolved per kilogram of solvent. The molarity is a measure of the moles of solute dissolved in a given volume of solution. If you know that a given solution has a molarity of 1.00, then you know there is 1.00 mole of solvent per liter of solution. Knowing the density will allow you to determine the mass of a solution. If the mass of the solute is subtracted from the mass of the solution, the result will be the mass of the solvent, which is required for the determination of molality.

52. **The correct answer is (B).** One important factor to remember (and one of the most frequently forgotten) is that molarity is the measure of the number of moles of solute per liter of solution. That means that the total volume of the solution must equal 5.00 L in this problem. In order to prepare a 0.1 molar solution, you must have 0.10 mole per liter of solution.

In this problem you must be careful of the total volume. The molarity, 0.10 M, tells us that we should be using 0.10 mole of solvent per liter of solution. In this problem, there are 5.00 L of solution, so we will need to use 5×0.10 mol to get the correct answer, which is shown below:

$$\left(\frac{0.10 \text{ mol Pb(NO}_3)_2}{1.00 \text{ L}}\right)\left(\frac{331 \text{ g Pb (NO}_3)_2}{1 \text{ mol Pb (NO}_3)_2}\right)(5.00 \text{ L})$$

$$= 165.5 \text{ g Pb(NO}_3)_2$$

If you add 165.5 g Pb(NO$_3$)$_2$ to a container (such as a volumetric flask) and add enough water to equal 5.00 L, you are making a 0.1 M solution.

53. **The correct answer is (E).** This question is checking your knowledge of colligative properties, more specifically boiling point elevation. When a nonvolatile solute is dissolved in a solvent, the vapor pressure of the solution decreases relative to the pure solvent. This decrease in vapor pressure causes a corresponding increase in the boiling temperature. The more solute particles that are present in the solvent, the higher the boiling point elevation. In this question, the solute particles are all ionic compounds, and the concentrations are all the same. The difference between each salt is the number of ions that each will form upon dissociation. The correct choice, Na$_2$SO$_4$, dissociates into three ions (two Na$^+$ and one SO$_4^{2-}$), which is the largest amount of any choice.

54. **The correct answer is (C).** There are two distracters imbedded in the problem. The problem is really a Charles's law problem, however, because the pressure is given, it appears like a combined gas laws problem. Because the pressure remains constant, it is not required in the equation. In addition, the temperature is given in degrees Celsius rather than

kelvin. Once you have identified the potential pitfalls, you should be able to solve this problem rather easily using the Charles's law equation:

$$\frac{V_1}{T_1} = \frac{V_2}{T_2}$$

$$\frac{2.00 \text{ L}}{350 \text{ K}} = \frac{4.00 \text{ L}}{x\text{K}}$$

$$2.00x = 1400$$

$$x = 700 \text{ K}$$

$$x = 700 - 273 = 427 \text{ °C}$$

55. **The correct answer is (D).** The solution of this problem requires a few steps. First, the rate determining step is the second step in the reaction mechanism, so the rate law can be set up as:

$$\text{Rate} = k_2[\text{N}_2\text{O}_2][\text{H}_2]$$

However, N$_2$O$_2$ is a reaction intermediate, which is not allowed in the rate law. In order to solve the problem, we will have to use the first step in the mechanism and find a suitable substitution for N$_2$O$_2$. In the first step, which is an equilibrium step, the rates of the forward and reverse reactions are identical. Therefore, we can set up an expression such that $k_1 = k_{-1}$. In this expression, we obtain the following equality:

$$k_1[\text{NO}]^2 = k_{-1}[\text{N}_2\text{O}_2]$$

If we rearrange this to set it equal to [N$_2$O$_2$], we will then have a suitable expression to substitute into the rate law.

$$[\text{N}_2\text{O}_2] = \frac{k_1}{k_{-1}}[\text{NO}]^2$$

The new rate law expression becomes:

$$\text{Rate} = k_2\frac{k_1}{k_{-1}}[\text{NO}]^2[\text{H}_2]$$

If you replace the expression $k_2\frac{k_1}{k_{-1}}$ with k, the experimental rate constant, the rate law is:

$$\text{Rate} = k[\text{NO}]^2[\text{H}_2]$$

56. **The correct answer is (B).** There are two levels of interpretation that you can make here. The first concerns only the definition of boiling point, which states that a liquid will boil when the vapor pressure equals the atmospheric pressure. What this means is that a substance with a low vapor pressure will have to be heated to a higher temperature to make the vapor pressure equal the atmospheric pressure.

Materials with higher vapor pressures won't need to be heated as much to boil.

The second way to interpret this is through the origins of vapor pressure. Substances that evaporate easily (are volatile) have weaker intermolecular forces than those that do not evaporate easily. Substances with higher vapor pressures are substances with weaker intermolecular forces. This means that they will also have lower boiling temperatures.

57. **The correct answer is (D).** This problem uses the free energy equation:

$$\Delta G° = \Delta H° - T\Delta S°$$

To solve this problem, we need to rearrange the equation to solve for $\Delta H°$:

$$\Delta H° = \Delta G° + T\Delta S°$$

When the given information is substituted in the equation, you obtain:

$$\Delta H° = 91.2 \text{ kJ} + (298 \text{ K})(135 \text{ J})\left(\frac{1 \text{ k J}}{1000 \text{ J}}\right)$$

$$= 131.4 \text{ kJ}$$

58. **The correct answer is (E).** In the $NaAsO_3$ molecule, you can determine the oxidation number of As by first determining the charges on the cation and anion. Since sodium always has a charge of 1^+, that means the AsO_3 must have a 1^- charge. Oxygen, with a 2^- charge contributes $3(2^-)$, or 6^- charge. In order to have a total charge of 1^-, arsenic must have an oxidative of $^+5$. This can be shown mathematically as: $-1 = 3(-2) + 5$

59. **The correct answer is (B).** The first thing that must be done is to calculate the molarity of the solution. This is accomplish using the grams of solute per liter data:

$$292 \text{ g Mg(NO}_3)_2 \times \frac{1 \text{ mol Mg(NO}_3)_2}{148.32 \text{gMg(NO}_3)_2}$$

$$= 1.969 \text{ mol Mg(NO}_3)_2$$

Next, we can use the density of the solution to determine the overall mass of the solution:

Mass of solution = density × volume
= 1.108 g/mL × 1.00 L × 1000 mL/L
= 1108 g

Using this mass of the solution, we can subtract the mass of the $Mg(NO_3)_2$ to determine the mass of the solvent (water).

Mass of solution – mass of solute = mass of solvent

$1108 \text{ g} - 292 \text{ g Mg(NO}_3)_2 = 816 \text{ g H}_2\text{O}$
$= 0.816 \text{ kg H}_2\text{O}$ (kg is the unit of molality)

Finally, we can calculate the molality.

$$\text{Molality} = \frac{\text{moles of solute}}{\text{kg of solvent}}$$

$$= \frac{1.969 \text{ mol Mg(NO}_3)_2}{0.816 \text{ kg H}_2\text{O}}$$

$$= 2.41 \text{ m}$$

60. **The correct answer is (A).** Li has been chosen because of the large jump between the first and second ionization energies. This means that the first electron was relatively much easier to remove than the second. This pattern is consistent with elements in Group IA since the second electron must be removed from a lower energy level, which has both less shielding and a higher effective nuclear charge than the first electron did.

61. **The correct answer is (B).** Gases are most soluble in liquids at low temperature. This is unlike most solids, which become less soluble at lower temperatures. In addition, high external pressures increase the solubility of gases in liquids. For solids, pressure has a negligible effect.

62. **The correct answer is (A).** The first step is to determine the number of moles of each substance present. From this we can determine the empirical formula, and later the molecular formula. When given percentages, you can assume a 100 g sample, which allows you to directly convert each percentage directly to an amount in grams. The number of moles of each substance can be calculated as shown below:

$$40.0 \text{ g C} \times \frac{1 \text{ mol C}}{12.011 \text{ g C}} = 3.33 \text{ mol C}$$

$$6.71 \text{ g H} \times \frac{1 \text{ mol H}}{1.01 \text{ g H}} = 6.64 \text{ mol H}$$

$$53.29 \text{ g O} \times \frac{1 \text{ mol O}}{16.00 \text{ g O}} = 3.33 \text{ mol O}$$

The next step is to divide each number by the smallest number of moles:

$$C = \frac{3.33}{3.33} = 1$$

$$H = \frac{6.64}{3.33} = 1.99 \cong 2$$

$$O = \frac{3.33}{3.33} = 1$$

These can be used as subscripts in the empirical formula.

$$CH_2O$$

The formula weight of the empirical formula can then be compared to the molecular weight to determine if any adjustment will be necessary. The formula weight of the empirical formula is

$$CH_2O = (1 \times 12.011\ g) + (2 \times 1.01\ g) + (1 \times 16.00) = 30.03\ g$$

Since the molecular weight is 60.5 g, that means that each subscript must be multiplied by two in order to obtain the molecular formula:

$$C_2H_4O_2$$

63. **The correct answer is (D).** This is a partial pressure problem. To solve it, you need to use two equations (both from chapter 9).

$$X_A = \frac{n_A}{n_t} \text{ and } P_A = P_t \cdot X_A$$

We can determine the mole fraction of NO_2 using the first equation. Next, knowing the total pressure, we can substitute the mole fraction into the second equation (along with the total pressure) to solve for the partial pressure of NO_2.

$$X_A = \frac{n_A}{n_t} = \frac{4.5\ mol}{6.0\ mol} = 0.75$$

$$P_{NO_2} = P_t \cdot X_A = (8.00\ atm)(0.75) = 6.0\ atm$$

64. **The correct answer is (D).** When calculating the oxidation numbers, the total numbers must add up to the charge of the species (whether it is an ion, molecule, or formula unit). In this case, for the formula:

$$Mn_2O_7$$

The oxidation state of oxygen is –2, which gives a total of –14. In order to balance this with two manganese atoms, the oxidation state on each must be +7.

65. **The correct answer is (B).** This is a mole to mole conversion. If you have a balanced equation to start, you can solve these in your head. The mole ratios from the balanced equation allow you to quickly convert between moles of substances. The ratio of Cl_2 to $SiCl_4$ is 2 to 1. That means you will produce only half as many moles of $SiCl_4$, or 1.92 mol. You can also solve the problem using a formula, as shown below:

$$3.84\ mol\ Cl_2 \times \left(\frac{1\ mol\ SiCl_4}{2\ mol\ Cl_2} \right) = 1.92\ mol\ SiCl_4$$

66. **The correct answer is (C).** The reaction is zero-order for CO. You can tell this because the rate law does not contain any information about it. As a result, the rate of the reaction is unaffected by the concentration of CO, provided that some is present.

67. **The correct answer is (C).** An important thing to remember about catalysts is that they do not affect the equilibrium of a system. They affect only the rates at which equilibrium is attained.

68. **The correct answer is (D).** A square planar configuration is achieved when an atom has 6 electron pairs, four of which are bonding pairs, and two of which are lone pairs. Because Xe is a noble gas, it can form four single bonds while still maintaining two lone pairs of electrons.

69. **The correct answer is (D).** Effective buffers consist of weak acids and their conjugate bases. This pairing consists of the weak acid HCO_3^-, and its conjugate, CO_3^{2-}

70. **The correct answer is (A).** This problem uses the equation for specific heat capacity:

$$q = mC_p\Delta T$$

The logic is that the heat lost by the metal as it is cooling is transferred to the water. This heat transfer causes an increase in the water's temperature. Because the heat lost by the metal is the same as the heat gained by the water, two equations can be set up and made equal to one another. This will allow us to solve for the unknown, the specific heat of the metal.

For water:

$$q = mC_p\Delta T = (100.0\ g)(4.18\ J/g^\circ C)(5\ ^\circ C)$$
$$= 2090\ J$$

This is the same amount of heat lost by the metal. While it is technically correct to assign the metal a negative sign (which would come as a result of the decrease in temperature, and the subsequent negative value for q), the sign has no impact on the final answer so we will use positive values.

For the metal:

$$q = mC_p\Delta T$$

$$C_p = \frac{q}{m\Delta T} = \frac{2090 \text{ J}}{(100.0 \text{ g})(70 \text{ °C})} = 0.30 \text{ J/g°C}$$

71. **The correct answer is (D).** The balanced equation is shown below:

$$4NH_3(g) + 5O_2(g) \rightarrow 4NO(g) + 6H_2O$$

72. **The correct answer is (B).** The change from 200 K to 400 K should stand out to you as a doubling of the absolute temperature. Of all the choices that are listed, pressure is the only one that is directly related to temperature (i.e., when temperature doubles, pressure doubles). The most tempting distracter is probably choice (C). While velocity does increase with increased temperature, you may remember from chapter 9 that it does so according to the equation

$$u_{rms} = \sqrt{\frac{3RT}{M}}$$

73. **The correct answer is (A).** The best strategy to solve problems like this is to look for patterns in the experimental data, particularly where the concentration of one reactant remains constant while the other changes. In this reaction, comparing experiments 1 and 2 doesn't provide a clear picture of the rate law. The concentration of A and B each double, while the initial rate increases by four times. Nothing clear can be concluded here, so check another.

Looking at experiments 2 and 3, we see a critical piece of the puzzle. The concentration of A doubles while B remains constant, and the initial rate also remains constant. This means that the reaction order for A is zero.

Going back to the data from experiments 1 and 2, we can now see that if the reaction is zero order for A, then it must be second order for B (to account for the fourfold increase in the initial rate). We can confirm this by comparing experiments 1 and 4. In these experiments, the concentration of B triples (we don't need to worry about what A is doing since

it is zero order), and the initial rate increase 3^2 times, or 9 times. The rate law must be Rate $= k[B]^2$.

74. **The correct answer is (A).** This is a mass-to-mass stoichiometric conversion. The first step in solving the problem is to determine the balanced equation for the reaction. This will be necessary to determine the mole ratios in the conversion. The balanced equation is:

$$3Mg(s) + N_2(g) \rightarrow Mg_3N_2(s)$$

At this point, you can set up the conversion from grams of Mg to grams of Mg_3N_2

$$1.22 \text{ g Mg} \times \left(\frac{1 \text{ mol Mg}}{24.30 \text{ g Mg}}\right)\left(\frac{1 \text{ mol Mg}_3N_2}{3 \text{ mol Mg}}\right)$$

$$\times \left(\frac{100.92 \text{ g Mg}_3N_2}{1 \text{ mol Mg}_3N_2}\right) = 1.69 \text{ g}$$

75. **The correct answer is (C).** The first thing to consider is the free energy. Reactions for which ΔG is negative will proceed spontaneously. This rules out three of the five choices. To determine the correct answer you need to use the relationship

$$\Delta G° = -RT \ln K \text{ or } \Delta G° = -2.303 \text{ } RT \log K$$

For this step, you need to recall that the when K is greater than 1, log K (or ln K) is positive, and therefore $\Delta G°$ is negative. When K is less than 1, log K (ln K) is negative, and $\Delta G°$ is positive. So, when K is greater than 1 (and therefore $\Delta G°$ is negative), the reaction will be spontaneous.

Section II

1.

(a) Propanoic acid will dissociate and establish the following equilibrium:

$$HC_3H_5O_2 \rightleftharpoons H^+ + C_3H_5O_2^-$$

The equilibrium constant expression, therefore, will be:

$$K_a = \frac{\left[H^+\right]\left[C_3H_5O_2^-\right]}{\left[HC_3H_5O_2\right]}$$

(b) To calculate the pH, we need to determine the concentration of hydrogen ions in the expression for K_a in part (a). We will need to set up an equilibrium table to do this.

	$HC_3H_5O_2$	H^+	$C_3H_5O_2^-$
Start	0.10	0	0
Δ	$-x$	$+x$	$+x$
Finish	$0.10 - x$	x	x

$$K_a = 1.3 \times 10^{-5} = \frac{\left[H^+\right]\left[C_3H_5O_2^-\right]}{\left[HC_3H_5O_2\right]}$$

$$= \frac{(x)(x)}{(0.10 - x)} = \frac{x^2}{0.10}$$

Rearranging to solve for x we obtain

$$x = \sqrt{1.3 \times 10^{-16}} = 1.1 \times 10^{-3} M$$

Since x is equal to $[H^+]$,

$$[H^+] = x = 1.1 \times 10^{-3} M$$

Finally, we can solve for pH, using the $[H^+]$

$$pH = -\log[H^+] = -\log(1.1 \times 10^{-3}) = 2.96$$

(c) To solve this problem requires a few steps. First, you need to decide whether the salt will be acidic or basic in solution. Since it is the salt of a strong base and a weak acid, it will be basic in solution. The propanoate ion ($C_3H_5O_2-$) will hydrolyze to yield $HC_3H_5O_2$ and $OH-$. Therefore, it will be basic in solution. Thus, in order to calculate the pH, we will need to solve the equilibrium expression for K_b and use this value to calculate the pH.

The reaction that will determine the pH is

$$C_3H_5O_2^- + H_2O \rightleftharpoons HC_3H_5O_2 + OH^-$$

To solve for OH⁻ (which will allow us to calculate the pH), we need to establish a value for K_b. This can be done as shown below:

$$K_b = \frac{K_w}{K_a} = \frac{1.0 \times 10^{-14}}{1.3 \times 10^{-5}} = 7.7 \times 10^{-10}$$

With this established, we can set up an equilibrium table to calculate the [OH⁻]

	$C_3H_5O_2^-$	$HC_3H_5O_2$	OH–
Start	0.10	0	0
Δ	$-x$	$+x$	$+x$
Finish	$0.10 - x$	x	x

The next step is to calculate K_b. This will allow us to determine the [OH⁻], which will allow us to calculate the pH.

$$K_b = 7.7 \times 10^{-10} = \frac{\left[HC_3H_5O_2\right]\left[OH^-\right]}{\left[C_3H_5O_2^-\right]}$$

$$= \frac{(x)(x)}{(0.10 - x)}$$

Again, we will assume that x is significantly smaller than 0.10. Therefore

$$\frac{x^2}{0.10} = 7.7 \times 10^{-10}$$

Solving for x, we obtain

$$x = \sqrt{7.7 \times 10^{-11}} = 8.77 \ 10^{-6}$$

Therefore, [OH–] = x = 8.77×10^{-6} M

To calculate the pH, there are a few different strategies we can use. We will use the technique of determining the [H⁺] from the [OH⁻], and then use the normal pH equation.

$$\left[H^+\right] = \frac{1.0 \times 10^{-14}}{\left[OH^-\right]} = \frac{1.0 \times 10^{-14}}{8.77 \times 10^{-6}} = 1.14 \times 10^{-9}$$

$$pH = -\log[H+] = -\log(1.14 \times 10^{-9}) = 8.94$$

(d) This problem will be similar to part (a) except this time, you will be starting with an amount of propanoate ion. The first thing to do is to set up an equilibrium table:

	$HC_3H_5O_2$	H^+	$C_3H_5O_2^-$
Start	0.100	0	0.100
Δ	$-x$	$+x$	$+x$
Finish	$0.100 - x$	x	$0.100 + x$

We can use the value, and equation for K_a that was given in part (a)

$$K_a = 1.3 \times 10^{-5} = \frac{\left[H^+\right]\left[C_3H_5O_2^-\right]}{\left[HC_3H_5O_2\right]}$$

$$= \frac{(x)(0.100 + x)}{(0.100 - x)}$$

At this point, we must make the assumption that x is much less than 0.100. Doing so allows us to rewrite the equation as

$$1.3 \times 10^{-5} = \frac{(x)(0.100)}{(0.100)}$$

Solving for x, we obtain

$$x = [H^+] = 1.3 \times 10^{-5}\ M$$

Finally, we can use the $[H^+]$ to solve for pH

$$pH = -\log[H^+] = -\log(1.3 \times 10^{-5}) = 4.89$$

2. **(a)** and **(b)** $Rate = k(p_{NO})^2(p_{Cl_2})$

Looking at the data, the differences between experiments 1 and 2 are not sufficient enough to make a judgment about the order since the partial pressures of each gas changes. However from experiments 1 and 3, the pressure of Cl_2 doubles, while the pressure of NO remains constant. This doubling of pressure causes a doubling of the rate, indicating that the reaction is first order for Cl_2.

Comparison of experiments 2 and 3 show that the concentration of NO decreases by one half, while the pressure of NO doubles (from experiment 3 to experiment 2), the initial rate increase by four times. This indicates that the reaction is second order for NO.

As a check, a comparison of experiments 1 and 2 where each NO and Cl_2 double should produce an eightfold increase in the initial rate, which it does.

(c) To calculate k, you just need to substitute data into the rate law. It doesn't matter which of the three experiments you pick, they will all come out the same.

$$Rate = k(p_{NO})^2(p_{Cl_2})$$

$$k = \frac{Rate}{\left(p_{NO}\right)^2\left(p_{Cl_2}\right)} = \frac{5.0 \times 10^{-3}\text{atm s}^{-1}}{\left(0.50\text{atm}\right)^2\left(0.50\text{atm}\right)}$$
$$= 4.0 \times 10\text{--}2\ \text{atm}^{-2}\ \text{s}^{-1}$$

(d) Equipped with the rate constant k from part (c), we can calculate the missing rate in experiment 4.

$Rate = k(p_{NO})^2(p_{Cl_2}) = (4.0 \times 10^{-2}\ \text{atm}^{-2}\ \text{s}^{-1})$

$(0.75\ \text{atm})^2(1.25\ \text{atm}) = 2.8 \times 10^{-2}\ \text{atm s}^{-1}$

3. **(a)** At the anode, chloride ions are oxidized to become chlorine gas, Cl_2. This will proceed according to the half–reaction:

$$2Cl– \rightarrow Cl_2(g) + 2e^-$$

(b) At the cathode, zinc ions will be reduced to zinc metal:

$$Zn^{2+} + 2e^- \rightarrow Zn(s)$$

(c) To determine the time required for the reaction, you need to consider the amount of zinc deposited at the cathode and the amount of current passed through the cell. From the amount of zinc deposited, you can determine how many moles of electrons will be required to allow this reduction. You can then determine how much current will have to pass through the cell to produce this many electrons.

$$24.5\ \text{g Zn} \times \frac{1\ \text{mol Zn}}{65.39\ \text{g Zn}} = 0.3747\ \text{mol Zn}$$

Because each zinc ion requires $2e^-$, the number of electrons required by the zinc will be

$$0.3747\ \text{mol Zn} \times \frac{2\ \text{mol } e^-}{1\ \text{mol Zn}} = 0.7494\ \text{mol } e^-$$

Using Faraday's constant, we can determine that the number of Coulombs required will be

$$0.7494\ \text{mol } e^- \times \frac{96\,500\ \text{C}}{1\ \text{mol } e^-} = 72317\ \text{C}$$

To determine how long a current of 3.0 A will have to be applied to produce this amount of charge, you need to use the equation

$$Charge = current \times time$$

The units of which are

$$Coulombs = Amps \times second$$

This can be rearranged to solve for the time

$$\frac{\text{Coulombs}}{\text{Amps}} = \text{seconds}$$

Substituting our data, we obtain

$$\frac{72.317 \text{ C}}{3.0 \text{ A}} = 24\,106 \text{ seconds, or } 402 \text{ minutes, or } 6.7$$

hours.

(d) The amount of chlorine liberated at the anode is solved in the same way, but the reverse direction. The first steps of the problem can be skipped because we already know how long the current is applied, how much charge is produced during this time, and how many electrons will be available at the anode for oxidizing the chloride ions. We can pick up the problem at that point.

$$0.7494 \text{ mol e}^- \times \frac{1 \text{ mol Cl}_2}{2 \text{ mol } e^-} = 0.3747 \text{ mol Cl}_2$$

This can now be converted to grams:

$$0.3747 \text{ mol Cl}_2 \times \frac{70.91 \text{ g}}{1 \text{ mol Cl}_2} = 26.57 \text{ g Cl}_2$$

4. **(a)** $PbS + O_2 \rightarrow PbO + SO_2$

This reaction, a first step in producing pure metals, involves an oxidation of sulfur and a reduction of oxygen.

(b) $KClO_3\ MnO_2 \rightarrow KCl + O_2$

This decomposition of potassium chlorate is a fairly common way to generate oxygen gas in the laboratory. The catalyst, written above the arrow, greatly facilitates this process.

(c) $Ag^+ + Cl^- \rightarrow AgCl$

A metathesis reaction where the reaction is driven by the formation of the insoluble salt, silver chloride.

(d) $Mg + Fe^{2+} \rightarrow Mg^{2+} + Fe$

Magnesium is above iron on the activity series of the metals, meaning it is more readily oxidized than iron. As a result, it will replace the iron in solution.

(e) $Sn^{2+} + H^+ + MnO_4^- \rightarrow Sn^{4+} + Mn^{2+} + H_2O$

The permanganate ion tends to act as an oxidizing agent in reactions, the manganese converting from its +7 oxidation state to a +2, the most common transformation for manganese. Acidic solutions allow for the reduction of manganese all the way to the +2 state.

(f) $H_2S + Cd^{2+} \rightarrow CdS + H^+$

Hydrogen sulfide is a strong reducing agent that will react with many substances to yield insoluble sulfides. It is frequently used as a step in qualitative analysis.

(g) $C_3H_7OH + O_2 \rightarrow CO_2 + H_2O$

This is a very typical combustion reaction. The answer above assumes an excess of oxygen during the reaction, as noted by the presence of CO_2. In the absence of adequate amounts of oxygen, the product CO will also be formed.

(h) $BCl_3 + NH_3 \rightarrow Cl_3BNH_3$

One thing to look out for whenever you see ammonia is its behavior as a Lewis base and its ability to form complexes. In this problem, you are also given boron trichloride, which is frequently cited as being an example of a molecule where the central atom has an incomplete octet. Although boron trichloride is stable, it readily reacts with ammonia.

5. **(a)** Your procedures may vary somewhat, but they should be similar to those listed here.

Start heating the water bath so it will be hot when needed.

Tightly cover the mouth of the Erlenmeyer flask with a small square piece of aluminum foil.

Poke a small hole in the mouth of the flask with the straight pin.

Weigh the empty flask (with the foil on it).

Remove the cap and place a 2–mL sample of the unknown liquid into the flask and replace the foil.

Using the clamp and ring stand immerse the flask into the water bath and heat.

When no more liquid is visible and no more condensate can be seen leaving the pinhole heat for about 30 more seconds and then remove the flask from the water bath. Record the temperature of the water bath just prior to removing the flask.

Allow the flask to cool to room temperature.

Dry the flask thoroughly, and reweigh.

Fill the flask with water and empty into a graduated cylinder (to determine the volume of the flask).

Use the barometer to measure the barometric pressure.

(b) You will need to record the following measurements:

1. Mass of the flask and foil (empty).

2. Mass of the flask, foil, and condensed vapor.

3. Volume of the flask.

4. Barometric pressure.

5. Temperature of the boiling water bath.

(c) Molecular mass = $\dfrac{mRT}{PV}$

Where m is mass. R must contain units consistent with all other units in the calculation. The most crucial is the unit of pressure, which will be determined by the units on the barometer. As an example, the value of the ideal gas constant might be 62.4 mm Hg L / mol K, where atmospheres have been converted to mm Hg.

The units of measure will set up as follows (if mm Hg is used):

Molecular mass = $\dfrac{(g)\left(mm\ Hg\ L\ mol^{-1}\ K^{-1}\right)(K)}{(mm\ Hg)(L)}$

The resulting units in the calculation will be g/mol, the desired units.

(d) If the liquid was not completely vaporized, the value of m in the equation in part (c) would be too high. This will cause the molar mass to be too high.

(e) Experimental error is always calculated the same way:

$$\dfrac{|your\ value - theoretical\ value|}{theoretical\ value} \times 100\%$$

$$\dfrac{130-125.5}{125.5} \times 100\% = error$$

6. **(a)** Ionization energy is determined by two main factors. The first is the amount of nuclear shielding between the nucleus and the outermost electrons in an atom. The more shielding, the more the attraction is affected, and therefore the weaker the attractive force. This means that as the amount of shielding increases, the ionization energy decreases. Shielding increases as you move down a group, meaning the group trend for ionization energy is that the ionization energy for an atom decreases as you move down a group. The second main trend is the periodic trend, which is determined by the effective nuclear charge acting on the outermost electrons. As you move from left to right across a period, the effective nuclear charge increases. This

is because the number of protons in the nucleus is increasing, while the shielding is remaining constant. As a result, the attractive force between the nucleus and the outermost electrons increases as you move left to right across a period. The periodic trend is that ionization energy increases from left to right. For this question, Rubidium has a higher first ionization energy than sodium because it is farther down a group. It therefore has more shielding and a weaker attraction on the outermost electrons.

(b) Both phosphorus and sulfur form negative ions. Phosphorus will gain three electrons when it ionizes, while sulfur will only gain two. Negative ions are larger than the element because when an atom gains electrons, the number of electrons exceeds the number of protons. As a result, there is a reduced overall attraction for each electron, which causes the ion to become larger. The more electrons that an atom gains, the larger the difference between the number of protons in the nucleus and the number of valence electrons.

Because phosphorus will gain three electrons compared to sulfur's two, it will form a larger ion.

(c) This is an example of a periodic trend for the atomic radius. A common misconception is to think that because an atom has a larger atomic number, it will naturally have a greater atomic size. This is incorrect. As you move down a group, atoms with larger atomic numbers have larger atomic radii. However, moving across a period, the increasing effective nuclear charge causes a greater attraction between the nucleus and the valence electrons. As a result, the atoms get smaller as you move left to right across a period.

(d) The magnesium atom has two valence electrons. Each one of these electrons can be removed with a relatively small amount of energy. However, once those outer electrons are removed from the 3s orbitals, the 2p orbitals contain the outermost electrons. These electrons in the 2p orbitals are isoelectronic to the noble gases and very stable. In addition, an atom like magnesium has two additional protons providing an even greater effective nuclear charge. As a result, there will be a tremendous difference between the ionization energies for the 2nd and 3rd electrons.

7. **(a)**

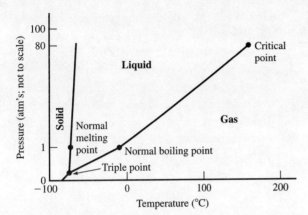

(b) For this change, SO_2 will change from a gas to a liquid (condense).

(c) The only changes to occur during this cooling is a lowering of temperature within the liquid phase. SO_2 remains in the liquid phase, but it is just getting cooler.

(d) Because the triple point lies to the left of the normal melting point, it can be ascertained that the slope of the solid-liquid transition line is slightly positive. This means that increases in pressure will increase the density of the substance (a line going straight up from the transition line will cause SO_2 to convert from the liquid phase to the solid phase).

8. **(a)** Ice is a rare substance that actually expands and becomes less dense as it freezes. As a result, applying pressure to solid ice at the freezing temperature will cause it to become slightly more dense and melt. CO_2, on the other hand, is more representative of other most substances that are more dense at colder temperatures. Substances like CO_2 will solidify when compressed.

(b) Rock salt, when it dissolves, lowers the freezing point of water (because of the colligative property of the freezing point depression). This allows for the slushy mixture to cool below the normal freezing temperature of ice.

(c) Helium, because it is a much lighter molecule than the components of air. As a result of this, and Graham's law, we know that the lighter He molecules will effuse more quickly from the balloons than air will.

(d) Gases are more soluble in liquids at lower temperatures. For the ice cubes made with hot water, most of the gases has already bubbled out of solution.

NOTES

NOTES

NOTES

NOTES

NOTES